Principles of Irish Employme

Principles of Irish Employment Law

By
Dr. Brenda Daly

BA(Hons), MA, PhD

Dr. Michael Doherty

LL.B (Dub), LL.M (Cantab), PhD (Dub),
Barrister-at-Law

CLARUS PRESS

Published by
Clarus Press Ltd,
Griffith Campus,
South Circular Road,
Dublin 8.

Typeset by
Datapage International Limited,
157 Rathmines Road Upper,
Rathmines,
Dublin 6.

Printed by
CPI Antony Rowe
Bumpers Farm Industrial Estate
Chippenham
Wiltshire
UK

ISBN
978-1-905536-31-3

Disclaimer
Whilst every effort has been made to ensure that the contents of this book are accurate, neither the publisher nor authors can accept responsibility for any errors or omissions or loss occasioned to any person acting or refraining from acting as result of any material in this publication.

This book is dedicated to the memory of my late grandparents,
Mick & Agnes Daly and George & Brigid Maxwell and
my late uncle Joe Maxwell.
(Brenda Daly)

For Bridie
(Michael Doherty)

FOREWORD

When I started in the practice of industrial relations, as a trade union official, in 1973 statute law had little bearing on the employment relationship. One was expected to be familiar with the Redundancy Payments Act 1967, the Holiday (Employees) Act 1961 and the newly enacted Minimum Notice and Terms of Employment Act 1973. There were some other statutes, such as the Conditions of Employment Act 1936, which were of some relevance to the employment relationship, but only marginally so. The dominant non-contractual source of the rights of workers, particularly those in manual occupations, and the concomitant obligations of their employers, was the collective agreement. Those rights and obligations were in turn the product of collective bargaining between trade unions and employers. Thus matters touching on rights and duties in employment were firmly in the province of trade unions and employers. That was a time when employment law, as a discrete topic for students, or as a field of practice for lawyers, was unknown.

All that has changed utterly. Trade union density, particularly in the private sector, has declined significantly and with it the incidents of collective bargaining. Parallel with the decline in collective bargaining there has been an explosion in the body of statute law governing key aspects of the employment relationship, much of it derived from the State's obligations as a member of the European Union. This has led to the emergence of a vast and complex jurisprudence centred in the statutory tribunals that have been given the adjudicative role in disputes concerning the rights and duties prescribed by this body of law. It is a novel, and for me a somewhat flattering experience, to read a learned legal text in which so many of the propositions of law discussed are derived from decisions of the Labour Court and other statutory tribunals rather than those of the Superior Courts.

As the authors have pointed out, the development of its extensive employment rights jurisdiction has significantly affected the role and procedures of the Labour Court. It was established not as a Court of law but, in the words of its first Chairman, as a Court of *"common sense and fair dealing"*. I hope that its decisions continue to be influenced by notions of common sense and fair dealing but they must be grounded firmly in the law as the Court finds it. In order to adequately discharge this relatively new role the Court has had to develop its own expertise in the application of complex principles of both domestic and European jurisprudence. It has also affected the profile of representation before the Labour Court. Whereas historically the Court was intended as a forum before which cases would be argued by trade union and employer representatives, in the discharge of its employment rights jurisdiction, the dominant representation is now by lawyers.

This book is directed at students of employment law and at legal practitioners in this speciality. It is a formidable work which provides a comprehensive and meticulous exposition of the current law governing the employment relationship. It provides the reader not just with a thorough understanding of the legal principles, rules and procedure involved but it explains with admirable clarity the political and socio-economic background against which they evolved.

To know the law requires far more than knowledge of relevant statutory provisions and the cases that appear to deal with a point in issue. It requires an understanding of the underlying rationale of decisions in point so as to adequately consider if they are truly apposite to what is being contended for. In this work the authors have undertaken a comprehensive and detailed analysis of the reasoning behind the decisions contained in the vast array of authorities which are examined. They have done so in a structured and lucid manner with clarity of language that makes their book a joy to read and a source of enlightenment even for those for whom the topic is part of their stock –in-trade.

In the application of employment law, perhaps more than in any other area of legal practice, an understanding of the law of the European Union is of particular importance. Many of the domestic statutory provisions which must be considered are derived from European Directives or Treaty provisions. It is well settled that national courts and tribunals must interpret and apply domestic law so as to achieve the result envisaged by European law. Hence, many of the cases decided in this jurisdiction, which are analysed in the chapters dealing with these issues, turned on the correct application of principles enunciated by the ECJ. Again this complex jurisprudence is explained with commendable lucidity.

I would commend this work not only to students and lawyers but also to practitioners in the field of industrial relations and human resource management. For them an understanding of the law applicable to the world of work is increasingly an integral and indispensable requirement of their job. This volume is so organised and written as to make the topic intelligible and accessible across a wide spectrum.

The authors have taken the perhaps brave step of departing from the customary practice of inviting a Judge of the Superior Courts to provide the foreword to their work. I am honoured and indebted to them for the opportunity to provide some introductory comments on this splendid and scholarly volume and I wish it the success it so richly deserves.

Kevin Duffy
Chairman
The Labour Court
31st August 2010.

PREFACE

We remember very clearly the moment the idea came to us to write this book. Another academic year beginning, more employment law courses to be taught, but, yet again, no comprehensive and up-to-date book to recommend to students. Despite the fact that employment is an area of law that is constantly changing and evolving (witness the explosion of legislative intervention in the employment relationship in recent years) and is of quite considerable scope and breadth, the number of Irish texts covering the subject has been surprisingly low. This is a vacuum that we hope to go some way towards filling with the publication of this book.

Employment law is, in many ways, the quintessential law student/ practitioner subject, encompassing, as it does, aspects of tort law, contract law, constitutional law, commercial law and criminal law. However, it is also an area of the law that strongly affects, and is affected by, prevailing economic, political and social trends and policies. Writing a text on employment law just a few years ago, at the height of the "Celtic Tiger" economic boom, we would probably have focused in a relatively minor way on issues like redundancy and industrial disputes. Now, in the context of an economic recession, these issues come before the courts and tribunals on a daily basis. For this reason, we have endeavoured, throughout the book, to set the law in its social and economic context, drawing, where appropriate, on criticisms and perspectives from a variety of disciplines.

We have also attempted to plot a route through the bewildering array of fora and institutions that exists for the resolution of employment disputes and to outline in a comprehensible fashion the remedies available to employment law litigants. Employment law study and practice requires a good understanding of the processes and procedures that affect the resolution of disputes, which lie outside the "regular" court system, as well as knowledge of the roles and functions of the various employment law actors (employers and employees, obviously, but also trade unions, state agencies, third party dispute resolution bodies and employer associations, to name but a few). The book attempts to explain these in a clear and meaningful fashion.

Naturally, in a work such as this, it is impossible to cover all areas of law that are pertinent to employment relations. For that reason, we have decided to concentrate on "core" issues that affect the employment relationship and treat these as comprehensively as we can. Inevitably, this leads to omissions of certain areas (for example, to do with pensions and social welfare, corporate insolvency, the relationship between trade unions and their members) in respect of which we can only direct readers to other, specialised texts.

The dynamism of employment law is reflected, too, in the fact that laws are passed, and decisions handed down, with bewildering frequency in this area. As we raced towards completion of the text, we endeavoured, as best we could, to incorporate late changes, from the relatively minor (for example, the renaming of Governmental departments) to the quite significant (see the European Court of Justice rulings on age discrimination, discussed in chapters 5 and 10). At the time of writing, a number of significant pieces of employment law legislation (on agency workers, employment rights compliance and industrial relations, for example) remain in Bill form and are discussed in those terms. Where possible, we have also indicated where employment tribunal decisions are under appeal. Employment law is never dull and ever changing!

We would like to express our thanks to a number of people for their help and support throughout the writing of the book. We are very grateful to our publishers, Clarus Press, and, in particular, to David McCartney who, despite signing a contract with us on April Fools' Day, remained resolutely good-humoured, positive and encouraging throughout the process. We would also like to apologise to David for the shock we gave him by delivering the book (more or less) on time. We wish to thank all those at Clarus Press responsible for proof-reading, correcting and indexing this book. We are also extremely grateful to Kevin Duffy, Chairman of the Labour Court, for taking time out of his incredibly busy schedule to write the foreword to the book and for his warm and generous comments.

We would like to thank our colleagues in the School of Law and Government at DCU for their support. In particular, we would like to thank Yvonne Daly and Elaine Dewhurst for their assistance and advice. A special thanks goes to Noelle Higgins: without Noelle's help and patience we would never get anything done! We also wish to thank the students at DCU for providing us with the idea and the impetus to write an accessible textbook to meet their demands to learn more about the peculiarities of employment law.

Brenda Daly would like to thank her parents, Kevin and Jean, and her brothers Colin, Shane and Eamonn for their constant support, understanding and encouragement. Thanks to Patrick for his support and good humour. Thanks to all my friends who have shared the writing experience and who listened to me talk endlessly about various chapters, especially my co-author Michael for his assistance and patience during the many different stages of the book. Thanks also to (the) Groove Armada for "Black Light", which turned out to be the soundtrack that got me through the final writing up process.

Michael Doherty would like to thank his parents, Brian and Nena for their love, support and updates on the Spanish labour market. Thanks also to all of my friends who listened to, and put up with, the (more than usually) incessant moaning while I was writing the book, particularly Dez, Suzanne, Jean, Carla, my favourite married couple, Brendan and Claire, and my co-author Brenda. Thanks to Ryan's for reducing the price of Beamish during the writing-up process and to the Trap for continuing to give me Hope. Thanks, always, to Bríd, the love of my life (*When my working day is through, I get my sweet reward, To be alone with you*).

Responsibility for the book (and any errors or omissions that occur within) is shared between us jointly and severally, but Brenda Daly assumes primary responsibility for chapters 4, 5, 6, 8, and 9 and Michael Doherty assumes primary responsibility for chapters 2, 3, 7, 10, 11 and 12.

We have attempted to state the law as it stands on 1st September 2010.

Brenda Daly and Michael Doherty

CONTENTS

Contents

TABLE OF CASES

Table of Cases

TABLE OF LEGISLATION

Constitutional Provisions

Statutes (Ireland)

Statutes (UK)

Statutory Instruments (Ireland)

Table of Legislation

Bills

EU DIRECTIVES AND REGULATIONS

Directives

Regulations

TREATIES AND CONVENTIONS

Treaties

Conventions

Codes of Practice

Other

CHAPTER 1
Introduction

I. Introduction

Employment law is one of the most challenging areas of the law with which the student (or, indeed, the practitioner) can engage. At the same time, it is one of the most dynamic and fast-moving areas of contemporary law. The modern workplace is a locus of seemingly constant change, influenced heavily by the political and socio-economic context of the wider society. The dynamism of this area of law can make its study sometimes look and feel quite daunting. However, the legal principles, rules and procedures that govern this area of law, while complex, also seem more concrete than other, more abstract, areas of legal study. Most of us (including, increasingly, second and third level students) have worked at some point in our lives and, so, have first-hand experience of the employment relationship that is not equalled by, say, our experience of corporate insolvency or the criminal law process (hopefully at least!). Thus, employment law intuitively "makes sense". While it has often been suggested by social theorists that, in contemporary society, work plays a much diminished role in the life experience,[1] the simple fact is that most of us spend a large proportion of our adult lives going to, coming from, completing, (or sleeping on) the job. Working fulfils for people important financial, but also personal (sense of worth, achievement, dignity, etc) and social (friendship and romance, for example) needs. Indeed, when asked the "the lottery question", that is "would you continue to work if there was no financial necessity to do so?", survey evidence in Ireland and internationally has consistently shown that more than two-thirds of people would, in fact, choose to do so and that this figure has *risen* in recent years.[2] However, the precise nature and implications of our rights and obligations when we work are less commonly understood and this is what we hope to address in this book.

[1–01]

---

[1] These are often referred to as the "end-of-work" prophets; see, for example, Beck, *The Brave New World of Work* (Polity, Cambridge, 2000); Bauman, *Work, Consumerism and the New Poor* (Open University Press, Buckingham, 1998); Sennett, *The Corrosion of Character. The Personal Consequences of Work in the New Capitalism* (WW Norton & Company Ltd, New York, 1998).
[2] O' Connell *et al*, *The Changing Workplace: A Survey of Employees' Views and Experiences* (ESRI/NCPP, Dublin, 2004); Noon and Blyton, *The Realities of Work* (Palgrave, Basingstoke, 2002).

[1–02]   Some of the things mentioned in the preceding paragraph may themselves be sufficient to scare the horses somewhat: in a legal text aimed at students and practitioners, why would the authors consider social theorists, life experiences and the socio-economic context? Well, in our view the study of employment law can only be properly understood if it also embraces insights from disciplines outside the law. These include sociology (and its understandings of how work is structured by society and perceived by individuals, as well as its conceptions of power relations); economics (particularly in the application of market theories to the labour market and in the working out of macroeconomic concepts like productivity and unemployment); political science (for example, the work of political scientists on governance in modern societies); feminist theory (particularly in the study of equality and diversity at work); and business studies (especially in the areas of human resources and theories of business organisation). The study of industrial relations is also particularly pertinent, bringing under its focus, as it does, questions of labour-capital relations, social welfare systems, the role of trade unions, wage policy and labour mobility. This is by no means an exhaustive list, but it is illustrative of our belief that employment law cannot be understood simply as a stand-alone conceptual and doctrinal subject, but needs to be understood also as a social and economic phenomenon.

[1–03]   Within the study of law itself, employment law straddles many areas. As we will see in chapter 2, the sources of employment law are varied and the student or practitioner requires at least a working knowledge of the law of contract, the law of torts, constitutional law and European Union law. The role of the common law, and particularly that of precedent, is also quite distinctive in studying employment law. As so many disputes are settled before employment tribunals (which, as we will see, do not operate as courts of law), often decisions tend to be quite specific to their own facts. It can, therefore, sometimes be more difficult to establish guiding principles from existing cases than it would be in other areas of law.

Here we are going to introduce some of the themes that will run through the book. Like the insights drawn from the disciplines mentioned above, these will not always be explicitly flagged. They do, however, inform the discussion of the law that follows.

II. General Themes

The Changing World of Work

[1–04]   Different "models" of employment relations exist throughout the world. Indeed, even in Europe, while there are certain features common to all European countries (the recognition of the rights of workers to organise, at least in the sense of a freedom to join trade unions, a degree of State intervention in the labour/capital relationship and the existence of a relatively developed welfare state, to name a few) it cannot be said that there is a "European model" of employment relations.[3] The Irish system of employment relations, derived as it is from that of the UK, has traditionally been classified as *adversarial* and *voluntarist*. "Adversarialism" refers to a situation where

---

[3] Crouch, *Industrial Relations and European State Traditions* (Clarendon Press, Oxford, 1993).

there is a strong "them and us" relationship between the two sides (capital — employers— and labour) and each side sees their interests as clearly divergent.[4] "Voluntarism" refers to a system where the preference is for joint trade union and employer regulation of employment relations and the relative absence of legal intervention.[5] Voluntarism is premised on freedom of contract (what Kahn-Freund referred to as the great "indispensible figment of the legal mind")[6] and freedom of association, whereby the employment relationship is essentially regulated by free collective bargaining between worker and employer representative groups.[7] In such a model, there is no *rejection* of public intervention or labour law but the role of the State is seen as primarily providing a supportive framework for collective bargaining and the "principal purpose of labour law is to regulate, support and restrain the power of management and organised labour".[8] The implications of this were that Irish (and British) employers and unions traditionally viewed with disfavour employment legislation, so that collective bargaining was a key element in the functioning of the employment relations system.

In recent years, the traditional pillars of adversarialism and voluntarism have come under stress. There has been much comment, both in Ireland and the UK, on the decline of the voluntarist model.[9] Principally, this is because trade union density has dropped considerably in Ireland over the course of the last twenty years and now stands at approximately 35 percent (in the private sector, the figure is approximately 20 percent).[10] Many organisations (particularly in the service industries) do not engage in collective bargaining and do not recognise trade unions. The decline in trade union density and presence in the workplace has been accompanied by a corresponding decline in industrial action (usually taken as a measure of adversarialism), prompting some to identify a new "individualism" amongst workers, which encompasses an ideological rejection of collective organisation and action.[11] However, this should not imply that employment disputes have gone away; on the contrary there has been a huge increase in the workload of the State's dispute resolution bodies, as we will see in

[1–05]

---

[4] Hyman, "Industrial Relations in Europe: Theory and Practice" (1995) 1(1) *European Journal of Industrial Relations* 17.

[5] The Irish "Anglo-Saxon" model can be contrasted, for example, with the "Roman-Germanic" model of France and Germany, where the State, through its labour laws, has an active and central role in labour market organisation; see Teague, "Deliberative Governance and EU Social Policy" (2001) 7(1) *European Journal of Industrial Relations* 26.

[6] Kahn-Freund, *Labour and the Law* (Stevens, London, 1977), p 18.

[7] Doherty, "Institutional Challenge: Tribunals, Industrial Relations and the Law" (2009) 2 ELRI 70.

[8] Kahn-Freund, *op.cit,* p 4.

[9] See, for example, Teague, "New Developments in Employment Dispute Resolution" (2005) 4 LRC Rev 5; Redmond, "The Future of Labour Law" (2004) 1 IELJ 3; Colling, "What Space for Unions on the Floor of Rights? Trade Unions and the Enforcement of Statutory Individual Employment Rights" (2006) 35(2) ILJ 140; Brown *et al*, "The Employment Contract: From Collective Procedures to Individual Rights" (2000) 38(4) *British Journal of Industrial Relations* 611.

[10] Sheehan, "Union Density Drops 10% in a Decade" (2005) 35 IRN.

[11] Beck, *The Brave New World of Work* (Polity, Cambridge, 2000); *cf.* Kelly, *Rethinking Industrial Relations: Mobilisation, Collectivism and Long Waves.* (Routledge, London, 1998).

chapter 2. At the same time, however, there are increasingly attempts by employers to individualise the employment relationship through the implementation of various human resource management (HRM) techniques, which often seek to bypass trade unions and foster employee commitment to the enterprise.[12] Growing antipathy, in some cases bordering on oppression, towards unions by some major employers has also been documented.[13] In certain cases, employer attention has shifted to the establishment of *non-union* structures for employee representation at work and, indeed, a number of obligations exist on employers in non-union settings to inform, and consult with, their workers.[14]

[1–06] However, while trade union presence and influence at workplace level has been on the wane, the union movement found for itself in recent years a new and crucial role in socio-economic governance at national level. Since 1987 a series of tripartite social pacts was concluded between the social partners (the State, unions, employers and some other representative interest groups) beginning with *The Programme for National Recovery* (PNR, 1987–1990) and encompassing most recently *Towards 2016* (agreed in 2006; reviewed in 2008). The agreements focus mainly on issues of pay (particularly in the public sector), tax reform and a range of other socio-economic issues.[15] As we will see in chapter 2, through partnership a number of legislative measures were agreed, which were then progressed through the normal legislative process. Although at the time of writing, the future of the process is somewhat uncertain, its legacy in terms of employment law remains important.

The Legislative Explosion

[1–07] The result of these changes (or, depending on one's perspective, a contributor to them) has been an explosion in the volume of employment legislation over the last 20 years or so. Teague and Thomas, for example, point to 16 major pieces of employment legislation enacted in the period 1990–2006 alone and this list is by no means exhaustive, as the authors do not include hugely important legislation like the Safety, Health and Welfare at Work Act 2005.[16] This has also been driven, to a significant extent, by Ireland's obligations as a Member State of the European Union. Much important employment legislation in recent years, as we will see throughout the book, has been driven by developments at EU level. Moreover, the changing nature of the (increasingly globalised) labour market has demanded and generated legislative responses. In particular the growth in private sector service employment and the demands by employers for "flexibility" in employment relations have seen an exponential growth in the numbers employed in "atypical" work (most commonly

---

[12] D'Art and Turner, *Irish Employment Relations in the New Economy* (Blackhall, Dublin, 2002).

[13] D'Art and Turner, "Union Recognition and Partnership at Work: A New Legitimacy for Irish Trade Unions?" (2005) 36(2) *Industrial Relations Journal* 121; O'Sullivan and Gunnigle, "Bearing All the Hallmarks of Oppression; Union Avoidance in Europe's Largest Low-cost Airline" (2009) 34(2) *Labor Studies Journal* 252.

[14] Doherty, *op.cit,* p 73.

[15] See Roche, "Social Partnership in Ireland and New Social Pacts" (2007) 46(3) *Industrial Relations* 395; Doherty and Erne, "Mind the Gap: National and Local Partnership in the Irish Public Sector" (2010) 41(5) *Industrial Relations Journal* (forthcoming).

[16] Teague and Thomas, *Employment Dispute Resolution and Standard Setting in the Republic of Ireland* (LRC, Dublin, 2008), pp 14-15.

part-time, fixed-term, temporary and agency work).[17] Given all of this, some commentators have argued that it is now inaccurate to describe the Irish employment relations system as voluntarist, due to the decline in trade union density and voluntary collective bargaining and the parallel expansion in individual employment rights, which has arguably resulted in a transition from a bargaining-based employment relations system to a rights-based system.[18]

The World of Irish Employment Law

We will encounter the issues outlined above throughout the book. However, an important feature of Irish employment law is not just the manner in which it responds to macro-level, global developments and trends, but also its localised peculiarities. In particular, here, it is important to note that the State has put in place an elaborate and distinctive system for the resolution of disputes and grievances that arise in the context of the employment relationship. While employees and employers (and trade unions or employer representative associations) have the same rights of access to the courts of the land as other citizens, specialised, expert tribunals and bodies have been set up to deal with employment relations issues and these have quite distinctive roles, procedures and powers of redress. Some tribunals deal with individual employment law claims (like the Employment Appeals Tribunal) and others deal with collective disputes that may, or may not, have a legal dimension (e.g. the Labour Court). Some contentious issues that arise in the context of the employment relationship are handled as "ordinary" legal claims, to be argued over by lawyers and adjudicated on by judges or others exercising judicial powers. Others, though, are in the nature of industrial relations claims, argued over by ordinary workers or trade union and HRM representatives that need to be handled, for example, by means of negotiation, conciliation or mediation by facilitators, who may have no powers to impose a legally binding settlement. Thus, it is vital for the student or practitioner of employment law to be able to "navigate" the system and know the appropriate forum in which to bring a particular employment law or industrial relations claim and the optimal remedy to seek, as well as understand the (to the classically trained lawyer) unusually informal procedures that apply before the employment tribunals.

[1–08]

III. Structure of the Book

It would not be possible to cover all of the areas of law applicable to the employment relationship in a book such as this. Nor is it possible to give a completely comprehensive account of *both* the substantive *and* procedural features of employment law. As a result, we have chosen to focus on some of the core issues that pertain to the employment relationship. We have also endeavored to give at least an overview of how the system operates procedurally and an account of the remedies available to employment law litigants.

[1–09]

Chapters 2 and 3 outline the overarching features of the employment law system, focusing on the sources of employment law, the institutional framework and the nature

[1–10]

---

[17] Castells, *The Rise of the Network Society* (Blackwell, Cambridge, Mass, 2006); *O' Connell et al*, *op.cit*, Doogan, "Insecurity and Long-term Unemployment" (2001) 15(3) *Work, Employment and Society* 419.

[18] Teague, "New Developments in Employment Dispute Resolution" (2005) 4 LRC Rev 5.

of the employment relationship. The bulk of the book then turns to the main incidents of the employment relationship. Chapter 4 examines the cornerstone of the rights and obligations that exist in the relationship: the contract of employment. The following chapters (5–9) then deal with the nature of these rights and obligations, looking at equality and discrimination in the workplace, "family-friendly" working, health, safety and welfare at work (including the right to a harassment-free place of work) and the rights of migrant workers. Chapter 10 examines the law in relation to the determination of the employment relationship, where the relationship, for whatever reason, has come to an end.

[1–11] Chapter 11 deals with collective employment law. This is a huge topic in and of itself, but the chapter focuses mainly on trade union rights, the law of trade disputes and collective employment law in a non-union context. Finally, in chapter 12, we have collected together in one chapter the various forms of redress that can be sought if a claim is successful. By gathering these in one chapter, rather than scattering them throughout the book, we hope readers will be better able to see the commonalties and differences between various (sometime overlapping) claims. This chapter should be read in conjunction with the other chapters.

CHAPTER 2
The Sources of Irish Employment Law and the Institutional Framework

I. Introduction

As with all areas of law, a starting point for any student or practitioner of employment law is to appreciate from where the relevant legal rules applicable to a particular scenario originate. It is also necessary to understand where the various legal rules fit into the overall system; is there a hierarchical framework if conflict arises and, if so, which legal rule will prevail over the others in the case of a conflict? Employment law is derived from a number of sources and the balance between these various sources is continuously changing.[1] As a result, employment law tends to be an area that is quite dynamic and is persistently evolving. While this can make it seem quite challenging (and even somewhat intimidating) the changing nature of the subject is key, as it reflects the reality that the employer-employee relationship itself is one that is constantly developing.[2] Adding to the complexity is the fact that, in addition to the regular courts, there is a variety of specific institutions and tribunals that deal with

[2–01]

---

[1] Regan, "Sources and Institutions" in *Employment Law* (Regan ed, Tottel, Dublin, 2009), p 3.
[2] Lockton, *Employment Law* (7th ed, Palgrave, Basingstoke, 2010), p 3.

claims relating to employment disputes. We will examine these in greater detail below, but first we need to identify the principal sources of employment law.

II. The Sources of Irish Employment Law

[2–02] In the Irish legal system we can identify four principal sources of law: the common law, legislation, the Constitution and European Union (EU) law. As well as these primary sources of law, other "influences" or secondary sources of law (such as international law or codes of practice) can be noted. These do not enjoy the force of law, *per se* but might prove to be significant either because they are incorporated into law by a law-making act or they influence the interpretation of a law by an adjudicative body.[3]

Common Law

[2–03] The common law consists of thousands of judicial decisions, resulting from cases arising before the courts, made down through the centuries. The doctrine of precedent (*stare decisis*) means that a court will decide a case by reference to earlier, similar decisions so that judicial decisions are, therefore, attributed the force of law. As much employment legislation has come on the statute books only relatively recently, the common law has been an important driving force in the development of many employment law principles. Furthermore, even where legislation exists, the courts retain an important role in its interpretation, meaning that they continue to play a vital role in developing key legal principles in the area.

[2–04] Certain areas of the common law are particularly important in the employment sphere. The law of *contract* plays a key role in the employment relationship, which has as its legal core the contract of employment between employer and employee, what Kahn-Freund referred to as the great "indispensible figment of the legal mind".[4] A contract of employment may be written or oral, can have express and implied terms, and either party can sue for breach. Some important implied contractual terms flow from the common law, for example, the mutual obligation on both the employer and employee to maintain trust and confidence in their relationship.[5] The rules of contract law apply in the employment context as they do in any other context. Therefore, for a contract to be valid there must be offer, acceptance, consideration and an intention to create legal relations.[6] Employment contracts, however, are subject to many conditions imposed by legislation.[7]

---

[3] See Byrne and McCutcheon, *The Irish Legal System* (5th ed, Bloomsbury, Dublin, 2009).

[4] Kahn-Freund, *Labour and the Law* (Stevens, London, 1977), p 18. Kahn-Freund argued that the individual contract of employment was something of a legal fiction, as the relationship between the parties arose generally where one party (the employer) was in a position of power, while the other (the employee) was in a position of subordination. This does not reflect the underlying basis of contract law, which sees two or more parties bargaining freely in order to come to agreement.

[5] *Berber v Dunnes Stores* [2009] ELR 61; see chapter 4.

[6] See, generally, Enright, *Principles of Irish Contract Law* (Clarus Press, Dublin, 2007).

[7] See chapter 4.

The law of *tort* is also important in employment law, as it imposes duties of care on parties to the employment relationship over and above any specified in the contract of employment. A tort is a legal wrong and the aim of tort law is primarily to compensate claimants for injury suffered as a result of the defendant's wrongdoing.[8] Beyond any contractual dealings, those involved in an employment relationship have an obligation to behave with reasonable care in their dealings and not to act negligently. Traditionally, the courts were somewhat slow to impose liability in tort on employers for injuries sustained by employees at work. This was because of their view that the employment relationship was primarily one of contract, in which employees could look after their own interests and could choose whether or not to take on dangerous employment for pay. This position has been firmly rejected, however, so that the duty of care that employers owe for their employees' safety at work is now seen as one of the most important obligations in the employment relationship.[9]   **[2–05]**

The law of *equity* also affects the employment relationship, primarily by providing the general principles governing the equitable remedies of injunction and specific performance (among others), which are available to claimants in situations where damages (financial compensation) are not an adequate remedy.[10] Certain categories of employees (like executive directors of companies) also owe fiduciary duties to their employers that go beyond the contract of employment and these are governed by the law of equity.   **[2–06]**

Legislation

The easiest legal rules to identify are those that are specifically created by a legislature. In Ireland, legislation consists principally of Acts of the Oireachtas (Art 15.2 of the Irish Constitution designates the Oireachtas as the sole law-making body of the State) and delegated or secondary legislation. Delegated legislation is enacted by bodies or individuals that are conferred with that power by statute.[11]   **[2–07]**

The historical traditions of the Irish system of employment relations are important to bear in mind here. As we saw in chapter 1, the Irish system has traditionally been classified as voluntarist, meaning that there is a preference for joint trade union and employer regulation of employment relations and the relative absence of legal intervention. However, as we have seen, two key factors, the weakening of voluntarism and Ireland's membership of the EU, have contributed greatly to an explosion of employment legislation over the last 30 years or so. While some of these legislative provisions address the implications of the changing context of industrial relations in Ireland,[12]   **[2–08]**

---

[8] See, generally, McMahon and Binchy, *Irish Law of Torts* (3rd ed, Butterworths, Dublin, 2000).

[9] See, for example, *Bradley v CIE* [1976] IR 217. The duty of care owed to employees in the context of psychiatric injury sustained at work has been the subject of a number of important recent decisions; see chapter 9.

[10] See chapter 12 and, generally, Delany, *Equity and the Law of Trusts in Ireland* (4th ed, Thomson Round Hall, Dublin, 2007).

[11] Byrne and McCutcheon, *op.cit,* chapter 13.

[12] See, for example, the Industrial Relations (Amendment) Acts 2001-2004 (see chapter 11).

many others are mandated by EU law.[13] This has proved controversial on occasions, where the Irish government has had to sponsor employment legislation before the Oireachtas, which it had opposed at EU level.[14] It is also important to remember that, as we saw in chapter 1, much legislation has been driven (at both domestic and EU level) by the need to respond to contemporary labour market changes, such as the increased participation of women and foreign nationals in the workplace[15] and the increased incidence of "atypical" working arrangements (e.g. agency work, part-time work and other "non-standard" employment relationships).[16] As noted above, aspects of employment legislation may be deemed to be part of an employment contract and can be enforced as such: legislative acts may also lay down specific procedures to be followed in the event of a breach of contract.

[2–09]   Delegated legislation, such as regulations and statutory instruments, is important in some areas of employment law. Although Art 15.2.1 of the Constitution talks of the "sole and exclusive" legislative power of the Oireachtas, the courts have accepted that legislative power may be delegated in order to supply the necessary detail to facilitate the implementation of the principles and policies, which have been enacted by the Oireachtas.[17] Many important regulations have been made pursuant to health and safety legislation, for example.[18] By and large, the use of delegated legislation is relatively uncontroversial. One area of debate, however, relates to the practice of implementing major pieces of legislation originating in the EU through the passing of regulations rather than by way of primary legislation. This occurred, for example, in relation to the transposition of the 2001 Acquired Rights Directive,[19] which was implemented in Ireland by the European Communities (Protection of Employees on

---

[13] For example, the Organisation of Working Time Act 1997, the Protection of Employees (Part-Time Work) Act 2001 and the Protection of Employees (Fixed-Term Work) Act 2003. These acts transpose, respectively, Directive 93/104 of 23 November 1993 concerning certain aspects of the organisation of working time [1993] OJ L307/18, Directive 97/81 of 15 December 1997 concerning the Framework Agreement on part-time work concluded by ETUC, UNICE and CEEP [1997] OJ L14/9, and Directive 1999/70 of 28 June 1999 concerning the framework agreement on fixed-term work concluded by ETUC, UNICE and CEEP [1999] OJ L175/43.

[14] For example, the Employees (Provision of Information and Consultation) Act 2006; see Doherty, "Hard Law, Soft Edge? Information, Consultation and Partnership" (2008) 30(6) *Employee Relations* 603.

[15] See chapter 6 on family friendly legislation and chapter 7 on migrant workers.

[16] See chapter 3.

[17] *Cityview Press Ltd v An Chomhairle Oiliúna* [1980] IR 38. The delegate must be expressly conferred with the power by an Act of the Oireachtas since it does not possess any inherent law-making capacity and that power must be exercised within certain limits; *Laurentiu v Minister for Justice, Equality and Law Reform* [1999] 4 IR 26.

[18] See the Safety, Health and Welfare (Construction) Regulations 2006 (SI No 504 of 2006) made pursuant to the Safety, Health and Welfare at Work Act 2005, s 58.

[19] Directive 2001/23 of 12 March 2001 on the approximation of the laws of the Member States relating to the safeguarding of employees' rights in the event of transfers of undertakings, businesses or parts of undertakings or businesses [2001] OJ L82/16.

Transfer of Undertakings) Regulations 2003.[20] This has been criticised, in particular, because the process of passing such regulations is less transparent than that involved in passing Acts of the Oireachtas. Sections 3 and 4 of the European Communities Act 1972 allow a Minister to make regulations in order to implement, in domestic law, any act of the EU institutions where that act required effect to be given to them in this way. In effect, this means that the sections confer on a Minister the power to amend an Act of the Oireachtas (primary legislation) by means of regulations (secondary legislation).[21] This practice can also make it difficult for lawyers and others trying to establish what the relevant provisions in a given area are, as some EU measures are implemented by way of regulations and others via the passing of statutes.

The Constitution

The Constitution, as the superior source of domestic law, impacts on employment law in many ways. Any law can be declared invalid if it is found to contravene a constitutional provision. The Employment Equality Bill 1996, for example, was found to be repugnant to the Constitution on a number of grounds.[22] However, as Forde notes, the "extent to which the Constitution affects relations between employers and workers outside the industrial action and trade union sphere is largely unexplored territory".[23] He argues that this may be due to the fact that legislation has been enacted to cover many areas where employer or worker rights might be affected by constitutional provisions (equality and non-discrimination at work, for example). **[2–10]**

Nonetheless, there are a number of constitutional provisions of direct relevance to the employment relationship, including Art 40.1 (all citizens are to be treated as equal before the law), Art 40.3.2 (property rights), Art 40.6.1° (freedom of expression, assembly and association) and Art 44.2.3° (freedom of religion). Article 45 sets out certain social policy principles (including the right to an adequate means of livelihood in Art 45.2.i) but these are "directive" principles only intended for the general guidance of the Oireachtas and not subject to the jurisdiction of the courts. **[2–11]**

A number of important rights affecting the employment relationship have been identified under Article 40.3.1°, under which the State "guarantees in its laws to respect, and, as far as practicable, by its laws to defend and vindicate the personal rights of the citizen". This article has been used as a basis to identify and protect fundamental rights other than those expressly protected by the Constitution and a number of these "unenumerated" rights recognised by the courts are of particular significance to employment law. In fact, even prior to the clear declaration of the **[2–12]**

---

[20] SI No 131 of 2003. The 2001 Directive replaced Directive 77/187 of 14 February 1977 on the approximation of the laws of the Member States relating to the safeguarding of employees' rights in the event of transfers of undertakings, businesses or parts of undertakings or businesses [1977] OJ L61/26, which itself had been transposed in Ireland by way of regulations; the European Communities (Safeguarding of Employees' Rights on Transfer of Undertakings) Regulations 1980 (SI No 306 of 1980).

[21] Byrne and McCutcheon, *op.cit,* chapter 16. The validity of s 3 was upheld by the Supreme Court in *Meagher v Minister for Agriculture* [1994] 1 IR 329.

[22] *Re Employment Equality Bill 1996* [1997] 2 IR 321.

[23] Forde, *Employment Law* (2nd ed, Round Hall, Dublin, 2001), p 9.

concept of unremunerated personal rights in the *Ryan* case,[24] the courts had hinted at such an interpretation of Art 40.3.1° in a number of cases involving the right to earn a livelihood.[25] This right was explicitly endorsed in *Murphy v Stewart*.[26] By virtue of the guarantee of private property in Art 40.3, there is also a fundamental right to carry on and manage a business without excessive State interference. In *Re Employment Equality Bill 1996*,[27] a provision seeking to ensure that employers provide any necessary facilities for disabled employees was struck down on the basis that it transferred the cost of solving one of society's problems onto one particular group (employers): the impugned provision was held to be an unjust attack on an employer's property rights and right to earn a livelihood. The constitutional guarantee of fair procedures outlined in cases like *Glover v BLN Ltd*[28] is also highly significant in the employment context, particularly as it applies to issues of discipline and, especially, dismissal.[29] Finally, although it has been suggested that the courts have recognised an unenumerated right to strike in cases like *Brendan Dunne Ltd v Fitzpatrick*[30] this cannot be definitively said to be the case: what is clear is that the Constitution *does* impose limitations on any such action by reference to the constitutional rights of others.[31]

European Union Law

[2–13]   Reference has already been made above to the significance for employment law of legislative developments at EU level.[32] In subsequent chapters, we will look in detail at the impact of various significant EU directives and regulations. At this point it suffices

---

[24]   *Ryan v Attorney General* [1965] IR 294.

[25]   Hogan and Whyte, *The Irish Constitution* (4th ed, LexisNexis, Dublin, 2003), p 1414.

[26]   [1973] IR 97. See also *Murtagh Properties v Cleary* [1972] IR 330 and *Re Employment Equality Bill 1996* [1997] 2 IR 321.

[27]   *ibid.* See Gwynn Morgan, *A Judgment Too Far? Judicial Activism and the Constitution* (Cork University Press, Cork, 2001), p 36.

[28]   [1973] IR 388.

[29]   See chapter 10. Note that Forde points out that, even in countries that do not have written constitutions guaranteeing fundamental rights, courts also imply fair procedures into employment contracts, *op.cit*, p 10.

[30]   [1958] IR 29.

[31]   Kerr and Whyte, *Irish Trade Union Law* (Professional Books Ltd, Abingdon, 1985), pp 246-247.

[32]   The "three-pillar" structure of the EU established by the Maastricht Treaty resulted in the creation of two pillars—Common Foreign and Security Policy and Justice and Home Affairs—which were of little real relevance to Irish employment law. The pillar structure was formally abolished on the entry into force of the Lisbon Treaty on 1 December 2009. As a result of the amendments introduced by that Treaty, the European Union now has a single legal personality and is founded on two treaties, the amended Treaty on European Union (the new TEU) and the Treaty on the Functioning of the European Union (TFEU). The Treaty of Lisbon renumbered the articles of the existing Treaties. As a result, case law of the Court of Justice (previously the European Court of Justice; ECJ) that dates from before the entering into force of the Treaty of Amsterdam (1 May 1999) refers to Treaty articles by their original Treaty of Rome numbering and case law after that date refers to Treaty articles by their Amsterdam numbering. In this book, we are going to refer to Treaty articles by their *new* Treaty of Lisbon numbering (referring also to their Amsterdam numbering). We are also going to refer to European Union (EU) law throughout (as opposed to European Community-EC-law). See, further, Craig and de Búrca, *EU Law: Text, Cases and Materials* (4th ed, Oxford University Press, Oxford, 2008), chapter 1.

to note a few important issues in relation to EU law.[33] First, as we will see in chapters 5 and 6, EU law has been an important source of rights in the area of equality and non-discrimination at work, most notably in relation to gender equality. For example, Art 157TFEU (ex-Art 141EC) provides for equal pay for equal work as between men and women. The provision for gender equality has been strongly enforced (and developed) by the European Court of Justice (ECJ). In *Defrenne v Sabena (No 2)*[34] an airhostess invoked the provision in an equal pay claim before the Belgian courts. The principle of equal pay was recognised by the ECJ as a fundamental right that served both an economic *and* a social function; namely to ensure social progress and to seek the constant improvement of the living and working conditions of the Union's citizens. More recently, equality legislation at EU level has moved to encompass many situations where there is potential for discrimination outside of the field of gender; for example, in relation to racial or ethnic origin,[35] religion, disability, age and sexual orientation,[36] as well as part-time and fixed-term work.[37]

Secondly, one of the core objectives of EU law is to provide for the free movement of labour within the Union: the pursuit of this objective has obviously resulted in the granting of significant rights to EU citizens who wish to work in other Members States, as we will see in chapter 7.[38] Thirdly, important legislation has been enacted in relation to other areas of social policy that impact on employment relations, such as employee rights on the restructuring of enterprises and health and safety and working conditions.[39] Finally, in the area of social policy the Treaty on the Functioning of the European Union, under Arts 151–156 (ex-Arts 136–140EC) grants the European social partners a unique legislative role not granted to other interest groups. The social partners are consulted twice (compulsorily) on potential EU social policy legislation, they are in a position to suspend (for nine months) the legislative procedure by jointly

[2–14]

---

[33] See, generally, Barnard, *EC Employment Law* (3rd ed, Oxford University Press, Oxford, 2006).

[34] Case 43/75 [1976] ECR 455.

[35] Directive 2000/43 of 29 June 2000 implementing the principle of equal treatment between persons irrespective of racial or ethnic origin [2000] OJ L180/22.

[36] Directive 2000/78 of 27 November 2000 establishing a general framework for equal treatment in employment and occupation [2000] OJ L303/16. This directive addresses discrimination on the specified grounds in the workplace. There is a proposal for a new directive extending the principle to also encompass non-discrimination outside of the labour market context, see Directive proposal SEC (2008) 2180.

[37] Above, n 13.

[38] See Art 45TFEU (ex-Art 39EC) and Directive 2004/38 of 29 April 2004 on the right of citizens of the Union and their family members to move and reside freely within the territory of the Member States [2004] OJ L229/35.

[39] See Directive 2001/23 of 12 March 2001 on the approximation of the laws of the Member States relating to the safeguarding of employees' rights in the event of transfers of undertakings, businesses or parts of undertakings or businesses [2001] OJ L82/16; Directive 98/59 of 20 July 1998 on the approximation of the laws of the Member States relating to collective redundancies [1998] OJ L225/16; Directive 80/987 of 20 October 1980 on the approximation of the laws of the Member States relating to the protection of employees in the event of the insolvency of their employer [1980] OJ L283/23; Directive 89/391 of 12 June 1989 on the introduction of measures to encourage improvements in the safety and health of workers at work [1989] OJ L183/1; and Directive 2003/881 of 4 November 2003 concerning certain aspects of the organisation of working time [2003] OJ L299/9.

exercising their right to enter into negotiations with a view to self-regulation[40] and, most significantly, they are entitled to enter into agreements, that, if endorsed by the Council, can be made binding on all Member States.[41]

[2–15] By virtue of Art 29.4 of the Irish Constitution, EU law takes primacy over any conflicting provision of national law, a principle that has been definitively accepted by the Irish courts.[42] In areas of employment law where the Union has competence to act, therefore, EU law is supreme.[43] Significant also is the role of the ECJ.[44] Article 267TFEU (ex-Art 234EC) permits a form of case stated[45] to the ECJ from any Irish court or tribunal in order to enable the domestic court or tribunal to reach a decision in accordance with the correct view of EU law. The term "tribunal" has been given a broad interpretation by the ECJ[46] and certainly includes important domestic employ-ment tribunals like the Labour Court and the Employment Appeals Tribunal.[47] By virtue of the nature of EU law, each domestic court or tribunal is also empowered to apply decisions of the ECJ even without the need for a preliminary reference, so that all the decisions of the ECJ regarding any area of EU law are binding precedents which must be followed in domestic courts.[48]

The European Convention on Human Rights

[2–16] Ireland was a founder member of the Council of Europe, established in 1949, which drafted the European Convention on Human Rights and Fundamental Freedoms (ECHR) in 1950. The Council was one of a number of institutions, including the United Nations, set up in the aftermath of World War II seeking to promote and protect human rights. Article 29.6 of the Irish Constitution, however, provides that "no international agreement shall be part of the domestic law of the State save as may be determined by the Oireachtas". International agreements, like the ECHR, do not, therefore, have any legal force in Ireland unless they have been incorporated into

---

[40] Art 154TFEU (ex-Art 138EC).

[41] Art 155TFEU (ex-Art 139EC). Two successfully concluded Art 155 agreements, which were later translated into directives, related to part-time work and fixed-term work; above, n 13.

[42] *Crotty v An Taoiseach* [1987] IR 713.

[43] Note that in Case C-268/06 *Impact v Minister of Agriculture* [2008] 2 CMLR 1265 the ECJ held that national courts or tribunals (in this case, the Labour Court) were required to apply directly effective provisions of EU law even if they had not been given express jurisdiction to do so under domestic law.

[44] Note that, under Art 251TFEU (ex-Art 221EC), the renamed Court of Justice of the European Union now comprises the Court of Justice (formerly the European Court of Justice), the General Court (formerly the Court of First Instance) and the Specialised Courts (formerly the Judicial Panels).

[45] This is a procedure whereby a lower court or tribunal can seek the opinion of a higher court in relation to a specific point of law. Once the latter has given its opinion, the matter is normally remitted to the referring court or tribunal for decision.

[46] The body or tribunal must exercise a *judicial function*, i.e. take legally binding decisions on the rights and duties of individuals, and exercise a *compulsory* jurisdiction; see Case C-516/99 *Walter Schmid* [2002] ECR I-4573 and Case 246/80 *Broekmeulen* [1981] ECR 2311.

[47] The situation of a body like the Equality Authority is less clear; see Fahey, *Practice and Procedure in Preliminary References to Europe* (FirstLaw, Dublin, 2007), pp 39-40.

[48] European Communities Act 1972, s 2. Case C-268/06 *Impact v Minister of Agriculture* [2008] 2 CMLR 1265.

domestic law by means of an Act of the Oireachtas. In 2003, the European Convention on Human Rights Act incorporated the ECHR into Irish law. The Act puts an obligation on "organs of the State" to perform their functions in a manner which is compatible with the Convention's provisions.[49] The term "organs of the State" includes any body established by law or which exercises any of the powers of the State, for example, local authorities, health boards and tribunals (like the Employment Appeals Tribunal). The Irish courts are obliged to interpret and apply any statutory provision or rule of law in a manner that is compatible with the country's obligations under the Convention.[50] Under s 5 of the Act the High Court and the Supreme Court have the power to make a declaration that a statutory provision is incompatible with the State's obligations under the Convention. However, this will not automatically mean that the law in question is invalid. The law may continue in force, but the Taoiseach must bring all such orders to the attention of the Oireachtas within 21 days.[51]

Given that, under the 2003 Act, the Convention is to be subject to the Constitution, the extent to which its incorporation will impact on Irish law remains to be seen. In any case, it has been noted by some commentators that the Convention itself deals primarily with civil and political rights and, so, has only a very limited direct impact on employment law.[52] However, there are a number of Convention provisions which could impact on the employment relationship: Art 6 (right to a fair trial);[53] Art 8 (right to privacy, family life and correspondence);[54] Art 9 (freedom of thought, conscience and religion); Art 10 (freedom of expression); and Art 14 (non-discrimination on grounds of sex, race, colour, language, religion, political or other opinion, national or social origin, association with a national minority, property, birth or other status). Article 11 of the Convention deals explicitly with employment, providing for the right to freedom of association with others, including the right to form and to join trade unions. We will look at the implications of this for collective employment law in chapter 11. Lastly, the decisions of the European Court of Human Rights are of persuasive precedential value in Irish courts and are treated as highly significant by the ECJ.[55]

[2–17]

---

[49] European Convention on Human Rights Act 2003, s 3.

[50] European Convention on Human Rights Act 2003, s 2.

[51] European Convention on Human Rights Act 2003, s 5(3).

[52] Palmer, "Human Rights Implications of Labour Law" (2000) 59 CLJ 168. See also Hogan, "The European Convention on Human Rights Act 2003" (2006) EPL 12(3) 331. Ireland has also ratified the European Social Charter, another Council Of Europe treaty, that explicitly protects social and economic rights (such as the right to work and the right to fair remuneration); the revised Charter of 1996 has not, however, been incorporated into domestic law. In addition, Ireland is party to a number of International Labour Organisation (ILO) Conventions, including ILO Convention No 98 Concerning the Application of the Principles of the Right of Organise and to Bargain Collectively and ILO Convention No 111 concerning Discrimination in Respect of Employment and Occupation ; see www.ilo.org. For a critical appraisal of the system for setting and enforcing international labour standards, see Creighton, "The Future of Labour Law: Is there a Role for International Labour Standards" in *The Future of Labour Law* (Barnard *et al* eds, Hart, Oxford, 2004), pp 253-275.

[53] This might impact on disciplinary procedures at work, for example.

[54] This could have implications for employers who wish to administer medical tests, for example.

[55] See Case 222/84 *Johnston v Chief Constable of the Royal Ulster Constabulary* [1986] ECR 1651.

Other Sources

[2–18]   It is important to note the existence of two other sources of employment rights, which, while they do not themselves enjoy the full force of law, have a significant influence in shaping Irish employment law.

[2–19]   *Codes of practice* are significant where they exist, as they can be taken into account in various ways by courts and tribunals. One of the most important functions of the Labour Relations Commission is the preparation of codes of practice under s 42 of the Industrial Relations Act 1990.[56] Codes are prepared, primarily, to give guidance to employers, employees and their representatives on the general principles which apply in a given area. So, for example, the Code of Practice on Grievance and Disciplinary Procedures[57] contains general guidelines on the application of grievance and disciplinary procedures and the promotion of best practice in giving effect to such procedures and is of particular relevance to situations of individual representation. This Code is cited regularly by the Labour Court in its recommendations and determinations and, in this, way represents an important "quasi-legal" source of employment rights. In cases taken under the 2001–2004 Industrial Relations (Amendment) Acts, for example, several legally binding Labour Court recommendations required the employer to comply with the provisions of the Code.[58] As we will see below, other bodies like the Equality Authority and the Health and Safety Authority also have an important role in preparing codes of practice.

[2–20]   A final area to consider is that of *social partnership*. Since 1987 a series of tripartite social pacts were concluded between the social partners (the government, unions, employers and some other representative interest groups): *The Programme for National Recovery* (PNR, 1987–1990); *The Program for Social and Economic Progress* (PESP, 1990–1993); *The Program for Competitiveness and Work* (PCW, 1993–1996); *Partnership 2000* (P2000, 1996–2000); *The Program for Prosperity and Fairness* (PPF, 2000–2003); *Sustaining Progress* (SP, 2003–2006); and *Towards 2016* (agreed in 2006). The contents of the agreements focus primarily on issues of pay (particularly in the public sector), tax reform and a range of other socio-economic issues.[59] Although, at the time of writing, the future of the process is somewhat uncertain, its legacy in terms of employment law remains important. This is because, through partnership, a number of legislative measures have been agreed, which were then progressed through the normal legislative process; these include legislation on the national minimum wage, trade union bargaining rights, collective redundancies and employment rights compliance.[60]

---

[56] See further below.

[57] SI No 146 of 2000.

[58] Doherty, "Representation, Bargaining and the Law: Where Next For the Unions?" (2009) 60(4) NILQ 383. See, further, chapter 11.

[59] See Roche, "Social Partnership in Ireland and New Social Pacts" (2007) 46 (3) *Industrial Relations* 395.

[60] Respectively the National Minimum Wage Act 2000, the Industrial Relations (Amendment) Acts 2001-2004, the Protection of Employment (Exceptional Collective Redundancies and Related Matters) Act 2007 and the Employment Law Compliance Bill 2008. At the time of writing the latter has not yet been passed into law.

III. The Institutional Framework

If a claimant wishes to pursue an action in respect of an alleged wrong related to his or **[2–21]** her employment, he or she can, of course, access the courts. However, a number of tribunals have been specifically established to deal with employment issues.[61] The nature of the claim will determine where an action should be taken, as particular statutes will indicate where the claim should begin and whether a choice of fora is available to the claimant.[62] A claimant can generally only claim a remedy in *one* forum. Nevertheless, the multiplicity of possible fora in which a claim can be initiated undoubtedly makes the system of employment rights quite difficult to navigate.[63]

It is important to remember, too, that a feature of contemporary employment, in **[2–22]** particular through human resource management (HRM) policies, is greater innovation in how workplace grievances and disputes are managed.[64] Thus, many employers will have in place various alternative dispute resolution (ADR) systems to attempt to deal with disputes "in-house": these can include interest-based bargaining systems, mediation, conciliation or arbitration.[65] In unionised workplaces, union-management bargaining or negotiation structures may be in place and employees may be able to rely on the assistance of trade union representatives in dealing with employment disputes.[66]

Finally, an important issue emerging in relation to the employment tribunals relates to **[2–23]** the manner in which they operate. As we will see below, procedure before the tribunals is less formal than would be the case before the regular courts. Nevertheless, the tribunals are required to comply with the constitutional guarantees of natural justice (including the guarantee of fair procedures) laid down in cases like *Kiely v Minister for Social Welfare*.[67] The tension between maintaining an informal, speedy and

---

[61] See Teague, "Path Dependency and Comparative Industrial Relations: The Case of Conflict Resolution Systems in Ireland and Sweden" (2009) 47(3) *British Journal of Industrial Relations* 499. See, also, Gennard, "UK Industrial Relations State Agencies" (2010) 32 (1) *Employee Relations* 5.

[62] As statutory bodies deriving their jurisdiction from specific pieces of legislation, employment tribunals have no inherent jurisdiction; see Kerr and McGreal, "Practice and Procedure in Employment Law" in *Employment Law* (Regan ed, Tottel, Dublin, 2009), p 827.

[63] Note that the Irish Times reported in early 2010 that the employment dispute resolution agencies had brought to the attention of the Minister of State for Labour Affairs the fact that they were concerned at the increase in "dispute shopping" by applicants (i.e. the practice of lodging a complaint with a second resolution body following a rejection of a claim by another body); "Agencies Warn of 'Dispute Shopping'" *The Irish Times*, 15 January 2010.

[64] Teague and Thomas, *Employment Dispute Resolution and Standard Setting in the Republic of Ireland* (LRC, Dublin, 2008), pp 19-22.

[65] See Vahey, "Conflict in the Workplace and the Role of Mediation" (2009) 6(4) IELJ 104.

[66] See Roche, *The Changing Landscape of Industrial Relations in the Republic of Ireland* (2005) available at: http://www.lrc.ie/viewdoc.asp?m =u&fn =/documents/publications/research conference/SeminarNov2005.htm.

[67] [1977] IR 267. See *also J & E Davy v Financial Services Ombudsman* [2008] 2 ILRM 507, where Charleton J noted that all administrative tribunals are required to act fairly and in accordance with the requirements of constitutional justice. They are entitled to latitude as to how they order their procedures but they may not imperil a fair resolution of a conflict in consequence of adopting a procedure which infringes fundamental principles of constitutional fairness; *Gallagher v The Revenue Commissioners* (No 2) [1995] 1 IR 55 at p 76 *per* Hamilton CJ.

inexpensive means of processing employment dispute claims and ensuring that procedures conform with constitutional principles has become one with which the various tribunals are increasingly grappling.

The Employment Appeals Tribunal

[2–24]   The Tribunal was established under s 39 of the Redundancy Payments Act 1967 and, up to 1977, was known as the Redundancy Appeals Tribunal.[68] In 1977, under s 18 of the Unfair Dismissals Act 1977, the name of the Tribunal was changed to the Employment Appeals Tribunal (EAT). The Tribunal was originally set up to adjudicate on disputes about redundancy between employees and employers and between employees or employers and the Minister for Labour or a Deciding Officer. The scope of the Tribunal was extended over the years and now it deals with disputes under the following legislation:

- Redundancy Payments Acts 1967–2007;
- Minimum Notice and Terms of Employment Acts 1973–2001;
- Unfair Dismissals Acts 1977–2007;
- Maternity Protection Acts 1994 and 2004;
- Protection of Employees (Employers' Insolvency) Acts 1984–2001;
- Payment of Wages Act 1991;
- Terms of Employment (Information) Acts 1994–2001;
- Adoptive Leave Acts 1995 and 2005;
- Protection of Young Persons (Employment) Act 1996;
- Organisation of Working Time Act 1997;
- Parental Leave Act 1998;
- Protections for Persons Reporting Child Abuse Act 1998;
- European Communities (Protection of Employment) Regulations 2000;
- European Communities (Protection of Employees on Transfer of Undertakings) Regulations 2003;
- Carer's Leave Act 2001;
- Competition Acts 2002–2006;
- Civil Service Regulation (Amendment) Act 2005;
- Chemicals Act 2008.

[2–25]   The Tribunal presently consists of a Chairman and 43 Vice-Chairmen and a panel of 80 other members, 40 nominated by the Irish Congress of Trade Unions (ICTU) and 40 by organisations representative of employers.[69] The Tribunal acts in Divisions, each consisting of either the Chairman or a Vice-Chairman and two other members, one drawn from the employers' side of the panel and one from the trade union side. The Tribunal is a quasi-judicial body. Its sole function is to adjudicate on disputes about individual employment rights that arise either during the course of employment or on the termination of the employment relationship.[70]

---

[68] See, generally, www.eatribunal.ie.

[69] http://www.eatribunal.ie/en/about_members.aspx.

[70] Doherty, "Institutional Challenge: Tribunals, Industrial Relations and the Law" (2009) 2 ELRI 70.

In some areas, the EAT has first instance jurisdiction. These include claims arising from the termination of the employment relationship under legislation relating to unfair dismissal,[71] redundancy[72] and minimum notice.[73] The Tribunal is, however, also an appellate body, adjudicating on appeals from the recommendations or decisions of Rights Commissioners under various pieces of employment rights legislation.[74] Unusually, claims for unfair dismissal can be made in the first instance *either* to the Tribunal *or* to a Rights Commissioner and in the latter case an appeal lies from the decision of a Rights Commissioner to the Tribunal.[75]

In 2008, over 5,400 cases were referred to the Tribunal, a massive 72 percent increase on 2007.[76] The EAT's annual report shows that the bulk of the Tribunal's work continues to be complaints under the Unfair Dismissals legislation,[77] claims under the Minimum Notice and Terms of Employment Acts, claims under the Redundancy Payments Acts and claims under Working Time legislation. Teague and Thomas note that it is a popular misconception that the Tribunal awards very high compensation to those who successfully claim unfair dismissal.[78] In fact, according to the Annual Report the average compensation awarded by the Tribunal for such claims in 2008 was just €11,476. However, a large number of claims are settled without a hearing. Anecdotal evidence from practitioners indicates many of these claims are settled for large sums of money.

[2–26]

The EAT aims to offer a speedy, inexpensive and relatively informal means for the adjudication of employment rights disputes under the various pieces of legislation that come within the Tribunal's remit. As a result, procedures before the EAT are not as formal as would be the case before a regular court.[79] A party to an application may "appear and be heard in person or be represented by counsel or solicitor or by a representative of a trade union or by an employers' association or, with the leave of the Tribunal, by any other person".[80] Any party to a case may have one or more representative(s) acting on his or her behalf. At the hearing, a party to an application may be invited to make an opening statement, call witnesses, cross-examine any witnesses called by any other party, give evidence on his/her own behalf and address

[2–27]

---

[71] Unfair Dismissals Act 1977, s 8(2).

[72] Redundancy Payments Act 1967, s 39(15).

[73] Minimum Notice and Terms of Employment Act 1973, s 11(1).

[74] See, for example, Payment of Wages Act 1991, s 7(1); Maternity Protection Act 1994, s 33(1) and Protection of Young Persons (Employment) Act 1996, s 19(2). See, generally, Kerr, *Employment Rights Legislation* (2nd ed, Round Hall, Dublin, 2006).

[75] Unfair Dismissals Act 1977, ss 8(2) and 9(1).

[76] EAT Annual Report 2008 available at http://www.eatribunal.ie/en/annual_reports.aspx.

[77] The EAT estimates that 85 percent of its total workload in terms of actual "time spent on cases" at hearings relates to unfair dismissal claims.

[78] *op.cit*, p 147. However, it may be the case that a trend is emerging towards the making of larger awards for former senior executives deemed to have been treated unfairly, which might reflect the straitened economic climate in the late 2000s; see, for example, *Mulligan v J2 Global (Ireland) Ltd* (UD 1369/2008) where the claimant was awarded €175,000 by the EAT and *Pickering v Microsoft Ireland Operations Ltd* [2006] ELR 65, where the High Court (in a constructive dismissal claim) awarded the plaintiff €340,000.

[79] See, generally, Kerr and McGreal, *op.cit.*

[80] Redundancy (Redundancy Appeals Tribunal) Regulations 1968 (SI No 24 of 1968).

the Tribunal at the close of the evidence.[81] The Tribunal has power to take evidence on oath and may administer oaths to persons attending as witnesses.[82] Penalties are prescribed by law for wilful and corrupt perjury by any person convicted in a court of law of wilfully giving false evidence or wilfully and corruptly swearing anything, which is false, at a hearing of the Tribunal.[83]

[2–28] A determination of the Tribunal is recorded in a document signed by the chairman and sealed with the seal of the Tribunal. Written determinations of the Tribunal are final and conclusive subject only to the appropriate avenue of legal appeal. So, for example, a determination of the Tribunal on any question referred to it under the Redundancy Payments Acts,[84] the Minimum Notice and Terms of Employment Acts,[85] or the Protection of Employees (Employers' Insolvency) Acts,[86] may be appealed by a dissatisfied party to the High Court on a point of law. A decision of the Tribunal given on appeal from a Rights Commissioner under the Payment of Wages Act 1991,[87] the Terms of Employment (Information) Act 1994,[88] the Protection of Young Persons (Employment) Act 1996,[89] the Parental Leave Act 1998,[90] the Maternity Protection Act 1994,[91] the Adoptive Leave Act 1995[92] and the Carer's Leave Act 2001,[93] may also be appealed on a point of law to the High Court.[94] Any such appeal to the High Court must be brought within 21 days of the date on which a copy of the decision of the Tribunal was given to the party appealing subject, however, to the proviso that the time within which the summons may be issued may be extended by the High Court.[95]

[2–29] A determination of the Tribunal under the Unfair Dismissals Acts may be appealed to the Circuit Court by a party within six weeks from the date of service of the determination.[96] Appeals to the Circuit Court are held *de novo* (that is, by way of a full re-hearing of the case). The Tribunal may not award costs against any party to an application except where, in its opinion, a party has acted frivolously or vexatiously.[97] Legal aid, under the Civil Legal Aid Act 1995,[98] may only be granted in relation to *court* proceedings and, therefore, not before tribunals like the EAT.

---

[81] *ibid.* These regulations are extended to most of the employment rights legislation.

[82] Redundancy Payments Act 1967, s 39(17)(a).

[83] Redundancy Payments Act 1967, s 39(17)(b).

[84] Redundancy Payments Act 1967, s 39(14).

[85] Minimum Notice and Terms of Employment Act 1973, s 11(2).

[86] Protection of Employees (Employers' Insolvency) Act 1984, s 9(5).

[87] s 7(4)(b).

[88] s 8(4)(b).

[89] s 19(4)(b).

[90] s 20(2).

[91] s 34(2).

[92] s 36(2).

[93] s 23(2).

[94] See Kerr and McGreal, *op.cit,* pp 865-866, where the authors outline in detail the relevant legislative provisions that allow for a question of law to be referred to the High Court.

[95] *ibid.*

[96] Unfair Dismissals (Amendment) Act 1993, s 11(1).

[97] Regulation 19(2) Redundancy (Redundancy Appeals Tribunal) Regulations 1968 (SI No. 24 of 1968).

[98] s 28(8).

In 2007, an EAT Procedures Revision Working Group was established to consider best **[2–30]** practice in improving the service the Tribunal provides to its client base. The Review Group reported later that year and identified a range of areas where improvements could be made to the Tribunal's services.[99] Key amongst its proposals is a recommendation that a preliminary process be introduced prior to the substantive hearing, which will streamline the process and allow maximum opportunity for settlement. This would take the form of a pre-examination of each case by a member of the Tribunal. All parties would be required to attend and give an outline of their respective positions. It further recommended that the objective of the procedures should be to ensure that they are speedy, inexpensive, fair and, as far as possible, informal. Other recommendations include: that Tribunal determinations should be issued without undue delay, made publicly available on the web and be legally consistent; that the Tribunal be given power to issue "consent determinations", i.e. to embody settlement agreements in a Tribunal determination thus rendering them enforceable in like manner to regular determinations of the Tribunal; that a standing Rules Review Group be established which would conduct periodic review of the procedures; and that time-limits be harmonised across all the pieces of legislation providing for the reference of disputes to the EAT.

A major criticism of the EAT relates to it being overly legalistic.[100] Browne, for **[2–31]** example, found that parties with legal representation tended to do better than those without.[101] Teague and Thomas report that approximately two-thirds of those appearing before the Tribunal in 2006 had legal representation.[102] This is an ongoing issue as an excessive focus on legalistic procedures inevitably impedes the mission of the EAT to provide a speedy, fair, inexpensive and informal means for individuals to seek remedies for alleged infringements of their statutory rights. The Report of the EAT review group[103] sums up the problem as follows:

> "the Tribunal has moved very substantially from the more informal inquisitor-ial model to a more long drawn out, over legalistic, adversarial, costly and, especially from the perspective of employees and unions, intimidating environment... it was never envisaged when the Tribunal was established that participation in what was supposed to be a relatively informal tribunal would frequently involve delays and adjournments and legal representation (counsel and solicitor) on both sides with court-like procedures (evidence on oath, examination, cross examination, re-examination and the adoption of rules of evidence) becoming the norm... it puts employees, especially those without union representation, and smaller firms which cannot afford legal representa-tion, at a distinct disadvantage. The frequent delays in Hearings and the cost of legal representation mean that the redress options of reinstatement or

---

[99] The report is available at: http://www.entemp.ie/publications/employment/2007/EATProceduresrevisiongroup.pdf.

[100] Doherty, "Institutional Challenge: Tribunals, Industrial Relations and the Law" (2009) 2 ELRI 70.

[101] See Browne, *The Juridification of the Employment Relationship* (Avebury, Aldershot, 1994).

[102] Teague and Thomas, *op.cit*, p 140.

[103] *op.cit*, p 3.

reengagement become less practicable and the maximum permissible award of two years' salary (subject to mitigation of loss) is eaten up in legal fees. It is a concern that over 70 percent of successful claimants, according to EAT Annual Report data, feel the need to have legal representation, the cost of which they must pay for from their own resources...".

However, the report goes on to note that:

> "the Tribunal is not bound to fully adopt court procedures or to strictly follow the rules of evidence in all cases...the Tribunal is much less formalised than a court and is helpful to all parties and all the members of the Tribunal are fully committed to fairness in process and outcome. For example, the Tribunal is especially careful to ensure that unrepresented parties are dealt with fairly and it adopts a more proactive and inquisitorial role in this situation. Tribunal proceedings are, however, frequently ones at which personal or professional character and reputation are at risk and the natural and constitutional rights of parties to vindicate their good names are reflected in SI No 24 of 1968 which provides for legal representation and cross-examination... While the Tribunal has no mediation role under its procedures, it does encourage settlement between the parties where it sees that it might be achieved...".[104]

[2–32] Research on the operation of the EAT, carried out by Teague and Hann, reported some interesting results in relation to "legalism" at the Tribunal.[105] They found that Irish nationals are disproportionately likely to appoint a solicitor while non-Irish nationals are more likely to be represented by a trade union official. Moreover, when an employee elects to be represented by a solicitor the response of the employer invariably is also to employ legal representation. They conclude that, given that employees who use representation are more likely to receive higher compensation, it is likely that the trend towards having legal representation will continue.

[2–33] The nature of the disputes with which the EAT must deal often involve the protection and vindication of important rights (claims relating to unfair dismissal in particular) and so it may not be surprising that the growth in employment legislation, the decline in trade union density and a more rights-based approach to the employment relationship has led to the growth of legalism at the Tribunal. However, the EAT must ensure that it does not become a "cold house" for litigants (on both sides) by approximating too closely a court of law. If it be otherwise, the very existence and continuing usefulness of such a tribunal must be called into question.[106]

The Equality Tribunal

[2–34] The Equality Tribunal is an impartial, quasi-judicial body set up under s 75 of the Employment Equality Act 1998 to decide, or mediate, complaints under three pieces of

---

[104] *ibid*, p 4.

[105] Reported in *Industrial Relations News*; "Employment Tribunal Holding Up Well in New Era of Individual Rights" (2008) 25 IRN.

[106] Doherty, "Institutional Challenge: Tribunals, Industrial Relations and the Law" (2009) 2 ELRI 70, p 78.

equality legislation: the Employment Equality Acts 1998–2008, the Equal Status Acts 2000–2008 and the Pensions Acts 1990–2004.[107] The Tribunal was originally know as the "Office of the Director of Equality Investigations", but was renamed under s 30 of the Equality Act 2004. Under the same legislation, the title of "Director of Equality Investigations" was changed to "Director of the Equality Tribunal". In addition to the Director, the Tribunal consists of Equality Officers, who consider and decide cases brought under equality legislation, as well as trained mediators.[108]

The Equality Tribunal's principal role is the investigation and mediation of complaints of discrimination in relation to employment and in relation to access to goods and services, disposal of property and certain aspects of education. As a result of s 46 of the Equality Act 2004, the Tribunal now also hears discriminatory dismissal claims: these were originally heard by the Labour Court under s 77(2) of the 1998 Act. If an employee who has been dismissed has referred the case of the dismissal to the Director of the Equality Tribunal under the equality legislation and either a settlement has been reached by mediation, or the Tribunal has begun an investigation, the employee is not entitled to seek redress under the Unfair Dismissals Acts in respect of the dismissal unless the Director, having completed the investigation, directs otherwise.[109] The processing of a claim both under unfair dismissals legislation and by a Rights Commissioner, or the Labour Court under industrial relations legislation, is prohibited. Note, however, that the Director can recommend (after an investigation is complete) that the case proceed under the unfair dismissals legislation: this may occur where the Director feels that the claimant was unfairly dismissed but not discriminated against. An action for wrongful dismissal at common law also precludes the taking of an action under the equality legislation.[110] **[2–35]**

The protection against discrimination applies to all nine grounds on which discrimination is prohibited under the equality legislation.[111] Where a complaint of discrimination is upheld, redress must be awarded.[112] An investigation is a quasi-judicial process carried out by a Tribunal Equality Officer, who will consider submissions from both parties before arranging a joint hearing, or hearings, of the case to enable him or her to reach a decision in the matter.[113] Any person who believes that he or she may have experienced discrimination may write to the person who may have discriminated against him or her asking for certain information, which **[2–36]**

---

[107] The last mentioned case arises where an employer fails to comply with the principle of equal treatment in relation to occupational benefit or pensions schemes. Claims of discrimination in relation to licensed premises are now dealt with in the District Court, under the Intoxicating Liquor Act 2003. See, generally, www.equalitytribunal.ie.

[108] The Director can appoint staff to be Equality Officers, mediators or both; s 75(4) Employment Equality Act 1998.

[109] Employment Equality Act 1998, s 101(2)(b) (as amended by Equality Act 2004, ss 42 and 46). Note that under the Unfair Dismissals legislation, one year's service is required before a claim can be made (except for pregnancy-related claims); this is not required under the Equality legislation (see chapter 10).

[110] Employment Equality Act 1998, s 101(4) (as amended by Equality Act 2004, s 42).

[111] See chapter 5.

[112] See chapter 12.

[113] Employment Equality Act 1998, s 79 (as amended by Equality Act 2004, ss 35 and 46).

will assist in deciding whether to refer a claim. Employers are not obliged to reply to any such requests, but an Equality Officer may draw such inferences as seem appropriate from an employer failing to reply or supplying false, misleading or inadequate information.[114] Investigations are conducted by trained Equality Officers, who have extensive powers to enter premises and to obtain information to enable them to conduct the investigation.[115] Hearings are held in private[116] and are inquisitorial (rather than adversarial) in that the Equality Officer will direct the hearing and can ask questions of the parties and any witnesses.[117] In *County Louth VEC v Equality Tribunal*[118] McGovern J held that an Equality Officer was entitled to run hearings under the legislation as he or she saw fit, provided that the hearing complied with the principles of natural and constitutional justice, emphasising that a hearing before the Tribunal is not a hearing in a court of law with all the formality that that would entail. Here, the VEC had sought a judicial review of the Officer's direction that a number of witnesses, other than the applicant's principal witnesses, be excluded from the hearing of a retired teacher's discrimination claim. McGovern J said he could easily understand how an Equality Officer might regard the exclusion of witnesses as a reasonable procedure, on the basis that complainants might feel intimidated by the employees against whom the complaint was being made were they all present in the same room. This would be permissible as long as the employees complained about were aware of the case being made against them and had an opportunity to confront the accuser and cross-examine him.

[2–37]   Decisions are binding and are published on the Tribunal's website. A party before the Tribunal may represent himself or herself or be represented by "any individual or body authorised by the party".[119] The Tribunal may not award costs, other than where it is of the opinion that a person is obstructing or impeding an investigation: that person may be ordered to pay a specified amount in respect of the travelling or other expenses reasonably incurred by another in connection with the investigation or appeal.[120]

[2–38]   Section 74 of the 1998 Act[121] prohibits the victimisation of an employee by the employer, which occurs as a result of the employee having made a complaint, supported a complaint, been used as a comparator, having been a witness, having opposed an unlawful act under the legislation or having given notice of an intention to

---

[114] Employment Equality Act 1998, s 81 (as amended by Equality Act 2004, s 46).

[115] Employment Equality Act 1998, s 94. The constitutionality of this section (originally Employment Equality Bill 2006, s 58) was upheld in *Re Employment Equality Bill 1996* [1997] 2 IR 321, where the Supreme Court held that the powers granted were reasonably necessary to enable the effective carrying out of investigations for the purpose of enforcing the relevant provisions of the legislation. It had been questioned whether the section was repugnant to Art 40.5 of the Constitution (which guarantees the inviolability of every citizen's dwelling).

[116] Employment Equality Act 1998, s 79(2).

[117] Kerr and McGreal, *op.cit,* p 845.

[118] [2009] IEHC 370.

[119] Employment Equality Act 1998, s 77(11) (as substituted by Equality Act 2004, s 32).

[120] Employment Equality Act 1998, s 99A (as inserted by Equality Act 2004, s 41).

[121] As amended by Equality Act 2004, s 29.

take a complaint. Equality Officers have stressed that victimisation is to be dealt with harshly:

> "the victimisation of a person for having in good faith taken a claim under the equality legislation is very serious as it could have the impact of undermining the effectiveness of the legislation and is completely unacceptable".[122]

Under s 98 of the 1998 Act dismissal of an employee in circumstances amounting to victimisation is a criminal offence, punishable by a fine.[123]

An innovation under the equality legislation allows the Director at any stage, with the consent of both parties, to appoint an Equality Mediation Officer, if the Director feels the case might be resolved in this way.[124] Mediation is used to assist the parties themselves, with the aid of an impartial third party, to reach a mutually acceptable agreement. Mediated agreements are binding and confidential. This provision represents an attempt to encourage the wider usage of alternative dispute resolution systems and procedures that can result in a speedier and less expensive resolution of the issues. This can result in a "win-win" situation, in that the settlement must be acceptable to both parties, and puts the parties themselves (rather than an adjudicator) in control of the outcome. Importantly, since 2004, the Director has opted to assign all cases to mediation (in the absence of an express objection from either party) making mediation the "default option" in relation to claims under the equality legislation: the process remains voluntary, in that either party can opt-out, but the onus is now on each to do so expressly.[125] Interestingly, Teague and Thomas note that, while parties have been increasingly represented by lawyers in the mediation process, this has not led to the process becoming over-legalistic as "to date the Tribunal has encountered no problems resulting from the involvement of the legal community in the mediation process".[126] In fact, by contrast with other tribunals, such as the EAT and the Labour Court, it is extremely rare for procedural issues relating to the Equality Tribunal to come before the higher courts.[127] **[2–39]**

The Equality Authority

The Equality Authority is an independent body set up under s 38(1) of the Employment Equality Act 1998 (although it is essentially the new name for what had been known as **[2–40]**

---

[122] *Dublin City Co v McCarthy* (DEC-E2001-015); here the complainant was awarded €25,000.
[123] As amended by Equality Act 2004, s 40.
[124] Employment Equality Act 1998, s 78 (as amended by Equality Act 2004, ss 34 and 46).
[125] Teague and Thomas, *op.cit*, p 111.
[126] *ibid*, p 129. A number of other groups, including trade unions, employer representative bodies, citizen advice centres and advocacy groups, has also participated in the process on behalf of claimants and respondents.
[127] A rare example is *County Louth VEC v Equality Tribunal* [2009] IEHC 370, discussed above and noted in Crompton and Dillon, "Equality Tribunal: Conduct at Hearings and Jurisdiction Reviewed by High Court" (2009) 6(4) IELJ 113. An issue as to the *jurisdiction* of the Tribunal arose in *Minister for Justice Equality and Law Reform v Director of the Equality Tribunal* [2009] IEHC 72, where the High Court found that the Tribunal, as a body whose powers are defined by statute, was not entitled to commence a hearing that has the result that it assumes a legal entitlement to overrule a statutory instrument made by the Minister where by law it is not entitled so to do.

the Employment Equality Agency).[128] It was established on 18 October 1999 and is to consist of "not less than 12 and not more than 16 members appointed by the Minister", one of whom is a chairperson.[129]

Under s 39 of the 1998 Act, the Equality Authority has five main functions:

a. To work towards the elimination of discrimination in relation to employment;
b. To promote equality of opportunity in relation to the areas covered by the legislation;
c. To provide information to the public on the working of the Parental Leave Act 1998;[130]
d. To provide information to the public on and to keep under review the working of the Employment Equality Act 1998, the Maternity Protection Act 1994 and the Adoptive Leave Act 1995, and make any necessary proposals for amendment;
e. To monitor and review the working of the Pensions Act 1990 as regards the principle of equal treatment and make any necessary proposals for amendment.

[2–41] Under s 39 of the Equal Status Act 2000, the Authority is also to provide information to the public on, and to keep under review the working of, the 2000 Act and make any necessary proposals for amendment. Under s 56 of the 1998 Act, the Authority can, if requested by the Minister for Justice, Equality and Law Reform,[131] draft codes of practice in relation to the elimination of discrimination and the promotion of equality in relation to the areas covered by the legislation. The first code of practice produced was on Sexual Harassment and Harassment at Work and was given legal effect by the Employment Equality Act 1998 (Code of Practice) (Harassment) Order 2002.[132]

[2–42] The Authority has an important research role and publishes information booklets on equality legislation[133] and can also carry out "equality reviews" of particular businesses or industries and produce "action plans" on foot of findings.[134] The Authority can also, where authorised by the Minister, carry out inquiries, during which it can call witnesses, request information and, ultimately, make recommendations to the Minister.[135]

---

[128] See, generally, www.equality.ie. Note that, at the time of writing, the future of the Authority is in question, as a result of Government proposals in 2009 to merge or abolish a number of state agencies.

[129] Employment Equality Act 1998, s 41 (as amended by Civil Law (Miscellaneous Provisions) Act 2008, s 82).

[130] Inserted by Parental Leave Act 1998, s 25(5).

[131] Note that, in early 2010, a reorganisation of Governmental departments resulted in the transfer of responsibility for equality, disability, integration and human rights matters from the Department of Justice to the new Department of Community, Equality and Gaeltacht Affairs; see www.justice.ie.

[132] SI No 78 of 2002.

[133] See http://www.equality.ie/index.asp?locID = 106&docID =-1.

[134] Employment Equality Act 1998, s 69.

[135] See Employment Equality Act 1998, ss 58-62 (as amended).

Another significant role undertaken by the Authority is in relation to giving assistance **[2–43]** to persons taking claims under the equality legislation, where it appears to the Authority that an "important matter of principle" is raised or "that it is not reasonable to expect the person making the request adequately to present the case without assistance".[136] In *Doherty v South Dublin County Council*[137] proceedings were brought by two older members of the Traveller community seeking habitable accommodation from their local housing authority, through the provision of a caravan. The applicants invited the Authority to appear as *amicus curiae*. This application was opposed by the respondents on a number of grounds including that, unlike the Irish Human Rights Commission, the Equality Authority was not given explicit power to apply to be appointed *amicus curiae*. The Supreme Court upheld an order granting liberty to the Authority to act as *amicus curiae* in the proceedings, noting that the Authority is authorised to work towards the elimination of discrimination and that the State did not seek to place limits on the scope of the power conferred by that provision. The power to act in such a role, to intervene in court proceedings in circumstances where the Authority considered that it could assist the court in reaching a conclusion, fell well within the scope of the general power of the Authority and was not merely ancillary or incidental.

The Labour Relations Commission

The Industrial Relations Act 1990 was the most significant piece of collective **[2–44]** employment law legislation passed in almost 50 years.[138] It became law in July 1990 and, in accordance with s 24 of the Act, the Labour Relations Commission (LRC) was established on 21 January 1991.[139] A general dissatisfaction with the manner in which the Labour Court was being used led to a reassessment of industrial relations (IR) policy at the end of the 1980s.[140] It was felt that the IR institutions needed to take a harder line in pushing the focus of dispute resolution back to the parties themselves and moving away from a culture of third party dependency and, in particular, the trend of seeing the Labour Court as a court of first, rather than last, resort.[141] The LRC was created as a new body that would take responsibility for promoting the conciliation process as a means of resolving labour disputes and have the general duty of improving industrial relations. The LRC has a chairperson appointed by the Minister for Enterprise, Trade and Employment[142] with six ordinary members, two nominated by trade unions, two by employer bodies and two by the Minister.[143] The Rights Commissioners Service is now part of the LRC.

---

[136] Employment Equality Act 1998, 67(2).

[137] [2006] IESC 57.

[138] See chapter 11.

[139] See, generally, www.lrc.ie

[140] http://www.lrc.ie/docs/History_of_the_LRC_Page_2/220.htm.

[141] See Wallace *et al, Industrial Relations in Ireland* (3rd ed, Gill & MacMillan, Dublin, 2004) p 94, *et seq*; Kerr, *The Trade Union and Industrial Relations Acts* (3rd ed, Round Hall, Dublin, 2007) pp 211-212.

[142] Note that, in early 2010, a reorganisation of Governmental departments resulted in the re-naming of the department, which is now known as the Department of Enterprise, Trade and Innovation; see www.entemp.ie.

[143] Industrial Relations Act 1990, s 24(3).

[2–45] The LRC's main functions are set out in s 25 of the Industrial Relations Act 1990. In addition to a general duty to improve industrial relations the LRC is to:

a. provide a conciliation service;
b. provide an industrial relations advisory service;
c. prepare codes of practice relevant to industrial relations after consultation with unions and employer organisations;
d. offer guidance on codes of practice and help to resolve disputes concerning their implementation;
e. select and nominate persons for appointment as rights commissioners and provide staff and facilities for the rights commissioner service;
f. conduct or commission research into matters relevant to industrial relations;
g. review and monitor developments in the area of industrial relations;
h. assist joint labour committees and joint industrial councils in the exercise of their functions.

[2–46] As a result, trade disputes are now normally referred to the Commission and its services in the first instance, meaning that the Labour Court does not investigate a dispute unless it receives a report from the Commission that it is unable to bring the issue to resolution.[144] Exceptions to this clause are where the Commission waives its conciliation function and the parties request the court to investigate the dispute and where the Court, after consulting the Commission, is of the opinion that there are exceptional circumstances.[145]

[2–47] The Commission also has an important role in the preparation of codes of practice, which, as we saw above, can be significant in the adjudication of employment disputes. In accordance with s 42 of the Industrial Relations Act 1990, the following codes have been completed:

- Code of Practice on Dispute Procedures, including Procedures in Essential Services[146];
- Code of Practice on Duties and Responsibilities of Employee Representatives and the Protection and Facilities to be Afforded them by their Employer[147];
- Code of Practice on Grievance and Disciplinary Procedures[148];
- Code of Practice on Compensatory Rest Periods[149];
- Code of Practice on Sunday Working in the Retail Trade[150];

---

[144] Industrial Relations Act 1990, s 26(1)(a).

[145] Industrial Relations Act 1990, ss 26(3) and (5).

[146] Industrial Relations Act 1990, Code of Practice on Dispute Procedures (Declaration) Order 1992 (SI No 1 of 1992).

[147] Industrial Relations Act 1990 Code of Practice on Employee Representatives (Declaration) Order 1993 (SI No 169 of 1993).

[148] Industrial Relations Act 1990 Code of Practice on Grievance and Disciplinary Procedures (Declaration) Order 2000 (SI No 146 of 2000).

[149] Organisation of Working Time (Code of Practice on Compensatory Rest and Related Matters) (Declaration) Order 1998 (SI No 44 of 1998).

[150] Organisation of Working Time (Code of Practice on Sunday Working in the Retail Trade and Related Matters) (Declaration) Order 1998 (SI No 444 of 1998).

- Code of Practice Detailing Procedures for Addressing Bullying in the Workplace[151];
- Enhanced Code of Practice on Voluntary Dispute Resolution[152];
- Code of Practice on Victimisation[153];
- Code of Practice on Access to Part-Time Work[154];
- Code of Practice on Persons Employed in Other Peoples' Homes[155];
- Code of Practice on Employees (Provision of Information and Consultation) Act 2006[156].

Section 42(4) of the Industrial Relations Act 1990 provides that a code of practice is admissible in evidence and should be taken into account, if considered relevant, in any proceedings before a court or employment tribunal.   **[2–48]**

In addition to "assisting" Joint Labour Committees (JLCs)[157] and Joint Industrial Councils,[158] the LRC also has a role in carrying out periodic reviews to ascertain whether, in its opinion, new JLCs should be established, the remit of existing committees should be changed, or if such committees should be abolished.[159]

In terms of mediation, the LRC has introduced a workplace mediation service aimed at providing a prompt, confidential and effective remedy to workplace conflicts, disputes and disagreements (e.g. interpersonal differences, conflicts, difficulties in working together, breakdown in a working relationship and issues arising from a grievance and disciplinary procedure, particularly before a matter becomes a disciplinary issue). Participation in mediation is voluntary and does not oblige any party to commit to any further procedure in the event that the problem remains following mediation.[160] The LRC also provides a conciliation service, whereby a professional external mediator   **[2–49]**

---

[151] Industrial Relations Act 1990 (Code of Practice Detailing Procedures for Addressing Bullying in the Workplace) (Declaration) Order 2002 (SI No 17 of 2002).

[152] Industrial Relations Act 1990 Enhanced Code of Practice on Voluntary Dispute Resolution (Declaration) Order 2004 (SI No 76 of 2004).

[153] Industrial Relations Act 1990 Code of Practice on Victimisation (Declaration) Order 2004 (SI No 139 of 2004).

[154] Industrial Relations Act 1990 Code of Practice on Access to Part-Time Working (Declaration) Order 2006 (SI No 8 of 2006).

[155] Industrial Relations Act 1990 (Code of Practice for Protecting Persons Employed in Other People's Homes) (Declaration) Order 2007 (SI No 239 of 2007).

[156] Industrial Relations Act 1990 (Code of Practice on Information and Consultation) (Declaration) Order 2008 (SI No 132 of 2008).

[157] JLCs are statutory bodies established under Industrial Relations Acts 1946-2001 to provide for the fixing of minimum rates of pay and the regulation of employment. They typically exist in employments where there is little or no collective bargaining and are designed to protect vulnerable workers; see chapter 11 and Wallace *et al*, *op.cit*, p 110.

[158] JICs are voluntary negotiating bodies for an industry or part of an industry and are designed to facilitate collective bargaining at industry level in certain sectors. They generally exist where a high level of unionisation exists. The most important at present is the Construction Industry JIC; see chapter 11.

[159] Industrial Relations Act 1990, s 39.

[160] See http://www.lrc.ie/ViewDoc.asp?fn =/documents/work/Workplace_Mediation_ Service.htm&CatID =54&m =w.

assists employers and their employees to resolve disputes when their efforts to do so have not succeeded.[161] The process can be described as a facilitated search for agreement between disputing parties. The Labour Relations Commission assigns a mediator, known as an "Industrial Relations Officer" (IRO),[162] who acts as an independent, impartial chairperson in assisting the parties to come to a mutually acceptable settlement to their dispute, which can be formalised in a conciliation agreement. If agreement cannot be reached, the parties have the option of referring the dispute to the Labour Court for a recommendation. The IRO, however, will not refer a dispute to the Labour Court unless the parties request this: the parties remain in control of the process. According to the LRC's annual report for 2008, the Conciliation Service in 2008 recorded an extremely high level of voluntary settlement in cases referred to it (just over 80 percent).[163]

[2–50]   The Advisory Service of the Commission (which under s 33 of the 1990 Act provides for Commission staff to "assist in the prevention and settlement of trade disputes" by giving advice on IR matters to employers, workers and their representatives) experienced a major growth in referrals relating to the "right to bargain" provisions under the Industrial Relations Amendment Acts 2001–2004 (and the accompanying Code of Practice on Voluntary Dispute Resolution).[164] However, as we will see, this may not continue to be the case following a significant Supreme Court judgment in the *Ryanair* case.[165] In research terms, the LRC conducts its own research projects as well as funding research projects on key areas of human resources management and various approaches to dispute resolution.[166] It also publishes reports and the *LRC Review* periodical journal.

[2–51]   The LRC, therefore, has a highly significant role in terms of the State's industrial relations machinery, as, unlike the EAT, which deals with cases involving individuals, the LRC typically deals with disputes that cover a large number of workers.

Rights Commissioners

[2–52]   The appointment of Rights Commissioners was provided for under s 13(1) of the Industrial Relations Act 1969, but since the 1990 Act the service has been brought within the remit of the LRC. Rights Commissioners investigate disputes, grievances and claims that individuals or small groups of workers refer, principally under the following legislation:

---

[161] Conciliation is similar to, but not the same as, mediation. In the latter, the third party actively seeks to assist the parties (often submitting proposals). In conciliation, the third party does not offer proposals and merely seeks to facilitate the parties themselves in so doing; see Salamon, *Industrial Relations: Theory and Practice* (4th ed, FT Prentice Hall, Essex, 2000) chapter 12; Vahey, *op.cit.*

[162] s 33(1) Industrial Relations Act 1990 allows the Commission to appoint members of staff to act as IROs.

[163] http://www.lrc.ie/documents/annualreports/2008/LRC_AR08.pdf. See also the Law Reform Commission Consultation Paper *Alternative Dispute Resolution* (LRC CP-50, 2008).

[164] Industrial Relations Act 1990 Enhanced Code of Practice on Voluntary Dispute Resolution (Declaration) Order 2004 (SI No 76 of 2004).

[165] *Ryanair v Labour Court* [2007] 4 IR 199. See below and chapter 11.

[166] A selection of research papers can be found at www.lrc.ie (Research Papers).

- Adoptive Leave Acts 1995–2005;
- Carers Leave Act 2001;
- Competition Acts 2002–2006;
- Employees (Provision of Information and Consultation) Act 2006;
- Employment Permits Act 2006;
- Industrial Relations Acts 1969–1990;
- Industrial Relations (Miscellaneous Provisions) Act 2004;
- Maternity Protection Acts 1994–2004;
- National Minimum Wage Act 2000;
- Organisation of Working Time Act 1997;
- Parental Leave Acts 1998 and 2006;
- Payment of Wages Act 1991;
- Protection of Employees (Fixed-Term Work) Act 2003;
- Protection of Employees (Part-Time Work) Act 2001;
- Protection of Young Persons (Employment) Act 1996;
- Protections for Persons Reporting Child Abuse Act 1998;
- Safety, Health and Welfare at Work Act 2005;
- Terms of Employment (Information) Acts 1994–2001;
- Unfair Dismissals Acts 1977–2007;
- Consumer Protection Act 2007;
- Health Act 2007;
- European Communities (Protection of Employment) Regulations 2000;
- European Communities (Safeguarding of Employees Rights on Transfer of Undertakings) Regulations 2003;
- European Communities (European PLC) (Employee Involvement) Regulations 2006.

Hearings before a Rights Commissioner usually take place in private[167] and are relatively informal and non-adversarial. Written submissions are not mandatory but a Rights Commissioner will usually invite both parties to make both oral and written submissions, will ask questions of the parties and, frequently, will speak to each party privately in the course of the hearing: essentially the conduct of the hearing is a matter for the Commissioner to decide.[168] Commissioners cannot take evidence under oath, compel the appearance of witnesses, or award costs. Rights Commissioners issue the findings of their investigations in the form of either decisions or non-binding recommendations, depending on the legislation under which a case is referred. A party to a dispute may object to a Rights Commissioner investigation where the case has been referred under the Industrial Relations Acts 1969–1990,[169] or under the Unfair Dismissals Acts 1977–2008.[170] Where such an objection is made, a Rights Commissioner cannot investigate the case. A right of appeal from a decision of a Commissioner exists, depending on the legislation under which a case is referred, to

[2–53]

---

[167] Public hearings may be held under the Payment of Wages Act 1991.

[168] Industrial Relations Act 1969, s 13(6), which also provides that a Rights Commissioner may provide for the cases in which persons may appear before him or her by counsel or solicitor and, except as so provided, no person shall be entitled to appear by counsel or solicitor before a Commissioner. See, generally, Wallace et al, *op.cit,* pp 103-106.

[169] Industrial Relations Act 1969, s 13(3).

[170] Unfair Dismissals Act 1977, s 8(3).

the Labour Court (in the case of an industrial relations dispute, for example) or the EAT (in the case of unfair dismissals claims, for example).

[2–54] According to the LRC Annual Reports, the number of cases referred to the Service in 2008 increased by 20 percent; this follows an increase of 26 percent in 2007. In 2008, the greatest number of claims heard related to payment of wages, working time and the Terms of Employment (Information) Acts 1994–2001. The 2008 Annual Report also indicates that a growing proportion of claimants are migrant workers, reflecting the changing profile of the Irish workforce: research in 2007 indicated that one-fifth of claimants who used the service in that year were from Central or Eastern Europe.[171] The growth in references to the service is a development that is running parallel to the decline in trade union density and industrial action. Thus, it appears that conflict at work has certainly not gone away but has become increasingly individualised.[172]

The Labour Court

[2–55] The Labour Court was established under s 10 of the Industrial Relations Act 1946 for the purposes of dealing with industrial relations disputes.[173] The Labour Court is not a court of law, but operates primarily as an industrial relations tribunal hearing both sides in a case and then issuing a non-binding recommendation, setting out its opinion on the dispute and the terms on which it should be settled. The Court, however, has acquired many extra functions in recent years as a result of specific roles being assigned to it under various pieces of employment legislation, under which it can make legally binding determinations.

[2–56] The Labour Court consists of nine full-time members: a chairman, two deputy chairmen and six ordinary members, three of whom are employers' members (nominated by the Irish Business and Employers' Confederation-IBEC) and three of whom are workers' members (nominated by the ICTU).[174] The Court operates in three separate divisions, although certain issues may require a meeting of the full Court. A division is made up of the chairman or a deputy chairman, an employers' member and a workers' member.[175]

[2–57] According to its mission statement the role of the Labour Court is to "find a basis for real and substantial agreement through the provision of fast, fair, informal and inexpensive arrangements for the adjudication and resolution of trade disputes".[176] The Court has been assigned functions in a number of discrete areas of employment law.

[2–58] Originally, the Court's primary role was seen to be in the industrial relations arena. The Court has a role to investigate trade disputes under the Industrial Relations Acts

---

[171] Teague and Hann reported in *Industrial Relations News*- "Employment law 2007-an Overview of Key Developments" (2008) 1 IRN; see also Hann *et al*, *Managing Workplace Conflict in Ireland* (Irish Stationary Office, Dublin, 2010).

[172] See Colling, "What Space for Unions on the Floor of Rights? Trade Unions and the Enforcement of Statutory Individual Employment Rights" 2006 35(2) ILJ 140.

[173] See, generally, www.labourcourt.ie.

[174] Industrial Relations Act 1969, s 2.

[175] Industrial Relations Act 1969, s 3.

[176] www.labourcourt.ie.

1946–2004. This includes the power to investigate a dispute referred by the LRC at the request of the parties to the dispute.[177] The Court may be requested by the Minister for Enterprise, Trade and Employment to investigate trade disputes affecting the public interest, or to conduct an enquiry into a trade dispute of special importance and report on its findings.[178] The Court also functions as an appellate forum in relation to Rights Commissioners' recommendations under the Industrial Relations Acts.[179] The Court can establish Joint Labour Committees and decide on questions concerning their operation,[180] register Joint Industrial Councils,[181] register, vary and interpret employment agreements and investigate complaints of breaches of registered employment agreements.[182] In relation to codes of practice, the Court can investigate complaints of breaches and give its opinion as to the interpretation of a code of practice made under the Industrial Relations Act 1990.[183] The Court has the power to investigate disputes and issue legally binding determinations under the Industrial Relations (Amendment) Acts 2001–2004.[184]

Outside of its traditional sphere of collective employment relations, the Court now hears appeals from decisions and recommendations of Equality Officers under the Employment Equality Acts 1998–2008[185] and the Pensions Act 1990[186] and from Rights Commissioners' decisions under s 28 of the Organisation of Working Time Act 1997, s 27 of the National Minimum Wage Act 2000, s 17 of the Protection of Employees (Part-Time Work) Act 2001, s 15 of the Protection of Employees (Fixed-Term Work) Act 2003 and s 29 of the Safety, Health and Welfare at Work Act 2005. In these cases, appeals are by way of re-hearing the entire case and the Labour Court can issue legally binding determinations.[187] [2–59]

We can see, therefore, that the Court increasingly has a significant role in relation to individual employment law disputes (although it is IR disputes that continue to make up the bulk of the Court's workload).[188] However, the fact that the Court must increasingly grapple with complex employment rights legislation and the fact that its decisions in many areas are now legally binding mean that, like the EAT, concerns exist that the Court will become overly legalistic.[189] Traditionally, while the Court has the [2–60]

---

[177] Industrial Relations Act 1990, s 26.
[178] Industrial Relations Act 1946, s 24 and Industrial Relations Act 1990, s 38. See, also, Kerr, *The Trade Union and Industrial Relations Acts* (3rd ed, Round Hall, Dublin, 2007) p 219.
[179] Industrial Relations Act 1969, s 13(9).
[180] Industrial Relations Act 1946, s 35. See chapter 11.
[181] Industrial Relations Act 1946, s 61. See chapter 11.
[182] Industrial Relations Act 1946, Part III.
[183] Industrial Relations Act 1990, s 43.
[184] See chapter 11.
[185] Employment Equality Act 1998, s 83.
[186] Pensions Act 1990, s 77.
[187] The Court has other significant functions under the working time and minimum wage legislation; see Regan, *op.cit,* pp 14-15.
[188] 890 out of 1,179 referrals in 2008 related to IR disputes— see Labour Court Annual Report 2008 available at http://www.labourcourt.ie/labour/labour.nsf/LookupPageLink/Home AboutUs.
[189] The Labour Court, for example, has in recent years needed to make quite sophisticated referrals to the ECJ in relation to issues arising from EU law; above, n 43.

power to take evidence on oath and require the production before it of persons or documents,[190] hearings are generally held in an atmosphere of informality and the procedure is inquisitorial rather than adversarial.[191] However, this informality has been thrown into some doubt by the decision in *Ryanair v Labour Court*.[192] This case centred around a dispute involving the company and pilots represented by the Irish Airline Pilots Association (IALPA, a branch of the Irish Municipal Public and Civil Trade Union, IMPACT), under the Industrial Relations (Amendment) Acts 2001–2004. The Supreme Court was quite critical of the informal procedures adopted by the Labour Court when hearing the case, in particular, the fact that neither a single pilot nor any other employee of Ryanair was called by the union to give evidence. The Supreme Court held that the Labour Court did not adopt fair procedures, first, by permitting complete non-disclosure of the identity of the persons on whose behalf the union was purporting to be acting and, secondly, by disbelieving the oral evidence of two senior management figures in Ryanair in the absence of hearing evidence from at least one relevant pilot who was an employee of Ryanair. The Labour Court had decided the issue against Ryanair to a large extent on foot of omissions in Ryanair documentation and on foot of a view put forward by the union that the company did not engage in collective bargaining. This, according to the Supreme Court, did not amount to sufficient evidence to justify the finding. Moreover, the Supreme Court was critical of what it referred to as the Labour Court's "mindset", which favoured the way particular expressions are used, and particular activities are carried out, by trade unions.[193]

[2–61] This aspect of the Supreme Court's judgment is somewhat surprising. The Superior Courts have traditionally been quite deferential to the Labour Court's expertise in relation to industrial affairs issues, as seen in another judgment dealing with the 2001–2004 Acts, *Ashford Castle v SIPTU*.[194] There, Clarke J noted that the Labour Court was an administrative body which was required, when exercising its role under industrial relations legislation, to bring to bear its own expert view on the approach to take to the issues. He held that "a very high degree of deference indeed needs to be applied to decisions which involve the exercise by a statutory body, such as the Labour Court, of an expertise which this (High) Court does not have".[195] The Supreme Court's criticism of the procedures adopted by the Labour Court will likely have the effect of encouraging a greater formality in respect of Labour Court hearings and perhaps

---

[190] Kerr and McGreal, *op.cit*, p 848.

[191] The Court publishes only one decision; dissenting opinions are not published (see Industrial Relations Act 1946, s 20(4)).

[192] [2007] 4 IR 199. The substantive aspects of this case will be examined in detail in chapter 11. See also Doherty, "Union Sundown? The Future of Collective Representation Rights in Irish Law" (2007) 4(4) IELJ 96.

[193] *ibid* at 215 *per* Geoghegan J.

[194] [2007] 4 IR 70.

[195] *ibid* at 85. See also the decision in *Calor Teoranta v Mc Carthy* [2009] IEHC 139, where Clarke J noted that, while the High Court can scrutinise the extent to which the Labour Court considered all necessary matters and excluded from its consideration any matters that were not appropriate, it should not interfere with a legitimate and sustainable judgment of the facts based on a proper consideration of all relevant materials. In *Russell v Mount Temple Comprehensive School* [2009] IEHC 533 Hanna J described the Labour Court as "a Tribunal possessed of formidable experience and expertise".

encourage a further "juridificiation" of the process.[196] The Labour Court has already drawn up a list of the key issues that arise out of the judgment and has laid down a set of guidelines that it will follow in future hearings, stressing the need for a "best evidence" rule.[197] As Kerr and McGreal point out, although the decision dealt with the Labour Court's jurisdiction under the 2001–2004 Acts, there seems to be nothing to suggest that the Supreme Court's comments would not apply equally to other employment tribunals and to the Labour Court when exercising other jurisdictions.[198]

National Employment Rights Authority

As part of the response to the increasing number of migrant workers employed in Ireland and, in particular, in response to large-scale disputes involving the exploitation of migrant workers at two companies, Gama and Irish Ferries,[199] the social partners agreed in the national partnership agreement, *Towards 2016*, a major new package of measures to deal with employment rights compliance. The resulting legislation, the Employment Law Compliance Bill 2008, was published in March 2008. It provides for the establishment of a new, statutory office dedicated to employment rights compliance: the National Employment Rights Authority (NERA).[200] Although at the time of writing the Bill has not yet been promulgated, NERA is currently operating, as it has been established on an interim basis. It has subsumed three former sections of the Department of Enterprise, Trade and Employment; the Labour Inspectorate,[201] the information unit, and the prosecution and enforcement section. The aim of the Authority is to establish a "national culture of employment rights compliance".[202] The 2008 Bill (in s 6) allows for NERA to have a Director and a tripartite Advisory Board. NERA has five primary functions[203]:

[2–62]

a. Information;
b. Inspection;
c. Enforcement;
d. Prosecution;
e. Protection of young persons at work.

---

[196] Browne, *op.cit.*

[197] Sheehan, "Labour Court's Guidelines for 2001-2004 Cases in Wake of 'Ryanair' Judgment" (2007) 14 IRN.

[198] Kerr and McGreal, *op.cit,* p 828.

[199] Krings, "A Race to the Bottom? Trade Unions, EU Enlargement and the Free Movement of Labour" (2009) 15(2) *European Journal of Industrial Relations* 49.

[200] See, generally, www.employmentrights.ie.

[201] See Cox *et al, Employment Law in Ireland* (Clarus Press, Dublin, 2009), pp 15-19. A further commitment in *Towards 2016* was that the number of labour inspectors would be trebled from 30 to 90. However, it has been reported that, because of the moratorium on recruitment and promotion in the public service announced in 2009, the number of labour inspectors has actually decreased since 2007 and that the commitment to employ 90 inspectors has not been met; "Inspectors Must Prosecute Firms that Exploit Migrant Labour" *Irish Examiner*, 12 January 2010.

[202] www.employmentrights.ie.

[203] Employment Rights Compliance Bill 2008, Part 2.

[2–63]   In terms of inspections, NERA has launched several sectoral campaigns (in relation to the contract cleaning, construction, security and mushroom sectors, for example) and targeted campaigns relating to protection of young persons and payment of the minimum wage.[204] Under NERA's prosecution and enforcement service, the Authority seeks to rectify breaches of employment law without recourse to legal proceedings where possible, but can refer cases (following inspections or on information supplied to the Authority) to the courts: in 2009, a total of 108 cases were referred to the Chief State Solicitor's Office for prosecution.[205] NERA can also seek to have certain Labour Court or Employment Appeals Tribunal determinations enforced through the courts, where a party has not complied with the determination.[206]

[2–64]   If the 2008 Bill is passed, NERA will have enhanced powers in the area of labour inspection (for example, to take evidence on oath, to allow inspectors greater access to premises, personnel and data and to empower inspectors to examine employment permits; see Part 4 of the 2008 Bill). The Bill, in s 59, also provides for greater penalties for employer offenders; in most cases fines of up to €5,000 and/or 12 months' imprisonment for summary offences and €250,000 and/or three years' imprisonment for indictable offences. Under s 62, there is also an Employment Law Offenders List, which is to be used to publicly name and shame employers who breach employment legislation, which will be periodically published by NERA. In Part 5, the Bill specifies a comprehensive list of documents which must be kept by the employer in respect of the most recent three-year employment period and must be retained by employers for a further two years after the employment relationship ends.

[2–65]   There has already been some significant criticism of the Bill.[207] In particular, there is a concern that the focus of the Bill is mostly on *criminal* offences, with 23 new offences created. Relatively minor breaches, such as the failure of an employer to keep a copy of a passport (or equivalent document) in respect of each and every employee, for example, are criminal offences under the Bill.[208] From an employee perspective, the focus on criminalising breaches of employment law has the effect of raising the standard of proof required for prosecution of such breaches (from the civil standard of balance of probabilities to the higher criminal standard of beyond all reasonable doubt). There is also concern about the extent of the powers given to NERA (the powers granted to take evidence on oath, demand access to premises, personnel and data, etc). Employers are concerned about the burdens the Bill will place on them. Record-keeping and administrative obligations are onerous and expense to the employer will undoubtedly increase. A good example of this is the new obligation on employers, under s 32, to display notices in the workplace outlining employees' entitlements under employment legislation and other specified information. Any

---

[204] See NERA Review of 2009 available at: http://www.employmentrights.ie/en/media/NERA%20Review%20of%202009.pdf. In 2008, over 8,000 inspections relating to the protection of young persons at work took place; just three breaches of legislation were detected.
[205] *ibid*, p 18.
[206] A total of 45 such cases were concluded in 2008, involving arrears totaling €17,419; *ibid*, p 4.
[207] See, Dobbins, "IBEC Want to Amend Employment Law Compliance Bill in National Talks" (2008) 25 IRN; "Employers Have Most to Fear from Employment Rights Bill" (2008) 28 IRN.
[208] Employment Rights Compliance Bill 2008, s 54.

employer with a high proportion of foreign national employees will most likely be required to translate information into appropriate language(s) and the Bill makes no financial or administrative allowance in terms of expense or in respect of small employers. In the context of what has been said above in relation to the EAT and the Labour Court, there is also a concern that the Bill represents a yet further juridification of employment relations. The range of new offences and their criminal nature inevitably means a shift away from the more informal procedures traditionally adopted by the dispute resolution bodies, more lawyer involvement and, inevitably, more cost and delay for the parties.

The Health and Safety Authority

Section 15 of the Safety, Health and Welfare at Work Act 1989 provided for the establishment of the National Authority for Occupational Health and Safety. Section 32 of the 2005 Safety, Health and Welfare at Work Act renamed this body the Health and Safety Authority.[209] Part 5 of the 2005 Act now outlines the Authority's main functions. These can be summarised as: **[2–66]**

- a. to make adequate arrangements for the enforcement of all legislation on occupational health and safety, particularly through workplace inspections;
- b. to keep existing legislation under review and conduct and commission research into occupational health and safety;
- c. to promote, encourage and foster the prevention of accidents and injury to health at work, particularly through promoting education and training in relation to occupational safety;
- d. to make arrangements for the provision of recommendations, information and advice on best practice to employers and employees, employer and employee representatives, and the Minister for Enterprise, Trade and Employment.

The Authority is also empowered, under s 60 of the 2005 Act, to prepare codes of practice to support the statutory provisions. These have special legal standing under s 61, as where, in criminal proceedings under the Act, a code of practice appears to the court to give practical guidance as to the observance of the requirement or prohibition alleged to have been contravened, it shall be admissible in evidence. Furthermore, where it is proved that any act or omission of the defendant alleged to constitute a contravention of health and safety legislation was a failure to observe a code of practice, that fact shall be admissible in evidence. A range of codes of practice has been produced; see, for example, the 2007 Code of Practice for Employers and Employees on the Prevention and Resolution of Bullying at Work.[210] Besides Acts of the Oireachtas, a wide range of occupational health and safety and dangerous substances legislation, is administered and enforced, in whole or part, by the Health and Safety Authority, including regulations implementing EU legislation.[211] **[2–67]**

---

[209] See, generally, www.hsa.ie and see chapter 8.

[210] See Byrne, *Safety, Health and Welfare at Work Act 2005* (Round Hall, Dublin, 2006), p 110.

[211] See the comprehensive list of all heath and safety legislation (and codes of practice) available at: http://www.hsa.ie/eng/Legislation/List_of_Legislation.pdf.

CHAPTER 3
The Employment Relationship

I. Introduction

Work remains one of the most importance sources of identity, meaning and social **[3–01]** affiliation in contemporary life.[1] The modern workplace is a locus of seemingly constant change and, as a result, people increasingly work under a variety of arrangements. This chapter looks at how the law regulates the formation and definition of the employment relationship. As we saw in the previous chapter, the common law has been an important driving force in the development of many employment law principles. In particular, the employment relationship has traditionally been founded on the individual contract of employment, with the result that the principles of contract law developed by the courts have had a significant impact on how the boundaries of the employment relationship have been defined. In the next chapter, we will consider in detail the formation, content and interpretation of the typical contract of employment. Here, however, we are concerned with how the law categorises relations in the employment sphere.

---

[1] Doherty, "When the Working Day is Through: the End of Work as Identity?" (2009) 23(1) *Work, Employment and Society* 84.

II. Classifying the "Employee"

[3–02] Kahn-Freund described the contract of employment as the cornerstone of the modern labour law system.[2] Great scope was given to the parties themselves by the common law courts to define the scope of the employment contract and, while this freedom is now circumscribed by the provisions of the Constitution, European law and domestic legislation, the result is that the "starting point for the analysis of legal obligations arising in the context of working relations must always be the terms of any contractual arrangement".[3] As we will see further below, this has resulted in the courts constructing a standard model of rules based on a "binary divide" between employment and self-employment, between subordinated labour (referred to as "servants" in the older case law) and independent or autonomous work relations (which would include work done by what we refer to nowadays as "independent contractors").[4] Those who fell within the former category could claim to work under a *contract of employment*, while others, who worked under a *contract for services*, fell outside of the "employee" categorisation. The primary basis for such a distinction was (or, at least, became in relatively modern times) that those in self-employment, those in business on their own, needed less protection against unemployment, sickness and old age than those in a "master-servant" relationship.

[3–03] It is important to note that this "binary divide" has come in for criticism in recent years, given the increasingly differentiated organisation of working life in the post-industrial era.[5] Freedland, in particular, has heavily criticised the "strict legal dichotomy" between the employed and self-employed.[6] He has powerfully advocated a conceptual shift away from the contract of employment model to a model based on what he refers to as a "personal work nexus". This refers to the

> "connection or connections, link or links, between a person providing a service personally and the persons, organisations or enterprises who or which are involved in the arrangements for, or incidental to, the personal work in question".[7]

---

[2] Kahn-Freund, *Labour and the Law* (Stevens, London, 1977).

[3] Collins *et al*, *Labour Law: Text and Materials* (2nd ed, Hart, Oxford, 2005), p 70.

[4] Deakin, "Does the 'Personal Employment Contract' Provide a Basis for the Reunification of Employment Law?" (2007) 36(1) ILJ 68, at p 70.

[5] See Deakin and Wilkinson, *The Law of the Labour Market* (Oxford University Press, Oxford, 2005); Davidov, "Who is a Worker?" (2005) 34(1) ILJ 57; Barmes, "The Continuing Conceptual Crisis in the Common Law of the Contract of Employment" (2004) 67(3) MLR 435; Grandi, "Would Europe Benefit From the Adoption of a Comprehensive Definition of the term 'Employee' Applicable in All Relevant Legislative Modes?" (2008) 24(4) Int J. Comp LLIR 495. For debates on the nature, form and implications of contemporary work organisation see, for example, Beck, *The Brave New World of Work* (Polity, Cambridge, 2000); Green, *Demanding Work: The Paradox of Job Quality in an Affluent Economy* (Princeton University Press, Princeton, 2006); Fevre, "Employment Insecurity and Social Theory: The Power of Nightmares'" (2007) 21(3) *Work, Employment and Society* 517; and Doherty, *op.cit.*

[6] Freedland, *The Personal Employment Contract* (Oxford University Press, Oxford, 2003), p 22.

[7] Freedland, "From the Contract of Employment to the Personal Work Nexus" (2006) 35(1) ILJ 1, p 16.

Essentially, Freedland argues that the employment relationship should be re-conceptualised so that employment law recognises (and offers protection to) a wider set of relationships categorised by personal service and economic dependence on the part of those working (even where these do not conform to the traditional model of contractual arrangement). This would necessitate the expansion of the idea of the traditional "employer" to include tri-lateral or multi-lateral arrangements, whereby different "employing entities" may have different and overlapping obligations to the same worker (as is the case in relation to agency work, for example).[8]

This debate has arisen, in large part, due to concerns about the conceptual and practical difficulties of drawing the distinction between a contract *of* service and a contract *for* services. This is exacerbated by the fact that there is no comprehensive statutory definition of either "employee" or "contract of employment". Instead, it has been left largely to the courts to define these concepts, a task with which, as we will see, they have struggled. **[3–04]**

However, the debate is also significant as many important implications flow from the classification of "employee". First, much employment legislation (particularly protective legislation), excludes from its coverage those who do not work under a contract of employment (for example, the Unfair Dismissals Acts discussed in chapter 10). Secondly, certain rights and duties are implied into the contract of employment that do not apply to contracts for services.[9] Thirdly, in the law of tort, the contract of employment has been used to fix the scope of the vicarious liability of employers for the negligent acts of employees done in the course of employment.[10] Fourthly, differing obligations arise under income tax and social security legislation depending on whether or not one is classified as an employee.[11] Fifthly, employees are preferential creditors in the event that their employer is wound-up or put into receivership.[12] Given these factors, the courts must always be alive to the possibility that it may be in the interest of one, other, or all of the parties to an employment relationship to seek to classify it as *not* involving a contract of employment. For example, the employer may try to evade taking on legislative **[3–05]**

---

[8] See also Waas, "The Legal Definition of the Employment Relationship" (2010) 1(1) *European Labour Law Journal* 45. The author examines the increasing complexity of the issue of determining the existence of an employment relationship between an organisation and a worker, with reference to the definitions of an employee under German and EU law. Waas considers the German law category of "quasi-salaried workers", self-employed persons who are economically dependent on a single entity.

[9] See chapter 4.

[10] See Cox *et al*, *Employment Law in Ireland* (Clarus Press, Dublin, 2009), p 87-106; Feeney, "The Supreme Court and Vicarious Liability- Implications for Employers" (2009) 6(2) IELJ 43. Note the decision in *Phelan v Coillte Teoranta* [1993] 1 IR 1, where the plaintiff employee was injured in the course of employment as a result of the negligence of a welder engaged as an independent contractor by the defendant. Barr J in the High Court, while suggesting that, in his view, the welder probably *was* an employee, said that it was not necessary for him to consider that issue because in the circumstances the degree of *control* exercised by Coillte over his work was such that vicarious liability would attach irrespective of the legal status of the worker. It seems there was a hint of a purposive interpretation of the statute at issue in the case, the Safety and Welfare at Work Act 1989, which was designed to ensure that employees are protected at work.

[11] Forde, *Employment Law* (2nd ed, Round Hall, Dublin, 2001), p 23.

[12] Companies Act 1963, s 285(2). See also *In Re Sunday Tribune* [1984] IR 505.

responsibilities in relation to notice or redundancy requirements, while the worker might seek to maximise his or her tax benefits. Employers may also seek to reduce their exposure to business risks by shifting these onto the worker through, for example, using a piece-work or performance-related remuneration system or offering work on a casual basis. The more risks the worker agrees to bear the less likely it will be that he or she will be classed as an employee at all.[13]

[3–06] We will look below at various, increasingly prevalent, forms of "atypical employment", such as fixed-term and part-time work, as well as various forms of employment relations. First, though, we need to look more closely at how the courts have grappled with the "binary divide" between employment and self-employment.

III. Employee or Independent Contractor?

[3–07] Who is classed as an "employee" varies depending on the piece of legislation in question. Virtually all employment legislation simply (and unhelpfully!) refers to an employee as someone who works under a "contract of employment". This, in turn, is typically defined in one of three ways. The Terms of Employment (Information) Act 1994 (s 1) defines a contract of employment as:

> "(a) a contract of service or apprenticeship, and
> (b) any other contract whereby an individual agrees with another person, who is carrying on the business of an employment agency within the meaning of the Employment Agency Act 1971, and is acting in the course of that business, to do or perform personally any work or service for a third person (whether or not the third person is a party to the contract)".

A similar definition is provided for in the legislation on statutory notice periods, unfair dismissal, redundancy, working time, maternity protection, adoptive leave, carer's leave, parental leave, protection of young workers, part-time work and transfer of undertakings.[14] This covers agency workers and apprentices, but excludes totally the self-employed and most casual workers.[15]

---

[13] Collins *et al, op.cit*, p 160.

[14] The Minimum Notice and Terms of Employment Act 1973 (although here there is no reference to agency workers); the Unfair Dismissals Act 1977 (as amended by the Unfair Dismissals (Amendment) Act 1993, s 13, which deems the end-user, rather than the agency to be the employer); Redundancy Payments Act 1967 (as amended by the Redundancy Payments Act 2003, s 3); Organisation of Working Time Act 1997; Maternity Protection Acts 1994 and 2004; Adoptive Leave Acts 1995 and 2005; Carer's Leave Act 2001; Parental Leave Acts 1998 and 2006; Protection of Young Persons (Employment) Act 1996; Protection of Employees (Part-Time Work) Act 2001; and European Communities (Protection of Employees on Transfer of Undertakings) Regulations 2003 (SI No 131 of 2003). Agency workers (unless they have a contract of employment with the agency) and apprentices are excluded from the scope of the Protection of Employees (Fixed-Term Work) Act.

[15] In *Aughney v Hays Specialist Recruitment* (RP 148/2009), in the context of an agency worker's claim for redundancy, the EAT held that the issue of whether or not the agency worker is an "employee" is largely irrelevant; it is enough under the Redundancy Payments Acts if the agency worker has agreed with the recruitment agency to perform any work or service on behalf of a third party and the agency is liable to pay the wages of the person concerned.

A wider definition applies in two acts relating to wages. Both the Payment of Wages Act 1991 and the National Minimum Wage Act 2000 apply to contracts where an individual has agreed with another person to do, or perform personally, any work or service for "a third person (whether or not the third person is a party to the contract) whose status by virtue of the contract is not that of a client or customer of any profession or business undertaking carried on by the individual" (1991 Act) or "that person or a third person (whether or not the third person is a party to the contract)" (2000 Act). A wider definition also applies in relation to the Employment Equality Act 1998 (as amended in 2004 by s 3 of the Equality Act 2004) which includes contracts whereby "an individual agrees with another person personally to execute any work or service for that person".[16] These wider definitions have given rise to much comment in the UK, where increasingly the concept of "worker" (formulated in the same terms as in those used in the Payment of Wages Act 1991) is being used in place of the traditional "employee".[17] The "worker" formulation may include, therefore, a group sometimes referred to as the "dependent self-employed"[18]; self-employed individuals who most likely enter into contracts to perform work personally for a single employer, who have a degree of dependence that is essentially the same as that of employees and who have no regular profession, or business of their own, to protect them. **[3–08]**

Aside from the equality legislation, the legislation that uses the wider definition relates to guaranteeing payment of wages (and in the UK, restricting excessive hours of work). Thus, the rationale appears to be that the type of self-employed workers mentioned above, or indeed casual workers, who do not fall within the traditional "employee" category should not be denied these basic protections, the primary purpose of which do not depend on the employment relationship being regular and long-term.[19] **[3–09]**

Before we move on to consider the core issues of how the courts construe a contract of employment, it should be noted that being classified as an "employee" does not necessarily afford automatic access to statutory rights. An important further threshold that must be crossed in many cases is that of continuity of employment. So, to acquire rights under unfair dismissals or redundancy legislation, for example, the employee must also demonstrate that he or she has been in continuous employment on a **[3–10]**

---

[16] This wider definition is required by EU law. In Case C-256/01 *Allonby v Accrington & Rossendale College and Others* [2004] IRLR 224 the ECJ held that the term "worker" in relation to equal pay under Art 141EC had to have an EU meaning and could not be defined by individual Member States' legislation. A worker, therefore, in the context of EU equal pay law means "a person who, for a certain period of time, performs services for and under the direction of another person in return for which he receives remuneration" but this does not include "independent providers of services who are not in a relationship of subordination with the person who receives the services" (paras 67-68).

[17] For example, in the National Minimum Wage Act 1998, s 54; the Working Time Regulations 1998, reg 2; and the Employment Relations Act 1996, s 230(3). See above, notes 4 and 5.

[18] See Burchell *et al*, *The Employment Status of Individuals in Non-standard Employment* (London, Department of Trade and Industry, 1999).

[19] Deakin and Morris, *Labour Law* (5th ed, Hart, Oxford, 2009), p 164. Note that, in the UK, some recent employment statutes (e.g. the Employment Relations Act 1999, s 21) delegate power to the Minister for Trade and Industry to extend the coverage of the legislation to other categories of workers of his designation.

full-time basis by the employer for a specified period (52 weeks under s 2(1)(a) of the Unfair Dismissals Act 1977, as amended, and 104 weeks under s 4(1) of the Redundancy Payments Act 1967).

The "Tests"— Control, Integration and Economic Reality

[3–11]   Given the lack of precision with which the legislature has defined a "contract of employment" it has fallen to the courts to flesh out the concept. The courts have developed a number of tests to use in deciding whether a contract of employment exists.[20] However, as we will see, while these tests provide a useful framework, and are helpful as reference points, ultimately the courts have not been able to develop a particularly sound conceptual distinction between employment and self-employment and cases tend to turn on their overall factual matrix.[21]

Control

[3–12]   One of the first tests to be developed by the courts focused on the extent to which, under the terms of the contract, the employer has control over the employee. In *Yewens v Noakes*[22] it was held that "a servant is a person subject to the command of his master as to the manner in which he shall do his work". In *Roche v Kelly*[23] Walsh J held that in a master-servant relationship, the master must have right to tell servant what to do and how to do it, whether or not he exercises that right. The main problem with this test, however, is that (especially in the case of skilled professionals) the employer may exercise very little actual, day-to-day control over the work done, but the relationship can still be classed as one of employment. This has been the case in relation to, for example, journalists,[24] hospital doctors,[25] university lecturers,[26] and so on. The idea of tight inspection and surveillance of employees that is implicit in the control test is somewhat anachronistic in much contemporary employment.[27] As a result the control test is now rarely used as a stand alone test.[28]

---

[20]   Barrett, "Employed v Self-employed Status" (2010) 23(1) *Irish Tax Review* 59.

[21]   Cox *et al* note that much seems to depend on the background policy considerations at play in a given case, for example, whether what is at issue relates to imposing vicarious liability (in which case *control* is often key) or whether the issue is one related to tax or insurance (in which case the parties' *financial arrangements* are heavily significant); *op.cit*, p 64.

[22]   (1880) 6 QBD 530, at 532 *per* Bramwell LJ.

[23]   [1969] IR 100.

[24]   *In Re Sunday Tribune* [1984] IR 505.

[25]   *O' Friel v St Michael's Hospital* [1990] ILRM 260.

[26]   *Cahill v DCU* [2007] ELR 113 (HC); [2009] IESC 80 (SC).

[27]   See *Beloff v Pressdram Ltd* [1973] 1 ALL ER 241, where Ungoed Thomas J (at 250) noted that the greater the skill required for an employee's work, the less significant control is in determining if there is a contract of service.

[28]   *Hogan v United Beverages*, Unreported, Circuit Court, Smyth J, 14 October 2005. However, the test was relied upon by the Supreme Court in *O' Keefe v Hickey* [2009] 1 ILRM 490, in deciding that a teacher in a state school was an employee of the school management rather than the Department of Education.

Integration

An alternative test looks at the extent to which an individual is employed as an integral part of the business. In the *Sunday Tribune* case[29] a freelance journalist who got commission in advance but was under no obligation to the newspaper to publish her work was held to be employed under a contract for services. By contrast a "staff" journalist working 50 weeks per year for the newspaper was an integral part of the newspaper and therefore had a contract of service. This case illustrates that the nature of the work itself is not always significant, as both journalists did the same *substantive* work (writing columns for the newspaper) but each had a different employment status. The problem with the integration test is that the courts have not spelt out clearly what is meant by "integration". While it applies quite well to professionals over whom the employer does not have direct control, it does not fit so well with others, such as outworkers or sub-contractors, who may be highly "integral" to the employer's business without necessarily being employees. This is particularly the case given the growth in the use of outsourcing by employers.[30]

[3–13]

Economic Reality

This test (sometimes referred to as the "enterprise test") essentially asks if the worker has engaged him or herself to perform the services, performing them as a person in business on his or her own account. This looks at a range of factors (whether the worker has helpers, whether he or she takes a financial risk, etc) and asks whether or not the worker is actually running a separate business. The test was outlined in the English case of *Market Investigations Ltd v Minister of Social Security*, where according to Cooke J[31]:

[3–14]

> "The fundamental test to be applied is this: 'Is the person who has engaged himself to perform these services performing them as a person in business on his own account?' If the answer to that question is 'yes' then the contract is a contract for services. If the answer is 'no' then the contract is a contract of service".

This test was noted with approval by Barr J in *O 'Coindealbhain v Mooney*.[32] Although this test has the attraction of clarity, in reality it is less of a conceptual categorisation and more of an approach, which encourages the courts to examine a range of features of the work relationship and come to a conclusion, on balance, as to how it should be categorised.[33] That no one test is determinative can be clearly seen in the key Irish and UK decisions in this area, to which we now turn.

---

[29] *In Re Sunday Tribune* [1984] IR 505.

[30] See Fevre, *op.cit.*

[31] [1969] 2 QB 173 at 184.

[32] [1990] 1 IR 422.

[33] Note, too, the comments of Edwards J in *Minister of Agriculture and Food v Barry* [2009] 1 IR 215, where he pointed out that this test could not be treated as being of universal application where the issue for determination involves the broader question as to what is the nature of a particular work relationship between two parties. This is because in certain cases a work relationship is not capable of being defined in terms of a simple choice as to whether it is governed by a contract of service or a contract for services (for example in the case of a statutory office holder).

Defining the Employment Relationship

[3–15] The question of whether or not a person is an employee is a mixed question of fact and law.[34] In *Ready Mixed Concrete (South East) Ltd v Minister for Pensions and National Insurance*[35] MacKenna J adopted an open-ended approach to the question of determining employee status. According to MacKenna J[36]:

> "A contract of service exists if these three conditions are fulfilled. (i) The servant agrees that, in consideration of a wage or other remuneration, he will provide his own work and skill in the performance of some service for his master. (ii) He agrees, expressly or impliedly, that in the performance of that service he will be subject to the other's control in a sufficient degree to make that other master. (iii) The other provisions of the contract are consistent with its being a contract of service....The servant must be obliged to provide his own work and skill. Freedom to do a job by one's own hands or by another's is inconsistent with a contract of service, though a limited or occasional power of delegation may not be...".

Although at first glance, this may appear to be a more comprehensive "test" than those outlined above, it arguably simply restates the control test (parts (i) and (ii)) and invites the court to consider all the other elements of the employment relationship (part (iii)) in coming to a conclusion. The final part of the quote relates to the idea of personal service to which we will return below.

[3–16] In the case, the question was whether an owner-driver of a vehicle used exclusively for the delivery of the company's concrete was engaged under a contract of service. The worker entered into a hire purchase agreement to purchase a lorry but the mixing equipment on the lorry was the company's property. The truck was painted in company colours and he wore a company uniform. He was also obliged to carry out the company's orders and was paid on a mileage basis, but the contract described him as an independent contractor. The Court concluded that he looked more like a small independent business than an employee.

[3–17] The leading Irish authority in this area is the Supreme Court decision in *Henry Denny & Sons v Minister for Social Welfare*.[37] Here, a worker was hired as in-house demonstrator, demonstrating and marketing the company's (Henry Denny & Sons) products in supermarkets. She was placed on a panel from which demonstrators were selected by the company. The demonstrator was employed by the company under yearly renewable contracts from 1991 to 1993. Her written contract of employment for 1993 described her as an "independent contractor" and purported to make her responsible for her own tax affairs. The demonstrator worked an average of 28 hours a week for 48 to 50 weeks a year and carried out approximately 50 demonstrations a year. The demonstrations were not carried out under the supervision of the company, but the demonstrator was required to comply with any reasonable directions given by

---

[34] See Regan, "The Contract and Relationship of Employment" in *Employment Law* (Regan ed, Tottel, Dublin, 2009), pp 41–42.

[35] [1968] 2 QB 497.

[36] *ibid* at 515.

[37] [1998] 1 IR 34.

the owner of the supermarket and she had been provided with written instructions as to how she was to carry out her work. She was supplied by the company with the materials for performing the demonstration (demonstration stand, uniform and products) and required the consent of the company prior to sub-contracting any of the demonstrations assigned to her. She was not a member of the company's pension scheme.

In 1992 both parties were required to fill out a form to determine whether she was an insurable person under the Social Welfare Acts 1993-1997 (if her contract was one of service she would be insurable). The social welfare officer decided she was an insurable person. The company appealed this decision and the appeals officer rejected the appeal. The company then appealed to High Court, where Carroll J also held that the worker was an insurable person. The company then appealed to Supreme Court. **[3–18]**

Keane J dismissed the appeal. He referred to the English decision of *Market Investigations v Minister of Social Security*,[38] where Cooke J noted that it was likely that no exhaustive list could be compiled of considerations which are relevant in determining the question of whether a person is, or is not, on business on his or her own account and nor could strict rules be laid down as to the relative weight which the various considerations should carry in particular cases. Keane J concluded that: **[3–19]**

> "while each case must be determined in the light of its particular facts and circumstances, in general a person will be regarded as providing his or her services under a contract of service and not as an independent contractor where he or she is performing those services for another person and not for himself or herself. The degree of control exercised over how the work is to be performed, although a factor to be taken into account, is not decisive. The inference that the person is engaged in business on his or her own account can be more readily drawn where he or she provides the necessary premises or equipment or some other form of investment, where he or she employs others to assist in the business and where the profit which he or she derives from the business is dependent on the efficiency with which it is conducted by him or her".[39]

In *Minister for Agriculture and Food v Barry*,[40] an appeal to the High Court on a point of law from the EAT, the respondents had worked as temporary veterinary inspectors (TVIs) at a meat factory in Cork. In order to become a TVI, each respondent had to apply for approval from the appellant. Once Departmental approval had been granted, each respondent had to apply in writing to the appellant for inclusion in a TVI panel, from which they would be periodically selected to do work in particular meat plants, assisting the permanent VI. When the Cork plant closed down, the respondents claimed entitlements under the legislation on redundancy and notice. The key issue was that any such entitlement was dependent on the respondents being employees of the appellant. The EAT decided that the respondents had all been employed under contracts of service and had therefore been employees of the appellant. The appellants appealed to the High Court. **[3–20]**

---

[38] [1969] 2 QB 173 at 184.

[39] [1998] 1 IR 34 at 50.

[40] [2009] 1 IR 215.

[3–21]   The High Court found, first, that the EAT had erred in law by formulating the issue as a straightforward choice between a contract of service or a contract for services. Edwards J noted that other possibilities should have been considered, such as whether the TVIs worked under a single contract (be it of service or for services), or whether on each occasion they worked they entered a new contract (again, be it of service or for services), or whether by virtue of a course of dealing over a lengthy period of time the relationship had become refined into an enforceable "umbrella" contract.

[3–22]   Secondly, Edwards J held that the EAT had erred in law in its approach to the correct tests to be applied. The EAT had first looked at whether a "mutuality of obligation" existed between the parties. This approach stresses that without the existence of reciprocal promises between the parties, their relationship lacks a genuine contractual character: it has been characterised by the House of Lords as "that irreducible minimum of mutual obligation necessary to create a contract of service".[41] While Edwards J felt that the mutuality of obligation approach was an "important filter", in that its absence meant the Court need not go further in examining the relationship, the existence of such an obligation could not be determinative of the issue. In any case, here, he felt the EAT had been incorrect in deriving a mutuality of obligation from an "implied agreement" as between the parties that the TVIs would carry out inspections on an ongoing basis where, he found, no such agreement existed.

[3–23]   Thirdly, Edwards J found that the EAT had misconstrued the decision of Keane J in *Henry Denny*. The EAT had referred to Keane J's judgment as providing a "single composite test", the enterprise test. The issues of control and integration were, according to the EAT, simply to be used as elements in applying the enterprise test. Edwards J found this to be a misreading of the *Henry Denny* decision:

> "I believe that this confusion derives primarily from misguided attempts to divine in the judgment the formulation of a definitive, 'one size fits all' test in circumstances where the learned judge was not attempting to formulate any such test... I think it can sometimes be unhelpful to speak of a 'control test', or of an 'integration test', or of an 'enterprise test', or of a 'mixed test', or of a 'fundamental test' or of an 'essential test', or of a 'single composite test' because, in truth, none of the approaches so labelled constitutes a 'test', in the generally understood sense of that term, namely, that it constitutes a measure or yardstick of universal application that can be relied upon to deliver a definitive result".[42]

[3–24]   Edwards J concluded by re-stating that every case must be considered in the light of its particular facts and it is for the court or tribunal considering those facts to draw the appropriate inferences from them. This requires the exercise of judgement and analytical skill and it is not, according to Edwards J, possible to arrive at the correct result by testing the facts of the case in some rigid, formulaic way. The judgment in *Barry* is useful in terms of clarifying that no one test can be determinative of the issue.

---

[41] *Carmichael v National Power PLC* [1999] ICR 1226 at 1230 *per* Lord Irvine.
[42] [2009] 1 IR 215 at 239.

However, essentially it asks the courts and tribunals to consider a range of factors in coming to its conclusion,[43] some of the most important of which we will now consider.

The Idea of Personal Service

At the core of the definition of a contract of employment is the requirement for the employee to "personally" execute the work. It has been suggested that the "boundary of labour law" should be fixed by this requirement that the work be performed *personally* as opposed to contracts that permit or expect the contractor to use *substitutes* or employ *others* to do the work.[44] The extent to which a party can delegate or sub-contract work has been a factor examined many times in the case law.

[3–25]

In *Henry Denny & Sons v Minister for Social Welfare* the Supreme Court noted that the inference that a person is engaged in business on his or her own account can be more readily drawn where he or she employs others to assist in the business.[45] In *Tierney v An Post*[46] the applicant was a sub-postmaster. McCracken J, in the High Court, noted that, while the applicant had the ability to employ an assistant, An Post had to approve of the assistant in advance. He held this to be indicative of a contract of service. On appeal, however, the Supreme Court said this was a contract for services. The Court noted that it was not normal to find a clause in a contract of service allowing an employee to hire assistants for the work he was employed to do.[47] The Court also noted that it was not surprising, in a situation like this, that An Post would wish to retain a right of veto over the appointment of persons who for any reason it might not be appropriate to employ in a post office; see also *McAuliffe v Minister for Social Welfare*.[48] However, very strict conditions regarding the use of substitutes might themselves be indicative of a high level of *control* by one party over the other; this could be indicative of an employer-employee relationship.[49]

[3–26]

Other Factors to Consider

As noted, the courts and tribunals need to engage in a "balancing exercise" in order to determine employment status. Under the 2000-2003 social partnership agreement (the *Programme for Prosperity and Fairness*) an Employment Status Group was set up. The group produced a Code of Practice (updated in 2007 by the Hidden Economy

[3–27]

---

[43] This has been rather pithily described by Wedderburn as the "elephant test"; the contract of employment has become "an animal too difficult to define, but easy to recognise when you see it"; Wedderburn, *The Worker and the Law* (3rd ed, Penguin, Harmondsworth, 1986), p 116. In the leading English case of *O' Kelly v Trusthouse Forte* [1983] ICR 728 the employment tribunal looked at *18* relevant factors in coming to its decision. See also the Labour Court decision in *Connaught Gold Co-op Society Limited* (AD 0818/2008).

[44] See Collins *et al, op.cit*, p 186 for a discussion of this idea.

[45] [1998] 1 IR 34 at 50 *per* Keane J.

[46] [2000] 1 IR 536.

[47] See also *Castleisland Cattle Breeding Society v Minister for Social and Family Affairs* [2004] IR 150, where the Supreme Court held that the inclusion of terms requiring the approval of the Minister to the appointment of any substitute inseminators did not indicate a "master/servant" level of control, but was required to comply with statutory regulations.

[48] [1995] 2 IR 238.

[49] See Regan, "The Contract and Relationship of Employment" in *Employment Law* (Regan ed, Tottel, Dublin, 2009), pp 33-34.

Monitoring Group, set up under the *Towards 2016* agreement) which lists criteria that the courts have indicated are useful in reaching a conclusion as to a party's employment status.[50] We will look at three factors here that have come before the courts and tribunals on many occasions.

Profit and Loss: Opportunity and Risk

[3–28] The extent to which a person has the opportunity to benefit financially from the work over and above a salary or wage, or, conversely, the extent of exposure to financial risk or loss will be important in determining if such a person is an employee. In *Henry Denny & Sons v Minister for Social Welfare*[51] the Supreme Court held that it is easier to infer that a person is engaged in business on his or her own account where the profit which he or she derived from the business was dependent on the efficiency with which it is conducted by him or her. In the case, the shop demonstrator's earnings were totally dependent on the extent to which the company used her services.

[3–29] By contrast, in *O' Coindealbhain v Mooney*[52] the worker was the branch manager of a social welfare office and was paid a fixed fee depending on volume of work performed. Blayney J concluded that Mr Mooney was, in fact, in business for himself, as the lower he kept his overheads the greater was his profit. Similarly, in *Tierney v An Post*[53] a postmaster of a sub-post office carried on the post office business in the same premises as his own business. The Supreme Court held that, while the extent to which he could maximise the profit which he derived from carrying on the post office business was relatively modest, it was nevertheless the case that any expenditure by him on improving the premises or employing assistants, which had the effect of increasing the volume of the post office business, would increase his own profit also. In *McAuliffe v Minister for Social Welfare*[54] the High Court was concerned with the status of two delivery men contracted to deliver newspapers. Two key factors were that the drivers were remunerated on the basis of a sum per delivery run (rather than a set wage) and were themselves responsible for damage, destruction or loss of goods carried for the appellant and for losses caused by any delays. As a result, their profits were determined to a significant extent by how they carried out their work and they were held to work under contracts for services.

It is important to distinguish opportunities for profit-making from contractual provisions to do with, for example, profit-sharing or commission payments. These are relatively common terms of employment that would not necessarily be incompatible with a contract of service.

---

[50] The Code states that it is vital that the job as a whole is looked at, but goes on to stress that the economic independence of the worker is the "overriding consideration"; see the comments, above, of Edwards J in *Minister for Agriculture and Food v Barry* [2009] 1 IR 215. The Code can be accessed at www.revenue.ie. Also note that, in the *Barry* case, the workers referred to the Code and, in their evidence to the EAT, claimed that the TVIs fit into the "employee" category under each and every relevant heading.

[51] [1998] 1 IR 34.

[52] [1990] 1 IR 422

[53] [2000] 1 IR 536.

[54] [1995] 2 IR 238.

Equipment and Materials

Generally, employers will be required to supply employees with the equipment and [3–30] materials necessary to perform the work. Where a worker supplies his or her own materials or equipment, this will point to a contract for services. In *McAuliffe v Minister for Social Welfare*[55] the delivery men owned the vehicles they drove and were responsible for the expenses involved in driving. They were also free to carry goods for other employers (albeit not at the same time as carrying goods for the appellant). By contrast, in *Henry Denny & Sons v Minister for Social Welfare*[56] the shop demonstrator was supplied by the company with the demonstration stand, uniform and products necessary for performing the demonstration. In both *O' Coindealbhain v Mooney*[57]and *Tierney v An Post*[58] the fact that the premises were provided and maintained by the workers in question was a significant factor in the courts concluding that neither were employees.

The Parties' Categorisation

In many contracts the parties themselves may use particular labels, most commonly [3–31] that one party is "an employee" or "an independent contractor". However, the courts will disregard such labels if they do not, in fact, correspond with reality. In *Henry Denny & Sons v Minister for Social Welfare*[59] the company argued that the appeals officer had erred in law in failing to have sufficient regard to the terms of the written contract between it and the store demonstrator, which expressly stated that the latter was "deemed to be an independent contractor" and nothing in the agreement should "be construed as creating the relationship of master and servant or principal and agents". Murphy J was satisfied that the appeals officer had been correct in his conclusion as he was required to consider "the facts or realities of the situation on the ground" to enable him to reach a decision. He was required to, and did, attempt to ascertain the true bargain between the parties, rather than merely rely on the "labels ascribed by them to their relationship".[60]

Similarly, in *Castleisland Cattle Breeding Society v Minister for Social and Family* [3–32] *Affairs*[61] the Supreme Court held that, notwithstanding the requirement to examine the terms of the written contract, in determining whether a contract was one of service, or for services, an appeals officer was bound to examine and have regard to what was the real arrangement, on a day-to-day basis, between the parties. A statement in a contract to the effect that a person was an "independent contractor" was not a contractual obligation but merely a statement which might or might not be reflective of the actual legal relationship between the parties. However, in this case, the Court found that, apart from matters of minor detail, the written contract, which was consistent with the worker being an independent contractor, seemed to have been the contract that was actually worked.

---

[55] [1995] 2 IR 238.
[56] [1998] 1 IR 34.
[57] [1990] 1 IR 422.
[58] [2000] 1 IR 536.
[59] [1998] 1 IR 34.
[60] *ibid* at 53. See also *In Re Sunday Tribune Ltd* [1984] IR 505.
[61] [2004] IR 150.

[3–33]   In *Millen v Presbyterian Church in Ireland* [62] the EAT determined that a minister of the
Presbyterian Church of Ireland was not an employee within the meaning of the Terms
of Employment (Information) Act 1994. The issuing of a P60 to the minister did not
determine the employment relationship regardless of the use of the descriptions
"employer" and "employee". In *Nyamhovsa v Boss Worldwide Promotions* [63] the
Equality Tribunal looked at the terms of the contract, which included a clause stating
"nothing contained in this agreement shall be construed as constituting any relationship of employer and employee". The Tribunal found, however, that most of the
remaining clauses in the contract were highly prescriptive of how the worker should
perform her tasks and held that a contract of service existed.

IV. Atypical Employment

[3–34]   The increasing regulation of the employment relationship has been driven to a
significant extent by the changing nature of contemporary employment. After World
War II, the "Fordist" model of employment predominated in most Westernised
countries, based on the idea of an employee working full-time, with standard hours
(generally conceived of as "9 to 5", five days a week) for a single employer and for a
fixed-wage. In our "post-Fordist" working world, [64] however, "atypical" or "non-
standard" work is more and more common and the forms of work in which
contemporary workers engage are becoming increasingly differentiated. Atypical
work refers to the use by employers of labour that is not regular or full-time or based
on indefinite employment contracts (or, indeed, all three) and refers, particularly, to
part-time, fixed-term and temporary work. [65] In response to the growing nature of such
work, and particularly concerns about the exploitation of atypical workers, there have
been some significant legislative interventions in this area in recent years, most of them
driven by EU law. [66] We will consider, next, three of the most prevalent forms of
atypical work.

Part-Time and Casual Work

[3–35]   Part-time work is not, by any means, a recent phenomenon but part-time workers make
up the biggest share of atypical workers in the EU. [67] In 1997, the Part-Time Workers

---

[62] [2000] ELR 292.

[63] DEC-E2007-072.

[64] Lash and Urry, *The End of Organised Capitalism* (Polity, Cambridge, 1987).

[65] See, for example, Bauman, *Work, Consumerism and the New Poor* (Open University,
Buckingham, 1998); Bosch and Lehndorff, *Working in the Service Sector: A Tale From
Different Worlds* (Routledge, London, 2005); Doogan, "Long-Term Employment and the
Restructuring of the Labour Market in Europe" (2005) 14(1) *Time and Society* 65; and above,
n 5. Note a recent report by the European Foundation for the Improvement of Living and
Working Conditions (Eurofound) focuses on what is referred to as "very atypical work", including
non-written employment contracts, contracts of less than 10 working hours a week and very short
fixed-term contracts of six months or fewer; Broughton *et al, Flexible Forms of Work: 'Very
Atypical' Contractual Arrangements* (Eurofound Report, 2010, available at www.eurofound.
europa.eu).

[66] See Middlemiss, "Legal Rights of Atypical Workers" (2005) 23 ILT 132.

[67] Corral and Isusi, *Part-time Work in Europe* (Eurofound Report, 2006, available at
www.eurofound.europa.eu).

Directive was adopted after almost 20 years of attempts to regulate atypical work at European level.[68] The Directive was adopted in accordance with the procedures relating to EU social dialogue under Arts 153-155TFEU (ex-Arts 137-139EC), which resulted in a Framework Agreement on part-time work concluded between the social partners at EU level.[69] The Directive was transposed into Irish law by means of the Protection of Employees (Part-Time Work) Act 2001. The Framework Agreement adopts the principle of equal treatment between part-time and full-time workers, but also allows for significant exceptions to this. The latter are partly a result of significant and sustained opposition to the Directive by some of the Member States (notably the UK), primarily on the grounds that regulation in this area would increase costs to employers and inhibit job creation.[70] It is important to note, also, that as the majority of part-time workers tend to be female, important issues of gender discrimination arise in this context.[71]

The Framework Agreement has the twofold aim of providing for the removal of discrimination against part-time workers and improving the quality of part-time work, as well as facilitating the development of part-time work on a voluntary basis and contributing to the flexible organisation of working time in a manner which takes into account the needs of employers and workers.[72] The Directive prohibits discrimination against part-time workers in relation to employment (as distinct from social security) matters, unless such discrimination can be justified on objective grounds.[73] Member States and national social partners are encouraged to identify and review obstacles of a legal or administrative nature, which may limit the opportunities for part-time work and, where appropriate, eliminate them, but the Directive emphasises that part-time work should be voluntary: a worker's refusal to transfer from full-time to part-time work, or vice-versa, should not constitute a valid reason for termination of employment.[74] The Directive has come in for criticism on the grounds that it gives insufficient weight to the interests of workers as against those of employers. According to Jeffrey: **[3–36]**

> "a requirement that employers should not treat part-time workers any worse than full-time workers, and a request that employers think about facilitating transfers between full-time and part-time work are *not* the same as a requirement that employers take workers' interests into account when setting

---

[68] Directive 97/81 of 15 December 1997 concerning the Framework Agreement on part-time work concluded by ETUC, UNICE and CEEP [1997] OJ L14/9. See Jeffrey, "Not Really Going to Work? Of the Directive on Part-time Work, 'Atypical' Work and Attempts to Regulate it" (1998) 27 ILJ 193.

[69] See Barnard, *EC Employment Law* (3rd ed, Oxford University Press, Oxford, 2006), chapter 2.

[70] Fitzpatrick *et al*, "The Commission Proposals on 'Atypical Work': Back to the Drawing-Board...Again" (1995) 24 ILJ 296.

[71] Bleijenbergh *et al*, "European Social Citizenship and Gender: The Part-time Work Directive" (2004) 10 (3) *European Journal of Industrial Relations* 309. See also chapter 5.

[72] Clause 1.

[73] Clause 4.

[74] Clause 5. In Case C-55/07 *Michaeler v Labour Inspectorate of the Autonomous Province of Bolzano* the ECJ found that Italian legislation requiring copies of part-time employment contracts be sent to the authorities within 30 days of their signature constituted an unjustifiable administrative obstacle likely to limit the opportunities for part-time work.

the working hours of part-time workers. This aim of the Directive turns out to be little more than a pious hope, combined with the uncritical repetition of an unsubstantiated argument about 'atypical work'; more usually put forward in order to support calls for 'de-regulation' and 'flexibility'".[75]

Nevertheless, the 2001 Act has been important in the sense that it granted part-time workers access to previously denied legislative rights (in particular under the Unfair Dismissals Act 1977).

The 2001 Act

[3–37] A part-time worker is defined in s 7(1) as an employee whose normal hours of work are less than the normal hours of work of a comparable employee in relation to him or her. "Normal hours of work" is defined as the average number of hours worked by the employee each day during a reference period. The reference period is a period of not less than seven days and not more than 12 months and must equate to a period of reference in which the comparable full-time employee has worked his or her normal hours. In *ESB v McDonnell*[76] the Labour Court held that this provision must be construed literally. The complainant here was a seasonal worker who had worked for over 30 years on a seven month per annum basis. The Court noted that the Act quite simply states that any one who works fewer hours in a reference period than those of a comparable full-time employee is a part-time employee. As the complainant in a 12-month period worked fewer hours than a comparable full time employee, the complainant was a part-time employee within the meaning of the Act. The Court was of the view that the contract of employment does not have to extend over the *entire* reference period for the employee to be considered a part-time employee under the Act.

[3–38] "Comparable employees" (s 7) are those who are employed by the same employer or associated employers or, if this condition cannot be satisfied, who are stipulated to be comparators for the purposes of the Act in a collective agreement or, if neither the preceding conditions can be satisfied, are employed in the same industry or sector of employment, as long as certain conditions are satisfied. The conditions to be satisfied for establishing a comparator are that:

a. both of the employees concerned perform the same work under the same or similar conditions, or each is interchangeable with the other in relation to the work;

b. the work performed by one of the employees concerned is of the same or a similar nature to that performed by the other and any differences between the work performed or the conditions under which it is performed by each, either are of small importance in relation to the work as a whole, or occur with such irregularity as not to be significant; and

c. the work performed by the relevant part-time employee is equal or greater in value to the work performed by the other employee concerned, having regard to such matters as skill, physical or mental requirements, responsibility and working conditions.

---

[75] *op.cit,* at p 199.
[76] PTD 081/2008.

Only one of these conditions needs to be satisfied. The kinds of issues that will be relevant in deciding whether or not the employees are engaged in "like work" include the skills and qualifications required (which could include entry standards, probationary standards, probationary training and ongoing training), the physical and mental requirements of the job, the responsibilities borne and the working conditions laid down in the contract of employment or collective agreement.[77] In *Matthews v Kent and Medway Towns Fire Authority and Ors*[78] the House of Lords (by a majority) allowed an appeal against a finding that retained firefighters were not engaged in the "same or broadly similar" work as full-time firefighters. The Court noted that the extent to which the work done by the different employees is *exactly the same* must be of great importance. If a large component of the work is exactly the same, the question is whether any differences are of such importance as to prevent their work being regarded overall as "the same or broadly similar".[79] In *Catholic University School v Dooley*[80] the claimant, a part-time teacher paid directly by the school, claimed he was paid less than his chosen comparator, a full-time permanent teacher employed by the school but paid by the Department of Education. The school argued that the choice of comparator was incorrect and that the claimant should have sought to compare himself with a permanent and/or full-time teacher employed by the school directly as a privately-paid teacher. This was because teachers paid by the Department had, *inter alia*, rights to incremental salary scales, the negotiation of terms and conditions of employment, being subject to redeployment, career breaks, job-sharing and the obligation to be in Department pension scheme, none of which applied to privately-paid teachers. The Labour Court referred to the decision of the High Court in *Minister for Finance v McArdle*[81] in which Laffoy J stated that comparability under the fixed-term workers' Act (and, therefore by extension, the part-time workers' Act) is defined not by reference to the status of the worker but by having the same employer and being engaged in like work. The Court confirmed the claimant's choice of comparator here.[82]

[3–39]

The 2001 Act, in s 9, provides that part-time employees shall not be treated less favourably than comparable, full-time employees in relation to conditions of employment, where such treatment is based on their part-time status. In *Dooley* the school argued that the presence within the employment of full-time and permanent teachers (directly paid by the school) who were treated similarly to the claimant was fatal to his case since it demonstrated that the treatment complained of was unrelated to his part-time status, which, according to the Framework Agreement, had to be the "sole" reason for the difference in treatment. The Labour Court rejected this argument, noting that the protection afforded by both the fixed-term and part-time Acts and Directives would be rendered nugatory if employers could claim that any factor, no matter how trivial, which influenced an employer in not applying the principle of equal treatment could operate as a full defence to a claim. There would rarely be a case in

[3–40]

---

[77] See *Bus Éireann v Group of Workers* (PTD 071/2008). See also the discussion of "like work" in chapter 5.
[78] [2006] UKHL 8.
[79] *ibid* at 26 *per* Baroness Hale.
[80] PTD 092/2009.
[81] [2007] 18 ELR 165.
[82] See also *Blackrock College v Browne* (PTD 091/2009).

which an employer could not point to some status-neutral consideration, which influenced an impugned decision, to avoid liability for what would otherwise be unlawful discrimination.

[3–41] However, less favourable treatment can be justified on objective grounds unrelated to that status. The less favourable treatment must seek to achieve a legitimate objective corresponding to a "real need" of the employer and must be appropriate and necessary to achieve that objective.[83] In *Louth VEC (Department of Education & Science) v A Worker* [84] the claimant (a part-time teacher) argued that she was treated less favourably in that she was not awarded incremental credit for previous unqualified service. She had taught part-time for many years prior to becoming fully qualified in 2003: it was only from that point that she received incremental credit. The Labour Court found that the difference in treatment of the part-time teacher was objectively justified by the real need on the part of the employer to ensure that all teachers had appropriate academic qualifications. The means to achieve this objective, a difference in incremental pay, was found to be appropriate and the Court noted that the claimant had not advanced any alternative means of achieving the objective that would have had a less discriminatory effect.[85]

[3–42] In *Boxmore Plastics Ltd v Curry*[86] the Labour Court found that a provision whereby part-time workers do not receive overtime payments until they have completed the standard number of hours under which a comparable full-time worker would be entitled to claim overtime is not unfavourable treatment and is not discriminatory. However, note that in *Voß v Land Berlin*[87] the ECJ held that the principle of *equal pay* (under Art 157TFEU, ex-Art 141EC) is infringed if a part-time civil servant is paid less for hours which are worked over and above his or her normal working hours, but which are not sufficient to bring the number of hours worked overall above the level of normal working hours for full-time civil servants, where the resulting difference in treatment affects a considerably higher number of women than men and cannot be justified by objective factors wholly unrelated to discrimination based on sex. In this case, a part-time teacher who gave additional classes was paid less for than a full-time teacher who worked the same number of hours.

[3–43] Employers cannot claim economic detriment as grounds for objective justification, since in every case in which it is necessary to implement principles of equality there is likely to be some cost to the employer.[88] In *Abbott Ireland Ltd v SIPTU*[89] "industry practice" was held not to be a reasonably objective ground for differential treatment.

[3–44] Under s 10 of the Act, part-time workers must have access to the same conditions of employment as full-time workers, although in certain respects these entitlements are on a

---

[83] The test laid down in an equality context by the ECJ in Case 170/84 *Bilka-Kaufhaus GmbH v Weber von Hartz* [1986] ECR 1607.

[84] PTD 051/2005.

[85] See also *Diageo Global Supply v Rooney* [2004] ELR 133.

[86] PTD 035/2003.

[87] Case C-300/06 [2007] ECR I-376.

[88] *Catholic University School v Dooley* (PTD 092/2009).

[89] PTD 43/2004.

pro rata basis. This means that, where conditions of employment in question are dependent on the number of hours worked, a part-time employee receives a benefit enjoyed by a full-time colleague only to the extent to which it is proportionate to the number of hours worked by the part-time employee relative to the full-time employee.[90] In *Department of Justice, Equality & Law Reform v Ennis*[91] the claimant was a part-time worker employed as a Traffic Warden with the Department. She claimed she received a lower rate of travel allowance (mileage) than her full-time colleagues. The employer argued that the mileage was an allowance in the nature of basic pay which forms part of the weekly remuneration package. The Labour Court, however, rejected that argument and held that such a payment was really a compensation for the time and expense involved in travelling to work, unconnected with the number of hours worked. The employer could not justify paying such an allowance on a pro rata basis.[92] In the recent *Land Tirol* case[93] an Austrian law provided that, in the event of a change in the working hours of an employee, the amount of annual leave not yet taken at the time of the change could be adjusted proportionally to the new working hours. This had the result that any worker who reduced his or her working hours from full-time to part-time, also had his or her entitlement to leave accumulated while working full-time reduced (or, as a part-time worker, could only take the annual leave with a reduced, pro rata, level of payment). The ECJ held that Clause 4 of the Framework Agreement on part-time work precluded any provision that would result either in a worker, who reduces his or her working hours from full-time to part-time, suffering a reduction in the right to paid annual leave that he or she has accumulated (but had not been able to exercise while working full-time), or in that worker being only entitled to take the leave on a reduced level of holiday pay.

The 2001 Act in s 11 makes provision for part-time workers who work on a casual basis. Under the Act a part-time employee is considered as working on a casual basis if: **[3–45]**

a. at that time he or she has been in the continuous service of the employer for a period of less than 13 weeks; and

b. that period of service and any previous period of service by him or her with the employer are not of such a nature as could reasonably be regarded as regular or seasonal employment; or

c. if he or she fulfils, at that time, the conditions specified in an approved collective agreement that has effect in relation to him and her and regards him or her, for the purposes of that agreement, as working on a casual basis.

Further, s 12(2) of the 2001 Act states that a ground which may not constitute an objective ground in relation to a part-time employee may constitute an objective ground with regard to a casual part-time employee. Under s 11 of the 2001 Act, a casual worker is defined as someone who has been in the "continuous service of the employer for a period of less than 13 weeks". It is probable that "continuous service", for the purposes of s 11 of the 2001 Act, would be interpreted by the courts in terms **[3–46]**

---

[90] Protection of Employees (Part-Time Work) Act 2001, s 10(2).

[91] PTD 041/2004.

[92] See also *Department of Education and Science v Gallagher* (PTD 047/2004).

[93] Case C-486/08 *Zentralbetriebsrat der Landeskrankenhauser Tirols v Land Tirol*.

similar to that of "continuous employment" for the purposes of s 9 of the Protection of Employees (Fixed-Term Work) Act 2003 (see below).

[3–47]   It is important to remember that there is no statutory *entitlement* to part-time work in this jurisdiction.[94] However, there is an obligation in s 13 of the 2001 Act for the Labour Relations Commission (LRC) and the Minister to keep under review any obstacles to part-time working in an industry and sector and recommend potential remedial action. The LRC has prepared a *Code of Practice on Access to Part-Time Work*, as requested by the social partners under clause 10.9 of the *Sustaining Progress* partnership agreement.[95] The Code seeks to encourage best practice and conformity with both the 2001 Act and equality legislation; promote the development of policies and procedures to assist employers, employees and their representative to improve access to part-time work for those employees who wish to work on a part-time basis; and stimulate employers to provide wider access to part-time work opportunities, where this is consistent with business requirements. Section 42(4) of the Industrial Relations Act 1990 provides that a code of practice is admissible in evidence and should be taken into account, if considered relevant, in any proceedings before a court or employment tribunal. While to date the Code has had a fairly limited impact in terms of cases brought to the tribunals,[96] it was cited before the Equality Tribunal in *Morgan v Bank of Ireland Group.*[97] The Tribunal found that, while the respondent had a procedure whereby workers could apply to transfer to part-time work, there was little indication that this corresponded with provisions of the Code of Practice in relation to consultation and discussion, a timely decision and response, and managing the outcome of the decision to the extent "that would be expected of an organisation the size of the respondent". The Tribunal found that, while flexible working arrangements are not an entitlement and are subject to the needs of the organisation, it is accepted that the significant majority of people taking up flexible working arrangements are female. It is therefore incumbent upon organisations to operate such arrangements according to fair procedures. Otherwise a prima facie case of indirect discrimination on gender grounds could arise. The Tribunal found for the claimant and ordered the respondent to implement a procedure for all part-time working applications that was fully in accordance with the Code of Practice.

---

[94] Clause 5(3) of the Framework Agreement calls for employers to give consideration to "measures to facilitate access to part-time work at all levels of the enterprise". However, as Jeffrey points out this clause creates no legal rights or obligations and he argues that the Directive constitutes "nothing more than a simple request to employers to think about taking unspecified measures in relation to the areas listed"; *op.cit*, p 197. A right to request flexible working arrangements (albeit it is difficult to claim that the ability to request something from an employer is a "right") was introduced in the UK in 2003 by virtue of the Employment Relations Act 2002, as part of a "work/life balance" campaign. Despite some controversy, the effect of this change has been fairly minimal; see Collins *et al*, *op.cit*, pp 382-387.

[95] Industrial Relations Act 1990 Code of Practice on Access to Part-Time Working (Declaration) Order 2006 (SI No 8 of 2006).

[96] By contrast, for example, with the Code of Practice on Grievance and Disciplinary Procedures (SI No 146 of 2000), which has featured in many binding Labour Court decisions under the Industrial Relations Acts 2001-2004. See chapter 11.

[97] DEC-E2008-029.

Section 15 of the 2001 Act prohibits the penalisation of employees for accessing, or attempting to access, rights under the legislation. Penalisation occurs where an employee is dismissed, suffers any unfavourable change in his or her conditions of employment or any unfair treatment (including selection for redundancy), or is the subject of any other action prejudicial to his or her employment.[98] However, s 15(2) provides that, where the action complained of results from the employee refusing to accede to a request by the employer to transfer from performing full-time work to performing part-time work, or vice versa, this will not constitute penalisation if:

[3–48]

a.   having regard to all the circumstances, there were substantial grounds both to justify the employer's making the request concerned and the employer's taking that action consequent on the employee's refusal; and
b.   the taking of that action is in accordance with the employee's contract of employment and the provisions of protective legislation generally.

The Labour Court found that an employer had penalised an employee by dismissing her when she refused to switch from part-time work to full-time work in *Beacon Automotive v A Worker.*[99]

Fixed-Term Work

Fixed-term work involves an employment relationship where the contract of employment is for a fixed period of time, i.e. has a start date and an end date, and terminates at the end date. A related form of work is fixed-purpose work. Here, the contract is for the duration of a specific purpose, for example, until the completion of a particular project, so that the duration of the contract is limited but cannot be precisely ascertained at its outset. The contract terminates when the purpose ceases and, generally, the employee can only carry out work related to the purpose for which they are employed.

[3–49]

There are various reasons why employers would choose to utilise fixed-term contracts. They may offer the employer greater flexibility in organising his or her workforce. Moreover, expiry of the term or purpose is *not* deemed to be an unfair dismissal.[100] For employees, the flexibility that fixed-term work offers may be an attraction if the employee does not wish to be tied to a particular employer, but, for example, instead wishes to engage in short-term and/or project work. However, there have been concerns, as the incidence of fixed-term contracts increases, about their use as a means of avoiding statutory regulation. As Collins puts it:

[3–50]

"Employers may choose between different forms of contract for acquiring labour, if they are efficient substitutes, on the basis of which contractual arrangement avoids legal incidents of employment law. One of the least satisfactory aspects of many employment law systems is the way in which the

---

[98]   Protection of Employees (Part-Time Work) Act 2001, s 15(2).
[99]   PTD 072/2007.
[100]   Unfair Dismissals Act 1977, s 2(2). Such contracts, however, must be in writing, signed by the employer and employee, and provide that the Act does not apply to a dismissal consisting of the expiry of the fixed-term or the cessation of the specified purpose: see also Unfair Dismissals (Amendment) Act 1993, s 3.

allocation of the risk of economic insecurity on to the worker also tends to exclude the worker from protection of employment rights".[101]

[3–51] In order to address this issue as it relates to fixed-term work, the Fixed-Term Workers Directive was adopted in accordance with the procedures relating to EU social dialogue under Arts 153-155TFEU (ex-Arts 137-139EC), which resulted in a Framework Agreement on fixed-term work concluded between the social partners at EU level.[102] The purpose of the Framework Agreement, as set out in Clause 1, is to:

a. improve the quality of fixed-term work by ensuring the application of the principle of non-discrimination;

b. establish a framework to prevent abuse arising from the use of successive fixed-term employment contracts or relationships.

[3–52] It is interesting to note that the Framework Agreement proceeds, in the "general considerations" section, on the basis that employment contracts of an indefinite duration are the "general form of employment relationships and contribute to the quality of life of the workers concerned and improve performance". Thus, while the Framework Agreement recognises that the use of fixed-term work is legitimate and valuable in certain circumstances, it is an exception to the (preferred) norm. In that respect, it could be argued that the objective of preventing abuse in the use of such contracts carries more weight than that of improving the quality of fixed-term work. The ECJ noted in *Angelidaki* that the aim of the Framework Agreement is to protect workers against "instability of employment" and to protect "the principle that contracts of indefinite duration are the general form of employment relationship".[103]

It is also important to note, first, that the Fixed-Term Directive (and the Irish transposing legislation) strongly reflects that of the part-time workers legislation.[104] Therefore, the interpretation given by courts and tribunals to one will often have implications for the other.[105] Secondly, as with part-time work, fixed-term workers

---

[101] Collins, *Employment Law* (Oxford University Press, Oxford, 2003), p 40. The ECJ has also noted that it is only in certain circumstances that fixed-term employment contracts are liable to respond to the needs of *both* employers and workers; Case C-212/04 *Adeneler and Others v Ellinikos Organismos Galakto* [2006] IRLR 716, at para 62. See also the comments of Advocate-General Jääskinen in Case C-98/09 *Sorge v Poste Italiane SpA*, where he noted that EU legislation in this area pursues "apparently contradictory objectives which therefore require compromises, that is to say, in particular, to achieve a better balance between flexible working time for companies and job security for workers, while also taking account of the realities of specific national, sectoral and seasonal situations" (para 20).

[102] Directive 1999/70 of 28 June 1999 concerning the framework agreement on fixed-term work concluded by ETUC, UNICE and CEEP [1999] OJ L175/43. See Barnard, *EC Employment Law* (3rd ed, Oxford University Press, Oxford, 2006), chapter 2.

[103] Joined Cases C-378/07 to C-380/07 *Angelidaki v Organismos Nomarkhiaki Aftodiikisi Rethimnis*, at para 99.

[104] Indeed, the Framework Agreement itself notes that, when it received the proposal for a Directive on part-time work, the European Parliament invited the Commission to submit immediately proposals for Directives on other forms of flexible work, such as fixed-term work and temporary agency work.

[105] This was explicitly recognised in *ESB v McDonnell* (PTD 081/2008).

tend to be disproportionately female (according to the Framework Agreement more than half of fixed-term workers in the EU are women) and therefore the legislation in both areas interacts with laws on equality as between women and men.

The 2003 Act

The Protection of Employees (Fixed Term Work) Act 2003 came into operation on 14 July 2003.[106] The Directive should have been implemented by July 2001 and the government's failure to meet the deadline has resulted in some complex questions relating to the direct effect of EU law in light of a State's failure to transpose Directives on time.[107]

[3–53]

The Act applies to fixed-term employees where the end of the contract of employment is determined by the arrival of a specific date, the completion of a specific task or the occurrence of a specific event.[108] The Act does not apply to: agency workers; apprentices[109]; employees in initial vocational training; employees with a contract of employment which has been concluded within the framework of a specific public or publicly-supported training, integration or vocational retraining programme; a member of the Defence Forces; a trainee Garda; or a trainee nurse.[110] In *Keehan & Flannery v Shannon Airport*[111] the Labour Court found that employees whose contracts engaged them on a "month-to-month" basis, with no specific termination date, were fixed-term workers. To exclude such contracts from legislative protection would mean that the "the purpose of the Framework Agreement would be subverted and the attainment of its object would be seriously compromised".

[3–54]

The Act provides that fixed-term workers are not to be treated less favourably than "comparable permanent employees". "Comparable employees" (see s 5) are those who are employed by the same employer or associated employers, or, if this condition cannot be satisfied, who are stipulated to be comparators for the purposes of the Act in a collective agreement, or, if neither the preceding conditions can be satisfied, are employed in the same industry or sector of employment, as long as certain conditions are satisfied. The conditions to be satisfied for establishing a comparator are that:

[3–55]

---

[106] See Meenan,"Protection of Employees (Fixed-Term Work) Act 2003-Recent Case Law" (2006) 3(2) IELJ 39.

[107] See discussion below and Ryan, "Fixed-Term Workers" in *Employment Law* (Regan ed, Tottel, Dublin, 2009), p 305. The author also notes that, despite the relatively recent introduction of the Act, it has been the subject already of a large volume of litigation. At least part of the reason for this probably relates to the fact that the Act has a big impact on the role of the State as an employer, as the State has tended to use fixed-term contracts widely in certain areas, for example, in the nursing and teaching professions.

[108] Protection of Employees (Fixed-Term Work) Act 2003, s 2.

[109] Although it seems the Labour Court will carefully examine contracts to be satisfied that they are, in fact, contracts of apprenticeship: *ESB Network v Group of Workers* (FTD 074/2007).

[110] Protection of Employees (Fixed-Term Work) Act 2003, ss 2 and 17.

[111] [2008] 19 ELR 281.

a. both of the employees concerned perform the same work under the same or similar conditions or each is interchangeable with the other in relation to the work;

b. the work performed by one of the employees concerned is of the same or a similar nature to that performed by the other and any differences between the work performed or the conditions under which it is performed by each, either are of small importance in relation to the work as a whole or occur with such irregularity as not to be significant; and

c. the work performed by the relevant part-time employee is equal or greater in value to the work performed by the other employee concerned, having regard to such matters as skill, physical or mental requirements, responsibility and working conditions.

Only one of these conditions needs to be satisfied. This section is framed in the same manner as s 7 of the Protection of Employees (Part-Time Work) Act and the same principles would apply (see discussion above).

[3–56]   Under the Act, fixed-term workers are entitled to equality of treatment with permanent workers in relation to conditions of employment. Section 6 of the Act provides that the fixed-term employee cannot in respect of his or her conditions of employment be treated in a less favourable manner than a comparable permanent employee.[112] This relates to, for example, annual leave, sick leave, maternity leave, overtime payments, training and remuneration.[113] In *Minister for Finance v McArdle*[114] the High Court found that the term "conditions of employment" under s 6 does not include the *duration* of the contract. Laffoy J found that while the defendant in the case, an "unestablished" (i.e. non-permanent) civil servant, was, under the Act, entitled to the same conditions of employment as an established civil servant doing like work, including pension entitlements and access to career break, this did not extend to tenure of employment, in the sense that she was not entitled to rules and procedures for termination of her contract on the same terms as those applicable to an established civil servant.[115]

[3–57]   There are, however, specified circumstances in which less favourable treatment is allowed. Section 6(5) provides that the right not to be treated in a less favourable manner than a comparable permanent employee shall not apply in relation to any pension scheme or arrangement to a fixed-term employee who normally works less

---

[112] Less favourable treatment, however, is not to be equated merely with different treatment; see *Eircom v McDermott* (FTD 051/2005) where the Labour Court found it was impossible to predict whether the claimant's treatment during the period in question was less favourable than that which applied to the named comparators in terms of their membership of the company's different pension schemes. Non-renewal of a fixed-term contract of itself does not amount to less favourable treatment: *Our Lady's Children's Hospital Crumlin v Khan* [2008] ELR 314.

[113] Case C-268/06 *IMPACT v Minister for Agriculture and Food & Others* [2008] 2 CMLR 1265.

[114] [2007] 2 ILRM 438.

[115] In Case C-307/05 *Yolanda Del Cerro Alonso v Osakidetza Servicio Vasco de Salud* [2007] ECR I-7019 the ECJ considered that the concept of "employment conditions" could act as the basis for a claim which sought the grant to a fixed-term worker of a length-of-service allowance that is reserved under national law solely to permanent staff.

than 20 percent of the normal hours of the comparable permanent employee. However, this provision does not prevent an employer and a fixed-term employee from entering into an agreement whereby that employee may receive the same pension benefits as a comparable permanent employee. Sections 6(6) and 6(7) apply the pro rata principle to any conditions of employment where the benefit or scope of these is related to the number of hours worked by the comparator employee.

Importantly, the Act provides in s 6(2) that a fixed-term employee may be treated in a less favourable manner than a comparable permanent employee where such treatment can be justified on "objective grounds". In s 7 the Act states that a ground would be considered as an objective ground for treatment in a less favourable manner (including the renewal of a fixed-term employee's contract for a further fixed-term), if it is based on considerations *other than* the status of the employee as a fixed-term employee and the less favourable treatment is for the purpose of achieving a legitimate objective of the employer and such treatment is appropriate and necessary for that purpose.[116] The totality of factors relevant to the working relationship must be assessed in making a determination on objective justification.[117] Employer claims relating to objective justification that have failed include those based on: cost; compliance with legislation; industrial relations harmony and different collective bargaining processes; successful arguments have been made out in respect of legitimate employment policy; labour market objectives; incentivising promotion; public pay policies; and requirement of flexibility of workers.[118] The employer will, in any case, need to demonstrate that there were no alternative means having a less discriminatory effect by which the legitimate objective being pursued could be achieved.[119]

[3–58]

Under s 7(2), less favourable treatment in relation to one or more specific matters may be justifiable if the terms of the fixed-term employee's contract of employment, taken as a whole, are at least as favourable as the terms of the comparable permanent employee's contract of employment; i.e. if the overall "package" of terms

[3–59]

---

[116] The test laid down in an equality context by the ECJ in Case 170/84 *Bilka-Kaufhaus GmbH v Weber von Hartz* [1986] ECR 1607. See also Case C-212/04 *Adeneler and Others v Ellinikos Organismos Galakto* [2006] IRLR 716.

[117] *28 Workers v Courts Service* [2007] 18 ELR 212.

[118] See Kimber, "Fixed-Term Workers-Where Are We Now?" (2007) 4(4) IELJ 103. In Case C-307/05 *Yolanda Del Cerro Alonso v Osakidetza Servicio Vasco de Salud* [2007] ECR I- 7019 the ECJ found that the Framework Agreement had to be interpreted as meaning that it precluded the introduction of a difference in treatment justified solely on the basis that it was provided for by statute or by a collective agreement. In Case C-486/08 *Zentralbetriebsrat der Landeskrankenhauser Tirols v Land Tirol* the ECJ rejected an argument by the Austrian Government that differences in treatment could be objectively justified on the grounds of the need for "rigorous personnel management". The Court held that this was a budgetary consideration and could not, therefore, justify discrimination.

[119] *Health Service Executive v Prasad* (FTD 062/2006). In *Biggart v University of Ulster* an industrial tribunal in Northern Ireland found that the claimant had been treated less favourably than his full-time colleagues as he was dismissed without the university considering redeployment; see Koukiadaki, "Case Law Developments in the Area of Fixed-Term Work" (2009) 38(1) ILJ 89.

of the fixed-term employee is at least as favourable as the overall "package" of the comparable permanent employee.[120]

[3–60] Where the employer proposes to determine a fixed-term contract, the employee must be informed in writing of the objective grounds justifying the determination (be it the completion of a specific task, occurrence of a specific event or the arrival of a specific date). Similarly, where the employer proposes to renew a fixed-term contract, the employee must be informed in writing of the objective grounds justifying the renewal and outlining the reasons why an indefinite contract is not being offered.[121] These written statements are important, as they are admissible as evidence in any proceedings under the Act.[122] It is also provided for in s 8(4) that a Rights Commissioner or the Labour Court may draw any inference considered just and equitable if it appears that an employer omitted to provide a written statement, or a written statement is evasive or equivocal. The Labour Court has emphasised that the provisions of s 8 are to be taken extremely seriously by employers. In *HSE v Ghulam*[123] the Court held that a failure to provide the written statement was "deplorable" conduct, which, in normal circumstances, will put employers in a position of considerable difficulty in defending claims under the Act.[124]

[3–61] The reason for the Court's stringent stance in relation to s 8 can, in large part, be explained by the importance of the section when read in conjunction with s 9, which deals with successive fixed-term contracts. As noted above, the 2003 Act and Directive 1999/70 have not only the aim of guaranteeing equal treatment for fixed-term workers, but also that of preventing abuse in the utilisation by employers of such contracts. Section 9(1) provides that where a fixed-term employee who completes, or has completed, his or her third year of continuous employment with his or her employer or associated employer, his or her fixed-term contract may be renewed by that employer on only one further occasion and for a fixed-term of no longer than one year. Where two or more continuous fixed-term contracts exist, the total duration must not exceed four years.[125] Where either provision is breached, a

---

[120] See *Minister for Finance v McArdle* [2007] 2 ILRM 438. See also the comments of Advocate-General Jääskinen in Case C-98/09 *Sorge v Poste Italiane SpA*, where he found that amendments made by national rules, which are intended to transpose Directive 1999/70 and the Framework Agreement, do not constitute a *reduction of the general level of protection* afforded to fixed-term workers within the meaning of Clause 8(3) of the Framework Agreement in so far as "they relate to a limited category of workers having entered into a fixed-term employment contract or may be offset by the adoption of other measures to protect workers having entered into such contracts, which it will be for the national court to ascertain" (para 57).

[121] Protection of Employees (Fixed-Term Work) Act 2003, ss 8(1-2).

[122] Protection of Employees (Fixed-Term Work) Act 2003, s 8(3).

[123] [2008] ELR 325.

[124] Note, however, in *Russell v Mount Temple Comprehensive School* (FTD 0815/2008) the Labour Court was satisfied that, while the School had failed to provide the claimant with a written statement of the objective grounds justifying the renewal of his contract, the renewal was grounded on a legitimate justification and that the claimant understood and accepted this to be the case.

[125] Protection of Employees (Fixed-Term Work) Act 2003, s 9(2).

contract of "indefinite duration" is deemed to exist.[126] The length of the initial contract can, however, exceed four years and on termination not lead to permanency. The renewal of a fixed-term contract in breach of s 9(1) and 9(2) can, however, be justified by the employer on objective grounds. It is in relation to making out a case of objective justification that the courts will carefully scrutinise the employer's compliance with s 8.[127] In *Minister for Finance v McArdle*[128] Laffoy J approved the Labour Court's explanation of the effect of s 9(3):

> "the expression 'contract of indefinite duration' should be understood in contradistinction to a contract of definite duration or a fixed-term contract. The terms and conditions of a contract of indefinite duration which comes into being by operation of s. 9(3) must therefore be the same as those in the fixed-term contract from which it is derived, as modified by s. 6, in all respects other than its fixed duration. Obviously, these terms will vary from one employment to another and every case will be decided mainly on its own facts".[129]

However, Laffoy found that the Labour Court had erred in law in concluding that the claimant had acquired security of tenure similar to the security of tenure enjoyed by an established civil servant. The Labour Court had wrongly accepted the view that the defendant's condition as to duration or tenure of her employment must not be less favourable than that of her chosen comparator. Laffoy J held that s 9(3) only impacts on one aspect of a contract of employment when it comes into play and that is to change the character of the contract from one of fixed-term duration to one of indefinite duration. All other aspects of the original contract (including terms relating to its termination) remain intact. Laffoy J essentially held, therefore, that one could not get a better contract than one already had: the operation of the rule simply deletes the automatic termination of the contract due to the expiry of time or due to the expiry of the purpose.[130] [3–62]

As noted, however, the renewal of a fixed-term contract, even after the four-year threshold has been passed, may be justified on objective grounds. The ECJ has noted that the concept of "objective reasons" for the purposes of clause 5(1)(a) of the Framework Agreement must be understood as referring to: [3–63]

> "precise and concrete circumstances characterising a given activity, which are capable, in that particular context, of justifying the use of successive fixed-term employment contracts. Those circumstances may result, in particular, from the specific nature of the tasks for the performance of which such contracts have

---

[126] *Sheehy v Ryan* [2008] 4 IR 258. See the discussion of "contracts of indefinite duration" and "permanency" in chapter 10.

[127] See *Khan v HSE* [2006] ELR 213.

[128] [2007] 2 ILRM 438.

[129] FTD 063/2006.

[130] See Kimber, *op.cit.*

been concluded and from the inherent characteristics of those tasks or, as the case may be, from pursuit of a legitimate social-policy objective of a Member State".[131]

[3–64] However, what will amount to objective justification will be analysed carefully on a case-by-case basis. Examples of successful arguments include significant restructuring for the purposes of economic viability[132] and the conclusion of fixed-term contracts for genuinely temporary needs.[133] However, in *UC Hospital Galway v Aswan*,[134] where the employer argued that it could not provide a consultant with a permanent consultant's contract due to the fact that statutory provisions in the Local Authorities (Officers and Employees) Act 1926 and the Health Act 1970 prevented conversion of a fixed-term post to a permanent post without the position being advertised, the Labour Court noted that the 2003 Act, required by EU Law, could not be derogated from by reliance on domestic law measures. In *Buckley v NUI Maynooth*[135] the claimant, a researcher working on a fixed-term contract, signed a contract containing the following term:

> "Renewal of your employment is justified by the fact that further temporary work has become available and that funding is available to support that work for a fixed period. The University is unable to offer a contract of indefinite duration as the funding in question is available for a fixed duration only".

[3–65] Before the Labour Court, the claimant argued that she did not realise the importance of what she was signing and that she feared if she did not sign, the University could refuse to host the research project on which she was working (which was externally funded). The Labour Court rejected her argument, stating that, had the claimant been in any doubt as to what the clause meant, then the logical course of action was surely to seek legal or trade union advice before signing the form.[136]

[3–66] An important question here relates to what constitutes a successive fixed-term contract? This question arose in the case of *Department of Foreign Affairs v Group of Workers*.[137] The case was brought by a group of clerical workers employed by the Department of Foreign Affairs on a number of fixed-term contracts between 2001 and 2006. In this case, the employer argued that the employee's continuity of employment (under s 9 of the 2003 Act) was broken upon the expiry of each fixed-term contract. In

---

[131] Case C-378/07 *Angelidaki v Organismos Nomarkhiaki Aftodiikisi Rethimnis*, at para 96. See also *Department of Foreign Affairs v Group of Workers* [2007] ELR 332. The ECJ confirmed that clause 5(1)(a) does not apply to the first or single use of a fixed-term employment contract or relationship.

[132] *Aer Lingus v Group of Workers* [2005] ELR 261.

[133] *Russell v Mount Temple Comprehensive School* [2009] IEHC 533; Case C-378/07 *Angelidaki v Organismos Nomarkhiaki Aftodiikisi Rethimnis*.

[134] [2008] ELR 64.

[135] FTD 092/2009.

[136] The claimant's union, the Irish Federation of University Teachers, has written to the European Commission to complain about the Labour Court decision, arguing that it represents a serious and fundamental undermining of the EU Directive (see IRN (2009) 31).

[137] [2007] ELR 332, noted in (2007) 4(2) IELJ 52.

each instance, the break between contracts was a number of weeks or months. It also argued that there were objective grounds justifying the renewal of the contracts, which were mainly to meet seasonal and fluctuating needs.

The Labour Court concluded that there was no mathematical approach that could be followed to compute the number of days that would break a "continuous employment". Instead, the Court looked at other factors including the reasons behind the use of fixed-term contracts and the expectation of the employees as to whether they would be re-employed. The Court found that an employee is continuously employed even where there are breaks of weeks or months between successive contracts, such breaks being considered as periods of lay-off, provided that the employee has a reasonable belief that he or she will be re-employed and is, in fact, re-employed. It was further held that the work being done by the employees was clearly meeting a continuing need as they had been employed for the "greater portion of recent years" and there were, therefore, no objective grounds based on seasonal or fluctuating needs, as advanced by the employer, justifying the continuing renewal of the contracts. **[3–67]**

The Labour Court's reasoning followed a consideration by the ECJ of this issue in *Adeneler*.[138] The ECJ held that the Directive is to be interpreted in light of its objective, which is to prevent the abuse of employment rights by employers. The ECJ held that it is not in the spirit or intention of the Directive to permit breaks between contracts to serve to prevent employees from accumulating the continuous employment required to obtain rights. The ECJ went on to hold that the national provision at issue, under which only fixed-term contracts that are separated by a period of time shorter than, or equal to, 20 working days were regarded as successive, compromised the object, the aim and the practical effect of the Framework Agreement. **[3–68]**

Taking into account the wide scope given to the concept of continuous employment by the Labour Court (one of the workers in question had a gap of 27 weeks between two of the contracts) it is unclear what length a gap between contracts would have to be to in order to break the continuity of the employment.[139] It seems that the approach of the Court will be to examine the *reasons* for the use of successive fixed-term contracts. Unless these reasons satisfy the objective test the fact that there is a break of weeks or months will not, of itself, be enough to protect the employer. **[3–69]**

Section 10 of the 2003 Act puts obligations on the employer to inform a fixed-term employee of any vacancies that become available to ensure that he or she shall have the same opportunity to secure a permanent position as other employees and to facilitate access by a fixed-term employee to appropriate training opportunities to enhance his or her skills, career development and occupational mobility.[140] **[3–70]**

---

[138] Case C-212/04 *Adeneler and Others v Ellinikos Organismos Galaktos* [2006] IRLR 716.
[139] Although note that in *Vassilakis* the ECJ held that clause 5 of the Framework Agreement on fixed-term employment is to be interpreted as not precluding, as a general rule, a national provision according to which only fixed-term employment contracts or employment relationships that are separated by a period of time shorter than three months can be regarded as "successive" for the purposes of that clause: Case C-364/07 *Vassilakis v Dimos Kerkyraion*.
[140] See *Henderson v Scoil Íosagáin* [2005] ELR 217.

[3–71]   Section 12 of the 2003 Act provides that, except where expressly provided otherwise in the Act, a provision in an agreement (whether a contract of employment or not and whether made before or after the commencement of the provision concerned of the Act) that purports to exclude or limit the application of, or is inconsistent with, any provision of the Act shall be void. However, in *Sunday Newspapers Limited v Kinsella*,[141] the High Court rejected the conclusion of the Labour Court that a severance agreement in full and final settlement of "any and all outstanding entitlements whether statutory or otherwise" and all claims under "all or any employment legislation" signed by the workers was void and of no legal effect. Smyth J was satisfied that there was some meaningful discussion and negotiation (which, he held, is not to be equated with interminable talks, documents and meetings) and professional advice of an appropriate character before the agreement was signed: thus, the employees had compromised their legislative rights under the Act.

Section 13 of the 2003 Act prohibits the penalisation of employees for accessing (or attempting to access), or upholding (or seeking to uphold) rights under the legislation. This would include dismissal at common law as well as a failure to renew a fixed-term contract.[142]

Direct Effect of Directive 1999/70[143]

[3–72]   Ireland's failure to meet the deadline for the transposition of Directive 1999/70 resulted in a number of claims being made relating to the period between 10 July 2001 (when the Directive should have been implemented) and 14 July 2003 (when it finally was implemented). Matters came to a head following a 2005 Rights Commissioner's decision on 91 fixed-term contract workers in the civil service, which was appealed to the Labour Court, both by the Government Departments involved and the union representing the workers, IMPACT. In early 2006 the Labour Court referred several questions regarding the cases to the ECJ. The ECJ gave its ruling in the case of *IMPACT v Minister for Agriculture and Food*.[144] The ECJ held, first, that national courts or tribunals (in this case, the Labour Court) were required to apply directly effective provisions of EU law, even if they had not been given express jurisdiction to do so under domestic law. Secondly, the Court held that clause 4(1) of the Framework Agreement, which bans discrimination against fixed-term workers arising from their fixed-term status, was sufficiently precise to be relied upon by an individual and applied in national courts. By contrast, clause 5, which protects against the abuse of successive fixed-term contracts, was not sufficiently precise as it allowed Member States to have one or more of three types of protection, with the choice left up to the Member State.

[3–73]   The third question asked of the Court was whether clause 5(1) of the Framework Agreement precluded a Member State, acting in its capacity as an employer, from renewing   a   fixed-term   employment   contract   for   up   to   eight   years   in

---

[141] [2007] 18 ELR 276.

[142] *Clare County Council v Power* (FTD 812/2008).

[143] On the meaning of direct effect see, generally, Craig and de Búrca, *EU Law: Text, Cases and Materials* (4th ed, Oxford University Press, Oxford, 2008), chapter 8.

[144] Case 268/06 [2008] 2 CMLR 1265. See Apps, "Major Impact" (2008) NLJ 158(7326), 875. The case is also noted at (2008) 5(3) IELJ 109.

the period between the deadline for transposing Directive 1999/70 and the date on which the legislation transposing that Directive enters into force. The ECJ held that such a renewal would be precluded, as an authority of a Member State, acting in its capacity as a public employer, could not adopt measures contrary to the objective pursued by the Directive as regards prevention of the abusive use of fixed-term contracts. This was the case here.[145]

Agency Work

We have already seen above some of the problems that can occur in defining the boundaries of the employment relationship. One of the most troublesome instances for the proper scope of labour regulation concerns agency workers.[146] Temporary agency work can be defined as:

[3-74]

> "a temporary employment relationship between a temporary work agency, which is the employer and a worker, where the latter is assigned to work for, and under the control of an undertaking and/or establishment making use of his or her services (the user company)".[147]

Thus, a temporary agency worker is employed by the temporary agency and is then, via a commercial contract, hired out to perform work assignments at the user firm. The said work is performed at the user company under the supervision of the user firm.[148] The basic common feature of all agency work is a "three-way relationship", sometimes called a "triangular employment relationship", between a user undertaking, an employee and an agency. Temporary agency work is increasing rapidly in almost all European countries, as part of the general movement towards increased flexibility in employment. It is estimated that the annual rate of growth is 10 percent and that about three million people in the EU currently work through temporary agencies.[149]

Agency work has become quite controversial in many countries in recent years, with trade unions accusing employers of using the practice of engaging temporary workers to undermine labour standards.[150] In Ireland, the issue exploded onto the

[3-75]

---

[145] As we have seen above, the ECJ also ruled that remuneration and pensions were included in the meaning of "employment conditions" referred to in clause 4(1). See also Cox *et al*, *op.cit*, pp 213-217.

[146] Collins *et al*, *op.cit*, p 187.

[147] See the European Industrial Relations Dictionary available at: http://www.eurofound.europa. eu/eiro/. As we will see, however, in Irish law the agency is not, in fact, always deemed the employer.

[148] *ibid.*

[149] It is estimated that there were 37,000 agency workers in Ireland in 2007; European Foundation for the Improvement of Living and Working Conditions, *Temporary Agency Work and Collective Bargaining in the EU* (2009) available at http://www.eurofound.europa.eu. However, the report itself notes (at p 6) that official data probably underestimates the extent of temporary agency work; "the problem is the highly fluid nature of the employment arrangement combined with uncertainty over who is the employer".

[150] McKay, *Agency and Migrant Workers* (Institute of Employment Rights, Liverpool, 2009).

national scene after a high-profile dispute involving agency workers at Irish Ferries.[151] At EU level, the European Commission's first proposal for a Directive regulating temporary agency work dates back to 1982. The EU social partners launched a social dialogue process at the end of the 1990s with the aim of reaching a framework agreement on the regulation of temporary agency work in the European Union. In May 2001 the negotiations ended in failure.[152] However, in June 2008 a draft Directive on agency working was finally agreed.[153] This will be examined below. First, though, the existing position in Irish law is considered.

Agency Workers at Common Law

[3–76] There is still considerable confusion and uncertainty in Irish law about the status of individuals who obtain work through employment agencies. In some cases, temporary agencies explicitly guarantee the persons they recruit the status of "employees", but in others temporary workers are regarded as being self-employed.[154] In *Minister for Labour v PMPA Insurance Company*[155] the High Court found that, where an agency assigns an agency worker to an end-user on a temporary basis, the worker is engaged under contract *sui generis*, a "unique" kind of contract.[156] In that case, a temporary typist was held not to be an employee of the end-user (PMPA) even though she worked under its control. As Regan points out, a series of British cases has suggested it is unlikely for the *agency* to be identified as the employer, as the agency generally exercises little or no control over the actual performance of the work: as a result, it is more likely that the end-user (at least in certain circumstances) would be found to be the employer.[157]

Agency Workers Under Employment Legislation

[3–77] Given the confusion at common law, various pieces of employment legislation also attempt to address the issue of agency workers. As argued above, the definition of "contract of employment" in several statutes includes contracts made between an agency and an agency worker. Here, the employer is deemed to be the person liable to pay the worker's wages.[158] Generally this is likely to be the agency. However, it should be noted that in *Diageo Global Supply v Rooney*[159] the Labour Court found a contract

---

[151] See Krings, "A Race to the Bottom? Trade Unions, EU Enlargement and the Free Movement of Labour" (2009) 15(2) *European Journal of Industrial Relations* 49.

[152] See the Commission's proposal for a Directive on working conditions for temporary workers for a legislative history of this issue; COM(2002) 149.

[153] COM(2002) 701.

[154] Note that this is somewhat unusual in European terms; in most EU Member States the temporary agency is generally regarded as the employer of the temporary worker, who is therefore an employee; see COM(2002) 149.

[155] [1986] 5 JISLW 215.

[156] Regan, "Agency Workers-Status and Rights" (2008) 5(3) IELJ 86.

[157] Regan, "The Contract and Relationship of Employment" in *Employment Law* (Regan ed, Tottel, Dublin, 2009), p 44. The cases include *Brook Street v Dacas* [2004] EWCA Civ 21; *McMeechan v Secretary of State For Employment* [1995] IRLR 461 and *James v Greenwich Council* [20008] EWCA Civ 35. See also Wynn and Leighton, "Agency Workers, Employment Rights and the Ebb and Flow of Freedom of Contract" (2009) 71(1) MLR 91.

[158] Above, n 14.

[159] [2004] ELR 133.

of service existed between a nurse and the place where she worked, even though her wages were supplied by an agency. The agency worker here was placed with Diageo as a part-time occupational health nurse. She sought to make a claim against the company under the Protection of Employees (Part-Time) Work Act 2001. The Court held that the claimant had entered into a contract of service with Diageo. She had been interviewed by an employee of Diageo and had agreed her hours of work, rate of pay and other particulars of duties and benefits with Diageo. The Court found that Diageo exercised such a degree of control over the worker in the performance of her work as to make the company her employer.

The general position, that the employer is deemed to be the person liable to pay the agency worker's wages, is subject to some important legislative exceptions. The most important of these are:

[3–78]

- The Unfair Dismissals Act 1977 (as amended by the Unfair Dismissals (Amendment) Act 1993, s 13) deems the end-user, rather than the agency, to be the employer[160];
- Agency workers (unless they have a contract of employment with the agency) are excluded from the scope of the Protection of Employees (Fixed-Term Work) Act;
- Under the Employment Equality Acts both the agency and the end-user have responsibilities for fulfilling the obligations of non-discrimination under the Acts;
- The 2005 Safety, Health and Welfare at Work Act makes it quite clear in s 2(1) that an employer/employee relationship under the Act arises where an employee is working in the capacity as an employee (regardless of *whose* employee he or she actually is) and is under an employer's direction and control; this includes temporary and fixed-term employees.

New Developments in the Regulation of Agency Work

Two major, recent developments aim to clarify the law in this area. In October 2008, the European Parliament adopted the Temporary Agency Work Directive.[161] Member States have until 11 December 2011 to implement the Directive. The Directive aims to ensure the protection of temporary agency workers and to improve the quality of temporary agency work, as well as to take into account the need to establish a suitable framework for the use of temporary agency work with a view to contributing effectively to the creation of jobs and to the development of flexible forms of working (Art 2).

[3–79]

A "temporary agency worker" is defined in Art 3 as a worker with a contract of employment, or an employment relationship with a temporary-work agency, with a view to being assigned to a user undertaking to work temporarily under its supervision and direction. Such an agency is defined as any natural or legal person who, in compliance with national law, concludes contracts of employment or employment

[3–80]

---

[160] Although, as Kimber points out, in practical terms, if the agency worker is truly only engaged on a temporary, casual or intermittent basis, claims for unfair dismissal will not arise, as the worker will not fulfil the requirement of having been continuously employed for one year, which is a precondition of the application of the Unfair Dismissals Acts; Kimber, "Agency Workers and Employers' Responsibilities" (2005) 2(3) IELJ 79.

[161] Directive 2008/104 of 19 November 2008 on temporary agency work [2008] OJ L327/9.

relationships with temporary agency workers in order to assign them to user undertakings to work there temporarily under their supervision and direction. A "user undertaking" means any natural or legal person for whom and under the supervision and direction of whom a temporary agency worker works temporarily. "Basic working and employment conditions" means working and employment conditions laid down by legislation, regulations, administrative provisions, collective agreements and/or other binding general provisions in force in the user undertaking relating to: (i) the duration of working time, overtime, breaks, rest periods, night work, holidays and public holidays; and (ii) pay. Rules in force in the user undertaking in relation to pregnancy and equality must also be complied with (Art 5(1)).

[3–81]   The core equal treatment principle of the Directive is laid down in Art 5, which states that the basic working and employment conditions of temporary agency workers shall be, for the duration of their assignment at a user undertaking, at least those that would apply if they had been recruited directly by that undertaking to occupy the same job. It is possible for Member States to derogate from this through collective agreements and through agreements between social partners at national level *but only* as long as the overall protection of temporary agency workers is respected. Member States may provide for a qualifying period before equal treatment rights can be enforced.[162]

[3–82]   Temporary agency workers must be informed about permanent employment opportunities in the user enterprise and given equal access to collective facilities (canteen, child care facilities, transport service, etc) as workers employed directly, unless the difference in treatment is justified by objective reasons (Art 6). Member States are to take suitable measures to promote dialogue between the social partners to improve temporary agency workers' access to training and child care facilities in periods *between* their assignments so to increase their employability.[163] Member States must put in place effective, proportionate and dissuasive penalties for non-compliance by temporary agencies and enterprises and ensure that adequate administrative or judicial procedures are available to enable the obligations deriving from the Directive to be enforced (Art 10).

[3–83]   Some weeks after the Directive was agreed the Irish social partners agreed a draft national agreement to succeed *Towards 2016*.[164] The social partners agreed, in section 8 of the agreement, to set up a process to develop a national framework on the

---

[162] The derogations and qualifying period were key demands of, in particular, the UK government, which, as ever, was concerned with protecting labour marker flexibility: see Barrow, "Minimising the expense" (2008) 93(Sep) *Emp LJ* 20; McKay, *op.cit.*

[163] This represents the EU's attempts to promote a "flexicurity" model of employment. This represents a policy approach that seeks a third way between the flexibility often ascribed to a liberal market economy (like that of the UK) and the social safety nets of the traditional Scandinavian welfare state. See the June 2007 Communication *Towards Common Principles of Flexicurity: More and Better Jobs Through Flexibility and Security* COM(2007) 359 final. See, generally, Wilthagan and Tros, "The Concept of Flexicurity: A New Approach to Regulating Employment and Labour Markets" (2004) 10(2) *Transfer, European Review of Labour and Research.*

[164] *Towards 2016* Review and *Transitional* Agreement 2008-2009 available at http://www.taoiseach.gov.ie. The status of this agreement is now open to question as the State and many employers have reneged on pay commitments made pursuant to it.

employment and rights of temporary agency workers, while prohibiting their use in the case of official strikes or lockouts. It seems the Government and the social partners will now use the national framework on the employment and rights of agency workers to negotiate a mutually acceptable transposition of the EU Directive.

As well as equal treatment rights for agency workers, existing commitments under the previous round of *Towards 2016* on the regulation of employment agencies resulted in the publication in July 2009 of the Employment Agency Regulation Bill 2009. This will repeal the Employment Agency Act 1971 and seeks to ensure that all recruitment agencies operating in Ireland are properly licensed. Under s 19 of the Bill it will be an offence for any individual to enter into an agreement with an employment agency that is not licensed in Ireland or is not a recognised agency from another EEA State. The Minister may appoint authorised officers to monitor compliance with the new law, who will have wide powers (in particular, in relation to inspection of records).[165]   **[3–84]**

While the main purpose of the Bill relates to licensing, it also makes provisions for prosecutions, in *absentia*, for offences under employment rights legislation in certain circumstances (s 26) and these include incidents where agencies based abroad do not turn up in court. Section 28 of the Bill provides for "administrative cooperation with foreign statutory" bodies in this regard. The Bill also provides for the protection of whistleblowers (ss 29–30) and the establishment of a code of practice for the recruitment sector (s 27).

V. Other Employment Relationships

This chapter concludes by having a brief (and by no means exhaustive) look at some other, less-common, types of employment relationship.[166] The important thing to note is that the full ambit of employment law, as it applies to employees, does not necessarily apply in relation to these other types of workers.   **[3–85]**

Office Holders

A person who holds a designated office is not an employee. The office is rather a position or place to which certain duties are attached. In *Glover v BLN Ltd* Kenny J in the High Court noted: **[3–86]**

> "The characteristic features of an office are that it is created by Act of the National Parliament, charter, statutory regulation, articles of association of a company or of a body corporate formed under the authority of a statute, deed of trust, grant or by prescription; and that the holder of it may be removed if the instrument creating the office authorises this. However, the person who holds it may have a contract under which he may be entitled to retain it for a fixed period".[167]

---

[165] Employment Agency Regulation Bill 2009, ss 24-25.
[166] See also Forde, *op.cit*, pp 35-40; Regan, "The Contract and Relationship of Employment" in *Employment Law* (Regan ed, Tottel, Dublin, 2009), pp 49-56.
[167] [1973] IR 1 388 at 414.

Generally, therefore, an office will be of a more or less public character, a position of trust or authority or service under a constituted authority. Many office holders work in the administration of government, the public service or in the direction of a corporation, company, or society. Administrative law, constitutional law and the rules of the office may confer rights of fair procedures on office holders similar to those implicit in the employment relationship.[168]

Apprentices

[3–87] Much employment legislation does include apprentices under the definition of "employee" (for example, apprentices are included under working time and unfair dismissals legislation), but some (for example, the Protection of Employees (Fixed-Term Work) Act 2003) do not. Where apprentices are not expressly included, it seems such workers are not employees. The rationale for this can be seen underpinning the case of *Sister Dolores v Minister for Social Welfare*[169] where it was held that student nurses were not employees. Their training was a means to an end, the end being "proper" employment.

Workers

[3–88] The Industrial Relations Acts 1946–2004 provide two definitions of the term "worker". In s 8 of the Industrial Relations Act 1990 "worker" means any person who is or was employed whether or not in the employment of the employer with whom a trade dispute arises, but does not include a member of the Defence Forces or of the Garda Síochána. This definition relates to the provisions of the Acts dealing with trade disputes. The High Court has not ruled out the possibility that this may apply to a person who is not employed under a contract of employment.[170] It would seem to exclude those seeking employment for the first time.[171] Section 23 of the Act (for the purposes of industrial relations generally in Part III of the Act, which deals with the Labour Court, the Labour Relations Commission, Registered Employment Agreements, Joint Labour Committees and Codes of Practice) defines "worker" as:

> "any person aged 15 years or more who has entered into or works under a contract with an employer, whether the contract be for manual labour, clerical work or otherwise, whether it be expressed or implied, oral or in writing, and whether it be a contract of service or of apprenticeship or a contract personally to execute any work or labour including, in particular, a psychiatric nurse employed by a health board and any person designated for the time being under *subsection (3)* [relating to the Defence Forces]..."

Excluded are persons employed by or under the State; teachers in a national or secondary school; and officers of a vocational education committee, or a school attendance committee. The section includes those working under a contract for

---

168 Regan, "The Contract and Relationship of Employment" in *Employment Law* (Regan ed, Tottel, Dublin, 2009), p 51. See also chapter 10.
169 [1962] IR 77.
170 *Daru Blocklaying Ltd v BATU* [2002] 2 IR 619.
171 See *dicta* of O'Higgins CJ in *Goulding Chemicals Ltd v Bolger* [1977] IR 211 at 230.

services.[172] It should be noted that most of those excluded under s 23(1) are covered by separate schemes of conciliation and arbitration for dealing with disputes relating to conditions of service.[173]

Home-workers

This refers to those who work at home, or work from home, for part of the week [3–89] (sometimes referred to as "out-workers"). In the past, this usually referred to low-paid, casual work but with advances in telecommunications technology all sorts of work can now be done remotely. This poses problems for traditional employment regulation, as issues of "control" here are difficult to define. It is also more difficult to ensure compliance with employment regulation in the case of such workers. There is specific regulation in the Telework sector, where the EU social partners negotiated in 2002 a voluntary Framework Agreement on Telework.[174]

Public Sector Employment

Finally, it should be noted that the State is the largest employer in the country. While [3–90] some public sector workers, like government ministers or judges, by virtue of their position as representatives of State power, are quite justifiably governed by special rules in relation to their employment, the expansion of the role of the State to cover large areas of administration and management of the economy has thrown up the issue of the extent to which many other public sector workers (like teachers or nurses, for example) should be treated differently to workers in the private sector.[175] In general, most employment legislation now applies to such workers.[176] However, as we will see in chapters 11 and 12, for example, some Acts continue to exclude certain categories of public sector workers.[177] It is worth remembering, though, that the public sector is heavily unionised, which may diminish somewhat the need for legislative protection.[178]

---

[172] *Mythen Brothers Ltd v BATU* [2006] ELR 237. In *TF Productions v A Worker* (LCR 19705/ 2010) the Labour Court recommended that a self-employed musician should receive compensation of €4,600 for the cancellation of her role in a tour with singer Tommy Fleming.

[173] Kerr, *The Trade Union and Industrial Relations Acts* (3rd ed, Round Hall, Dublin, 2007), p 211.

[174] See http://ec.europa.eu/employment_social/news/2002/oct/teleworking_agreement_en.pdf.

[175] See Morris and Fredman, "Is There a Public/Private Labour Law Divide?" (1993) 14 *Comp Lab Law J* 115 and Freedland, "Status and Contract in the Law of Public Employment" (1991) 20 ILJ 72.

[176] See Forde, *op.cit,* chapter 13.

[177] However, we will also see in chapters 10 and 12 that public sector workers may have additional routes by which to obtain redress (such as judicial review) in cases of dispute; we will also see that many cases relating to fair procedures and disciplinary procedures relate to public sector employment.

[178] According to Central Statistic Office (CSO) data approximately 80 percent of public sector workers are members of a trade union.

CHAPTER 4
The Employment Contract

I. Introduction

The legal regulation of the employment contract is a relatively recent phenomenon. **[4–01]**
Historically, the notion existed that employers and employees could freely negotiate the terms and conditions of the individual contract, under the principles of *laissez faire* prevalent within contract law in the 19th century. However, it is somewhat questionable as to whether, in reality, employees are in a position of any power to freely negotiate terms and conditions. Kahn-Freud contends that:

> "...there can be no employment relationship without a power to command and a duty to obey, that is without this element of subordination in which lawyers rightly see the hallmark of the 'contract of employment'. However, the power to command and the duty to obey can be regulated. An element of co-ordination can be infused into the employment relationship."[1]

In more recent times, it is Ireland's membership of the European Union that has had **[4–02]**
the most significant impact on the development of Irish employment law and the regulation of the employment contract. This is very evident with the raft of employment legislation that has been introduced in Ireland since it joined the EU. The purpose of this chapter is to examine the nature and formation of an employment contract. This takes into account the reality that very often employment contracts are not written and acknowledges that, even where a written contract does exist, terms besides those expressly contained therein may be incorporated into the employment contract by other methods.

---

[1] Kahn-Freund, *Labour and the Law* (Stevens, London, 1977), p 7.

II. Nature of the Employment Contract

[4-03] The employment contract sets out the main terms and conditions of employment. The formation of an employment contract is identical to the formation of any other type of contract. Thus, an employment contract must comprise all elements necessary to create a valid, legally binding contract. There must be an offer, acceptance of the offer, an intention to create legal relations and consideration.[2] The term "contract of employment" is defined in many pieces of legislation: according to s 1 of the Unfair Dismissals Act 1977, for example, a contract of employment is a "contract of service or of apprenticeship, whether it is express or implied and (if it is express) whether it is oral or in writing".

[4-04] There is a notion that employment contracts can be, and are, freely negotiated by both the employer and the employee. This is certainly possible. However, the drafting of employment contracts can be, and very often is, fettered by a variety of constraints and rules. Employment contracts are primarily governed by the rules of contract law but are also subject to the provisions of the Constitution and subject to legislation, such as the Terms of Employment (Information) Act 1994. There is a variety of statutes which regulate certain minimum standards that have to be applied to employment contracts, such as the National Minimum Wage Act 2000 and the Organisation of Working Time Act 1997. As a result, both the employer and employee are subject to certain duties and obligations under the provisions of an employment contract which may not be expressly set out in the contract itself (these will be examined in greater detail below).

[4-05] Very often employers will use a standard form contract for each individual employment contract, with the employees having no opportunity whatsoever to negotiate or change the particular terms.[3] As Kahn-Freund aptly puts it:

> "[t]he individual employee or worker...has normally no social power, because it is only in the most exceptional cases that, as an individual, he has any bargaining power at all".[4]

[4-06] Therefore, in the majority of situations, the person seeking employment will have no option but to accept the majority of terms and conditions presented. In circumstances where a recognised trade union exists, there may be some opportunity for discussion between employers and the unions regarding terms and conditions of employment.[5] Agreements made by employers and trade unions are known as "collective agreements". As Ireland has traditionally operated a voluntarist system of employment relations, whereby employers and trade unions worked together to regulate the

---

[2] For further information on the formation of a contract, see Enright, *Principles of Irish Contract Law* (Clarus Press, Dublin, 2007); Purdy, "Changing the Contract of Employment— What are the Issues to Consider?" (2005) 2(3) IELJ 74.

[3] Collins, "Legal Responses to the Standard Form Contract of Employment" (2007) 26 (1) ILJ 2, at p 3; Holland and Burnett, *Employment Law— Legal Practice Course Guide* (Oxford University Press, Oxford, 2005), p 3.

[4] Kahn-Freund, *op.cit* p 6.

[5] Collins, *op.cit* p 3.

operation of the relationship, such collective agreements would be a normal feature of employment law in Ireland.[6]

Oral Contracts

As with any other type of contract, an employment contract can be in either oral or written form and oral employment contracts remain commonplace. Oral terms are of equal importance as the written terms of a contract and very often contracts contain a mix of both oral and written terms.[7] A significant disadvantage of an oral contract lies in *proving* what it was each party actually said during negotiations and what both parties ultimately agreed to do.[8] Therefore, to better avoid later misinterpretations, it is advisable that the parties reduce the terms of employment to writing.[9] The Terms of Employment (Information) Acts 1994 and 2001 now require all employees to be provided with a written statement of particulars detailing the terms and conditions of the employment contract. This can include information relating to pay, working hours, annual leave entitlements, sick pay and so on.[10]

[4-07]

Written Contracts

The provision of a written employment contract is a relatively recent phenomenon. There are no statutory requirements stipulating that all employment contracts must be in a written format. In fact, there are only two specific types of employment contract that legislation requires to be in writing: the articles of agreement for hiring merchant seamen,[11] and articles of apprenticeship for apprentice solicitors[12] or apprentice seamen.[13]

[4-08]

The first piece of legislation to provide any regulation in Ireland in regard to written contracts was the Minimum Notice and Terms of Employment Act 1973.[14] This legislation applied to those on contracts of service as well as apprentices, employment agency personnel, public sector employees, members of the civil service, An Garda Siochána and the defence forces. However, this legislation did not make it mandatory for employers to provide employees with a written employment contract. Under s 9 of the 1973 Act, employers only had to provide employees with details of the terms and conditions of employment *if* employees made a formal request for this information. Part-time and short-term employees were not afforded protection by this legislation.

[4-09]

As a consequence of Directive 91/533 on an employer's obligation to inform employees of the conditions applicable to the contract or employment relationship,[15] the

[4-10]

---

[6] Although "voluntarism", as we have seen, is under some strain; see chapter 1.

[7] Friel, *The Law of Contract* (2nd ed, Round Hall, Dublin, 2000), p 167.

[8] Forde, *Employment Law* (2nd ed, Round Hall, Dublin, 2001), p 45.

[9] This does not mean that successful claims for breach of oral contractual terms cannot be brought; see *Carey v Independent Newspapers (Ireland) Ltd* [2004] ELR 45.

[10] See below for a consideration of the Acts.

[11] Merchant Shipping Act 1894, s 114.

[12] Solicitors Act 1954, ss 24-39.

[13] Merchant Shipping Act 1894, ss 105-109.

[14] See Purdy, *op.cit* p 74.

[15] [1991] OJ L288/32.

Minimum Notice and Terms of Employment Act 1973 was amended by the Terms of Employment (Information) Act 1994. Again, under s 3 of the 1994 Act employment contracts do not have to be in written format, but the employer is legally obliged to provide employees with a written statement of the terms and conditions of employment within two calendar months from the beginning of the contract of employment. This written statement of particulars is not an employment contract, although it is possible for both parties to subsequently agree that this written statement should amount to a contract.[16] The written statement of particulars is quite simply the employer's record of the agreed terms. No legal obligation exists that requires employees to sign the written statement of particulars: however, where employees have acknowledged this written statement as "an accurate summary of the main employment terms", the courts will recognise that these form part of the contract of employment.[17]

[4–11]   The written employment contract in itself is not always definitive. It is not necessary for every term of the contract to be included in the written contract. Very often the written employment contract contains references to other documentation that employees will need to be aware of, including documents such as staff manuals, health and safety policies, policies on dismissal, complaints and disciplinary procedures.[18] These are sometimes referred to as "works rules", which may also contain specific rules on the times of work, breaks during the working day, sick pay, holiday leave, remuneration and grievance and disciplinary procedures. It can be a common practice in larger organisations for such employment policies to be contained within a staff manual. Employees must be made aware of the existence of these other documents and, where possible, they should be provided with a copy of the policies, or at the very least be informed of where such policies are kept so that they can consult them whenever necessary. Information about such policies should be given to all new staff commencing employment as part of their induction process and to existing staff as part of any refresher course. To ensure that staff manuals and other such policies are incorporated into the employment contract, the employer may require the employee to accept that the terms contained within the policies form an additional part of the written contract.[19]

[4–12]   In *Kenny v An Post*[20] an agreement had been made between the superintendent and the representative union in 1969 that a 15-minute break would be allowed for those postal sorters who regularly worked on the overtime shift from 8.30pm to 11.30pm and also that these workers would be paid at the ordinary overtime rate for the break period between 9.30pm and 9.45pm. The purpose of this break was to minimise disruption of work. In 1983, a decision was taken by a new superintendent to curtail this practice. The plaintiffs took action seeking a declaration from the High Court that the break period was a term of the employment contract and also seeking payment of monies deducted in relation to the break period. O'Hanlon J found that this arrangement,

---

[16] Walshe, "The Terms of the Employment Contract" in *Employment Law* (Regan ed, Tottel, Dublin, 2009), p 60.

[17] Lewis & Sargeant, *Essentials of Employment Law* (Chartered Institute of Personnel and Development, London, 2007), p 15.

[18] Collins, *op.cit* p 3.

[19] Sprack, *Employment Law and Practice* (Sweet and Maxwell, London, 2007), para 3.01.

[20] [1988] 1 IR 285.

regarding the break period and the payment of overtime for the break period, was not a term of the employment contract. The case does recognise the importance of work practices, however, as O'Hanlon J noted that:

> "[a]lteration of, and adjustment to, work practices may have to take place constantly in the sphere of employment where large numbers of people are working on the same premises and it seems to me that where a particular change in the terms of employment is intended to be regarded as binding contractually the parties should take some positive steps to achieve this object".[21]

III. Terms of Employment

The employment contract between employers and employees sets out the specific terms and conditions of the agreement. It is not necessary for the employment contract to contain all specific duties and obligations that are to be undertaken by the employee. The reality is that it would not be possible to draft such a prescriptive and detailed contract to cover every eventuality.[22] There are two different types of terms contained in an employment contract: "express terms" and "implied terms". Again the general contract law rules on express terms and implied terms are applicable.

[4–13]

Express Terms

Express terms are the terms that have been specifically agreed between the parties to a contract.[23] Express terms take precedence over terms that can be implied by way of custom or practice and terms implied by the common law.[24] Express terms cannot, however, override terms implied by legislation or by the Constitution. Generally, when a dispute arises between the employer and employee regarding the contract of employment, the court will examine the written terms to determine what both parties had agreed to do. The advantage of having a written employment contract containing express terms is that it is much easier for the parties to prove precisely what was agreed upon.[25] The court will interpret the terms and conditions within the context of the contract, using generally applicable legal rules of interpretation. Very often employers will use a standard form contract with, for example, some differences in terms of the rate of pay and nature of work. In some instances, the employment contract will be very detailed and specific, depending upon the nature of the job.[26] Two common terms which may be written into the employment contract as express terms relate to probation and confidentiality.

[4–14]

Probation and Confidentiality

The employer may require the employee to undergo a probationary period upon commencing the contract of employment. Periods of probation should be specified as

[4–15]

---

[21] *ibid* at 288. See also *Rafferty v Bus Eireann* [1997] 2 IR 424.

[22] Collins, *op.cit* p 5.

[23] Forde, *op.cit* p 45.

[24] Lewis & Sargeant, *op.cit* p 12.

[25] Collins, *op.cit* p 4.

[26] Walshe, *op.cit* p 60.

an express term within the employment contract before the period of employment begins.[27] Employers have a right to extend probationary periods if necessary and again the employment contract should include a provision to allow for an extension. Some employers may include an express term imposing a duty of confidentiality on the employee. A duty of confidentiality may be necessary, for example, where the employee is working for someone who is in the public eye, who may have concerns regarding their privacy and the potential disclosure of their private life in the media. Employers who are working on developing new technologies, for example, new treatments for curing cancer, may require a duty of secrecy as the disclosure of this information to competitors would be damaging for business. A controversial term that is sometimes included in employment contracts is a "restrictive covenant" clause. Restrictive covenants are terms or conditions in a contract of employment that place restrictions on the right of employees to compete with their employer after their employment has ceased *or* that protect the proprietary interest of the employer in trade secrets, confidential information or information relating to customer/supplier relations given to the employee in the course of the employment.[28] In some cases it may be felt that there is a confidential relationship between that parties that justifies an obligation being put on one party not to abuse that relationship. In *House of Spring Gardens v Point Blank*[29] the Court found that where a confidential relationship exists, and where the owner of information has expended skill, time and labour in compiling it, use of the information may be confined for a specific purpose. The employer must show a legitimate commercial interest capable of protection and any express restriction on the employee must go no further than is necessary to protect that interest.[30] An employer cannot prevent a former employee from using information or skills that are ordinarily used in the course of trade.[31]

[4–16]   Three types of express restrictions are common: restrictions as to trade or subject matter of employment; time[32]; and geographical location.[33] These must be reasonable to be effective. As these clauses are a restriction of rights, they must not go further than is necessary to protect the employer's legitimate interests. In *Murgitroyd v Purdy*[34] the defendant, a patent agent worked out of the plaintiff's Dublin office but subsequently left and commenced practising as "Purdy & Associates". Clarke J held that a service agreement between the parties and the "restraint of trade" clause contained therein was operative at the time the defendant terminated his employment. Clarke J held that on the facts of this particular case that, first, a geographical restriction preventing the defendant from operating in the Irish State was reasonable (as there were at the time only ten patent attorneys operating in Ireland and they all operated from Dublin); secondly, that providing the defendant could not operate as a patent agent for a period of 12 months was not unreasonable (having regard to the specialised nature of the business); but, thirdly, that the prohibition in the clause on

---

[27] *ibid* p 61.

[28] Walshe, *op.cit* p 67.

[29] [1985] FSR 387.

[30] *Meadox Medicals Inc v VPI Ltd*, Unreported, High Court, Hamilton J, 1981.

[31] *Faccenda Chickens v Fowler* [1981] ILRM 345.

[32] *Hollis & Co v Stocks* [2000] IRLR 712.

[33] *Mulligan v Corr* [1925] IR 169.

[34] Unreported, High Court, Clarke J, 1 June 2005.

the defendant dealing with *potential*, as opposed to *actual*, customers of the plaintiff was too wide. Clarke J held that a non-compete clause will not be enforced unless it meets a two fold test: that it is reasonable as between the parties; and that it is consistent with the interests of the public.[35] In *European Paint Importers v O'Callaghan*[36] Peart J, *obiter*, considered the situation of a clause that the plaintiff claimed restricted the former employee from soliciting *and* doing business with his clients, or former clients, *even if* the latter approached the former employee independently. This would be "an unwarranted restriction, and serve only to unreasonably and unjustifiably place an obstacle in the way of a fledgling company" trying to get off the ground.

Other common express terms might relate to job specification, discipline and grievance procedures and email and internet use. As regards the use of facilities like the internet, as noted in chapter 2, the influence of the European Convention on Human Rights on Irish employment law may be felt particularly in the area of privacy in the workplace.[37]   [4-17]

Implied Terms

The terms of the employment contract may comprise a combination of both express terms and implied terms.[38] The courts will not always confine the terms of the agreement to what the parties have specifically said or written, but are sometimes prepared to "read in" some implied terms. Generally, the courts will imply terms into the contract of employment to ensure justice and fairness. Terms can be implied into an employment contract in a number of different ways. Terms may be implied by legislation, from the facts, by common law (contract or tort law), by custom and practice of a certain trade, by the Constitution or by collective agreements. Certain terms will be implied into every employment contract (such as those implied by legislation). By implying a term as a matter of common law, the court is laying down a general rule that, in contracts of this type, a particular term will exist unless the express terms or special circumstances of a case indicate otherwise.   [4-18]

Terms Implied by the Constitution

According to Art 40.3.1° of Bunreacht na hÉireann: [4-19]

> "The State guarantees in its laws to respect, and as far as practicable, by its laws to defend and vindicate the personal rights of the citizen".

---

[35] See also *Macken v O'Reilly* [1979] ILRM 79. In *Cantor Fitzgerald Ltd v Wallace* [1992] IRLR 215 the English High Court held that an employer could not protect the "customer connection" an employee had built up during employment where that connection is a function of the employee's personal qualities (e.g. personality, temperament, ability to get on with others, etc).

[36] Unreported, High Court, Peart J, 10 August 2005.

[37] See Cox *et al*, *Employment Law in Ireland* (Clarus Press, Dublin, 2009), chapter 18; McGreal, "Workplace Privacy and Data Protection" in *Employment Law* (Regan ed, Tottel, Dublin, 2009), chapter 6.

[38] Terms of Employment (Information) Act 1994, s 1(1).

Under Art 40.3.1°, the courts have identified a number of constitutional rights pertinent to the employment relationship.[39] The first case to consider the unenumerated constitutional right to work was *Murtagh Properties Ltd v Cleary*.[40] Here a picket was organised by trade union members at the plaintiff's property protesting against the employment of staff who were non-union members. The plaintiffs sought an injunction to restrain the trade union members from picketing at their property. The trade union was representative of men only and refused to allow any women to become members. In essence, the picket was against the employment of women as part-time bar waitresses by the plaintiff, which the trade union claimed was in breach of an existing agreement in place between the employer and trade union. Kenny J referred to the equal right of men and women to work as contained in Art 45.2.i of the Constitution,[41] which states:

> "The State shall, in particular direct its policy towards securing...that the citizens (all of whom, men and women equally, have the right to an adequate means of livelihood) may through their occupations find the means of making reasonable provisions for their domestic needs".

[4–20] As a consequence, the High Court held that to exclude women was a breach of their constitutional right to earn a livelihood. The Supreme Court in *Murphy v Stewart* endorsed the right to work as an unenumerated right deriving from Art 40.3.1°.[42] The courts are anxious to protect the unenumerated constitutional right to earn a livelihood. In *Parsons v Kavanagh*, an injunction was granted to the plaintiff to prevent the defendants from competing with the plaintiff's passenger bus service, as the defendants were operating without a licence. O'Hanlon J held that:

> "...the constitutional right to earn one's livelihood by any lawful means carries with it the entitlement to be protected against any unlawful activity on the part of another person or persons which materially impairs or infringes that right".[43]

[4–21] The Supreme Court subsequently endorsed O'Hanlon J's decision in *Lovett v Gogan*.[44] The facts of this case are similar to that of *Parsons*. The plaintiff had an occasional passenger licence permitting him to operate road passenger services on Fridays and Sundays between Dublin and County Clare. The plaintiff sought an injunction to prevent the defendants from operating a similar service as they were not in possession of the occasional passenger licence. The Supreme Court held that an injunction could be granted as it was evident that this was the only means of protecting the plaintiff's constitutional right to earn a livelihood by lawful means against the unlawful activities of the defendants in operating a similar service without the necessary licence.

---

[39] See chapter 2.

[40] [1972] IR 330.

[41] As noted in chapter 2, Art 45.2.i is a "directive" principle only in that it is intended to be for the guidance of the Oireachtas and is not subject to the courts' jurisdiction.

[42] [1973] IR 97.

[43] [1990] ILRM 560 at 565.

[44] [1995] 3 IR 132.

Article 40.6.1°(iii) protects the freedom of expression, assembly and association. The [4–22] freedom to associate has been recognised as a further constitutional right that can be implied into the contract of employment. The Irish courts have, however, recognised that a corollary of the right to associate is the right to *dissociate*. One of the first decisions to acknowledge the existence of such a right was *Educational Company of Ireland v Fitzpatrick*.[45] This case arose as a result of efforts by members of the Irish Union of Distributive Workers and Clerks, who worked for the plaintiff, to persuade nine of the plaintiff's workers who were not union members to join the union. These nine members refused to join. The union requested that the company make membership of the union mandatory, with dismissal the consequence of any failure to join. The plaintiff company refused to take such action and consequently the union picketed the plaintiff's premises. The plaintiffs successfully sought an injunction to end the picket. The decision in *Meskell v CIE* firmly established the constitutional right to dissociate.[46] Meskell had been employed by CIE for 15 years, during which time he was a member of a trade union. CIE dismissed all of their employees and offered new contracts of employment that contained a mandatory condition that the employees become members of a particular trade union. Meskell refused to take up this new contract of employment. All other terms of the new employment contract were the same as before, except for this mandatory requirement to join the representative trade union. Meskell was dismissed because he refused to join the union and thus took legal action against CIE for his dismissal and for the breach of his constitutional right to dissociate. The Supreme Court found that this mandatory term was a breach of his constitutional right to dissociate. Walsh J held that dismissal of an employee, or even the mere threat of dismissal, for exercising his or her constitutional right to associate *or* right to dissociate, would render the employer liable to pay damages.

The courts have interpreted Art 40.3 as implying a constitutional guarantee of fair [4–23] procedures in the contract of employment: see *In Re Haughey*.[47] Thus, the principle of *audi alteram partem* (everyone should have a right to be heard) is relevant. In *Glover v BLN Ltd*[48] the Supreme Court considered this constitutional right to fair procedures. This case arose following the dismissal of the plaintiff (who was a director of the company), without notice, for serious misconduct. Among the terms of employment was the right to dismiss the plaintiff for serious misconduct if the board was of the opinion that such behaviour would be damaging to the company's business. The plaintiff was dismissed but the board of directors did not provide him with either notice or any explanation for his dismissal. The Supreme Court held that the failure to provide reasons for the dismissal was a breach of the constitutional principle of natural justice. According to Walsh J:

> "[i]t is sufficient to say that public policy and the dictates of constitutional justice require that statutes, regulations or agreements setting up machinery for

---

[45] [1961] IR 323.
[46] [1973] IR 121.
[47] [1971] IR 217.
[48] [1973] IR 388.

taking decisions which may affect rights or impose liabilities should be construed as providing for fair procedures".[49]

[4–24]   As such, failure to provide the plaintiff with the opportunity to present his side of the case was a breach of the implied constitutional term that the dismissal procedure would be conducted fairly, even if there was substantial evidence to justify the dismissal. The importance of ensuring fair procedures was emphasised by Walsh J, who stated that "[t]he obligation to give a fair hearing to the guilty is just as great as the obligation to give a fair hearing to the innocent".[50] Similarly, in *State (Gleeson) v Minister of Defence,*[51] the Supreme Court stipulated that the rules of natural justice must be adhered to when dismissing an employee. This requires provision of "due notice of the intention to discharge" and also of providing "a reasonable opportunity of presenting [the employee's] response to that notice".[52] However, judges should be cautious when trying to imply terms into a contract of employment by reference to the Constitution. Friel is critical of implying terms in this manner, as he argues that to imply constitutional terms into the contract of employment is "excessive ... to remedy a defect" in that contract.[53]

Terms Implied by Legislation

"Employers and workers... must expect the law to play a part in regulating their mutual obligations and rights".[54]

[4–25]   Even though Kahn-Freund recognises the employer's power in regards to being able to determine the terms and conditions of the employment contract, the nature of employment law in modern society is such that this "power" is fettered by the law:

"The law is expected to have a share in the regulation of normal behaviour in relations between employers and employed. Examples abound. Think of safety and health, of hours of work, of minimum wages and guarantees against loss through abnormal events, of periods of notice and redundancy payments and remedies for unfair dismissal, and an untold number of other things".[55]

[4–26]   The amount of legislation that now regulates the employment relationship in Ireland has increased dramatically as a consequence of Ireland's obligation to implement EU Directives. The relevant legislation includes, for example, the Terms of Employment (Information) Acts 1994 and 2001; the Equality Act 2004; the Organisation of Working Time Act 1997; the Protection of Young Persons (Employment) Act 1996; the Protection of Employees (Part-Time Work) Act 2001; the Protection of Employees (Fixed-Term) Act 2003; the Maternity Protection Act 1994 and the Maternity

---

[49] *ibid* at 425.
[50] *ibid* at 429.
[51] [1976] IR 280.
[52] [1976] IR 280 at 296. See also chapter 10.
[53] Friel, *op.cit* p 189.
[54] Kahn-Freund, *op.cit* p 20.
[55] *ibid* p 20.

Protection (Amendment) Act 2004; the Parental Leave Act 1998; the Adoptive Leave Act 1995; the Carer's Leave Act 2001; and the Safety, Health and Welfare at Work Act 2005.[56] Parties to the employment contract cannot override the obligations implied by way of legislation by the inclusion of an express term to the contrary.

Written Statement of Particulars and Terms of Employment (Information) Acts 1994 and 2001

The first significant piece of Irish legislation attempting to regulate the form of the employment contract itself (as distinct from the substantive terms of employment) was the Minimum Notice and Terms of Employment Act 1973. Section 9 of the 1973 Act introduced the requirement that an employee could request written details of the main terms and conditions of employment from his or her employer.[57] Upon such a request, employers were legally obliged to provide this information within one month after the employee commenced employment.[58] If an employer did not provide a written statement of the terms of employment within the timeframe, the employer was deemed guilty of an offence.[59] [4-27]

Sections 9 and 10 have since been repealed by the Terms of Employment (Information) Act 1994.[60] This Act applies to any person working under a contract of service or apprenticeship, workers who have a contract with an employment agency, or workers holding office, or in the service of the State.[61] However, the 1994 Act did not initially apply to all types of workers. Part-time employees who worked for fewer than eight hours per week, or who had been employed for less than a month by the employer were excluded from the protection of the 1994 Act.[62] This position has changed since the enactment of the Protection of Employees (Part-Time Work) Act 2001, which extends the remit of the 1994 Act to include anyone who works for fewer than eight hours a week.[63] To take these changes into account, the Acts are now referred to as the Terms of Employment (Information) Acts 1994 and 2001. To benefit from the protection under the Terms of Employment (Information) Acts 1994 and 2001, the employee must have at least one month's continuous service. Any person who has worked for less than one month does not qualify for the rights and benefits accruing from this legislation. [4-28]

Under s 3(1) of the Terms of Employment (Information) Acts 1994 and 2001, an employer must now provide employees with a written statement of particulars of the terms of employment within two months of the commencement of the employee's [4-29]

---

[56] Further discussion and analysis of this legislation will occur in the relevant chapters throughout the book.

[57] s 9(2) of the Minimum Notice and Terms of Employment Act 1973 also provided that the Minister "may by order provide that employees may require their employers to furnish such further or other particulars of their contracts of employment".

[58] Minimum Notice and Terms of Employment Act 1973, s 5.

[59] Minimum Notice and Terms of Employment Act 1973, s 10.

[60] This Act was introduced to implement Directive 91/533; see above, n 15.

[61] Terms of Employment (Information) Act 1994, ss 1(1)(a) and (b).

[62] Terms of Employment (Information) Act 1994, s 2(1).

[63] The purpose of this Act was to implement Directive 97/81 of 15 December 1997 concerning the Framework Agreement on part-time work concluded by ETUC, UNICE and CEEP [1997] OJ L14/9: see chapter 3.

employment for those contracts entered into on, or after, 16 May 1994. This is in contrast to the provisions under s 9 of the 1973 Act, which originally required the employer to provide a written statement "at the request of the employee". The legislation stipulates that the employer must provide a written statement that includes the specific information listed below[64]:

a. the full names of the employer and the employee;
b. the employer's address or principal place of business or the registered address of the employer in accordance with the provisions of the Companies Act 1963;
c. the place of work, or a statement requiring the employee to work at various locations where there is no main place of work, or in the event of flexible working arrangements to allow the employee to work somewhere other than the main place of work;
d. the job title or nature of the work;
e. the date of commencement of the contract of employment;
f. in the case of a fixed-term contract, the date on which the contract expires or the duration of a temporary contract;
g. the rate of remuneration or method of calculating remuneration and the reference period as required by the National Minimum Wages Act 2000[65];
h. the employee may ask the employer to provide a written statement of the average hourly rate of pay for any pay reference period under s 23 of the National Minimum Wages Act 2000[66];
i. the frequency of remuneration-weekly, fortnightly, monthly or other;
j. the hours of work including overtime;
k. terms and conditions relating to paid leave (other than paid sick leave);
l. terms and conditions relating to incapacity to work as a consequence of sickness or injury, paid sick leave, and pensions and pension schemes;
m. the period of notice that an employee is required to give or receive;
n. a reference to any collective agreements which impact on the terms and conditions of the employment contract.

[4-30] Employers have a legal obligation to provide employees with information regarding the times and duration of rest periods and breaks within two months after the employment contract commences.[67] The employer must also provide details to the employee if there is a requirement that the employee works outside the State for the duration of at least a month as part of the employment contract. This information must be given to the employee before the employee leaves the State. The employer must provide the

---

[64] Terms of Employment (Information) Act 1994, s 3(1)(a)-(m).

[65] The method of calculating remuneration may be subject to pre-determined agreements such as collective agreements, agreements registered with the Labour Court or Labour Court Employment Regulation Orders. Employment Regulation Orders are commonly used within certain sectors (e.g. hairdressing, hotel, and manufacturing industries); see chapter 11.

[66] This refers to any pay reference period in the preceding 12 months that is different from the employee's current pay reference period.

[67] Terms of Employment (Additional Information) Order 1998 (SI No 49 of 1998). This Order was enacted to ensure that ss 11, 12 and 13 of the Organisation of Working Time Act 1997 were implemented.

employee with all of the required details as listed above under s 3(1)(a) to (m) and in addition to this, information regarding:

a. the period of employment outside the State;
b. the currency in which the employee is to be remunerated for the period of employment outside the State;
c. any benefits in cash or in kind for the employee as a consequence of working outside the State;
d. the terms or conditions, where appropriate, governing the employee's repatriation.[68]

Employers who employ children or young people under the age of 18 also have a legal duty to provide these employees with a copy of the abstract of the Protection of Young Persons (Employment) Act 1996, in addition to the written statement of particulars within a month from the date the employment contract begins.[69]

Under the provisions of Directive 91/533 employers must notify employees of any terms which form an essential part of the employment contract. The ECJ in *Lange v Georg Schünemann GmbH,*[70] a case arising from a requirement to work overtime, held that to ensure compliance with Art 2(1) of the Directive an obligation is placed on employers to notify employees of: **[4–31]**

> "... any element which, in view of its importance, must be considered an essential element of the contract or employment relationship of which it forms part...That applies in particular to a term under which an employee is obliged to work overtime whenever requested to do so by his employer".[71]

As Lewis and Sargeant contend, the rationale for providing clear written statements of the terms of employment is to reduce the risk of disputes arising between the employer and employee.[72]

It is possible for an employer to make changes to the details of the terms of the written statement of particulars furnished. In the event that this should occur, the employer must notify the employee of these changes within one month of the changes taking effect.[73] The employer has a duty to inform employees of a change, which is consequent on the employee being required to work outside the State for a period of more than one month, at the time of the employee's departure.[74] Some employment contracts may include an express term to enable the employer to vary the terms of the contract, or even to allow for the renegotiation of certain terms of employment, although such terms will be carefully scrutinised by the courts to ensure they are **[4–32]**

---

[68] Terms of Employment (Information) Act 1994, s 4(1)(a)-(d).
[69] Terms of Employment (Information) Act 1994 (Section 3 (6)) Order 1997 (SI No 4 of 1997).
[70] Case C-333/20 *Lange v Georg Schünemann GmbH* [2001] IRLR 244.
[71] *ibid* at para 25.
[72] Lewis & Sargeant, *op.cit* p 12.
[73] Terms of Employment (Information) Act 1994, s 5(1)(a)-(b). The employer does not have to notify the employee of changes that are made due to changes in legislation: s 5 (1)(c).
[74] Terms of Employment (Information) Act 1994, s 5(1)(b).

reasonable. Variation of the employment contract by the employer may be implied into the contract of employment where no written agreement exists between the employer and the employee. Circumstances where this could arise include those where the employer unilaterally varies a term of the employment contract and the employee continues to work without any objection to the variation of the term of employment.[75] If an employee feels that the employer is in breach of the provisions of the legislation on the terms of employment, for example, if the employer refuses to provide the written statement or refuses to include details about rest periods and breaks, the employee may submit a complaint to a Rights Commissioner.[76]

Terms Implied by Common Law

[4–33]   Terms can also be implied by common law. However, the courts will only imply those terms necessary to give effect to the employment contract. Maguire explains that the courts will imply terms into an employment contract "to achieve justice between the parties".[77] The courts will apply the "officious bystander" test, or the related "business efficacy" test. Essentially what this means is that the courts will imply terms into the employment contract to give effect to the unexpressed, but assumed, presumptions of the parties. Lord Justice McKinnon in *Shirlaw v Southern Foundries (1926) Ltd* explains that this:

> "... is something so obvious that it goes without saying; so that, if while the parties were making their bargain, an officious bystander were to suggest some express provision for it in their agreement, they would testily suppress him with a common, 'Oh, of course'".[78]

[4–34]   However, other criteria have to be met before a term can be implied into an employment contract. It is insufficient for the term merely to be *reasonable*. First, the term has to be both reasonable and equitable. Secondly, it must be necessary to give business efficacy to the contract. Thirdly, the term must be so obvious that it goes without saying. Fourthly, the term must be capable of clear expression. Finally, the term must not contradict any express term of the employment contract.[79] Courts will also take into account the conduct of the parties subsequent to the conclusion of the contract.

Duty to Maintain Mutual Trust and Confidence

[4–35]   An important example of a term implied into a contract of employment is that both the employer and the employee have a duty to maintain mutual trust and confidence in the relationship. In recent years, the implied duty of mutual fidelity, trust and confidence in the employment relationship has emerged as a major area of employment

---

[75] Purdy, *op.cit* p 79.

[76] Terms of Employment (Information) Act 1994, s 7(1); for further information on this issue of available remedies refer to chapter 12.

[77] Maguire, "Implied Terms and Conditions and the Contract of Employment" (2004) 1(5) IELJ 146, p 153.

[78] [1939] 2 KB 206 at 227.

[79] *McGrath v Trintech Technologies* [2005] 4 IR 382.

litigation.[80] According to Freedland, it is now "undoubtedly the most powerful engine of movement in the modern law of employment contracts".[81] Increasingly, the Irish Superior Courts have referred to the "mutual trust and confidence" that exists in the employment relationship. In *Berber v Dunnes Stores*,[82] for example, the High Court considered the issue of breach of contract by the defendant in the context of the implied term of the plaintiff's contract that both the employer and employee would maintain mutual trust and confidence. There Laffoy J described the obligation of fidelity as "a two-way street". The emergence of this implied term can be attributed primarily to recent developments in the English courts. In *Imperial Group Pension Trust Ltd v Imperial Tobacco Co*[83] the Court referred to an "implied obligation of good faith" in relation to the management by employers of occupational pensions. This was endorsed in *Malik v Bank of Credit & Commerce Int'l SA*[84] where the House of Lords upheld employees' claims that there was an implied term in their contracts that the company they worked for would not be managed in a corrupt manner: the Court referred to an "implied term of trust and confidence". The House of Lords held that if the employer's conduct was a breach of the duty to maintain trust and confidence which detrimentally affected an employee's future employment prospects so as to give rise to continuing financial loss, and it was reasonably foreseeable that such loss was a serious possibility, damages would, in principle, be recoverable if injury to reputation (and hence future employment prospects) could be established as being a consequence of the breach. In *Cronin v Eircom Ltd* the Irish High Court held that:

> "[a]s a matter of principle a contractual term of mutual trust and confidence... should be implied into each contract of employment in this jurisdiction by operation of law".[85]

Even though both parties to the employment contract may not specifically identify this duty, the courts recognise that the duty has a central place in the employment relationship. This is clearly evident in the Supreme Court decision in *Berber v Dunnes Stores*,[86] which emphasised the importance and significance of this duty of mutual trust and confidence in employment contracts.[87] In this case, the plaintiff had been employed by Dunnes Stores as a trainee manager in 1980. The plaintiff suffered from an ongoing bowel condition, Crohn's Disease. In 1988, he moved to a position of buyer within Dunnes Stores until late 2000, when there was a request by management that he transfer back to store management in the Blanchardstown store. The plaintiff agreed to

[4–36]

---

[80] See Bolger and Ryan, "The Mutual Duty of Fidelity in the Contract of Employment: Significant Recent Developments" (2007) 4(4) IELJ 112; Callanan, "Mutual Trust and Confidence in the Workplace: A Concept or an Obligation" (2007) ELRI 9; Brodie, "Mutual Trust and Confidence: Catalysts, Constraints and Commonality" (2008) 37(4) ILJ 329; Fudge, "The Spectre of *Addis* in Contracts of Employment in Canada and the UK" (2007) 36(1) ILJ 51.
[81] Freedland, *The Personal Employment Contract* (Oxford University Press, Oxford, 2003), p 166.
[82] [2007] ELR 1 (HC).
[83] [1991] 1 WLR 589 at 597.
[84] [1998] 2 AC 20.
[85] *Cronin v Eircom Ltd* [2007] ELR 84 at 103 *per* Laffoy J.
[86] *Berber v Dunnes Stores* [2009] 20 ELR 61.
[87] See Redmond, "The Implied Obligation of Mutual Trust and Confidence-A Common Law Action for 'Unfair' Dismissal?" (2009) 6(2) IELJ 3.

this transfer upon receiving assurances that he would be eligible to be "fast-tracked" for appointment as a store or regional manager within six to 12 months of taking up this transfer. A dispute arose between the parties regarding these assurances, resulting in Berber refusing to transfer to store management. He was suspended from work by the defendants as a consequence. Berber sent a letter to his employer alleging that the employer's conduct had caused him to become ill because of stress.

[4-37]　By the end of December 2000, Berber did report for work. However, there were continual disagreements between both parties regarding the terms and conditions of the employment contract. Berber sent a letter to Dunnes Stores claiming that his contract was at an end because the company had repudiated the terms of the contract. The case initially was heard by Laffoy J in the High Court, who awarded damages for wrongful dismissal and personal injuries. Dunnes Stores appealed this decision to the Supreme Court, which allowed the appeal. However, the Supreme Court recognised the existence of an implied term of mutual obligation in contracts of employment. According to Finnegan J:

> "[t]here is implied in a contract of employment a mutual obligation that the employer and the employee will not without reasonable and proper cause conduct themselves in a manner likely to destroy or seriously damage the relationship of confidence and trust between them. The term is implied by law and is incident to all contracts of employment unless expressly excluded. The term imposes reciprocal duties on the employer and the employee. In assessing whether there has been a breach by the employer what is significant is the impact of the employer's behaviour on the employee rather than what the employer intended. Having regard to the mutuality of the obligation the impact of an employee's behaviour is also relevant. The test is an objective one: if conduct objectively considered is likely to cause serious damage to the relationship between employer and employee a breach of the implied obligation may arise...".[88]

[4-38]　Thus, neither party to an employment contract should behave in such a way as to undermine this mutual duty of trust and confidence. According to Finnegan J's judgment, as outlined above, the courts will apply an objective test to determine whether there has been a breach of this duty. The conduct of both parties will be taken into consideration as part of this objective test and the courts will look at the "cumulative effect" of the parties' behaviour. Finnegan J stipulated that:

> "The conduct of the employer complained of must be unreasonable and without proper cause and its effect on the employee must be judged objectively, reasonably and sensibly in order to determine if it is such that the employee cannot be expected to put up with it".[89]

The importance of the implied term of mutual confidence in the context of the law on dismissal will be discussed further in chapter 10.

---

[88] *Berber v Dunnes Stores* [2009] 20 ELR 61 at 73.

[89] *ibid* at 76. The Supreme Court's focus on the mutual obligation of the employee to act reasonably is noteworthy, and the objective nature of the tests "makes the hurdle higher for the employee to jump"; Kimber, "Editorial" (2009) 6(1) IELJ 2.

Terms Implied by Custom and Practice

Traditionally, custom and practice played an important role in implying terms into employment contracts when written employment contracts were not normally issued.[90] The advent of written employment contracts and the issuing of written statements in accordance with statutory obligations have still not eradicated the need to imply terms into an employment contract by way of custom and practice. Whincup contends that in certain situations "even the express terms of the contract are of secondary importance..." to terms arising from a particular custom and practice.[91] Furmston *et al* endorse this view that a contract, including contracts of employment, may include terms implied by custom.[92] According to Walshe, terms that "relate to paid sick leave, *ex gratia* redundancy payments or leaves of absence" are the most common forms of term implied by way of custom or practice.[93] Such a term must be in common usage within a particular industry, or locality, for it to be incorporated into a contract.[94] The terms that may be implied by custom or practice must not contradict the express terms of the employment contract. The purpose of custom is "not to destroy but to fulfil the law".[95] In essence what this means is that the incorporation of a custom into an employment contract is to supplement the express terms contained therein.

[4-39]

For a term to be implied into a contract of employment, by way of custom and practice, it must satisfy four requirements: essentially the custom and practice must be notorious, certain, reasonable and must be regarded as imposing an obligation. For example, in *Meeks v Port of London Authority* it was held by the English courts that in a situation where an employer paid an employee's income tax, this could not be regarded as a custom, rather, it was deemed to be an "apparent bounty".[96] In addition to this, employees must be fully aware of the custom or rule. The custom or practice must be such that it almost goes without saying that this should form a part of the employment contract.

[4-40]

The Irish courts have implied terms by way of custom and practice into employment contracts in a number of cases. In *O' Reilly v Irish Press*, McGuire P considered whether there was a custom that chief sub-editors working for a newspaper had an entitlement to six months' notice of termination of employment.[97] It was found that no such custom or practice existed, although due to his position of chief sub-editor and night editor, the plaintiff was entitled to six months' notice as reasonable notice. In his judgment, McGuire P held that a custom or usage of any kind is a difficult thing to establish. The courts would need to be satisfied that it is so "notorious, well-know and acquiestine" that in the absence of agreement in writing it is to be taken as one of the

[4-41]

---

[90] Lewis & Sargeant, *op.cit* p 18.

[91] Whincup, *Modern Employment Law* (6th ed, Heinemann Professional Publishing, Oxford, 1990), p 35.

[92] Furmston *et al, Cheshire, Fifoot and Furmston's Law of Contract* (Butterworths, London, 1991) p 133.

[93] Walshe, *op.cit* p 80.

[94] Enright, *op.cit* p 167.

[95] Furmston *et al, op.cit* p 135.

[96] *Meeks v Port Authority of London* [1918] 1 Ch 415.

[97] *O'Reilly v Irish Press* [1937] ILTR 194.

terms of agreement between the parties. In *O' Connail v The Gaelic Echo*,[98] a Dublin journalist sought holiday pay even though there was no specific term in his contract of employment referring to such an entitlement. The Court found that the custom and practice in the Dublin newspaper industry was to pay journalists for holidays. The High Court decision in *Carroll v Dublin Bus* discussed the existence of a custom and practice of rehabilitating employees in the workplace after an illness or accident.[99] Carroll was an employee of Dublin Bus. He had been involved in a road traffic accident at work and, as a consequence, there was a recommendation that he return to work undertaking lighter duties. The question arose in the High Court as to whether there was an implied term in the contract of employment by way of "a sufficiently well-established custom and practice" entitling employees to be given rehabilitative work.[100] In the circumstances, the High Court found that there was a well-established custom and practice within Dublin Bus that alternative, rehabilitative, work would be provided for the plaintiff while he was unable to undertake his contractual duties and that this custom and practice was an implied term of the contract of employment.

Collective Agreements

[4–42]   Collective agreements refer to those agreements that have been negotiated between an employer (or an employer representative group) and a trade union representative of the employees. Collective agreements are often "normative" in so far as these agreements will set out certain terms and conditions of the contract of employment that are aspirational in nature, for example, productivity targets or industrial peace clauses. However, collective agreements may also set out certain terms and conditions of the contract of employment, for example, the hours of work, rate of pay, organisation of holidays and so on. Where such an agreement exists, its terms may become express terms of the employment contract.[101] If a term of a collective agreement is incorporated into the employment contract, any breach of the term will amount to a breach of contract. Terms of collective agreements can be incorporated into the employment contract in a number of ways. First, they may be incorporated by the trade union reaching an agreement with the employer while acting as an *agent* of the employees; secondly, by way of express incorporation; and thirdly, such terms can be incorporated by way of implication.

[4–43]   In *O'Rourke v Talbot*[102] the plaintiffs were a group of foremen who had formed a small committee to "discuss with the company matters of a common interest". The company was experiencing financial difficulties and this group of foremen sought assurances from the company that their jobs would be guaranteed. The company issued assurances that compulsory redundancies would not take place, in the form of a written document. A further document was issued by the company, at the insistence of the plaintiffs, to guarantee against compulsory redundancy until 1984 (in which the company, at the request of the foremen, changed the word "assurance" to "guarantee"). Due to the decline of business in 1980, the company had to make these

---

[98] [1958] 92 ILTR 156.
[99] [2005] 4 IR 184.
[100] *ibid* at 195-196 *per* Clarke J.
[101] Forde, *op.cit* p 53.
[102] [1984] ILRM 587.

employees redundant, thus breaching the guarantee. As a result, the foremen sued. The High Court found that the company had breached its agreement with the foremen and that this particular guarantee, concerning redundancy, had been incorporated effectively into the contract of employment, as it was clear and unambiguous and it was intended to be legally binding by the committee representing all foremen. Collective agreements, however, do not automatically bind all employees within a workplace where a collective agreement has been negotiated by the employer and trade union.[103] It was held in *Goulding Chemicals Ltd v Bolger* that a collective agreement will not be binding on those employees who have clearly indicated that they do not wish to be bound by such an agreement.[104]

IV. Duties of the Employer

This section will consider one of the most fundamental terms of employment found in the employment contract: that relating to remuneration. The next section will look at the equally important issue of working time. These areas are now regulated by various pieces of employment legislation (described below). It is important to remember that various other duties exists (for example, relating to health and safety) that are discussed elsewhere in the book. Also, in an employment relationship and under the employment contract, the *employee* clearly has also to fulfil certain obligations (to obey lawful orders, for example).   [4-44]

Pay

The employment contract will almost always specify the remuneration of the employee. The method and rate of pay is regulated by two key pieces of legislation: the Payment of Wages Act 1991 and the National Minimum Wage 2000.   [4-45]

The Payment of Wages Act 1991 provides protection for employees regarding the method of payment, the right to a written statement of wages, as well as deductions from wages. This legislation applies to all employees working under a contract of service from the first day of their employment. For the purposes of the Act, an employee is defined as "a person of any age who has entered into, or works or has worked under, a contract of employment".[105] This Act was introduced to allow for the payment of wages using non-cash methods, enabling employers to pay wages electronically, or by way of cheque. Employees must provide consent to any alternative forms of wage payment. It is perhaps more common in today's world for wages to be paid by means of electronic transfer into the employee's bank account. Cheques are becoming a less frequently used method of payment, which can probably be explained by the fact that banks are phasing out the issuing of cheque books to customers and even in everyday life, many retailers, for example, will no longer accept cheques as a form of payment.[106]

---

[103] Purdy, *op.cit* p 79.
[104] [1977] IR 211. See also *Reilly v Drogheda Borough Council* [2008] IEHC 357. For further discussion and analysis of the role of collective agreements and the employment relationship refer to chapter 11.
[105] Payment of Wages Act 1991, s 1. See chapter 3.
[106] The Irish Payments Services Organisation has called for the elimination of cheques by 2016 – for further information go to www.ipso.ie.

[4-46]   Wages are defined under s 1 of this legislation as any payment in return for work done. This includes regular basic pay, overtime pay, bonuses and commission, holiday pay, maternity leave pay, sick leave pay, shift payments and payment in lieu of notice. This definition of wages does not include expenses incurred by employees during the course of their employment, redundancy payments, benefits in kind, pensions, or any payment to the employee in a capacity other than that of employee. Employers must provide employees with a written statement of wages at the time of payment, which indicates the nature and amount of any deductions made from their gross wages.[107] It should be made clear within the employment contract what the rate of pay is and also when the employee is to be paid, whether this is on a weekly, fortnightly or monthly basis. Under s 5 of the Act deductions from wages are unlawful, unless the deductions are required by legislation,[108] are specified under the employment contract,[109] or specified within a written agreement.[110] Deductions may be applied in situations arising from the acts of employees in the course of their employment (e.g. breakages) or the need for employees to possess certain equipment to carry out their employment (e.g. a uniform). Certain rules are in place which must be satisfied for deductions to be lawful. First, the contract of employment must specifically provide for the deduction. Secondly, the employee must be provided with written details of this provision for deduction of wages in the contract. Thirdly, the amount deducted must be fair and reasonable.[111]

[4-47]   This issue of unlawful deduction of wages arose in *Ryanair v Downey*.[112] This case was an appeal by Ryanair against the findings of the Rights Commissioner that it was in breach of the Payment of Wages Act 1991. Under the contract of employment in dispute, there was a clause outlining that if the employee failed to complete the "Aircraft Engineer's Type Training" training course, or if the employee's contract of employment was terminated before the end of two years' service after completion of this course, the employee would be liable for the costs incurred by Ryanair in providing this training. This amounted to €5,000 in costs. Under the contract of employment, a further clause allowed Ryanair to deduct this amount from the employee's wages within six months of completion of the course, as long as a week's notice in writing was given to the employee. Ryanair failed to provide the required notice and the deductions were made *after* this six month time period. The Employment Appeals Tribunal (EAT) held that Ryanair had not provided the employee with one week's written notice of the deduction of wages, as required by s 5(2)(iv) of the Payment of Wages Act 1991. The EAT also found that the deduction was not fair and reasonable in accordance with s 5(2) of the 1991 Act and that a further breach had arisen as the deduction of wages had not been made within six months of the employee completing the course.

[4-48]   Certain deductions can be made from the wages of employees who go on strike or participate in some other forms of industrial action. This seems to be based on the notion that, where the employee refuses to perform the tasks contracted for, the employer can make deductions from his or her wages. So, in the English case of *Sim v*

---

[107] Payment of Wages Act 1991, s 4.
[108] For example, PRSI and PAYE.
[109] For example, pension contributions.
[110] For example, health insurance or trade union membership dues.
[111] Payment of Wages Act 1991, s 5.
[112] [2006] ELR 347.

Rotherham Council,[113] secondary school teachers refused to provide cover for absent colleagues as part of action relating to an industrial dispute. As this was in breach of their contracts, the employer was held entitled to "set off" the damages that would have been received if the employees had been sued against the wages of those involved. It seems there is no inherent right, though, to withhold wages for bad work or as a disciplinary measure.[114]

National Minimum Wage Act 2000

This Act applies to all full-time, part-time, temporary and casual workers. Under s 11 of the Act, the Minister for Enterprise, Trade and Employment has the power, after taking into account the impact the proposed rate may have on employment, the overall economic conditions in the State and national competitiveness, to declare a national minimum hourly rate of pay.[115] From 1 July 2007, the national minimum hourly rate of pay is €8.65 for an experienced adult worker. For those employees under 18 years of age, the minimum hourly rate of pay is €6.06. The Act does not apply to all types of employee (see s 5) as close relatives of the employer and apprentices, within the meaning of the Industrial Training Act 1967 and Labour Services Act 1987, are excluded from its provisions. Thus, it is possible that an apprentice, as defined by the legislation above, or indeed an employee of a family relative, could be paid less than the statutory minimum rate of pay. It is quite common for agreements to have been made by Joint Labour Committees or Joint Industrial Councils within certain industries to regulate the minimum rate of pay.[116]   **[4-49]**

Employees have a right to be paid a minimum wage under the 2000 Act. The amount of pay must meet the minimum legislative amount as prescribed by the Act. Pay has been defined (under s 2) as: **[4-50]**

> "... all amounts of payment, and any benefit-in-kind specified in Part 1 of the Schedule, made or allowed by an employer to an employee in respect of the employee's employment".

Under s 22 of the 2000 Act, the employer is required to keep records indicating its business is in compliance with its obligations under the Act. These records must be retained by the employer for at least three years from the date of their making. There is an "inability to pay" mechanism under the Act, whereby an employer in financial difficulty may be exempted from the obligation to pay minimum wage rates.[117] The Labour Court must approve the exemption, but the employer must first have reached agreement with the majority of the employees (or their representatives) in order to   **[4-51]**

---

[113] [1987] 1 Ch. 216.

[114] See Kerr, "Industrial Relations" in *Employment Law* (Regan ed, Tottel, Dublin, 2009), pp 685-688.

[115] ss 12 and 13 provide for a role, respectively, for the social partners (in the form of negotiating a national economic agreement) and the Labour Court (employer and worker representative bodies can ask the Court for a recommendation for a change in the rate to be made to the Minister).

[116] See also chapters 2 and 11.

[117] National Minimum Wage Act 2000, s 41. Such an exemption shall be for a period not exceeding one year and not less than three months.

make the Labour Court application.[118] The provision has yet to be invoked by an employer.

[4–52] As a consequence of an investigation in 2005 by the Minister for Enterprise, Trade and Employment into alleged breaches of legislative requirements, it emerged that a Turkish company, Gama Construction, had failed to pay employees the national minimum wage.[119] Indeed, foreign-national, unskilled construction workers were being paid between €2 and €3 per hour basic pay. Skilled workers received just over €3 per hour.[120] Failure to pay the national minimum wage as set out under the 2000 Act is a complete breach of an employer's statutory duty and amounts to an offence under the legislation.[121] The Gama case, in part, contributed to the negotiation of a new employment rights compliance regime under *Towards 2016*, which included the establishment of the National Employment Rights Authority (NERA) and the publication of the Employment Law Compliance Bill 2008.[122]

Sick Pay

[4–53] Under the provisions of the Terms of Employment (Information) Acts 1994 and 2001, employers have to provide employees with information regarding any entitlement to sick leave and to sick pay. There is no statutory duty for employers to pay employees for any sick leave: this is at the employer's discretion.[123] Where an employer does decide that employees will be entitled to sick pay, details of this must be stipulated in the employment contract.[124]

Payment of Bonuses

[4–54] The payment of bonuses is also a matter for negotiation between employers and employees. Agreements to pay bonuses are often part of a performance-related reward system for employees, designed to incentivise and reward actual performance against the achievement of specific goals and agreed objectives.[125] Bonus payments are not an entitlement but are based on an assessment of performance and, as such, are usually at the discretion of the employer. However, a recent line of cases in the UK has illustrated that any such discretion should be exercised rationally, in good faith and, where criteria are to be applied to the discretion, these must be open and transparent.[126] A question about payment of a *deferred* bonus to a former employee arose before the Irish High Court in *Finnegan v J & E Davy*.[127] In this case, no specific reference was made to

---

[118] National Minimum Wage Act 2000, s 41(6).

[119] See *Gama Construction v Minister for Enterprise* [2007] 3 IR 472. See chapter 12 for a discussion of this case. See also Krings, "A Race to the Bottom? Trade Unions, EU Enlargement and the Free Movement of Labour" (2009) 15(2) *European Journal of Industrial Relations* 49.

[120] This case also dealt with breaches of the Payment of Wages Act 1991, the Organisation of Working Time Act 1997 and the Industrial Relations Acts 1946 to 2000.

[121] National Minimum Wage Act 2000, s 35. See chapter 12.

[122] See chapter 2.

[123] Cox *et al, op.cit* p 147.

[124] See Shubotham, "Illness and Incapacity in the Workplace" (2004) 1(1) IELJ 6.

[125] See for example *An Post v AHCPS* (LCR 14094/2009).

[126] See Ryan and Ryan, "Bonus Points: Employers' Discretion in the Determination of Bonus Payments" (2007) 14(8) CLP 166.

[127] [2007] 18 ELR 234.

payment of any bonuses in the employment contract. The employee did, however, receive a "performance-related bonus" at the end of each year. After a certain period of employment, Mr Finnegan was informed that he would receive only a portion of his bonus in the year to which it related and that the balance would be deferred until the following year. He was also told that if he left his employment before the balance fell due, he would not be paid that balance. The High Court noted that the rules of the bonus scheme had not been reduced to writing: the scheme, therefore, had to be interpreted through the (conflicting) oral evidence of the parties. The Court found that the decision to defer part of the bonus was a unilateral change to the terms and conditions of the plaintiff's employment and he had not accepted this change.

Conditions

In accordance with the Terms of Employment (Information) Act 1994, employers must provide employees with certain information regarding their employment contract, such as their rates of pay, entitlement to annual leave and so on. In addition to the statutory conditions that must be included, employers may also insert additional conditions of employment particular to the type of job to be undertaken by the employee. In *Hurd v Leitrim County Council*[128] the claimant was employed as a part-time retained fire fighter by the respondents. Among his conditions of employment was the requirement that he reside and work "within distances from the Fire Station which are acceptable to the Fire Authority". The reason for this was the necessity for part-time fire fighters to respond quickly to any emergency call outs. The claimant took up a new full-time job located 16 miles away from the fire station and this was deemed to be in breach of the residence condition of his employment contract. The claimant took action against his employers claiming that he had been unfairly dismissed, but his claim was rejected by the EAT.

[4–55]

Complaints and Disciplinary Procedures

Reference to any complaints procedures available to employees should also be included within the employment contract. Employers should appoint a suitable person within the workforce to deal with any complaints that may arise. For example, if an employee feels that he or she is being subject to harassment or bullying within the workplace, the employee should be able to utilise the complaints procedure that is in place to voice any concerns.[129]

[4–56]

V. Working Time

The Organisation of Working Time Act 1997 regulates various aspects of employees' working hours, imposing minimum requirements regarding rest periods, breaks during the working day, night work, annual leave entitlement and public holidays. Details of rest periods, holidays, leave entitlement and so on must be documented within the written statement of particulars that the employer must give employees in accordance with the Terms of Employment (Information) Acts 1994 and 2001 and the Terms of Employment (Additional Information) Order (SI NO 49 of 1998). The 1997 Act

[4–57]

---

[128] UD 840/2007.
[129] See chapter 2 on the role of codes of practice, especially the Code of Practice on Grievance and Disciplinary Procedures (SI No 146 of 2000).

implements Directive 93/104 concerning certain aspects of the organisation of working time, which defines working time as:

> "[a]ny period during which the worker is working, at the employer's disposal and carrying out his activity or duties, in accordance with national laws and/or practice".[130]

[4–58]   It is clear that the 1997 Act and the EU Directive have their roots in health and safety concerns. Indeed, Directive 93/104 was subject to a controversial challenge by the UK government, which argued that the Directive should not have been adopted as a health and safety measure under the Treaty (under which it was adopted by a qualified majority vote), but pursuant to Treaty provisions relating to the common market (which would have required unanimity).[131] The ECJ rejected this argument. However, the Directive, and the ECJ's interpretation of it, has continued to cause controversy. An ongoing issue relates to "on-call workers". In *Jaeger* the applicant was a doctor in the surgical department of a hospital in Kiel who spent three-quarters of his normal working hours on call.[132] The ECJ ruled that the time spent at the workplace on-call and on the premises of the employer (even while asleep in a bed provided by the employer) constituted working time:

> "in contrast to a doctor on stand-by, where the doctor is required to be permanently accessible but not present in the health centre, a doctor who is required to keep himself available to his employer at the place determined by him for the whole duration of periods of on-call duty is subject to appreciably greater constraints since he has to remain apart from his family and social environment and has less freedom to manage the time during which his professional services are not required. Under those conditions an employee available at the place determined by the employer cannot be regarded as being at rest during the periods of his on-call duty when he is not actually carrying on any professional activity".[133]

Neither could such activity count as a "rest period":

> "In order to be able to rest effectively, the worker must be able to remove himself from his working environment for a specific number of hours which must not only be consecutive but must also directly follow a period of work in

---

[130]   Art 2, Directive 93/104 [1993] OJ L307/18. This Directive has been subsequently amended by Directive 2000/34 of 22 June 2000 amending Council Directive 93/104/EC concerning certain aspects of the organisation of working time to cover sectors and activities excluded from that Directive [2000] OJ L195/45. The legislation was codified by Directive 2003/88 of 4 November 2003 concerning certain aspects of the organisation of working time [2003] OJ L299/9. While it seemed political agreement had been reached on a new Working Time Directive in 2008 (http://www.eurofound.europa.eu/eiro/2008/07/articles/EU0807049I.htm), at the time of writing the proposal remains stalled. The Commission has, however, begun first-phase consultation of the social partners at EU level under Art 154TFEU (ex-Art 138EC): see COM(2010) 106 final.

[131]   Case C-84/94 *UK v Council* [1996] ECR I-5755.

[132]   Case C-151/02 *Landeshauptstadt Kiel v Jaeger* [2003] ECR I-08389.

[133]   *ibid* at para 65.

order to enable him to relax and dispel the fatigue caused by the performance of his duties. That requirement appears all the more necessary where, by way of exception to the general rule, normal daily working time is extended by completion of a period of on-call duty".[134]

In June 2008, a political agreement was reached on changes to the Working Time Directive, but as noted, this has not been progressed. Among the proposals was a provision to "split" on-call time into active and inactive on-call time. Active on-call time would be counted as working time while inactive on-call time could be counted as rest time *or* as working time (if national laws or national social partners agree).[135]   **[4-59]**

The 1997 Act lays down rules relating to maximum weekly working hours and minimum holiday and rest periods. Certain categories of employees are excluded from the Act, or from some of its terms, for example, the Garda Síochána, the Defence Forces, doctors in training[136] and persons whose working time is determined by themselves. Certain provisions, also, do not apply to shift workers.   **[4-60]**

Certain specified activities are also exempt (including, under s 24, work in respect of which the Labour Court has approved a collective agreement that includes terms in breach of the Act). These are mainly provided for in the Organisation of Working Time (General Exemptions) Regulations 1998[137]:   **[4-61]**

a. An activity in which the employee is regularly required by the employer to travel distances of significant length, either from his or her home to the workplace or from one workplace to another workplace;

b. An activity of a security or surveillance nature the purpose of which is to protect persons or property and which requires the continuous presence of the employee at a particular place or places, and, in particular, the activities of a security guard, caretaker or security firm;

c. An activity falling within a sector of the economy or in the public service, in which it is foreseeable that the rate at which production or the provision of services, as the case may be, takes place will vary significantly from time to time, or the nature of which is such that employees are directly involved in ensuring the continuity of production or the provision of services (including, for example, the provision of services relating to the reception, treatment or care of persons in a residential institution, hospital or similar establishment, the production in the press, radio, television, cinematographic, postal or telecommunications industries, the provision of ambulance, fire and civil protection services, the production, transmission or distribution of gas, water or electricity, the collection of household refuse or the operation of an incineration plant, and any industrial activity in which work cannot, by reason of considerations of a technical nature, be interrupted).

---

[134] *ibid* at para 95.

[135] See http://www.eurofound.europa.eu/eiro/2008/07/articles/EU0807049I.htm.

[136] But see European Communities (Organisation of Working Time) (Activities of Doctors in Training) Regulations 2004 (SI No 494 of 2004).

[137] SI No 21 of 1998.

[4–62] Employees that fall under these provisions are entitled to "compensatory" periods, however. In *Tribune Printing & Publishing Group v Graphical Print and Media Union*[138] the Labour Court held that an employer was under a positive duty to ensure employees took breaks (i.e. putting in place procedures to ensure breaks were taken rather than simply stating that employees could take a break if they wished).

Maximum Hours and Rest periods

[4–63] The core aspect of the legislation provides for a maximum working week: s 15 states that an employer shall not permit an employee to work, in each period of seven days, more than an average of 48 hours, calculated over a period ("the reference period") that does not exceed four months (although this can be exceeded in specific circumstances laid down in s 15).[139] Under s 15(4) the reference period cannot include any period of annual leave granted to the employee (unless such leave exceeds the minimum period of annual leave required by the Act), any absences from work by the employee authorised under legislation relating to parental leave, *force majeure* leave, carer's leave, the Maternity Protection Act 1994, or the Adoptive Leave Act 1995, or any sick leave taken by the employee. Cox *et al* point out that the obligations on the employer created by this section are strict liability in nature: the fact that the employer neither knows nor is negligent as to whether an employee is exceeding the maximum number of working hours is irrelevant.[140]

[4–64] Section 11 of the 1997 Act provides that employees are entitled to a daily rest period of at least 11 consecutive hours every 24 hours. During the course of the working day, employees are also entitled to rests and interval breaks. As a minimum, an employee is entitled to a 15 minute break every four and a half hours, or 30 minutes every six hours.[141] These breaks cannot be taken at the end of the working day. Employees are also legally entitled to weekly rest periods. Section 13 provides that employees are entitled to a weekly rest period of at least 24 consecutive hours in each period of seven days, or 48 hours in every period of 14 days.

[4–65] Employees have a right to complain under the 1997 Act if they feel that they are being forced to work excessive hours. In *IBM Ireland v Svoboda*[142] the employee complained that she had been required to work excessively long hours. This case was heard by the Labour Court, which found that, in fact, the employer did not require the employee to work excessively long hours. The reality in this case was that the employee herself was working beyond her contractual hours, but not at the behest of the employer. However, even though the Labour Court found that the employer was not forcing this employee to work extra hours, it was held that the employer had a duty to ensure that she did not work beyond the hours stipulated in her contract. It is somewhat difficult to reconcile the outcome of the case with the logic of this approach by the Labour Court. Nevertheless, breaches of legislation relating to daily rest periods and excessive working hours will lead to awards of compensation for the employee. For example, in

---

138 DWT 047/2004.
139 Note that special provisions are laid down for night work (s 16) and Sunday working (s 14).
140 Cox et al, *op.cit* p 389.
141 Organisation of Working Time Act 1997, s 12.
142 DWT 0818/2008, noted in (2008) 5 IELJ 101.

Bridford Properties Ltd v Smilgys[143] the employee was awarded €1000 for breaches of the legislation in relation to daily rest periods, and €862.88 for breaches of annual leave entitlement provisions.

Annual Leave

Article 7 of Directive 2003/88 provides that employees have an entitlement to paid annual leave. The 1997 Act provides for a statutory minimum period of holidays to which the employee is entitled. Section 19 provides for four weeks' paid annual leave for a leave year in which the employee works at least 1,365 hours, in addition to public holidays. Under ss 19 (1) (b) and (c) of the 1997 Act, employees who work at least 117 hours will be entitled to at least one-third of a working week for each month in the leave year or eight percent of the hours worked by the employee up to a maximum of four working weeks. There is no statutory definition of a "working week". Section 19(6) of the 1997 Act interprets a working week within the context of s 19 "as references to the number of days that the employee concerned usually works in a week". The Labour Court considered the meaning of this phrase "working week" in *Irish Ferries v Seamen's Union of Ireland*.[144] It held that the entitlement to annual leave must correspond to the amount of time which the employee would normally be required to work in each work cycle.

[4–66]

Section 20 addresses the questions of the timing of, and pay for, annual leave. The employer can determine when annual leave is to be taken, but must have due regard for family responsibilities and ensuring that employees have an adequate opportunity to rest. Annual leave must be taken within the leave year, or within six months of the leave year with the consent of the employee. In the event of the termination of the employment contract, the employee must be paid for any outstanding holidays due.[145] The only circumstance where payment in lieu of statutory holidays is permissible is in the event that the employment relationship has terminated.[146]

[4–67]

The European Court of Justice in the joined cases of *Schultz-Hoff* and *Stringer* has recently considered the issue of employee's entitlement to paid annual leave during a period of unpaid sick leave.[147] The ECJ found that employees can accrue annual leave while sick, even during long-term sick leave. The Court outlined that the entitlement to paid annual leave must be regarded as a particularly important principle of EU law from which there can be no derogations. The ECJ held that it is for the Member States to lay down, in their domestic legislation, conditions for the exercise and implementation of the right to paid annual leave. However, where an employee is *incapable* of exercising his or her right to paid annual leave, due to illness for example, the entitlement to paid annual leave cannot be extinguished at the end of the leave year and/or of a carry-over period laid down by national law. Moreover, on the termination of the employment relationship, such a worker is entitled to be paid *in lieu* of paid

[4–68]

---

[143] DWT 0822/2008. See, further, chapter 12.
[144] DWT 35/2001.
[145] Organisation of Working Time Act 1997, s 23(1).
[146] Case C-173/99 *BECTU* [2001] ECR I-4881.
[147] Joined Cases C-350/06 and C-520/06 *Schultz-Hoff v Deutsche Rentenversicherung Bund* and *Stringer v Her Majesty's Revenue and Customs* [2009] 2 CMLR 27.

annual leave not taken. Unsurprisingly, this ruling has led to critical commentary from organisations representative of business, given the potential cost implications.[148] The decision could be of huge significance: under the ruling, there is a possibility that an employee who has been off sick for a decade could accrue over 40 weeks holiday with full pay once, or if, he or she returns to work. The ECJ, nevertheless, has confirmed its decision in *Pereda v Madrid Movilidad SA*.[149] The ECJ reiterated that that the purpose of the entitlement to paid annual leave is to enable the worker to rest and to enjoy a period of relaxation and leisure. The purpose of the entitlement to sick leave is different. It is given to the worker so that he or she can recover from being ill. Therefore, if a worker decides not to take annual leave during a period of illness, he or she must be granted a replacement holiday period.[150]

Public Holidays

[4-69] Section 21 of the 1997 Act deals with public holidays. There are nine public holidays in Ireland, Christmas Day, St Stephen's Day, 1 January, St Patrick's Day, Easter Monday (Good Friday is not regarded as a public holiday for the purposes of the legislation), the first Monday in May, the first Monday in June, the first Monday in August and the last Monday in October. An employee who ceases to be employed during the week ending on the day before a public holiday is entitled to be paid for that public holiday if that person has worked for four consecutive weeks preceding this.[151] To be entitled to a public holiday, the employee must have worked at least 40 hours in the previous five weeks. A qualifying employee must be given a day off or a day's pay within that month. Alternatively, the employee can be given an additional day of annual leave or an additional day's pay. Any absence of 52 weeks by reason of occupational injury, or 26 weeks by reason of other injury or illness, or 13 weeks for any other reason will disentitle an employee from the benefit of a public holiday falling within that period.

---

[148] O'Mara "Have Employees an Entitlement to Paid Annual Leave During Unpaid Sick Leave?" (2009) 6(1) IELJ 30.

[149] Case C-277/08.

[150] The ECJ also addressed the issue of annual leave in Case C-486/08 *Zentralbetriebsrat der Landeskrankenhauser Tirols v Land Tirol*. The Court found that the provisions of Directive 96/34 of 3 June 1996 on the framework agreement on parental leave concluded by UNICE, CEEP and the ETUC [1996] OJ L145/4 (discussed in chapter 6), must be interpreted as precluding a national provision under which workers exercising their right to parental leave of two years lose, following that leave, their right to paid annual leave accumulated during the year preceding the birth of their child.

[151] Organisation of Working Time Act 1997, s 23(2).

CHAPTER 5
Equality Law and Employment Rights

I. Introduction

Employers have to make daily choices about which persons to hire for particular jobs.   **[5–01]**
Decisions will also need to be made regularly in relation to the selection of particular
employees for promotion, re-grading, termination and redundancy.[1] All of these
decisions will necessitate some element of *discrimination*, the choosing of certain job
applicants or employees over others, which will be completely legitimate.[2] At common

---

[1] Forde, *Employment Law* (2nd ed, Round Hall, Dublin, 2001), p 123.
[2] Cox *et al*, *Employment Law in Ireland* (Clarus Press, Dublin, 2009), p 241.

law, employers historically had the discretion to discriminate against members, or prospective members, of the workforce "for the most capricious, malicious or morally reprehensive motives".[3] However, since the 1970s, the development of legislative protections prohibiting discrimination in the workplace has significantly fettered this discretion.

[5–02] Discrimination, therefore, involves the making of a selection between different options or the drawing of some type of distinction and is unproblematic.[4] *Unlawful* discrimination will occur, however, where the employer refuses, or fails, to make a decision on who to employ or how to treat employees that is based on objective criteria (such as qualifications or expertise necessary for the job) and instead bases this decision on the *characteristics of the person*. Under Irish law, the general rule is that an employer is not entitled to make decisions relating to employment that are based primarily on the following characteristics: age, race, disability, gender, family status, marital status, religious beliefs, sexual orientation or membership of the travelling community.

[5–03] It is important to note, then, at the outset, that "discrimination" can have many different meanings. Connolly points out that the concept encompasses three types of mistake:

> "The first is an incorrect view that people in certain groups possess certain characteristics. The second is a belief that many members of a group have certain characteristics when in fact only a few of them do. The third mistake is a reliance on fairly accurate group-based generalisations when more accurate (and not especially costly) classifying devices are available".[5]

Why the law should prohibit discriminatory treatment in employment, and how the legislature should go about doing so, are not unproblematic issues. So, from a human rights perspective, for example, it may be felt that all persons should be treated equally, irrespective of inherent characteristics, such as race or gender. From an economics perspective, however, the argument might be that it is necessary to prohibit employment-based discrimination, not because of its effects on individuals, but because to discriminate is *inefficient*, for example, on the grounds that an irrational decision based on a person's characteristics (rather than his or her ability to do a particular job) will ultimately be of detriment to the employer's business.[6]

---

[3] *Allen v Flood* [1898] AC 1 at 172-173 *per* Davey J.

[4] Bamforth *et al*, *Discrimination Law: Theory and Context* (Thomson Sweet & Maxwell, London, 2008), p 17.

[5] Connolly, *Discrimination Law* (Thomson Sweet & Maxwell, London, 2006), p 2. The author is himself referring to Sunstein, "Three Civil Rights Fallacies" (1991) 79 *California Law Review* 752.

[6] See Davies, *Perspectives on Labour Law* (2nd ed, Cambridge University Press, Cambridge, 2009), chapter 7. Of course these arguments can be (and have been) challenged. A different economic perspective, for example, might argue that it *is* efficient for employers to discriminate. An employer seeking to hire a person for a job that requires heavy lifting, for example, might simply decide to exclude all female applicants from consideration. While this might exclude certain females who could do the job effectively, it also saves the employer the time and cost involved in carrying out an objective assessment of all the applicants. See, generally, Becker, *The Economics of Discrimination* (2nd ed, University of Chicago Press, Chicago, 1971).

Similarly, what anti-discrimination laws should seek to achieve is a matter of considerable **[5–04]** debate. One view of equality is that all persons should be treated according to their own merits (excluding irrelevant factors like race or gender). As a result, the law should ensure that women be treated like men and ethnic minorities like whites: this approach, the "formal equality model", assumes that all persons (be they male or female, white or black, etc) are equal and should be paid and treated in the same manner, irrespective of any dissimilarities that they possess.[7] A model based on "substantive equality", however, focuses on achieving equality of *outcome or results*. This approach does not see certain characteristics, such as gender or race, as being irrelevant, as certain groups (e.g. women, ethnic minorities, the disabled) have suffered a historical disadvantage due to their possession of these characteristics. Therefore, radical action needs to be taken to remedy this historical disadvantage (going beyond mere "equal treatment"). As the responsibility for discrimination, on this view, rests with the dominant group in *society as a whole*, it is this group that should bear the costs of change.[8] Such an approach, therefore, recognises that "positive action" (or "affirmative action") measures, which give more favourable treatment to disadvantaged groups in the workforce are permissible. Such measures will, of course, often come at the expense of formal equality.[9]

II. The Development of Equality Law in Ireland

Article 40.1 of the Irish Constitution provides a guarantee of equality of all citizens **[5–05]** before the law:

> "All citizens, shall, as human persons, be held equal before the law. This shall not be held to mean that the State shall not in its enactments have due regard to differences of capacity, physical and moral, and of social function".

The Constitution also specifically prohibits discrimination on the grounds of religious or political beliefs,[10] or on the basis of an individual's membership of a family unit.[11] Clearly, however, these constitutional guarantees do not focus solely on equality *in the workplace*. Indeed, relatively few cases initiated under these particular provisions have related to individuals seeking to assert their constitutional rights to equality at work.[12]

Given the fact that the Constitution has been invoked relatively infrequently in this area, **[5–06]** it is unquestionably Ireland's membership of the European Union that has been the most significant influence on the development of the principle of equality in Irish employment law.[13] Article 2 of the Treaty on European Union (TEU) states that the Union is founded on certain core values, including respect for human dignity, freedom and equality. Article 2 states that these values are common to the Member States "in a society in which

---

[7] Barnard, *EC Employment Law* (3rd ed, Oxford University Press, Oxford, 2006), p 333.

[8] Connolly, *op.cit*, p 11.

[9] See Fredman, "Reversing Discrimination" (1997) 113 LQR 575.

[10] Arts 44.2 and Art 40.6.1°.

[11] Art 41.

[12] See, generally, Hogan and Whyte, *The Irish Constitution* (4th ed, LexisNexis, Dublin, 2003), Part 7.

[13] Although the removal of the "marriage bar", the ban on married women continuing to work in the Irish public service in the 1970s, is an example of an important domestic legislative change: see the Civil Service (Employment of Married Women Act) 1973.

pluralism, non-discrimination, tolerance, justice, solidarity and equality between women and men prevail". Article 8 of the Treaty on the Functioning of the European Union (TFEU) states that, in all its activities, the Union shall aim to eliminate inequalities and to promote equality between men and women. Article 10TFEU states that, in defining and implementing its policies and activities, the Union "shall aim to combat discrimination based on sex, racial or ethnic origin, religion or belief, disability, age or sexual orientation". The Charter of Fundamental Rights also provides that all persons are equal before the law (Art 20) and that equality between women and men must be ensured in all areas, "including employment, work and pay" (Art 23). Article 21(1) provides that:

> "Any discrimination based on any ground such as sex, race, colour, ethnic or social origin, genetic features, language, religion or belief, political or any other opinion, membership of a national minority, property, birth, disability, age or sexual orientation shall be prohibited".

Finally, Art 26 of the Charter states that the Union recognises and respects the right of persons with disabilities to benefit from measures designed to ensure their independence, social and occupational integration and participation in the life of the community.

[5–07]   While the inclusion of many of the strong equality and non-discrimination provisions in the Treaties noted above date from relatively recently (in particular, following the amendments introduced by the Treaty of Amsterdam), the goal of achieving equality in employment as between men and women has been recognised since the foundation of the Union. What was originally Art 119 of the EEC Treaty, now Art 157TFEU (ex-Art 141EC), recognised the principle of equal pay for equal work for men and women in the workplace. From the outset, it was clear that the rationale for such a provision was both economic and social.[14] On an economic level, gender equality was necessary in order to prevent distortions in the common market as between Member States with equal pay laws (particularly France) and those without such laws. Secondly, gender equality provided a relatively uncontroversial area of social policy in which the EU could act without allegations of trampling on Member State sovereignty. Thirdly, it provided the EU with law-making competence in an area of direct concern to ordinary citizens of the Member States.[15]

[5–08]   Secondary legislation, in the form of the Equal Pay and Equal Treatment Directives,[16] soon followed and was incorporated into Irish law by means of the Anti-Discrimination

---

[14] Barnard, *op.cit*, p 298.

[15] Craig and de Búrca, *EU Law: Text, Cases and Materials* (4th ed, Oxford University Press, Oxford, 2008), p 875.

[16] Directive 75/117 on the approximation of the laws of the Member States relating to the application of the principle of equal pay for men and women [1975] OJ L45/19 and Directive 76/207 on the implementation of the principle of equal treatment for men and women as regards access to employment, vocational training and promotion and working conditions. [1976] OJ L39. The Directives (as amended) on equal pay and equal treatment have now been consolidated into Directive 2006/54 (to be transposed by August 2010), the aim of which is to simplify, modernise and improve EU legislation on equal treatment between men and women by bringing together in a single text the relevant passages of the Directives on this subject to make the provisions clearer and more practical for all citizens: Directive 2006/54/EC on the implementation of equal opportunities and equal treatment of men and women in matters of employment and occupation [2006] OJ L204/23 (hereinafter referred to as "the Recast Equal Treatment Directive").

(Pay) Act 1974 (which was the first piece of domestic legislation to specifically prohibit discrimination in the workplace) and the Employment Equality Act 1977. The primary focus of both these pieces of legislation was to prevent gender discrimination and to provide for equality between men and women in the workplace.

The Employment Equality Act 1998 replaced both the Anti-Discrimination (Pay) Act 1974 and the Employment Equality Act 1977 and consolidated Irish equality law into one single Act. The 1998 Act, which was introduced before the Treaty of Amsterdam came into force in 1999, was an innovative piece of equality legislation as it went beyond an exclusive focus on gender and extended the grounds upon which employment-related discrimination was prohibited to include family status, marital status, religion, disability, age, race, membership of the Traveller Community and sexual orientation (so, including gender, these are referred to in the legislation as the nine "discriminatory grounds").[17] The Treaty of Amsterdam subsequently also provided for the extension of protection against workplace discrimination at EU level to include religion or belief, racial or ethnic origin, disability, age and sexual orientation.[18] As a consequence of the various changes introduced by the Treaty of Amsterdam, amendments were made to the equal pay and equal treatment Directives and two new Directives were introduced: Directive 2000/78 establishing a general framework for equal treatment in employment and occupation[19] and Directive 2000/43 dealing specifically with race discrimination.[20] To ensure compliance with EU equality legislation introduced after 1998, the 1998 Act was amended by the Equality Act 2004. Therefore, Irish employment equality law is now regulated by the Employment Equality Acts 1998–2008 (hereinafter "the Employment Equality Acts").[21]

[5–09]

The Equality Act 2004 introduced significant amendments to some of the key definitions in the 1998 Act. While the most important of these will be discussed throughout the chapter, some are briefly mentioned some here. These amendments included new definitions of key terms such as "direct" and "indirect" discrimination, "harassment", "victimisation" and "reasonable accommodation" and a number of changes to procedure and jurisdiction, in particular, the transfer of jurisdiction for discriminatory dismissal cases from the Labour Court to the Equality Tribunal.[22] The definitions of an "employee" and a "contract of employment" are also extended by the

[5–10]

---

[17] See Darcy, "Achieving De Facto Equality between Men and Women-Making the Employment Equality Act 1998 Work" (2004) 22 ILT 199.

[18] In Art 13EC (now Art 19TFEU).

[19] Directive 2000/78 of 27 November 2000 establishing a general framework for equal treatment in employment and occupation [2000] OJ L303/16.

[20] Directive 2000/43 of 29 June 2000 implementing the principle of equal treatment between persons irrespective of racial or ethnic origin [2000] OJ L180/22. For an excellent and comprehensive overview of the ECJ's case law post-Amsterdam see Costello and Davies, "The Case Law of the ECJ in the Field of Sex Equality Since 2000" (2006) 43(6) CMLR 1567.

[21] The 2004 Act also updated and amended the Equal Status Act 2000, which prohibits types of discrimination in relation to the provision of goods and services.

[22] See chapter 2 for a full discussion of the role of the Equality Tribunal and the Equality Authority.

2004 Act.[23] This Act now applies to persons employed in a self-employed capacity and to partners and partnerships.

[5–11]   There was no extension of the nine protected grounds of discrimination, although the 2004 Act does extend the scope of some of the existing grounds: most notably the legislation now states that discrimination on the gender ground shall occur where a female employee is subject to discrimination on the basis of her maternity leave or pregnancy.[24] A further key amendment was the extension of "positive action" provisions to all nine grounds under the Act (see below). The 2004 Act also provided for the narrowing of the exclusion of employment in private households.[25] A person who applies for a position in another person's home will not be afforded protection from discrimination under the legislation when applying for the job. However, once that person is employed in the private household, he or she will be fully protected.[26] Another significant amendment under the 2004 Act relates to the requirement imposed on employers in relation to employing a person with a disability. Employers now have an obligation to provide "reasonable accommodation" for persons with disabilities, subject to it not imposing a "disproportionate burden" on the employer (rather than a "nominal" cost as was previously the case).[27]

III. Direct Discrimination

[5–12]   The ECJ in *Gillespie v Health and Social Services Board*[28] defines unlawful discrimination as "the application of different rules to comparable situations or the application of the same rule to different situations". More recently, Art 2(1) of the Recast Equal Treatment Directive defines direct discrimination as occurring where "one person is treated less favourably on the grounds of sex than another is, has been or would be treated in a comparable situation". The definition of discrimination under the Employment Equality Acts, which extends to protection against discrimination on any of the nine discriminatory grounds, is contained in s 6(1):

> "...discrimination shall be taken to occur where –
> (a) a person is treated less favourably than another person is, has been or would be treated in a comparable situation on any of the grounds specified in subsection (2) (in this Act referred to as the 'discriminatory grounds') which –
> (i) exists,
> (ii) existed but no longer exists,

---

[23] See chapter 3. Note that in *Dunbar v ASTI* (DEC-E2009-054) the Equality Tribunal, in upholding a claim of victimisation against the respondents, held that the definition of *employer* under the Acts included a trade union of which the complainant was a member (but which was not his direct employer). This decision is currently under appeal.

[24] See chapter 6.

[25] Employment Equality Acts, s 2.

[26] Kerr, *Employment Equality Legislation* (2nd ed, Round Hall, Dublin, 2005), p L-166.

[27] Employment Equality Acts, s 16(3).

[28] Case C-342/93 *Gillespie v Health and Social Services Board* [1996] ECR 475, para 16. See chapter 6 for further discussion of this decision.

(iii) may exist in the future, or

(iv) is imputed to the person concerned".[29]

"'Less favourable treatment" constitutes what is generally referred to as "direct discrimination".[30] To determine whether a person has been treated less favourably than another person, there is a need to find a *comparator*; that is, what must be assessed is whether the complainant has, in fact, been disadvantaged *in comparison with* another employee in a similar position to the claimant. Locating a comparator is, of course, in itself insufficient evidence of discrimination: it is also necessary to demonstrate that the complainant has been treated *less favourably* than the comparator *and* that the reason for this difference in treatment is connected with one or more of the nine discriminatory grounds.[31]

[5–13]

The comparator must be chosen by the person complaining that he or she has been subject to discrimination,[32] however, the Tribunal will consider the reasons for selecting the particular comparator chosen.[33] For equal pay claims, the comparator must be a real person (a hypothetical comparator will not suffice) undertaking the same or similar work as the complainant.[34] It is not necessary to have a real comparator for claims of discrimination concerning issues other than pay. Section 6(1)(a) of the Employment Equality Acts permits the claimant to identify a hypothetical comparator, as discrimination is defined as including situations where a person "would be" treated less favourably. This point was made clear in *Ntoko v Citibank*,[35] where the Labour Court held that a hypothetical comparator could be used where no actual comparator existed to establish whether the claimant had been subject to discrimination on the grounds of race in relation to his dismissal. The Equality Tribunal applied the test of the hypothetical comparator in *Gorys v Igor Kurakin Transport Limited*[36] to determine if the complainant, a Lithuanian truck driver, had been discriminated against on the grounds of race, in a situation where he had not been provided with a contract of employment, time sheets or payslips. The Tribunal compared the complainant with a hypothetical worker of Irish nationality and found that, in the circumstances, the complainant had not been treated less favourably than such a worker would have been treated. The respondent company had only recently been established and other employees had not yet been provided with the relevant

[5–14]

---

[29] Note that vicarious liability is provided for in s 15(1) of the Employment Equality Acts, which states that anything done by a person in the course of his or her employment shall, in any proceedings brought under the Act, be treated for the purposes of the Act as done also by that person's employer, whether or not it was done with the employer's knowledge or approval. s 15(3) provides a defence to the employer where it can show it took such steps as were reasonably practicable to prevent the prohibited acts from occurring.

[30] Bolger and Kimber, "Employment Equality" in *Employment Law* (Regan ed, Tottel, Dublin, 2009), p 416.

[31] Cox *et al, op.cit*, pp 247–248.

[32] *Wilton v Steel Company of Ireland Ltd* [1999] ELR 1; *National University of Ireland v Ahern* [2005] 2 IR 577.

[33] *National University of Ireland v Ahern* [2005] 2 IR 577; *Department of Justice, Equality and Law Reform v CPSU* [2008] ELR 140.

[34] See below for further discussion on the need for a comparator in relation to equal pay claims.

[35] *Ntoko v Citibank* [2004] 15 ELR 116.

[36] *Gorys v Igor Kurakin Transport Limited* (DEC-E2008-014).

documentation. The ability to identify a hypothetical comparator is extremely important; the *inability* to choose a hypothetical comparator in claims for equal pay, for example, has made it extremely difficult to tackle the issue of occupational sex segregation in workplaces and sectors that traditionally have very few, if any, male employees.[37]

[5–15] It should also be noted that the definition of discrimination extends to prohibit less favourable treatment of any person who is *attributed* with any of the characteristics under the nine identified grounds in s 6(2).[38] This means that an employee will be protected from discrimination on any of the nine grounds if an employer *mistakenly* believes that that person possesses any of the characteristics associated with any of those grounds. So, for example, if the employer believes that the employee is married with a family when in reality the employee is single and childless, discrimination will occur if that employee is treated less favourably as a result of the employer's mistaken belief. Cox *et al* argue that this provision is likely to be of particular benefit to those employees who have been subject to discrimination on the grounds of sexual orientation.[39]

[5–16] Section 14A of the Employment Equality Acts provides that it shall constitute discrimination under the legislation to harass, or sexually harass, a worker. Harassment is defined as "any form of unwanted conduct in relation to any of the discriminatory grounds". Sexual harassment is defined as "any form of unwanted verbal, non-verbal or physical conduct of a sexual nature". In either case, it will constitute discrimination under the legislation where such conduct has the "purpose or effect of violating a person's dignity in creating an intimidating, hostile, degrading, humiliating or offensive environment for the person". Harassment and sexual harassment will be looked at in detail in chapter 9. However, as will be seen from the case law discussed throughout the present chapter, many claims under the Acts include references to harassment on one of the discriminatory grounds.

[5–17] Section 74(2) of the Employment Equality Acts offers protection against victimisation by an employer.[40] This can arise where dismissal or other adverse treatment of an employee by his or her employer occurs as a reaction to:

    i.   a complaint of discrimination made by the employee to the employer;
    ii.   any proceedings by a complainant;
    iii.   an employee having represented or otherwise supported a complainant;
    iv.   the work of an employee having been compared with that of another employee for any of the purposes of the Acts;
    v.   an employee having been a witness in any proceedings under the Acts or the Equal Status Act 2000;
    vi.   an employee having opposed by lawful means an act which is unlawful under the Acts or the Equal Status Act 2000;

---

[37] Bolger and Kimber, *op.cit*, p 465; Steele, "Tracing the Single Source: Choice of Comparators in Equal Pay Claims" (2005) 34(4) ILJ 338.
[38] Employment Equality Acts, s 6(1)(a)(iv).
[39] See Cox *et al*, *op.cit*, pp 251-252.
[40] Curran, "'Victimisation': A New Remedy for Employees" (2008) 5(1) IELJ 4; Bolger and Kimber, *op.cit*, pp 436-441.

vii. an employee having given notice of an intention to take any of the actions mentioned in the preceding paragraphs.

Discrimination by Association

Section 6(1)(b) of the Employment Equality Acts prohibits discrimination *by association*. Under this provision, discrimination is taken to occur where a person who is associated with another person:

[5–18]

> "(i) is treated, by virtue of that association, less favourably than a person who is not so associated is, has been or would be treated in a comparable situation, and
> (ii) similar treatment of that other person on any of the discriminatory grounds would, by virtue of paragraph (*a*), constitute discrimination".

Although the Framework Directive does not contain any reference to protection from discrimination by association, the ECJ in *Coleman v Attridge Law*[41] held that the Directive does provide for protection against discrimination for associated persons. Here, Ms Coleman claimed that she was unfairly dismissed from her job as a legal secretary and treated less favourably than other employees because she was the primary carer for her disabled son. Ms Coleman submitted that she was not permitted to resume her old job when she returned to work after her maternity leave period ended. Additionally, her employer refused to provide her with the same flexibility in relation to working arrangements as was provided to her colleagues with non-disabled children. The ECJ held that it did not follow from the provisions of Directive 2000/78 that the principle of equal treatment is limited to people who *themselves* have a disability within the meaning of the Directive. On the contrary, the Court held that the purpose of the Directive, as regards employment and occupation, is to combat all forms of discrimination on grounds of disability: the principle of equal treatment enshrined in the Directive, therefore, applies not to a *particular category of person* but by reference to *the grounds* protected.[42] Thus,

> "[w]here an employer treats an employee who is not himself disabled less favourably than another employee is, has been or would be treated in a comparable situation, and it is established that the less favourable treatment of that employee is based on the disability of his child, whose care is provided primarily by that employee, such treatment is contrary to the prohibition of direct discrimination laid down by Article 2(2)(a)".[43]

Exemptions to the Prohibition on Discrimination

Discrimination on any of the specified grounds may be permissible in certain circumstances. Some of the exemptions to the general principle of non-discrimination apply to particular *types* of employment, some apply to *all* kinds of employment, some

[5–19]

---

[41] Case C-303/06 *Coleman v Attridge Law* [2008] IRLR 722.

[42] At para 38.

[43] At para 56. See also Pilgerstorfer and Forshaw, "Transferred Discrimination in European Law" (2008) 37(4) ILJ 384; Eriksson, "European Court of Justice: Broadening the Scope of European Non-discrimination Law" (2009) 7(4) *International Journal of Comparative Law* 731.

apply to *particular grounds* and some apply to provisions in *other legislation.* Some of the main exemptions are summarised here.[44]

[5–20]   An employer is not required to employ, train or promote a person who will not undertake the necessary duties or is not fully competent or capable of doing the job.[45] Thus, the section can provide a complete defence to a claim of discrimination on the disability ground where it can be shown that the employer genuinely believed that the complainant was not fully capable of performing the duties for which he or she was employed.[46]

[5–21]   Under s 25 of the Employment Equality Acts a difference in treatment based on gender in relation to access to employment may be permitted. Similarly, under s 37 a difference in treatment based on a characteristic related to any of the other grounds may be permitted. However, in both cases, the difference in treatment shall not constitute discrimination *only* where, by reason of the particular occupational activities concerned, or of the context in which they are carried out, the characteristic constitutes *a genuine and determining occupational requirement* and the objective is legitimate and the requirement *proportionate.* In terms of gender, for example, discrimination would be permissible if the job required the employer to hire a female fashion model or a female dancer. In terms of other discriminatory grounds, authenticity for the purpose of the job may require an employer to discriminate on one of the prohibited grounds. So, for example, it might be permissible to discriminate on the grounds of race by requiring a black actor to play the role of Othello in the Shakespeare play, or by requiring a chef or a waiter in an ethnic restaurant to be of a particular nationality.

[5–22]   Section 36 permits discrimination in relation to residency, citizenship and language requirements for certain State employees. Section 36(4) allows requirements in relation to the holding of specified educational, technical or professional qualifications, which are generally accepted qualifications in the State for the post in question.[47] Section 34(1) provides that it will not constitute discrimination if an employer provides a benefit to an employee in respect of the employee's family or family events (such as giving the employee a wedding present, for example) or in relation to the provision of childcare or other care provision, which is connected with his or her family or marital status.[48]

[5–23]   A number of important exemptions from the general principle of non-discrimination apply to specific grounds.[49] Section 27 of the Employment Equality Acts allows for

---

[44] See also the Equality Authority's explanatory booklet on the Employment Equality Acts 1998 and 2004, available at www.equality.ie.

[45] Employment Equality Acts, s 16(1).

[46] Note that s 16(3) requires "reasonable accommodation" to be provided in order to enable persons with disabilities to be capable of doing the job. See, further, below for a full discussion of the disability ground.

[47] See Smith, "Side-stepping Equality? Disability Discrimination and 'Generally Accepted Qualifications'" (2008) 30 DULJ 279. See, for a US perspective on this issue, Shorter *et al*, "Can Employers Use Gender in Hiring Decisions: The Discrimination Bona Fide Occupational Qualification Applied to Health Care" (2007) 33(2) *Employee Relations Law Journal* 55.

[48] Cox *et al, op.cit*, p 266.

[49] The provisions relating to pregnancy, maternity and other "family-friendly" legislation will be looked at in chapter 6.

gender discrimination in relation to certain posts in the Garda Síochána and the prison service.[50] In relation to the religion ground, s 37(1) permits discrimination where it is necessary to maintain the religious ethos of a religious, educational or medical institution that is under the control and direction of a body set up for religious purposes, or which has the purpose of providing services in an environment promoting certain religious values.[51] Under s 37(1), therefore, it would appear to be permissible for a school under the control and direction of a Catholic religious order to refuse to appoint a person who was of a different religious belief.[52] Failure to comply with the religious ethos of a school has previously resulted in the dismissal of an employee. In *Flynn v Power*[53] Ms Flynn, an unmarried woman, was dismissed because she failed to end her relationship with a married man at the request of the nuns in charge of the convent school where she was employed as a schoolteacher. Costello J upheld her dismissal on the grounds that her behaviour (the extra-marital affair) was in breach of the "norms of behaviour and religious tenets" that the school sought to promote.[54]

In relation to the disability ground there is an exemption allowing for the provision of a particular rate of remuneration for work of a particular description where, due to disability, the amount of work done during a particular period is less than the amount of similar work done, or which could reasonably be expected to be done, over that period by an employee without a disability.[55]   **[5–24]**

In relation to the age ground, an employer may impose an age criterion for admission to any occupational benefits scheme, and can also take an employee's age into account for actuarial calculations and for the purposes of making severance payments.[56] An employer can also use age as an objectively justifiable reason to provide different employees with different rates of pay, or indeed different terms and conditions of employment, provided that the reason for this difference is related to the employee's length of service.[57] An employer is also permitted under the legislation to set different ages for the retirement of employees and may, in certain circumstances, set a maximum age for recruitment[58]; see however chapter 10 for a discussion of recent ECJ case law on age discrimination in relation to mandatory retirement and recruitment ages.   **[5–25]**

Positive Action

An employer can take "positive action" to promote equal opportunities for men and women in relation to access to employment, vocational training and promotion and   **[5–26]**

---

[50] See also ss 37(3)-(6).
[51] See Coen, "Religious Ethos and Employment Equality: A Comparative Irish Perspective" (2008) 28(3) *Legal Studies* 452.
[52] Cox *et al*, *op.cit*, p 265.
[53] [1985] IR 648.
[54] See, also, chapter 10.
[55] Employment Equality Acts, s 35(1).
[56] Employment Equality Acts, s 34(3).
[57] Employment Equality Acts, s 34(7). Although see Case C-17/05 *Cadman v HSE* [2006] ECR I-9583, discussed below.
[58] Employment Equality Acts, ss 34(4)-(5).

working conditions.[59] Positive action measures are designed to redress imbalances in the workforce and, in particular, to address the problem of occupational segregation by gender.[60] Section 24 of the Employment Equality Acts permits an employer to adopt measures:

  i. to make it easier for an under-represented sex to pursue a vocational activity; or
  ii. to prevent or compensate for disadvantages in professional careers.

However, the ECJ has ruled that it would not be possible to justify measures that guarantee that women have unconditional and absolute priority for appointment or promotion.[61] An employer must ensure that any positive action measures to promote equal opportunities between men and women must be proportionate and take into account the individual qualities of the relevant candidates.[62]

IV. Indirect Discrimination and Objective Justification

[5–27] The legislation also prohibits what is known as "indirect discrimination" on any of the nine discriminatory grounds. Indirect discrimination is defined in a number of sections in the Acts.[63] Section 19(4) of the Employment Equality Acts prohibits indirect discrimination on the gender ground in relation to pay:

> "Indirect discrimination occurs where an apparently neutral provision puts persons of a particular gender (being As or Bs) at a particular disadvantage in respect of remuneration compared with other employees of their employer".[64]

Under s 22, indirect discrimination on the gender ground will be deemed to have occurred where an apparently neutral provision puts a person, who is protected by the Act, at a particular disadvantage in respect of any matter (other than pay) in comparison with other employees. Section 31 prohibits indirect discrimination against a person on any of the other discriminatory grounds.

---

[59] Employment Equality Acts, s 24(1). s 33 also renders lawful positive action measures designed to prevent or compensate for disadvantages linked to any of the other discriminatory grounds; to protect the health or safety at work of persons with a disability, or to create or maintain facilities for safeguarding or promoting the integration of such persons into the working environment.

[60] For critical discussion of the concept of occupational segregation see Breen and Whelan, "Gender and Class Mobility: Evidence from the Republic of Ireland" (1995) 29(1) *Sociology* 1; Hakim, "Explaining Trends in Occupational Segregation: The Measurement, Causes, and Consequences of the Sexual Division of Labour" (1992) 8(2) *European Sociological Review* 127; Hakim, "Lifestyle Preferences as Determinants of Women's Differentiated Labour Market Careers" (2002) 29(4) *Work and Occupations* 428.

[61] Case 450/93 *Kalanke v Frei Hansestadt Bremen* [1995] ECR I-3051.

[62] Case C-407/98 *Abrahamsson v Fogelqvist* [2000] ECR I-5539. See Caruso, "Limits of the Classic Method: Positive Action in the European Union After the New Equality Directives" (2003) 44 *Harvard Law Review* 331.

[63] Although the broad concept remains the same; Bolger and Kimber, *op.cit*, p 417. See Cunningham, "Indirect Discrimination: Between the Wheat and the Chaff" (2009) 38(2) ILJ 209.

[64] Under the 1998 Act (before the 2004 amendments) complainants needed to demonstrate that "a substantially higher proportion of persons of the same gender" were disadvantaged by the provision.

Indirect discrimination, therefore, occurs where a rule or provision, which on its face [5–28] appears to affect all employees equally, in fact, favours or disfavours a particular category of employees, which is protected from discrimination under s 6 of the Employment Equality Acts. In *Nathan v Bailey Gibson*[65] Ms Nathan claimed that she had been indirectly discriminated against because of a "closed shop" agreement that was in place between her employer and the Irish Print Union.[66] Ms Nathan had been employed as an assistant to a machine operator and she applied for his job after his retirement. An unemployed male member of the union was appointed, as the employer had a closed shop agreement in place with the union, which provided that the employer would fill any vacancies with a member of the union if that vacancy became available due to the departure of a union member. The union had an overwhelmingly male membership. The Supreme Court held that:

> "A requirement, relating to employment or membership of a body which is not an essential requirement for such employment or membership and in respect of which the proportion of persons of the other sex or (as the case may be) of a different marital status but of the same sex able to comply in substantially higher numbers may amount to indirect discrimination".[67]

The crucial distinction between direct and indirect discrimination is that an employer [5–29] can explain the imposition of any provision that indirectly discriminates as being *objectively justifiable*; this is not permissible for direct discrimination, which can only be justified by reference to the legislation itself (see the exemptions outlined above) and, therefore, seems to attract strict liability.[68]

Objective justification is not defined in any detailed way in the Employment Equality [5–30] Acts, but s 19(4) states that indirect discrimination on the grounds of gender will not occur where the provision is "objectively justified by a legitimate aim and the means of achieving that aim are appropriate and necessary". This reflects the test set out by the ECJ in *Bilka-Kaufhaus*.[69] In this case, the employer imposed a requirement that only those workers who had worked a minimum period of full-time employment could access the occupational pension scheme. Ms Weber initiated legal proceedings against Bilka-Kaufhaus claiming that this requirement was in breach of Art 157TFEU (then Art 119EEC) in relation to equal pay. The employer argued that the reasons for the rule were to discourage part-time work and to make full-time work more attractive, as part-time workers generally refused to work in the late afternoon or on Saturdays. The ECJ held that such a rule was capable of being justified by economic factors. According to the ECJ in *Bilka-Kaufhaus*, an indirectly discriminatory measure may be justifiable if it is necessary to meet a real need on the part of the employer, if it is

---

[65] [1998] 2 IR 162.
[66] See chapter 11 for a discussion of closed shop agreements.
[67] [1998] 2 IR 162 at 177 *per* Hamilton CJ.
[68] Bolger and Kimber, *op.cit*, p 418. However, this point may not be as clear cut as traditionally assumed; see Barnard, *op.cit,* p 322; Bowers and Moran, "Justification in Direct Sex Discrimination Law: Breaking the Taboo" (2002) 31 ILJ 307; Gill and Monagahan, "Justification in Direct Sex Discrimination Law: 'Taboo Upheld' "(2003) 32(2) ILJ 115.
[69] Case C-170/84 *Bilka-Kaufhaus GmbH v Karin Weber von Hartz* [1986] ECR 1607.

appropriate with a view to achieving the objective pursued and if it is necessary to meet that objective.

[5–31]   In *Department of Justice, Equality and Law Reform v Civil Public and Services Union*[70] the Labour Court adopted the test for objective justification outlined by the English EAT in *Barton v Investec PC Henderson Crosthwaite Securities Ltd.*[71] Under this test, it is necessary to establish:

i.   that there were objective reasons for the difference;
ii.   unrelated to sex;
iii. corresponding to a real need on the part of the undertaking;
iv.   appropriate to achieving the objective pursued;
v.   that it was necessary to that end;
vi.   that the difference conformed to the principle of proportionality; and
vii. that that was the case throughout the period during which the differential existed.

[5–32]   In the *CPSU* case, the complainants were clerical officers who were employed by the Department of Justice, Equality and Law Reform and assigned to undertake clerical duties in An Garda Síochána. The identified comparators were members of An Garda Síochána, who undertook certain clerical and administrative work. Certain posts within An Garda Síochána are reserved for members of the force (as opposed to civilians) and are referred to as "designated posts". The majority of the comparators identified held one of these designated posts: 279 of which were held by male employees and 74 by female employees. However, a clear majority of the 761 clerical officers deployed in An Garda Síochána were female. Applying the test outlined above, the Labour Court found that the respondent was *not* indirectly discriminating against the female clerical officers by paying them a lower rate than the male comparators who held a designated post, as there were objective justifications for this pay difference unrelated to gender. In particular, the respondent successfully argued that there were *genuine operational reasons* for deploying members of An Garda Síochána in clerical posts (the need for police knowledge and training in the discharge of functions connected to the post or, where that was not the case, the need to extend the process of civilianisation in a manner and at a pace which would attract the agreement of the Garda representative bodies). It was also deemed essential to have members of An Garda Síochána undertaking clerical work to ensure the continuity of service at all times, as these officers could not go on strike or engage in industrial action. Thus the Labour Court concluded that:

> "...the deployment of members of An Garda Síochána on rates of pay appropriate to their rank is an appropriate, necessary and proportionate means of achieving the objective which the practice is intended to pursue".[72]

---

[70] [2008] ELR 140.

[71] [2003] IRLR 332.

[72] This case is currently the subject of a referral to the ECJ on the grounds that that the use of industrial relations considerations as an objective justification for indirect discrimination is contrary to EU law; see "Garda Clerical Equal Pay Case to be Referred to Europe" (2009) 17 IRN.

V. The Burden of Proof

Section 85A of the Employment Equality Acts deals with the burden of proof on a [5–33] claimant taking an action under the legislation. The section gives effect to the Burden of Proof Directive,[73] which itself reflects ECJ jurisprudence on this issue. As in all civil law claims the burden of proof rests with the complainant and the standard is on a "balance of probabilities". However, the legislation and case law recognises that, unlike in other civil cases, it is rare for there to be explicit and direct evidence of discrimination. Furthermore, the complainant is required to establish that he or she was treated less favourably *because of* gender, race, or another prohibited ground: this, however, "is something which is almost exclusively within the knowledge (and therefore) control of the discriminator".[74] Consequently, as proof of discrimination usually must be inferred from other primary facts, the burden of proof is partly shifted to the employer.[75] Section 85A provides that:

> "(1) Where in any proceedings facts are established by or on behalf of a complainant from which it may be presumed that there has been discrimination in relation to him or her, it is for the respondent to prove the contrary...
> (4) In this section 'discrimination' includes-
> (*a*) indirect discrimination,
> (*b*) victimisation,
> (*c*) harassment or sexual harassment,
> (*d*) the inclusion in a collective agreement to which section 9 applies of a provision which, by virtue of that section, is null and void".

In *Southern Health Board v Mitchell*[76] the Labour Court considered the issue:

> "The first requirement is that the claimant must establish facts from which it may be presumed that the principle of equal treatment has not been applied to them. This indicates that a claimant must prove, on the balance of probabilities, the primary facts on which they rely in seeking to raise a presumption of unlawful discrimination...It is only if these primary facts are established to the satisfaction of the Court, and they are regarded by the Court as being of sufficient significance to raise a presumption of discrimination, that the onus shifts to the respondent to prove that there was no infringement of the principle of equal treatment".

In that case the "primary facts" upon which the complainant sought to rely were that [5–34] he was continually assigned more work than other financial administrators with whom he worked and that different standards of scrutiny and supervision were applied to the work of the complainant relative to that of others. The complainant was not able to

---

[73] Directive 97/80 of 15 December 1997 on the burden of proof in cases of discrimination based on sex [1998] OJ L14/6. The burden of proof in cases of discrimination is also addressed in the other main equality Directives as seen above; the Recast Equal Treatment Directive 2006/54 (Art 19); the Race Directive 2000/43 (Art 9) and the Framework Directive 200/78 (Art 10).

[74] Bamforth *et al, op.cit*, p 1185.

[75] See Cunningham, "Discrimination Through the Looking-Glass: Judicial Guidelines on the Burden of Proof" (2006) 35(3) ILJ 279.

[76] [2001] ELR 201.

satisfy the test here, as witnesses on behalf of the respondent gave evidence of the methods by which work was allocated within the employment and as to the supervisory structures and practices: they told the Court that the manner in which the complainant was treated in respect of those matters was identical to that of all the other employees with whom he worked.

VI. Equal Pay

[5–35] Article 157TFEU (ex-Art 141EC) enshrines the principle that male and female workers are entitled to equal pay for equal work, or work of equal value. Although, as discussed above, economic reasoning was important in terms of the provision for equal pay being included in the Treaty of Rome, the principle is now predominantly regarded as having a *social* objective: that of vindicating the fundamental human right of equality as between the sexes.[77] The ECJ has stressed many times that this provision is the cornerstone of the Treaty provisions that relate to employment law.[78] The Court's decision in *Defrenne v Sabena*[79] confirmed that Art 157TFEU (ex-Art 141EC) has both horizontal and vertical direct effect. As a result individuals can rely directly on their rights under the provision before their national courts.[80]

[5–36] The principle of equal pay as between the sexes was originally implemented in Ireland by the Anti-Discrimination (Pay) Act 1974, but is now provided for in Part III of the Employment Equality Acts. Section 19(1) of the Employment Equality Acts provides that:

> "It shall be a term of the contract under which A is employed that, subject to this Act, A shall at any time be entitled to the same rate of remuneration for the work which A is employed to do as B who, at that or any other relevant time, is employed to do like work by the same or an associated employer".[81]

Section 2(1) of the Employment Equality Acts defines remuneration as "any consideration, whether in cash or in kind, which the employee receives, directly or indirectly, from the employer in respect of the employment". Such remuneration does not include equal rights to a pension as this is dealt with under specific legislation governing pensions and pension rights.[82] The ECJ has defined "pay" in an extremely broad manner, so that it includes:

> "... any consideration, whether in cash or in kind, whether immediate or future, provided that the worker receives it, albeit indirectly, in respect of his employment from his employer, and irrespective of whether the worker receives

---

[77] See, for example, Docksy, "The Principle of Equality between Men and Women as a Fundamental Right under Community Law" (1991) 20 ILJ 258.

[78] Barnard, *op.cit*, p 339.

[79] Case C-43/75 *Defrenne v Société anonyme belge de navigation aérienne Sabena* [1976] ECR 455.

[80] See Craig and de Búrca, *op.cit*, p 878.

[81] s 29 of the Employment Equality Acts mirrors this section and provides for an entitlement to equal pay as between employees who differ in respect of any of the other eight prohibited grounds of discrimination; see Kerr, *op.cit*, p L-186.

[82] Pensions Acts 1990-2009, ss 67, 70 and 74. See Kenny and Smith, "Pay, Pensions and Benefits" in *Employment Law* (Regan ed, Tottel, Dublin, 2009).

it under a contract of employment, by virtue of legislative provisions or on a voluntary basis".[83]

Like Work

The principle of equal pay applies where the employees in question are engaged in "like work". Section 7(1) of the Employment Equality Acts defines "like work" as being: [5–37]

i.   the same work undertaken by another person under the same or similar conditions;

ii. where the work is of a similar nature (and any differences between the work performed or the conditions under which it is performed either are of small importance in relation to the work as a whole, or occur with such irregularity as to be insignificant to the work as a whole); or

iii. the work is of equal value taking into consideration such matters as skill, physical or mental requirements, responsibility and working conditions.[84]

Section 7(3) provides that the principle of equal pay also prohibits a difference in pay where the *lower* paid worker does work that is of *higher* value: this incorporates into the Acts the ECJ decision in *Murphy v Bord Telecom Eireann*.[85] [5–38]

Section 7 requires that, for the purposes of any comparison, the work undertaken must actually be "performed". This confirms the approach adopted by the Labour Court in *Department of Posts and Telegraphs v Kennefick*,[86] where the Court held that the nature of the work undertaken by two post and telegraph clerks was essentially the same, despite the fact that the job description for one of the clerks included additional responsibilities. However, in the "Austrian Psychotherapists Case" [87] a group of mainly female psychotherapists (with degrees in psychology) sought wage parity with medical doctors, who were employed as psychotherapists. While the ECJ did acknowledge that both groups of psychotherapists undertook "seemingly identical activities" it found that the doctors who were employed as psychotherapists were also qualified, by virtue of possessing medical degrees, to undertake other tasks. Furthermore, both groups possessed different disciplinary skills and knowledge. Consequently, the ECJ held that the differences in the professional training and qualifications meant that they could not be treated as being in a comparable situation.

In assessing if the parties are engaged in "like work", however, there is no necessity for the claimant to be employed contemporaneously with the comparator.[88]

---

[83] Case C-360/90 *Arbeiterwohlfahrt der Stadt Berlin v Bötel* [1992] ECR I-3589, at para 12. This would include things like sick pay, concessions, bonuses and so on; see Deakin and Morris, *Labour Law* (5th ed, Hart, Oxford, 2009), p 608.

[84] See also the discussion of "like work" in the context of the legislation on fixed-term and part-time workers in chapter 3.

[85] Case 167/86 *Murphy v Bord Telecom Eireann* [1988] ECR 673.

[86] EP 9/1979.

[87] Case C-309/97 *Angestelltenbetriebsrat der Wiener Gebietskrankenkasse v Wiener Gebietskrankenkasse* [1999] ECR 2865.

[88] Case 129/79 *Macarthys Ltd v Smith* [1980] ECR 1275, where the applicant compared the work she was doing with that done by her (male) predecessor.

[5–39]   The employer's belief, or indeed intention, that the work is equal in value is irrelevant for the purposes of s 7. Barron J confirmed this in *C & D Food Ltd v Cunnion*,[89] where he held that it is not up to the employer to determine what constitutes "like work"; rather this responsibility rests with the relevant court or tribunal.

The Comparator

[5–40]   The definition of "like work" clearly requires that a complainant seeking equal pay must be able to *compare* his or her work to that of another. The ECJ held in *MacCarthys*[90] that there is a need for an *actual* comparator (not a hypothetical one): "comparisons are confined to parallels which may be drawn on the basis of concrete appraisals of the work actually performed by employees of different gender within the same establishment or service".[91] This judgment was endorsed in *Brunnhofer*,[92] where the ECJ held that the principle of equal pay applies to men and women who are "in identical or comparable situations" and that this necessitates a concrete evaluation as to whether the employees concerned are performing the same work or work to which equal value may be attributed. Budd J in the High Court approved this approach in *Brides v Minister for Agriculture*[93] holding that the complainant would need to find an actual, concrete real life comparator of the other gender.[94] As a result, women in an all-female employment cannot use the legislation to secure "the male rate for the job".[95]

[5–41]   It is not essential for the comparator to be in employment within the same establishment or service *at the same time* as the person claiming discrimination.[96] However, the comparator must undertake the same work for the same or associated employer.[97] In *Lawrence*[98] the ECJ said that, in principle, there was nothing in Art 157TFEU (ex-Art 141EC) to prevent comparisons between men and women working for different employers but went on to say that:

> "where, as in the main proceedings here, the differences identified in the pay conditions of workers performing equal work or work of equal value cannot be attributed to *a single source*, there is no body which is responsible for the inequality and which could restore equal treatment. Such a situation does not come within the scope of Article 141(1) EC. The work and the pay of those workers cannot therefore be compared on the basis of that provision".[99]

---

[89] [1997] 1 IR 147 at 151.

[90] Case C-129/79 *MacCarthys Ltd v Smith* [1980] ECR 1275.

[91] *ibid* at para 15.

[92] Case C-381/99 *Brunnhofer v Bank der österreichischen Postsparkasse AG* [2001] ECR 4961.

[93] *Brides v Minister for Agriculture* [1998] 4 IR 250.

[94] See also *Power v Blackrock College* (DEC-E2008-72), where the failure to identify a real comparator in an identical situation to the complainant resulted in the failure of the claim for discrimination on the grounds of age (relating to the non-payment of redundancy).

[95] See Wynn, "Equal Pay and Gender Segregation" (1994) LQR 556.

[96] Case C-129/79 *MacCarthys Ltd v Smith* [1980] ECR 1275.

[97] Employment Equality Acts, s 19(1). In addition, s 19(3) requires that the comparator undertaking work for an associated employer must have the same or reasonably comparable terms and conditions of employment.

[98] Case C-320/00 *Lawrence and Others* [2002] ECR I-7325.

[99] *ibid* at para 18 (emphasis added).

A "single source" would appear to exist in cases where the claimant and comparator [5–42] work for the same legal person; for public authorities operating under joint control; or where pay is governed by legislation or collective agreements. This decision has been criticised for creating a situation where employers can side-step equal pay laws by changing the organisational structure of the business, or the status of the workers, through out-sourcing or contracting out work rather than employing workers directly: this was precisely the case in *Lawrence*.[100]

While the ECJ has acknowledged the right of the complainant to chose the comparator [5–43] in equal pay claims, in *Dansk Industri*[101] the Court held that the two groups being compared had to encompass all the workers who could be considered to be in a comparable situation, taking into account the nature of the work, training requirements and working conditions. It clearly indicated that the choice of comparator must not be based on "purely fortuitous or short-term factors or to differences in the individual output of the workers concerned".[102]

Once the comparator is identified the claimant must still show that any difference in [5–44] pay is due to discrimination that is *related to* one of the prohibited grounds. It was noted above that discharging the burden of proof in discrimination cases can present particular difficulties for claimants. In recognition of this fact the ECJ has held in *Jämställdhetsombudsmannen*[103] that, where there is a *prima facie* case of discrimination, it is for the *employer* to show that there are objective reasons for the difference in pay. The Court held that workers would be deprived of the means of securing compliance with the principle of equal pay before national courts if evidence establishing a *prima facie* case of discrimination did not have the effect of imposing on the employer the onus of proving that the difference in pay is not, in fact, discriminatory.[104] In *Danfoss*[105] the ECJ held that where an employer applies a system of pay which is totally lacking in transparency, it is for the *employer* to prove that his practice in the matter of wages is not discriminatory, where a female worker establishes, in relation to a relatively large number of employees, that the average pay for women is less than that for men.[106]

Objective Justification and Pay Differentials

Under s 19(5) of the Employment Equality Acts, employers may pay different rates of [5–45] remuneration to men and women but this must be justifiable on grounds other than

---

[100] The ECJ has nevertheless endorsed the "single source" test in Case C-256/01 *Allonby v Accrington & Rossendale College* [2004] ECR I-873; see Fredman, "Marginalising 'Equal Pay Laws'" (2004) 33(3) ILJ 281; Barnard, *op.cit*, pp 352-354.
[101] Case C-400/93 *Specialarbejderforbundet i Danmark v Dansk Industri* [1995] ECR I-1275.
[102] *ibid* at para 38.
[103] Case C-236/98 *Jämställdhetsombudsmannen v Örebro läns landsting* [2000] ECR I-2189.
[104] At para 53. See also Art 19 of the Recast Equal Treatment Directive 2006/54.
[105] Case C-109/88 *Handels- og Kontorfunktionærernes Forbund I Danmark v Dansk Arbejdsgiverforening* [1989] ECR 3199.
[106] This may occur, for example, where "basic pay" in an organisation is supplemented by a range of bonuses, share options, benefits-in-kind, etc so that it can be difficult to establish exactly what the comparator (or comparator group) is *actually* being paid.

gender.[107] In *Department of Justice, Equality and Law Reform v Civil Public and Services Union*,[108] discussed above, the use of Gardaí in clerical posts, who were paid more than civilian clerical officers, was justifiable on grounds other than gender (it was necessary for "genuine operational reasons"). Similarly, in *NUI Cork v Ahern*[109] the Supreme Court held that a pay differential between male security guards and female telephone operators was justifiable. The Court found that, while the parties were engaged in like work, the female telephone operators were being paid more for doing less work. This was not, however, because of gender. The telephone operators had initially been doing more work, but due to family responsibilities, had been facilitated by the employer in doing less work whilst retaining the higher rate of pay.[110]

[5–46]　Furthermore, as noted above, a difference in treatment on a discriminatory ground that amounts to *indirect discrimination* may be capable of being objectively justified by the employer. In such circumstances, the employer will not discriminate unlawfully where unequal pay rates can be "objectively justified by a legitimate aim and the means of achieving that aim are appropriate and necessary".[111] Many justifications for unequal pay rates have been put forward by employers: some examples of these will be considered here.

[5–47]　It seems that *collective bargaining agreements or negotiations* can constitute an objective justification for different rates of pay.[112] In *Flynn v Primark*[113] female sales assistants sought to be paid the same as male store-room workers. They were unsuccessful in their claim because the employer was able to justify the difference in pay on the grounds that the male workers belonged to a union with substantial industrial relations strength, which had secured higher levels of pay by negotiating productivity agreements. The High Court confirmed the Labour Court's determination that the pay differential was objectively justifiable on economic grounds.

[5–48]　*Market forces* and the need to attract suitable candidates for a particular job can constitute an objective justification for a difference in pay. The ECJ accepted that "the needs of the market" was an objective justification for explaining why female speech therapists were paid less than male pharmacists and psychologists in *Enderby*. The ECJ stated that an employer could objectively justify a difference in pay where a higher rate of pay is necessary in order to attract suitable candidates for a particular job.[114]

---

[107] The same principle also applies to the other grounds of discrimination; Employment Equality Acts, s 29(5).

[108] [2008] ELR 140.

[109] [2005] 2 IR 577.

[110] See also *McManus v Diageo Ireland* (DEC-E2007-021).

[111] Employment Equality Acts, s 19(4).

[112] Case C-400/93 *Specialarbejderforbundet i Danmark v Dansk Industri* [1995] ECR I-1275. Note that the ECJ took a different approach in *Enderby*. In that case, the ECJ held that the fact that rates of pay were decided by collective bargaining processes conducted separately for male and female groups of workers could *not* be relied upon as a justification for differences in pay. Otherwise, the Court held, an employer could easily circumvent the equal pay rules by using different collective bargaining processes; Case C-127/92 *Enderby v Frenchay Health Authority and Secretary of State for Health* [1993] ECR 5535.

[113] *Flynn v Primark (No.2)* [1999] ELR 89.

[114] Case C-127/92 *Enderby v Frenchay Health Authority and Secretary of State for Health* [1993] ECR 5535.

However, the ECJ has been reluctant to accept arguments by employers that it simply costs too much to secure equal pay.[115]

It appears that an employer could objectively justify pay differentials between men and women based on *length of service or seniority*. The ECJ has acknowledged that the application of length of service as a criterion to make pay awards indirectly discriminates against female workers. This is because female workers tend to accrue service more slowly, as they are more likely to take periods away from work for family and caring reasons. The ECJ, however, held in *Danfoss* that an employer does "not have to provide special justification for recourse to the criterion of length of service".[116] The ECJ took a different view to the use of length of service to justify a difference in pay in a number of subsequent cases,[117] but appears to have recently reverted to its earlier approach. In *Cadman*[118] the Court held that an employer can rely on length of service as a decisive factor to determine levels of pay and does not have to establish the importance it has in the performance of specific tasks entrusted to the employee. However, the ECJ did emphasise that an employee could *challenge* the use of length of service to determine pay where it is evident that greater length of service does not necessarily mean that the employee is better able to perform his or her duties. In such circumstances, the onus will fall back on the employer to prove that the experience acquired from greater length of service is necessary for the particular job.[119]

[5-49]

VII. Equal Treatment on Grounds of Gender

Prior to the Treaty of Amsterdam, Art 157TFEU (ex-Art 141EC) did not contain any reference to the equal treatment of men and women, other than in the context of equal pay. However, a number of Directives on equal treatment provided for equality in employment for matters other than equal pay, namely access to employment and promotion, vocational training and working conditions.[120] Equal treatment will be looked at in the context of the other discriminatory grounds below, but first equal treatment on the grounds of gender will be examined.

[5-50]

Section 21 of the Employment Equality Acts provides for the insertion of a gender equality clause into a contract of employment (where such a clause does not exist). Section 22 of the Acts prohibits indirect discrimination on the gender ground as it relates to equal treatment in employment, vocational training, by an employment agency or by a trade union or professional body. As Bolger and Kimber note, given the

---

[115] Case C243/95 *Hill and Stapleton v Revenue Commissioners* [1998] ECR I-3739.

[116] Case 109/88 *Handels-og Kontorfunktionaerernes Forbund I Danmark v Dansk Arbejdsgiverforening, acting on behalf of Danfoss* [1989] ECR 3199, para 25.

[117] See, for example, Case C-243/95 *Hill and Stapleton v Revene Commissoners* [1998] ECR I-3739.

[118] Case C-17/05 *Cadman v HSE* [2006] ECR I-9583.

[119] *ibid* at para 38.

[120] Council Directive 76/207/EEC on the implementation of the principle of equal treatment for men and women as regards access to employment, vocational training and promotion and working conditions [1976] OJ L39; Council Directive 2000/78/EC establishing a general framework for equal treatment in employment and occupation [2000] OJ L303/16; Directive 2006/54/EC on the implementation of equal opportunities and equal treatment of men and women in matters of employment and occupation [2006] OJ L204/23.

length of time that the equal treatment legislation has been in place, it is nowadays rare to see litigation where an employer has engaged in blatant gender discrimination.[121] Much litigation tends to revolve around disputes relating to pregnancy and maternity and other leave entitlements (see chapter 6). However, one area of gender discrimination that does still generate a significant amount of case law relates to access to employment and/or promotion, where a complainant challenges an interview or selection process. In these cases, the courts and tribunals have stressed that, where a competitive interview process takes place, the issue for consideration is whether or not the gender of the complainant affected the decision: it is *not* for the court or tribunal to decide who was the more *meritorious candidate*.

[5–51] In *Medical Council v Barrington*[122] the claimant was a single female who alleged that she was asked at an interview whether or not she was "thinking of getting married". This question had not been asked of either male, or married female, candidates. In *Trinity College Dublin v McGhee*[123] a married female was asked about whether or not she was planning to have any more children and about her husband's attitude to her applying for the job. In both cases the questions asked were adjudged to be discriminatory.

[5–52] In *Dublin City University v Horgan*[124] Ms Horgan alleged that she had been subject to discrimination on the grounds of her gender in relation to an internal promotional process. Ms Horgan was a Senior Lecturer at Dublin City University when she applied for an internal promotion to the position of Associate Professor. She was short listed along with four other candidates, all of whom were male. The other four candidates were successful and subsequently appointed as Associate Professors. Ms Horgan claimed she had been discriminated against on grounds of her gender at all stages of the selection process and particularly in relation to the referees that she had nominated. The University rejected her referees, including one referee with whom she had collaborated, even though this referee had been accepted on behalf of one of the male candidates. The Labour Court determined that Ms Horgan did possess better qualifications on paper than the other male candidates who were appointed to the position of Associate Professor and, furthermore, accepted that the University's rejection of her referee raised inferences of discrimination, which had not been rebutted. The Labour Court upheld the findings of the Equality Tribunal that Ms Horgan had been discriminated against on the grounds of her gender during the selection process.

[5–53] The Court stipulated that, in such cases, the respondent must provide cogent evidence to discharge the burden of proof in relation to discrimination.[125] Thus, employers would be well advised to make and retain interview notes. The Labour Court in *Horgan*, in fact, recommended that the members of any interview panel keep

---

[121] Bolger and Kimber, *op.cit*, p 441.
[122] EE 9/1988.
[123] EE 1/1989.
[124] EDA 715/2007.
[125] See the discussion above on the burden of proof in discrimination claims.

"contemporaneous notes" of all interviews and that these notes be retained for a minimum period of 12 months.[126]

In *Rotunda Hospital v Gleeson*[127] the Labour Court, in determining whether a case of unequal treatment could be made out, referred, *inter alia,* to the following:

[5–54]

> "One of the interviewers stated that the appellant's major career development appeared to have occurred during the years when she had her babies. This remark, whether intended as complimentary or not, clearly identifies the appellant by reason of her sex and could give rise to a prima facie finding of discrimination".

Where no difference in treatment with a comparator can be established, however, no claim for discrimination can be made out. In *Savage v Federal Security*[128] the male complainant, who wore his long hair in a ponytail, stated that he was asked at interview about cutting his hair. The employer argued that, as the complainant's hair was hip length, it was too long to fit under the cap guards were required to wear as part of their uniform. All security guards were required to be neat in appearance and long hair, whether on men or women, was to be worn either under the cap or in a bun. The Equality Tribunal found that a female applicant would have been treated the same as the complainant and so found no evidence of discrimination.

VIII. Areas of Discrimination

Section 8(1) of the Employment Equality Acts prohibits discriminatory treatment in relation to:

[5–55]

   i.   access to employment;
   ii. conditions of employment;
   iii. training or experience for or in relation to employment;
   iv. promotion or re-grading; or
   v. classification of posts.

Access to Employment

Section 8(1) renders it unlawful to discriminate against an employee, prospective employee or agency worker in relation to access to employment.[129] An employer will be taken to discriminate against an employee or prospective employee in relation to any discriminatory arrangements that the employer sets out to determine which person should be made an offer of employment. Furthermore, discrimination will arise if the

[5–56]

---

[126] See also *South Eastern Health Board v Burke* (EDA 041/2004); *Department of Health and Children v Gillen* (EDA 0412/2004). In the latter case, the Labour Court stressed that interview boards, both internal and external, should be trained, and apply strict promotion criteria agreed in advance with adequate markings. See, below, the discussion in relation to access to employment.

[127] [2000] ELR 206 at 210.

[128] DEC-E2007-064.

[129] The case law discussed above on the correct conduct of interviews for jobs or promotions is obviously relevant here. See also Turner, "Access to Employment: Discrimination on Grounds of Disability" (2009) 6(1) IELJ 23.

employer stipulates that one person or class of persons must meet specific entry requirements, which other persons or classes or persons do not need to meet.[130]

[5–57] However, it is possible in certain circumstances for employers to impose *eligibility requirements*, which may be indirectly discriminatory, so long as these pursue a legitimate objective, are necessary to achieve that objective and are proportionate. So, for example, the ECJ in *Groener*[131] recognised the important objective of affording special protection to the promotion of national languages. Here, a Dutch national applied for a job in an Irish Vocational College. Section 23 of the Vocational Education Act 1930 required that any person appointed to a permanent full-time position in specified areas of teaching had to demonstrate his or her knowledge of, and proficiency in, the Irish language. Ms Groener failed to pass the required examination in Irish and attempts to obtain an exemption for her from this language requirement were also unsuccessful. The ECJ held that it was not contrary to EU law for a Member State to have a policy in place that promotes the national and first official language of the State, as long as such language requirements were proportionate in relation to the implementation of the language policy.

[5–58] The Labour Court applied this decision in the case of *NUI Galway v McBrierty*.[132] Proficiency in the Irish language was one of the stipulated eligibility requirements for those candidates seeking appointment to permanent secretarial and clerical positions at NUI Galway. The complainant, a UK national, received notification that she was deemed ineligible for such a position, as it was a requirement that she possess the Leaving Certificate qualification in Irish. The Labour Court acknowledged that, in principle, the imposition of a language requirement did have a discriminatory effect on non-Irish nationals, but held that the imposition of the language requirement in this situation was reasonable and justifiable given NUI Galway's statutory obligations to promote the Irish language, the proximity of the university to the Gaeltacht areas and its special relationship with those Gaeltacht areas.

[5–59] In *Czerski v Ice Group*[133] the respondent employment agency advertised for applications for positions as production operatives. Applicants were required to provide two references. The complainant successfully argued before the Equality Tribunal that this amounted to discrimination on the grounds of race, as she was only able to produce one employment-related reference from an Irish referee. The Tribunal accepted that an employer is absolutely entitled to place a requirement for the furnishing of two references on job applicants, but was satisfied that the application of such a requirement operated to the disadvantage of a non-Irish national, as the requirement could be complied with by a substantially smaller number of non-Irish national, as compared to Irish national, prospective employees. The Labour Court, on appeal, found against the complainant on the facts, as it found that one of the references could be a *character* (as opposed to an employment-related) reference.[134]

---

130 Employment Equality Acts, s 8(5).

131 Case C-379/87 *Groener v Minister for Education* [1987] ECR 3967.

132 EDA 091/2009.

133 DEC-E2006-027.

134 EDA 0812/2008. See Reynolds, "When Equal Treatment is not Enough—A Review of Recent Decisions in the Management of International Workers" (2008) 5(3) IELJ 94.

However, the Labour Court indicated that, had the rigid rule not been relaxed in this way with regard to individual circumstances, there may well have been a breach of the provisions of the Acts.

In terms of interviews for recruitment or promotion, the employer must take care to make the process as clear, fair and transparent as possible. Two decisions involving claims of discrimination on the grounds of age, in relation to promotional interviews, illustrate this point. The Labour Court in *County Louth VEC v Johnson*[135] praised the employer's interview process as being an example of best practice: there were clear selection criteria set out; clear procedures; independent panel members (who were experienced and trained in anti-discrimination law and policy); a pre-interview panel meeting to establish the ground rules; and marks were awarded based on pre-determined criteria. By contrast, the complainant was successful in *Fagan v Revenue Commissioners*,[136] where the interview panel in question had not recorded minutes of the interviews and had no record of the existence of any pre-set criteria for the position.   [5–60]

In *A Complainant v A Health Board*[137] a British social worker alleged that he was discriminated against by a health board on the ground of race when he was unsuccessful at an interview for a permanent post. The record of the interview recorded a comment that "the candidate needs to orientate himself to the legislative and cultural framework in which he is working" and that the complainant "needs more experience in Irish statutory childcare services". The Tribunal found that the many references to differences in culture seemed designed to mark out the complainant as "different" and found the complainant had been discriminated against on the ground of race.   [5–61]

Conditions of Employment

Section 8(6) of the Employment Equality Acts prohibits discrimination on any of the discriminatory grounds in relation to conditions of employment. "Conditions of employment" relate to terms of employment (except for those terms relating to pay and pension rights)[138]; working conditions; and treatment in respect of overtime, shift work, short time, transfers, lay-offs, redundancies, dismissals and disciplinary measures. In *Zhang v Towner Trading*[139] Ms Zhang, a Chinese national, claimed that she had been discriminated against on the grounds of her race with regard to her conditions of employment and her dismissal. The employer had accused Ms Zhang of stealing 21 bus tickets from behind the shop counter. The employer contacted her about the theft by text message, saying that there was proof of her stealing the bus tickets and threatening to contact the police. Ms Zhang met with the employer and denied the allegations of theft. After this, Ms Zhang alleged that she was treated differently than an Irish national would have been in the same circumstances, because she received a text the day after the meeting to notify her that she had been removed   [5–62]

---

[135] EDA 0712/2007.
[136] DEC-E2008-004.
[137] DEC-E2004-010.
[138] See Kimber and Lynch, "Age Discrimination and Pensions" (2007) 4(2) IELJ 47.
[139] DEC-E2008-001.

from the staff rota and informed that she no longer had a job. Her employer did not instigate any formal disciplinary procedures before her dismissal. The employer denied Ms Zhang's claims of discrimination on the grounds of race as there were other employees working in the shop who were also Chinese nationals. The Equality Tribunal accepted the evidence submitted by the employer showing that the bus tickets were missing and acknowledged that theft would constitute gross misconduct and could justify the dismissal of an employee. However, the Tribunal ruled that the lack of any investigation by the employer in relation to the theft of the bus tickets, in conjunction with the fact that Ms Zhang not being given the opportunity to officially repudiate the allegations made against her, constituted less favourable treatment.

[5–63] In *58 Named Complainants v Goode Concrete Limited*[140] the complainants were found to have been discriminated against on the grounds of race, on the basis that they had not received contracts of employment in a language understandable to them.[141] In *Cers & Eimas v Securazone Manhour Ltd (in liquidation)*[142] the complainant (a security worker) successfully claimed he received less favourable treatment on the grounds of nationality on the basis that his Irish colleagues were offered the "best sites" for security duties. The Tribunal found that, while Irish national workers were allocated sites that were convenient to reach from their homes, non-Irish workers would be rostered for duty on sites which could be an hour or more from their homes. Furthermore, the employer would "allocate day shifts to Irish workers, where possible, whereas the non-Irish workers were allocated night shifts almost exclusively".

In terms of dress codes at work, having different codes for men and women seems not to be discriminatory *per se*. In *3 Male Employees v Powers Supermarkets*[143] a ban on male employees wearing earrings was held to be discriminatory. However, the Equality Tribunal indicated a ban on men wearing lipstick or skirts could be commercially justifiable and not discriminatory.

Training or Experience

[5–64] It is unlawful to discriminate against any person or class of persons in regards to training or experience for, or in relation to, employment. In *A Worker v An Engineering Company*[144] the complainant was a British citizen who was selected for redundancy by the employer. There were a number of different aspects to his claim, one of which being that he had been not been permitted access to a training programme on the grounds of his nationality or race. The Equality Tribunal rejected his claim that he had been subject to discrimination: the reason he was not allowed to undertake the training programme was because he was about to be made redundant.

---

[140] DEC-E2008-020.

[141] This case is under appeal. See also *Stukonis v Coalport Building Company* (DEC-E2009-122) and chapter 8.

[142] DEC-E2009-116.

[143] EE 9/1994. See Flynn, "Gender Equality Laws and Employers' Dress Codes" (1994) 24 ILJ 255; Kerr, *op.cit*, p L-171. For a discussion of an issue that is slowly emerging in the Irish workplace, that of religious dress, see Tahzib-Lie, "Controversies over Religious Symbols in the Workplace: Workforce Diversity Versus 'Androgynous, Mechanical Clones'"? (2007) 25(4) *Netherlands Quarterly of Human Rights* 563.

[144] DEC-E2008-038.

Promotion or Re-grading

It is also unlawful for an employer to discriminate on any of the nine grounds in [5–65] relation to any promotion or re-grading opportunities. Such discrimination will occur where an employer refuses or deliberately omits to offer the employee access to promotional opportunities in the same manner as other eligible and qualified employees.[145] In *A Female Employee v A Printing Company*[146] the complainant successfully claimed that she was discriminated against on the grounds of her gender in relation to a promotional opportunity. The promotion was instead was offered to one of her male colleagues, who did not have the requisite experience or skills. The Equality Tribunal accepted there was evidence that the employer had favoured the successful male candidate before the selection process for promotion began. In *Ms Z v A Transport Company*[147] the complainant was also discriminated against on the grounds of her gender in relation to access to promotional opportunities: the complainant was awarded compensation of €189,000. In addition to this award, the respondent was ordered to provide the complainant with "meaningful work consistent with her skills and experience".

In *Fagan v Revenue Commissioners*[148] the Equality Tribunal found that the complai- [5–66] nant had been denied access to promotional opportunities on the grounds of his age. The complainant was not promoted despite having previously been deemed by his direct supervisor to be a suitable candidate for promotion under the organisation's annual performance management and development review system.

Classification of Posts

A difference in how a particular employee's post is classified may be permissible if the [5–67] employer can demonstrate that the comparator's post involves additional duties that are not undertaken by the complainant; *Kane v Sligo Leitrim Home Youth Liaison Services Ltd*.[149]

IX. The Discriminatory Grounds

Equality legislation has developed significantly over the past four decades. As noted [5–68] above, while initially the primary focus of such legislation was gender-specific, the Employment Equality Acts now provide protection against discrimination on eight additional grounds: marital status; family status; sexual orientation; religious belief or outlook; age; disability; race; and membership of the travelling community. This chapter has examined the general principles of equality law that are common to all of the grounds. The final section considers, in more detail, some of the specific issues pertaining to each. It should also be noted that the Minister for Justice, Equality and

---

[145] Employment Equality Acts, s 8(8).

[146] DEC-E2008-022.

[147] DEC-E2009-105. A challenge, by way of judicial review proceedings, to this decision was dismissed by the High Court; High Court, Hedigan J, 27 July 2010.

[148] DEC-E2008-004.

[149] DEC-E2007-038. See also *Quilter v Kerry Agri Business* (DEC-E2003-043).

Law Reform has been given the power to review the nine listed grounds of discrimination in order to assess if further grounds should be added to this list.[150]

Gender

[5–69] The law on gender discrimination has been looked at extensively throughout this chapter. As noted above, given the longevity of legislation prohibiting gender discrimination in the workplace, claims of direct discrimination on the grounds of gender are no longer common: instead it is more likely for a gender discrimination claim to be linked to other grounds, such as discrimination on the grounds of marital or family status. As noted above, under the Employment Equality Acts, less favourable treatment that arises from the employee's pregnancy or maternity leave constitutes direct discrimination on the gender ground.[151] It is also possible for a person who has undergone, or is undergoing, gender reassignment to claim discrimination on the grounds of gender. In *P v S and Cornwall County Council*[152] the ECJ held that the scope of the Equal Treatment Directive:

> "...cannot be confined simply to discrimination based on the fact that a person is of one or other sex. In view of its purpose and the nature of the rights which it seeks to safeguard, the scope of the directive is also such as to apply to discrimination arising, as in this case, from the gender reassignment of the person concerned".

Race

[5–70] Section 6(2)(h) of the Employment Equality Acts provides that it is unlawful to discriminate against any person because he or she is of different race, colour, nationality or ethnic or national origin. However, such discrimination may be justifiable if a difference in treatment is a genuine occupational requirement.[153]

[5–71] The protection against discrimination on the grounds of race in s 6(2)(h) is broader in scope than the protection against race discrimination set out in Art 2 of the Race Directive, which provides that "there shall be no direct or indirect discrimination based on racial or ethnic origin" but does not extend to provide protection against discrimination on the grounds of the person's nationality.[154] The ECJ has recently ruled on a controversial aspect of the Race Directive in *Feryn*.[155] The Court held that a

---

[150] Employment Equality Acts, s 6(4). Note that, in March 2010, as part of a reorganisation of Governmental Departments, the responsibility for equality, disability, integration and human rights matters moved from the Department of Justice to the new Department of Community, Equality and Gaeltacht Affairs. The new Department will become responsible for a number of existing Agencies, including the Equality Tribunal, the Equality Authority and the National Disability Authority.

[151] Employment Equality Acts, s 6(2A). See chapter 6.

[152] Case C-13/94 *P v S and Cornwall County Council* [1996] ECR 2143 at para 20.

[153] See discussion above.

[154] Council Directive 2000/43/EC implementing the principle of equal treatment between persons irrespective of racial or ethnic origin [2000] OJ L180/22. See Guild, "The EC Directive on Race Discrimination: Surprises, Possibilities and Limitations" (2000) 29(4) ILJ 416.

[155] Case C-54/07 *Centrum voor Gelijkheid van Kansen en voor Racismebestrijding v Firma Feryn NV* [2008] ECR I-05187.

public statement made by an employer regarding his policy of not recruiting Moroccans because they would "damage his business" amounted to direct discrimination contrary to the Race Directive, even though there was no identifiable complainant (the complaint was taken by the Belgian centre for equal opportunities and combating racism). The ECJ held that the objective of fostering conditions for a socially inclusive labour market would be hard to achieve if the scope of the Directive were to be limited to only those cases in which an unsuccessful candidate for a post, considering himself or herself to be the victim of direct discrimination, brought legal proceedings against the employer.

As regards the burden of proof, the ECJ held that public statements, by which an employer lets it be known that under its recruitment policy it will not recruit any employees of a certain ethnic or racial origin, were sufficient for a presumption of the existence of a recruitment policy, which is directly discriminatory. It is for the employer to prove that there was, in fact, no breach of the principle of equal treatment: for example, by showing that the undertaking's actual recruitment practice does not correspond to those statements. Lastly, the ECJ considered what sanctions may be considered to be appropriate for employment discrimination established on the basis of an employer's public statements. In a case where there is no direct victim of discrimination, the Court indicated that sanctions, which must be effective, proportionate and dissuasive, might include an anti-discrimination publicity campaign (the cost of which should be borne by the defendant); a prohibitory injunction ordering the employer to cease the discriminatory practice; and, where appropriate, a fine.[156]   **[5–72]**

Claims of race discrimination now account for almost a half of all discrimination claims brought before the Equality Tribunal.[157] Bolger and Kimber argue that this is probably attributable to the broad scope of s 6(2)(h) under which any person of any nationality can bring claims of discrimination (including, by virtue of s 14A, claims for harassment) on the grounds of race.[158] So for example, in *Glennon v Bormac*[159] Ms Glennon, an Irish national, claimed that her dismissal was discriminatory on the grounds of her race. She was informed that the reason for her dismissal was that there was no work available for her, but a week after her dismissal she found out that her position had been filled by a non-Irish national. The Equality Tribunal found that she had been dismissed because of her nationality.   **[5–73]**

Discrimination on the grounds of race can occur not only where different rules are applied to comparable situations, but also where the same rule is applied to different situations.[160] The Labour Court considered this issue in *Campbell Catering Ltd v Rasaq.*[161] The claimant, a Nigerian national, worked as a catering assistant for the respondent in a hostel for refugees and asylum seekers. During her induction course   **[5–74]**

---

[156] s 10 of the Employment Equality Acts expressly prohibits the advertising of a job in such a way that the advertisement could reasonably be interpreted as indicating an intention to discriminate. Claims are to be brought by the Equality Authority (s 85); see below.

[157] Equality Tribunal Annual Report 2009; available at www.equalitytribunal.ie.

[158] Bolger and Kimber, *op.cit*, p 427.

[159] DEC-E2009-99.

[160] Case C-279/93 *Finanzamt Koln-Alstadt v Schumacker* [1995] ECR 1225.

[161] [2004] ELR 310.

the manager informed her that employees were permitted to take as much food as they wanted for consumption on the premises, but that the removal of any food from the premises would constitute a serious disciplinary matter. The claimant took three bananas from the kitchen at the end of her shift with the intention of consuming the bananas in the locker room before she left the premises. Other staff had frequently taken food to eat in either the locker room or TV room. The manager requested that the complainant return the bananas, which she did before she left the premises. The following day, the claimant was summarily dismissed for theft of the bananas. The claimant was not given the opportunity to respond to the allegations of serious misconduct prior to her dismissal. On this basis, the Labour Court found that the claimant had been treated less favourably than other employees facing such allegations were, or would have been, treated. Referring to the ECJ decision in *Schumacker,* the Labour Court emphasised that discrimination could occur in circumstances arising from the application of the same rule to different situations, especially in situations concerning non-national workers who, because of differences in language and culture, may not be aware of their statutory and contractual employment rights. The claimant had not been provided with a written contract of employment, an employee handbook, or details of the company's disciplinary and grievance procedure. As such, the Labour Court found that:

> "[i]n the case of disciplinary proceedings, employers have a positive duty to ensure that all workers fully understand what is alleged against them, the gravity of the alleged misconduct and their right to mount a full defence, including the right to representation. Special measures may be necessary in the case of non-national workers to ensure that this obligation is fulfilled and that the accused worker fully appreciates the gravity of the situation and is given appropriate facilitates and guidance in making a defence. In such cases, applying the same procedural standards to a non-national workers as would be applied to an Irish national could amount to the application of the same rules to different situations and could in itself amount to discrimination".

[5–75] As seen above, under s 85A(1) of the Employment Equality Acts, the complainant in a race discrimination case will have to establish the facts, which infer that he or she has been subject to discrimination, before the onus of proof shifts to the respondent.[162] The key test to be applied in this area was laid down by the House of Lords in *Glasgow City Council v Zafar*[163] and subsequently adopted in this jurisdiction by Quirk J in *Davis v Dublin Institute of Technology.*[164] In *Zafar* Lord Browne-Wilkinson pointed out that where there is a difference in treatment and a difference in race there is *prima facie* evidence of discrimination and it is for the respondent to provide a non-discriminatory

---

[162] According to the Labour Court in *Melbury Developments v Valpeters* (EDA 0917/2009), however, s 85A places the burden of establishing the primary facts fairly and squarely on the complainant: "they must be established as facts on credible evidence. Mere speculation, or assertions, unsupported by evidence, cannot be elevated to a factual basis upon which an inference of discrimination can be drawn".

[163] [1998] 2 All ER 953.

[164] Unreported, High Court, 23 June 2000.

explanation. This approach was adopted by the Labour Court in *Ntoko v Citibank*[165] wherein the Court explained its underlying rationale as follows:

> "This approach is based on the empiricism that a person who discriminates unlawfully will rarely do so overtly and will not leave evidence of the discrimination within the complainant's power of procurement. Hence, the normal rules of evidence must be adapted in such cases so as to avoid the protection of anti-discrimination laws being rendered nugatory by obliging complainants to prove something which is beyond their reach and which may only be in the respondent's capacity of proof".[166]

In *Nyamhovsa v Boss Worldwide Promotions*[167] the Tribunal found that the claimant **[5–76]** had established a *prima facie* case of discrimination on grounds of race. In particular, the Tribunal concluded that verbally admonishing a black female employee in front of a trainee for the "trifling matter" of leaving an identification badge behind constituted harassment on the ground of race, as it had the effect of "violating her dignity and creating a humiliating environment". The Tribunal was satisfied that:

> "...the respondent would not have made such an undermining remark to a white, Irish man in front of a trainee...While the respondent might have commented on such a man's forgetfulness, he would have been conscious of not undermining that man's authority in front of a subordinate".

Age

Section 6(2)(f) of the Employment Equality Acts prohibits discriminatory treatment **[5–77]** on the ground of age. However, differential treatment on the ground of age differs in nature to, say, such treatment being based on (inherent) racial characteristics. Being relatively old or relatively young *can* in some cases affect an individual's ability to do a particular job.[168] Therefore, in relation to age discrimination the underlying approach adopted is not to *ignore* a person's age for employment purposes (as one should generally do in relation to a person's race or gender) but to ensure that stereotypes and blind assumptions regarding age should be avoided.[169] As a result of this approach, there are a number of specific exemptions to the general rule of non-discrimination, which are laid out in s 6(3) of the Employment Equality Acts.[170] The age ground is only applicable to any person who is above the statutory age at which he or she must attend school.[171] For some jobs, an employer may stipulate that applicants for the post must be of a minimum age, not exceeding 18 years.[172] It is also possible for an

---

[165] [2004] ELR 116.

[166] For a general analysis of how courts and tribunals approach the burden of proof in race claims in the UK, see Brown and Erskine, "A Qualitative Study of Judgments in Race Discrimination Employment" (2009) 31(1) *Law and Policy* 142.

[167] DEC-E2007-072.

[168] See Weller, "Discrimination, Labour Markets and the Labour Market Prospects of Older Workers: What can a Legal Case Teach Us?" (2007) 21(3) *Work, Employment and Society* 417.

[169] Bolger and Kimber, *op.cit*, p 489; Swift, "Justifying Age Discrimination" (2006) 35 (3) ILJ 228.

[170] See also the outline of the exemptions contained in s 34, discussed above.

[171] Employment Equality Acts, s 6(3)(a).

[172] Employment Equality Acts, s 6(3)(b).

employer to offer a fixed-term contract to any person or class of persons over the compulsory retirement age for that employment without this constituting discrimination on the ground of age.[173] The issue of whether there is an upper age limit at which employees can be forced to retire is one that has created much recent controversy. Section 34(4) of the Employment Equality Acts states that it shall not constitute discrimination on the age ground to fix different ages for the retirement (whether voluntarily or compulsorily) of employees or any class or description of employees. In *Calor Teoranta v Mc Carthy*[174] the Labour Court noted that there were serious questions concerning the proper interpretation of s 34(4) of the Act having regard to the jurisprudence of the ECJ. Employers should now, at the very least, stipulate what the normal retirement age is within their organisation in the employee handbook or contract of employment to avert claims of unfair dismissal for attempting to retire an employee.[175]

[5–78]   In *Hawkins v Irish Life and Permanent*[176] the Tribunal made it clear that it was not enough just to demonstrate a difference upon which one can ground a complaint under the legislation, such as the fact that there is a difference in age between the successful candidate and the complainant. To make out a claim for discrimination in relation to the age ground, the complainant must demonstrate that there was a difference in treatment between persons *that resulted from* a difference in their ages. In *Portroe Stevedores v Nevins*[177] the Labour Court stated in relation to age discrimination:

> "Evidence of discrimination on the age ground will generally be found in the surrounding circumstances and facts of the particular case. Evidence of it can be found where job applications from candidates of a particular age are treated less seriously than those from candidates of a different age. It can also be manifest from a conclusion that candidates in a particular age group are unsuitable or might not fit in, where an adequate appraisal or a fair assessment of their attributes has not been undertaken. Discrimination can also be inferred from questions asked at interview which suggest that age is a relevant consideration".

[5–79]   The Labour Court went on to find that a question put to one of the complainants at interview concerning his age (and the data presented concerning the age profile of those recruited by the respondent since the complainants' interviews) established an evidential nexus between the unfair treatment of the complainants and their age. These were facts of sufficient significance to establish a *prima facie* case of discrimination and so shift the probative burden to the respondent.

[5–80]   Clearly, there must be a difference in age between the complainant and his or her comparator(s). The question is, however, how much of a difference must there be? In *Limerick City Council v Reynolds*[178] the complainant alleged that he had been

---

[173]   Employment Equality Acts, s 6(3)(c).
[174]   ED 089/2008, upheld on appeal to the High Court on a point of law; [2009] IEHC 139.
[175]   See chapter 10 for a full discussion of the ECJ case law on mandatory retirement ages.
[176]   DEC-E2004-009.
[177]   EDA 051/2005.
[178]   EDA 248/2004.

discriminated against on the grounds of his age in respect of a promotion competition in the respondent organisation. According to the complainant (aged 45 at the time of the competition) he was better qualified and had more experience for the vacant position than the person who was successful in the competition (aged 38 at the time of the competition) and the person who was placed second on the list (aged 37 at the time of the competition). The Labour Court noted that in the case of *Superquinn v Freeman*[179] it was held that a gap in age of three years was too small to sustain a claim of age discrimination. Here, the gap was more significant (especially when the gap between the youngest and the oldest candidate was a total of 12 years) and the Court found that an age difference of eight years between the complainant and the candidate placed second on the panel was sufficiently significant to sustain a claim of age discrimination. In *Department of Health & Children v Gillen*[180] the complainant was able to prove he had been discriminated against in two competitions for promotion because he was over 50. He produced figures to prove that no candidate over 50 was successful in such competitions between 1999 and 2003. It was also shown that the age profile of the successful candidates in the competitions *did not* reflect the age profile of the applicants.

As noted above in relation to the gender ground, many cases relate to access to employment and/or promotion, where a complainant challenges an interview or selection process. In these cases, the courts and tribunals have stressed that, where a competitive interview process takes place, the issue for consideration is whether or not the age of the complainant affected the decision: it is *not* for the court or tribunal to decide on who was the more *meritorious candidate*. So, in *O'Neill v St Gabriel's National School*[181] the complainant, in an interview for a vacant Deputy Principal position at the school, was asked by the Chairman of the interview board "considering that you have been teaching for 27 years, why would you now be bothered with the hassle of the job of Deputy Principal?" The complainant argued this comment was a clear reference to her age and that the panel felt she had left it too late in life to seek such a post. The successful candidate was under 30 years of age. The Chairman of the interview board stated that the purpose of the question was to put the candidate at ease. He realised from the complainant's reaction that he had made a mistake but reiterated that as far as he was concerned there was no ageist connotation in the question. The Tribunal found that, whatever the Chairman's intention, coming as it did at an early stage in the interview, the question could have impacted on the complainant's performance. Such a question was deemed to be discriminatory. **[5–81]**

Employers should be careful not to discriminate against any person on the grounds of age when advertising positions. In *Equality Authority v Ryanair*[182] the Equality Authority initiated a case against the airline Ryanair because of an advertisement that specified that the company was seeking to hire a "young and dynamic professional". The Equality Tribunal ruled that the use of the word "young": **[5–82]**

---

[179] DEE 0211/2002.
[180] EDA 0412/2004.
[181] DEC-E2005-007.
[182] [2001] ELR 107.

"...might reasonably be understood as indicating, an intention to exclude applicants who were 'not young', i.e. applicants who were 'middle aged' or 'old'. Furthermore I find that the use of the word 'young' to describe the type of person required for the position indicated, or might reasonably have been understood as indicating, an intention to discriminate against a person who was 'not young'. It is my view that the use of the word 'young' as a requirement in this employment advertisement constitutes clear discrimination".

Note that individuals cannot refer a claim of discrimination in relation to advertisements. Section 85(1)(d) of the Employment Equality Acts specifies that the Equality Authority has the power to refer to the Tribunal any claims relating to discrimination arising from advertisements or displays.[183]

[5–83] An interesting recent decision in relation to indirect discrimination on the grounds of age can be seen in *Mary Immaculate College v Sister Loye.*[184] Here, the complainant, a member of a Religious Order, was employed on successive fixed-term contracts as an Assistant Lecturer with the respondent. She applied for a permanent position in 2001, but of the seven academics who applied for consideration, was the only person not to be promoted. The process was not competitive as between the candidates: the candidates "competed" only against criteria tailored to their own areas and departments. The complainant was the oldest candidate (11 years older than the second oldest candidate) and she was 27 years older than average age of the other applicants. The Labour Court found for the complainant. The Court decided that her employers regarded Sister Loye as "of her time" and felt that she would not "fit in" with the modern image the College wanted to project. Although the Court found that the employer did not specifically take her age into account, the latter considered that her *approach* and *ethos* were "of a different era". Since the complainant's approach to teaching and her ethos were inextricably linked to her age and the era in which she grew up, the respondents did discriminate against the complainant on the grounds of her age.

Disability

[5–84] The inclusion of discrimination on the grounds of disability in equality legislation has proven to be contentious.[185] The Employment Equality Bill 1996, in fact, was referred to the Supreme Court under Art 26 of *Bunreacht na hÉireann* in order to test its constitutionality.[186] The Supreme Court ruled that the requirement for an employer to do all that was reasonably necessary to accommodate the needs of a disabled worker and to accept the full costs of doing so, unless it gave rise to "undue hardship", was

---

[183] *Burke v FÁS* (DEC-E2004-016). In the Equality Authority's 2007 Annual Report, mention is made of four cases where advertisements were run seeking "young" applicants. In all cases, the Authority wrote to the organisations in question and in all four the organisation apologised for the breach and re-advertised the posts (no-one had been appointed on the basis of the original advertisements): available at www.equality.ie.

[184] EDA 082/2008.

[185] See McCrann and Kelleher, "Disability Discrimination under the Employment Equality Act 1998 and the Equality Bill 2004" (2004) 1(2) IELJ 42; Gallagher, "When the Employee becomes a Legal Dilemma" [2008] ELRI 2.

[186] *In the matter of Article 26 of the Constitution and in the matter of the Employment Equality Bill 1996* [1997] 2 IR 321.

unconstitutional. The Supreme Court ruled that the Bill, by requiring the employer to bear the full cost of all special treatment or facilities which the disabled person might require to carry out the work, unless the cost of the provision of such treatment or facilities would give rise to undue hardship, imposed a disproportionate burden on employers. Subsequently, however, the wording adopted in the 1998 Act, that an employer could refuse to provide facilities to reasonably accommodate a person with a disability on the grounds that it gave rise to more than a "nominal cost", was perceived as being too weak to provide sufficient protection to disabled persons against employment-related discrimination.[187] As a result, the Employment Equality Acts now provide that an employer must take appropriate measures to reasonably accommodate the needs of disabled workers, unless this would impose a "disproportionate burden" having regard to the circumstances of the employer.[188]

The concept of "reasonable accommodation" recognises the fact, as noted above in relation to the age ground, that a disability *can* affect a person's ability to do a particular job.[189] While employers are required by law to be "colour-blind", for example, by not discriminating on the grounds of racial prejudice, employing a person with a disability might require positive action by the employer to enable that person to do a job, which, without the employer's accommodation, he or she may not otherwise be able to do. What is required of employers will be looked at in more detail below. **[5–85]**

Section 6(2)(g) of the Employment Equality Acts stipulates that it is unlawful to discriminate against a person on the grounds of disability. Section 2 of the Employment Equality Acts defines disability as: **[5–86]**

> "(a) the total or partial absence of a person's bodily or mental functions, including the absence of a part of a person's body;
> (b) the presence in the body of organisms causing, or likely to cause, chronic disease or illness;
> (c) the malfunction, malformation or disfigurement of a part of a person's body;
> (d) a condition or malfunction which results in a person learning differently from a person without the condition or malfunction; or
> (e) a condition or malfunction which results in a person's thought processes, perception of reality, emotions or judgement or which results in disturbed behaviour, and shall be taken to include a disability which exists at present, or which previously existed but no longer exists, or which may exist in the future or which is imputed to a person".

There is no definition of "disability" in Directive 2000/78, but it seems the definition laid down in the Employment Equality Acts is wider than that contained in the Directive. This is as a result of the ECJ decision in *Navas*.[190] In this case, the Court's view was that a disability in the context of the Directive had to be understood **[5–87]**

---

[187] Cox *et al, op.cit*, p 338.
[188] Employment Equality Acts, s 16(3).
[189] Deakin and Morris, *op.cit,* p 666; *Bolger* and Kimber, *op.cit,* p 508.
[190] Case C-13/05 *Navas v Eurest Colectividades SA* [2006] ECR I-6467.

"as a limitation which results in particular from physical, mental or psychological impairments and which hinders the participation of the person concerned in professional life".[191] The ECJ also noted that, when setting out the protection contained within the Framework Directive, the legislature had deliberately chosen to use a term that differed from "sickness". This implied that sickness and disability were not synonymous and that they should not be treated as the same thing.[192]

[5–88]   The Irish courts and tribunals have diverged strongly from this view and have taken a very broad view of what constitutes a disability.[193] For example, the Labour Court has deemed alcoholism to constitute a disability.[194] The Court has also found that persons suffering from eating disorders come with the scope of the provision.[195] In *Government Department v A Worker*[196] the Labour Court considered, in great detail, a considerable amount of evidence presented by the medical experts for the parties and concluded that the complainant in the case did suffer from a depressive illness and that such an illness was a disability for the purposes of the Acts.

[5–89]   *Imputing* a disability to a person can also fall foul of the legislation. In *Ms X v An Electronic Component Company*[197] the claimant successfully applied for the position of temporary process operator with the respondent. She completed a medical examination and a pre-employment medical questionnaire in which she disclosed her medical history. She stated that she did not suffer back pain or sciatica on the questionnaire because, in her view, she did not have a back problem. Once she began the job, the claimant was called upon not to slouch on a few occasions. The claimant explained she had difficulty sitting straight because she was heavy-chested but that it was a cosmetic issue. The following day she received a telephone call from the occupational health nurse informing her that she should have disclosed her back problem in the pre-employment questionnaire. The claimant was dismissed on the basis of non-disclosure of medical information. The Equality Tribunal found that the company had imputed a disability to the claimant and that this was a significant factor in the decision to dismiss her. The Tribunal found that operation of pre-employment medical examinations or questionnaires are not *per se* unlawful but that employers must exercise caution when using information obtained from such procedures so as not to fall foul of employment equality legislation.

[5–90]   More recently, there has been discussion as to whether obesity constitutes a disability under Irish equality law.[198] The Equality Tribunal had to address this issue in *A Health*

---

[191] At para 43.

[192] See Hosking, "A High Bar for EU Disability Rights" (2007) 36(2) ILJ 228.

[193] Note, too, the UK's Disability Discrimination Act 2005 (s 18) brings within the definition of "disabled" any person suffering with "cancer, HIV infection or multiple sclerosis". See, also, Pereira, "HIV/AIDS and Discrimination in the Workplace: the Cook and the Surgeon Living with HIV" (2010) 17(2) *European Journal of Health Law* 139.

[194] *Government Department v An Employee* (EDA 062/2006); this was so even though the claimant in the case had not drunk alcohol for 10 years.

[195] *Humphries v Westwood Fitness Club* [2004] 15 ELR 296.

[196] EDA 094/2009.

[197] DEC-E2006-042.

[198] Morgan, "Disability Discrimination—How Far Does It Extend?" (2009) 6(3) IELJ 70.

Service Employee v The Health Service Executive.[199] The claimant was a nurse, who failed a medical examination for a vacant position as a staff nurse on the grounds of obesity. The claimant had been given medical clearance six months earlier for her then job as a care attendant, which required her to undertake duties similar to those of a staff nurse and she had also lost weight during that period. A second medical opinion was sought and the claimant was declared fit for the position as staff nurse. Consequently the claimant took action against her employer on the grounds that she had been attributed with a disability. The Equality Tribunal declined to deal with the issue of whether obesity constituted a disability within the meaning the Employment Equality Acts. However, the Tribunal held that the employer did discriminate against the employee by *imputing* that she had a disability because of her weight. Morgan notes that, although the case is not definitive as to whether obesity in and of itself constitutes a disability, it does indicate a willingness on the part of the Tribunal to accept that "obesity can be an imputed disability under the legislation depending on the treatment by an employer of its overweight employees".[200]

Clearly, it is not necessary in order to make out a claim of disability-related discrimination to show that the employer had an *intention* to discriminate. In *A Technology Company v A Worker*[201] the Labour Court pointed out that: **[5–91]**

> "A person with a disability may suffer discrimination not because they are disabled *per se*, but because they are perceived, because of their disability, to be less capable or less dependable than a person without a disability. The Court must always be alert to the possibility of unconscious or inadvertent discrimination and mere denials of a discriminatory motive, in the absence of independent corroboration, must be approached with caution".[202]

Note, too, that the scope of disability has been extended by the ECJ in *Coleman v Attridge Law*[203] to include workers with disabled dependents: this case is discussed in detail above.[204]

Reasonable Accommodation
As noted, under the current legislative framework, an employer may only refuse to provide "reasonable accommodation" to a disabled worker where to do so would impose a "disproportionate burden" on the employer.[205] It is the interpretation of these terms that will be crucial in determining what facilities will be provided to persons with disabilities by employers to enable such persons to take up, or remain in, **[5–92]**

---

[199] DEC-E2009-013.

[200] Morgan, *op.cit*, p 71.

[201] EDA 0714/2007.

[202] See also the decision of the European Court of Human Rights in *DH and Others v the Czech Republic* [2007] ECHRR 57325.

[203] Case C-303/06 *Coleman v Attridge Law* [2008] IRLR 722.

[204] See also Roberts, "Caring for the Disabled? New Boundaries in Disability Discrimination" (2009) 72(4) MLR 635.

[205] Employment Equality Acts, s 16(3).

Principles of Irish Employment Law

employment.[206] The Acts provide that, in assessing what "burden" is to be imposed on employers, the financial and other costs to the employer of putting in place appropriate measures; the scale and financial resources of the employer's business; and the availability of public funding or other sources of financial assistance will be taken into consideration.[207] The measures taken should enable a person with a disability to have access to employment; to participate or advance in employment; or to avail of any training opportunities.[208] "Appropriate measures":

"(a) means effective and practical measures, where needed in a particular case, to adapt the employer's place of business to the disability concerned,
(b) without prejudice to the generality of paragraph (a), includes the adaptation of premises and equipment, patterns of working time, distribution of tasks or the provision of training or integration resources, but
(c) does not include any treatment, facility or thing that the person might ordinarily or reasonably provide for himself or herself".[209]

[5–93] The test to determine what constitutes reasonable accommodation was set out in *Humphries v Westwood Fitness Club*.[210] Here, the Labour Court, while accepting that s 16 of the Employment Equality Acts could afford a complete defence to an employer who formed a *bona fide* belief that the employee was not fully capable of performing the required duties, stressed that such an employer would need to make adequate enquiries to establish fully the factual position in relation to the employee's capacity. An employer must conduct a two-stage enquiry. The first stage of this process is to determine the "factual position concerning the employee's capability including the degree of impairment arising from the disability and its likely duration", which should be based on medical evidence made available to the employer. Secondly, if it is established that the employee is not fully capable of undertaking the duties associated with the position, the employer has a statutory obligation to consider "what if any special treatment or facilities may be available" to assist the employee to become fully capable of undertaking such duties, taking into consideration the cost of providing special treatment or facilities.

[5–94] In the case of *A Worker v A Health and Fitness Club*[211] the claimant was dismissed as she suffered from anorexia and, consequently, her employer stated that she was unsuitable for working in a childcare facility. The Labour Court found that the employer did not obtain any medical or psychiatric advice in relation to the complainant's disorder and nor did it undertake any form of risk assessment in relation to her condition. In *Boyle v*

---

[206] See Smith, "A Pandisability Analysis? The Possibilities and Pitfalls of Indirect Disability Discrimination" (2009) 60(3) NILQ 361. Here, the author argues that the relatively scant jurisprudence on indirect disability discrimination in the US, the UK and Ireland is due to the association between indirect discrimination and the reasonable accommodation duties contained within those jurisdictions' disability discrimination legislation.
[207] Employment Equality Acts, s 16(3)(c).
[208] Employment Equality Acts, s 16(3)(b).
[209] Employment Equality Acts, s 16(4).
[210] [2004] 15 ELR 296 at 300-301.
[211] EDA 059/2003.

142

Department of Social and Family Affairs[212] the complainant was employed in the Civil Service and suffered from a serious eye condition, which meant she was unable to undertake certain work involving computers. Originally, this was not a problem as much of the work was carried out manually, but many aspects of the job were subsequently computerised and the complainant was unable to carry out these tasks. She applied for a promotion and, despite being the most senior candidate, was not offered the position on the grounds of "poor performance". The complainant contended that the reason she was not recommended for promotion was directly related to her eye condition. The Equality Tribunal referred to the Labour Court determination in the case of *An Employer and A Worker* where the Court held[213]:

> "Prima facie [s 16(1)(b)] allows an employer to treat a person with a disability less favourably than others. An applicant for promotion or for training may be rejected... if an existing employee, by reason of disability, is no longer fully able to do the job for which he or she was employed, they can lawfully be dismissed for lack of capacity. Moreover, in certain circumstances, the contract of employment may come to an end by operation of law due to frustration..."

However, the Court went on to hold that:

> "The provision of special treatment or facilities is not an end in itself. It is a means to an end and that end is achieved when the person with a disability is placed in a position where they can have access to, or as the case may be, participate in, or advance in employment or to undergo training. This can involve affording the person with a disability more favourable treatment than would be accorded to an employee without a disability.... The scope of the duty is determined by what is reasonable, which includes consideration of the costs involved. This is an objective test which must have regard to all the circumstances of the particular case".

Ms Boyle was successful on the basis that she had no prior notice of local management concern about her performance such that it would not recommend her for promotion. The Tribunal complimented the employer for taking certain steps, such as relieving the complainant of the obligation to perform computer tasks, but held that the employer should have addressed the implications of this, where it had the potential to adversely affect her promotion prospects. Furthermore, while the employer had organised an assessment of the complainant's condition by the National Council for the Blind, this should have occurred much earlier. **[5–95]**

Note that under s 35(2) of the Acts, it is not unlawful for the employer to provide special treatment or facilities for persons with disabilities in relation to, for example, training or the working environment.

Marital Status and Family Status
Section 6(2)(b) of the Employment Equality Acts provides that where two persons, who are of different marital status, are treated differently, this will constitute unlawful **[5–96]**

---

[212] DEC-E2005-032.
[213] [2005] ELR 159 at 168-169.

discrimination. Section 6(2)(c) prohibits discrimination between any two persons who have a different family status, where one person has family status and the other does not. It is unusual for claims to be taken *solely* under either of these grounds: instead, claimants often plead discrimination on *both* grounds, or plead discrimination on one or both grounds *in addition to* the gender ground. For example, the Labour Court in *Inoue v NBK Designs Ltd*[214] found that Ms Inoue had been subject to indirect discrimination because of her marital status *and* her family status. Ms Inoue was a lone parent with a child of school-going age. She was employed by NBK Designs Ltd as a part-time secretary/personal assistant, which was a job-sharing position with another employee. The employer decided to merge the two part-time positions into one full-time post, which was offered to Ms Inoue. Ms Inoue was not in a position to take up this offer due to her childminding responsibilities. She was given four weeks' notice of her dismissal when she turned down the offer of the full-time job. The respondent claimed that the reason for merging the two part-time positions into one full-time position was to improve efficiency in the workplace. The Labour Court found that the requirement for the secretary/personal assistant to work full-time was not necessary, appropriate or objectively justifiable in the circumstances.

[5–97] In *Long v Hanley Group*[215] the claim was brought on the grounds of discrimination, harassment, discriminatory dismissal and victimisation on the grounds of the complainant's family status. The complainant commenced her employment as a sales and marketing manager in 2006. During the recruitment process, she informed the employer that she was unavailable to work outside normal office hours and that she would also be unavailable for travel because of her parental responsibilities. The hotel manager conducting the interview assured her that this would not cause any problems. The appointment of a new manager led to a change in her duties and responsibilities at work, however, whereby Ms Long was required to travel for the purpose of generating corporate business for the hotel. After raising the fact that she thought her legal rights had been infringed with her manager and unsuccessfully requesting a copy of the company's grievance procedures, she was informed that she was to be let go. Another person was appointed to the sales manager role shortly after Ms Long's dismissal, with less specific travel requirements than those indicated to Ms Long as being essential as part of the job. Ms Long's successor also had a different family status as she had no children at the time of her appointment. The Equality Tribunal found that the complainant had been discriminated against on the grounds of family status.

Sexual Orientation

[5–98] Under s 6(2)(d) of the Employment Equality Acts, it is unlawful to discriminate between any two persons on the grounds that they are of a different sexual orientation.[216]

---

[214] [2003] ELR 98.

[215] DEC-E2010-015.

[216] See also Case C-267/06 *Maruko v Versorgungsanstalt der Deutschen Buhnen* [2008] ECR I-1757, where the ECJ held that the combined provisions of Arts 1 and 2 of Framework Directive 2000/78 preclude legislation under which, after the death of his gay life partner, the surviving partner does not receive a survivor's benefit equivalent to that granted to a surviving spouse, even though, under national law, life partnership places persons of the same sex in a situation comparable to that of spouses so far as concerns that survivor's benefit.

Section 2 of the Employment Equality Acts defines sexual orientation as meaning "heterosexual, homosexual or bisexual orientation". The Employment Equality Act 1998 introduced protection against unlawful discrimination on the grounds of a person's sexual orientation into Irish law.[217]

The definition does not extend so far as to include persons who have undergone gender reassignment or who are transsexuals.[218] However, as noted above, the ECJ in *P v S and Cornwall County Council* has established that persons who are transsexuals, or are in the process of undergoing gender reassignment, could bring a claim of unlawful discrimination based on the ground of gender.[219]   [5–99]

Religious Belief

Unlawful discrimination will occur if a person is treated differently because of his or her religious belief, or lack of religious belief.[220] Religious belief includes a person's religious background or outlook.[221] As noted above, s 37(1) of the Employment Equality Acts permits discrimination where it is necessary to maintain the religious ethos of a religious, educational or medical institution that is under the control and direction of a body set up for religious purposes, or which has the purpose of providing services in an environment promoting certain religious values.   [5–100]

Membership of the Traveller Community

Section 6(2)(i) provides that it is unlawful to discriminate between any two persons on the grounds that one is a member of the traveller community and the other is not. "Traveller community" means the community of people who are commonly called "Travellers" and who are identified (both by themselves and others) as people with a shared history, culture and traditions including, historically, a nomadic way of life on the island of Ireland.[222]   [5–101]

---

[217] Cox *et al, op.cit*, p 324.

[218] *ibid.*

[219] Case C-13/94 *P v S and Cornwall County Council* [1996] ECR 2143.

[220] Employment Equality Acts, s 6(2)(e). See Pitt, "Religious Freedom, Religious Discrimination and the Workplace" (2009) 38(2) ILJ 242.

[221] Employment Equality Acts, s 2.

[222] Employment Equality Acts, s 2. This definition was inserted by virtue of s 39 of the Equal Status Act 2000.

CHAPTER 6
Family Friendly Working and the Law

I. Introduction

[6–01] There is much comment in contemporary debates on employment regulation of the importance of "work-life" balance.[1] It has been long recognised that, to ensure full implementation of the equality principle in the employment field, it is necessary to put in place measures to enable workers (male and female) to reconcile occupational and family obligations.[2] As a result, in addition to protecting rights to non-discriminatory treatment in the workplace based on the grounds looked at in the preceding chapter, a number of statutory rights and entitlements are conferred on employees in accordance with their family or care obligations. While initially these focused on protecting the rights of the "traditional family" and particularly those of mothers,[3] in more recent times legislative rights have been extended not only to parents, but also to those employees who might require time off work to care for a sick or elderly spouse or relative.[4] The impetus for what are termed "family friendly" policies and legislation has its origins in European Union law.[5] The EU has a commitment to the promotion of work-life balance and the need to safeguard family life.[6] This is enshrined in Art 33(2) of the EU Charter of Fundamental Rights:

> "To reconcile family and professional life, everyone shall have the right to protection from dismissal for a reason connected with maternity and the right to paid maternity leave and to parental leave following the birth or adoption of a child".[7]

[6–02] This chapter discuss the range of rights and entitlements accruing to employees by virtue of their family status. Specific legislation that applies to adoptive parents and carers will be examined first. The rights of natural parents (in terms of time off work to care for, and bond with, their children) will then be looked at in detail. Lastly, legislation relating to maternity rights will be considered. This will lead to a focus on the particular difficulties confronting a pregnant employee in the workplace. The special protection and rights afforded to the pregnant employee under EU and Irish law are outlined within the final sections.

---

[1] See, for example, Felstead *et al*, *Changing Places of Work* (Palgrave, Basingstoke, 2005); Hakim, *Work-Lifestyle Choices in the 21st Century: Preference Theory* (Oxford University Press, Oxford, 2000); Crompton (ed), *Restructuring Gender Relations and Employment* (Oxford University Press, Oxford, 1999); Caracciola di Torella and Reid, "The Changing Shape of the 'European Family' and Fundamental Rights" (2002) 27 ELRev 80.

[2] Kerr, *Employment Rights Legislation* (2nd ed, Round Hall, Dublin, 2006), p C-52; Lewis, "Balancing 'Time to Work' and 'Time to Care': Policy Issues and the Implications for Mothers, Fathers and Children" (2009) 21(4) *Child and Family Law Quarterly* 443.

[3] See, for example, the Maternity Protection of Employees Act 1981.

[4] For an overview of leave entitlements in Irish law generally, see Inverarity, "Leave Matters" (2005) 2(2) IELJ 44. See also Barry, "The Task Force on Small Business and the Working Group on Child Care Facilities for Working Parents" (1994) 12 ILT 125.

[5] See Fay, "An Overview of the European Union's Influence on Employees' Rights and Industrial Relations within Ireland" (2004) 22 ILT 282.

[6] Barnard, *EC Employment Law* (3rd ed, Oxford University Press, Oxford, 2006), p 445.

[7] The Charter now has binding legal status following the entry into force of the Treaty of Lisbon on 1 December 2009.

II. Adoptive Leave

Adoptive leave is governed by the Adoptive Leave Acts 1995 and 2005. The Adoptive Leave Act 1995 introduced entitlement to leave from employment for the purposes of adoption, essentially seeking to grant the same rights to adoptive parents as those that accrue to natural parents.

[6–03]

Entitlement to Adoptive Leave

Section 6(1) of the Adoptive Leave Acts 1995 and 2005 (hereinafter referred to in this section as "the Acts") provides that:

[6–04]

> "...an employed adopting mother (or sole male adopter) shall be entitled to leave (to be known as 'adoptive leave') from the employee's employment".

An employed adopting mother, or sole male adopter, is entitled under the Acts to a minimum of 24 weeks adoptive leave[8] and an additional adoptive leave period up to a maximum of 16 additional weeks.[9] An "adopting mother" is defined under the Acts as:

> "...a woman, including an employed adopting mother, in whose care a child (of whom she is not the natural mother) has been placed or is to be placed with a view to the making of an adoption order, or to the effecting of a foreign adoption or following any such adoption".[10]

It is set out clearly in the Acts that an adopting father will only acquire entitlement to adoptive leave where the adopting mother has died. An "adopting father" is defined by s 2(1) as:

[6–05]

> "...a male employee in whose care a child has been placed or is to be placed with a view to the making of an adoption order, or to the effecting of a foreign adoption or following any such adoption, where the adopting mother has died".

In the event of the adopting mother's death, the adoptive father is entitled to a period of 24 weeks adoptive leave from the date of placement and the date of the adopting mother's death.[11] The Acts permit the adoption of a child solely by a male employee. Section 2(1) of the Acts describes a "sole male adopter" as:

> "...a male employee who is not an adopting father within the meaning of this Act and in whose sole care a child has been placed or is to be placed with a view to the making of an adoption order, or to the effecting of a foreign adoption or following any such adoption".

---

[8] s 6(2), as amended by the Adoptive Leave Act 1995 (Extensions of Periods of Leave) Order (SI No 52 of 2006).
[9] *ibid.*
[10] s 2(1).
[11] s 9(1) as amended by Adoptive Leave Act 1995 (Extensions of Periods of Leave) Order (SI No 52 of 2006), Art 10.

Notification of Adoptive Leave

[6–06]   The employee must, as soon as is reasonably practicable, but no later than four weeks before the expected date of placement of the child with the employee, give his or her employer notification of the intention to take adoptive leave.[12]

Entitlement to Additional Adoptive Leave

[6–07]   The employed adopting mother, or sole male adopter, is entitled under the Acts to a further leave period up to a maximum of 12 weeks.[13] The employee who wishes to avail of additional adoptive leave must provide the employer with written notice of an intention to do so at the same time notification is provided of his or her intention to avail of adoptive leave, or, at most, no later than four weeks before the employee's scheduled date of return to work.[14] It is possible for the employee entitled to additional adoptive leave to revoke the period of additional adoptive leave before it commences on giving the employer the required notification.[15] In the case of foreign adoptions, the adopting parent(s) are entitled to take some or all of the additional adoptive leave period before the day of placement of the child "for the purposes of familiarisation with the child".[16] Adopting fathers are also entitled to avail of additional adoptive leave up to a maximum of 24 weeks leave.[17] Again, if it is a foreign adoption, the adopting father is able to take additional adoptive leave before the day of placement of the child.[18]

[6–08]   If the adopting parent becomes sick during a period of additional adoptive leave, he or she may notify the employer in writing and ask the employer to terminate this additional leave period and request that the employer treat the adopting parent's absence as sick leave.[19] However, if the employer agrees to terminate the period of additional adoptive leave and treats this as sick leave, the employee will not be entitled to avail of any additional adoptive leave that has not already been taken.[20]

[6–09]   The Adoptive Leave Act of 2005 inserted a new entitlement for adopting parents to take paid time off work to attend pre-adoption classes and meetings that the adopting parents are required to attend as part of the adoption process.[21] Employees must notify the employer of the dates and times of these classes and meetings at least two weeks before the date of the first class.[22]

---

[12] s 7(1).

[13] Adoptive Leave Acts, s 8(1) as amended by Adoptive Leave Act 1995 (Extensions of Periods of Leave) Order (SI No 52 of 2006).

[14] ss 8(2)-(4).

[15] s 8(4).

[16] s 8(5).

[17] Adoptive Leave Acts, s 10(1) as amended by Adoptive Leave Act 1995 (Extensions of Periods of Leave) Order (SI No 52 of 2006), Art 11.

[18] s 11(1).

[19] s 11B.

[20] ss 11B and 11D.

[21] s 11A(1).

[22] s 11A (3)(b)(i)-(ii).

The adopting parent(s) may postpone the adoptive leave, or additional adoptive leave, period if the adopted child is hospitalised.[23] Postponement of such leave does not mean that the employee's entitlement to adoptive leave or additional adoptive leave comes to an end. An amendment under the 2005 Act provides that in such circumstances, the employee will be entitled to take the leave once the child is discharged from hospital, beginning no later than seven days from the date of discharge, or at an alternative date agreed between the employer and employee.[24]

[6–10]

Protection of Employment Rights

Employees who take time off work for the purposes of adoptive leave will, under the Acts, have their employment rights protected.[25] The employee who avails of adoptive leave or additional adoptive leave will be treated as if he or she is still in employment for the duration of the leave period.[26] The period of adoptive leave or additional adoptive leave will not constitute a break in the employee's continuity of service.[27] The employment rights of the employee will not be affected by any time taken off work in connection with adoptive leave, additional adoptive leave, or time to attend pre-adoption classes or meetings. Adoptive leave or additional adoptive leave is not to be treated as forming part of any other leave period, such as annual leave, sick leave, or *force majeure* leave, to which the employee is entitled.[28] The employer has the right to suspend any training, probation or apprenticeship of the employee for the duration of the adoptive leave or additional adoptive leave period and the employee will have to complete this training, probation or apprenticeship upon his or her return to work following the end of the leave period.[29]

[6–11]

Return to Work

Under the Acts, employees who have taken time off work for adoptive leave, or additional adoptive leave, must provide their employer with at least four weeks' written notice of the intention to return to work before the scheduled date of return.[30] Employees who have taken adoptive leave, or additional adoptive leave, are entitled to return to work for the same employer, or, if there has been a transfer of ownership, the new employer at the end of the leave period. Where possible, employees are entitled to return to the same job as the one they held prior to the commencement of the adoptive leave period.[31] The employee is entitled to return to work under the same contract of employment that was in place before the adoptive leave began.[32] The terms and

[6–12]

---

[23] s 11C.

[24] s 11C(2)(d).

[25] s 15.

[26] s 15(1)(a)-(b) and s 15(2)(a)-(b).

[27] s 15(2).

[28] s 15(4).

[29] s 15(6).

[30] s 20(1).

[31] s 18(1).

[32] In *McCormack v Ark Fashions (Dundrum Limited)* (UD115/2007) the employee successfully sued for constructive dismissal, having returned to work following adoptive leave to find her terms of employment had been substantially altered: she was not given the hours that she had always previously worked and she was not now in a position to work afternoons, due to childcare commitments.

conditions of the contract of employment must not be any less favourable and will also take into account any improvements that the employee would be entitled to before the leave period.[33] If it is not feasible for the employee to return to the same job after the adoptive leave period has ended, the employer must provide a new contract of employment offering suitable alternative employment.[34] The terms and conditions of the new contract of employment must not be less favourable to the employee than those contained in the contract of employment in place before the commencement of the adoptive leave period and must also include any improvements to these terms and conditions to which the employee would have been entitled if he or she had not taken adoptive leave.[35]

III. Carer's Leave

[6–13]   The Carer's Leave Act 2001 (hereinafter referred to in this section as the "2001 Act") provides for the temporary absence from employment of an employee to provide full-time care to any person who requires such care. The minimum period of leave an employee can take under the 2001 Act is 13 weeks, up to a maximum of 104 weeks.[36] Carer's leave is unpaid, although a Carer's Benefit is available to an employee if he or she has made sufficient PRSI contributions; employees who do not qualify for the Carer's Benefit may be eligible to claim for a Carer's Allowance, subject to means testing.[37]

Entitlement to Carer's Leave

[6–14]   To be entitled to take carer's leave under the 2001 Act, an employee must have been working for his or her employer for a period of 12 months' continuous service and leave is only to be taken to provide full-time care and attention to a "relevant person".[38] If an employee wishes to take carer's leave, he or she must apply to the Minister for Social, Community and Family Affairs[39] for a decision by a Deciding Officer that the person the employee intends to provide full-time care and attention for is a relevant person as prescribed by legislation.[40] Any employee who wishes to avail of carer's leave must not be engaged in any employment or self-employment during the leave period.[41]

Relevant Person

[6–15]   Section 99 of the Social Welfare (Consolidation) Act 2005 defines a "relevant person", for the purposes of the 2001 Act, as "a person who has such a disability that he or she requires full-time care and attention". The relevant person who needs full-time care and attention must have a disability that means he or she needs constant supervision

---

[33] s 18(1)(c)(i)-(ii).

[34] s 19(1).

[35] s 19(2)(b)(i)-(ii).

[36] s 6(1) as amended by Social Welfare Law Reform and Pensions Act 2006, s 48(1). This is an increase from 65 weeks as originally set out under the 2001 Act.

[37] For further information see http://www.citizensinformation.ie/categories/employment/employment-rights-and-conditions/leave-and-holidays/carers_leave_from_employment.

[38] s 6(1).

[39] Now called the Minister for Social Protection.

[40] s 6(4).

[41] s 6(1)(d).

and frequently requires assistance during the day in connection with "normal bodily functions", such as getting dressed, washed, eating or drinking, and also needs constant supervision to "avoid danger to themselves".[42]

Carer

A carer is deemed to be anyone over the age of 16 years that has not reached [6–16] pensionable age. A carer can be someone who resides with the relevant person in need of full-time care and attention: in some situations, the carer who provides full-time care and attention does not have to reside with the relevant person for the purposes of the 2001 Act.[43]

Manner of Carer's Leave

Under the 2001 Act an employee is not entitled to avail of carer's leave if someone else [6–17] is also taking time off work to provide full-time care and attention to the same person.[44] However, it is possible for the employee who is on carer's leave to apply for carer's leave for another person who resides with the relevant person,[45] with both periods of leave not amounting to more than 208 weeks leave in total.[46] Section 8 of the 2001 Act provides that the leave period can be taken as one block of 104 weeks, or alternatively leave can be taken in periods which do not amount to more than 104 weeks in total from the date that the employee's carer's leave began. However, if carer's leave is not taken in a block of 104 weeks but in separate blocks, the employee can only commence the next period of carer's leave for a relevant person has ended six weeks after the end of the previous period.[47] An employer can refuse on "reasonable grounds" to allow an employee to take carer's leave for less than a period of 13 weeks; however, reasons for such refusal must be given in writing.[48] There must be a gap of six months between the date that an employee's carer's leave for a relevant person has ended before he or she can commence carer's leave for a different relevant person.[49]

Notice of Carer's Leave

An employee must provide his or her employer with written notice six weeks before the [6–18] date of commencement of the proposed carer's leave period under the 2001 Act.[50] The employee must also include details of the proposed date that he or she intends to commence the carer's leave period and whether the leave is to be taken in one continuous 104 week block, or in separate blocks of leave.[51] Where an emergency or exceptional circumstances arise necessitating the employee to take immediate carer's leave, where prior notice has not been given to the employer, the employee should give

---

[42] Social Welfare (Consolidation) Act 2005, s 99(2).
[43] Social Welfare (Consolidation) Act 1993, s 82A(1) (b) (as inserted by the Social Welfare Act 2000).
[44] s 6(3).
[45] s 7(2).
[46] s 7(4), as amended by Social Welfare Law Reform and Pensions Act 2006, s 48(1).
[47] s 8(3).
[48] s 8(2).
[49] s 8(4).
[50] s 9(1).
[51] s 9(1)(c).

notice as soon as is reasonably practicable.[52] An employee may revoke any notice of proposed carer's leave, in writing, before the commencement date of the confirmation document.[53] An employee who has taken carer's leave must also provide the employer with written notice of his or her intention to return to work at least four weeks before the date of return.[54] Both the employee and employer must sign a confirmation document at least two weeks before the proposed carer's leave is to begin, setting out details of the date of commencement, the period of leave and the manner in which it is to be taken.[55] Carer's leave can come to an end in a variety of different ways. The period of carer's leave will finish in one of the following ways: on the specified date of termination set out in the confirmation document; on an alternative date agreed by both parties; if the person that the employee has taken leave for is no longer deemed a "relevant person"; if the employee no longer qualifies as a "carer" for the purposes of the legislation; or in the event of the death of the relevant person.[56]

Protection of Employment Rights

[6–19] Part 3 of the 2001 Act provides safeguards to protect the employment rights of the employee for the duration of any leave period. Section 13(1) stipulates that an employee who has taken carer's leave is to be regarded as still in employment and any related rights or duties connected with his or her employment shall not be affected as a consequence of taking carer's leave, apart from rights related to remuneration, annual leave, public holidays, superannuation benefits and any obligations to pay contributions in, or in respect of, employment.[57] Carer's leave is treated as being distinct from any other leave from employment, such as annual leave, sick leave, maternity leave, adoptive leave, parental leave or *force majeure* leave, to which the employee is entitled.[58] If an employee seeking to avail of carer's leave is on probation, undertaking training or on a contract of apprenticeship, the employer may suspend the probation, training or contract of apprenticeship for the duration of the carer's leave period and may require the employee to complete probation, training or the apprenticeship when he or she has returned to work.[59]

Return to Work

[6–20] An employee who has taken carer's leave under the 2001 Act is entitled to return to work with the same employer once this leave period has come to an end.[60] Section 14(1)(a) also provides that the entitlement to return to work extends to cover circumstances where there has been a change in ownership of the undertaking in which the person was employed. The employee has a right to return to the same job that he or she held before taking carer's leave and the employee is entitled to return to work under the same contract of employment, with the same terms and conditions,

---

[52] s 9(2).
[53] s 9(3).
[54] s 9(6).
[55] s 10(1).
[56] s 11(1)(a)-(f).
[57] s 13(1)(a)(i)-(iv) and s 13(1)(b).
[58] s 13(4).
[59] s 13(5)(a)-(b).
[60] s 14(1).

that was in place before he or she went on carer's leave.[61] It may not always be possible to return to the same job after the carer's leave period has ended; however, the employer has a legal obligation under the 2001 Act to offer the employee suitable alternative work under a new contract of employment should this situation arise.[62] Section 15(2) of the 2001 Act defines "suitable alternative work" as work that is suitable for the employee, and is also appropriate work for the employee. The terms and conditions of the new contract of employment for suitable alternative work must not be any less favourable than those contained within the employee's contract of employment prior to start of the employee's carer's leave period.[63] Provision of a new contract of employment for suitable alternative work will not be deemed a break in the employee's continuity of service.[64]

Protection from Penalisation

Employers are prevented from penalising employees for seeking to avail of, or having already availed of, their entitlement to carer's leave under the 2001 Act.[65] Section 16(2) of the 2001 Act stipulates that penalisation includes:

[6–21]

a. dismissal of the employee;
b. unfair treatment of the employee, including selection for redundancy; and
c. an unfavourable change in the conditions of employment of the employee.

If an employee is dismissed on the grounds that he or she sought to take carer's leave, or that the employer refuses to allow the employee to return to work after taking carer's leave, he or she will be able to initiate proceedings under the Unfair Dismissals Acts.[66]

IV. Parental Leave

The Parental Leave Act 1998 was introduced in order to implement Directive 96/34 on parental leave.[67] The 1998 Act was amended by the Parental Leave (Amendment) Act 2006 (the Parental Leave Acts 1998 and 2006 are hereinafter referred to in this section as "the Acts"). The purpose of Directive 96/34 is twofold. First, it provides both female and male employees with time off work to facilitate them in their parental responsibilities following the birth or adoption of a child. The second objective of the Directive is the provision of the right for employees to take *force majeure* leave in the event of a crisis within the family due to illness or an accident.[68]

[6–22]

---

[61] s 14(1)(b)-(c).

[62] s 15(1).

[63] s 15(2)(b).

[64] s 15(2)(c).

[65] s 16(1).

[66] s 16(3)-(4). See chapter 10.

[67] Directive 96/34 of 3 June 1996 on the framework agreement on parental leave concluded by UNICE, CEEP and the ETUC [1996] OJ L145/4. See Boyle, "The Parental Leave Act 1998" (1999) 17 ILT 124.

[68] O' Boyle and Ní Longáin, "Protective Leave" in *Employment Law* (Regan ed, Tottel, Dublin, 2009), p 139.

[6–23] In Ireland, the Acts mirror the provisions of the Directive by granting employees the right to parental leave to care for a child for a period of three months, until the child is eight years old.[69] Employees who have a child with a disability are entitled to parental leave under the Acts until the child concerned reaches 16 years of age, or the disability ceases.[70] The extension of the parental leave entitlement for employees with a disabled child was introduced by the 2006 Act. The Acts now define disability as meaning "an enduring physical, sensory, mental health or intellectual impairment of the child".[71]

[6–24] On 8 March 2010, the Council adopted a new Directive which repeals Directive 96/34 and extends the rights of employees to parental leave from three months to four months for each parent.[72] This Directive actively seeks to encourage *fathers* to take time off work for the purpose of parental leave by refusing to allow the transfer of at least one of the four months leave entitlement to the other parent: if the time is not taken, it will be lost. This new Directive provides clarification that all workers are entitled to parental leave, including any worker who has a fixed-term, part-time or temporary agency contract with the employer.[73] Under the provisions of the new Directive, workers applying for parental leave, or those who have already taken time off work for parental leave, cannot be treated less favourably at work for so doing. It will now be possible for those workers who have taken parental leave to request a change to working hours for a limited period upon their return to work. The employer now has a duty to consider and reply to any such requests although the employer is not obliged to grant this request.[74] Member States will have two years in which to transpose the new Directive into national law.

Entitlement to Parental Leave

[6–25] The 1998 and 2006 Acts govern the rights and entitlements of parents, who are employees, to time off work to look after a child. Under the Acts, anyone deemed a "relevant parent" is entitled to leave of up to fourteen weeks to look after a child.[75] Section 6(1) defines a "relevant parent" as any person who is the natural parent, adoptive or adopting parent, or any person who acts in *loco parentis* to the child.

[6–26] To benefit from the entitlements and protection under the parental leave legislation, the relevant parent must have completed one year's continuous service with the employer.[76] Anyone who has been employed for less than one year will not be entitled to claim fourteen weeks off work for parental leave reasons, although the legislation does provide limited entitlements for any employee with more than three months' continuous service to one week of parental leave for every month of continuous

---

[69] This was five years of age before the 2006 amendments.

[70] s 6(2)(c)(i) and (ii).

[71] s 6(9).

[72] See O'Mara, "Parental Leave" (2010) 7(1) IELJ 33.

[73] Council of the European Union, "Council Extends Parental Leave." Europa Press Release, PRES/10/33, 8 March 2010.

[74] *ibid.*

[75] s 6(1).

[76] s 6(3).

service.[77] There is no legal duty imposed on employers to pay employees on parental leave, although employers may do so at their own discretion.

If both parents work for the same employer, it is now possible for one parent to transfer parental leave entitlements to the other.[78] There is considerable evidence in EU Member States to show that it is more usual for the female employee to take time off work on parental leave.[79] As discussed above, the new Directive on Parental Leave seeks to restrict these rights of "transferring leave" to encourage greater use of the leave entitlements by male employees.

[6–27]

Section 7 of the Acts provides that the parental leave may be taken as separate blocks of leave or by reduced working hours. Employees may take two separate periods of parental leave of not less than six weeks. However, there must be a lapse of at least ten weeks before the second six week period of parental leave can be taken.[80] Days taken for parental leave do not include any public holidays, sick leave, maternity leave, adoptive leave or *force majeure* leave.[81] Employees must provide their employer with reasonable notice in writing at least six weeks before the parental leave is due to commence.[82] Both the employer and the employee have to sign a confirmation document four weeks prior to the commencement of the parental leave period agreeing when, and in what manner, the leave will be taken.[83] Section 10 provides that either party may postpone the parental leave even after the confirmation document has been signed (for example if the employee becomes ill): in the event of postponement, any parental leave that is not taken can be taken at another time.[84]

[6–28]

Postponement by the Employer of Parental Leave

Section 11(1) of the Acts provides that an employer may also postpone any period of parental leave once, without the consent of the employee. Postponement of parental leave can occur under the section if the employer deems that the leave would have a "substantial adverse effect on the operation of his or her business, profession or occupation". The parental leave can only be postponed for a period of six months after the initial date of commencement specified in the notice to the employer. The employer must also provide the employee with written notice at least four weeks before the parental leave is to start. [85]

[6–29]

Parental leave under the Acts is only to be used to take care of a child. Employers have a legal right to terminate any parental leave if they believe that the employee is using the leave for any other purpose.[86] The employer has to give the employee seven days'

[6–30]

---

[77] s 6(7).

[78] s 6(6).

[79] Barnard, *op.cit*, p 466. See, also, Hakim, *op.cit*.

[80] s 7(1)(a)(i)-(ii).

[81] s 7(2)(b).

[82] ss 8(1) and 9(1).

[83] s 9(1).

[84] s 10(3).

[85] s 11(1).

[86] s 12(1).

written notice of the intention to terminate the parental leave period, which must include the reasons for the termination.[87]

An employer has a right to refuse to grant parental leave to an employee who has provided written notice of his or her intention to take such leave if the employer has "reasonable grounds" to believe that the employee does not qualify for parental leave.[88] The employer must provide written notice, with reasons explaining its refusal to grant parental leave.[89]

Force Majeure Leave

[6–31] Section 13(1) of the Acts provides that employees are entitled to take *force majeure* leave from employment to care for any person identified under s 13(2) who has become ill or injured, where the employee's presence at the place the person in question is located (usually the family home) is indispensible. This leave period is to facilitate employees when a family crisis occurs. Employees who take *force majeure* leave are entitled to be paid during this period.[90] An employee who is a parent or an adoptive parent can avail of *force majeure* leave to care for: a child in his or her care; the employee's spouse or person with whom the employee is living as husband or wife; any person to whom the employee is in *loco parentis*; the employee's brother or sister, parent or grandparent; or any person who resides with the employee in a relationship of domestic dependency.[91] A relationship of domestic dependency is one where a person, who lives with the employee, is dependent upon the employee to make arrangements to care for the person: the sexual orientation of persons in a relationship of domestic dependency is immaterial for the purposes of the section.[92] Employees are entitled to three *force majeure* leave days in any period of twelve consecutive months, or five days over a period of 36 months.[93] Employers should be provided with written notice of the employee's *force majeure* leave as soon as is reasonably practicable and should also receive a copy of the medical certificate pertaining to the family member's illness or accident.[94] In *Carey v Penn Racquet Sports Ltd*[95] the High Court held that questions of urgency and indispensability in relation to *force majeure* leave are not to be judged with hindsight, but from the employee's point of view at the time the decision was made not to go to work.[96]

Protection of Employment

[6–32] Section 14 of the Acts provides that the employment status of any employee who has taken parental leave will be protected. Any period of parental leave will not constitute a

---

[87] s 12(2).
[88] s 12(4).
[89] s 12(5).
[90] s 13(1).
[91] ss 13(2)(a)-(f). The category of "domestic dependency" was inserted pursuant to s 8 of the 2006 Act.
[92] s 13(2A).
[93] s 13(4).
[94] s 13(3).
[95] [2001] 3 IR 32.
[96] See also *Quinn v J Higgins Engineering Galway Ltd t/a APW Enclosures System* [2000] ELR 102.

break in the employee's continuity of service, which has consequences for an employee's ability to avail of other statutory protection measures in relation to redundancy and unfair dismissal.[97] In addition, the employee's pay and benefits will not be affected.[98] Parental leave will not be treated as constituting part of any other statutory leave entitlement such as annual leave, sick leave, adoptive leave, maternity leave or *force majeure* leave.[99] In the *Land Tirol* case[100] a question was referred to the ECJ regarding the interpretation of Clause 2.6 of the Framework Agreement on parental leave (annexed to Directive 96/34), which states that "rights acquired or in the process of being acquired by the worker on the date on which parental leave starts shall be maintained as they stand until the end of parental leave". The Court held that this clause must be interpreted as precluding a national provision such as that at issue in the case, under which workers exercising their right to parental leave of two years lost, following that leave, their right to paid annual leave accumulated during the year preceding the birth of their child. The ECJ noted that it was apparent from both the wording of Clause 2.6 and its context that the provision was intended to avoid the loss of, or reduction in, rights derived from the employment relationship, so as to ensure that, at the end of the leave period, with regard to those rights, the worker would find himself or herself in the same situation as that which pertained before the leave. As the right to paid annual leave is, the Court noted, particularly important, it is undoubtedly one of the rights derived directly from the employment relationship of every worker (both male and female).

Note that if an employee has not completed his or her probation, training or apprenticeship before taking parental leave, the employer may suspend probation, training or the contract of apprenticeship for the duration of the employee's parental leave.[101]

Section 15(1) of the Acts provides that an employee who has taken parental leave to care for a child will be entitled to return to work with his or her employer when this leave period comes to an end. Section 15(1) also protects the employee's right to return to work in the event that there has been a change of ownership of the undertaking while the employee is on parental leave. The employee has a right to return to the same job that he or she was in prior to the commencement of the parental leave period,[102] except in the situation where this job was not the "normal or usual" job of the employee.[103] Section 9 of the 2006 Act amended s 15 of the 1998 Act to include further protection regarding the employee's right to return to work where there has been a transfer of ownership. In the event of this occurring, the employee's contract of

[6–33]

---

[97] Indeed, in Case C-116/08 *Meerts v Proost NV* the ECJ held that full-time workers who are on part-time parental leave, and are dismissed without notice during the leave, are entitled to compensation calculated on their *full-time*, rather than their *part-time*, salary. To hold otherwise, the Court held, would mean that the entitlement to rights and benefits would be compromised, with the result that workers might be discouraged from taking their leave and employers might be encouraged to dismiss workers on parental leave rather than other workers.

[98] s 14(1).

[99] s 14(2).

[100] Case C-486/08 *Zentralbetriebsrat der Landeskrankenhauser Tirols v Land Tirol.*

[101] ss 14(3)(a)-(b).

[102] s 15(1)(b).

[103] s 15(2). The employee is entitled to return to the "normal or usual" job.

employment cannot be changed to include terms, which would be less favourable to the employee than those under the original contract; however, the employee will be entitled to any improvements to the terms and conditions of employment subsequent to the transfer of ownership.[104] If it is not possible to allow the employee to return to work under s 15, the employee is entitled to be offered suitable alternative employment under a new contract of employment by the employer.[105] Section 16A of the Acts (inserted by s 11 of the 2006 Act) aims to safeguard the employee from penalisation by his or her employer for "proposing to exercise or having exercised his or her entitlement to parental leave or *force majeure* leave".[106] As a consequence of this amendment, employees have protection from dismissal, unfair treatment, or any unfavourable changes to the employment contract. In *O'Kane v Dunnes Stores Limited*[107] the EAT found that the claimant was justified in terminating her employment following the breakdown of trust and confidence between the claimant and the employer after she returned from parental leave. She had been transferred to work in a different store and in a different role that she viewed as a demotion; she was also confronted by a human resources manager at a meeting of which she had no prior notice. Any employee who is dismissed in relation to his or her entitlement to parental leave is therefore eligible to initiate legal proceedings under the Unfair Dismissals Act.[108] The 2006 Act also inserted a new s 22A, which allows the Minister to request the Equality Authority to draw up a statutory code of practice on the manner in which parental leave and *force majeure* leave might be taken and the manner in which the employer can terminate parental leave.

V. Maternity Leave

[6–34] Directive 92/85 (the Pregnancy Directive) was introduced in an attempt to deal with issues concerning pregnant women in the workplace; in particular, in relation to entitlement to maternity leave, equal treatment in the workplace and the protection of pregnant employees in respect of health and safety.[109] The introduction of the Pregnancy Directive was significant in recognising the entitlement of protection for pregnant workers as of *right* rather than as a part of sex equality.[110] It should also be noted that the passing of the Directive was not without controversy: it was eventually introduced on the basis of Art 118A of the EEC Treaty (now Art 154TFEU) as a measure to protect the health and safety of workers rather than on the (more usual) employment equality law basis of Art 119 (now Art 159TFEU).[111] A recent amendment to the Directive has been proposed, which, if passed, would provide for

---

[104] s 15(1)(c).

[105] s 16(1).

[106] s 16A(1).

[107] [2005] 16 ELR 337.

[108] s 16A(3).

[109] Directive 92/85 of 19 October 1992 on the introduction of measures to encourage improvements in the safety and health at work of pregnant workers and workers who have recently given birth or are breastfeeding [1992] OJ L348/1. See Barnard, *op.cit*, pp 447 and 455.

[110] Bolger, "Protective Measures for Pregnant Workers" (2009) 6(3) IELJ 74, p 78.

[111] This was likely done to avail of the majority voting procedures provided for by Art 118AEEC; measures under Art 119EEC required unanimity; see Ellis, "Protection of Pregnancy and Maternity" (1993) 22 ILJ 63.

payment of 100 percent of the woman's salary while on maternity leave, subject to the possibility of a Member State setting a ceiling at the level of national sick pay.[112] However, Bolger notes that the proposals are facing strong opposition from a number of Member States "primarily on grounds of cost and to a lesser extent, on grounds of limiting parental rights to mothers rather than to fathers and creating obstacles to the recruitment of women in the workforce".[113]

The Maternity Protection Act 1994, as well as repealing the earlier Maternity **[6–35]** Protection Acts of 1981 and 1991, incorporated Directive 92/85 into Irish law.[114] The Maternity Protection (Amendment) Act 2004 introduced further amendments regarding entitlement to maternity leave; entitlement of pregnant workers to attend ante-natal classes without loss of pay; entitlement to time off work for the purposes of breastfeeding; and fathers' rights to time off work to attend ante-natal classes without loss of pay. The Maternity Protection Acts 1994 and 2004 are hereinafter referred to in this section as "the Acts". Two statutory instruments have been enacted granting pregnant women the right to paid time off work to attend ante-natal classes,[115] and extending the period of maternity leave.[116]

Entitlement to Maternity Leave

The ECJ in *Hofmann*[117] explains that the objective of maternity leave is: **[6–36]**

> "...to protect a woman's biological condition and the special relationship between a woman and her child over the period which follows pregnancy and childbirth, by preventing that relationship from being disturbed by the multiple burdens which would result from the simultaneous pursuit of employment".

The 1994 Act initially entitled pregnant employees to 14 weeks' maternity leave: this was extended to 18 weeks' leave by the 2004 Act and the statutory entitlement to maternity leave has been increased again by the Maternity Protection Act 1994

---

[112] COM (2008) 637 final.

[113] Bolger, *op.cit*, p 80. Note also that, under proposed legislation endorsed by EU governments on 7 June 2010 *self-employed* workers and their partners will enjoy better social protection, including, for the first time, the right to at least 14 weeks' maternity leave. Member States will have to decide whether paying for membership of social insurance schemes (covering maternity leave, sickness, invalidity and old age) must be mandatory for self-employed women or whether they can access this system voluntarily. They must also decide whether this social protection can also be "proportional to the participation in the activities of the self-employed worker". Member States will have two years to implement the changes to the Directive, or up to four years "if Member States find difficulties" in so doing; see the European Parliament Press Release "Wives of Self-Employed Should Have Similar Maternity Leave Rights to Employees" available at http://www.europarl.europa.eu.

[114] Masselot, "Implementation of the Pregnant Workers Directive in the Republic of Ireland" (1997) 15 ILT 96.

[115] Maternity Protection (Time Off for Ante-Natal Classes) Regulations 2004 (SI No 653 of 2004).

[116] Maternity Protection Act 1994 (Extension of Periods of Leave) Order 2006 (SI No 51 of 2006).

[117] Case 184/83 *Hofmann v Barmer Ersatzkasse* [1984] ECR I-3047 at para 25. See also Case C-411/96 *Boyle v EOC* [1998] ECR I-6401.

(Extensions of Periods of Leave) Order 2006, which provides that pregnant employees are now entitled to 26 weeks' maternity leave.[118]

Notification of Maternity Leave

[6–37]   Under the Acts, the pregnant employee has a duty to provide the employer with written notice of her intention to take maternity leave as soon as reasonably practicable and at least four weeks before the date of commencement of maternity leave.[119] In conjunction with this written notice, the pregnant employee must also provide the employer with a medical certificate that confirms her pregnancy and also indicate the expected week of birth.[120] The pregnant employee may revoke in writing any notification of her intention to take maternity leave or notification regarding confirmation of her pregnancy or due date of birth.[121]

Commencement of Maternity Leave

[6–38]   The Acts stipulate that the pregnant employee must begin her period of maternity leave at least two weeks before the expected week of birth.[122] In those cases where the pregnant employee may give birth four weeks or more before the expected date of birth, she will still be entitled to the full 26 weeks of maternity leave. Her period of maternity leave will commence on either the first day of maternity leave or from the date of the baby's birth.[123] The employee will have to give her employer written notice of her intention to take maternity leave within 14 days of the birth.[124]

Additional Maternity Leave

[6–39]   The pregnant employee also has a statutory entitlement to take a period of additional maternity leave. This period has been extended to allow pregnant employees to take a maximum of 16 consecutive weeks.[125] This period of additional maternity leave must commence as soon as the ordinary period of maternity leave comes to an end.

Termination of Additional Maternity Leave Due to the Mother's Illness

[6–40]   In the event of the mother's illness during the period of additional maternity leave, she can seek to terminate this period of leave under the Acts by notifying her employer in writing.[126] Subject to the employer's consent, the additional maternity leave period will

---

[118] Maternity Protection Acts 1994 and 2004, s 8(1) as amended by Maternity Protection Act 1994 (Extension of Periods of Leave) Order 2006 (SI No 51 of 2006), Art 8.

[119] s 9(1)(a).

[120] s 9(1)(b).

[121] s 9(1)(c).

[122] s 10(1).

[123] ss 13(1)-(2).

[124] s 13(1).

[125] Maternity Protection Acts 1994 and 2004, s 14(1)(a), as amended by Maternity Protection Act 1994 (Extension of Periods of Leave) Order 2006 (SI No 51 of 2006), Art 10. The Maternity Protection Act 1994 originally provided for four consecutive weeks of additional maternity leave under s 14, which was extended to eight consecutive weeks by the Maternity Protection Act 1994 (Extension of Periods of Leave) Order 2001 (SI No 29 of 2001), Art 6.

[126] ss 14A (1)(a)-(b).

come to an end on the date agreed by both the employer and employee.[127] The employer is obliged to inform the employee in writing of its decision as soon as is reasonably practicable after it receives the employee's request to end the additional maternity leave period.[128] Where additional maternity leave is terminated due to the mother's sickness, the period of leave will then be treated as sick leave: it is not possible for the employee to resume a period of additional maternity leave at a later date once this period has been terminated.[129]

Postponement of Maternity Leave or Additional Maternity Leave

The Acts provide that the employee taking maternity leave or additional maternity **[6–41]** leave is entitled to ask her employer to postpone all or part of this leave if the child to whom she has given birth is hospitalised.[130] The employee must already have taken 14 weeks of her maternity leave, four of which must have been taken at least four weeks after the child's birth, before requesting to postpone her maternity leave or additional maternity leave.[131] The employer has to give the employee written notice of its decision as soon as is reasonably practicable.[132] The employer is not legally obliged to consent to postponement of maternity leave or additional maternity leave: it retains discretion as to whether to agree to the employee's request. Where the employer does approve the request to postpone the employee's leave, both parties must agree a date upon which the employee is to return to work. This date cannot be any later than the date that the leave is scheduled to end.[133]

The employee has the right to resume all or part of the maternity leave or additional **[6–42]** maternity leave period once her child is discharged from hospital. This is referred to in s 14B(c) of the Acts as "resumed leave". The employee's entitlement to resumed leave is conditional on her having given her employer written notice of her intention to resume her leave as soon as is reasonably practicable.[134] The employee may not have to provide such notice if the employer waives its right to receive notice regarding resumed leave.[135] If the employee becomes ill when she begins the resumed leave period, she can notify the employer in writing as soon as possible that she does not wish to continue with resumed leave because of her sickness.[136] This will mean that her absence from work will constitute sick leave, and, furthermore, she will no longer be entitled to continue with the resumed leave period.[137]

Time Off Work for Ante-Natal or Post-Natal Care

The legislation places emphasis on the care of pregnant employees, as well as those **[6–43]** employees who have recently given birth. Section 15(1) of the Acts provides that

---

[127] s 14A(2).
[128] s 14A(3).
[129] ss 14A(4)(a)-(b).
[130] s 14B.
[131] s 14B(2).
[132] s 14B(5).
[133] s 14B(4)(a).
[134] s 14B(8).
[135] s 14B(10).
[136] s 14B(6).
[137] ss 14B(6)(a)-(b).

pregnant employees, or those employees who have recently given birth, can take time off work with no loss of pay for the purposes of receiving ante-natal or post-natal care. The details of the general entitlements to time off work for these reasons are set out in the Maternity Protection (Time Off for Ante-Natal and Post-Natal Care) Regulations 1995.[138] Under the 1995 Regulations, ante-natal care is defined as that which deals with the "existing pregnancy of the employee", while post-natal care concerns any care that the employee receives after she gives birth and is "consequential on that birth".[139] The employee who is seeking to take time off work for such purposes has a duty to provide her employer with notification in writing of the time and date of her medical appointment as soon as is reasonably practicable, and at least two weeks before the scheduled date of the appointment.[140] Under the Maternity Protection Acts, both pregnant employees and expectant fathers are entitled to take time off work with pay to attend ante-natal classes.[141] The general obligations of both the expectant mother and father in regards to seeking time off work for the purposes of attending ante-natal classes are set out in the Maternity Protection (Time Off for Ante-Natal Classes) Regulations 2004.[142]

Time Off Work or Reduction of Working Hours for Breastfeeding

[6–44] In recent years, it has been widely acknowledged that there are significant health benefits to breastfeeding babies.[143] To facilitate mothers who decide to breastfeed their babies, the Maternity Protection (Amendment) Act 2004 introduced an entitlement for employees to time off work, or a reduction of working hours,[144] for the purposes of breastfeeding up to the twenty-sixth week after the mother gave birth.[145] Breastfeeding is defined under the Acts as:

> "...breastfeeding a child or expressing breast milk and feeding it to a child immediately or storing it for the purpose of feeding it to the child at a later time".[146]

[6–45] Section 15B(1) of the Acts provides that employees who are breastfeeding are entitled to paid time off work to breastfeed where the employer has breastfeeding facilities in the workplace. If there are no facilities for breastfeeding in the workplace, the employee is entitled to a reduction in her working hours, again with no loss of pay, to enable her to breastfeed her baby. Employers have no legal obligation to provide breastfeeding facilities in the workplace where this would incur a cost greater than a nominal cost.[147]

---

[138] SI No 18 of 1995.

[139] Art 2.

[140] Art 4(1).

[141] s 15A.

[142] SI No 653 of 2004.

[143] Department of Health and Children National Committee on Breastfeeding, *Breastfeeding in Ireland – A Five-year Strategic Action Plan* (Department of Health and Children, Dublin, 2005).

[144] Now s 15B of the Acts.

[145] Maternity Protection (Protection of Mothers who are Breastfeeding) Regulations 2004 (SI No 654 of 2004), Art 2.

[146] s 15B(4).

[147] s 15B(2).

The details of the general entitlements of employees under s 15B of the Acts are set out in the Maternity Protection (Protection of Mothers who are Breastfeeding) Regulations 2004.[148]

Paternity Leave

The father of a child does not have any statutory right to paternity leave under the Acts when his child is born, except in those cases where the mother dies after she has given birth, at any stage before her maternity leave period expires.[149] In such circumstances, the father will then be entitled to begin his leave within seven days of the mother's death.[150] The father of the child will also be entitled to take additional leave from employment up to a maximum of 12 consecutive weeks.[151] The father will be entitled to similar leave entitlements as the mother of the child, for example, he will be able to terminate the statutory leave if he becomes sick during this period.[152] Similarly he will be able to postpone this leave period if the child is hospitalised.[153] The father will have to comply with any statutory notification requirements regarding commencement of his leave period and provision of documentation regarding the mother's death, requests to take additional leave and intention to return to work.[154]

[6–46]

Right to Pay During Maternity Leave

Employers are not legally obliged under the Acts to pay employees for the period of maternity leave.[155] However, the employee may be paid as normal during the maternity leave period, subject to the provisions of the contract of employment.[156] O' Boyle and Ní Longáin note that it is commonplace for employers to pay the employee on maternity leave as normal, deducting any maternity benefit payments to which the employee is entitled.[157] Some employers may stipulate that employees will only be entitled to full pay during maternity leave after completing one year's continuous service with the employer.[158] Employers do not have a statutory obligation to pay the employee any superannuation benefits and contributions when the employee is on additional maternity leave, father's leave (subsequent to the mother's death), or additional father's leave.[159]

[6–47]

---

[148] SI No 654 of 2004.

[149] s 16(1).

[150] s 16(3).

[151] s 16(4)(a), as amended by Maternity Protection Act 1994 (Extension of Periods of Leave) Order 2006 (SI No 51 of 2006), Art 7(b)(i).

[152] s 16A.

[153] s 16B.

[154] ss 16(2), (5) and (6).

[155] s 22.

[156] Kerr, *Employment Rights Legislation* (2nd ed, Round Hall, Dublin, 2006), p C68/7.

[157] O' Boyle and Ní Longáin, *op.cit*, p 134.

[158] *ibid.*

[159] Equality Authority, *About the Maternity Protection Acts 1994 and 2004—Information on Entitlements under Maternity Legislation.* Available at http://www.equality.ie/index.asp?locID=106&docID=53.

Protection of Employment Rights

[6–48]   Employees who are absent from work for the purposes of maternity leave under the Acts will be treated as still being in the employment of the employer. This period of absence will not be treated as a break in the employee's continuity of service.[160] This includes absences for additional maternity leave; father's leave (in the event of the mother's death); additional father's leave; time off for ante-natal or post-natal care; time off to attend ante-natal classes; time off work or reduction in working hours for breastfeeding; and health and safety leave. The employee's rights or obligations arising under the contract of employment, or from legislation, will not be affected by this period of absence, other than the right to pay during this leave period.[161] Absence from work for the purposes of maternity leave, or other such associated leave as listed above, cannot be treated as constituting sick leave or annual leave.[162] The employer cannot compel the employee to take annual leave for the purposes of attending ante-natal classes.

[6–49]   Section 23 of the Acts prohibits the purported dismissal of the employee during any absences from work connected with maternity leave; absences for the purposes of natal care; absences whereby the employee is attending ante-natal classes; or absences for the purposes of breastfeeding.[163] Employers are also not allowed under the Acts to give an employee any notice of a proposed termination of employment, or proposed suspension of the employee's employment, during the maternity leave period, or periods of absence for natal care, ante-natal classes, or breastfeeding.[164] If notice of termination, or suspension, of employment has been given to the employee before the employer has been provided with notification from the employee regarding entitlement to leave, this shall be extended by the duration of the protective leave period, or period of leave for the purposes of natal care, attendance at ante-natal classes or breastfeeding, if this is due to end during the leave period.[165] In *Paquay*[166] the ECJ confirmed that the Pregnancy Directive should be interpreted as prohibiting not only notification of a decision to dismiss on grounds of pregnancy and/or the birth of a child during the period of the protected leave, but also the taking of such a decision to dismiss in preparing the permanent replacement of such a worker before the expiry of that period. In *Pontin*[167] the ECJ considered the Luxembourg legislation implementing the Pregnancy Directive, which provided that a legal action brought by a pregnant employee dismissed during her pregnancy and seeking to annul the decision to dismiss had to be brought within 15 days of the termination of the contract. The ECJ held that Arts 10 and 12 of the Pregnancy Directive must be interpreted as not precluding such legislation provided that the rules laid down were not framed in such a way as to render practically impossible the exercise of rights conferred by EU law. The ECJ felt that a 15-day limitation period did not appear to meet that condition, but that this was a matter for the national court to determine.

---

[160]   s 22(2).
[161]   s 22.
[162]   s 22(4).
[163]   s 23. See below (on pregnancy dismissal) for further discussion of this issue.
[164]   s 23.
[165]   s 24.
[166]   Case C-460/06 *Paquay v Société d'Architectes Hoet & Minne SPRL* [2007] ECR 1-851.
[167]   Case C-63/08 *Pontin v T-Comalux SA*.

An employee who is on probation, or undergoing training in relation to the job, or is **[6–50]** employed under a contract of apprenticeship, will have this period suspended for the duration of the protective leave. Upon return to work after such absence, the employee will have to complete the probationary period, training, or apprenticeship.[168]

An employee who has taken protective leave from work is entitled to return to work in **[6–51]** the same job he or she held, with the same employer, or with the employer's successor where there has been a change in ownership during the period of protective leave.[169] The employee has a right to return to work under the same terms and conditions of his or her contract of employment before the protective leave period began: any improvement to the terms and conditions of the contract of employment, which the employee would have been entitled to if he or she had not been absent on protective leave, must also be incorporated into the contract upon the employee's return to work.[170] In *Gardiner v Mercer Human Resource Consulting*[171] the Equality Tribunal found that the complainant had not returned to the same job as that which she held before the commencement of maternity leave as, although her salary and job title were the same, in practice her job had changed. Her replacement had remained in the company and was performing some of the tasks the complainant had previously performed. Furthermore, the Tribunal found that the fact that the complainant now had a young child significantly influenced the employer's decision to restructure her job and remove certain tasks from her.

If it is not reasonably practicable for the employee to return to the job that he or she held **[6–52]** before the protective leave period commenced, the employee must be offered suitable alternative work under a new contract of employment by the employer, or the employer's successor if there has been a change of ownership, or an associated employer.[172] Section 27(2) of the Acts defines "suitable alternative work" as work that is "suitable in relation to the employee concerned and appropriate for the employee to do in the circumstances". The terms and conditions of any new contract offering suitable alternative work must not be less favourable than those contained in the original contract, and the new contract should also incorporate any improvements to which the employee would have been entitled if he or she had not taken protective leave from work.[173]

Notification of Intention to Return to Work

Employees who have taken any leave entitlements under the provisions of the Acts have a **[6–53]** legal obligation to notify the employer of their intention to return to work no later than four weeks before the date of return.[174] The employee's entitlement to return to work, or

---

[168] s 25(1).

[169] s 26.

[170] ss 26(1)(c)(i)-(ii).

[171] DEC-E2006-007. While complaints under the Acts are normally referred to a Rights Commissioner in the first instance (see chapter 12) the Equality Tribunal was satisfied it had jurisdiction here, as the maternity protection legislation does not prevent an employee from referring a complaint of discriminatory treatment in respect of pregnancy or maternity-related issues to the Equality Tribunal.

[172] s 27(1).

[173] ss 27(2)(b)(i)-(ii).

[174] s 28.

to be offered suitable alternative work, is subject to his or her compliance with the statutory notification requirements.[175] Where an employee becomes ill during a period of resumed leave, he or she also has a statutory duty to notify the employer in writing of the intention to return to work and the date he or she expects to return to work.[176]

[6–54] If the employee fails to provide written notification of the intention to return to work as required under the Acts, he or she may be granted an extension of time if, in the opinion of a Rights Commissioner or the EAT, there are reasonable grounds for the failure to do so within the prescribed time limits.[177] Failure to provide written notification of the intention to return to work, in the absence of any reasonable grounds, will be taken into consideration by a Rights Commissioner, the EAT or the Circuit Court when determining any rights arising in regards to the remedies of re-instatement, re-engagement or compensation.[178]

Health and Safety Leave

[6–55] Special provision is made under the Acts to protect the health and safety of pregnant employees, employees who have recently given birth and employees who are breastfeeding.[179] These measures aim to protect this group of employees from any risks or activities arising within the workplace which could pose a threat to their health and safety and also the health and safety of the unborn child, or breastfeeding child.

[6–56] Part III of the Maternity Protection Acts prescribes that pregnant employees, employees who have recently given birth and employees who are breastfeeding may have an entitlement to leave on health and safety grounds.[180] However, it is unlikely that employees who have recently given birth or employees who are breastfeeding will be at work for the purposes of taking health and safety leave given the legal definitions of both categories of employee.[181] According to s 2(1) of the Acts, an "employee who has recently given birth" is an employee whose date of confinement was not more than 14 weeks' earlier, who has notified the employer of her condition. An "employee who is breastfeeding" means an employee whose date of confinement was not more than twenty-six weeks earlier, who is breastfeeding and who has informed her employer of her condition.

[6–57] The Safety, Health and Welfare at Work (General Application) Regulations stipulate that employers have a duty to conduct a risk assessment of any activities in the workplace that are likely to pose a risk of exposure to certain agents, processes or working conditions, which could potentially harm the health and safety of this particular category of employees.[182] This particular risk assessment is in addition to the general risk assessment that must normally be conducted by an employer under the

---

[175] s 28(1A).
[176] s 28(1B).
[177] s 28(2).
[178] s 28(3). These remedies are discussed in detail in chapter 12.
[179] s 17.
[180] s 18.
[181] O' Boyle and Ní Longáin, *op.cit*, p 128.
[182] Safety, Health and Welfare at Work (General Application) Regulations 2007 (SI No 299 of 2007), Reg 149.

Safety, Health and Welfare at Work Act 2005. Under the 2007 Regulations, the employer must implement any necessary preventive and protective measures to protect the safety, health and welfare of pregnant employees, breastfeeding employees or employees who have recently given birth and to prevent any potential effect on the pregnancy or breastfeeding.[183] If it is not feasible for the employer to introduce preventive or protective measures to ensure the safety, health and welfare at work of the employee, the Regulations provide that the employer must temporarily adjust the working conditions and/or working hours of the qualifying employee so as to ensure that the employee avoids any exposure to the risk.[184] In circumstances where it may not be technically or objectively practicable to adjust either the employee's working conditions or working hours to avoid exposure to the risk, the employer must then provide the employee with other suitable work, which does not give rise to any risks.

Under the Maternity Protection Acts, the employer may grant health and safety leave to such employees if it is not technically or objectively feasible to move the employee to other work, there are no substantiated grounds to justify such a move, or the other work to which the employer proposes to move the employee is not suitable.[185] "Suitable work" is defined as work that is suitable to the employee in question and also appropriate for her to perform in the circumstances.[186] Where an employee has been given health and safety leave, she must be provided with a certificate specifying the reasons why she has been granted such leave and the certificate must also contain details regarding the date of commencement, duration of the health and safety leave period and any other necessary information regarding this leave.[187] The Maternity Protection (Health and Safety Leave Certification) Regulations stipulate that this certificate must identify the risk posed to the employee, explain why it is not feasible to eradicate this risk and must also verify that it is not possible to undertake other work.[188] Under the Maternity Protection Acts, the employee will be entitled to be paid as normal for the first 21 days of the health and safety leave period.[189] The employee may qualify for social welfare benefits if the health and safety leave period is for more than 21 days.[190]   **[6–58]**

Pregnant employees, employees who have recently given birth, or employees who are breastfeeding cannot be required to undertake night work during the pregnancy or during the 14 weeks after they have given birth, if the employees' doctor certifies that they should not work at night to protect their health and safety. The employer must transfer any such employees to "day-time work", or if it is not possible to do so, then the employees should be granted health and safety leave or else have the period of maternity leave extended.[191]   **[6–59]**

---

[183] Reg 149(b).

[184] Reg 150(a).

[185] s 18(1).

[186] s 18(3).

[187] s 18(2).

[188] Maternity Protection (Health and Safety Leave Certification) Regulations (SI No 19 of 1995).

[189] s 18(4). See also the 1995 Regulations.

[190] Social Welfare (Consolidation) Act 2005, s 52.

[191] Safety, Health and Welfare at Work (General Application) Regulations 2007 (SI No 299 of 2007), Reg 151.

[6–60] Under the Maternity Protection Acts, the period of health and safety leave will be terminated once the employee's maternity leave period commences.[192] If the health and safety leave period is granted due to the employee breastfeeding her child, this period will cease once the employee stops breastfeeding the child.[193] If the employee in question is on a fixed-term contract, the period of health and safety leave will come to an end on the day of expiry of the contract.[194] The employee has an obligation to provide the employer with written notification at the earliest practical time if she is no longer breastfeeding or if she believes that her condition is no longer at risk from exposure to agents, processes or working conditions.[195] Once the employer receives this notification from the employee and it has no grounds to believe that the employee remains vulnerable to exposure to the risks in the workplace, the employer must take all reasonable steps to ensure that the employee can return to work in the job that she was in immediately prior to the start of the health and safety leave period. The employer must then notify the employee in writing that she can return to work.[196]

[6–61] The health and safety leave period may also be terminated if the employer is able to implement measures to protect the employee from exposure to any risks that may arise, or is in a position to offer suitable alternative work. Where the employer is able to do this, written notice must be given to the employee informing her that she can return to work and that she will not be exposed to the identified risks, or that she will be offered suitable work instead.[197] The employee's health and safety leave period will end seven days after receiving this written notification, or it may end earlier if she returns to work or takes up the other work before this date.[198]

VI. Pregnancy Discrimination and EU Law

[6–62] Prior to the introduction of the Pregnant Workers' Directive,[199] there were no specific EU laws in place to provide protection for pregnant workers other than provisions preventing pregnant employees from undertaking work at night under the Equal Treatment Directive 76/207 (the primary purpose of which were to protect the health and safety of both the pregnant worker and the unborn child).[200] Article 2(2)(c) of the Recast Equal Treatment Directive 2006/54 now provides that discrimination includes:

---

[192] s 19(1)(a).
[193] ss 19(1) and 20(1).
[194] s 19(1).
[195] s 20(2).
[196] ss 20(3)(a)-(b).
[197] ss 20(4)(a)-(b).
[198] s 20(4).
[199] Directive 92/85 of 19 October 1992 on the introduction of measures to encourage improvements in the safety and health at work of pregnant workers and workers who have recently given birth or are breastfeeding [1992] OJ L348/1.
[200] Directive 76/207 of 9 February 1976 on the implementation of the principle of equal treatment for men and women as regards access to employment, vocational training and promotion and working conditions [1976] OJ L39/40. This has been repealed by the Directive 2006/54 on the implementation of the principle of equal opportunities and equal treatment of men and women in matters of employment and occupation [2006] OJ L204/23. See Barnard, *op.cit*, p 446.

"...any less favourable treatment of a woman related to pregnancy or maternity leave within the meaning of Directive 92/85/EEC".

However, as the original Equal Treatment Directive did not contain specific **[6–63]** provisions for pregnant workers, it was left to the ECJ to develop principles relating to the treatment of such workers.[201] The ECJ first addressed the issue of pregnancy discrimination in *Dekker*.[202] The Court was asked by the Supreme Court of the Netherlands to determine whether a refusal to employ a pregnant woman constituted direct discrimination on the grounds of sex and was, therefore, in breach of Arts 2(1) and 3(1) of the Equal Treatment Directive, if the only reason for refusing to appoint the woman was the fact of her pregnancy. Dekker had applied for a position at the employer's training centre for young adults in June 1981. She informed the committee responsible for processing the applications on 15 June 1981 that she was three months' pregnant at the time. This committee, in full knowledge of her pregnancy, recommended her to the board of selection as the most suitable candidate among all the applicants for the job. The employer subsequently notified Mrs Dekker that she would not be appointed to the post. The employer argued that its actions were justified as its insurers would not cover the cost of her absence during maternity leave and, as a consequence, the company would be unable to afford to pay for a replacement worker. All the other applicants for the job in question were female. However, despite the fact that all applicants were female and, therefore, there was no male with whom Dekker could compare herself, the ECJ held that the refusal to employ Dekker because she was pregnant constituted direct discrimination on the grounds of sex as:

"...only women can be refused employment on the grounds of pregnancy and such a refusal therefore constitutes direct discrimination on the grounds of sex".[203]

The decision of the ECJ to identify pregnancy discrimination as direct discrimination on **[6–64]** the grounds of sex was a hugely significant development.[204] Prior to this, courts had tried to "fit" pregnancy discrimination within the framework of gender discrimination law generally: this led to the illogical approach of comparing a pregnant woman to a hypothetical "sick male" in order to establish whether a woman treated less favourably on grounds of her pregnancy was, in fact, a victim of unlawful discrimination on grounds of her sex.[205] Also significant was the fact that the ECJ in *Dekker* dismissed the employer's argument that if it appointed a pregnant woman it would suffer a financial loss:

"A refusal of employment on account of the financial consequences of absence due to pregnancy must be regarded as based, essentially, on the facts of

[201] See Bolger and Kimber, *Sex Discrimination Law* (Round Hall, Dublin, 2000); Bamforth *et al*, *Discrimination Law: Theory and Context* (Thomson Sweet & Maxwell, London, 2008), chapter 10.
[202] Case C-177/88 *Dekker v Stichting Vormingscentrum voor Jong Volwassen* [1992] ICR 325.
[203] At para 12.
[204] Bolger and Kimber, "Employment Equality" in *Employment Law* (Regan ed, Tottel, Dublin, 2009), p 447.
[205] See Barry, "Direct Discrimination, Pregnancy and Maternity Leave and the Sick Male Comparison" (1993) 11 ILT 94; Flynn, "Pregnancy and Dismissal: Rejecting the 'Sick Male' Comparison" (1994) 12 ILT 257; Flynn, "Gender Blindness in the Face of Real Sex Differences" (1993) 15 DULJ 1.

pregnancy. Such discrimination cannot be justified on grounds relating to financial loss which an employer who appointed a pregnant woman would suffer for the duration of her maternity leave".[206]

[6-65] In *Mahlburg*[207] the ECJ also held that the refusal to appoint a pregnant woman to a post because of financial loss accruing to the employer for the duration of her pregnancy was not justifiable. Furthermore, the ECJ held that the existence of a statutory prohibition on pregnant women undertaking night-time work did not provide justification for the employer's refusal to appoint a pregnant woman to a post for an indefinite period, even though the statutory prohibition prevented her appointment to the post from the outset and from working in the post for the duration of her pregnancy.

Dismissal of Pregnant Employees

[6-66] In *Hertz*[208] the ECJ had to consider if the dismissal of a pregnant employee was also in contravention of the Equal Treatment Directive. The Court held that the dismissal of a female employee because of her pregnancy amounted to direct discrimination on the grounds of sex. The Court also drew a clear distinction between *pregnancy* and *illness*: the latter is not an issue that falls under the protection afforded to pregnant employees *even where* the illness is attributable to pregnancy, but manifests itself after the maternity leave. The ECJ held that there is no reason to distinguish such an illness from any other illness.

[6-67] The ECJ confirmed its decision in *Hertz* that dismissal of a pregnant employee is direct discrimination on the grounds of sex in *Habermann-Beltermann*.[209] Mrs Habermann-Beltermann had applied for a job as a night attendant in home for the elderly. She was appointed to the post and signed the employment contract on 23 March 1992. The commencement date of the contract was 1 April 1992. The employment contract was for an indefinite period and one of the specific terms of the contract was that Mrs Habermann-Beltermann was to undertake night-time work only. From 29 April to 12 June 1992, Mrs Habermann-Beltermann was off work due to illness. According to a medical certificate dated 29 May 1992 she was pregnant. The pregnancy commenced on 11 March 1992, although she was unaware that she was pregnant when she signed her contract of employment. Her employer sought to terminate the contract of employment because of the German law prohibition on pregnant employees being assigned night-time work. The national court held that this statutory prohibition rendered the employment contract void. Thus, the employer was not seeking to dismiss the employee solely on the grounds of her pregnancy: rather it was as a consequence of the legislation in place to protect pregnant workers. However, the ECJ ruled that despite the existence of this statutory prohibition, the employer could not dismiss Mrs Habermann-Beltermann on the grounds of her pregnancy as her contract was for

---

[206] At para 12.
[207] Case C-207/98 *Mahlburg v Land Mecklenburg-Vorpommern* [2000] ECR I-549.
[208] Case C-179/88 *Handels- og Kontorfunktionaererernes Forbund I Danmark (Hertz) v Dansk Arbedjdsgiverforening* [1990] ECR I-3979.
[209] Case C-421/92 *Habermann-Beltermann v Arbeiterwohlfahrt, Bezirksverband Ndb./Opf, e.V* [1994] ECR I-01657.

an indefinite period. Therefore the statutory prohibition would not apply to the entire duration of her contract of employment. Thus, to dismiss her because of her temporary inability to perform her contract, due to pregnancy, would contravene the provisions of the Equal Treatment Directive.

The ECJ held in *Webb*[210] that dismissal of an employee on account of her pregnancy [6–68] was in breach of the Equal Treatment Directive. In this case, Mrs Webb had initially been hired to cover the maternity leave of another employee, Mrs Stewart, but was to continue in the job after Mrs Stewart's return from her maternity leave. Two weeks after she accepted the post she discovered that she was pregnant. She was dismissed when she informed the employer of her pregnancy. The employer claimed that Mrs Webb was dismissed due to her unavailability to work during the period she was needed to cover Mrs Stewart's maternity leave and that the dismissal was not connected with her pregnancy. The ECJ, in applying its earlier decision in *Hertz*, rejected the employer's argument, on the grounds that Mrs Webb's contract was for an indefinite period and it was not a fixed-term contract. The ECJ held that the:

> "...dismissal of a pregnant woman recruited for an indefinite period cannot be justified on grounds relating to her inability to fulfil a fundamental condition of her employment contract".[211]

The ECJ also held that the fact that Mrs Webb had been hired on a contract to [6–69] specifically cover maternity leave before she became pregnant could not justify the dismissal.[212]

As noted above, one of the difficulties arising from pregnancy discrimination claims under equality law in the past had been that there was no clear male comparator for a pregnant woman and this very often led to the pregnant woman being compared to a hypothetical "sick male". It was in *Webb* that the ECJ conclusively ruled that pregnancy was a condition unique to women and therefore not comparable to any hypothetical male illness or other "pathological condition".[213]

The ruling of the ECJ in *Webb* did cause concern that it could give rise to employers [6–70] being able to justify the dismissal of a pregnant employee employed on a *fixed-term* contract.[214] However, the ECJ ruled in *Tele-Danmark*[215] that a pregnant woman could

---

[210] Case C-32/93 *Webb v EMO Cargo (UK) Ltd* [1994] ECR I-3567. See Flynn, "Webb's Edge: Fixed Term Contracts and Pregnancy" (1995) 13 ILT 81.
[211] At para 26.
[212] At paras 26 and 28.
[213] At paras 24-25. Note that in Case C-63/08 *Pontin v T-Comalux SA*, the ECJ held that the Equal Treatment Directive precludes legislation of a Member State, such as that at issue in the case, which denies a pregnant employee who has been dismissed during her pregnancy the option to bring an action for damages, whereas such an action is available to any other employee who has been dismissed, where such a limitation on remedies constitutes less favourable treatment of a woman related to pregnancy.
[214] Barnard, *op.cit,* p 448.
[215] Case C-109/00 *Tele-Danmark A/S v Kontorfunktionaerernes Forbund I Danmark* [2001] ECR I-6993.

not be dismissed on the grounds that her contract of employment was for a fixed-term. In this case, the woman was employed on a six-month fixed-term contract. She spent two months on a training course. After commencing employment, she informed her employer that she was pregnant and was subsequently dismissed. Her employer argued that she could not perform a substantial part of her duties and that, by failing to mention her pregnancy before she was employed, there had been a violation of the principle of good faith. However, it was held that the employee is under no legal obligation to inform the employer of her pregnancy, as an employer has no legal right to be made aware of pregnancy at the time of appointment. The ECJ held that:

> "[s]ince the dismissal of a worker on account of pregnancy constitutes direct discrimination on grounds of sex, whatever the nature and extent of the economic loss incurred by the employer as a result of her absence because of pregnancy, whether the contract of employment was concluded for a fixed or an indefinite period has no bearing on the discriminatory character of the dismissal. In either case the employee's inability to perform her contract of employment is due to pregnancy."[216]

The ECJ confirmed that the duration of the employment relationship has no bearing on the extent of the protection guaranteed to pregnant workers by EU law.

[6–71]   The ECJ confirmed that Art 10 of the Pregnancy Directive prohibits the dismissal of pregnant workers, irrespective of the duration of the employment contract, in *Jimenez Melgar*.[217] Here, the ECJ had to consider whether the non-renewal of a fixed-term contract was justifiable under Art 10 of the Directive where the employee in question was pregnant. The ECJ ruled that the non-renewal of a fixed-term contract does not *automatically* breach Art 10 of the Pregnancy Directive: it is only where it is evident that the reason for the non-renewal of the fixed-term contract is the employee's pregnancy, i.e. where the non-renewal could amount to a refusal to employ the pregnant worker, that the Article is breached. As such, the non-renewal would constitute direct discrimination on the grounds of sex in contravention of the Equal Treatment Directive. The ECJ's decision in *Jimenez Melgar* is a clear signal that Art 10 of the Pregnancy Directive 92/85 supersedes the ECJ's earlier decisions on pregnancy-related dismissals under the Equal Treatment Directive.[218]

Pregnancy-Related Illness and Dismissal

[6–72]   The ECJ has not always provided pregnant women with complete protection from less favourable treatment or indeed dismissal when those women are suffering from pregnancy-related illness. In *Hertz*[219] the applicant had taken a considerable amount of

---

[216] At para 31.

[217] Case C-438/99 *Jimenez Melgar v Ayuntamiento de Los Barrios* [2001] ECR I-6915. Art 10 of the Pregnancy Directive prohibits the dismissal of workers during the period from the beginning of pregnancy until the end of maternity leave, save in exceptional circumstances unconnected with pregnancy.

[218] Deakin and Morris, *Labour Law* (5th ed, Hart, Oxford, 2009), p 639. See also Case C-460/06 *Paquay v Société d'Architectes Hoet + Minne SPRL* [2007] ECR 1-851.

[219] Case C-179/88 *Handels- og Kontorfunktionaererernes Forbund I Danmark (Hertz) v Dansk Arbedjdsgiverforening* [1990] ECR I-3979.

time off work as sick leave because she suffered from complications during her pregnancy. After her return to work at the end of her maternity leave period, she had to take a further period of sick leave, a total of 100 days, due to pregnancy-related illness. She was dismissed. The ECJ made a clear distinction between the period of maternity leave and the period immediately after the end of the maternity leave period. As such, the ECJ ruled that a pregnant woman is protected from dismissal during any period of maternity leave due to absences caused by pregnancy-related illness. The ECJ refused to extend protection from dismissal for illness, whether connected to the pregnancy or other illness, for the period after the maternity leave period has come to an end. The ECJ held that the dismissal of a woman because of repeated absences from work due to illness not connected to her pregnancy or birth does not amount to direct discrimination on grounds of sex, provided that a male worker in a comparable situation would also be dismissed.[220] Barnard is critical of the ECJ's decision in *Hertz,* as she argues that dismissal on the grounds of pregnancy-related illness should also be considered to be direct discrimination on the grounds of sex.[221] Nevertheless, the restrictive approach of the ECJ regarding dismissals due to absences from work because of pregnancy-related illness, regardless of whether the illness began during or after the period of maternity leave, is also evident in its decision in *Larsson.*[222] The ECJ held in this case that the Equal Treatment Directive did not prohibit employers from dismissing a female worker who had been absent from work due to a pregnancy-related illness, even if the illness initially occurred during the maternity leave period and continued after it had ended.

The ECJ reconsidered its approach to dismissals arising from pregnancy-related illness in *Brown v Rentokil.*[223] The ECJ ruled that a woman could not be dismissed at any time during her pregnancy for absences arising from pregnancy-related illnesses. In this case, Mrs Brown was employed as a driver for Rentokil. She informed her employer of her pregnancy in August 1990. Subsequent to this, she suffered complications associated with her pregnancy. She submitted medical certificates from 16 August onwards detailing the pregnancy-related illnesses. She did not work after this date. In her contract of employment with Rentokil, there was a clause that provided that an employee who was absent from work due to illness for a continuous period of 26 weeks or more would be dismissed. Mrs Brown was informed on 9 November 1990 that her contract of employment would be terminated if she did not return to work by 8 February 1991. Mrs Brown did not return to work in February 1991 and consequently was dismissed. In its decision, the ECJ recognised that pregnancy can give rise to "disorders and complications", which may necessitate either strict medical supervision or complete rest for the pregnant employee for all or part of her pregnancy.[224] The ECJ held that pregnant employees who are absent from work because of pregnancy-related illness should be afforded protection from dismissal. Consequently, the ECJ held that the employer could not take into account

[6–73]

---

[220] At para 17.

[221] Barnard, *op.cit,* p 451.

[222] Case C-400/95 *Larsson v Fotex Supermarked* [1997] ECR I-2757.

[223] Case C-394/96 *Brown v Rentokil* [1998] ECR I-4185.

[224] At para 22.

Mrs Brown's absences from work where these were due to pregnancy-related illness. According to the ECJ the:

> "...dismissal of a female worker during pregnancy for absences due to incapacity for work resulting from her pregnancy is linked to the occurrence of risks inherent in pregnancy and must therefore be regarded as essentially based on the fact of pregnancy. Such a dismissal can affect only women and therefore constitutes direct discrimination on grounds of sex".[225]

[6–74] However, the ECJ did not extend the protection against dismissal for pregnancy-related illness to the period immediately after the ending of maternity leave. During this period, if a female employee becomes ill (irrespective of whether this is related to her pregnancy or not), is absent from work and is dismissed because of this absence, such a dismissal will not amount to a breach of the Equal Treatment Directive, provided that the female employee is treated in the same manner as any comparable male worker who is absent from work because of illness.[226]

[6–75] Recently, in *Mayr*[227] the ECJ had to consider the meaning of a "pregnant worker" in the context of the dismissal of an employee, who was undergoing in vitro fertilisation treatment. Ms Mayr underwent a course of in vitro fertilisation (IVF) treatment and hormone treatment over a period of one and a half months. On 8 March 2005, she underwent a follicular puncture. Ms Mayr's doctor certified that she was sick for the period from 8 to 13 March 2005. Ms Mayr's employer, Flockner, told her by telephone on 10 March 2005 that she was dismissed, with her dismissal taking effect from 26 March 2005. At the time of the IVF treatment, Ms Mayr's ova had been fertilised but had not been implanted into her uterus. On the same day, Ms Mayr sent a letter to Flockner informing her employer that as part of her IVF treatment, the implantation of the fertilised ova into her uterus was scheduled to take place on 13 March 2005. Ms Mayr claimed that she was entitled to protection against dismissal under the provisions of Austrian legislation from the date of the implantation of the fertilised ova. Furthermore, she sought payment of her salary and pro rata annual remuneration from Flockner. Flockner rejected her claim for payment on the basis that she was not pregnant at the time of her dismissal.

[6–76] The question before the ECJ in this case was whether the definition of a pregnant worker under Art 2(a) of Directive 92/85 extended to include a worker, undergoing IVF treatment, who has not yet had the fertilised ova implanted into her uterus and, consequentially, if the prohibition on the dismissal of pregnant workers covered such workers. The ECJ ruled that the Pregnancy Directive does not provide protection from dismissal for a worker who has not yet had the fertilised ova implanted into her uterus. The ECJ's explanation for its decision was based on the principle of legal certainty on the grounds that any extension of the protection against dismissal under the Pregnancy Directive to this category of workers could confer the benefits of this protection *even where* the transfer of the fertilised ova has not taken place, or is postponed for a number of years, or is postponed indefinitely.

---

[225] At para 24.

[226] Case C-394/96 *Brown v Rentokil* [1998] ECR I-4185, para 26.

[227] Case C-506/06 *Mayr v Backerei und Konditorei Gerhard Flockner OHG* [2008] ECR I-1017.

However, the ECJ did indicate that the worker undergoing IVF treatment in such [6–77] circumstances could rely on the protection afforded by the Equal Treatment Directive 76/207 on the grounds of sex discrimination. As only female workers can receive IVF treatment, the ECJ ruled that the dismissal of the female worker because she is in undergoing a course of such treatment amounts to direct discrimination on the grounds of sex: therefore, dismissal on this basis contravenes Arts 2(1) and 5(1) of the Equal Treatment Directive.[228] While the ECJ's decision in this case does not extend the remit of the Pregnancy Directive to include workers undergoing IVF treatment, but who have not yet had the fertilised ova transferred into the uterus, the ECJ did send out a very clear message that dismissal of pregnant workers is in breach of the Pregnancy Directive 92/85 and that:

> "...Article 10 of Directive 92/85 does not provide for any exception to, or derogation from, the prohibition of dismissing pregnant workers, save in exceptional cases not connected with their condition where the employer justifies the dismissal in writing..."[229]

Terms and Conditions of Employment

The ECJ has ruled that discrimination in relation to pregnant workers can arise not [6–78] only in relation to issues surrounding dismissal, but also with regards to other terms and conditions of employment.[230]

Informing Employers of Pregnancy

A pregnant woman does not have a legal obligation to inform prospective employers [6–79] of her pregnancy, nor does she have to inform the employer of her pregnancy during her contractual period of employment. This question of whether a pregnant woman has a legal obligation to inform the employer, or prospective employer, of her condition arose for consideration in *Busch*.[231] Ms Busch gave birth to a child in June 2000 and began a period of parental leave, which was to last for three years. She became pregnant again in October 2000. She got permission from her employer to terminate her period of parental leave in January 2001 and returned to work in April 2001. She informed her employer that she was seven months pregnant the day after her return to work. Pregnant women were prevented from working in certain circumstances under German law and Ms Busch's employers argued that she was unable to perform her duties due to her pregnant condition. As a consequence, Ms Busch's employers withdrew their consent to her return to work on grounds of fraudulent misrepresentation and mistake. However, the ECJ held that to refuse to allow an employee to return to work because of her pregnancy constituted direct discrimination on the grounds of sex. The ECJ in *Busch*, basing its judgment on *Tele-Denmark*, also confirmed that a woman is under no obligation to tell an employer that she is pregnant prior to accepting a job offer, or prior to returning to work, as the employer is not permitted to take this into consideration when

---

[228] At paras 50-54.

[229] At para 37. See Douglas, "Discrimination: Assisted Reproduction Treatment" (2008) 38 *Fam Law* 512.

[230] See Pitt, *Employment Law* (7th ed, Sweet & Maxwell, London, 2009), chapter 6.

[231] Case C-320/01 *Busch v Klinikum Neustadt GmbH & Co. Betriebs KG* [2003] ECR I-2041.

appointing someone to a job or deciding if the employee can return to work. Furthermore, similar to its decision in *Habermann-Beltermann*, the ECJ stated that the existence of a legislative prohibition in German law preventing pregnant women from working in certain circumstances could not justify the discrimination on the grounds that the pregnant employee would be temporarily unable to perform all of her duties. The ECJ made it very clear that employers could not justify discrimination against pregnant workers because of any financial loss that the employer would incur. The ECJ stated that the extra cost arising from Ms Busch receiving a maternity allowance, which was higher than the parental leave allowance, along with the supplementary allowance paid to her by the employer, could not justify discrimination on the grounds of sex because of her pregnancy.[232]

[6–80] The ECJ's decision in *Busch* tested the boundaries of the principle of non-discrimination, especially as the issues arising in this case concerned Ms Busch's request to return to work from parental leave without informing the employer that she was pregnant or that she would then also require maternity leave. The overriding principle of non-discrimination was upheld by the ECJ in this case, as it made very clear that it was unacceptable for an employer to take the employee's pregnancy into account when deciding whether the employee could return to work.[233]

Appraisals, Bonuses and Service Periods

[6–81] That the ECJ has taken an increasingly pro-worker approach to the treatment of pregnant women in the workplace can be seen in its decision in *Thibault*.[234] In this case, Mrs Thibault was employed in 1983 by CNAVTS. She had been absent from work due to illness on three different occasions (4-13 February; 3-16 March; 16 May-12 June), before going on maternity leave for the period between 13 June and 1 October for which she was entitled to claim full pay. This was followed immediately by a period of maternity leave on half pay from 3 October to 16 November 1983. CNAVTS refused to assess Mrs Thibault's performance for this period on the basis that she had not been present at work for at least six months of the year, which was a requirement of the CNAVTS standard service regulations. The primary reason for Mrs Thibault's absence was her period of maternity leave. The ECJ held that a failure to conduct a performance assessment of a female employee who had been absent from work because of her pregnancy constituted direct discrimination on the grounds of sex. The ECJ explained in this case that:

> "[t]he principle of non-discrimination requires that a woman who continues to be bound to her employer by her contract of employment during maternity leave should not be deprived of the benefit of working conditions which apply to both men and women and are the result of that employment relationship. In circumstances such as those of this case, to deny a female employee the right to have her performance assessed annually would discriminate against her merely in her capacity as a worker because, if she had not been pregnant and had not taken the maternity leave to which she was entitled, she would have been

---

[232] At para 46.

[233] Bolger, *op.cit*, p 75.

[234] Case C-136/95 *CNAVTS v Thibault* [1998] ECR I-2011.

assessed for the year in question and could therefore have qualified for promotion".[235]

Accordingly, a woman who is absent from work for the purposes of maternity leave retains her right to have an annual assessment of her performance in the workplace and should not be denied the opportunity of promotion due to such absence. Failure of the employer to conduct this annual appraisal of the employee, or indeed to overlook the female employee for promotion, for reasons connected with her pregnancy or maternity leave will constitute direct discrimination on the grounds of sex. [6–82]

In *Lewen*[236] the ECJ held that an employer could not take periods of maternity leave into account when deciding to grant a Christmas bonus, so as to reduce the benefit pro rata. To do so would be direct discrimination on the grounds of sex.

The ECJ further strengthened the protection afforded to pregnant workers under the Equal Treatment Directive in *Sarkatzis Herrero*.[237] This case concerned a woman who was initially employed in a temporary post. Ms Sarkatzis Herrero was successful in a competition to recruit permanent staff and was appointed to the post of administrative assistant, which she had to commence within one month. At the time of her appointment, she was on maternity leave and she asked the employer to defer the commencement of the post until the end of her maternity leave period. She also sought to have her period of maternity leave taken into account for the purposes of calculating her seniority from the date of her initial appointment and not from the date that she actually began her post at the end of the maternity leave period. The employer allowed her to defer the start of her post until the end of the maternity leave period, but did not grant her request regarding the calculation of her seniority from the date of her appointment to the new post. The ECJ held that failing to take her maternity leave period into account for the purposes of calculating her seniority of service from the date of her appointment was discriminatory and in breach of the Equal Treatment Directive. [6–83]

Payment During Pregnancy

There is no automatic entitlement to full pay during the period of maternity leave. The ECJ considered the issue of payment during maternity leave in *Gillespie*.[238] In 1988, the applicants, who were employees of various health services, took maternity leave and were paid less than their normal full rate of pay. A pay increase was awarded in November 1988 in the health services and this was backdated to 1 April 1988. The employees in question, however, did not receive this increase and claimed that they were discriminated against on the grounds of sex. The questions before the ECJ concerned whether women on maternity leave were entitled to receive full pay and if they also had an entitlement to any pay increases granted before or during their period of maternity leave. In acknowledging that maternity benefit did constitute "pay" under [6–84]

---

[235] At para 29.

[236] Case C-333/97 *Lewen v Lothar Denda* [1999] ECR I-07243. See Kimber, "Equal Treatment for Employees on Leave and Bonus Payments" (2005) 2(2) IELJ 53.

[237] Case C-294/04 *Sarkatzis Herrero v Instituto Madrileño de la Salud (Imsalud)* [2006] ECR I-1513.

[238] Case C-342/93 *Gillespie v Northern Health and Social Services Board* [1996] ECR I-5723.

the provisions of both Art 119EC (now Art 157TFEU) and also Art 1 of the Equal Pay Directive 75/117,[239] the ECJ ruled that there was no requirement that women should continue to receive full pay for the duration of the maternity leave period, nor were there any specific guidelines to calculate the amount of maternity benefit to be paid. However, the ECJ did stipulate that:

> "... [t]he amount payable could not, however, be so low as to undermine the purpose of maternity leave, namely the protection of women before and after giving birth".[240]

[6–85]   The ECJ stated that, in determining whether the amount payable is adequate, the length of the maternity leave period and any other means of social protection provided for by national law for "justified absence from work" had to be taken into consideration. Furthermore, the ECJ ruled that the amount to be paid had to take into account any pay rise awarded from the beginning of the maternity leave period to the end of that period.[241]

[6–86]   In *Boyle*[242] the ECJ had to consider whether an employer could include a condition in an employee's contract of employment requiring the employee to return to work for at least one month after the child is born in circumstances where the employee has taken time off work for maternity leave, but where the rate of maternity pay is higher than the statutory payments for maternity leave. The ECJ in *Boyle* held that the provisions of Art 119EEC (now Art 157TFEU), Art 1 of the Equal Pay Directive 75/117 and Art 11 of the Pregnancy Directive 92/85 do permit an employer to make maternity payments conditional on the employee's return to work for at least one month. Furthermore, if the employee fails to return to work for this period, the employer can require the employee to repay the difference between the amount of maternity pay she received during her maternity leave period and the statutory rate of maternity pay.

[6–87]   The protection of pregnant employees from discrimination does not include a right to sick pay when the pregnant woman has taken an extensive amount of time off work as a result of pregnancy-related illness.[243] In *McKenna*[244] the question before the ECJ was whether a reduction in pay to a female worker who was absent from work because of pregnancy-related illness constituted sex discrimination. Ms McKenna had taken long-term sick leave during her pregnancy as a consequence of pregnancy-related illness. Initially, she received full pay during her pregnancy but, in accordance with the employer's sick pay provisions, she was then placed on half pay. Ms McKenna submitted that she was unfairly treated in regards to being put on half pay and that this was a breach of her entitlement to equal pay. She also contended that, by taking her

---

[239] Directive 75/117 of 10 February 1975 on the approximation of the laws of the Member States relating to the application of the principle of equal pay for men and women [1975] OJ L45/19, now repealed and replaced by the Recast Equality Directive 2006/54.

[240] At para 20.

[241] At paras 20-25.

[242] Case C-411/96 *Boyle v EOC* [1998] ECR I-6401.

[243] Bolger and Kimber, "Employment Equality" in *Employment Law* (Regan ed, Tottel, Dublin, 2009), p 448.

[244] Case C-191/03 *McKenna v North Western Health Board* [2005] ECR 1-7631.

pregnancy-related illness into consideration when determining her right to sick pay in the future, the employer had subjected her to less favourable treatment on grounds of her pregnancy. The ECJ ruled that the Equal Treatment Directive did not apply in this case as it concerned the right to equal pay. This signalled immediately that the ECJ was adopting a restrictive approach, as the Court has traditionally taken a more pro-worker line in dealing with the equal treatment of pregnant workers than it has in equal pay matters.[245] The ECJ came to the same conclusion as in *Gillespie* and ruled that a woman did not have an automatic entitlement to full pay during the period of her maternity leave and, by the same token, a woman who was absent from work due to pregnancy-related illness did not have an automatic right to full sick pay. Thus, the conclusion of the ECJ was that the reduction of pay, or the reduction of sick pay, of female workers during maternity leave did not constitute discrimination:

> "If a rule providing, within certain limits, for a reduction in pay to a female worker during her maternity leave does not constitute discrimination based on sex, a rule providing, within the same limits, for a reduction in pay to that female worker who is absent during her pregnancy by reason of an illness related to that pregnancy also cannot be regarded as constituting discrimination of that kind".[246]

Bolger and Kimber submit that the introduction of the Recast Equality Directive 2006/54, which replaces the Equal Treatment and Equal Pay Directives, could enable the ECJ to adopt a more liberal attitude towards equal pay matters concerning pregnant workers, as this Directive includes "pay" within the concept of "working conditions". However, this optimism is tempered by the fact that the economic motivation behind the judgment in *McKenna* may render any fundamental rethink by the Court unlikely.[247]   [6–88]

VII. Pregnancy Discrimination and Irish Law

The Equality Act 2004 introduced a definition of pregnancy discrimination into Irish law for the first time. Section 6(2A) of the Employment Equality Acts 1998-2008 provides that "discrimination will occur on the gender ground where a female employee is subject to discrimination on the basis of her maternity leave or pregnancy". Thus, under s 8 of the Acts, employees cannot be discriminated against on the grounds of their pregnancy in relation to: access to employment; conditions of employment; training or experience for or in relation to employment; promotion or re-grading; or classification of posts. The Equality Tribunal and the Labour Court have been very proactive in protecting the rights of pregnant employees in the workplace.   [6–89]

Dismissal of Pregnant Employees

Under the Unfair Dismissals Acts 1977-2007, an employee's dismissal is deemed to be automatically unfair if the dismissal is due to her pregnancy, unless there are substantial grounds justifying the dismissal.[248] Pregnant employees may, however, be   [6–90]

---

[245] Craig and de Búrca, *EU Law: Text, Cases and Materials* (4th ed, Oxford University Press, Oxford, 2008), chapter 24; Bamforth *et al, op.cit,* chapter 10.

[246] At para 60.

[247] Bolger and Kimber, "Employment Equality" in *Employment Law* (Regan ed, Tottel, Dublin, 2009), p 449.

[248] See also chapter 10.

dismissed by way of redundancy. In *Mason v Winston's Jewellers*[249] the claimant was employed as a sales assistant from September 2000. She notified her employer that she was pregnant in May 2001 and agreed that she would return from her maternity leave period four weeks early to work during the Christmas period. Before the commencement of her maternity leave period, Ms Mason went on sick leave due to pregnancy-related illness. While she was absent from work at this time, she was sent her P45 and informed in writing of the termination of her contract of employment. The reasons given were that there had been a decrease in business as a consequence of increased competition resulting from the opening of a new shopping centre, which had three jeweller's shops, 500 metres from Winston's Jewellers. Ms Mason brought her claim to the Labour Court on the grounds that she had been dismissed for reasons connected with her pregnancy. The Labour Court disagreed and held that she had not been discriminated against, that the reasons for the termination of her contract of employment were genuine and not in any way connected with her pregnancy. The Labour Court took into account evidence of the employer's financial difficulties and was satisfied that a genuine redundancy situation existed.

[6–91]   In *Gleeson v L'Oreal Luxury Products Ltd*[250] the claimant was employed as an Account Development Executive (ADE) for L'Oreal Luxury Products. In 2004, two of the four account development executives were made redundant and, following a review of this role, Gleeson's position was made redundant in 2006. Gleeson had been absent from work because of a pregnancy-related illness from April 2006. Gleeson claimed that the reason for her being selected for redundancy was as a consequence of her informing the employer of her intention to start a family. She also claimed that freelance artists were engaged to conduct her job as ADE after she left the company and that an offer of alternative work, effectively, was a demotion from her position as ADE. The EAT dismissed Gleeson's claim on the grounds that a genuine redundancy situation existed because of re-structuring that had taken place within the company. The EAT held that Gleeson's pregnancy was not a contributory factor in her being made redundant and that her redundancy was in fact "fair, reasonable and genuine", taking into account the offer made to Gleeson of alternative work within the company.

[6–92]   A similar situation arose in *Kearney v Lettertec Ireland Limited*.[251] Ms Kearney began work as an administrative assistant for Lettertec in May 2005. She notified her employer that she was pregnant in November. After this, Ms Kearney claimed that there was an immediate change to the terms and conditions of her employment regarding her duties and workload, causing her to suffer a stress-related illness for which she had to take time off work. Ms Kearney subsequently decided to resign in December because of her stress, with her resignation to take effect at the start of the Christmas holidays, although she had indicated that she was prepared to continue working until the end of January 2006. The employer had officially accepted her resignation, but in January Lettertec offered Ms Kearney a contract allowing her to work three days a week under the same terms and conditions as before. She returned to work under this new contract. Six weeks before the date of commencement of her

---

[249]   [2003] ELR 108.
[250]   UD 115/2008.
[251]   DEC-E2008-054.

maternity leave period, she was informed of the termination of her employment because of redundancy. Ms Kearney alleged that she was dismissed for reasons connected with her pregnancy. Her claim was rejected as the employer was able to produce evidence demonstrating that there were justifiable reasons for the termination of her contract that were not related to her pregnancy. There had been a significant decrease in the sales and profits of the business. Coupled with this financial uncertainty was the fact that her revised contract was temporary and part-time and its renewal was dependent upon the company's commercial performance. In addition, the company's practice regarding selection for redundancy was based on "last in, first out" and there had been a reduction of both male and female employees in the workforce.

Availability for Work

The unavailability for work of an employee is not a sufficient justification for the [6–93] dismissal of a pregnant employee in Ireland. In *Fox v National Council for the Blind*,[252] the issue concerned a pregnant employee, who had a fixed-term contract of employment stating that she had to be available for a period of essential training. This training period was due to occur during her maternity leave period. Due to her unavailability to undergo the necessary training at this time, Ms Fox was dismissed. She submitted a claim on the grounds that she had been discriminated against because of her pregnancy. Both the Equality Tribunal and the Labour Court held that she had not been subject to discrimination on the grounds of her sex, arising from her pregnancy, by making a distinction in this case between a fixed-term contract and a contract of indefinite duration, such as arose in the ECJ's decision in *Webb v EMO Air Cargo*.[253] However, the shift in approach to pregnancy discrimination claims relating to fixed-term contracts is evident in *Rabbitte v EEC Direct*.[254] Here, Ms Rabbitte's contract of employment began on 21 November 2005. She informed her employer of her pregnancy on 28 November 2005 and was dismissed. The employer's rationale for the dismissal was that the employee was specifically appointed on a fixed-term contract for the duration of another employee's maternity leave but, because of her pregnancy, Ms Rabbitte would no longer be available to provide this cover. The Equality Officer noted the ECJ decision in *Webb,* whereby the dismissal of an employee in such circumstances was held to constitute discrimination. Consequently, the Equality Tribunal held that the dismissal of Ms Rabbitte was discriminatory as it was due to her pregnancy. The Equality Tribunal issued an award of €18,000 compensation; €2,000 of this was for Ms Rabbitte's loss of earnings.

Health and safety concerns can also affect a pregnant employee's availability to work. [6–94] As discussed above, employers have a legal obligation to protect the safety, health and welfare at work of pregnant employees under the Pregnancy Directive and also the provisions of the Safety, Health and Welfare at Work Act 2005. Employers must ensure that a pregnant employee is not subject to unlawful discrimination because of pregnancy when deciding whether it is necessary to place that employee on health and safety leave. In *Doorty v University College Dublin*[255] a pregnant employee who was

---

[252] [1995] ELR 74.
[253] See above for further discussion of the *Webb* case.
[254] DEC-E2008-07.
[255] DEC-E2004-043.

placed on health and safety leave brought a claim of discrimination on the grounds of pregnancy. Dr Doorty was appointed on 1 October 2000 as a Post-Doctoral Research Fellow on a fixed-term contract of employment for two years to undertake laboratory work as part of a research project in the Department of Pharmacology in UCD. She notified the Senior Lecturer in charge of the research project of her pregnancy in January 2002 and informed him of her doctor's concerns regarding her undertaking laboratory work handling known teratogenic drugs, which could cause the unborn child to develop malformations. A risk assessment, undertaken on 28 January 2002, verified the high risk factors to both the pregnant employee and her unborn child, concluding that the laboratory and her office were not suitable places for her to continue working. Consequently, it was recommended that Dr Doorty be either offered alternative duties away from the laboratory, or be placed on health and safety leave in accordance with the Maternity Protection Act 1994. Dr Doorty was informed that she was being placed on health and safety leave from 11 March 2002. Dr Doorty brought a challenge on the grounds that she should not have be placed on health and safety leave as she had been working full-time in the weeks prior to this. The respondent, UCD, denied that the placing of Dr Doorty on health and safety leave was discriminatory given that the recommendation based on the risk assessment was that there was no suitable alternative work that she could carry out during her pregnancy because of the potential risks to both her and her unborn child. However, the Equality Tribunal held that UCD did not sufficiently consider the available options which would have allowed Dr Doorty to continue with the duties that she was still able to perform: failure to take into account Dr Doorty's ability to conduct alternative work did amount to discrimination on the grounds of gender, relating to her pregnancy.[256]

Pregnant Employees, Disciplinary Procedures and Dismissal

[6–95] To justify the dismissal of a pregnant employee, the employer has to demonstrate that there exist circumstances grounding dismissal that are not connected with her pregnancy. In *Bermingham v Colour's Hair Team*[257] Ms Bermingham had worked for the employer, a hair salon, for almost a year when she notified her supervisors of her pregnancy. Subsequent to this Ms Bermingham claimed that both the director and manager of the salon ignored her, that she was prevented from going for lunch with other colleagues, that colleagues stopped talking to her and that her regular clients were assigned to someone else. She was dismissed without prior warning. The employer indicated that the reason for her dismissal was based on disciplinary problems (including a lack of motivation, commitment and professionalism, a failure to turn up to work on a number of occasions, lateness and customer complaints) and was not in any way related to her pregnancy, as it had employed pregnant workers in the past and some of the existing staff had small children. Ms Bermingham did acknowledge the employer's account regarding her conduct in the workplace, but contended that she was not made aware that these constituted disciplinary matters, as she had only been given one verbal warning and had never been provided with a written warning. The Tribunal ruled that the employer had failed to prove that the reason for dismissing the employee was unconnected to her pregnancy. The decision in this case highlights the importance of implementing any internal disciplinary procedures before dismissing an

---

[256] See also *LW Associates v Lacey* (HSD 085/2008).
[257] DEC-E2008-040.

employee. In *McGuirk v Irish Guardian Publishers*[258] similar problems arose concerning the employee's alleged poor performance, but here the employer had undertaken appraisals with the employee and disciplinary meetings had been conducted to discuss the employee's performance, at which she was informed of the consequences should her performance not improve. Ms McGuirk notified her employer of her pregnancy. Her contract of employment was terminated shortly after this. Ms McGuirk claimed that the reason for her dismissal was her pregnancy. However, the Tribunal ruled that the decision to dismiss her was not connected with her pregnancy and instead was justified because of her poor performance. The fact that the employer had implemented the disciplinary process to deal with her poor performance enabled the employer to discharge the burden of proof in this case. The importance of not only implementing disciplinary procedures, but also keeping a record of the matters dealt with as part of the process, can, therefore, be critical in establishing whether the dismissal is for reasons other than pregnancy. The timing of dismissal, where it occurs after the employer is notified of the employee's pregnancy, should not automatically imply that pregnancy is the reason for dismissal.[259]

Access to Employment and Pregnant Employees

Rejecting a job applicant on the grounds of pregnancy constitutes a breach of the Equality Acts.[260] In *Costello v Pamela Scott*[261] Ms Costello had gone for a first interview for the position of manager at Pamela Scott after being referred by a recruitment agency. She was invited to a second interview four days later. Ms Costello informed the recruitment agency of her pregnancy on the day before the second interview. The recruitment agency notified her that the second interview was cancelled shortly after this time. Ms Costello claimed she was informed that Pamela Scott was unwilling to appoint a pregnant woman to a managerial position. The Equality Tribunal found that no effort had been made to cancel the interview prior to the recruitment agency notifying the respondent of Ms Costello's pregnancy. Therefore, the Tribunal found that Ms Costello had been discriminated against because of her pregnancy and awarded €7,000 for the distress Ms Costello suffered as a result of this discrimination.

[6–96]

Promotion and Re-grading

Pregnancy should not be a reason to treat an employee less favourably in regards to the possibility of promotion or the re-grading of posts.[262] The Equality Tribunal in *Lane v MBNA*[263] found that Ms Lane had been subject to discrimination due to pregnancy when the employer did not offer her a promotional position, for which she had applied during her maternity leave. Ms Lane further claimed that she had been victimised for complaining about this. Ms Lane worked as a customer service assistant for MBNA and she had discussed promotional opportunities with her manager before she began

[6–97]

---

[258] DEC-E2007-031.
[259] Bolger and Kimber, "Employment Equality" in *Employment Law* (Regan ed, Tottel, Dublin, 2009), p 453.
[260] Employment Equality Acts, s 8(1)(a).
[261] DEC-E2003-048.
[262] Employment Equality Acts, s 8(1)(d).
[263] DEC-E2008-051.

her maternity leave period. When she returned to work, her manager did not discuss the possibility of promotion again, cancelling any meetings set up to do so. Ms Lane claimed that there was a reduction in her duties and responsibilities and also that an external candidate was appointed to the position that she had discussed with her manager with a view to her promotion to this post. The external candidate was unmarried, did not have any children and also had no previous relevant experience. Ms Lane had been told that previous relevant experience was essential for the position. Ms Lane officially complained that she was treated unfairly, but her department manager informed her that there had simply been miscommunication regarding the promotional position. Ms Lane became pregnant for a second time and the employer rejected her official complaint shortly after this. Ms Lane then took stress-related sick leave and was absent from work until the commencement of her maternity leave period. A review of Ms Lane's performance was undertaken during this period and the manager expressed concern about her performance and attitude in the workplace. Ms Lane received a letter from MBNA on 15 March 2007 informing her that she was to be made redundant. Ms Lane was then told that if she waived her right to pursue any claims against MBNA that she would be given an enhanced redundancy package. Ms Lane refused to agree to this offer as it meant that she would be unable to continue with her claim before the Equality Tribunal. Consequently, she was given a reduced redundancy package. As a result, the Tribunal ruled that Ms Lane had been subject to discrimination as the employer failed to objectively justify why she was not offered the promotion. Ms Lane was issued with an award of €56,315.[264]

---

[264] See also *Devereux v Bausch and Lomb* (DEC-E2005-020).

CHAPTER 7
Migrant Workers

I. Introduction

In the second half of the 20th century, international migration has emerged as one of the **[7–01]** main factors in social transformation and development in all regions of the world. The International Organisation for Migration (IOM) estimates that there are now about 192 million people living outside their place of birth, meaning that approximately one of every 35 persons in the world is a migrant.[1] In many cases, people choose to migrate in search of better employment opportunities. As a result, this unprecedented level of movement poses challenges to existing models of employment regulation in receiving (host) countries.[2] In Ireland, the "Celtic Tiger" economic boom of the late 1990s and early 2000s precipitated a quite unprecedented influx of foreign workers into the country; while foreign nationals accounted for around two percent of the employed labour force in 1994, this had jumped to 17 percent by 2006.[3] Up to 2004, the majority of labour migrants to Ireland came under a work permit system targeted at unskilled occupations

---

[1] Castles, "International Migration at the Beginning of the Twenty-first Century: Global Trends and Issues" (2000) 11(165) *International Social Science Journal* 269.

[2] See Shia, "Immigration and its Imperatives" (2009) 15(6) ELJ 683; McGovern, "Immigration, Labour Markets and Employment Relations: Problems and Prospects" (2007) 45(2) *British Journal of Industrial Relations* 217; Krings, "A Race to the Bottom? Trade Unions, EU Enlargement and the Free Movement of Labour" (2009) 15(2) *European Journal of Industrial Relations* 49.

[3] Central Statistics Office, *Census 2006* (CSO, Dublin, 2007).

and administered by the Department of Enterprise, Trade and Employment (DETE).[4] However, the accession of ten new Member States (EU10) to the EU in 2004 heralded a major change in immigration patterns, as the granting of full access to the Irish labour market to citizens of the EU10 led to a dramatic increase in the inflow of migrant workers from these new Member States.[5] It is undoubtedly the case that the scale and speed of the increase in labour-related migration to Ireland came as a surprise to the governments of the day (as well as other labour market actors, principally trade unions and employer groups). As a result, immigration policy has developed over the last number of years on a "somewhat ad hoc basis under a less than satisfactory legislative regime".[6] Linked with the question of immigration are issues of residency and citizenship rights, as foreign workers may apply for Irish citizenship on the basis of the Irish Naturalisation and Citizenship Acts 1956-2004.

[7-02] This chapter is structured as follows. First, the rights of nationals of the European Economic Area (EEA) to live and work in Ireland will be examined. This is substantially governed by European Union law, in particular Art 45TFEU (ex-Art 39EC). Secondly, the next section will look at the same rights in respect of non-EEA citizens. Finally, the last section will set out briefly the issue of transnational employment, where people work, often temporarily, on an international and cross-border basis.

II. EEA Nationals

[7-03] The European Economic Area is an area of free trade and free movement of peoples comprising the Member States of the European Union, as well as Norway, Iceland and Liechtenstein.[7] As a general rule (and subject to specific exceptions discussed below) EEA nationals do not require permission to enter, or take up employment in, the Republic of Ireland.

The EU Treaties and Direct Effect

[7-04] Articles 45-48TFEU (ex-Arts 39-42EC) deal with the free movement of workers.[8] Article 45(1)TFEU provides that "freedom of movement for workers shall be secured within the

---

[4] Ruhs, *Managing the Immigration and Employment of Non-EU Nationals in Ireland* (The Policy Institute/Trinity College, Dublin, 2005). Note that, in early 2010, a reorganisation of governmental departments resulted in the re-naming of the department, which is now known as the Department of Enterprise, Trade and Innovation; see www.entemp.ie.

[5] Barrett, *EU Enlargement and Ireland's Labour Market* (Institute for the Study of Labour (IZA), Bonn, 2009). Ireland was one of only three countries (the others were Sweden and the UK) to allow full labour market access to citizens from the EU10 from 2004; other existing Member States availed of the opportunity to impose the "transitional restrictions" allowed by the Accession Treaties; see Currie, *Migration, Work and Citizenship in the Enlarged European Union* (Ashgate, London, 2008).

[6] Buckley and Connolly, "Immigration" in *Employment Law* (Regan ed, Tottel, Dublin, 2009), p 715.

[7] Note also that the European Communities and Swiss Confederation Act 2001 enables the free movement of workers between Switzerland and Ireland, without the need for employment permits. Unless otherwise stated in this chapter "EEA nationals" will also be taken to refer to Swiss nationals.

[8] See, generally, Craig and de Búrca, *EU Law: Text, Cases and Materials* (4th ed, Oxford University Press, Oxford, 2008); Barnard, *EC Employment Law* (3rd ed, Oxford University Press, Oxford, 2006).

Union". While the original provisions very much reflected the economic basis of the Union's founding Treaties, the ECJ, from early on, recognised that the worker was not to be seen solely as a "mere source of labour, but as a human being".[9] The Court (and indeed the Commission) has viewed the free movement principle as being the source of not simply an *economic*, but also a *social*, right. This broad view of free movement has particular implications in terms of the rights of movement of the worker's family. The amendments introduced by Treaty on the European Union (1992; now amended by the Treaty of Lisbon) also saw a shift in focus away from the economic foundations of the Union to a more social basis. This was reflected in the establishment of the concept of European citizenship, now found in Art 20TFEU (ex-Art 17EC), which, subject to the limitations and conditions laid down in the Treaties and secondary legislation, entitles EU nationals to move and reside throughout the EU without references to economic status (Art 21TFEU, ex-Art 18EC).

Article 45TFEU (ex-Art 39EC) is the essential Treaty provision under which the free movement of workers is secured within the Union. The Article requires the abolition of any discrimination based on nationality between workers of the Member States in relation to employment, remuneration, and other conditions of work and employment. Article 45(3)TFEU states that a worker has the right to free movement in order to: [7–05]

a. accept offers of employment actually made;
b. move freely within the territory of Member States for this purpose;
c. stay in a Member States for the purpose of employment under the same provisions laid down by law, regulation or administrative action governing employment of nationals of that Member State; and
d. remain in the territory of a Member State after employment in that State, subject to conditions contained in secondary legislation.

The right to free movement is directly effective,[10] and has both *vertical* (*Bosman*)[11] and *horizontal* (*Angonese*)[12] effect. It may be invoked by the employee and the employer.[13] The ECJ has used Art 18TFEU (ex-Art 12EC) on the principle of non-discrimination on grounds of nationality, in conjunction with Art 45TFEU, to ensure that nationals of all Member States receive equal treatment with the host Member State's nationals in the context of employment rights. [7–06]

The right to free movement may be subject to limitations imposed by a Member State on grounds of public policy, public health or public security and the provisions do not apply to employment in the public service (Art 45(4)TFEU). Article 46TFEU (ex-Art 40EC) allows for secondary legislation to be passed. The European Parliament and the Council can, in accordance with the ordinary legislative procedure and after consulting [7–07]

---

[9] As noted by Advocate General Trabucchi in Case 7/75 *Mr and Mrs F v Belgian State* [1975] ECR 679.
[10] On the meaning of direct effect see, generally, Craig and de Búrca, *op.cit,* chapter 8.
[11] Case C-415/93 *Union Royal Belge des Societies de Football Association v Bosman* [1995] ECR I-4921.
[12] Case C-281/98 *Angonese Cassa di Risparmio di Bolanzo SpA* [2000] ECR I-4139.
[13] Case C-350/96 *Clean Car Autoservice* [1998] ECR I-2521.

the Economic and Social Committee, issue directives or make regulations setting out the measures required to bring about freedom of movement for workers, as defined in Art 45TFEU. As will be seen below, a number of important directives and regulations in this area have been passed under ex-Art 40EC.

[7–08] It should also be noted that new Title V of the TFEU (the Area of Freedom, Security and Justice) replaces the old title IV of the EC Treaty on visas, asylum, integration and other free movement of persons policies.[14] The aim of Title V is to ensure the absence of internal border controls for persons and to frame a common policy on asylum, immigration and external border control, based on solidarity between Member States, which is fair towards third-country nationals.[15]

Who is a "Worker"?

[7–09] It is important to determine the employment status of an individual (particularly whether he or she is classed as an employee, or is deemed to be self-employed) in order to establish whether or not particular legislative rights can be accessed was noted in chapter 2. The Treaties and secondary legislation at EU level do not define the term "worker", so it has been left to the ECJ to shape the meaning of the term in a series of Art 267TFEU (ex-Art 234EC) references. In *Levin*[16] the ECJ held that the definition of a worker must be an EU one and could not be determined by the laws of the Member States. The ECJ held that, as the free movement of persons is a fundamental freedom, it must be broadly interpreted. As such, the *purpose or motive* of the worker is immaterial as long as he or she is pursuing a *genuine and effective* economic activity (to the exclusion of activities that are on such a small scale as to be regarded as purely *marginal or ancillary*). As a result, the Court found in the case that "worker" would encompass persons engaged in part-time and seasonal work, provided the work was "real" work of an economic nature. The Court explicitly recognised the role of part-time work as an effective means of improving a worker's living conditions. In *Lawrie-Blum*[17] the ECJ found that the essential characteristic of a worker is the performance of services under the direction of another in return for remuneration during a certain period of time. Here, a trainee teacher was a worker for the purposes of Art 45TFEU (ex-Art 39EC).

[7–10] In *Steymann*[18] a member of a religious community paid "keep" and pocket money but not paid formal wages was held to be a worker, where the commercial activity (in this case the person in question did plumbing work for a religious community) was a genuine and inherent part of membership. Somewhat contradictorily, in

---

[14] Protocols attached to the TFEU explicitly allow the UK to "opt out" of provisions in Arts 26 and 77TFEU and maintain border controls. The same applies to Ireland as long as the "common travel area" between the countries is maintained. The Protocols also provide that Ireland and the UK will not take part in the adoption by the Council of proposed measures pursuant to Title V. No decision of the Court of Justice of the European Union interpreting such provisions or measures adopted under Title V will be binding upon, or applicable in, the UK or Ireland. Both countries may "opt in" at a later stage (subject to the agreement of the other Member States). The two countries can also "opt in" to specific measures adopted. See, further, below.

[15] Art 67TFEU.

[16] Case 53/81 *Levin v Staatsecretaris van Justitie* [1982] ECR 1035.

[17] Case 66/85 *Lawrie-Blum v Land Baden-Wurttemberg* [1986] ECR 2121.

[18] Case 196/87 *Steymann v Staatsecretaris van Justitie* [1988] ECR 6159.

Bettray[19] a person who was paid for activities carried out as part of a state-run drug rehabilitation scheme was held *not* to be engaged in real and genuine economic activity, as the activities performed did not seem to serve some economic purpose. However, in *Trojani*,[20] a man living in a Salvation Army hostel was given board, lodging and some pocket money in return for doing various jobs for about 30 hours a week as part of a personal socio-occupational reintegration programme. The ECJ established that he did perform services under the direction of the hostel and he was remunerated. It was for the national court to ascertain if the paid activity in question was real and genuine. In doing so, it would have to consider whether the services actually performed were capable of being regarded as forming part of the normal labour market (looking at the status and practices of the hostel, the content of the social reintegration programme, and the nature and details of performance of the services). In *Kurz*[21] the ECJ summarised some of the principles established in earlier cases by saying that the classification of the employment relationship under national law, the level of productivity of the person concerned, the origin of the funds from which the remuneration is paid, or the limited amount of remuneration would *not* have any consequence in deciding whether or not the person is a worker. These ideas were reiterated in *Vatsouras*,[22] where a German Court referred questions to the ECJ on the assumption that the applicants were not workers, as the "brief minor" professional activity engaged in by the first did not "ensure him a livelihood" and the activity pursued by the second "lasted barely more than one month". The ECJ ruled that, independently of the limited amount of the remuneration and the short duration of the professional activity, it could not be ruled out that such professional activity, following an overall assessment of the employment relationship, could be considered by the national authorities as real and genuine, thereby allowing its holder to be granted worker status.

In *Antonissen*[23] the ECJ took a purposive approach to Art 45TFEU (ex-Art 39EC), to [7–11] include as workers those who are *seeking* work. However, the Court found that the status of such workers is not the same as someone actually employed; for example, rights to unemployment insurance could be restricted and Member States could expel a job seeker after a period of time without invoking Art 45(3)TFEU (ex-Art 39(3)EC). However, this must now be read in the light of the growing jurisprudence on EU citizenship.[24] For example, in *Collins*,[25] the ECJ held that financial payments, such as a job-seeker's allowance, would now fall among payments that were to be granted to all EU citizens on an equal basis (overturning previous decisions like *Lebon*).[26] Here, an Irishman arrived in the UK and immediately applied for a job-seeker's allowance. He was refused as he did not satisfy the requirement of being "ordinarily resident" in the

---

[19] Case 344/87 *Bettray v Staatsecretaris van Justitie* [1989] ECR 1621.

[20] Case C-456/02 *Trojani v Centre public d'aide sociale de Bruxelles* [2004] ECR I-7573.

[21] Case C-188/00 *Kurz v Land Baden-Württemberg* [2002] ECR I-10691.

[22] Joined Cases C-22/08 and C-23/08 *Vatsouras and Koupatantze v Arbeitsgemeinschaft.*

[23] Case C-292/89 *R v Immigration Appeal Tribunal (ex parte Antonissen)* [1991] ECR I-1745.

[24] See Craig and de Búrca, *op.cit*, p 866; Chalmers and Monti, *EU Law Updating Supplement* (Cambridge University Press, Cambridge, 2008), pp 128 *et seq.*

[25] Case C-138/02 *Collins* [2004] ECR I-2703.

[26] Case 316/85 *Lebon* [1987] ECR 2811.

UK. The ECJ held that the UK was allowed to require a job-seeker establish a connection between his claim to such an entitlement and the Member State employment market. However:

> "...while a residence requirement is, in principle, appropriate for the purpose of ensuring such a connection, if it is to be proportionate it cannot go beyond what is necessary in order to attain that objective. More specifically, its application by the national authorities must rest on clear criteria known in advance and provision must be made for the possibility of a means of redress of a judicial nature. In any event, if compliance with the requirement demands a period of residence, the period must not exceed what is necessary in order for the national authorities to be able to satisfy themselves that the person concerned is genuinely seeking work in the employment market of the host Member State".[27]

[7–12]   The key factor here appears to be a "solidarity principle"; the idea that because of the *fact* of EU citizenship there exists a sufficient degree of solidarity between nationals of one Member State, lawfully resident in another, to enable those citizens to claim equal treatment with the host state's own nationals.[28] The concept of equal treatment will be discussed further below. First, it is necessary to consider the explicit restrictions on freedom of movement.

Derogations from the Principle of Free Movement

[7–13]   The free movement provisions do not apply to employment in the public service (Art 45(4)TFEU; ex-Art 39(4)EC). This has been an area of some controversy, as the Member States have consistently argued for a wide interpretation of what constitutes "public service" on the grounds that "the functioning of the public service is an exercise of full State sovereignty".[29] The ECJ, meanwhile, has been concerned to interpret this limitation on free movement as restrictively as possible, given that it is a constraint on the exercise of rights under a fundamental Treaty provision. The Court has made it clear that it, and not the Member States, will define the scope of the exception; the Member States, merely by designating a post as being in the "public service", will not necessarily bring it within the scope of the exemption.[30] In *Commission v Belgium*[31] the Court held that public service posts would require a specific bond of allegiance and mutuality of rights and duties between State and employee; this would involve participation in the exercise of powers conferred by public law and would entail duties designed to safeguard the general interests of the state. The sort of state functions envisaged probably include the armed forces, police,

---

[27] At para 72.

[28] O'Gorman, "The Evolution of the Concept of 'Financial Solidarity' in EU Law" (2006) 6(1) *Hibernian Law Journal* 229.

[29] Mancini, "The Free Movement of Workers in the Case Law of the European Court of Justice" in *Constitutional Adjudication in European Community and National Law* (Curtin and O'Keefe eds, Butterworths, Dublin, 1992), p 67.

[30] Case 152/73 *Sotgiu v Deutsche Bundespost* [1974] ECR 153.

[31] Case 149/79 *Commission v Belgium* [1980] ECR 3881.

judiciary and tax authorities; those probably not included might be nursing and teaching in public establishments.[32]

Outside of the specific area of the public service, Art 45(3)TFEU (ex-Art 39(3)EC) allows Member States to limit free movement for workers on grounds of public policy, public health, and public security.[33] A similar proviso for the self-employed is made in Art 52TFEU (ex-Art 46EC). These derogations do not apply to the *type of work involved* but to the specific *characteristics of particular persons*. Chapter VI of Directive 2004/38[34] governs the exercise by Member States of the derogations and applies to all "measures" taken by Member States concerning entry into the territory of the Member States, issue or removal of residence permits, or expulsion from the territory of Member States on grounds of public policy, public security or public health. Measures cannot be taken on economic grounds. In *Bouchereau*[35] the ECJ defined "measures" as any action affecting the rights of persons coming within the field of application of Art 45TFEU (ex-Art 39EC) to enter and reside freely in a Member State on the same conditions as the nationals of the host Member State. This would cover not only national legislation but also individual decisions taken.   **[7–14]**

Under Art 29 of Directive 2004/38, the diseases justifying restricting freedom of movement are those with epidemic potential, as defined by the relevant instruments of the World Health Organisation, and other infectious diseases or contagious parasitic diseases if they are the subject of protection provisions applying to nationals of the host Member State. The right of residence, after three months, may never be contested on grounds of health. Article 29(3) of the Directive restricts the existing practice in certain Member States of carrying out medical examinations on beneficiaries of the right to residence by requiring there be "serious indications" these are necessary and specifying that they are not to be "routine".   **[7–15]**

The public policy derogation has proven to be the most contentious of the grounds for restricting free movement. In *Van Duyn*[36] the ECJ held that the concept of public policy varies from Member State to Member State and over time. However, the ECJ held that a Member State could not define the term unilaterally, without the input of the Union institutions. Similar points have been made in relation to public security; it is to that extent a "national concept" within the framework of an overall EU approach. In *Rutili*[37] the ECJ held that restrictions on the movement of an EU national under Art 45(3)TFEU (ex-Art 39(3)EC) may not be imposed unless the behaviour of the individual constitutes a *genuine and sufficiently serious threat* to public policy. This principle gives effect to Arts 8 to 11 of the European Convention on Human Rights, which do not permit restrictions in the interests of national security or public safety unless they are necessary to protect those interests in a democratic State.   **[7–16]**

---

[32] Craig and de Búrca, *op.cit,* p 768.

[33] See generally Craig and de Búrca, *op.cit,* pp 783-788; Chalmers *et al, European Union Law* (Cambridge University Press, Cambridge, 2006), pp 584-588.

[34] Directive 2004/38 of 29 April 2004 on the right of citizens of the Union and their family members to move and reside freely within the territory of the Member States [2004] OJ L158/77.

[35] Case 30/77 *R v Bouchereau* [1977] ECR 1999.

[36] Case 41/74 *Van Duyn v Home Office* [1974] ECR 1337.

[37] Case 36/75 *Rutili v Ministre de l'Interieur* [1975] ECR 1219.

[7–17] Measures taken on grounds of public policy or public security must be based exclusively on the *personal conduct* of the individual concerned; Art 27(2) of Directive 2004/38 specifically requires the application of the principle of "proportionality". In *Adoui and Cornaill*[38] two prostitutes were refused residence permits in Belgium (where prostitution was not illegal). The ECJ held that Member States are not entitled to refuse residence to non-nationals on account of conduct that is not illegal for nationals of the host Member State. It seemed to suggest that there would have to be evidence of the need to take *genuine and effective* repressive measures against the conduct of Member State nationals if the same conduct is to be used as a justification for denying entry to non-nationals. A rare example of the derogation being successfully invoked was in *Van Duyn*,[39] against a Dutch national who was a member of the Church of Scientology.

[7–18] Chapter VI of Directive 2004/38 provides important safeguards for parties claiming rights of entry or residence in Member States. Article 28(1) of the Directive requires Member States, before ordering the expulsion of Union citizens or their family members, to take account of the person's degree of integration in the host country and of certain other criteria such as age, state of health and family and economic situation. Article 30 of the Directive specifies the manner in which the person concerned must be notified of any decision restricting their free movement rights and governs various procedural safeguards allowing a right of appeal against such a decision.

Employment and Equal Treatment

[7–19] Workers would not travel from one Member State to another to take up employment if such workers could be discriminated against under the host State's laws. Article 45(2)TFEU (ex-Art 39(2)EC) prevents this by abolishing any discrimination based on nationality between workers of Member States in employment, remuneration and other conditions of work and employment. As will be seen below, the ECJ has also held that measures, which do not in themselves discriminate on the grounds of nationality, but which impede access to the market and are an obstacle or hindrance to free movement, are also prohibited.

[7–20] Regulation 1612/68[40] implements this aspect of the Treaty. The Regulation requires equality of treatment in all matters relating to the actual pursuit of activities of employed persons and the elimination of obstacles to the mobility of workers, particularly the right to be joined by family members and integration of the family into the host Member State. The equality principle applies to eligibility for, and access to, employment, equality of treatment in relation to working conditions whilst in employment (including, *inter alia,* remuneration, dismissal and reinstatement or re-employment on becoming unemployed) and extends certain rights to the worker's family members.

---

[38] Joined Cases 115 and 116/81 *Adoui and Cornaill v Belgian State* [1982] ECR 1665.

[39] Case 41/74 *Van Duyn v Home Office* [1974] ECR 1337.

[40] Regulation 1612/68 of 15 October 1968 on freedom of movement for workers within the Community [1968] OJ L257/2. This regulation has been updated and amended by Directive 2004/38 (see, further, below). In May 2010, the Commission proposed a new Regulation to undertake a codification of Regulation 1612/68. The new Regulation will supersede the various Acts incorporated in Regulation 1612/68 but will fully preserve the content of the Acts being codified (COM (2010)204 final).

Article 24(1) of Directive 2004/38 lays down the principle of equal treatment of Union   **[7–21]** citizens with respect to host country nationals. It broadly takes up the conclusions of the Court of Justice in *Martinez Sala*[41] and establishes a direct link between the principle of non-discrimination and the right of residence (Arts 18 and 21TFEU; ex-Arts 12 and 18EC). The same right is expressly extended to family members, entitled to rights of residence, who are third-country nationals (TCNs). An exception to the right to equal treatment, under Art 24(2) of the Directive, concerns access to social assistance during the first three months of residence or where the person in question has the status of a job-seeker. Under this provision, the host Member State is not obliged to confer entitlement to social assistance on job-seekers for the longer period during which they have the right to reside there. In *Collins*,[42] however, the ECJ ruled that it was not possible to exclude from the scope of Art 45(2)TFEU (ex-Art 39(2)EC) a benefit of a financial nature intended to facilitate access to employment in the labour market of a Member State, although it was legitimate for a Member State to ensure that there is a "genuine link" between an applicant for an allowance and the employment market in question.[43] In *Vatsouras*[44] the ECJ ruled that it is for the competent national authorities not only to establish the existence of a real link with the labour market but also to assess the constituent elements of the benefit, in particular, its purposes and the conditions subject to which it is granted. The objective of the benefit must be analysed according to its results and not according to its formal structure. Therefore, benefits of a financial nature which, independently of their status under national law, are intended to facilitate access to the labour market could not be regarded as constituting "social assistance" within the meaning of Art 24(2) of Directive 2004/38.

EU citizens, therefore, are guaranteed the right to take up and pursue employment in   **[7–22]** the territory of another Member State under the same conditions as nationals of that Member State. Member States are prohibited from discriminating either *directly* or *indirectly* against non-nationals. Directly discriminatory rules (for example, restriction by number or percentage of non-host state EU nationals employed in any particular activity or area)[45] will be prohibited, unless they can be justified by Member States under the explicit derogations outlined above. Rules that are indirectly discriminatory, i.e. rules that appear on their face to be nationality-neutral but in fact favour national, over migrant, workers tend to generate more controversy.[46]

The ECJ has found that workers have been disadvantaged in a number of cases involving   **[7–23]** indirect discrimination. In *Ugliola*[47] the ECJ held that legislation which recognised periods of national service in the home state but not in another Member State for calculating job seniority was indirectly discriminatory. In *Köbler*[48] the applicant was an Austrian academic whose salary was based on length of service. The Austrian courts

---

[41] Case C- 85/96 *Maria Martínez Sala v Freistaat Bayern* [1998] ECR I-26891.
[42] Case C-138/02 *Collins* [2004] ECR I-02703.
[43] Case C-224/98 *D'Hoop* [2002] ECR I-6191.
[44] Joined Cases C-22/08 and C-23/08 *Vatsouras and Koupatantze v Arbeitsgemeinschaft*.
[45] Case 167/73 *Commission v France (Re French Merchant Seamen)* [1974] ECR 359.
[46] See Barnard, *op.cit*, p 190 *et seq.*
[47] Case 15/69 *Südmilch v Ugliola* [1969] ECR 363.
[48] Case C 224/01 *Köbler v Republik Österreich* [2003] ECR I-10239.

upheld a national law which did not take into account periods of service in other Member States. Köbler claimed this ruling was in breach of EU law. The ECJ held that such a regime is likely to impede freedom of movement for workers because, first, it operates to the detriment of migrant workers who are nationals of Member States other than Austria and, secondly, because it would deter workers established in Austria from leaving the country to exercise that freedom. Consequently, such a measure is likely to constitute an obstacle to freedom of movement for workers. In *O'Flynn*[49] the ECJ held that, for indirect discrimination to be established, it was not necessary to prove that a particular measure in practice affected a higher proportion of foreign workers but merely that the measure was "intrinsically liable" to affect migrant workers more than nationals. As noted in *O' Flynn*, however, indirectly discriminatory measures are capable of being objectively justified; such provisions can be saved if they are:

> "...justified by objective considerations independent of the nationality of the workers concerned, and if they are proportionate to the legitimate aim pursued by the national law".[50]

[7–24]   Thus, in *Groener*[51] the Irish State's requirement that teachers in vocational schools in Ireland should be proficient in the Irish language was held to be permissible in light of the national policy on promotion of the Irish language.

It is increasingly apparent, however, that it is not just rules that are overtly discriminatory that can be held to be in breach of the free movement provisions; non-discriminatory rules that impede access to the market may also be caught by Art 45TFEU (ex-Art 39EC) and the secondary legislation.[52] This can be seen in *Bosman*,[53] where a rule that required a football club seeking to sign an out-of-contract player to pay a "transfer fee" to his former club was challenged. The rule was not discriminatory on the grounds of nationality, as it applied equally to transfers between clubs belonging to the same national association as to transfers between clubs belonging to different national associations. Nevertheless, the ECJ held that such a rule directly affected players' access to the employment market in other Member States and was thus capable of impeding freedom of movement for workers. This type of "market impediment" rule, therefore, must be objectively justifiable in order to be lawful.[54]

Article 7(2) of Regulation 1612/68

[7–25]   EU workers from other Member States are entitled to the same "social and tax advantages" as national workers (Art 7(2) of Regulation 1612/68). The ECJ has

---

[49] Case C-237/94 *O'Flynn v Adjudication Officer* [1996] ECR I-2617.

[50] At para 19.

[51] Case 379/87 *Groener v Minister for Education* [1989] ECR 3967.

[52] See, generally, Craig and de Búrca, *op.cit*, p 760; Chalmers *et al*, *op.cit*, p 730; Barnard, *op.cit*, p 192.

[53] Case C-415/93 *Union Royal Belge des Societes de Football Association v Bosman* [1995] ECR I-4921.

[54] See Johnson and O'Keefe, "From Discrimination to Obstacles to Free Movement: Recent Developments Concerning the Free Movement of Workers" (1994) 31 CMLRev 1313. See also the Opinion of Advocate General Sharpston in Case C-325/08 *Olympique Lyonnais v Bernard* on the "objective justification" test laid down in *Bosman*.

interpreted social and tax advantages in a wide manner and, as a result, this provision has been a fruitful source of rights for EU workers and their families. In *Fiorini*[55] an Italian man employed in France had claimed the special French train fare reduction card issued to the parents of large families. After his death, his Italian widow claimed the card but was refused on grounds of nationality. The ECJ held that Art 7(2) of Regulation 1612/68 covers all social and tax advantages, whether or not these derive from contracts of employment. Since the family were lawfully resident in France, family members were entitled to equal "social advantage" under Art 7(2). This approach was followed in *Even*,[56] where the ECJ held that Art 7(2) of Regulation 1612/68 applies to any benefit, whether or not linked to a contract of employment, payable by virtue of an individual's status as a worker, by virtue of residence on national territory and taking into account the benefit's suitability in facilitating mobility within the EU. However, discriminatory rules may be justified. Here, a pension increase granted to Belgians with a war service pension did not fall within Art 7(2) as the purpose in granting the benefit was to compensate these individuals for services rendered, and hardship suffered, for their country. Similarly, the ECJ held, in *Bachmann*,[57] that the need to preserve the cohesion of the national tax system could justify discriminatory treatment in some cases.

Under Art 7(3) of Regulation 1612/68, workers are entitled to access vocational **[7–26]** training on the same terms as Member State nationals. In *Gravier*[58] "vocational training" was defined broadly to include any form of education that prepares for a qualification or provides the necessary training or skills for a profession, trade or employment. Since access to training was likely to promote free movement of workers, the ECJ held that conditions of access fell within the scope of the Treaty. As a result, if a Member State charged a registration fee to migrant students, but not to its own nationals, it would breach Art 18TFEU (ex-Art 12EC).[59]

Directive 2004/38: Entry and Residence Rights

The secondary legislation governing rights of entry, movement and residence for EU **[7–27]** migrant workers consisted, until relevantly recently, of two Regulations and nine Directives.[60] Directive 2004/38 on the right of citizens of the Union and their family members to move and reside freely within the territory of the Member States amends

---

[55] Case 32/75 *Fiorini v SNCF* [1975] ECR 1075.

[56] Case 207/78 *Even* [1979] ECR 2019.

[57] Case C-204/90 *Bachmann v Belgium* [1992] ECR 1-249.

[58] Case 293/83 *Gravier v City of Liege* [1985] ECR 593.

[59] The question of access to maintenance grants (as opposed to fees) has provoked considerable controversy; see, for example, Case 39/86 *Lair v Universitaet Hannover* [1988] ECR 3161; Case C-209/03 *The Queen (on the application of Dany Bidar) v London Borough of Ealing, Secretary of State for Education and Skills* [2005] ECR I-2119; Case C-158/07 *Forster v Hoofddirectie van de Informatie Beheer Groep* [2009] 1 CMLR 32. See, also, Dougan, "Fees, Grants, Loans and Dole Cheques: Who Covers the Costs of Migrant Education Within the EU?" (2005) 42(4) CMLRev 943; Van der Mei, "Union Citizenship and the Legality of Durational Residence Requirements for Entitlement to Student Financial Aid" (2009) 16(4) *Maastricht Journal of European and Comparative Law* 477.

[60] See Craig and de Búrca, *op.cit*, p 770 *et seq.*

Regulation 1612/68 on the free movement of workers and codifies the remaining complex body of previous legislation into one single instrument.[61]

[7–28] The Directive applies to all citizens (not just the economically active) and, basically, creates three "categories" of migrants; those staying in the host Member State for up to three months, those residing for up to five years, and those residing for more than five years (permanent residence).[62] The rights that accrue become more significant the longer a migrant is resident in a Member State. Under the Directive the only requirement for EU citizens in residence for fewer than three months is the possession of a valid identity document (Art 6). Article 7 provides a right of residence of more than three months for EU citizens that are workers or self-employed persons, have sufficient resources not to be a burden on the host Member State, or are students. The same rights and conditions apply to family members who are third-country nationals.[63]

[7–29] Residence may not be withdrawn because a worker is temporarily unable to work (Art 14) through illness or accident or through *involuntary* unemployment. This reflects the ECJ decisions in *Antonissen*[64] and in *Collins*,[65] where the Court ruled that the right of residence that persons seeking employment derive from the Treaty may be limited in time and that, in the absence of EU provisions prescribing a period during which EU nationals who are seeking employment may stay in their territory, the Member States are entitled to lay down a reasonable period for this purpose. In *Antonissen* the Court considered that the period of six months laid down in the national legislation did not appear, in principle, to be insufficient to enable the persons concerned to appraise themselves of offers of employment corresponding to their qualifications and to take, where appropriate, the necessary steps in order to be engaged and, therefore, did not

---

[61] Member States were given until 30 April 2006 to transpose the new Directive; see, generally, Carrera and Faure Atger, "Implementation of Directive 2004/38 in the context of EU Enlargement: A Proliferation of Different Forms of Citizenship?" (2009) *Centre for European Policy Studies Special Report* available at www.ceps.eu. In Ireland, the Directive was transposed by virtue of the European Communities (Free Movement of Persons) (No. 2) Regulations 2006 (SI No 656 of 2006), as amended by the European Communities (Free Movement of Persons) (Amendment) Regulations 2008 (SI No 310 of 2008).

[62] Articles 6, 7, 16, 17 and 18 of Directive 2004/38. Note that nationals of Bulgaria and Romania, both of which joined the Union on 1 January 2007, who come to Ireland must have an employment permit for a continuous period of 12 months. After that they do not need an employment permit to work in Ireland. This is because Ireland has chosen to impose transitional arrangements (permitted as part of the accession arrangements for these countries) on Bulgaria and Romania. This stands in stark contrast to the open approach taken in relation to the EU10 (see above, n 5). The decision to impose the restrictions is to be kept under on-going review and will be assessed comprehensively before the end of 2011; http://www.entemp.ie/labour/ workpermits/bulgariaromania.htm. Nationals from the other countries of the European Economic Area (EEA), that is, Norway, Iceland and Liechtenstein, and those from Switzerland, do not need employment permits to work in Ireland.

[63] See Fahey, "Third-Country National Spouses and the Citizens Rights Directive in Irish Law" (2008) 2 *Irish Journal of Family Law* 32.

[64] Case C-292/89 *R v Immigration Appeal Tribunal (ex parte Antonissen)* [1991] ECRI-1745.

[65] Case C-138/02 *Collins* [2004] ECR I-02703.

jeopardise the effectiveness of the principle of free movement. However, if, after the expiry of that period, the person concerned provides evidence that he or she is continuing to seek employment and that he or she has genuine chances of being engaged, such a person may not be required to leave the territory of the Member State. In *Collins* the ECJ found that a residence requirement was justifiable only where based on objective considerations that are independent of the nationality of the persons concerned and proportionate to the legitimate aim of the national provisions.

Directive 2004/38 introduces, in Art 16, the right of *permanent residence* for EU citizens after five years of continuous residence. Such citizens will no longer be subject to any conditions on the exercise of their right of residence, with virtually complete equality of treatment with nationals. The right of permanent residence may only be lost through absences of more than two consecutive years. Article 18 provides that third-country family members, who have kept their right of residence after the Union citizen died, or after the termination of their marriage or partnership, acquire a permanent right of residence after five years. [7–30]

The worker and his or her family have the right to leave any Member State (Art 4) but a valid identity card or passport must be produced and must be valid for all Member States through which the holder must pass when travelling. There is a right to enter the territory of another Member State (Art 5) on the production of a valid identity card or passport. Member States may only demand entry visas for family members who are not EU nationals; Art 5(2) provides for an exemption from the visa requirement for the holders of a residence card issued by a Member State. [7–31]

Rights of Family Members

Workers would be extremely unwilling to move from one Member State to another if they were not entitled to bring their families with them and have a proper family life.[66] Regulation 1612/68 was designed to facilitate the right of a worker to have his or her family travel from one Member State to another and reside there. The legislation does not in itself create rights, but protects and facilitates the exercise of rights granted by the Treaty.[67] While the Regulation defines a family as including a worker's spouse and descendants who are under 21 years of age or dependent and dependent relatives in the ascendant line of the worker and his or her spouse, Directive 2004/38 expands the definition to include, for the first time, registered partners under the legislation of a Member State, if the legislation of the host Member State treats registered partnerships as equivalent to marriage. This extends the same rights to such a partner's dependent relatives and children. [7–32]

Member States must also "facilitate" the entry and residence of other family members who, in the country from which they have come, are dependants or members of the household of the Union citizen or where serious health grounds strictly require the [7–33]

---

[66] De Hart, "Love Thy Neighbour: Family Reunification and the Rights of Insiders" (2009) 11(3) *European Journal of Migration and Law* 235; Tryfonidou "Family Reunification Rights of (Migrant) Union Citizens: Towards a More Liberal Approach" (2009) 15(5) Emp LJ 634.
[67] Case 48/75 *Procureur du Rol v Royer* [1976] ECR 497.

personal care of the family member.[68] Member States will also have to facilitate the entry and residence of any partner with whom the EU citizen has a durable relationship, duly attested (Art 3(2)). The host Member State shall undertake an extensive examination of the personal circumstances and shall justify denial of entry or residence to these persons. It is important to realise that the rights of families are "parasitic" on the EU citizen's rights; only full workers, or specifically listed family members, can benefit from the substantive rights in the secondary legislation. Article 13 addresses the situation of marital (or partnership) breakdown. Family members who are themselves Union citizens have a residence entitlement in their own right, which is not affected by the termination of a marriage or registered partnership, provided they satisfy the conditions for the exercise of the right of residence as established by Art 7(1) (i.e. show that they are workers or self-employed persons, or that they have sufficient resources for themselves and their family members not to become a burden on the social assistance system of the host Member State). Article 13(2) creates a new right to retain the right of residence for family members who are third-country nationals when the marriage or registered partnership ends. Conditions for retaining the right of residence are, however, strict.

[7–34] As noted above, Art 24 lays down the principle of equal treatment of Union citizens with respect to host country nationals. The same right is expressly extended to family members entitled to a right of residence, who are third-country nationals. The exceptions to the right to equal treatment concern access to social assistance during the first three months of residence or where the person in question has the status of a job-seeker. Article 23 provides that, irrespective of nationality, family members of an EU citizen who have the right of residence or permanent residence in a Member State may take up employment or self-employment there.

[7–35] Despite these provisions, it has been argued that "citizens of the Union who exercise their free movement rights when accompanied by family members who are *also* citizens of the Union encounter far less difficulties" than when they seek to be accompanied (or joined) by third-country national family members.[69] In *Metock*[70] a national of Cameroon married a UK national, who had been living and working in Ireland since late 2006. Mr Metock applied for residence in Ireland as the spouse of an EU national. He was refused as, under the legislation implementing Directive 2004/38, the European Communities (Free Movement of Persons) (No 2) Regulations 2006, Irish law would not grant residence to a non-national spouse of an EU citizen unless that spouse was first "lawfully resident in another Member State". The ECJ, in ruling that the Irish legislation was in breach of the Directive, noted that the Directive did not make reference to any "prior lawful residence" condition. The ECJ held that a refusal to grant rights of entry and residence to spouses of EU citizens represented an

---

[68] In Case 316/85 *Lebon* [1987] ECR 2811 the ECJ held that dependency is a matter of fact; a dependent is a member of the family who is supported by the worker. There is no need for an applicant to establish why the dependent needs support or whether he or she could support himself or herself by working. See also Case C-1/05 *Jia v Migrationsverket* [2007] ECR-I 1 and Case C-291/05 *Minister voor Vreemdelingenzaken en Integratie v Eind* [2007] ECR I-10719.
[69] Carrera and Faure Atger, *op.cit*, p 17.
[70] Case C-127/08 *Metock and Others v Minister for Justice, Equality and Law Reform*.

impediment to such citizens' exercise of their free movement rights. It was for the Union, and not individual Member States, to determine the entry and residence rights of TCN spouses. In response to Member State arguments that the Court's interpretation would prevent the Member States from controlling immigration levels, the ECJ said that Member States may, where this is justified, refuse entry and residence on grounds of public policy, public security or public health, where such a refusal is based on an individual examination of the particular case. Moreover, in accordance with Art 35 of Directive 2004/38, Member States may adopt the necessary measures to refuse, terminate or withdraw any right conferred by the Directive in the case of abuse of rights or fraud, such as marriages of convenience, it being understood that any such measure must be proportionate and subject to the procedural safeguards provided for in the Directive.[71]

III. Non-EEA Nationals

For those not automatically entitled to work in Ireland, permission to do so must be sought through the rather Byzantine employment permit system established under the Employment Permits Acts 2003 and 2006.[72] There are four different types of employment permit: the Green Card Permit, the Work Permit, the Intra-Company Transfer Permit and the Spousal/Dependant Work Permit. These will be considered below, but first it is necessary to examine the general legislative framework.

[7-36]

The Employment Permits Acts

Certain rules apply generally to the granting of employment permits. For example, ss 6 and 7 of the Employment Permits Act 2006 set out the information that must be included on each application form (e.g. nature of the employment; the place at, or in, which the employment concerned is to be carried out; the qualifications, skills or experience required; remuneration; information to do with the foreign national's immigration status, etc). Either the prospective employer or the prospective employee may apply to the Department for Enterprise, Trade and Employment (DETE) for the permit.[73] Applications from recruitment agencies, agents, intermediaries or companies who intend to outsource or subcontract the prospective employee to work in another company are not accepted. Irrespective of who makes the application for the grant of the permit, the foreign national is the grantee of permit.[74] The issue of an employment permit requires a job offer from a prospective Irish employer who has made every

[7-37]

---

[71] See Costello, "Metock: Free Movement and 'Normal Family Life' in the Union" (2009) 46(2) CMLRev 587. Note the European Communities (Free Movement of Persons) (Amendment) Regulations 2008 (SI No 310 of 2008) were made for the purpose of amending the 2006 Regulations in order to reflect the decision in *Metock*.

[72] See Cashman, "Migrant Workers and the Law" (2005) 2(2) IELJ 40.

[73] Employment Permits Act 2006, s 4. A foreign national may not make an application under the section in respect of his or her employment in the State unless an offer of employment in the State has been made in writing to him or her within such period preceding the application as may be prescribed; s 4(3).

[74] Employment Permits Act 2006, s 5. Under s 9, the original of any employment permit granted is issued to the foreign national, with the proposed employer receiving a copy.

effort to recruit an Irish or EEA national for the post.[75] There is also a limit to the proportion of the employer's workforce which can hold an employment permit; permits are not granted to employers where the result of granting the permit would be that more than 50 percent of employees in the firm would be non-EEA nationals.[76] The holder of an employment permit is only permitted to work for the employer and in the employment stated on the permit; it is an offence for both an employer and an employee to be party to the employment of a non-EEA national without a valid employment permit.[77] If the employment is terminated, the permit must be surrendered to the Minister within four weeks of the date of termination.[78]

[7–38]   The legislation also places a number of obligations on employers; these relate, in particular, to record-keeping,[79] proper use of the permit (for example, the obligation not to transfer it to another person or use it in respect of an employment other than the employment in respect of which it has been granted)[80] and the prohibition on penalisation of foreign national employees, in particular where such an employee is accessing or vindicating rights under the 2003 and 2006 Acts.[81] Enforcement of the Acts occurs generally through the use of criminal prosecutions; labour inspectors have a large role in monitoring, and ensuring compliance with, the legislation and both summary prosecutions and prosecutions on indictment are provided for in the legislation.[82]

[7–39]   It is important to realise that this is a sensitive and controversial area of employment law in which political and public policy considerations (many, but crucially not all, of which relate to the employment relationship *per se*) weigh heavily. It is also an area in which Ministerial regulations and administrative discretion play a large role, which means that precise rules on the granting of permits (and related matters) are subject to frequent change. The first of these points can be illustrated by looking at some of the issues the Minister is to consider in deciding whether or not to grant a permit; for example, the extent to which a decision to grant the permit would be consistent with the current economic policy of the Government.[83] There is a great concern in this general policy area to "manage" immigration carefully, in line with the expectations of the indigenous population and in order to prevent abuses of the system (particularly in relation to employment-related welfare and benefits).[84] So, there is a range of

---

[75] Employment Permits Act 2006, s 10(2)(a). This is referred to as the "Labour Market Needs Test"; it does not apply to Green Card Permits or to Intra-company Transfer Permits (see below).
[76] s 10(2)(b).
[77] s 19.
[78] s 24.
[79] s 27.
[80] s 19.
[81] s 26.
[82] s 32.
[83] s 11(1)(a). The Minister can refuse to grant a permit where in his or her opinion it is in the public interest to do so (s 12(1)(f)).
[84] See Cornelissen, "Third-Country Nationals and the European Coordination of Social Security" (2008) 10(4) *European Journal of Social Security* 347; Hammarberg, "It is Wrong to Criminalise Migration" (2009) 11(4) *European Journal of Migration and Law* 383; and above, ns 2 and 4.

provisions in the legislation dealing with potential fraud and/or misrepresentation; s 11(2) of the 2006 Act, for example, empowers the Minister to "take such steps as he or she considers necessary to establish the accuracy or authenticity of the information provided in respect of the application".

Secondly, the Minister is empowered under s 14 of the 2006 Act to make regulations [7–40] (for a period not exceeding two years) relating to a range of areas,[85] such as the maximum number of employment permits that may be granted in respect of a specified economic sector and the qualifications or skills that foreign national applicants are required to possess in order for a grant of a permit to be made. In making these regulations, the Minister is required to have regard only to matters outlined in s 15 of the 2006 Act. These include, for example, the qualifications or skills that, in the opinion of the Minister, are required for economic and social development and competitiveness; and the qualifications or skills that, in the opinion of the Minister, are required for the proper functioning of particular economic sectors (and whether these might be in short supply). In addition to regulations, many aspects of this area of employment law are subject to administrative discretion. As the focus of the employment permits regime is on responding to labour market developments, rules and criteria for eligibility tend to change rapidly.[86] For example, a number of important changes to the employment permits system were made in 2009 (mainly as a response to the rapidly deteriorating economic climate and growing unemployment). In the main, these were measures designed to strengthen the qualifying conditions for the granting of new Work Permits to non-EEA nationals for occupations requiring low levels of skills or qualifications and vacancies which could increasingly be filled by Irish or EEA citizens. New procedures for dealing with Work Permit holders placed on short-time working, as well as those made redundant, were also introduced.[87] Cox *et al* point out (and this will be seen below) that the impact of policy decisions and administrative schemes (as opposed to primary or secondary legislation) has been so enormous that these have, in large measure, come to represent the law in this area; the authors express strong reservations as to whether this is either appropriate or, indeed, legitimate.[88]

It should also be stressed, before looking at the various types of employment permit in [7–41] more detail, that foreign nationals working legally in Ireland have exactly the same rights under employment legislation as indigenous workers. Section 9(2) of the 2006 Act requires that the employment permit contains a statement of the rights and

---

[85] See, for example, the Employment Permits Act 2006 (Prescribed Fees and Miscellaneous Procedures) Regulations 2006 (SI No 683 of 2006).

[86] Up-to-date information on the currently operating rules and procedures can be found at www.entemp.ie.

[87] http://www.entemp.ie/labour/workpermits/whatsnew.htm. One important change means that it will not now be necessary for those who have been working lawfully and who have held an employment permit for five consecutive years to have an employment permit to remain in employment. In those circumstances, the Department of Justice and Law Reform will give immigration permission to the foreign national to reside in Ireland and to work without the need for an employment permit. This will apply to those made redundant after five years working on a permit and to those still in employment.

[88] Cox *et al, Employment Law in Ireland* (Clarus Press, Dublin, 2009), p 164 and, generally, chapter 5.

entitlements of the worker, including information about when and how the worker may change employment and details of pay, rights under the national minimum wage legislation and any deductions which it is proposed to make from that pay.[89] Employers are not allowed to deduct expenses associated with recruitment from the employee's pay and are not allowed retain any of the worker's personal documents.[90] All applications must conform to Joint Labour Committee (JLC) and Registered Employment Agreement (REA) rates of pay.

[7–42]   However, foreign nationals working in Ireland and, in particular, those in low-pay, low-skill occupations constitute an especially vulnerable group. Although recent policy initiatives (which remain, remember, largely a matter of Ministerial and administrative discretion) relating to redundancy have sought to introduce some "breathing-space" for foreign nationals made redundant[91] or who have become undocumented through no fault of their own,[92] the situation for foreign nationals who are unfairly dismissed, or whose rights under the Employment Permits legislation or other employment legislation are breached, remains precarious. Frequently, the only remedy (if any) will be financial compensation, which may be of little use to a worker whose immigration status depends on ongoing *employment*. As a result, migrant workers are less likely to take claims for breaches of employment legislation; recent research has shown that between 2005 and 2007 (a period in which the numbers of foreign nationals working in Ireland increased dramatically) just four percent of claimants before the Employment Appeals Tribunal were non-EEA citizens.[93] The proportion of foreign nationals pursuing claims before Rights Commissioners is also relatively small (albeit higher than before the EAT). In such cases a "disturbing trend" has been noted by Teague and Thomas, in that where claims *are* pursued by migrant workers before the Rights Commissioners the employee tends to list multiple complaints of legislative infringement, suggesting that certain employers are transgressing on employee rights to a significant extent.[94]

---

[89] A common deduction made for foreign national employees newly arrived in the country, for example, relates to accommodation costs. The national minimum wage legislation allows for certain deductions to be made from the statutory minimum pay of an employee if the employee is provided with board and/or lodgings; National Minimum Wage Act 2000, s 11(2).

[90] Employment Permits Act 2006, s 23.

[91] Above, n 87.

[92] In October 2009, the Department of Justice and Law Reform announced details of an administrative scheme for undocumented immigrant workers formerly holding employment permits who have become undocumented through no fault of their own, but through the action or inaction of their employer. Note that in *Dubyna v Hourican Hygiene Services* (UD 781/2004) the EAT considered it to be an implied term of an employment contract that one's employer would process an application for a work permit in a proper and diligent manner. This decision was made at a time when only the *employer* could apply for a permit.

[93] Hann and Teague, *The Employment Appeals Tribunal* (Queen's University Belfast, 2008).

[94] Teague and Thomas, *Employment Dispute Resolution and Standard Setting in the Republic of Ireland* (LRC, Dublin, 2008), p 61. A similar picture has been revealed in UK research looking at the extent to which migrant workers pursue claims before employment tribunals; see Colling, "What Space for Unions on the Floor of Rights? Trade Unions and the Enforcement of Statutory Individual Employment Rights" (2006) 35(2) ILJ 140.

As discussed in chapter 2, following concerns over the possible exploitation of migrant workers and the "displacement" of indigenous workers, which crystallised around large-scale disputes involving migrant workers at two companies, Gama and Irish Ferries, the social partners agreed, in the national partnership agreement *Towards 2016*, a major new package of measures to deal with employment rights compliance.[95] Chief among these were the establishment of the National Employment Rights Authority (NERA) and the publication of the Employment Law Compliance Bill 2008. Although neither exclusively targets migrant workers, both aim to increase compliance with employment law generally and, particularly, aim to vindicate the rights of vulnerable groups; see chapter 2 for further details. **[7–43]**

Categories of Employment Permits

Green Card Permits

The Employment Permits Acts 2003 and 2006 allowed the establishment of a Green Card Scheme for occupations where high-level strategic skills shortages exist, replacing the previous working visa/work authorisation system.[96] This scheme basically covers highly-skilled migrant workers. Green Card Permits are available to two categories of worker; those with specified skills in a restricted list of occupations in the salary range of €30,000 to €59,999 (including, for example, information technology and healthcare professionals)[97] and people in almost any occupation (other than those which are contrary to the public interest) where the salary range is €60,000 or above. Green Card Permits are issued for an initial period of two years and are only issued in respect of job offers of two years' duration. Successful applicants can apply for immediate family re-unification (and spouses and dependents legally resident in the State are free to seek employment and apply for a Spousal/Dependant Work Permit). No Labour Market Needs Test must be satisfied prior to making an application. The issue of a Green Card Permit is contingent on a job offer from a *bona fide* employer registered with the Companies Registration Office and the Revenue Commissioners and trading in Ireland. As noted above, a Green Card Permit will not be granted to companies where a consequence of granting the Permit would be that more than 50 percent of employees in the firm would be non-EEA nationals. **[7–44]**

Green Card Permit holders, although they must have an *offer* of at least two years' employment in order to apply, are not *guaranteed* continuous employment for two years; their employment may be terminated in the usual manner (e.g. by way of appropriate notice) and they are entitled to the same protections as Irish nationals **[7–45]**

---

[95] See, also, O'Sullivan and Wallace, "Protecting Migrant Workers: The Case of Ireland" (2010, forthcoming) *International Migration*; Krings, *op.cit.*

[96] See the DETE's Guide to Green Card Permits available at http://www.entemp.ie/publications/labour/2009/guidelines-greencards-sept2009.pdf.

[97] The Green Card list is reviewed periodically to ensure that it meets current labour market demands. So, for example, a review in April 2009 revealed that skills shortages no longer existed in respect of certain occupations, which had been covered by the scheme; these were then removed from the Green Card eligible list and included healthcare professionals such as physiotherapists, psychologists, social workers, medical physicists and speech and language therapists (http://www.entemp.ie/labour/workpermits/revisedgreencard.htm).

under dismissal and anti-discrimination legislation.[98] Under rules established in August 2009, Green Card Permit holders who are made redundant have six months to find alternative employment; at that stage, if another job has not been found, they are obliged to contact the immigration authorities to establish immigration status beyond that period.[99]

Work Permits

[7–46] Work Permits may be issued to foreign nationals who need employment permits for those occupations (other than those which are contrary to the public interest) to which the Green Card Permit scheme does not apply and where the salary is €30,000 or more.[100] There are certain occupations for which Work Permits are not considered.[101] Work Permits may be issued, in exceptional cases only, where the salary range in question is below €30,000.[102] Work Permits are issued for an initial period of two years, can be renewed for a further three years and, after five years, can be renewed indefinitely.

[7–47] The Labour Market Needs Test must be satisfied.[103] Any vacancy in respect of which an application for a Work Permit is being made must be advertised with the FÁS/ EURES employment network for at least eight weeks and additionally in local and national newspapers for six days. This is to ensure that a national of the EEA (including a national of Bulgaria or Romania) cannot be found to fill the vacancy.

[7–48] Successful applicants, who applied for a Permit before 1 June 2009, can apply for immediate family re-unification (and spouses and dependents legally resident in the State are free to seek employment and apply for a Spousal/Dependant Work Permit). For applications made after that date, the spouse or dependant must apply for a Work Permit in his or her own right, according to standard Work Permit eligibility criteria. The issue of a Work Permit is contingent on a job offer from a *bona fide* employer registered with the Companies Registration Office and the Revenue Commissioners and trading in Ireland. As noted above, a Work Permit will not be granted to companies where a consequence of granting the Permit would be that more than 50 percent of employees in the firm would be non-EEA nationals.

[7–49] Under rules established in August 2009, Work Permit holders who are made redundant have six months to find alternative employment; at that stage, if another job has not been found, they are obliged to contact the immigration authorities to establish immigration status beyond that period.[104]

---

[98] Buckley and Connolly, *op.cit*, p 735.

[99] http://www.entemp.ie/labour/workpermits/whatsnew.htm.

[100] See the DETE's Guide to Work Permits available at http://www.entemp.ie/publications/labour/2009/guidelines-workpermits-oct2009.pdf.

[101] These are generally low-skill and low-pay occupations; for example, clerical and administrative workers, labourers and general operatives and domestic workers (see http://www.entemp.ie/publications/labour/2009/guidelines-workpermits-oct2009.pdf).

[102] This is essentially a matter of discretion for the Minister.

[103] Employment Permits Act 2006, s 10(2)(a).

[104] http://www.entemp.ie/labour/workpermits/whatsnew.htm.

Intra-Company Transfer Permit

This scheme is designed to facilitate the transfer of senior management, key personnel, or trainees who are foreign nationals (who need an employment permit) from an overseas branch of a multinational corporation to its Irish branch.[105] Only these three categories of applicant will be considered and they must also satisfy the criteria of earning a minimum annual salary of €40,000 and have been working for a minimum period of 12 months with the overseas company prior to transfer. Buckley and Connolly note that, given the significant amount of foreign businesses with operations in Ireland, the scheme has proven to be extremely popular.[106] Intra-Company Transfer Permits are issued for a defined period depending on the reason for transfer, but applications may be granted for a maximum period of up to 24 months in the first instance and may be extended upon application to a maximum stay of five years. The employee/transferee cannot work for any employer other than that named in the Permit. **[7–50]**

Successful applicants, who applied for a Permit before 1 June 2009, can apply for immediate family re-unification (and spouses and dependents legally resident in the State are free to seek employment and apply for a Spousal/Dependant Work Permit). For applications made after that date, the spouse or dependant must apply for a Work Permit in his or her own right, according to standard Work Permit eligibility criteria. **[7–51]**

Normally the number of Intra-Company Transferees should not exceed five percent of the total Irish workforce in a firm, although in exceptional circumstances (e.g. small firms or start-up companies) a higher percentage may be permitted on a strictly temporary basis. In accordance with the Employment Permits Act 2006, however, there is an absolute limit of 50 percent of non-EEA staff.[107] No Labour Market Needs Test must be satisfied prior to making an application. **[7–52]**

The foreign branch of the organisation in question must be *bona fide* and engaged in substantive business operations in the foreign country in question. The Irish company to which the transfer is sought must have a direct link with the overseas company by common ownership (e.g. either one company must own the other, or else both must be part of a group of companies controlled by the same parent company). The application can only be made by the host company in Ireland. **[7–53]**

Spousal/Dependant Work Permits

As ever, workers will be more reluctant to migrate for employment purposes if they are unable to bring family members with them.[108] Such family members themselves may wish to work in the host country and, so, a scheme has been established whereby spouses and dependants of employment permit holders may be granted a Work Permit. Spouses **[7–54]**

---

[105] See the DETE's Guide to Intra-Company Transfer Permits available at http://www.entemp.ie/publications/labour/2009/guidelines-ict-april2009.pdf.

[106] Buckley and Connolly, *op.cit*, p 738.

[107] Employment Permits Act 2006, s 10(2)(b).

[108] See the DETE's Guide Spousal/Dependent Permits available at http://www.entemp.ie/publications/labour/2009/guidelines-spousals-july2009.pdf.

and eligible dependent unmarried children,[109] who have been admitted to the State as family members of an employment permit holder (who must be working within the terms of his or her employment permit) may apply under this scheme.

[7–55]   This Permit has the advantage of allowing successful applicants to apply for a permit in respect of most occupations and does not require the employer to undertake a Labour Market Needs Test. As noted above, a Permit will not be granted to companies where a consequence of granting the Permit would be that more than 50 percent of employees in the firm would be non-EEA nationals. A Permit under this Scheme is normally issued up to the expiry date of the GNIB (Garda National Immigration Bureau) Card of the existing employment permit holder.

Other Categories of Applicant

[7–56]   It should be noted that there are further rules governing the right of non-EEA nationals to work in Ireland, which apply to other, specific situations. These relate, primarily, to certain categories of workers (e.g. nurses, doctors and sports professionals); students seeking to work while undertaking educational courses; third-level graduates seeking employment; persons who are not employees seeking to relocate to Ireland for business purposes (e.g. the self-employed); and those visiting Ireland for temporary business reasons (e.g. a business conference).[110]

Developments in Immigration Law

Immigration, Residence and Protection Bill 2008

[7–57]   The Immigration, Residence and Protection Bill was published in January 2008 but, at the time of writing, has yet to be passed into law.[111] This Bill sets out a legislative framework for the management of inward migration to Ireland. The Bill proposes a new visa scheme for non-EU nationals seeking to live, work, study or visit relatives in Ireland. Section 10 contains provisions whereby the Minister may designate a foreign national as exempt from the need to have a visa; one of the factors the Minister may have regard to in deciding to designate a foreign national as "visa-exempt" is "occupation".

The Bill also makes provision for the granting of Long-term Residence Permits. Under s 36, these will be granted to foreign nationals who fulfil the following requirements:

---

[109] The scheme is available, on an exceptional basis, to dependants who have reached the age of 18. These applications will be dealt with strictly on a case-by-case basis and can only be considered for dependants who arrived in the State while still minors and whose immigration status in the State is in order.

[110] See Buckley and Connolly, *op.cit,* pp 740-743 for an analysis of the rules applicable in these situations.

[111] Indeed, in May 2010, the Government announced that the Bill was to be withdrawn and that a new Bill to reform immigration law in the State would be published before autumn 2010. So many amendments were proposed to the Bill at Committee Stage that the Government felt it would be better to re-draft the Bill totally rather than seek to accommodate the amendments within its original framework; see "Amended Immigration Bill Expected Before Autumn" *Irish Times,* 1 June 2010. At the time of writing, it appears that many of the changes to be made relate to the asylum process and, so, do not impact hugely on the aspects of it that concern this chapter. However, this section should be read in conjunction with the new Bill if and when this is published.

i.   the foreign national has been lawfully resident in the State for periods totalling at least five out of the six years prior to the date of application;
ii. the foreign national is of good character;
iii. the foreign national is in compliance with his or her obligations in relation to the payment or remittance of any taxes, interest or penalties required to be paid or remitted by law;
iv. the foreign national can demonstrate, in such manner as may be prescribed, a reasonable competence for communicating in the Irish or English language, and has satisfied the Minister, in such manner as may be prescribed, that he or she has made reasonable efforts to integrate into Irish society, and has, during his or her presence in the State, been supporting himself or herself and any dependants without recourse to such publicly-funded services as are prescribed.

Granting of such a Permit entitles the foreign national to reside in the State and to access the same rights of travel as those to which Irish citizens are entitled. The foreign national and his or her dependants lawfully resident in the State are entitled to seek and enter employment, to engage in economic activity, to have access to education and training in the State and to receive social welfare benefits in the same manner as Irish citizens are so entitled.   **[7–58]**

Section 37 deals with "qualified long-term residence permission" for foreign nationals who do not meet the five-year residence requirement. The Minister may grant Qualified Long-term Residence Permits to such persons that entitle them to reside in the State for a period of two years and to access the same rights of travel as those to which Irish citizens are entitled. The foreign national and his or her dependants lawfully resident in the State are entitled to seek and enter employment and to engage in economic activity in the same manner as Irish citizens are so entitled. Permit holders may apply for a Long-term Residence Permit. The foreign national shall be deemed to have satisfied the standard five-year requirement if he or she had, at the time of the application for the long-term residence permission, been resident in the State for a period of not less than 21 months of the two-year period for which the Qualified Long-term Residence Permit was granted. The applicant must satisfy the other requirements listed in s 36(4)(ii-iv) (above).   **[7–59]**

These provisions aim to encourage those with experience, skills or qualifications that are in short supply to come and work in Ireland.[112] However, the Bill also contains provisions, in Part 6, for detention in Garda stations or prisons of those suspected of being in the State illegally, who may be deported without notice if they are not in possession of explicit permission to reside, subject to the protections afforded by international law. These provisions have been criticised by many commentators as being overly repressive.[113]   **[7–60]**

---

[112] Buckley and Connolly, *op.cit,* p 749.
[113] See, for example, Becker, *Offences and Penalties in the Immigration, Residence and Protection Bill 2008– Do the Punishments Fit the Crimes?* (paper delivered at the ACJRD Eleventh Annual Conference, Dublin, October 10 2008; available at http://www.immigrantcouncil.ie/images/8470_091008_ACJRDpaper.pdf).

The EU and Migrant Workers: Recent Developments

[7–61]   Significant recent developments in relation to the regulation of third-country national migrant workers have occurred at EU level.[114] As with the 2008 Bill discussed above, these have essentially focused on two areas; sanctions relating to illegal migrants and methods of attracting high-skilled workers to the EU.

[7–62]   Directive 2008/115 sets out common standards and procedures to be applied in Member States for returning illegally staying third-country nationals, in accordance with fundamental rights principles of EU law, as well as international law, including refugee protection and human rights obligations. It contains information on termination of illegal stay, procedural safeguards, and definitions for the purpose of removal.[115] Directive 2009/52 establishes a general prohibition on the employment of third-country nationals who do not have the right to be resident in the EU, accompanied by sanctions against employers who infringe that prohibition.[116] Sanctions include financial fines and contributions to the costs of returning illegally staying third-country nationals, together with the possibility of reduced financial sanctions on employers who are natural persons where the employment is for their private purposes. The Directive provides for minimum standards and Member States remain free to adopt or maintain stricter sanctions and measures and impose stricter obligations on employers. As regards high-skill workers, Directive 2009/50 (the "Blue Card Directive") sets out the conditions of entry and residence for more than three months in the territory of the Member States of third-country nationals for the purpose of highly qualified employment, as EU Blue Card holders, and of their family members.[117] It also sets out the conditions for entry and residence of such third-country nationals and of their family members in Member States other than the first Member State of residence. A third development took place in December 2007, when an additional nine Member States became part of the Schengen area, which permits nationals of Member States to travel across the borders of participating countries without having to show a passport or identification.

[7–63]   All three developments can be seen as part of a broad attempt to frame a common EU-wide approach to migration and employment. However, Protocols attached to the TFEU[118] explicitly allow the UK to "opt out" of provisions under Art 26 (which aims to establish an internal market comprising of an area without internal frontiers) and Art 77 (which aims to develop a Union policy ensuring the absence of any controls on persons, whatever their nationality, when crossing internal borders) of the TFEU and maintain border controls. The same applies to Ireland as long as the "common travel area" between the two countries is maintained. The Protocols also provide that Ireland and the UK will not take part in the adoption by the Council of proposed measures

---

[114] See Peers, "EC Immigration and Asylum Law: Attracting and Deterring Labour Migration - the Blue Card and Employer Sanctions Directives" (2009) 11(4) *European Journal of Migration and Law* 387.

[115] Directive 2008/115 of 16 December 2008 on common standards and procedures in Member States for returning illegally staying third-country nationals [2008] OJ L348/98.

[116] Directive 2009/52 of 18 June 2009 providing for minimum standards on sanctions and measures against employers of illegally staying third-country nationals [2009] OJ L168/27.

[117] Directive 2009/50 of 25 May 2009 on the conditions of entry and residence of third-country nationals for the purposes of highly qualified employment [2009] OJ L155/17.

[118] See Protocols 20 and 21.

pursuant to Title V (the Area of Freedom, Security and Justice). No decision of the Court of Justice of the European Union interpreting such provisions or measures adopted under Title V will be binding upon, or applicable in, the UK or Ireland. Both countries may "opt in" at a later stage (if other Member States agree). They can also "opt in" to specific measures adopted. Protocol 19 (attached to the TFEU) also notes that Ireland and the UK do not participate in all of the provisions of the Schengen *acquis*. Ireland has chosen not to opt-in to any of the Directives discussed and remains outside of the Schengen area.[119] The Irish position, therefore, leads to a rather fragmented position for third-country foreign nationals coming to work in the Union; whether the somewhat anomalous Irish approach will be maintained in the face of deepening European integration remains to be seen.

IV. Transnational Employment

Given the internationalisation of business, trade and employment, it is increasingly common for employees to work in different legal jurisdictions. This section looks at some of the important employment law issues that can arise when employees do not exclusively work in Ireland, but spend some (or most) of their time working abroad.

[7–64]

Jurisdictional Issues

Where an employee's work takes him or her to two or more states, questions arise as to which State's laws govern the employment relationship and which courts have jurisdiction to hear the case in the event of a dispute arising.[120] Generally, parties to such a relationship would be advised to address the issue of governing law in the contract of employment itself.[121] The parties' choice will generally be respected, and given effect, by the courts (subject to the contract's compliance with any mandatory local legal requirements). It should be noted that, in some cases, the employer will simply send the employee abroad for a period but the employment relationship remains otherwise intact. In other cases, however, the employee may be "seconded" to another employer or may be directly employed by a foreign employer for a defined period. In these situations, the question might arise as to who is the employer for legal purposes.[122] It should be noted that the employer must, under the Terms of Employment (Information) Act 1994, provide details to the employee if there is a requirement that the employee works outside the State for the duration of at least a month as part of the employment contract. This information must be given to the employee before the employee leaves the State and must include information regarding the period of employment outside the State, the currency in which the employee is to be remunerated for the period of employment outside the State, any benefits in cash or in kind for the employee as a consequence of working outside the State and the terms or conditions, where appropriate, governing the employee's repatriation.[123]

[7–65]

---

[119] At present the only EU countries that remain outside Schengen are Ireland, the UK, Cyprus, Bulgaria and Romania.

[120] See Forde, *Employment Law* (2nd ed, Round Hall, Dublin, 2001), chapter 11.

[121] See Dunne, "International Employment" in *Employment Law* (Regan ed, Tottel, Dublin, 2009), p 757 for an extensive examination of the issues such a contract should address.

[122] See, for example, *Lynch v Palgrave* [1962] IR 150.

[123] Terms of Employment (Information) Act 1994, s 4(1). See also chapter 4.

The Rome Convention

[7–66]   The Rome Convention on the law applicable to contractual obligations 1980 (the "Rome Convention") was transposed into Irish law by the Contractual Obligations (Applicable Law) Act 1990.[124] The Convention applies to contractual obligations in situations involving a choice of laws, where the parties have not made an explicit choice of applicable law. In such a situation, the contract is governed by the law of the country with which it is most closely connected. In the case of employment contracts, this is generally the law of the country in which the employee habitually carries out his or her work.[125] If this cannot be determined, the applicable law is that of the country in which the company that employed the worker has its place of business. Where it appears from the circumstances as a whole that the contract is more closely connected with a country other than that indicated by either of the preceding, the applicable law is that of the country with which the employment contract is most closely associated.[126] If the parties decide to select another law to apply to the contract, this choice may not be at the expense of the protection of the worker. Therefore, employment contracts are subject to all applicable provisions of local law, from which the parties cannot derogate. These are referred to in Art 9 of Regulation 593/2008 as "overriding mandatory provisions".[127] They are defined as "provisions the respect for which is regarded as crucial by a country for safeguarding its public interests, such as its political, social or economic organisation". In Ireland, the requirements of the Unfair Dismissals Acts would be regarded as mandatory for this purpose.[128] The Convention has universal application; it is not limited to Contracting States or to EU Member States.[129]

The Brussels Convention

[7–67]   The rules governing the appropriate jurisdiction for a case to be heard were set out, at European level, in the Brussels Convention on Jurisdiction and the Enforcement of Judgments in Civil and Commercial Matters 1968 (the "Brussels Convention"). The Convention was implemented in Irish law by the Jurisdiction of Courts and Enforcement of Judgments Act 1998. The Convention has been updated by Regulation 44/2001[130] (the "Brussels Regulations"), which was transposed into Irish law by the European Communities (Civil and Commercial Judgments) Regulations 2002.[131]

---

[124] The Convention has been consolidated and modernised as a result of Regulation 593/2008 of 17 June 2008 [2008] OJ L177/10 (the "Rome I Regulations").

[125] See Linden, "Employment Protection for Employees Working Abroad" (2006) 35(2) ILJ 186; Smith and Cromack, "International Employment: The Applicable Law" (1993) 22(1) ILJ 1.

[126] Art 8 of Regulation 593/2008.

[127] Dunne, *op.cit*, p 769.

[128] Forde, *op.cit*, p 255.

[129] Art 82 of Regulation 593/2008. However, as provisions of EU law, the rules can only be enforced by a court within the EU.

[130] Regulation 44/2001 of 22 December 2000 on jurisdiction and the recognition and enforcement of judgments in civil and commercial matters [2001] OJ L124/1. The Regulation applies in all Member States (except Denmark). Similar rules are in place with some EEA countries; the 1988 Lugano Convention governing the same subject matter binds the Member States (including Denmark) and Iceland, Norway, and Switzerland.

[131] SI No 52 of 2002.

The core principle of Regulation 44/2001 (as laid down in Art 2(1)) is that persons domiciled in a Member State shall, whatever their nationality, be sued in the courts of that Member State. "Domicile" means ordinarily resident; a person will be considered domiciled in a particular jurisdiction if he or she is ordinarily resident in that State.[132] Under Art 60, a company or other legal person or association of natural or legal persons is domiciled at the place where it has its statutory seat, its central administration, or its principal place of business.

[7–68]

Section 5 of Regulation 44/2001, however, contains specific rules relating to individual contracts of employment. In essence, these seek to protect employees (usually the weaker party in an employment relationship) by making the available forum as convenient as possible for them. Article 19, therefore, allows an employee to sue in his or her country of domicile, in the country in which he or she habitually carries out work (or in the country where he or she last did so), or, if the employee does not, or did not, habitually carry out his or her work in any one country, in the country where the business which engaged the employee is, or was, situated. Article 18 further provides that, where an employee enters into an contract of employment with an employer who is not domiciled in a Member State but has a branch, agency or other establishment in one of the Member States, the employer shall, in disputes arising out of the operations of the branch, agency or establishment, be deemed to be domiciled in that Member State. Under Art 20, however, the employer may only issue proceedings against an employee in the employee's place of domicile. Article 21 allows the parties to agree what jurisdiction will apply to the contract of employment but only where such an agreement is entered into after the dispute has arisen, or allows the employee to bring proceedings in courts other than those otherwise indicated. Where the possible jurisdictions for hearing the dispute are all outside of the EU, the Regulation does not apply.

[7–69]

Application of Irish Law Abroad

As a general principle of International Law, the principle of territoriality holds that a State's regulatory legislation does not usually apply to events occurring outside its borders.[133] However, this is not the case where a piece of legislation itself purports to have an extra-territorial reach. Although this is unusual in Irish employment law, two important examples can be found in the Redundancy Payments legislation and the Unfair Dismissals Acts.[134]

[7–70]

Posted Workers

As seen above the abolition of obstacles to the free movement of persons and services constitutes one of the most fundamental objectives of the European Union. However, the promotion of the transnational provision of services can also raise concerns about fair competition. Service providers in Member States with relatively high remuneration

[7–71]

---

[132] Dunne, *op.cit,* p 766.

[133] See, generally, Brownlie, *Principles of Public International Law* (7th ed, Oxford University Press, Oxford, 2008).

[134] s 25 of the Redundancy Payments Acts 1967-2007 and s 2(3) of the Unfair Dismissals Acts 1977-2007; see Dunne, *op.cit,* pp 777-778.

rates or labour standards, for example, may be placed at a competitive disadvantage when compared to providers in other Member States with lower wages and labour standards.[135]

[7–72] The issue came before the ECJ in *Rush Portuguesa*.[136] Here, a Portuguese-owned company won a sub-contract to carry out work in France. The company arranged for its own Portuguese employees to travel to France to carry out the work but the company's right to do this was challenged by the French Immigration Board. Furthermore, after establishing that Rush Portuguesa had not complied with the requirements of the French Labour Code relating to the activities of employed persons carried on in France by nationals of non-member countries, the Board sought payment of a special contribution, which an employer employing foreign workers in breach of the provisions of the Labour Code was liable to pay. The ECJ ruled that the principle of free movement of services precluded a Member State from prohibiting a service-providing company established in another Member State from moving freely on its territory with its entire staff for the duration of the services. However, the Court went on to rule that Member States would be permitted to extend and apply all of their labour legislation or collective agreements to any person who is employed, even temporarily, within their territory, irrespective of where the employer is established.[137]

[7–73] Following the decision, Directive 96/71 of 16 December 1996 concerning the posting of workers in the framework of the provision of services was passed.[138] The recital to the Directive explicitly states that its purpose is to promote a climate of fair competition, measures guaranteeing respect for the rights of workers and the co-ordination of Member State laws in order to lay down a nucleus of mandatory rules for minimum protection to be observed in the host country by employers who post workers to perform temporary work in the territory of a Member State where the services are provided. The Directive, therefore, applies to virtually all employers based in the Union who provide cross-border services. This includes situations where the contract remains with the home employer, where it is with an undertaking in another Member State owned by the home employer, or where an agency or temporary employment undertaking hires out a worker to an undertaking in another Member State.[139] A "posted worker" (Art 2) means a worker who, for a limited period, carries out work in

---

[135] This concern was the reason, for example, behind the inclusion in the Treaty Establishing the European Economic Community of what is now Art 157TFEU (ex-Art 141EC) on equal pay as between men and women. This principle (originally Art 119EEC) was incorporated in the Treaty of Rome, principally at the insistence of the French government. France already had equal pay legislation in place and was concerned that, in a common market, if other countries were not also obliged to enforce equal pay rights, French industry would be a competitive disadvantage; see Barnard, "The Economic Objectives of Article 119" in *Sex Equality Law in the European Union* (O' Keefe and Hervey eds, Wiley, Chichester 1996).

[136] Case C-113/89 *Rush Portuguesa v Office National d 'Immigration* [1990] ECR 1-1417.

[137] See De Vos, "Free Movement of Workers, Free Movement of Services and the Posted Workers Directive: a Bermuda Triangle for National Labour Standards?" (2006) 7(3) *ERA Forum* 356.

[138] [1996] OJ L18/1.

[139] Article 1(3).

the territory of a Member State other than the State in which he or she normally works; the definition of a "worker" is that which applies in the law of the Member State to the territory of which the worker is posted.

Article 3 of the Directive requires that Member States ensure that posted workers are guaranteed the same terms and conditions of employment as apply to domestic employees in the following areas: [7–74]

a. maximum work periods and minimum rest periods;
b. minimum paid annual holidays;
c. the minimum rates of pay, including overtime rates (excluding supplementary occupational retirement pension schemes);
d. the conditions of hiring-out of workers, in particular the supply of workers by temporary employment undertakings;
e. health, safety and hygiene at work;
f. protective measures with regard to the terms and conditions of employment of pregnant women or women who have recently given birth, of children and of young people;
g. equality of treatment between men and women and other provisions on non-discrimination.

However, the Directive only covers such matters where they are laid down by law, regulation or administrative provision and/or by collective agreements or arbitration awards which have been declared universally applicable in the Member State. [7–75]

It is this issue that has recently provoked controversy before the ECJ. In *Laval*[140] a Latvian company posted several dozen workers from Latvia to building sites in Sweden. Swedish unions took action against Laval over the company's refusal to sign a collective agreement and to respect Swedish collective agreements on working conditions and minimum wages. The Swedish Labour Court referred the case to the ECJ.

The Court pointed out that the Posted Workers Directive does not allow the host Member State to make the provision of services in its territory conditional on the observance of terms and conditions of employment which go beyond the mandatory rules for minimum protection. The Directive expressly lays down the degree of protection which undertakings established in other Member States must guarantee, in the host Member State, to the workers posted to the territory of the latter. The Court stated that it would be a restriction on the free movement of services if service providers established in another Member State were forced into negotiations of unspecified duration with trade unions in the host Member State in order to ascertain minimum wage rates and to sign a collective agreement, the terms of which went beyond the minimum protection guaranteed by the Directive. This is because it would be liable to make it less attractive, or more difficult, for such undertakings to carry out construction work in the host Member State. As Sweden did not have a system of declaring collective agreements to be universally applicable (as envisaged under the [7–76]

---

[140] Case C-341/05 *Laval v Svenska Byggnadsarbetareförbundet* [2007] ECR I-11767.

Directive), the posted workers in question were not covered by the terms of the local collective agreements.

[7–77]   Similarly, in *Rüffert*,[141] the ECJ ruled that in circumstances where a Member State recognises a system for declaring the rate of pay fixed by a collective agreement to be universally applicable, but fails to make such a declaration to this effect, a legislative measure of that Member State relating to the regulation of public contracts and tenders cannot impose a requirement on providers of cross-border services who post workers to that Member State to comply with that rate of pay. Although Germany had a system for declaring collective agreements to be of universal application, the ECJ found that no such declaration appeared to have been made in respect of the collective agreement at issue in the case.

[7–78]   The Directive, in Art 3(10), allows Member States to apply to cross-border service providers terms and conditions of employment on matters other than those specified above in the case of "public policy provisions" (as long as these are applied equally to domestic workers). In *Commission v Luxembourg*[142] the issue revolved around what constituted "public policy" under the Directive. Luxembourg had implemented the Directive in such a manner that considered virtually *all* "laws, regulations and administrative provisions and those resulting from collective agreements which have been declared universally applicable or an arbitration decision with a scope similar to that of universally applicable collective agreements" to constitute mandatory provisions falling under national public policy. This included, for example, the requirement of an automatic adjustment to rates of pay to reflect changes in the cost of living. According to the ECJ, the public policy exception was a derogation from the fundamental freedom to provide services and, so, must be interpreted strictly and relied on only if there is a "genuine and sufficiently serious threat to a fundamental interest of society". As a result, Member States could not rely on the public policy exception in order to apply to undertakings posting staff on its territory the requirement relating to the automatic adjustment of wages, other than minimum wages, to reflect changes in the cost of living.

[7–79]   These cases have provoked much comment, as they seem to restrict the power of Member States and, particularly, trade unions to enforce against cross-border service providers negotiated terms and conditions of employment that exceed statutory minima.[143] These cases will be considered further in chapter 11 to examine the ramifications for the taking of industrial action. It should be noted that, prior to *Laval*, the Directive had been seen as a somewhat neglected EU social policy instrument.[144]

---

[141] Case C-346/06 *Rüffert v Land Niedersachsen* [2008] IRLR 467.

[142] Case C-193/05 *Commission v Luxembourg* [2006] ECR 1-8673.

[143] See, for example, Kilpatrick, "Laval's Regulatory Conundrum: Collective Standard-Setting and the Court's New Approach to Posted Workers" (2009) 34(6) ELRev 844; Deakin, "The Labour Law Perspective: the Economic Implications of the Decisions" (2007-08) 10 *CYELS* 463; Barnard, "Viking and Laval: A Single Market Perspective" in *The New Spectre Haunting Europe-The ECJ, Trade Union Rights and the British Government* (Ewing and Hendy eds, IER, Liverpool, 2009); Davies, "One Step Forward, Two Steps Back? The Viking and Laval Cases in the ECJ" (2008) 37(2) ILJ 126.

[144] Davies, "The Posted Workers Directive and the EC Treaty" (2002) 31(3) ILJ 298, p 298.

One reason for this is that employers generally are not concerned with the issues raised unless they themselves are posting workers abroad.[145] The impact of the Directive on Irish employers (and posted) employees, therefore, depends more on how *other* Member States implement the Directive, as opposed to anything the Irish Government does. The Directive was transposed into Irish law by s 20 of the Protection of Employees (Part-Time) Work Act 2001, which extended all Irish employment protection legislation to eligible workers.

---

[145] Although, as Dunne notes, Irish employers engaging subcontractors from outside the jurisdiction would need to be concerned, for industrial relations reasons, that the latter are complying with relevant local standards; *op.cit,* p 775.

CHAPTER 8
Health and Safety in the Workplace

I. Introduction

The management of safety, health and welfare in the workplace is a hugely important **[8–01]** issue for both employers and employees. In fact, it is an employment law issue that has increasingly become a focus of debate not only for lawyers but also doctors, psychologists, trade unions, economists, politicians and policy makers.[1] This is for several reasons. In the first place, in every conceivable type of workplace, there is the potential risk of injury, or at worst death, occurring as a consequence of a work-related accident. Should this risk materialise there are obviously important physical and psychological effects that can result for employees (and their families) and employers.[2] Secondly, industrial accidents and work-related ill-health also carry a significant financial cost. For the employer, this might include, *inter alia*, initial costs associated with the accident (e.g. to repair damage or pay for medical care), rising insurance costs, disruption to production, bad publicity, administrative costs, legal costs and lost workdays.[3] The Indecon Report of 2006, for example, estimated the total cost to the

---

[1] Jacobson and Mottiar, "Legal Implications of the Economics of Occupational Health and Safety" (1998) 16 ILT 309, p 309. See also Ichino, "The Changing Structure and Contents of the Employer's Legal Responsibility for Health and Safety at Work in Post-Industrial Systems" (2006) *International Journal of Comparative Labour Law and Industrial Relations* 603.
[2] See Hrymak and Perezgonzalez, *The Costs and Effects of Workplace Accidents: Twenty Case Studies from Ireland* (Health and Safety Authority Research Series 02/2007, 2007) available at www.hsa.ie.
[3] See Mossink and De Greef, *Inventory of Socioeconomic Costs of Work Accidents* (European Agency for Safety and Health at Work, 2002) available at http://osha.europa.eu/en/publications/reports/207.

State of occupational accidents and ill-health to be approximately 2.5 percent of total national income (€3.3 billion in 2006 terms).[4] Therefore, the issue of health and safety at work raises important regulatory issues, particularly in relation to the burdens to be imposed on business. The European Commission argues that higher health and safety standards, while initially imposing higher costs on organisations, in the long run work to reduce the costs to business and increase competitiveness, by reducing the number of accidents and occupational diseases.[5]

[8-02] It is also the case that regulation of workplace health and safety must take account of the fact that the problem is more acute in some sectors and types of organisations than in others and affects certain groups of workers more than others. The Health and Safety Authority (HSA) reports that, in 2008, 7,658 non-fatal incidents were notified to the Authority by employers; in addition, the Authority recorded 57 work-related fatalities. Some sectors, though, account for a disproportionately high share of work-related accidents; these are, in particular, construction, manufacturing and agriculture. Furthermore, larger organisations accounted for the bulk of incident reports in 2008, with almost 70 percent coming from organisations employing more than 50 employees. Lastly, accidents tend to disproportionately befall *male* workers and *younger* workers, especially those in the 20-24 age bracket.[6] Factors such as these must be taken into account by regulators when formulating policy in this area.

[8-03] As will be seen in chapter 12, much of health and safety law operates through the imposition of regulatory duties upon employers, which are enforced through the powers of a designated health and safety inspectorate (the HSA) and, ultimately, the sanction of the criminal courts.[7] However, the employer may also owe a duty to its employees at common law; this can arise in negligence for breaching a duty of care to an employee or by virtue of breaching an implied or express contractual term.[8] Thus, assessing the penalties to be imposed on those who breach health and safety laws, as well as the redress for those affected by such breaches, is not an uncomplicated matter.

[8-04] For all these reasons, therefore, it is essential that both employers and employees are aware of the key provisions of health and safety legislation and of their respective duties arising under this legislation to reduce the possibility of accidents, injuries or deaths occurring. This chapter will look at the regulation of health and safety in the workplace by considering the main provisions of the Safety, Health and Welfare at Work Act 2005. First though, its predecessor, the Safety, Health and Welfare at Work Act 1989 will be briefly considered. It should also be noted at this point that various provisions of EU law deal with the issue of occupational health and safety. Article 153TFEU (ex-Art 137EC)

---

[4] *Report on Economic Impact of the Safety, Health and Welfare at Work Legislation* (available at www.entemp.ie).

[5] See Barnard, *EC Employment Law* (3rd ed, Oxford University Press, Oxford, 2006), p 539.

[6] *Summary of Workplace Injury, Illness and Fatality Statistics 2007-2008* (HSA, 2009) available at www.hsa.ie.

[7] Deakin and Morris, *Labour Law* (5th ed, Hart, Oxford, 2009), p 294.

[8] See McMahon and Binchy, *Irish Law of Torts* (3rd ed, Butterworths, Dublin, 2000), chapters 18 and 43. The duty of an employer to provide a safe working environment for the employee is an implied term of the employment contract. See, generally, Shannon, *Health and Safety: Law and Practice* (2nd ed, Round Hall, Dublin, 2007).

provides that the Union shall support and complement the activities of the Member States in improving the "working environment to protect workers' health and safety"; Art 156TFEU (ex-Art 140EC) allows the Commission to encourage cooperation between the Member States and facilitate the coordination of their action in matters relating to both "the prevention of occupational accidents and diseases" and "occupational hygiene"; and Art 31 of the Charter of Fundamental Rights guarantees every worker the right to "working conditions which respect his or her health, safety and dignity". The most important legislative measure adopted by the EU in this area is the Framework Health and Safety Directive.[9]

II. Safety, Health and Welfare at Work Act 1989

The notion of regulating health and safety in the workplace first emerged during the period of the Industrial Revolution when legislation was introduced in an attempt to improve the working environment within factories and mills.[10] Until the 1989 Act, the legislation in this area tended to be very *prescriptive* and *detailed* and, moreover, focused on certain *specific* types of working environments; see, for example, the Office Premises Act 1958 and the Mines and Quarries Act 1965.[11] The Safety, Health and Welfare at Work Act 1989, enacted as a result of the Barrington report of 1983,[12] however, differed significantly from the legislation that it repealed as it set out very *general* duties to be adhered to in *all* types of workplaces. [8–05]

The 1989 Act was the first codified piece of Irish legislation governing health and safety in the workplace.[13] This legislation set out general principles regulating safety, health and welfare in all places of work and general duties were imposed on a wide range of persons, including employers, the self-employed, employees, manufacturers, suppliers, designers and builders. These general duties are outlined in ss 6 to 11 of the 1989 Act. These sections set out the duties of the employer to employees; the general duties of employers and the self-employed to third parties; duties of those who have control over places of work; duties of employees and other persons; duties of manufacturers and suppliers of articles and substances for use at work; and the duties of designers and builders of places of work. The Act focused on the need to ensure *management* of safety, health and welfare at work, requiring all organisations with more than three employees to compile a "safety statement".[14] The purpose of the [8–06]

---

[9] Directive 89/391 of 12 June 1989 on the introduction of measures to encourage improvements in the health and safety of workers in the workplace [1989] OJ L183/1.

[10] Forde, *Employment Law* (2nd edition, Round Hall Sweet & Maxwell, Dublin, 2001), p 107.

[11] For further discussion on the pre-1989 legislation, refer to Forde, *op.cit*, pp 107-109.

[12] *Report of the Committee of Enquiry on Safety, Health and Welfare at Work* (1983; available at www.lawreform.ie).

[13] See Shannon, "Employer's Liability and Safety Management" (1998) 5(9) CLP 224 (Part I) and (1998) 5(10) CLP 262 (Part II); Binchy and Byrne, "The Extension of the Scope of Breach of Statutory Duty for Accidents at Work" (1995) 13 ILT 4; Murphy, "Irish Law on Health, Safety and Welfare at Work" (1995) 1(1) MLJI 24.

[14] Jacobson and Mottiar note that "in general discussion, as well as within firms themselves, health and safety is often dealt with as a separate matter, a sort of add-on to the way firms are run"; the authors argue that "in fact it is most appropriate to study health and safety as part of the general management and business strategy of the firm"; *op.cit*, p 309.

safety statement was to identify hazards within a workplace and also to undertake an assessment of any risks to safety and health in the workplace.

[8–07]   While the 1989 Act set out very broad principles, provision was made for this legislation to be supplemented with more detailed regulations, such as the Safety, Health and Welfare at Work (General Application) Regulations 1993.[15] Other significant Regulations made under the 1989 Act included the Safety, Health and Welfare at Work (Children and Young Persons) Regulations 1998[16]; the Pregnant Employees Regulations 2000[17]; and the Construction Regulations 2001.[18] The 1989 Act also provided for the establishment of an independent enforcement body, the National Authority for Occupational Health and Safety.[19] The 1989 Act was repealed and replaced by the Safety, Health and Welfare at Work Act 2005, which introduces a number of key changes that will be discussed in more detail below.[20]

III. Safety, Health and Welfare at Work Act 2005

[8–08]   The Safety, Health and Welfare at Work Act 2005 (hereinafter "the Act") places responsibility on all stakeholders for the protection of health and safety in the workplace. Schedule 3 of the Act, which sets out the "general principles of prevention", underscores the key aims and focus of this legislation. The general principles of prevention are:

i.   the avoidance of risks;
ii.   the evaluation of unavoidable risks;
iii. the combating of risks at source;
iv.   the adaptation of work to the individual, especially with regard to the design of places of work, the choice of work equipment and the choice of systems of work, with a view, in particular, to alleviating monotonous work and work at a predetermined work rate and to reducing the effect of this work on health;
v.   the adaptation of the place of work to technical progress;
vi.   the replacement of dangerous articles, substances or systems of work by safe or less dangerous articles, substances or systems of work;
vii. the giving of priority to collective protective measures over individual protective measures;

---

[15] SI No 44 of 1993, as amended by SI No 188 of 2001, which transposed, in part, requirements of Directive 89/391 of 12 June 1989 on the introduction of measures to encourage improvements in the health and safety of workers in the workplace [1989] OJ L183/1 and those of Directive 91/383 of 25 June 1991 on measures to improve the safety and health of workers with a fixed-duration or temporary employment relationship [1991] OJ L206/19.

[16] SI No 504 of 1998.

[17] Safety, Health and Welfare at Work (Pregnant Employees Etc) Regulations 2000 (SI No 11 of 2000).

[18] Safety, Health and Welfare at Work (Construction) Regulations 2001 (SI No 481 of 2001).

[19] Renamed the Health and Safety Authority under the 2005 Act; see chapter 2.

[20] Health and safety law is a huge and complex area of study in and of itself. For a comprehensive overview see Shannon, *Health and Safety: Law and Practice* (2nd ed, Round Hall, Dublin, 2007). For a comprehensive review of the 2005 Act in particular, see Byrne, *Safety, Health and Welfare at Work Act 2005* (Round Hall, Dublin, 2006). See, also, Cox *et al*, *Employment Law in Ireland* (Clarus Press, Dublin, 2009), chapter 16.

viii. the development of an adequate prevention policy in relation to safety, health and welfare at work, which takes into account technology, organisation of work, working conditions, social factors and the influence of factors related to the working environment;

ix. the giving of appropriate training and instructions to employees.

The Act, therefore, has at its core a focus on *risk* (the evaluation and avoidance of); **[8–09]** *adaptation* (of work to the worker, of the workplace to new technology and the replacement of unsafe by safe systems of work); *prevention* (through training); and the need for effective *collective measures* (involving employer and employee representatives). Interestingly, the Act does not define health, safety or welfare.[21] However, it is clear from the decision of the ECJ in *UK v Council*[22] that the concepts are to be widely interpreted. In rejecting the UK's challenge to the legal basis of the Working Time Directive,[23] the Court referred to the World Health Organisation's definition of health as "a state of complete psychic, mental and social well-being ... [which] does not merely consist of an absence of disease or infirmity".[24] The scope of health and safety, therefore, includes the protection of the worker's well-being; social and psychological as well as physical. Many factors thereby fall within the scope of health and safety. *Social* well-being may be affected by the organisation of work itself (e.g. the work space, working time patterns, isolation in the workplace), while *psychological* well-being (psychosocial hazards) may be affected by factors such as work-load and speed, stress at work, monotony, lack of social contacts, absence of collective representation, unfair remuneration and so on.[25] Byrne notes that "welfare" is probably the vaguest of the three concepts and most likely relates to the provision of "comfort" items, such as sanitary and washing facilities.[26]

The 2005 Act also introduces a number of significant changes to take into account the **[8–10]** changing nature of the workplace over the years since the 1989 Act was put in place; for example, the 2005 Act now deals with the issue of intoxicants in the workplace. The 2005 Act is supplemented by the Safety, Health and Welfare at Work (General Application) Regulations 2007.[27]

IV. General Legislative Duties of the Employer

The employer's general duties are outlined in ss 8 to 12 of the Act. It is clear from the **[8–11]** definition of an "employer" in s 2(1) that an employer-employee relationship under the Act arises where an employee is working in the capacity as an employee (regardless of *whose* employee he or she is) and is under an employer's direction and control. Therefore, if an employer uses an employee from another business for temporary purposes, the employer bears responsibility for a safe working environment for that

---

[21] Nor did the 1989 Act; Byrne, *op.cit*, p 16.

[22] Case C-84/94 *UK v Council* [1996] ECR I-5755.

[23] Directive 93/104 of 23 November 1993 concerning certain aspects of the organisation of working time [1992] OJ L307/19.

[24] Case C-84/94 *UK v Council* [1996] ECR I-5755, at para 15.

[25] See Noon and Blyton, *The Realities of Work* (3rd ed, Palgrave, Basingstoke, 2006). See also http://www.eurofound.europa.eu/areas/industrialrelations/dictionary/dictionary8.htm.

[26] Byrne, *op.cit*, p 16.

[27] SI No 299 of 2007.

employee. Note also that under s 8(5) every employer must ensure that any measures taken by it relating to safety, health and welfare at work do not involve financial cost to its employees.

General Duties

[8–12]   Section 8(1) provides that every employer shall ensure, so far as is reasonably practicable, the safety, health and welfare at work of its employees. The 2005 Act contains many of the same duties set out in the 1989 Act (and the Regulations made thereunder).[28] The Act, however, also imposes a number of new duties on employers; for example the employer now has a duty under s 8(2)(a) to manage and conduct work activities in a manner so as to ensure the health and safety of employees in the workplace, so far as is reasonably practicable; and, under s 8(2)(b), to prevent, so far as is reasonably practicable, any improper conduct or behaviour that is a potential risk to the safety, health and welfare at work of any employees. The inclusion of these duties means that the employer must endeavour to prevent unacceptable behaviour that endangers occupational safety, health and welfare. This provision also extends to cover bullying and harassment in the workplace.[29] Employers have a duty to outline what constitutes unacceptable behaviour and also to identify the disciplinary processes to be utilised to deal with any incidents of such behaviour that arise; the consequence of this new duty is that it places a responsibility on employers to ensure that there is a comprehensive safety management *system* in place.

[8–13]   The 2005 Act does not provide a definition of "improper conduct or behaviour". According to Shannon, "improper conduct" may include behaviour that could be classified as "horse play", the dangerous or unsafe use of any workplace equipment, or hazardous work practices.[30] Consideration of the case law relating to employers' liability in tort provides some indication of how this statutory provision may be interpreted.[31] In *Hough v Irish Base Metals Ltd*[32] the plaintiff was injured as he jumped away from a gas fire that had been placed near him by a fellow employee in the repair shop where they both worked. This type of behaviour had begun to occur a short period before the accident and had only occurred on a relatively small number of previous occasions. None of the previous incidents had been reported to the work supervisor and, until this accident, it had been considered, the Court was told, to be a "bit of devilment". The Supreme Court found that the company had not breached its duty in providing a reasonable level of supervision and, thus, the plaintiff was unsuccessful in his claim for compensation. In comparison, the English High Court in *Hudson v Ridge Manufacturing Co Ltd*[33] held the employer had failed to prevent one employee from engaging in "habitual horseplay", such as tripping up other employees (including the plaintiff). This behaviour had been ongoing over a period of four years before the accident occurred. The employee responsible for engaging in such horseplay

---

[28] Shannon, "The Safety, Health and Welfare At Work Act 2005: An Update" (2006) 1 QRTL 23.

[29] Bullying and harassment will be discussed in detail in chapter 9.

[30] Shannon, *Health and Safety: Law and Practice* (2nd ed, Round Hall, Dublin, 2007), p 18.

[31] See McMahon and Binchy, *Irish Law of Torts* (3rd ed, Butterworths, Dublin, 2000), chapter 18.

[32] Unreported, Supreme Court, 8 December 1967.

[33] [1957] 2 WLR 948.

had been reprimanded on many occasions by the foreman in charge and also had been warned that this behaviour was liable to injure someone. The plaintiff sustained injuries as a consequence of this employee taking hold of him from behind and forcing the plaintiff to the ground. The English High Court held that the company had breached its duty of care to its employees by failing to take proper steps to prevent this behaviour from recurring. According to Streatfeild J:

> "...upon principle it seems ... that if, in fact, a fellow workman is not merely incompetent but, by his habitual conduct, is likely to prove a source of danger to his fellow employees, a duty lies fairly and squarely on the employers to remove that source of danger".[34]

The 1989 Act provided that the employer's health and safety duties were applicable only where the employer had *control* over the place of work.[35] The 2005 Act does not contain any reference to the employer having specific control over a workplace with the result that the employer's duty to protect the safety, health and welfare of employees in the workplace also extends to places *other than* the principal place of work.[36] **[8–14]**

Section 8(2)(c)(i) of the Act imposes an obligation on the employer to ensure that the design, provision and maintenance of the workplace is in a condition that will not endanger the safety, health and welfare of the employees. Consequential to this is the duty to ensure that there is a safe way into and out of the workplace.[37] **[8–15]**

Employers also have a statutory obligation to ensure that any plant or machinery or other articles for use in the workplace will not pose a threat to the safety, health and welfare of employees.[38] In *Deegan v Langan*[39] the employer required all carpenters to use a particular type of steel masonry nail, which was known to disintegrate when hit with a hammer! The plaintiff was using this nail during the course of his employment when it disintegrated, resulting in him losing the sight of one eye. The employer was found responsible for providing faulty equipment and therefore liable for the injury sustained by the plaintiff. In *Heeney v Dublin Corporation*[40] the employer was held liable for failing to provide firemen with breathing equipment, which had been made available to other fire brigades in the country. However, even if the employer provides the proper equipment, this is not sufficient on its own to ensure that the employer has complied fully with its statutory obligations. Under s 8(2)(c)(iii) of the Act, the employer also has a duty to *maintain* plant and machinery. Thus, the equipment initially provided may comply with health and safety standards; however, a defect could subsequently arise which could render the equipment dangerous. The employer in *Burke v John Paul & Company Ltd*[41] was deemed to be negligent for failing to foresee that the blades on the cutting equipment used by the plaintiff would become blunt, **[8–16]**

---

[34] *ibid* at 949.

[35] Safety, Health and Welfare at Work Act 1989, s 6(2)(a).

[36] s 2(1). See Shannon, *Health and Safety: Law and Practice* (2nd ed, Round Hall, Dublin, 2007), p 20.

[37] See *Kielthy v Ascon Ltd* [1969] IR 122.

[38] s 8(2)(c)(iii).

[39] [1966] 1 IR 373.

[40] Unreported, High Court, Barron J, 16 May 1991.

[41] [1967] IR 277.

requiring him to use additional force when utilising this equipment (which ultimately resulted in the plaintiff suffering a hernia). In *Mackay v Iarnród Éireann*[42] the plaintiff was exposed to excessive diesel fumes and cleaning chemicals in the course of his employment. The employer was found liable for failing to provide proper protective equipment, namely a facemask and gloves.

[8–17] In *Marsella v J & P Construction Ltd*[43] the main contractor was held liable for failing to ensure that scaffolding was properly set up. The plaintiff, working for a sub-contractor, fell off a scaffolding platform when he was plastering a ceiling in a school corridor and sustained severe injuries. Peart J found that the main contractor had the primary responsibility for ensuring that the scaffolding in place was safe to use. The employer in *DPP v Kilkenny Limestone*[44] breached s 8(2)(a) by not providing an adequate machine guard on the fly wheel of the diamond rope-saw used for cutting dimensional stone blocks. An employee was struck on the back when the diamond tip of the steel rope failed to operate.

[8–18] Section 8(2)(e) of the Act imposes a duty on employers to provide systems of work for employees that are planned, organised, performed, maintained and revised as appropriate so as to be, so far as is reasonably practicable, safe and without risk to health. The 2005 Act introduces a new requirement that employers must "revise as appropriate" systems of work. This means that employers must undertake measures to review existing systems to ensure that these comply with the legislation and, if necessary, to amend those systems of work. No indication is given in this statutory provision as to how regularly such reviews should occur, other than that it should occur "as appropriate", leaving this aspect to the discretion of the employer.

[8–19] Again, guidance can be taken from the case law on employers' liability at common law in relation to the duty to provide a safe system of work.[45] For example, in *Guckian v Cully*[46] the employer was held liable for failing to provide a safe system of work for the plaintiff. The plaintiff's job was to feed dough into a machine. The dough had to be pushed into the machine in order for the blade in the machine to cut it. The plaintiff had to stand on a stool and use his hands to push the dough into the machine. On the day of the accident, the plaintiff was standing on a shaky stool when he fell and injured himself. While the employer was found liable, the Court also found the plaintiff to be guilty of contributory negligence (for using a faulty stool) and his compensation was reduced by 20 percent. In *Daly v GPA Ltd*[47] liability was imposed on the employer when a plaintiff walked through a glass panel, which was not sufficiently noticeable. In *Mackay v Iarnród Éireann*[48] the employer was found liable for not providing a safe system of work by failing to install adequate ventilation in a maintenance shed, thus exposing the employee to excessive diesel fumes. In *Barclay v An Post*[49] the employer

---

[42] [2001] IEHC 96.

[43] [2004] IEHC 369.

[44] Reported in (2008) 13(4) *Health and Safety Review*, p 18.

[45] McMahon and Binchy, *op.cit*, pp 511-523.

[46] Unreported, Supreme Court, 23 February 1972.

[47] Unreported, High Court, 13 February 1998.

[48] [2001] IEHC 96.

[49] [1998] 2 ILRM 385.

was found not to be liable for exposing the plaintiff to a back injury caused by delivering post to houses which had letter boxes at foot height. An Post had discharged its duty because it offered training in safe manual handling to all of its employees.[50]

In *McCann v Brinks Allied*[51] the plaintiffs were security men delivering cash to a bank. The delivery van was unable to get any closer than 47 feet to the door of the bank because the forecourt had not been designed to sustain the weight of vehicles. This meant that the plaintiffs had to carry the cash to the front door of the bank. On this occasion, raiders attacked the security men when they were delivering cash. The security men sued Brinks Allied and the bank on the grounds of negligence in failing to enable safe delivery of cash to the bank. Brinks Allied contended that it was prevented from guaranteeing a safe system of work for those employees, as the bank had failed to take all reasonable steps to remove the danger posed by the lack of closer access. The High Court dismissed this argument. Morris J found that Brinks Allied had failed to fulfil its obligations; first, in failing to provide a safe system of work and, second, in not ensuring that all proper and reasonable precautions for the employees' safety had been put in place. The Court found it significant that this failure had occurred despite the occurrence of two earlier attacks on security men delivering cash to the bank, of which Brinks Allied was aware. In *Rogers v Bus Átha Cliath*[52] bus drivers had been subjected to a number of assaults on particular routes. The employer had previously acknowledged that there was an increase in the number of attacks on bus drivers and had made efforts to address the problem, including the fitting out of new buses with extra security features. Unfortunately for the plaintiff, his bus had not yet been fitted out by the time of the assault on him; however, McMahon J found that the employer had discharged its duty in the provision of a safe system of work as it had both acknowledged the problem that had arisen and was in the process of addressing the situation. [8–20]

Employers have a duty to provide employees with protective clothing or equipment under s 8(2)(i) of the 2005 Act in those circumstances where it has not been possible to eradicate or control risks. For example, this could be the provision of breathing apparatus for fire service personnel or the provision of goggles and gloves for employees using dangerous cutting equipment. [8–21]

Information for Employees

Under s 8(2)(g) of the Act, employers must provide information, instruction, training and supervision for employees. All new employees should be given health and safety information upon commencement of their contract of employment. Section 9 deals more specifically with the type of information that employers must provide. Section 9 (1) states that: [8–22]

> "...every employer shall, when providing information to his or her employees under that section on matters relating to their safety, health and welfare at work ensure that the information –

---

[50] However, An Post was found to have breached its duty when the plaintiff was assigned to overtime duties to deliver to an estate with 350 low-level letter boxes, resulting in *further* back injury.
[51] Unreported, High Court, Morris J, 12 May 1992; [1997] 1 ILRM 461 (SC).
[52] Circuit Court, McMahon J, 9 January 2000.

(a) is given in a form, manner and, as appropriate, language that is reasonably likely to be understood by the employees concerned...".

[8–23]   It is important that all information regarding safety, health and welfare in the workplace should be translated into an understandable format and language. Accordingly, employers may be required to translate any safety, health and welfare manuals into languages other than English. Section 9 states, however, that such information is translated into an understandable language "as appropriate"; therefore, employers are presumably not under a legal obligation to translate information into *all* languages spoken by *all* employees. However, in *58 Named Complainants v Goode Concrete Limited*[53] the Equality Tribunal found that the complainants were treated less favourably on the grounds of race when all safety documentation was not translated into a language they understood. Here the company had endeavoured to communicate safety documentation to all of its employees irrespective of their nationality with the provision of some documentation in both English and Russian (and a Health and Safety Seminar in a local hotel at which a Russian interpreter was present). However, the Tribunal held that there was an onus on the respondent to ensure that *all* safety documentation was set out in whatever language or languages that all employees would understand.[54]

[8–24]   The Health and Safety Authority has also noted that the scope of s 9 imposes on employers a duty to ensure that employees who may not be literate understand information on safety, health and welfare at work.[55] Dissemination of this information could, for example, be through the use of pictures or diagrams to highlight hazards and also to demonstrate what steps are to be taken to avoid such hazards or, if the hazard does occur, what steps are necessary to mitigate risks to the safety, health and welfare of the employee.[56] The legislation is clear about the type of information that employees should be given regarding safety, health and welfare at work. Section 9(1)(b) stipulates that employees should be given information regarding any hazards arising in that workplace and, in particular, of risks identified as part of the risk assessment procedures. Employers must also inform employees of the protective and preventive measures to be taken concerning safety, health and welfare at work. Employees must be given the names of the designated persons to contact in the case of an emergency and also of the workplace safety representatives. Failure to comply with section 9 will result in criminal proceedings.[57] The employer's duty to provide the information on safety, health and welfare at work, as noted above, extends to employees of other undertakings working at the employer's premises[58] and also to any temporary or fixed-term employees.[59]

---

[53] DEC-E2008-020.

[54] This case is currently under appeal. In *Kelly v Algirdas Girdzius* (HSD 081/2008) the Labour Court rejected a claim that a failure to provide proper health and safety training in an appropriate language which the employee could understand amounted, in and of itself, to penalisation under s 27 of the Act. See chapter 12.

[55] HSA, *A Guide to the Safety, Health and Welfare at Work Act 2005* (available at www.hsa.ie).

[56] See, for example, HSA, *Safe System of Work Plan for Construction* (available at www.hsa.ie).

[57] s 77(2)(a).

[58] s 9(1)(2).

[59] s 9(4)(a)-(b).

Instruction, Training and Supervision for Employees

Section 10 of the Act deals with the instruction, training and supervision of employees. **[8–25]**
This must be in a form, manner and, as appropriate, language that is reasonably likely
to be understood.[60] All employees are entitled to paid time off work to attend training
and instruction sessions on emergency measures.[61] Under s 10(1)(c), the employer must
ensure, in relation to any specific task assigned to an employee, that his or her
capabilities in relation to safety, health and welfare are taken into account. In the case
of groups of particularly sensitive employees and employees covered by specific
legislation, such as persons with disabilities, pregnant workers or young persons, the
employer must ensure they are protected against the specific dangers that affect them.[62]
The English case of *Harrison v Michelin Tyre Co Ltd*[63] demonstrates that it is necessary
to show that the employer had *knowledge* that the employee was not competent to
undertake a particular task. However, this can be evidence of *actual* or *constructive*
knowledge of the employee's lack of competence (in the latter case, where it can be
shown that a reasonable employer should have been aware of the lack of competence);
evidence of a negligent system of "no questions asked"; or late discovery by the
employer of the lack of competence followed by continuance of the employment.

Employees must undergo training in relation to safety, health and welfare at work **[8–26]**
upon commencement of their employment.[64] The Act also provides that employers
have a duty to allow employees to take time off work, without loss of earnings, to
attend any training courses necessary for particular types of work.[65] Training may be
necessary if the employee has been given different responsibilities; if the employee will
be using new equipment; following the implementation of a new system of work; or if
the employee will be using new technology in the workplace.[66] Employers must ensure
that employees of another employer carrying out work at their place of work (for
example, maintenance contractors at a manufacturing plant or specialised sub-
contractors at a construction site) must receive appropriate instruction in any risks
associated with that place of work.[67] Short induction presentations may be a suitable
way of giving this information. Section 10(2) requires employee training to be
periodically reviewed and updated.

Emergencies and Serious and Imminent Dangers

Under s 11 of the Act, the employer has a duty to prepare plans, procedures and **[8–27]**
measures for dealing with emergencies or serious and imminent dangers. The nature of
these measures will differ significantly according to the size and nature of the
workplace. Section 11 stipulates that certain provisions must be implemented in
regards to first aid, fire fighting and the evacuation of employees or any other persons

---

[60] s 10(1)(a).

[61] s 10(1)(b).

[62] Shannon, *Health and Safety: Law and Practice* (2nd ed, Round Hall, Dublin, 2007), p 24.

[63] [1985] All ER 918.

[64] s 10(3)(a).

[65] s 10(4).

[66] s 10(3)(a)-(d).

[67] s 10(5).

present in the workplace in the event of an emergency. The employer will also have to liaise with the emergency services.

Duties to Other Persons

[8–28] Section 12 of the 2005 Act provides that:

> "Every employer shall manage and conduct his or her undertaking in such a way as to ensure, so far as is reasonably practicable, that in the course of the work being carried on, individuals at the place of work (not being his or her employees) are not exposed to risks to their safety, health or welfare".

[8–29] Section 12 sets out the duty that employers, including the self-employed, owe to those who are not their employees but who may be exposed to risks to their health or safety at the place of work while work is being carried on. The section applies to multi-occupancy workplaces (for example, shopping centres), where the duty holder would have to determine if his or her undertaking exposes the other occupiers and employees to risk. Section 12 has even greater significance when contractors are brought into a place of work. Under this section, the duty holder would have to make an appropriate assessment of the competence of a *contractor* to undertake a particular task, where there is the potential for exposure to risk. For example, in the construction industry, which makes extensive use of sub-contracting, these issues are addressed in the design and management provisions of the Safety, Health and Welfare at Work (Construction) Regulations 2006.[68] Situations where contractors are used are generally characterised by the retention of a high degree of control over the place of work by the duty holder; the contractor would, therefore, be expected to conform to certain site rules that may apply to the undertaking.[69] In *DPP v JRD Developments*[70] the defendant, the main contractor, was fined €25,000 for a breach of s 12 of the 2005 Act. This incident arose after an accident in which an employee of the subcontractor was electrocuted by overhead power lines and sustained injuries. The subcontractor was acquitted on the grounds that it had undertaken a risk assessment in relation to working near overhead power lines and details of this were contained in the safety statement. It had also provided its employees with appropriate training and instruction.

[8–30] Section 12 applies where the public has access to the place of work while work is in progress (this might include trespassers). The provision of appropriate measures to prevent access by the public and, in particular, children, to comparatively high-risk workplaces such as construction sites, factories, on farms or in hospitals, needs to be considered.[71] In *DPP v Grade Development*[72] the employer was fined for a breach of s 12 due to a failure to properly secure a construction site. Children entered the construction site through an unfenced section of the perimeter. One of the children sustained head injuries after climbing scaffolding and falling off. It was found that the

---

[68] SI No 504 of 2006 (as amended).
[69] Byrne, *op.cit*, p 45.
[70] Circuit Court, reported in (2009) 14(4) *Health and Safety Review*, p 15.
[71] See McMahon and Binchy, *op.cit*, chapter 12.
[72] District Court, reported in (2009) 14(9) *Health and Safety Review*, p 17.

employer had not undertaken a risk assessment to ascertain risks posed to persons other than employees.

Note that the definition of "place of work" contained in s 2(1) of the Act includes "a location at, in, upon or near which work is carried on"; the duty would, therefore, extend to members of the public in the immediate *vicinity* of a place of work.

[8–31]

V. General Legislative Duties of the Employee

Section 13 of the 2005 Act details the general duties imposed on employees in relation to workplace health and safety. Employees have a duty to comply with all relevant statutory provisions and to take reasonable care during the course of employment to ensure their own safety, health and welfare in the workplace as well as that of any other person who may be affected by their acts or omissions at work.[73] There has been a number of significant changes under the 2005 Act regarding employees' duties in the workplace, one of the most notable of which is the duty that an employee should ensure that he or she is not under the influence of an intoxicant to the extent that he or she is in such a state as to endanger his or her own safety, health and welfare at work, or that of any person.[74] Section 2(1) of the Act defines an intoxicant as including alcohol and drugs and any combination of drugs, or of drugs and alcohol. This definition does not make a distinction between prescription, non-prescription or illegal drugs. No indication is given in the 2005 Act as to what amount of alcohol or drugs would be unacceptable.[75] Section 13(1)(c) states that employees shall, if reasonably required by the employer, submit to any appropriate, reasonable and proportionate tests for intoxicants by, or under the supervision of, a registered medical practitioner.

[8–32]

This was one of the most controversial provisions in the 2005 Act, attracting significant criticism from civil liberty groups.[76] The (then) Minister for Labour Affairs, Tony Killeen, in announcing the new Act said:

[8–33]

> "...the requirement for testing for intoxicants will not come into force until the HSA has consulted the Social Partners and other interested groups. It is intended that the regulations, which have to be made, will bring in the testing requirement in *safety critical* situations and then only on a *sectoral* basis. It is important to allay fears that testing will be a requirement across all employments. There is no such intention".[77]

To date, regulations have not been introduced by the Minister to clarify the procedures employers will be able to use to test for intoxicants or even the levels of intoxicant which would be in breach of s 13(1)(b). Testing for intoxicants at work will be problematic. Shannon points out that one of the key difficulties arises if an employer requires employees to submit to tests for intoxicants on the grounds of safety, health and welfare

[8–34]

---

[73] s 13(1)(a).

[74] s 13(1)(b).

[75] Shannon, "The Safety, Health and Welfare At Work Act 2005: An Update" (2006) 1 QRTL 23, p 24.

[76] Byrne, *op.cit*, p 47.

[77] "Minister Tony Killeen Signs Commencement of the Safety, Health and Welfare at Work Act 2005" (available at www.entemp.ie); emphasis added.

at work, as this could amount to a violation of an employee's constitutional right to liberty under Art 40.1.4 of the Constitution.[78] Further pragmatic difficulties arise as the 2005 Act does not provide sufficient detail regarding the type of intoxicants that employees can be tested for, neither does it indicate the method employers can utilise to test for intoxicants.[79] There is also a danger that, if the employer requests that an employee submit to testing for intoxicants, the employee could bring a claim under the provisions of the Employment Equality Acts on the ground that, by selecting the particular employee, the employer is acting in a discriminatory manner.[80] Selecting employees for testing could also create problems for the employer where an employee may *appear* to be under the influence of an intoxicant but where the reality is that the employee's behaviour is due to an underlying medical condition or disability.[81] Employers must also be cautious in selecting employees for testing for intoxicants to ensure that the mode of selection does not result in an action on the grounds of victimisation.[82] The *reliability* of tests for intoxicants generates additional problems, particularly those used for testing for illegal substances.[83]

[8–35] In *Wretlund v Sweden*[84] a Swedish national objected to the drug testing programme used by her employer to detect the presence of cannabis. The applicant was employed as an office cleaner at a nuclear power plant. A collective agreement was in place between the employer and three of the four trade unions operating within the company specifying that employees could be subject to drug tests. As part of this agreement, employees would be given a week's notice in advance of any tests. Employees would have to provide a urine sample in private, which would then be sent to a hospital laboratory for analysis. There was a requirement under this agreement that the employee would have to consent to the test and also provide information regarding any medication that had been taken in the previous week. The employee would also have to give permission for disclosure of the test results to the occupational health service and his or her immediate supervisor. The agreement on the employer's drug policy programme stipulated that failure to provide a sample would be treated as a positive result.

[8–36] There was no legislation in place in Sweden governing employees' legal obligations to undergo drug tests. In this case, the applicant was a member of the one trade union that had not accepted the collective agreement in question. The trade union representing the applicant argued that the employee was not legally obliged to submit

---

[78] Shannon, "The Safety, Health and Welfare At Work Act 2005: An Update" (2006) 1 QRTL 23, p 24. The author also notes that enactment of the ECHR Act 2003 is also relevant as it arguably gives added impetus to the constitutional protection; see, also, Cox *et al*, *Employment Law in Ireland* (Clarus Press, Dublin, 2009), chapter 18; McGreal, "Workplace Privacy and Data Protection" in *Employment Law* (Regan ed, Tottel, Dublin, 2009), chapter 6.

[79] Shannon, *Health and Safety: Law and Practice* (2nd ed, Round Hall, Dublin, 2007), p 28.

[80] See chapter 5 for further discussion of discrimination in the workplace.

[81] Doran, "Drug and Alcohol Testing Under the Safety, Health and Welfare at Work Act 2005" (2006) 3(2) IELJ 36.

[82] Shannon, "The Safety, Health and Welfare At Work Act 2005: An Update" (2006) 1 QRTL 23, p 24.

[83] Byrne, *op.cit*, p 48.

[84] (2004) 39 EHRR SE5.

to drug testing, as there was no provision for such testing in her individual contract of employment. The applicant contended that the drug testing constituted a violation of her right to personal integrity and, as such, contravened Art 8 of the European Convention on Human Rights (ECHR). The applicant also submitted that drug testing was not proportionate given the nature of her employment; she was an office cleaner and did not have access to controlled, security-sensitive areas of the power plant. The European Court of Human Rights dismissed the applicant's claim on the grounds that the requirement to undergo drug testing was necessary and proportionate to ensure the security of the nuclear power plant. The Court held that there had been no breach of the applicant's right to personal integrity under Art 8 of the ECHR, as all employees were subject to this testing. Byrne suggests that the decision most likely indicates that "something along the lines" of the provisions in the 2005 Act is compatible with the ECHR but that it underlines the need to ensure *reasonable measures* (that should be risk-related) and the need to ensure accuracy of testing procedures.[85] Shannon notes that the nature of the employee's work must be taken into account, as this will impact upon the risk to the employee's safety, health and welfare at work and the potential risk of harm to other persons (for example, if the employee operates dangerous machinery or is responsible for driving vehicles in the workplace).[86]

In addition to the employee's duty to comply with health and safety legislation, [8–37] employees must also co-operate, when necessary, in assisting the employer or others to ensure that there is compliance with occupational health and safety legislation in the workplace in question.[87] Employees' statutory duties include a duty not to behave improperly in the workplace.[88] This means that employees should not behave in such a way as to place the safety, health and welfare of others, or indeed themselves, in danger. This duty mirrors that of the employer under s 8(2)(b) (discussed above). Employees also have an obligation under the Act, where health and safety training related to a particular task is required by the employer, or by legislation, to attend and undergo, as appropriate, any reasonable assessment required by the employer and not to misrepresent their level of prior training in health and safety to the employer.[89]

Under the 2005 Act, employees also have a duty to report any potential dangers to [8–38] safety, health and welfare to the employer, or "any other appropriate person", arising from the work "being carried on, or likely to be carried on".[90] Shannon suggests that the "other appropriate person" could be interpreted as meaning the HSA although, as he acknowledges, there is no clarification of this within the legislation.[91] Employees are legally obliged to report any defects in the workplace, problems with systems of work,

---

[85] Byrne, *op.cit*, p 48. It is unclear if an employee wrongly accused of being under the influence of intoxicants when the test results are negative will be able to sue his or her employer; it is certainly feasible that such legal action could arise; Doran, *op.cit*, p 38.

[86] Shannon, *Health and Safety: Law and Practice* (2nd ed, Round Hall, Dublin, 2007), p 29.

[87] s 13(1)(d).

[88] s 13(1)(e).

[89] ss 13(1)(f) and 13(2).

[90] s 13(1)(i).

[91] Shannon, *Health and Safety: Law and Practice* (2nd ed, Round Hall, Dublin, 2007), p 27.

or defective articles or substance to the employer if these pose a potential threat to the safety, health and welfare of the employees or to any other person who may be present in the workplace.[92] The 2005 Act imposes an additional obligation on employees to report any breaches of the legislation which "may endanger the safety, health and welfare at work of the employee or that of any other person".[93] Consequentially, an employee must be cognisant of the dangers in the workplace that may pose a risk to him or her and to others; the employee cannot ignore any breaches of the legislation that pose a threat to the safety, health and welfare of others in the workplace simply because there is no immediate risk to him or her personally.

[8–39] Section 14 of the Act prohibits any person from intentionally or recklessly interfering with, misusing or damaging anything provided under health and safety legislation, or provided to protect the safety, health and welfare of persons at work, or to place at risk the safety, health or welfare of persons in connection with work activities, without reasonable cause. An example of the application of this section would be a duty to refrain from misusing personal protective equipment supplied to employees at a place of work. Note that the section applies to *persons* and not just to *persons at work*. A member of the public who intentionally damages a barrier surrounding an excavation site or a fence designed to prevent access by children onto a hazardous construction site could be held to be liable under this provision. In other examples, the section could also apply to students if they behaved recklessly in a school or college laboratory, to persons removing a lifebuoy for fishermen or to persons interfering with, or removing, equipment such as fire extinguishers.[94] Section 15 of the Act applies to persons in control of places of work that are made available for others to work in. The duties under the section require such a person to ensure, so far as is reasonably practicable, that the place of work, access and egress and any article or substance is safe and without risk to health. This section would apply, for example, where an employee is working in a premises that is not under the control of his or her employer.[95]

VI. The Duty and Standard of Care

[8–40] Most of the duties set out in ss 8 to 17 of the 2005 Act are restricted by the requirement that the employer, employee or other persons subject to the legislation must only do what is "reasonably practicable". For the first time, a statutory definition of "reasonably practicable" is set out in the 2005 Act. Section 2(6) provides that:

> "[f]or the purposes of the relevant statutory provisions, 'reasonably practicable', in relation to the duties of an employer, means that an employer has exercised all due care by putting in place the necessary protective and

---

[92] s 13(1)(h)(ii).
[93] s 13(1)(h)(iii).
[94] HSA, *Guide to the Safety, Health and Welfare at Work Act 2005*, p 20 (available at www.hsa.ie).
[95] Note that Chapter 3 of the 2005 Act outlines the general legislative duties of "Other Persons". s 16 relates to the general duties of designers, manufacturers, importers and suppliers of articles and substances to ensure these are safe and comply with relevant standards. s 17 specifies duties related to the commissioning or procurement of construction work (i.e. that the project is properly designed, capable of being built and maintained safely.)

preventive measures, having identified the hazards and assessed the risks to safety and health likely to result in accidents or injury to health at the place of work concerned and where the putting in place of any further measures is grossly disproportionate having regard to the unusual, unforeseeable and exceptional nature of any circumstance or occurrence that may result in an accident at work or injury to health at that place of work".

Section 2(6) is limited to *employers* and their duties under the Act. It is also associated with s 8, which places the onus of proof on anyone accused of a breach of the Act to demonstrate that all reasonably practicable measures were implemented.[96]

Prior to the 2005 Act, it had been left to the courts to develop the meaning of "reasonably practicable" in the health and safety context. One of the most widely-cited formulations was handed down by the English Court of Appeal in *Edwards v National Coal Board*.[97] This case arose after the side of a road in a mine collapsed due to a hidden defect. Under s 49 of the Coal Mines Act 1911, mine owners had a duty to support a roof. The mine owners had not provided this support and they failed to prove that the cost of providing such support was grossly disproportionate to the risk of the roof collapsing. It was held that what is "reasonably practicable" is linked to a question of risk. According to Asquith LJ: **[8-41]**

" 'Reasonably practicable' is a narrower term than 'physically possible', and seems to me to imply that a computation must be made by the owner in which the quantum of risk is placed on one scale and the sacrifice involved in the measures necessary for averting the risk (whether in money, time or trouble) is placed on the other, and that, if it be shown that there is a gross disproportion between them – the risk being insignificant in relation to the sacrifice – the defendants discharge the onus on them".[98]

Effectively, what this means is that the duty holder is deemed to have done all that is "reasonably practicable", even if there are other measures that could have been taken to prevent harm or injury, where it can be shown, in relation to the risk involved, that the measures, which are technically possible, are disproportionately expensive or troublesome.[99] **[8-42]**

The employer's duty to do all that is reasonably practicable to ensure the safety, health and welfare at work of employees was considered by the Irish superior courts in *Boyle v Marathon Petroleum (Irl) Ltd.*[100] Mr Boyle worked on the Kinsale offshore gas platform, *Platform Alpha*. He was injured when he hit his head against a girder hanging from a mezzanine floor. The mezzanine floor had been installed following complaints by employees, who previously had to use a ladder to check valve and pressure gauges that were located at a height. Using the ladder was quite difficult as the floor of the **[8-43]**

---

[96] See chapter 12.

[97] [1949] 1 KB 704.

[98] *ibid.* at 712.

[99] See also *Marshall v Gotham Co Ltd* [1954] AC 360.

[100] *Boyle v Marathon Petroleum (Irl) Ltd* [1995] *Irish Current Law Monthly Digest* 330 (High Court).

platform also contained fire-fighting equipment and electrical equipment and was quite cluttered. Therefore, the employer installed the mezzanine floor that enabled the employees to check the valves and gauges from a standing position. Mr Boyle was cleaning the bottom floor of the platform when he struck his head on one of girders protruding downwards from the mezzanine floor. At the time of the accident, Mr Boyle was wearing a protective helmet, which also had a visor. Given the lack of headspace between the bottom and middle floors, Mr Boyle had to bend down to clean the floor. He claimed that the visor on his protective helmet made it difficult for him to see properly. Accordingly, he took action against his employer on the grounds of a breach of the common law duty of care and also a breach of the Safety, Health and Welfare (Offshore Installations) Act 1987, which provided under s 10(5) that the installation manager had a duty to ensure that every workplace on the installation is made and kept safe "so far as is reasonably practicable".

[8–44] The High Court rejected the plaintiff's claim. While the Court acknowledged the difficulties arising from working on the bottom floor of the gas platform, which was inconvenient and to "some degree hazardous", the Court took into account the fact that the bottom floor was used infrequently (Mr Boyle worked on the bottom floor around six times a year) and recognised that the middle floor was inserted by the employer following earlier concerns about the dangerous working conditions. There had been no complaints about the middle floor for the 10 years that the gas platform was in operation until Mr Boyle's accident. As such, the High Court found that the employer had done all that was reasonably practicable by inserting the middle floor in this workplace. On appeal, the Supreme Court upheld the High Court's decision. O'Flaherty J stated that:

> "...the onus of proof does rest on the defendants to show that what they did was reasonably practicable. I am also of the opinion that this duty is more extensive than the common law duty which devolves on employers to exercise reasonable care in various respects as regards their employees. It is an obligation to take all practicable steps. That seems to me to involve more than that they should respond, that they, as employers, did all that was reasonably to be expected of them in a particular situation. An employer might sometimes be able to say that what he did by way of exercising reasonable care was done in the 'agony of the moment', for example, but that might not be enough to discharge his statutory duty under the section in question.
>
> However as against the requirement of a higher duty, it must be noted that the statutory duty extends to 'every workplace' on the installation; not just the particular place where the accident happened to occur. As far as the facts of this case were concerned, a balance had to be struck. If the middle floor had not been installed, then undoubtedly the low height hazard would have been removed. On the other hand, the men would have had to go to the lower level to reach the valves much oftener and thus run the risk of tripping over the various obstacles that were there so much more frequently."[101]

---

[101] *ibid* at 466-467.

Byrne notes that the Supreme Court approach involves three elements:

> "...the onus of proof is shifted to the duty holder; the duty is higher than the common law duty of care; cost is not always to be a factor in determining whether 'reasonably practicable' precautions have been taken, but equally a balance has to be struck between the high risk removed by a particular precaution (in the installation of the mezzanine floor) and the remaining low risk created for the plaintiff".[102]

Thus, it is crucial to note that the term "reasonably practicable" does *not* have the same meaning as in the law of negligence; this must be borne in mind when applying the principles derived from the negligence case law discussed above to the fulfilment of duties under the Act.[103] It seems that the definition set out in s 2(6) of the Act conforms to the general meaning of "reasonably practicable" as set out by the Supreme Court in *Boyle*.

[8–45]

VII. Protective and Preventative Measures

Part 3 of the Act deals with protective and preventive measures. Section 18 sets out in greater detail the requirements on employers in s 8 to appoint "competent persons". The employer must appoint one or more competent persons to assist it in complying with safety and health legislation. In this context a competent person, depending on the risks involved and the size of the undertaking, could include a person who is able to give informed and appropriate general advice on health and safety to management, as well as a person with specialised technical knowledge of matters such as electrical work, lifting operations and so on. The competent person should certainly be able to demonstrate knowledge of current best practice in the sector concerned, be aware of any gaps in training and be prepared to supplement those shortfalls. Competent persons must be given enough time, without financial cost or other loss of remuneration, to perform their functions and to be able to keep up to date with relevant information.[104]

[8–46]

Section 19 provides that every employer must identify the hazards at the place of work, assess the risks from those hazards and have a written assessment (referred to under the Act as a "risk assessment") of those risks. This includes an assessment of the risks as they apply to all of the employees and to any single employee or group of employees who may be exposed to any unusual risks, including anything specified by safety and health legislation.[105] Particular consideration may need to be given to "vulnerable workers"; for example, young or inexperienced workers, new and expectant mothers, night time workers and those who work alone. The degree of detail in the risk assessment would need to be proportionate to the risk. For a small business with comparatively insignificant hazards, a simple risk assessment would be sufficient; larger undertakings that present a wide range of hazards would be required to adopt a

[8–47]

---

[102] Byrne, *op.cit,* p 18.

[103] Although, clearly, the employer continues to owe a common law duty of care to its employees; see McMahon and Binchy, *op.cit*, chapter 18.

[104] s 18(2).

[105] s 19(1).

more thorough and sophisticated approach.[106] In order to assist in the identification of hazards, the employer may have to consult various sources of advice and information, such as suppliers' and manufacturers' manuals, legal guidance and competent, specialised sources. Note that under s 26 the employer must consult with employees, or their representatives, on the risk assessment. Under s 21, employers who share a place of work must inform each other of risks arising from the work activity. Employers and persons in control of places of work must carry out a risk assessment in relation to their duty to persons other than their employees as regards s 12 and s 15, respectively. In carrying out the risk assessment it is necessary, therefore, to consider *all* those who might be affected by the undertaking's activities.

[8–48] Section 20 provides that every employer must have a written "safety statement" based on the hazards identified and the risk assessment under s 19 and setting out how the safety, health and welfare of employees will be secured and managed. This is a core requirement under the Act as it emphasises the role of proper planning and management in preventing, and protecting against, threats to health and safety in the workplace. Section 20(2) provides that every employer must ensure that the safety statement specifies:

a) the hazards identified and the risks assessed;
b) the protective and preventive measures taken and the resources provided for protecting safety, health and welfare at the place of work to which the safety statement relates;
c) the plans and procedures to be followed and the measures to be taken in the event of an emergency or serious and imminent danger, in compliance with ss 8 and 11;
d) the duties of his or her employees regarding safety, health and welfare at work, including co-operation with the employer and any persons who have responsibility under the relevant statutory provisions in matters relating to safety, health and welfare at work;
e) the names and, where applicable, the job title or position held of each person responsible for performing tasks assigned to him or her pursuant to the safety statement; and
f) the arrangements made regarding the appointment of safety representatives and consultation with, and participation by, employees and safety representatives, in compliance with ss 25 and 26, including the names of the safety representative and the members of the safety committee, if appointed.

Thus the aims of the safety statement are[107]:

i. to involve management up to the highest level by assigning clear responsibilities in the control of safety, health and welfare at the place of work;
ii. to ensure that appropriate steps are taken to comply with the relevant statutory provisions and that those measures are monitored and reviewed on a regular basis;

---

[106] HSA, *A Guide to the Safety, Health and Welfare at Work Act 2005* (available at www.hsa.ie).
[107] *ibid.*

iii. to identify hazards and prioritise risks;

iv. to ensure sufficient resources are allocated to safety management;

v. to ensure all at the workplace are informed and involved in the control of safety, health and welfare; and

vi. to ensure systematic follow-up of problems as they arise.

The employer must bring the safety statement, in a form, manner and, as appropriate, language that is reasonably likely to be understood, to the attention of its employees at least once a year; at any time when it is amended; to newly-recruited employees upon commencement of their employment; and to any other persons at the place of work who may be exposed to any specific risk to which the safety statement applies.[108] It must be brought to the attention, specifically, of employees exposed to "serious risks".[109]   **[8–49]**

The statement must be reviewed, as appropriate, and a copy must be available for inspection at the workplace.[110] Employers and persons in control of places of work must prepare a safety statement in relation to their duty to persons other than their employees as regards ss 12 and 15.[111] There is an innovation in the Act, which removes the requirement for an employer with three or fewer employees to have an up-to-date safety statement[112]; instead, it will be sufficient for such employers to comply with HSA codes of practice.[113]   **[8–50]**

Section 22 of the Act requires employers to ensure that health surveillance relevant to the risks to safety, health and welfare identified by risk assessments prepared under s 19, and any particular health surveillance required by relevant legislation, is available to employees. This could be construed as requiring an employer to make available a counselling service or an employee assistance programme. In *Hatton v Sutherland*[114] it was held that an employer who offers a confidential advice service, with referral to appropriate counselling or treatment services, is unlikely to be found in breach of duty as regards health surveillance. In *Maher v Jabil Global Services*[115] it was held that the employer company did not breach its duty of care in circumstances where the company provided a confidential advice service with a referral to appropriate counselling services, despite its knowledge of the plaintiff's psychiatric vulnerability. The Court did, however, go on to say that a confidential advice service must be one of *substance* rather than form and that the Court will look at each case carefully as it arises. There is a close relationship between the duty regarding health surveillance and the carrying out of the risk assessment, again emphasising the need for careful planning and management in relation to occupational heath and safety. It would be appropriate to carry out health surveillance when, for example, the nature   **[8–51]**

---

[108] s 20(3).

[109] s 20(4).

[110] ss 20(5) and (7).

[111] s 20(9).

[112] s 20(8).

[113] See, for example, *Construction Safety Code of Practice for Contractors with Three or Less (sic) Employees 2008*.

[114] [2002] 2 All ER 1.

[115] [2008] 1 IR 25. See also chapter 9.

of the particular work is associated with an identifiable disease or adverse health condition, there is a reasonable likelihood that the disease or condition may occur under the particular circumstances, or health surveillance is likely to further the protection of the employees.[116]

[8–52]   Section 23 (subject to the making of specific regulations), gives the right to the employer to require employees to be assessed by a registered medical practitioner, nominated by the employer, as to fitness to carry out work which presents critical risks to the safety, health and welfare of persons at work. If the registered medical practitioner is of the opinion that an employee is unfit to perform such work, he or she must tell the employer and indicate the likelihood of early resumption of work for rehabilitative purposes; the registered medical practitioner must also tell the employee and give him or her the reasons for that opinion.[117]

[8–53]   Sections 24 to 26 emphasise that the management of health and safety in the workplace should be a collective endeavour, involving all stakeholders.[118] Section 24 provides that trade unions and bodies representing employers may make agreements setting out practical guidance on safety, health and welfare and the requirements of safety and health legislation and may apply to the HSA for approval of such an agreement or its variation. The Authority may approve a joint safety and health agreement if the parties have consented to the approval being sought, the agreement does not conflict with safety and health legislation and is in a form suitable for approval.[119] If the agreement stipulates that it applies to all employees in a particular class of employment and their employers, and the Authority is satisfied with this, the agreement will also apply to employers and employees who are not members of the trade unions or the bodies representing employers carrying out work in this class of employment.

[8–54]   Section 25(1) permits employees to appoint a safety representative who will act on their behalf to consult with the employer regarding any issues concerning safety, health and welfare at work. The remit of the safety representative extends beyond a consultative role, as s 25(2) provides that the safety representatives have a right to conduct an inspection of the "whole or any part of the place of work" after providing the employer with reasonable notice. The safety representative may conduct an immediate inspection of the workplace "in the event of an accident, dangerous occurrence or imminent danger or risk to the safety, health and welfare of any person", without the need to give notice to the employer.[120] The safety representative can undertake an investigation in response to complaints from employees with concerns about safety, health and welfare at work, provide assistance to HSA inspectors undertaking investigations and can attend any interviews undertaken by HSA inspectors.[121] One of the key functions of the safety representative is to put forward any issues or concerns relating to safety, health and welfare in the workplace to the employer, on behalf of the employees, in

---

[116] HSA, *A Guide to the Safety, Health and Welfare at Work Act 2005* (available at www.hsa.ie).
[117] s 23(3).
[118] See the discussion of employee consultation rights in chapter 11.
[119] s 24(2).
[120] s 25(2)(a)(ii).
[121] s 25(2)(c)-(f).

either oral or written format.[122] The employer is legally obliged to take into consideration any representations made to it by the safety representative on the employees' behalf and the employer has a duty to act on these representations as appropriate.[123] Section 25(5) provides that the safety representative is entitled to paid time off work to undergo training necessary to assist him or her to properly undertake the functions and duties under the 2005 Act. Section 26 provides for the consultation and participation of employees in all discussions relating to matters of health and safety. The employer should, in relation to such matters, consult with its employees, their safety representatives or both, as appropriate, "in advance" and in "good time".[124] Section 26(3) provides for the establishment of a health and safety committee (subject to the employer's agreement).

The enforcement of the Act and the liabilities that can be imposed thereunder are discussed in chapter 12.

---

[122] s 25(2)(g) and (h).
[123] s 25(4).
[124] s 26(1)(b).

CHAPTER 9

Bullying and Harassment in the Workplace

I. Introduction

The remit of the equality legislation examined in chapter 5 extends beyond issues of discrimination in relation to pay, working conditions and dismissal in the workplace: it also provides protection from the "more aggressive, predatory conduct" that can exist.[1] Sexual harassment, harassment on the basis of any of the nine discriminatory grounds and bullying are all examples of this type of conduct.

[9–01]

The EU has only introduced prohibitions on harassment and sexual harassment on the discriminatory grounds within the past decade. The Recast Equal Treatment Directive, Race Directive and Framework Directive all provide that harassment on any of the discriminatory grounds is unlawful.[2] The introduction of prohibitions on harassment and sexual harassment in the workplace by the Employment Equality Act 1998 is yet another indicator of the pioneering nature of this piece of equality

[9–02]

---

[1] Eardley, *Sex Discrimination at Work* (FirstLaw, Dublin, 2002), p 129.

[2] Directive 2006/54 on the implementation of equal opportunities and equal treatment of men and women in matters of employment and occupation [2006] OJ L204/23 (hereinafter referred to as the "Recast Equal Treatment Directive"); Directive 2000/43 on Race Discrimination [2000] OJ L180/22 (hereinafter referred to as the "Race Directive"); Council Directive 2000/78 establishing a general framework for equal treatment in employment and occupation [2000] OJ L303/16 (hereinafter referred to as the "Framework Directive").

legislation.[3] Section 23 of the 1998 Act provided that sexual harassment was unlawful and s 32 stipulated that harassment on any of the nine discriminatory grounds was also unlawful. The Equality Act 2004 repealed both ss 23 and 32, replacing them with a new section (s 14A) and also introduced changes to the definitions of harassment and sexual harassment, so that the occurrence of either will constitute unlawful discrimination by the victim's employer in relation to the conditions of employment.[4] As will be seen, one single incident can give rise to a claim of harassment or sexual harassment in the workplace.

[9–03] Cases of bullying in the workplace have been on the rise over the past ten years, with an increasing number of plaintiffs taking legal action against employers for personal injuries on the grounds of work-related stress caused by bullying behaviour.[5] It is recognised that there are huge financial and human costs caused by bullying, as such behaviour can have a very damaging impact on the victim's physical and mental health. In addition, from the employer's perspective, such behaviour can create a negative working environment with a potential to affect performance and output.[6]

This chapter examines the available avenues of redress for employees subjected to sexual harassment, harassment or bullying in the workplace.

II. Harassment and Sexual Harassment

[9–04] Harassment is a specific form of discrimination in relation to conditions of employment, which is based on one or more of the nine discriminatory grounds specified in s 6 of the Employment Equality Acts: gender, marital status, family status, sexual orientation, religion, age, disability, race or membership of the traveller community.[7] Section 14A(7)(a) defines harassment and sexual harassment:

> "(i) references to harassment are to any form of unwanted conduct related to any of the discriminatory grounds, and
> (ii) references to sexual harassment are to any form of unwanted verbal, non-verbal or physical conduct of a sexual nature,
> being conduct which in either case has the purpose or effect of violating a person's dignity and creating an intimidating, hostile, degrading, humiliating or offensive environment for the person".

---

[3] See Darcy, "Achieving De Facto Equality between Men and Women- Making the Employment Equality Act 1998 Work" (2004) 22 ILT 199.

[4] As in chapter 5, the 1998 Act, as amended by the 2004 Act, will be referred to as "the Employment Equality Acts". The prohibition on harassment and sexual harassment at work is now contained in s 14A of the Employment Equality Acts.

[5] See, for example, Stewart *et al*, "Bullying and the Workplace" (2008) 5(4) IELJ 114; Barrett, "Psychiatric Stress - an Unacceptable Cost to Employers" (2008) 1 *Journal of Business Law* 64; Cox, "Employer's Liability for Workplace Stress" (2006) 1(2) QRTL 10.

[6] *Health and Safety Authority Code of Practice for Employers and Employees on the Prevention and Resolution of Bullying at Work* (Health and Safety Authority, 2007). See, also, Hrymak and Perezgonzalez, *The Costs and Effects of Workplace Accidents: Twenty Case Studies from Ireland* (Health and Safety Authority Research Series 02/2007, 2007) available at www.hsa.ie.

[7] See chapter 5.

The Employment Equality Acts provided a definition of sexual harassment for the first time in Irish legislation. Originally, under the 1998 Act, an objective test was used to determine what constituted sexual harassment, as s 23(3) required that "the act, request or conduct is unwelcome and could *reasonably be regarded* as sexually offensive, humiliating or intimidating" (emphasis added). Section 14A of the Employment Equality Acts redefines sexual harassment to ensure compliance with the definitions contained in the various EU Directives. This amended definition replicates the definition of sexual harassment set out in Art 2(1)(c) of the Recast Equal Treatment Directive. Similarly, the definition of harassment in the Acts now reflects those contained within the Race Directive and the Framework Directive. However, the definition of harassment stipulates that it is unwanted conduct that must be "related to" any of the discriminatory grounds. As a result, the complainant taking a claim for harassment will have to prove that the harassment that occurred related in some way to any of these nine grounds.[8]

[9–05]

In a claim for harassment or sexual harassment, it must be shown that the conduct complained of was unwelcome. The employee must decide what is unwelcome and from whom, if anyone, such behaviour is welcome or unwelcome. In *A Company v A Worker*,[9] for example, the Labour Court stated that a sexual relationship between consenting adults does not imply that the consent of the parties is unlimited as regards time, duration, or what acts may take place between the parties.

[9–06]

Unwelcome conduct must have the purpose or effect of violating a person's dignity and creating an intimidating, hostile, degrading, humiliating or offensive environment for the person. As a result, the *intention* of the perpetrator of the harassment or sexual harassment is largely irrelevant. The fact that the perpetrator has no intention of harassing or sexually harassing the employee is no defence: it is the *effect* of the behaviour on the employee that is important. Therefore, it is now necessary to analyse the conduct from the perspective of the victim alone.[10]

[9–07]

As regards sexual harassment, conduct will likely not be considered to be "unwelcome" if it is *reciprocated*, for example if the complainant responds positively to any physical, verbal or non-verbal conduct which is of a sexual nature and/or encourages the other's advances or behaviour.[11]

---

[8] Cox *et al*, *Employment Law in Ireland* (Clarus Press, Dublin, 2009), p 366.

[9] [1990] ELR 187.

[10] Bolger and Kimber, "Employment Equality" in *Employment Law* (Regan ed, Tottel, Dublin, 2009), p 423. Note, though, that the authors refer to the decision in *Scanlon v St Vincent's Hospital* (DEC-E2004-284), where the English complainant alleged that he was subjected to harassment on the grounds of his nationality. In particular, the complainant relied on an incident where his supervisor made derogatory remarks about England losing a football match. The Tribunal found the complainant had not established a prima facie case, as the supervisor, at the time of making the comments, was unaware that the complainant was English. This was despite the Tribunal seeming to accept the complainant's evidence that the *effect* of the comments was to make him feel he was working in an offensive and hostile environment.

[11] Cox *et al*, *op.cit*, p 358. This, however, is often a contentious issue of fact before the courts and tribunals (see below).

The unwanted conduct that could amount to harassment or sexual harassment can take the form of "acts, requests, spoken word or gestures or the production, display or circulation of written words, pictures or other material".[12]

[9–08] Further regulation of harassment and sexual harassment in the workplace is provided for by the Employment Equality Act 1998 (Code of Practice) (Harassment) Order 2002, which gives statutory effect to the Code of Practice on Sexual Harassment and Harassment at Work.[13] It was noted by the Equality Tribunal in *A Female Employee v A Recruitment Company*[14] that the Code is an approved Code of Practice in accordance with s 56(4) of the Employment Equality Acts and, therefore, admissible in evidence in any proceedings to help determine any questions that arise.[15]

Victimisation

[9–09] Section 74(2) of the Employment Equality Acts provides that:

> "... victimisation occurs where dismissal or other adverse treatment of an employee by his or her employer occurs as a reaction to –
> (a) a complaint of discrimination made by the employee to the employer,
> (b) any proceedings by a complainant,
> (c) an employee having represented or otherwise supported a complainant...".

If an employee makes a complaint to the employer of discrimination on the grounds that he or she has been subject to harassment or sexual harassment and is treated differently as a consequence of complaining (or is dismissed) the complainant can initiate a claim of victimisation.[16] The Equality Tribunal in *Ms A v A Contract Cleaning Company*[17] found that the complainant had been subject to victimisation by her employer for reporting an incident of sexual harassment. In this case, Ms A was informed by her immediate supervisor, who had been a witness to the incident of sexual harassment, that Ms A would be dismissed if she continued to pursue her claim.

Similarly, a claim of victimisation could arise because the complainant has brought a claim to the Equality Tribunal or indeed provided representation or support for another employee taking a claim of harassment or sexual harassment.[18] In *A Female Employee v A Recruitment Company*[19] the complainant alleged that she had been victimised by her employer when she complained about sexual harassment, as she was dismissed shortly after making her complaint. The Equality Tribunal found that she had been victimised and the complainant was awarded €15,000 compensation for the effects of the victimisation.

---

[12] Employment Equality Acts, s 14A(7)(c).
[13] SI No 78 of 2002.
[14] DEC-E2008-015.
[15] See chapter 2 for a discussion of the status of Codes of Practice in Irish employment law.
[16] See Curran, "Victimisation: A New Remedy for Employees" (2008) 5(1) IELJ 4.
[17] DEC-E2004-068.
[18] *McCarthy v Dublin Corporation* [2001] ELR 255.
[19] DEC-E2008-015.

Protection under the legislation is also afforded to an employee who is treated **[9–10]** differently in the course of his or her employment (for example, as regards to any opportunities for promotion or access to training opportunities) subsequent to the employee's *rejection or acceptance* of any harassment or sexual harassment that occurs.[20] The Equality Tribunal in *Ms Z v A Hotel*[21] found that the complainant had been adversely treated for rejecting the advances of her general manager, Mr A. At a work party, Mr A had told the complainant that she "looked gorgeous" that evening and suggested that they should share a taxi home together. The complainant subsequently informed Mr A that she found his behaviour unacceptable. Shortly after, her contract of employment was terminated, allegedly on the grounds that she had used abusive language when making her complaint to Mr A. The Equality Tribunal, while noting there was contradictory evidence relating to the alleged incident at the party, held that the comments made by Mr A to the complainant did constitute sexual harassment. The Tribunal found that the termination of the complainant's contract was linked to her rejection of Mr A's advances.

III. The Scope of the Prohibition

According to s 14A(1)(a) of the Employment Equality Acts, harassment or sexual **[9–11]** harassment can occur at the employee's place of work, or otherwise in the course of his or her employment.[22] The Code of Practice on Sexual Harassment and Harassment at Work provides that the prohibition on harassment and sexual harassment extends to work-related events, which take place outside the workplace, or events that employees attend in the course of employment, such as conferences, workshops, business trips or training events. In *A Limited Company v One Female Employee*,[23] for example, the complainant alleged that she had been sexually harassed when she was attending a residential company training programme in a hotel.

The prohibition also extends to non-workplace harassment or sexual harassment that **[9–12]** occurs at work-related *social* events, particularly if such events have been officially organised by the employer. In *A Female Employee v A Recruitment Company*[24] the complainant received lewd and sexually suggestive texts from her manager after a work night out. The Equality Tribunal referred to its earlier decision in *Maguire v North Eastern Health Board*,[25] where the Tribunal determined that harassment which took place at an office Christmas party constituted discrimination within the scope of the legislation. Considering both the earlier decision in *Maguire* and the Code of Practice,

---

[20] Employment Equality Acts, s 14A(3). See *Maguire v North Eastern Health Board* (DEC-E2002-039).

[21] DEC-E2007-14.

[22] See Ryan and Ryan, "Vicarious Liability of Employers- Emerging Themes and Trends and their Potential Implications for Irish Law" (2007) 4(1) IELJ 3, where the authors speculate on whether the scope of what constitutes "in the course of employment" will expand, following the decision of the House of Lords in *Lister v Hesley Hall* [2002] 1 AC 215.

[23] EE 10/1988.

[24] DEC-E2008-015.

[25] DEC-E2002-039. In this case, the complainant successfully argued that he had been discriminated against on the grounds that he was a member of the Traveller Community. He also successfully argued that he had been subject to harassment for this at the Christmas party, on the basis that he was referred to by a colleague as a "knacker".

the Tribunal held that, even though the night out in question had been arranged by the *employees* and was not an official night out organised by the *employer*, it did fall under the scope of the legislation: the complainant would not have been present if she had not been employed by the respondent company. The Equality Tribunal further stated that the actions of the complainant's manager (and another colleague, who it seemed sent the messages from the manager's phone) were conducted in the course of their employment.[26]

[9–13] An employer who provides funding for social events could, therefore, potentially be held liable for any harassment or sexual harassment that occurs at such events.[27] However, in *Ms O'N v An Insurance Company*[28] the respondent was found not to be liable for sexual harassment that occurred at a social club function, which was part-funded by the employer. The Tribunal concluded that, while an incident of sexual harassment did occur at a pub quiz, on the night in question the complainant had not been attending the social club in the course of her employment.

Who are the Harassers?

[9–14] An employer can be held *vicariously liable* for the harassment or sexual harassment of its employees.[29] Section 15(1) of the Employment Equality Acts provides that:

> "... [a]nything done by a person in the course of his or her employment shall, in any proceedings brought under this Act, be treated for the purposes of this Act as done also by that person's employer, whether or not it was done with the employer's knowledge or approval".

Essentially, therefore, the principle of vicarious liability means that a defendant employer can be held liable for the wrongdoing of its employee: "in this respect the principle is a species of strict liability, in that it is not necessary at all to prove any fault or moral blameworthiness on the part of the defendant employer".[30] The rationale for this principle was summarised well by Lord Nicholls in *Majrowski v Guy's and St Thomas's NHS Trust*[31]:

> "... [the] common law principle of strict liability for another person's wrongs finds its rationale today in a combination of policy factors....Stated shortly, these factors are that all forms of economic activity carry a risk of harm to others, and fairness requires that those responsible for such activities should be liable to persons suffering loss from wrongs committed in the conduct of the enterprise. This is 'fair', because it means injured persons can look for recompense to a source better placed financially than individual wrongdoing

---

[26] This decision is discussed further below. See also *Ms Z v A Hotel* (DEC-E2007-14).

[27] But see Connolly, "Bullying and Harassment in the Workplace- Recent Developments" (2002) 9(6) CLP 123.

[28] DEC-E2004-52.

[29] See Ryan and Ryan, *op.cit.*

[30] Ryan, "Vicarious Liability" in *Employment Law* (Regan ed, Tottel, Dublin, 2009), p 265.

[31] [2006] 3 WLR 125 at 128.

employees. It means also that the financial loss arising from the wrongs can be spread more widely, by liability insurance and higher prices. In addition, and importantly, imposing strict liability on employers encourages them to maintain standards of 'good practice' by their employees. For these reasons employers are to be held liable for wrongs committed by their employees in the course of their employment".

Section 15(3) of the Employment Equality Acts, however, provides a defence to the employer where it can show it took such steps as were "reasonably practicable" to prevent the prohibited acts from occurring.

Section 14A(1) of the Employment Equality Acts protects employees from harassment **[9–15]** or sexual harassment by the employer or another employee of the employer. It also protects employees from harassment or sexual harassment by a client, customer or other business contact of the victim's employer: this includes "any other person with whom the employer might reasonably expect the victim to come into contact in the workplace or otherwise in the course of his or her employment".[32]

The broad scope of this prohibition is evident from the decision of the Equality **[9–16]** Tribunal in *Ms A v A Contract Cleaning Company*.[33] The complainant alleged that she had been sexually harassed by an employee of a security firm who worked in the same shopping centre. The Tribunal held that the alleged harasser was a person that the respondent might reasonably expect the complainant to come into contact with either in her workplace or in the course of her employment. The Tribunal, therefore, held the respondent liable for acts of sexual harassment carried out by this person, even though he was not an employee of the respondent.

"Other business contacts of the victim's employer" could include, for example, **[9–17]** suppliers, delivery persons, interns, and so on. In *BH v A Named Company*[34] the complainant alleged that she had been subject to sexual harassment by a number of cab drivers who provided services for the respondent company. Even though the complainant did not provide any evidence to confirm whether the cab drivers who had carried out these acts were employees of the company, or whether they were self-employed, the Tribunal held that the drivers did fall within the scope of the legislation, either as employees *or* as business contacts with whom the employer might reasonably expect the complainant to come into contact in the workplace or otherwise in the course of her employment. In *Atkinson v Carty*[35] the employer was held liable for sexual harassment carried out by a person who was not an employee but an independent contractor who provided accountancy services to the employer.

IV. Proving a Claim

In accordance with s 85A of the Employment Equality Acts, the burden of proof in **[9–18]** harassment and sexual harassment claims initially rests with the complainant, who must establish prima facie evidence that the harassment or sexual harassment did, in

---

[32] Employment Equality Acts, s 14A(4).
[33] DEC-E2004-068.
[34] DEC-E2006-026.
[35] [2005] 16 ELR 1.

fact, take place. The focus then shifts to whether the employer is liable, that is, did it take reasonable steps to prevent the harassment or sexual harassment.[36]

[9–19] The Tribunal frequently faces an extremely difficult task in harassment and, particularly, sexual harassment claims, as often there will be no witnesses to the alleged incident and it will be the claimant's word against that of the alleged perpetrator. The Tribunal, in such instances, must, on the balance of probabilities, come down on the side of the party before it that presents the most credible evidence.

[9–20] A perfect example of the difficulties that often arise can be seen in *Ms CL v CRM*.[37] Here, the complainant alleged that she had been subject to both physical and verbal sexual harassment in the workplace. The complainant worked as a junior sales adviser for the respondent. As part of her duties, she would, on occasion, deliver and collect cars for the respondent. On one such occasion, a colleague, Mr A, provided her with a lift back to the workplace. According to the complainant, Mr. A grabbed her and sexually harassed her. She alleged that he said "come on... how about we pull over for a quickie", to which she replied "I don't think so". The complainant also alleged that Mr A put his hand on her breast and said "give me a go". This incident was reported to a supervisor, however, it was further alleged that Mr A sent the complainant text messages of a sexual nature on a number of subsequent occasions.

[9–21] Mr A responded to the claims by alleging that *he* was the one constantly being harassed by the *complainant*. On one occasion when he travelled with the complainant, he claimed she made the comment that he had missed out as "we could have gone for a quickie". Mr A further claimed that the complainant texted and phoned him on a regular basis both during and after work, asking him to go for lunch or for a drink and that her text messages were of a sexual nature. According to Mr A, the complainant regularly called him "big boy" in front of other members of staff and was "constantly flirting" and "bragging about sexual encounters". The Tribunal acknowledged the clear conflict in the evidence and held that, on the balance of probabilities, the complainant was subjected to sexual harassment by Mr A.

[9–22] It seems the Tribunal will look favourably on evidence that the complainant swiftly *reported* any incident of alleged sexual harassment. In *Ms A v A Cleaning Company*[38] the complainant reported the incident to both her husband *and* to the Gardaí almost immediately after it occurred: the complainant was awarded the maximum amount of compensation available (104 weeks' remuneration).

V. Sexual Harassment

[9–23] Section 14A(7) of the Employment Equality Acts provides that references to sexual harassment are references to any form of behaviour which includes physical, verbal or non-verbal conduct of a sexual nature. The Code of Practice on Sexual Harassment and Harassment at Work also provides a description of the type of behaviour that may amount to sexual harassment. It is the *sexual nature* of the conduct, therefore, that

---

[36] *Mr A v A Hotel* (DEC-E2009-003). See the discussion of the burden of proof in equality claims in chapter 5.
[37] DEC-E2004-02.
[38] DEC-E2004-068.

distinguishes it from other forms of harassment, which must be connected in some way with any of the nine discriminatory grounds. Indeed, one of the most significant changes to the definition of sexual harassment introduced by the 2004 Act is that a claim can now be brought in relation to harassment by someone of the same sex as the complainant.[39]

Physical Conduct of a Sexual Nature

Under the Code of Practice on Sexual Harassment and Harassment at Work, unwanted physical conduct of a sexual nature includes any "unnecessary touching, patting or pinching or brushing against another employee's body, assault and coercive sexual intercourse". Thus, in accordance with this definition, a person placing his or her hand on the shoulder of a colleague could constitute sexual harassment.[40] [9–24]

In *Ms A v A Cleaning Company*[41] the complainant was employed as a cleaner by the respondent. Part of her work involved carrying out cleaning duties at a shopping centre. According to the complainant, she was subject to sexual harassment by Mr B, who was a security guard employed by a company that provided security services for the shopping centre. The complainant alleged that Mr B made crude and sexually offensive remarks to her and other female colleagues. On one occasion, while she was cleaning, the security guard pulled the waistband of her trousers and commented on her wearing "flowery knickers". On another occasion, the complainant alleged that she was approached by Mr B, who pinned her arms behind her back, pulled down her trousers and underwear and slapped her a number of times on her bare bottom. The Tribunal held this incident did amount to sexual harassment and, moreover, deemed it to be "the most appalling attack on [the complainant's] personal dignity". Similarly, in *Ms A v A Gym*[42] the Tribunal held that the complainant was sexually harassed when she received a "robust slap" on her bottom from a male colleague. On complaining to her manager, the latter immediately began to investigate the matter and tried to arrange shifts so that the complainant did not have to encounter her male colleague. However, the manager informed the complainant that she could not take the matter further, due to a lack of witnesses. The Tribunal held this was an inadequate response and ordered the respondent to immediately implement a full and fair complaints procedure.[43] [9–25]

Verbal Conduct of a Sexual Nature

Verbal conduct of a sexual nature is defined in the Code of Practice as including "unwelcome sexual advances, propositions or pressure for sexual activity, continued [9–26]

---

[39] Cox *et al, op.cit*, p 358. See *A Construction Worker v A Construction Company* (DEC-E2008-48), where a male complainant alleged he was subject to harassment on the grounds of his sexual orientation. He was awarded compensation in excess of €50,000. The case is currently under appeal.

[40] *A Worker v A Company* [1992] ELR 73. Although the context in which such an act takes place will, of course, be crucial.

[41] DEC-E2004-068.

[42] DEC-E2004-11.

[43] Such a procedure should probably be based on the provisions of the Code of Practice on Sexual Harassment and Harassment at Work. See below for further detail on employer defences to harassment actions.

suggestions for social activity outside the work place after it has been made clear that such suggestions are unwelcome, unwanted or offensive flirtations, suggestive remarks, innuendos or lewd comments". The use of crude language as part of office "banter" or "repartee" could, therefore, be deemed to constitute sexual harassment under this definition. For example, the Tribunal found in *Ms A v A Gym*[44] that, in addition to being sexually harassed physically (as seen above), the complainant was sexually harassed *verbally* by her male colleague. Prior to slapping the complainant, the male colleague had been heard making comments to the effect that he felt the complainant had "lovely legs" and a "lovely" bottom. These comments made to the victim (and, about her, to others) constituted sexual harassment.

[9–27]   In *An Office Worker v A Security Company*[45] the complaints of sexual harassment related to incidents whereby the managing director of a company made offensive comments about the complainant, told her "dirty jokes" and frequently made offensive and sexually explicit remarks to her. The complainant was awarded compensation for the distress and effects of both discrimination and sexual harassment, because the impugned conduct had been ongoing, had occurred at an early stage in her employment and had created a "degrading, humiliating and offensive work environment", which led to the complainant suffering from a stress-related illness.

Non-Verbal Conduct of a Sexual Nature

[9–28]   Non-verbal conduct of a sexual nature is defined by the Code of Practice as including "the display of pornographic or sexually suggestive pictures, objects, written materials, emails, text-messages or faxes...leering, whistling or making sexually suggestive gestures". In *An Office Worker v A Security Company*[46] the company managing director had put up a picture of a naked woman in the complainant's office and refused to remove it. The respondent claimed that the picture was a replica of a painting in the National Gallery but was unable to identify the "genesis of the original painting". The Tribunal found that this behaviour fell within the statutory definition of sexual harassment. In *A Worker v A Company*[47] the impugned non-verbal conduct included the display of an offensive calendar and a Christmas card message that had sexual connotations. The respondent submitted that these displays, along with the use of crude language with a sexual connotation, were part of the "office banter, repartee and jest". The Labour Court rejected the respondent's submissions as a defence for such behaviour, finding that it did constitute sexual harassment.

[9–29]   Sending text messages with sexually suggestive content will constitute non-verbal conduct of a sexual nature. In *A Female Employee v A Recruitment Company*[48] the complainant received a number of lewd and sexually suggestive text messages from a colleague, Mr C, shortly after his departure from a work night out. The complainant was subsequently informed by another colleague that, while the messages had been

---

[44] DEC-E2004-11.
[45] DEC-E2010-002.
[46] *ibid.*
[47] [1992] ELR 73.
[48] DEC-E2008-015.

sent from Mr C's phone, they had been sent by a friend of his as a "prank". The Tribunal found, nevertheless, that the receipt by the complainant of text messages sent from her manager's phone amounted to unwanted conduct as defined by s 14A(7)(b) of the Employment Equality Acts. The complainant was awarded €10,000 for the effects of the discrimination arising from her dismissal, plus a further €15,000 for the effects of sexual harassment. The respondent was ordered to prepare a policy to prevent sexual harassment and harassment in the workplace.

Sex-Based Conduct

The Code of Practice defines sexual harassment as including any sex-based conduct. Sex-based conduct is defined as conduct that "denigrates or ridicules or is intimidatory or physically abusive of an employee because of his or her sex such as derogatory or degrading abuse or insults which are gender-related". **[9–30]**

VI. Harassment

The Code of Practice on Sexual Harassment and Harassment at Work also identifies different types of conduct that may be deemed to amount to harassment in the workplace. This type of conduct includes verbal harassment, written harassment, physical harassment, intimidatory harassment, visual displays, isolation or exclusion from social activities or pressure to behave in a manner perceived by the employee to be inappropriate. The Code specifically states that an employee can be subjected to harassment on the basis of a range of attributes that he or she might possess, for example a physical or social feature like an accent, hair colour, dietary regime or dress code. In *BH v A Named Company*[49] the complainant was subjected to harassment, *inter alia*, on the grounds of her weight, when the perpetrators placed laxative tablets and steroids in an office kettle that the complainant and other colleagues used. The protection against harassment also extends to situations where the employee does *not* have the relevant characteristic but the perpetrator believes that he or she does, for example, where the harasser wrongly thinks the employee is gay and subjects him or her to harassment on that basis. **[9–31]**

Physical harassment would include any jostling, shoving or any form of physical assault. Verbal harassment could comprise jokes, comments, songs or ridicule. In *A Worker v An Engineering Company*[50] the complainant, who was an English national, brought a successful claim of harassment as a consequence of the complainant's colleagues persistently singing anti-British rebel songs at work. He also complained that his colleagues would make negative comments in relation to the nuclear plant at Sellafield and about the English football team's performance during the World Cup in Germany. The complainant felt so intimidated and excluded in the workplace that a fortnight after he commenced employment with the respondent, he began to have his lunch in his car. **[9–32]**

Intimidatory harassment could take the form of intimidatory gestures, posturing or poses. Visual displays can include emblems, badges or posters. Isolation or exclusion from work-related social activities may also amount to harassment. In *Odion v* **[9–33]**

---

[49] DEC-E2006-026.
[50] DEC-E2008-038.

Techniform (Waterford) Ltd[51] the complainant alleged that he had been harassed because of his race in the course of his employment. The complainant was a Nigerian national. The harassment took the form of abusive comments (including racially abusive comments) and isolation, for example when he sat down to eat his lunch, the other employees would get up and leave. The Equality Tribunal found that the complainant had been subject to harassment on the grounds of his race. Moreover, the Tribunal highlighted its concern regarding the respondent's failure to ensure that the complainant was not isolated in the workplace, given the fact that the complainant was the only black employee and it was evident that there were cultural differences between employees.

Pressure to behave in a manner that the employee thinks is unsuitable might, for example, include a requirement to dress in a manner unsuited to a person's ethnic or religious background or belief.[52]

VII. Employers' Defences

[9–34]   Section 14A(2) of the Employment Equality Acts provides that the employer will have a defence to a claim of harassment or sexual harassment if it can prove that it took "such steps as are reasonably practicable":

> "(*a*) to prevent the person from harassing or sexually harassing the victim or any class of persons which includes the victim, and/or
> (*b*) to prevent the victim from being treated differently in the workplace or otherwise in the course of the victim's employment and, if and so far as any such treatment has occurred, to reverse its effects".

It is evident from many of the decisions of the Equality Tribunal regarding claims of harassment or sexual harassment that the failure of employers to implement a comprehensive and effective *policy* to prevent harassment and sexual harassment in the workplace can have serious consequences, both in terms of the number of employees bringing such claims and in relation to financial cost to the employer.[53]

[9–35]   Such a policy should reflect the provisions of the Code of Practice on Sexual Harassment and Harassment at Work and should include, at least: a definition of harassment and sexual harassment; a procedure for reporting and/or complaining about incidents of harassment and sexual harassment; and a statement that management and others in positions of authority have a particular responsibility to ensure that incidents of harassment and sexual harassment do not occur and that complaints are addressed speedily.

[9–36]   The mere *existence* of a workplace policy, however, is not sufficient on its own. The Equality Tribunal has made it clear on numerous occasions that such policies must be

---

[51] DEC-E2007-018.

[52] See Tahzib-Lie, "Controversies over Religious Symbols in the Workplace: Workforce Diversity Versus 'Androgynous, Mechanical Clones'"? (2007) 25(4) *Netherlands Quarterly of Human Rights* 563.

[53] See, Middlemiss, "Liability of Employers for Verbal Harassment in the Workplace" (2009) 6(1) IELJ 8.

meaningfully and effectively *implemented*. The employer has a responsibility to ensure that the employees have been made aware of the policy and any related grievance procedure. In *A Worker v An Engineering Company*[54] the complainant alleged that he had been discriminated against on the grounds of his race because he was persistently harassed by his colleagues for being an English national. The complainant stated that he felt that he could not complain about this behaviour, as his supervisor had taken no action to stop it when he observed what was going on and, on occasion, had also engaged in harassing conduct. The respondent submitted that a policy to prevent bullying and harassment did exist within the company. However, the Equality Tribunal found that the respondent had failed to demonstrate how this policy had been disseminated among the staff. The respondent was deemed liable for the harassment as the policy had not been effectively implemented and also because the supervisor who had been aware of the harassment had failed to take any steps to prevent it from occurring.

In *Ms A v A Gym*[55] the complainant made a verbal and written complaint to her manager that she had been slapped on the bottom by a colleague. The Tribunal found that the manager did not know how to deal with an allegation of sexual harassment, that there was no internal grievance procedure or code of practice on such a matter and that the respondent had not introduced any procedures to comply with its responsibilities under equality legislation. Therefore, the respondent had not taken such steps as were reasonably practicable to provide it with a defence to the finding of discrimination. The respondent was ordered to introduce a policy to deal with complaints of sexual harassment. **[9–37]**

In *A Construction Worker v A Construction Company*[56] the complainant alleged that he had been subject to discriminatory treatment on the grounds of sexual orientation, sexual harassment and victimisation. The complainant did complain to his foreman after he had been subject to harassment on a number of occasions. However, the complainant was subjected to further harassment after this, at which stage he made a formal complaint informing the respondent that he was having suicidal thoughts due to the level of abuse and harassment. The respondent stated that the complainant was subsequently removed from working at heights and redeployed to a ground-level site to protect the safety, health and welfare of the complainant and other employees. The Tribunal found that the complainant had established a prima facie case of discrimination on the grounds of sexual harassment, as the respondent accepted that incidents of harassment had arisen. However, the respondent had failed to show that there was any formal policy or procedure in place to deal with complaints or grievances relating to sexual harassment. Consequently, the Tribunal held that the lack of a policy or a complaints procedure rendered it impossible for the employer to rely on the statutory defence. In addition to paying a significant amount of compensation to the victim, the respondent was also instructed to ensure that its policies in relation to preventing harassment and sexual harassment complied with the Code of Practice on Sexual Harassment and Harassment. **[9–38]**

---

[54] DEC-E2008-038.
[55] DEC-E2004-011.
[56] DEC-E2008-048.

Effective implementation of a policy to prevent harassment and sexual harassment in the workplace will, however, significantly strengthen an employer's ability to defend such claims.[57]

VIII. Bullying and Stress at Work

[9–39] Claims by employees alleging that they have been the victims of bullying in the workplace have increased significantly over the past decade and, as a result, the issue has garnered a significant amount of attention.[58] This is, not least, because of the fact that some cases have resulted in extremely large awards of compensation being paid to victims.[59]

[9–40] It is important, first, to distinguish bullying from harassment. While neither form of behaviour is tolerable in the workplace, an employee, as seen above, will gain a right of action following just one single incident of harassment. An employee who has been subject to bullying, on the other hand, will have to demonstrate that this behaviour occurred more than once before he or she can initiate a claim. Moreover, an employee alleging that he or she has been subject to harassment will have to show that the mistreatment received was *related to* one or more of the nine discriminatory grounds. This is not a requirement for taking an action on the grounds of bullying.

[9–41] Moreover, while actions for harassment or sexual harassment are taken under the Employment Equality Acts, there is no one specific avenue of redress for employees taking a claim against employers for bullying in the workplace.[60] Claims of bullying could be taken under the Safety, Health and Welfare at Work Act 2005.[61] Equally, however, an employee who has been subjected to bullying in the workplace and, as a result, feels that he or she has no option but to quit could claim constructive dismissal under the Unfair Dismissals Acts.[62] A third route of redress available to a victim of bullying is that he or she could sue the perpetrator in negligence for the effects of the bullying or, alternatively, could sue the employer on the basis of vicarious liability. In addition, the victim of bullying could sue for breach of contract, for example, on the basis of a breach of the implied contractual term of mutual trust and confidence.[63] Increasingly, it seems, most claims of bullying are now, in practice, being brought as personal injury actions against the employer.[64]

---

[57] *Mr A v A Hotel* (DEC-E2009-003). Although, see *A v A Health Board* (DEC-E2005-016).

[58] Stewart *et al*, "Bullying and the Workplace" (2008) 5(4) IELJ 114; Neligan, "Jurisdictions and Causes of Action: Commercial Considerations in Dealing with Bullying, Stress and Harassment Cases" (2008) 15(1) CLP 3 and (2008) 15(2) CLP 38.

[59] See the feature by McMahon on recent awards in the UK and Ireland; "Time for Workplace Bullies and Harassers to Step Back?..." (2009) 43 IRN.

[60] Bolger, "Claiming for Occupational Stress, Bullying and Harassment" (2006) 3(4) IELJ 108; Cox, "Employer's Liability for Workplace Stress" (2006) 1(2) QRTL 10.

[61] See chapter 8.

[62] See chapter 10.

[63] *Berber v Dunnes Stores Ltd* [2009] ELR 61. See, also, chapter 4.

[64] Ryan, "Bullying, Harassment and Stress at Work" in *Employment Law* (Regan ed, Tottel, Dublin, 2009), p 231.

What is Bullying?

The commonly accepted definition of workplace bullying is: [9–42]

> "... repeated inappropriate behaviour, direct or indirect, whether verbal, physical or otherwise, conducted by one or more persons against another or others, at the place of work and/or in the course of employment, which could reasonably be regarded as undermining the individual's right to dignity at work. An isolated incident of the behaviour described in this definition may be an affront to dignity at work but, as a once off incident, is not considered to be bullying".[65]

The Industrial Relations Act 1990 (Code of Practice detailing Procedures for Addressing Bullying in the Workplace) (Declaration) Order 2002[66] and the Health and Safety Authority (HSA) Code of Practice for Employers and Employees on the Prevention and Resolution of Bullying at Work 2007 have both adopted this definition of bullying. The definition has also been approved and adopted by both the High Court and Supreme Court in *Quigley v Complex Tooling and Moulding.*[67]

The HSA Code of Practice provides an indicative list of behaviour that could amount to   [9–43]
bullying. This includes: physical abuse; verbal abuse; intimidation; aggression; less favourable treatment than other employees; excessive monitoring of work; repeated manipulation of a person's job content and targets; exclusion with negative consequences; menacing behaviour; humiliation; intrusive behaviour (stalking, spying or pestering); withholding work-related information; or blame for things beyond the individual's control.[68] Banter, "slagging" or horseplay clearly might be reasonably regarded as bullying behaviour in the workplace necessitating the employer to take action to stop it from happening and to implement measures to eradicate such behaviour.[69]

Safety, Health and Welfare at Work

Section 8(2)(b) of the Safety, Health and Welfare at Work Act 2005 imposes an   [9–44]
obligation on the employer to manage and conduct work activities:

> "... in such a way as to prevent, so far as is reasonably practicable, any improper conduct or behaviour likely to put the safety, health and welfare at work of his or her employees at risk".[70]

Bullying is one example of improper conduct or behaviour that poses a risk to the safety, health and welfare at work of employees. As such, employers must endeavour to prevent bullying behaviour or conduct in the workplace. Employers have a duty to take action to prevent bullying from occurring in the first instance, such as implementing a bullying

---

[65] See the Report of the Taskforce on the Prevention of Workplace Bullying, *Dignity at Work: The Challenge of Workplace Bullying* (Health and Safety Authority, Dublin, 2001).

[66] SI No 117 of 2002.

[67] [2005] ELR 305 (HC); [2008] ELR 297.

[68] Note also that, in April 2007, the EU social partners signed a framework agreement to combat harassment and violence at work (available at www.etuc.org).

[69] Eardly, *op.cit*, p 82. See also chapter 8.

[70] See chapter 8 for further discussion of this statutory obligation.

prevention policy, and also to ensure that there is a code of practice detailing the measures in place for dealing with bullying behaviour. Such policies should take into consideration the Code of Practice detailing Procedures for Addressing Bullying in the Workplace[71]; the Code of Practice on Sexual Harassment and Harassment at Work[72]; and the HSA's Code of Practice for Employers and Employees on the Prevention and Resolution of Bullying at Work 2007. Furthermore, an employer should ensure that an appropriate complaints procedure for handling employee grievances about bullying behaviour is put in place. Indeed, the HSA recommends that employers include procedures for dealing with bullying in the safety statement required under s 20 of the Safety, Health and Welfare at Work Act 2005.

[9–45] Other measures that an employer could implement to prevent bullying in the workplace include training and instruction for employees, which should aim at developing an "anti-bullying culture" in the work environment.[73] The HSA's Code of Practice also recommends that employers provide clearly defined job descriptions identifying each employee's role and responsibilities, as the absence of such descriptions can be a factor in workplace bullying.

[9–46] The onus for preventing bullying in the workplace does not rest solely on the employer, however. Section 13(1)(e) of the Safety, Health and Welfare at Work Act 2005 provides that *employees* have a duty not to engage in improper conduct or behaviour in the workplace that could potentially endanger their own safety, health and welfare or that of others in the workplace.

Very often in *negligence* actions, the courts will take into consideration the employer's obligations to prevent workplace bullying that arise under the Safety, Health and Welfare at Work Act 2005. However, it remains to be seen fully what impact the provisions of 2005 Act will have on such claims.[74]

Constructive Dismissal

[9–47] Bullying in the workplace is very often cited as an important factor in constructive dismissal cases.[75] The issue arose for consideration in the leading case of *Allen v Independent Newspapers*.[76] The plaintiff, who was a journalist, alleged that she had been subject to continuous bullying and harassment at work, resulting in her suffering from work-related stress and illness. Moreover, she claimed that she was effectively isolated at work, resulting in her confidence being undermined to such an extent that she could no longer bear to continue working in such an environment. For these

---

[71] Industrial Relations Act 1990 (Code of Practice detailing Procedures for Addressing Bullying in the Workplace) (Declaration) Order 2002 (SI No 17 of 2002).

[72] Employment Equality Act 1998 (Code of Practice) (Harassment) Order 2002 (SI No 78 of 2002).

[73] See Eardly, *op.cit*, p 83.

[74] In actions for bullying, harassment and stress, breach of statutory duty (by reference to the 2005 Act) is almost always pleaded in addition to negligence. It remains to be seen how the developing jurisprudence on the 2005 Act will inform the "contours of the negligence action"; Ryan, *op.cit*, pp 234-235.

[75] See chapter 10 for further discussion of constructive dismissal.

[76] [2002] ELR 84.

reasons, the claimant alleged that she was left with no choice but to resign from her position. The Employment Appeals Tribunal (EAT) upheld her claim, finding that, not only had the claimant been significantly undermined at work, but that her supervisors had failed to address her complaints in any meaningful way. The claimant was awarded the not insignificant sum of £70,500 (Irish pounds) in compensation.

The EAT applied the decision in *Allen* in the case of *Monaghan v Sherry Brothers Ltd.*[77] The complainant claimed that he was constructively dismissed as a consequence of the employer's failure to adequately deal with his complaint of bullying and intimidation and that, essentially, he had no other option but to quit his job. The EAT found that the complainant had been subjected to "systematic teasing and isolation" and also that the employer had failed to deal with an incident whereby another employee tried to run the complainant off the road. The EAT stated that, subsequent to the judgment in *Allen,* it had to consider two questions: first, whether the complainant had reported the alleged incidents of bullying to the employer; and, if so, whether the employer's response to this report had been satisfactory. In this case, the EAT found that the complainant had notified the employer of the incidents, but the employer had failed to adequately deal with the complaint.

[9–48]

Bullying, Stress and Psychiatric Injury

The issue of the employer's liability for bullying and work-related stress that results in psychiatric injury to the employee has been one of the main growth areas of Irish employment law in recent years.[78] This is certainly in part a result of the greater recognition in contemporary working life of the threat of psychological, as opposed to physical, injury.[79] The general principles of the law of negligence apply in this area[80]; of particular importance is the extent to which an employer owes a *duty of care* to employees for personal injuries resulting from bullying or work-related stress.

[9–49]

This issue began to arise more frequently in the English courts in the 1990s.[81] The Irish High Court had to consider the circumstances in which occupational stress resulting in psychiatric injury will give rise to employers' liability in *McGrath v Trintech Technologies Ltd.*[82] The plaintiff was employed as a senior project manager for a multinational company specialising in information technology and, as part of his job, was required to work abroad from time-to-time. The plaintiff had suffered ill-health during the first two and a half years of his employment. When he was absent from work on sick leave, the plaintiff was contacted by his employer in relation to a possible secondment in Uruguay. The plaintiff agreed to the secondment but, while in Uruguay, he claimed that he suffered psychological injuries as a result of work-related stress. Upon his return from Uruguay, the plaintiff was again absent from work on sick leave. The plaintiff was notified in August 2003 that he was being made redundant. The

[9–50]

---

[77] UD 376/2002.

[78] For an excellent and comprehensive review of this area, see Cox *et al, op.cit,* chapter 17; Ryan, *op.cit.*

[79] See Best, "The Law of Psychiatric Damage and the 'Irrational' Fear of Floodgates" (2006) 24 ILT 58.

[80] See McMahon and Binchy, *Irish Law of Torts* (3rd ed, Butterworths, Dublin, 2000).

[81] See, for example, *Walker v Northumberland County Council* [1995] 1 ALL ER 737.

[82] [2005] 4 IR 382.

plaintiff claimed that the employer was liable for the psychological injuries he had suffered, which he alleged were caused by work-related stress.

[9–51] Laffoy J, in the High Court, extensively reviewed the Irish and English case law in this area. In particular, she considered and approved the 16 "practical propositions" laid down by Hale LJ in the English Court of Appeal decision in *Hatton v Sutherland*,[83] as providing helpful guidelines in Irish law to determine the employer's liability for claims of psychiatric injury caused by bullying or stress at work. In *Hatton*, the Court of Appeal confirmed that the ordinary principles of negligence were applicable to any claims of work-related stress. Hale LJ set out 16 practical propositions to be taken into account when establishing liability. These are as follows:

"(1) There are no special control mechanisms applying to claims for psychiatric (or physical) illness or injury arising from the stress of doing the work the employee is required to do. The ordinary principles of employer's liability apply.
(2) The threshold question is whether this kind of harm to this particular employee was reasonably foreseeable: this has two components (a) an injury to health (as distinct from occupational stress) which (b) is attributable to stress at work (as distinct from other factors).
(3) Foreseeability depends upon what the employer knows (or ought reasonably to know) about the individual employee. Because of the nature of mental disorder, it is harder to foresee than physical injury, but may be easier to foresee in a known individual than in the population at large. An employer is usually entitled to assume that the employee can withstand the normal pressures of the job unless he knows of some particular problem or vulnerability.
(4) The test is the same whatever the employment: there are no occupations which should be regarded as intrinsically dangerous to mental health.
(5) Factors likely to be relevant in answering the threshold question include:
(a) the nature and extent of the work done by the employee. Is the workload much more than is normal for the particular job? Is the work particularly intellectually or emotionally demanding for this employee? Are demands being made of this employee unreasonable when compared with the demands made of others in the same or comparable jobs? Or are there signs that others doing this job are suffering harmful levels of stress? Is there an abnormal level of sickness or absenteeism in the same job or the same department?
(b) Signs from the employee of impending harm to health. Has he a particular problem or vulnerability? Has he already suffered from illness attributable to stress at work? Have there recently been frequent or prolonged absences which are uncharacteristic of him? Is there reason to think that these are attributable to stress at work, for example because of complaints or warnings from him or others?
(6) The employer is generally entitled to take what he is told by his employee at face value, unless he has good reason to think to the contrary. He does not

---

[83] [2002] 1 ICR 613.

generally have to make searching inquiries of the employee or seek permission to make further inquiries of his medical advisers.

(7) To trigger a duty to take steps, the indications of impending harm to health arising from stress at work must be plain enough for any reasonable employer to realise that he should do something about it.

(8) The employer is only in breach of duty if he has failed to take the steps, which are reasonable in the circumstances, bearing in mind the magnitude of the risk of harm occurring, the gravity of the harm which may occur, the costs and practicability of preventing it, and the justifications for running the risk.

(9) The size and scope of the employer's operation, its resources and the demands it faces are relevant in deciding what is reasonable; these include the interests of other employees and the need to treat them fairly, for example, in any redistribution of duties.

(10) An employer can only reasonably be expected to take steps which are likely to do some good: the court is likely to need expert evidence on this.

(11) An employer who offers a confidential advice service, with referral to appropriate counselling or treatment services, is unlikely to be found in breach of duty.

(12) If the only reasonable and effective step would have been to dismiss or demote the employee, the employer will not be in breach of duty in allowing a willing employee to continue in the job.

(13) In all cases, therefore, it is necessary to identify the steps, which the employer both should and could have taken before finding him in breach of his duty of care.

(14) The claimant must show that the breach of duty has caused or materially contributed to the harm suffered. It is not enough to show that occupational stress has caused the harm.

(15) Where the harm suffered has more than one cause, the employer should only pay for that proportion of the harm suffered which is attributable to his wrongdoing, unless the harm is truly indivisible. It is for the defendant to raise the question of apportionment.

(16) The assessment of damages will take account of any pre-existing disorder or vulnerability and of the chance that the claimant would have succumbed to a stress related disorder in any event".[84]

Accordingly, Laffoy J found that the effect of the English cases was to amalgamate the principles of negligence that govern the employer's liability for both physical *and* psychiatric injury in circumstances where the employee claims that his or her working conditions created stress and pressure that resulted in psychiatric injury. She concluded that a similar approach could be adopted in Irish law to assist with the assessment of [9–52]

---

[84] *Hatton v Sutherland* [2002] 1 ICR 613 at 632. In *Barber v Somerset County Council* [2004] UKHL 13, the House of Lords held that, in connection with stress claims brought by employees, the various practical propositions set out by the Court of Appeal in *Hatton* were correct, save that *greater emphasis* should be placed on the duty of employers to be on the look out for signs of stress in their employees and to keep themselves abreast of developing knowledge of occupational stress and protective measures which can be taken to alleviate it.

liability. However, Laffoy J emphasised that the *Hatton* propositions are helpful as guidance only and that each case must be evaluated on its own particular facts.[85] Applying the principles of negligence, and taking into account the *Hatton* propositions, Laffoy J held that the employer was not liable as it was not reasonably foreseeable that the plaintiff would suffer psychological harm as a consequence of the stress he suffered at work.

[9–53]   It was established that the defendant did not know that the plaintiff was susceptible to psychological harm or injury. The Court acknowledged that the plaintiff had undergone a medical assessment before he commenced his employment with the defendant and there was no reference to any risk of injury in that assessment. Furthermore, the plaintiff had been an employee for two and half years with the defendant (and had assumed numerous foreign assignments) with no indications that he had previously suffered stress-related or psychological problems or that he was vulnerable to such problems. According to the defendant, the plaintiff appeared to possess the necessary characteristics pertaining to the job and there was no suggestion made to the defendant that this was not the case. Laffoy J, in applying the *Hatton* propositions, therefore held that the defendant had discharged its duty of care to the employee insofar as the defendant had done everything that reasonably could be done in the circumstances.[86]

[9–54]   In *Maher v Jabil Global Services Ltd*[87] Clark J set out a "three questions" approach to ascertain whether an employer should be held liable for psychological injuries that result from work-related stress. These questions are:

> "(a) Has the plaintiff suffered an injury to his or her health as opposed to what might be described as ordinary occupational stress?; (b) if so is that injury attributable to the workplace; and (c) if so was the harm suffered by the particular employee concerned reasonably foreseeable in all the circumstances?".

It seems increasingly apparent that plaintiffs taking these types of claims are finding it difficult to overcome the second and third stages of this test, relating to causation and foreseeability.[88] In *Maher,* for example, the plaintiff was not able to demonstrate that his injuries were foreseeable.[89]

---

[85]   *McGrath v Trintech Technologies Ltd* [2005] 4 IR 382, at 416.

[86]   For further analysis of this judgment, see Ryan, *op.cit*, pp 248-250, where the author points out that it seems, on the basis of Laffoy J's judgment, that the Irish courts will apply a more *objective* test to claims of bullying as compared with claims of harassment and sexual harassment: in the latter cases, as noted above, a *subjective* approach (considering only the plaintiff's perspective), is taken.

[87]   [2008] 1 IR 25 at 39.

[88]   See Cox and Ryan "Bullying, Harassment and Stress at Work: The Implications of the Supreme Court Decisions in *Quigley* and *Berber*" (2009) ELRI 17.

[89]   Here, Clarke J found that the employer did not breach its duty of care in circumstances where it provided a confidential advice service for employees, with the possibility of a referral to appropriate counselling services. The Court did however go on to say that a confidential advice service must be one of *substance* rather than *form*.

The decision in *Quigley v Complex Tooling and Moulding*[90] is evidence of the difficulties   **[9–55]**
plaintiffs face in trying to establish causation in these types of cases. The plaintiff, a
factory operative, had been subjected to bullying, harassment and victimisation at
work. The plaintiff submitted undisputed evidence demonstrating that he had been
subject to unfair and humiliating treatment and excessive scrutiny by management.
Moreover, nine fellow employees were prepared to testify on the plaintiff's behalf,
despite the fact that these witnesses were no longer employees of the defendant (as it
had ceased to trade). The High Court found the plaintiff had been the victim of "a
campaign of bullying which had repercussions on the mental health of the plaintiff"
and consequently held the defendant liable.

The defendant appealed to the Supreme Court challenging the plaintiff's evidence and   **[9–56]**
claiming that there was insufficient evidence to prove causation. The Supreme Court
upheld the appeal regarding causation, basing its decision principally on medical
reports submitted as evidence. These medical reports did not contain any reference to
the plaintiff's depression having been caused by bullying or harassment at work.
Instead, the medical evidence indicated that the plaintiff's *dismissal* and the subsequent
unfair dismissal proceedings were the main causative factors of his depression.[91]
Therefore, the Supreme Court found that the plaintiff had failed to prove that the
bullying and harassment he suffered in the course of his employment *caused* his
depression.

The Supreme Court had to consider, in *Berber v Dunnes Stores Ltd*,[92] whether it is   **[9–57]**
possible for an employee to claim damages for psychological injury caused by stress in
the workplace, where the stress is *not* linked to the alleged bullying.[93] The plaintiff in
Berber initiated proceedings for breach of the implied contractual term of mutual trust
and confidence[94] and damages for personal injuries. The plaintiff commenced
employment as a trainee manager for Dunnes Stores in 1980 and thereafter as store
manager. He suffered from a chronic bowel condition, Crohn's disease. Between 1988
and 2000, the plaintiff transferred to the position of buyer. In late 2000, the company
requested that he transfer back to store management in Blanchardstown. The plaintiff
agreed to this transfer as he had been assured that he would be eligible to be "fast-
tracked" for appointment as a store or regional manager within six to 12 months of
taking up the transfer. A dispute arose between the parties regarding these assurances,
resulting in Berber refusing to transfer back to a store position. The defendants
subsequently suspended Berber from work. Berber sent a letter to his employer alleging
that the employer's conduct had caused him to become ill because of stress.

The three-question approach set out in *Maher* was followed by Laffoy J in the High   **[9–58]**
Court. Based on these criteria, the High Court concluded that the defendant was liable
for Berber's work-related stress. The defendant appealed to the Supreme Court, which

---

[90] [2008] ELR 297.
[91] See Cox and Ryan, *op.cit*, pp 17-20. See also Ryan and Ryan, "Employers' Liability in
Negligence: Recent Approaches in the Irish Courts" (2008) 3(2) QRTL 1.
[92] [2009] ELR 61.
[93] Cox *et al*, *op.cit*, p 601. See, also, Cox, "Recent Developments in the Rules Relating to Workplace
Stress: the Supreme Court Decision in Berber v Dunnes Stores" (2008/9) 3(3) QRTL 17.
[94] This case is also discussed in chapters 4 and 10.

upheld the appeal on the grounds that the plaintiff's injury was "unforeseeable". This was because the employer had taken reasonable action in dealing with the plaintiff's vulnerabilities.

[9–59]   What is evident from the Supreme Court judgments in both *Quigley* and *Berber* is that plaintiffs face significant hurdles to overcome the burden of proof in negligence claims for psychiatric injury that results from bullying and/or work-related stress. The difference of approach between the High Court and Supreme Court in *Berber* also reveals the difficulties in attempting to predict the outcomes of such cases.[95]

---

[95] Ryan, *op.cit*, p 255.

Chapter 10
Termination of Employment

I. Introduction

One of the most controversial areas of employment law, and one which gives rise to   **[10–01]** more litigation than any other, relates to the termination of employment. Frequently, this is because a situation of confrontation has been reached by the parties, so that an agreed or negotiated solution (as may be possible in relation to other areas of discord, such as disagreements over wages or time off) becomes increasingly difficult to achieve. However, it is important to remember that a contract of employment can be terminated in several ways and not all of these lead to disputes. A crucial distinction to make is that between termination of employment at *common law* and *statutory* termination of employment. The latter is primarily governed by the Unfair Dismissals Acts 1997–2007. At common law, the issue is essentially one of contract.

II. Termination Without Controversy

As is the case with most contracts, the parties themselves may agree to the termination   **[10–02]** of a contract of employment at any time and upon any terms (subject to any statutory or constitutional limitations that may exist). Occasionally, a period of notice may be required by the contract before termination takes place. In other cases, in relation to fixed-term contracts, for example, the contract simply expires without notice at the end of the term. Of course, it must be conclusively shown that the "agreement" is, in fact, genuine and not the result of undue pressure from either side.[1] If there is genuine agreement between the parties to bring the employment contract to an end, the parties are entitled to waive any contractual rights to notice; furthermore, the employee may accept payment in lieu of notice.[2] In a situation where the parties' relationship has broken down, this can be an attractive option for both sides. Voluntary redundancy is a common means by which the parties agree to end the relationship.

[10–03] An employee can terminate a contract by resigning from the job. In the majority of cases, the employee will resign to take up another job elsewhere and, provided that proper notice has been given, this is perfectly fine. Under s 6 of the Minimum Notice and Terms of Employment Act 1973 an employer is entitled to at least one week's notice from an employee who has been employed by the employer for 13 weeks or more and who proposes to give up his or her job. The employer will oftentimes waive all or some of the notice period required because an employee who is set to leave can prove disruptive (intentionally or otherwise). As this is a minimum requirement, any contract of employment that provides for a longer notice period will displace the statutory provision.[3] Again, however, the employee's decision to resign must be freely made. In *O'Reilly v Minister for Industry and Commerce*,[4] for example, a civil servant with over 45 years' service resigned because of a mistaken belief that he would be dismissed if he did not do so. The Court found that the plaintiff had effectively been forced to resign, as the Minister should have corrected the obvious error that the plaintiff had made. In some cases resignations can be generated by the employer's bad faith; in such circumstances issues of constructive dismissal may arise. In circumstances where the business is in trouble, voluntary redundancies and early retirement may be sought. These issues will be addressed below.

[10–04] As is the case with a dismissal, where the words used by resigning employees are clear and unambiguous there are no problems. However, where there is any ambiguity, the employer may be wise to seek confirmation in writing of the resignation. As with dismissals, resignations can occur in the heat of the moment and in periods where the parties are feeling under pressure. For example, in *Kwik-Fit GB v Lineham*[5] an employee used a depot toilet while returning home from the pub and set off the alarm. A company director (mistakenly) felt this was a breach of the rules and issued a disciplinary warning in front of a junior employee. The plaintiff threw his keys down, walked out and did not return the following day. Nevertheless, the English Employment Appeals Tribunal (EAT) found that, in special circumstances such as existed here, the employer should not have assumed the resignation was genuine.

---

[1] The English courts have long cautioned that tribunals should be careful when finding a mutual agreement to terminate and should, in particular, be convinced that the employee is aware of any and all financial implications of termination; see *McAlwane v Broughton Estates Ltd* [1973] ICR 470.

[2] Redmond, *Dismissal Law in Ireland* (2nd ed, Tottel, Dublin, 2007), p 58.

[3] Similarly, a longer notice period may be implied by common law or custom and practice; see chapter 4.

[4] [1997] ELR 48.

[5] [1992] IRLR 156.

Notice

The contract of employment can, of course, also be lawfully terminated by either party **[10–05]** on the giving of proper notice. At common law, the employer can dismiss for any reason, subject to giving the required notice. It was to protect against abuses of this common law position that the Unfair Dismissals Act 1977 was enacted. Proper notice is determined according to the terms (express or implied) of the contract. Any contractual period of notice will need to exceed the statutory minimum to be valid. The Minimum Notice and Terms of Employment Act 1973 lays down minimum periods of notice to be given by employers when terminating a contract of employment. The Act applies to "employees", defined in s 1 as anyone who has entered into or works under a contract with an employer, whether the contract be for manual labour, clerical work or otherwise, whether it be expressed or implied, oral or in writing and whether it be a contract of service or of apprenticeship or otherwise.[6] The notice period to be given varies according to the employee's period of service:

- 13 weeks to 2 years—1 week
- 2 years to 5 years—2 weeks
- 5 years to 10 years—4 weeks
- 10 years to 15 years—6 weeks
- More than 15 years—8 weeks

Continuity of service is not usually affected by lay-offs or lock-outs, by dismissal followed by immediate re-employment, or by the transfer of a trade or business from one person to another.[7]

Where a contract does not expressly state the notice period, the courts may have to imply **[10–06]** a term. The courts will order a "reasonable" notice period.[8] In *Lyons v MF Kent & Co International Ltd*[9] a senior accountant employed by a large construction company, who worked on a number of projects throughout Europe, was held entitled to one year's notice. There was no express agreement between the parties regarding termination of employment. When the case came to trial, the defendant conceded that the plaintiff had been wrongly dismissed so that the issue to be determined was the appropriate length of notice (which was necessary to ascertain the appropriate amount of damages). The plaintiff submitted that he was entitled to 12 months' notice on the basis of his remuneration and responsibilities within the company. The defendant argued that five years of service warranted notice of two weeks (the minimum period required under notice legislation) and that notice of one year was excessive. Costello P found that no custom existed within the company regarding a reasonable length of notice and that the appropriate notice had to be determined according to what was reasonable in the circumstances, in particular, the plaintiff's status and responsibilities in the company. Given the plaintiff's professional qualifications, the fact that he carried out his profession independently prior to taking up this position and the fact

---

[6] See chapter 3 for further discussion of who is an "employee".

[7] Minimum Notice and Terms of Employment Act 1973, First Schedule.

[8] Although this does not apply in the context of a dismissal for misconduct; see Stewart and Dunleavy, *Compensation on Dismissal* (FirstLaw, Dublin, 2007), p 54.

[9] [1996] ELR 103.

that he had to work abroad, a 12-month notice period was deemed appropriate.[10] Similar conclusions were reached in *Carvill v Irish Industrial Bank Ltd*,[11] where the managing director of a small bank was held to be entitled to one year's notice and in *McDonnell v Minister for Education*,[12] where a teacher was deemed to be entitled to six months' notice. It appears from the case law that those in well-paid or prestigious jobs can expect relatively lengthy notice periods. It is important to remember that notice periods under the 1973 Act (as amended) are *not* deemed to be a part of the employment contract. Instead, applications can be made under s 11 to the EAT for failure to give the required notice and the EAT may award compensation. Breach of any *contractual* term relating to notice can be pursued through the courts as a contract law case.[13]

[10–07]   The fact that a job is described as "permanent" and/or "pensionable" employment does not mean it cannot be terminated by reasonable notice. In *Walsh v Dublin Health Board*[14] it was held that a carpenter employed on a permanent and pensionable basis could be dismissed. The court found that "permanent" did not necessarily equate to "a contract for life". According to Budd J:

> "The word 'permanent' has various shades of meaning. Generally, it means something lasting, as distinct from temporary. In the case of a contract of service, a person may be said in one sense of the word to be 'permanently' employed when he is employed for an indefinite period on the regular staff of the employer, as distinct from persons taken on for a temporary or defined period. That does not necessarily mean that such a person has a contract of employment for life. On the other hand a person may be given 'permanent' and pensionable employment in the sense that under his contract he holds his employment for life or for life subject to the right of his employer to dismiss him for misconduct, neglect of duty or unfitness or again it may mean that his employment is to last until he reaches full pensionable age, subject to the rights of the employer just mentioned. As to what is meant, and should be implied as being in the contemplation of the parties, depends upon the true construction of the whole contract viewed in the light of the surrounding circumstances and all relevant matters".[15]

[10–08]   In *Grehan v North Eastern Health Board*[16] Costello J indicated that there are circumstances in which a term providing for termination on reasonable notice will not be implied into a contract of service, where this is not justified having regard to the terms of the contract as a whole. Here, a medical practitioner had been employed under terms negotiated between the Department of Health and the Irish Medical Organisation. There were very detailed terms as regards dismissal. The Court refused to imply a further term that the plaintiff could be dismissed on being given "reasonable

---

10 See Redmond, *op.cit*, pp 53-54.
11 [1968] IR 325.
12 [1940] IR 316.
13 See chapter 12.
14 98 ILTR 82.
15 *ibid* at 86-87.
16 [1989] IR 422.

notice". The terms of the relevant collective agreement had been the subject of extensive negotiations, so the Court was able to infer that a term on reasonable notice had not been intended to feature.[17]

In *Sheehy v Ryan*[18] the High Court held that, while the claimant had been offered a permanent, pensionable job, "there was no express or implied condition or promise that it would be a job for life or until age 65". This was upheld in the Supreme Court.[19] Ms Sheehy was employed by Bishop Ryan and then Bishop Lennon as a secretary. Ms Sheehy was eventually told that she was being made redundant. The plaintiff argued that, in view of the fact that her employment was described as "permanent and pensionable", she was entitled to remain in her position until she reached retirement age, in the absence of serious illness or misbehaviour. However, Geoghegan J dismissed this view. Justice Geoghegan considered some of the case law advanced in connection with the proposition that an offer of a permanent and pensionable position in this case was the equivalent of the offer of a job to the claimant up until she reached the age of 65 (being the most common meaning of the words "job for life"). However, he made it clear that each case should be determined on its own facts:

[10–09]

> "I would take the view that every contract of employment is different and that case law is of marginal assistance only, in construing the terms of any given contract …In this particular case, there is no written contract of that kind which has to be construed. What constitutes the contract is a mixture of express oral terms and implied terms. I am satisfied that the general rule applied and that the agreement could be terminated on reasonable notice".[20]

In *Cahill v DCU*[21] the plaintiff occupied a post of Associate Professor at Dublin City University (DCU). After informing the DCU President that there was a "high probability" that he would be moving to another university, he received a letter from DCU giving him three months' notice of termination of his contract of employment. The dismissal was due to take effect in September 2006. Clarke J ruled that the dismissal was contrary to the provisions of the Universities Act 1997. One of the key matters at issue concerned the meaning of "tenure". The applicant argued that "tenure", when used in the educational (and in particular, the university) context, conveyed a level of permanence, which would only permit the person concerned to be removed from office for stated reasons involving misconduct or incapacity. DCU argued that tenure merely carried with it a connotation of the term of office and did not bear any necessary requirement that the term of office have any significant degree of permanency. Clarke J noted that it was clear from the evidence that most of the officers of the University had a contract in broadly similar terms to that held by Professor Cahill and were, therefore, subject to dismissal on the giving of a relatively

[10–10]

---

[17] See Forde, *Employment Law* (2nd ed, Round Hall, Dublin, 2001), pp 167-168.
[18] [2004] 15 ELR 87.
[19] [2008] 4 IR 258.
[20] *ibid* at 267.
[21] [2007] IEHC 20.

short period of notice (three months).[22] Clarke J contrasted the way Europeans view "tenure" with the approach adopted in the United States:

> "It would certainly seem that in the United States at least, it is not normally considered possible to terminate the office of a tenured member of the academic staff save for reasons such as serious misconduct, or incapacity... It is not, however, quite so clear that the term only has that meaning in those European countries (such as the UK and Ireland) which have a broadly similar university structure to that of the United States".

[10–11]   Although, ultimately, the case was not decided on the grounds of what constituted "tenure", Clarke J noted that s 14 of the 1997 Act, which provides for academic freedom and requires a university, in performing its functions, to preserve and promote the traditional principles of academic freedom in the conduct of its internal and external affairs, required the Court, in construing any provision of the Act, to favour a construction which would have the effect of the promotion of the principles of academic freedom.[23]

Summary Dismissal

[10–12]   It should be noted that an employer is, in certain circumstances, entitled to dismiss an employee without giving the notice to which the employee is entitled by virtue of the contract of employment. This is known as "summary dismissal". The decision to dismiss must be communicated to be effective: this can be in written or oral form. It is virtually impossible to define the reasons that will be regarded as sufficient to justify a summary dismissal.[24] As a result, it is perhaps prudent for an employer to specify in the contract some (non-exhaustive) grounds that may justify such a dismissal.[25]

[10–13]   In *Carvill v Irish Industrial Bank Ltd*[26] Kenny J held that the grounds relied on in such cases must be actions or omissions by the employee that are inconsistent with the performance of the express or implied terms of his contract of service. Some examples might include (but will depend on the exact circumstances) refusal to obey a lawful order; failure to cooperate; dishonesty; assault; gross negligence; drunkenness at work; disclosing confidential information, and so on. According to Kenny J in *Glover v BLN Ltd*[27]:

> "It is impossible to define the misconduct which justifies immediate dismissal... (misconduct) must be decided in each case without the assistance of a definition or a general rule. Similarly, all that one can say about serious misconduct is that it is misconduct which the court regards as being grave and

---

[22] Contrast this with the decision in *McDonnell v Minister for Education* [1940] IR 316, discussed above, where a notice period of three months for a teacher was deemed insufficient.

[23] On appeal, the Supreme Court upheld the decision of wrongful dismissal but did not feel it necessary to address the issue of tenure; [2009] IESC 80.

[24] Lockton, *Employment Law* (7th ed, Palgrave, Basingstoke, 2010), pp 222-224.

[25] See Stewart and Dunleavy, *op.cit,* p 59, where the authors point out that some grounds specified in contracts have included sleeping, smoking and spitting while at work.

[26] [1968] IR 325.

[27] [1973] IR 388 at 405.

deliberate. And the standards to be applied in deciding the matter are those of men and not of angels".

In this case, the plaintiff was a company director who held shares in another company [10–14] (managed by his son) involved in a goods transaction with a subsidiary of the defendants, BLN. There was an allegation of misconduct in relation to this potential conflict of interest. The plaintiff had also had work done on his own cars by BLN employees without charging himself and had gotten company employees to work for several weeks on his private house without paying. The first charge was held *not* to be misconduct as it had been disclosed to his employers and there was no evidence of any losses suffered by the company. The second charge was held to constitute misconduct, but not serious enough to justify dismissal, while the third charge was held to amount to serious misconduct. Walsh J noted that "misconduct, if known but not used as a ground for dismissal at the time, cannot be relied upon afterwards in an effort to justify the dismissal".[28] This, obviously, implies that conduct *not* known at the time (but discovered subsequently) also cannot be used to justify a dismissal.

III. Frustration

Frustration occurs in situations where the parties to a contract can no longer perform [10–15] their contractual obligations due to circumstances beyond the control of either party.[29] This could occur in the employment context where one of the parties, through no fault of his or her own, is unable to continue with the employment contract (e.g. due to the death of one of parties, or where performance becomes illegal). Frustration automatically brings the contract to an end. To determine whether a contract has been frustrated, it is necessary to construe the obligations assumed and the circumstances in which the parties had undertaken them. In *Herman v Owners of the SS Vica*[30] it was held that frustration depends on the terms of the contract and the surrounding circumstances of each case, as some kinds of "impossibility" may not discharge the contract at all.

The event which frustrates the contract must be unexpected and not within the parties' [10–16] contemplation. In *Zuphen v Kelly Technical Services (Irl) Ltd*[31] technicians were recruited from South Africa to work in Ireland. The employers had thought the men would be working on a contract job to be obtained from the telecommunications company eircom, but two months after they arrived they were told the contract was lost and that there was no work for them to do. The Court rejected the argument that the contract had been frustrated. The men had not been specifically hired to work on the eircom contract and had been hired before the employers had finalised that contract.

Determining when a contract has become incapable of being performed is a difficult [10–17] exercise. It is important to bear in mind that, by successfully pleading frustration, the employer is relieved of statutory obligations in relation to dismissal. Courts will be

---

[28] *ibid* at 426.
[29] See Enright, *Principles of Irish Contract Law* (Clarus Press, Dublin, 2007), chapter 22.
[30] [1942] IR 305.
[31] [2000] ELR 277.

conscious of the resulting impact this may have on employees. In *Taylor v Caldwell*[32] Blackburn J stated that a contract would not be construed as absolute where the parties must, from the beginning, have known that its fulfilment was dependent on the continued existence of some particular thing and, therefore, must have realised that this continuing existence was the foundation of the contract. Here, the plaintiffs and defendants entered into a contract for the use of a concert hall, which was destroyed by fire before the first concert could be held. The Court found that the fire had discharged the parties from their obligations under the contract.

[10–18]   *Imprisonment* or some other form of compulsory detention can cause a contract to become frustrated. Commencement of a long sentence will almost always bring a contract to an end. In *Shepherd v Jerrom*[33] an apprentice plumber was sentenced to six months' borstal for his involvement in a fight in which another was killed. The employer insisted on a termination of the apprenticeship contract. The contract was held to be frustrated. A potential problem was that this was possibly an example of "self-induced frustration"; that is, that the frustrating event (imprisonment) was the *fault* of the apprentice. However, the court found that the frustrating event was the imposition of the sentence, rather than the apprentice's own conduct. In these cases, much will depend on duration of the detention, the nature of the job and the terms of the contract.[34]

[10–19]   An employee's *illness* can result in the contract becoming frustrated, but this depends on, in particular, the nature of the job, the nature of the illness and the terms of the contract.[35] Again, the courts will be conscious of the implications of allowing a plea of frustration in the context of illness or incapacity; this could, for example, effectively amount to allowing a dismissal on grounds of disability. In *Condor v Barron Knights Ltd*[36] Condor, a drummer, was contracted to play seven nights per week with the Barron Knights pop group. He had a minor nervous breakdown and was advised by a doctor that to continue the demanding tour schedule might well lead to a major breakdown. As a result the contract was held to be frustrated. In the case of *Poussard v Spiers & Pond*[37] an actress/singer had contracted to take the lead role in an operatta for a whole season. She was unable to take up this position for the first week of the season due to a cold and the producers had to employ someone else, who insisted on a contract exceeding the period of illness. When the original singer did arrive, the producers purported to terminate her contract and she sued for breach of contract. However, it was held that her absence for the first week of the season was sufficient to allow the producers to terminate the contract as the opera was not due to run for a long period, the first week of the season was so important and because of the contractual demands of her replacement.

---

[32]   (1863) 3 B & S 826.

[33]   [1987] 1 QB 301.

[34]   See Forde, *op.cit*, p 165.

[35]   See *Donegal County Council v Langan* (UD 143/1989), where the EAT held that the clearest possible evidence must be produced in order for a contract to be frustrated due to illness.

[36]   [1966] 1 WLR 87.

[37]   (1876) 1 QBD 410.

A contract cannot be frustrated by the *risk* of an employee's health deteriorating. Redmond gives the example of a person with full-blown AIDS (where the contract probably is frustrated) as against a person who has contracted the HIV Virus (where it is unlikely the contract would be held to be frustrated).[38]

[10–20]

Two other instances where frustration is pleaded are in relation to the dissolution of partnership (and thus employment contracts with the partnership) and receivership and liquidation.[39]

IV. Repudiation

A contract can be repudiated in a number of ways as a result of the conduct of either the employer or the employee. For example, the employer may repudiate the contract by reducing the remuneration it was agreed would be payable or by unilaterally changing the entire nature of the job; an employee may repudiate the contract by unambiguously leaving the job or point-blank refusing to do the work agreed.[40] If it is the conduct of the employer that is repudiatory, the employee, even if he or she resigns as a result of the employer's conduct, may pursue a claim for wrongful dismissal at common law or for constructive dismissal under the unfair dismissals legislation (see below). If the employer is the innocent party, and the employee's repudiatory breach brings the contract to an end, the employee is dismissed.[41]

[10–21]

The issue is problematic, however, for a number of reasons. First, what amounts to "repudiatory conduct" is difficult to define. In *Woodar Investment Development Ltd v Wimpy Construction UK Ltd*[42] repudiation was said to be a drastic conclusion that should only be held to arise in clear cases of refusal, in a matter going to the root of the contract, to perform contractual obligations. However, what conduct goes to the "root of the contract" will differ according to, *inter alia*, the terms of the contract, the nature of the employment and the nature of the employment relationship.[43] Secondly, there is the issue of the precise time at which the contract comes to an end. As Lockton points out[44]:

[10–22]

> "...[a] breach which is repudiatory rejects the original contract and may produce a variety of results. It may reject the original contract and bring into

---

[38] Redmond, *op.cit*, p 306.

[39] Forde, *op.cit,* pp 165-166.

[40] *ibid* at pp 160-161. "It has long been part of our law that a person expudiates the contract of service if he willfully disobeys the lawful and reasonable orders of his master. Such a refusal fully justifies an employer in dismissing him summarily"; *Pepper v Webb* [1969] 2 All ER 216 at 218 *per* Karminski LJ, cited with approval and adopted by Hamilton J (as he then was) in *Brewster v Burke* [1985] 4 JISLL 98 at 100.

[41] *Industrial Yearns Limited v Greene* [1984] ILRM 15.

[42] [1980] 1 WLR 277.

[43] See *Carvill v Irish Industrial Bank Ltd* [1968] IR 325 and *Glover v BLN Ltd* [1973] IR 388 (discussed above). See also the conflicting views of the High Court and Supreme Court as to what constitutes repudiatory conduct on the part of the employer in *Berber v Dunnes Stores* [2009] ELR 61 (SC); [2007] ELR 1 (HC).

[44] Lockton, *op.cit,* p 218.

play new terms. The innocent party has two options in this case: he can reject the new terms or he can accept them and continue the relationship".

[10–23] Thus, a repudiatory breach will not automatically bring the contract to an end. If the breach is accepted by the injured party the contract is terminated; if not, however, the employment relationship may continue. This was made clear in *Pickering v Microsoft Ireland Operations Ltd.*[45] The company here effected a large-scale reorganisation of its operations and agreed with the plaintiff that she would be a party to the resolution of any difficulties which might arise as a result of the reorganisation. The plaintiff claimed that such assurances amounted to an express term of her contract with the defendant that had been breached as, subsequent to the reorganisation, she claimed she was being undermined and isolated in her role within the company. Esmond Smyth J agreed that the contractual term, which was breached by the defendant, was one which went to the root of the plaintiff's contract of employment with the defendant. Esmond Smyth J went on to state:

> "However, the mere fact that there has been a breach of contract does not, of itself, alter the obligation of either party under the contract; what it may do, is to justify the injured party, if she chooses, in regarding herself as absolved or discharged from the further performance of the contract. It does not automatically terminate her obligation. She could still have the option of either treating the contract as still in existence or to regard herself as discharged".[46]

[10–24] The question of repudiation, and whether and when this had been accepted by the plaintiff, was crucial to the assessment of liability in the case. The defendants submitted that, in relation to constructive dismissal, if an employee succeeds in making a claim for constructive dismissal at common law or repudiatory breach, the employee's claim in such circumstances is limited to the damages available for wrongful dismissal. This would be the period of notice to which the plaintiff was entitled. The defendants also submitted that the plaintiff had continued to affirm the contract for approximately seven months after the alleged repudiatory breach and that that period was in excess of any period of notice to which she would have been entitled. The Court rejected the defendant's contention that the plaintiff's claim was, in effect, a claim for damages for the manner of her dismissal. Esmond Smyth J was satisfied here that the plaintiff had acquired a cause of action at law for breach of contract, which was unimpaired by the subsequent repudiation of her contract; the breach constituted a separate and antecedent wrong.

V. Wrongful Dismissal

[10–25] Dismissal ranges from "being given the sack" through to resignations that are *deemed* to be dismissals by the courts or tribunals. This is an area of legal technicalities, which can lead to confusion. An employee cannot claim wrongful dismissal, unfair dismissal or redundancy unless he or she is actually *dismissed*. Dismissal can be defined as a "unilateral termination of the contract by the employer; by word or by deed, the

---

[45] [2006] ELR 65.
[46] *ibid* at 125.

employer tells the employee that their relationship has or shall come to an end".[47] Where the employer does not give the agreed notice of dismissal, for example, it repudiates one of the most fundamental obligations under the contract, which is to pay wages in return for work done. At common law, the question of whether or not an employee has been dismissed is one of contract. Employers are entitled to dismiss employees for any (or no) reason as long as there are no constitutional issues involved and the required notice is given.[48] Simply put, therefore, a wrongful dismissal at common law amounts to a dismissal that is in breach of contract.

As already seen above, there is a number of ways in which a dismissal can be held to be wrongful at common law; i.e. where notice has not been given in accordance with contractual or statutory rights, where a summary dismissal is held to be unlawful and where there has been a breach of the employment contract, but this has not brought about the termination of the relationship. Here, situations where a dismissal is deemed wrongful due to a breach of an express or implied term of an employment contract will be examined. Special attention will also be paid to the influence of constitutional guarantees of fair procedures.

Breach of Contractual Terms

In some cases, an employment contract will contain express provisions governing the procedures that should apply before any purported dismissal can be effected.[49] Any breach of such a term will normally render a dismissal unfair. In *Glover v BLN Ltd*[50] the plaintiff's contract contained a term stating that he could only be summarily dismissed in the case of "serious misconduct" which, in the unanimous opinion of the board of directors, injuriously affected the reputation, business or property of the employer. As a result, the Court found that the issue was not whether he was, or was not, guilty of serious misconduct but whether the misconduct approximated that envisaged in the express terms of the contract.

[10–26]

As outlined in chapter 4, the courts will, on occasion, imply terms into contracts of employment.[51] In recent years, the implied duty of mutual fidelity, trust and confidence

[10–27]

---

[47] Forde, *op.cit*, p 160.

[48] Fennel and Lynch, *Labour Law in Ireland* (Gill & Macmillan, Dublin, 1993), p 207. Although note that the emerging jurisprudence around the implied term of mutual trust and confidence in the employment relationship seems to impose obligations on both parties to the employment relationship not to act in a manner that might seriously damage the relationship of trust and confidence between them. This may have important implications for the common law rules on dismissal. This is discussed further below. See also chapter 4 and Redmond, *op.cit*, chapter 5.

[49] In fact, it is probably true to say that most employment lawyers would advise employers to specifically incorporate such a term into individual contracts of employment; Stewart and Dunleavy, *op.cit*, p 47.

[50] [1973] IR 388.

[51] So, for example, a dismissal that is in breach of a term implied by virtue of the Constitution, such as the implied right to freedom of association (or dissociation) or the implied right to work, can be invalidated by the courts: see chapter 4; Stewart and Dunleavy, *op.cit*, chapter 15; and Redmond, *op.cit*, chapter 10.

in the employment relationship has emerged as a major area of employment litigation.[52] According to Freedland, it is now "undoubtedly the most powerful engine of movement in the modern law of employment contracts".[53] In *Imperial Group Pension Trust Ltd v Imperial Tobacco Co*[54] the English courts referred to an "implied obligation of good faith" in relation to the employer's duties to manage properly occupational pension schemes. This was endorsed in *Malik v Bank of Credit & Commerce Int'l SA*,[55] where the House of Lords upheld employees' claims that there was an implied term in their contracts by which the company would not be managed in a corrupt manner; the Court referred to an "implied term of trust and confidence". The House of Lords held that if the employer's conduct was a breach of the duty to maintain trust and confidence, which detrimentally affected an employee's future employment prospects so as to give rise to continuing financial loss, and it was reasonably foreseeable that such loss was a serious possibility, damages would, in principle, be recoverable if injury to reputation (and hence future employment prospects) could be established as being a consequence of the breach. The Supreme Court, in *Berber v Dunnes Stores Limited*,[56] confirmed that Irish law recognised the existence of an implied term of mutual obligation in contracts of employment.

[10–28]   However, the future scope and ambit of any implied term of mutual trust and confidence remains somewhat uncertain,[57] particularly in relation to its interaction with the law on termination of employment.[58] In *Johnson v Unisys*[59] the applicant alleged that as a result of his dismissal he had sustained psychiatric stress, resulting in financial loss as his employment prospects had been badly affected. In particular, he alleged, the *manner* of his dismissal (he had not received a fair hearing and the disciplinary procedures laid down in his contract had not been followed) amounted to a breach of the employer's implied duty of trust and confidence. The House of Lords rejected his argument, principally on the basis that a statutory regime of unfair dismissal existed (indeed, Mr Johnson had already successfully pursued an unfair dismissals claim) and, therefore, this implicitly precluded the development of a common law remedy for wrongful dismissal based on the manner in which an employee is dismissed. Therefore, according to the House of Lords in *Johnson*, the implied duty of mutual trust and confidence would only apply *during* the employment relationship and would not extend to matters involving the employee's dismissal.

---

[52] See Bolger and Ryan, "The Mutual Duty of Fidelity in the Contract of Employment: Significant Recent Developments" (2007) 4(4) IELJ 112; Callanan, "Mutual Trust and Confidence in the Workplace: A Concept or an Obligation" (2007) ELRI 9; Brodie, "Mutual Trust and Confidence: Catalysts, Constraints and Commonality" (2008) 37(4) ILJ 329; Fudge, "The Spectre of *Addis* in Contracts of Employment in Canada and the UK" (2007) 36(1) ILJ 51.

[53] Freedland, *The Personal Employment Contract* (Oxford University Press, Oxford, 2003), p 166.

[54] [1990] 1 WLR 589 at 597.

[55] [1998] 2 AC 20.

[56] [2009] 20 ELR 61.

[57] Brodie, "Legal Coherence and the Employment Revolution" (2001) 117 LQR 604.

[58] Note Lord Steyn's *dicta* in *Malik* where he pointed out that, given the employee's traditional implied obligation to not act contrary to the employer's interests, the major importance of the implied duty of trust and confidence lies in its impact on the *employer's* obligations; [1998] 2 AC 20 at 46.

[59] [2001] ICR 480. See Redmond, *op.cit*, p 79 for criticism of the decision.

In subsequent cases, the English courts have expanded the potential of the mutual duty [10–29] of implied trust and confidence to assist employees. In *Eastwood v Magnox Electric plc*[60] the two claimants successfully pursued common law claims for breach of trust and confidence on the grounds that the employer had pursued a campaign to humiliate and undermine them prior to their dismissals (including a flawed disciplinary procedure). The House of Lords held that the employer's actions had been a breach of the implied term of trust and confidence; however, *Johnson* was distinguished here as both claimants alleged that they were suffering from depressive illness (brought on by the employer's conduct) *prior* to the disciplinary hearing. *Johnson* was also distinguished in *Gogay v Hertfordshire County Council*,[61] where the employer was found to have breached the implied duty of trust and confidence by suspending an employee without reasonable grounds for suspicion or a proper investigation (this case involved wrongful allegations of sexual abuse against the claimant). Again, as the case did not involve dismissal, but rather a suspension, it was held to fall outside the scope of *Johnson*.

To date, the Irish courts seem to have adopted the *Johnson* position. In *McGrath v* [10–30] *Trintech*[62] Laffoy J refused to accept an argument by the plaintiff that the mutual duty of trust and confidence could imply into the contract a term that the defendant would not be dismissed without due cause or reasonable notice and consultation. In *Pickering v Microsoft Ireland Operations Ltd*[63] Esmond Smyth J held that an implied term, such as that of mutual trust and confidence, could not be relied on to circumvent the principle that an employer at common law was free to dismiss an employee for any or no reason (on giving reasonable notice); nor could such a term be relied on to circumvent the principle that damages for the manner of dismissal are confined to those to which the employee is entitled by reference to the notice period.[64] However, some commentators have suggested that the criticism of *Johnson* and the English courts' willingness to limit its application in subsequent cases might suggest that the Supreme Court will take a more expansive view of the role of the implied duty of mutual trust and confidence in relation to wrongful dismissal.[65]

Breach of Procedures

The procedures to be followed in order for a purported dismissal to be effective will [10–31] often be set out in the employment contract, relevant collective agreement or works

---

[60] [2005] 1 AC 503.

[61] [2000] IRLR 703.

[62] [2005] ELR 49.

[63] [2006] ELR 65.

[64] Although see Bolger and Ryan's discussion of the decision in *Quigley v Complex Tooling* [2005] ELR 325; *op.cit*. See also Brodie, "The Beginning of the End for *Addis v The Gramophone Company?*" (2009) 38(2) ILJ 228.

[65] See Brodie, "Mutual Trust and Confidence: Catalysts, Constraints and Commonality" (2008) ILJ 37(4) 329; Deakin and Morris, *Labour Law* (5th ed, Hart, Oxford, 2009), pp 385-388 for an assessment of the position of the English Courts. See Redmond, "The Implied Obligation of Mutual Trust and Confidence- A Common Law Action for 'Unfair' Dismissal?" (2009) 6(2) IELJ 3; Bolger and Ryan, *ibid*; Redmond (2007), *op.cit*, at pp 85-89, all of whom refer to remarks made in the Supreme Court case of *Maha Lingham v Health Service Executive* [2006] ELR 137.

rules.[66] Procedures laid down in the contract itself must be followed. In *McLoughlin v Great Southern Railways Co*[67] the plaintiff was summarily dismissed on suspicion of having stolen goods. The Court found that he could be dismissed for misconduct or breach of duty. However, as a result of collective agreements in place, this could only take place after affording him a hearing; the agreed procedure had to be followed for the dismissal to be effective. Note that giving due notice will not be a proper substitute for failing to follow the procedures laid down.[68]

[10–32]   In *Mooney v An Post*[69] the Supreme Court noted that where the employee is an office-holder, or where dismissal procedures are provided for in the contract, the courts, guided by the Constitution, will imply minimum standards of fairness to the conduct of these procedures in accordance with the rules of natural and constitutional justice. If the contract does *not* specify any procedures to be followed, but allows the employee to be dismissed for misconduct, the position is less clear-cut. The general terms of employment and the circumstances surrounding the purported dismissal will be key; the minimum entitlement to be afforded the employee is to be informed of the charges against him or her and be given the opportunity to answer them and to make submissions.[70]

[10–33]   Two core principles of natural justice, in particular, are frequently cited[71]:

---

[66] Employers would be well advised to have a written disciplinary policy that covers the procedures to be adopted in the case of dismissal for misconduct; Stewart and Dunleavy, *op.cit*, p 333. This should be based on the Code of Practice on Grievance and Disciplinary Procedures (SI No 146 of 2000), implementation of which, as seen in chapter 2, has been imposed on employers by the Labour Court in certain cases. See Cox *et al*, *Employment Law in Ireland* (Clarus Press, Dublin, 2009), chapter 18 for a comprehensive overview of the law (and practice) relating to procedural fairness and the conduct of disciplinary action in the workplace.

[67] [1944] IR 479.

[68] Forde, *op.cit*, p 174.

[69] [1998] 4 IR 288 (SC).

[70] *ibid* at 298 *per* Barrington J. See also McCrann, "Investigations in the Workplace" (2006) 3(3) IELJ 68.

[71] See, generally, Hogan and Morgan, *Administrative Law in Ireland* (3rd ed, Round Hall, Dublin 1998). Note also the comments of Barrington J in *Mooney*, where he noted that, due to the nature of the employment relationship and the power resources involved, it may not be easy to adhere to these principles, as they imply the existence of an impartial judge to hear both sides of the argument. However, some of the literature on human resource management and contemporary work relations notes the increasing emergence of Alternative Dispute Mechanisms or quasi-judicial mechanisms and fora of various kinds (such as review panels and arbitrators) that are established *within* (predominantly large) firms; see, for example, Ewing, *Justice on the Job: Resolving Grievances in the Nonunion Workplace* (Harvard Business Press, Harvard, 1989). See also Finkin, "Privatisation of Wrongful Dismissal Protection in Comparative Perspective" (2008) 37(2) ILJ 149, where the author examines the reasons for the acceptability in the United States of employment disputes relating to the dismissal of an employee being dealt with by private arbitration systems set up unilaterally by employers and considers the policy reasons why this is not allowed in the UK, where such matters, as in Ireland, are generally dealt with by public tribunals.

- *audi alteram partem* — the employer must hear the employee's side of the argument before deciding to dismiss. This will require the employee to be given knowledge of the case for dismissal and time to prepare a defence[72];
- *nemo iudex in sua causa* — no one should be a judge in his own case; i.e. an unbiased enquiry should be held.[73]

What is precisely required by principles of natural justice will, however, depend on the facts of the case.[74] Plainly the first port of call is the contract of employment and its disciplinary rules. Where procedures are laid down therein, questions that arise might include whether there is a right to an oral hearing; whether there is a right to silence during the hearing; and whether there is a right to cross-examine witnesses. If no express reference is made to dismissal procedures in the contract, it will depend upon the circumstances as to what fairness will require. For example, unless the contract expressly requires ordinary rules of evidence to be applied, their application by a disciplinary tribunal is not necessary.[75] By contrast, if it is stipulated that an employee is entitled to an oral hearing before an independent board or arbitrator before he or she can be dismissed then such a hearing should be held and held in accordance with principles of natural and constitutional justice.[76]   [10–34]

In *Mooney*, the Supreme Court reiterated that if the contract or statute governing a person's employment contained a procedure providing for the termination of the contract, it would usually be enough for the employer to demonstrate that it had adhered to such a procedure. Here, the plaintiff was a postman who had been accused of tampering with the post. He was acquitted of criminal charges but, subsequently, An Post informed him that he was to be dismissed pending his making representations to the company. Mr Mooney did not make any representations and was dismissed. He subsequently alleged his dismissal was unlawful, as he had not been afforded an oral hearing before an independent arbitrator and had not had the opportunity to cross-examine those prepared to give evidence. The Supreme Court found that, in the context of Mr Mooney refusing to engage with the employer's proposed procedures and refusing even to make a statement to the employer, he was not entitled to an oral hearing. The Court also found that Mr Mooney, in the context of a non-criminal disciplinary procedure, had no implied right to remain silent.   [10–35]

Whether or not an employee can claim a right to cross-examine his or her accusers will depend on the circumstances of the case and nature of the enquiry; it seems, however, that where the charges against the employee are serious or substantial that such a right should be afforded.[77] In *Shortt v Royal Liver Assurance Ltd*[78] the plaintiff alleged a breach of his right to fair procedures in that, in the course of the disciplinary process,   [10–36]

---

[72] *State (Gleeson) v Minister of Defence* [1976] IR 280.

[73] *O' Donoghue v Veterinary Council* [1975] IR 398.

[74] Factors likely to be relevant, for example, might include the seriousness of the consequences for the employee and the seniority of the employee; Cox *et al*, *op.cit*, p 659.

[75] *Flynn v Great Northern Railways Co (Ire) Ltd* 89 ILTR 46 (1955); *Kiely v Minister for Social Welfare* [1977] IR 267.

[76] Redmond, (2007), *op.cit*, p 533.

[77] *Gallagher v Revenue Commissioners* [1995] ILRM 108.

[78] [2008] IEHC 332.

he was neither afforded the opportunity to cross-examine the complainant nor provided with an alternative means of testing her evidence. Given the serious nature of the charges of intimidation against him, he argued this was warranted. Laffoy J, while accepting the conduct of the disciplinary process had not been perfect, concluded that the defendant was entitled to proceed on the basis that the refusal to allow cross-examination was "not likely to imperil a fair hearing or a fair result".[79]

[10-37]   In *Glover v BLN Ltd*[80] the plaintiff was not informed of the charges against him nor was he given an opportunity to defend himself. Thus, there was a violation of the employer's obligation to proceed fairly. The Court found that, even if the employer would have come to the same conclusion after following the proper procedures, this did not validate a dismissal made in breach of those procedures.

[10-38]   In *Carroll v Dublin Bus*[81] the plaintiff was employed as a bus driver by the defendant. At an initial disciplinary hearing, the defendant proceeded in the plaintiff's absence and concluded, *inter alia*, that, as he was involved in union activities at a time when he was certified as unfit for work, he should be dismissed. The plaintiff subsequently appealed that decision to an appeals board. He applied, *inter alia*, for a declaration that his purported dismissal was void as being in breach of fair procedures. Clarke J emphasised that it was not the case that an employer may not, in an appropriate case, deal with a disciplinary process on the basis that an employee is not engaging with the process.[82] However, he went on to hold that whether it can be said that an employee has by his conduct placed himself in a position where it is reasonable for the employer to infer that he is no longer interested in dealing with a disciplinary process depends on all the circumstances of the case. In circumstances where an employee had, in effect, no real first instance hearing at the initial stage of the disciplinary procedure, it would be unfair to require him to have the first substantive hearing at the appeal stage, no matter how fairly that appeal hearing may be conducted. However, different considerations might well apply in circumstances where there was a substantive initial hearing, which was flawed in some material but relatively technical respect.[83]

[10-39]   In the case of *John White*[84] a soldier won a High Court action to prevent his discharge from the Army after testing positive for drugs. The applicant claimed the positive test was due to his having eaten a pizza which, unbeknownst to him, had been "spiked" with cannabis resin by a friend as a prank. On being informed by the prankster what had happened, the applicant gave the information to his commanding officer who asked for the names and addresses of anyone involved and for the matter to be

---

[79] Laffoy J held that the defendant was further entitled to take into account the likelihood of a detrimental effect on the *complainant* by being cross-examined by the plaintiff. On the evidence, the Judge was satisfied that the defendant was entitled to conclude that such a detrimental effect was likely.

[80] [1973] IR 388.

[81] [2005] 4 IR 184.

[82] In *Murphy v College Freight Limited* (UD 867/2007) the EAT noted that it was not open to an employee to be "coy" throughout the investigative or disciplinary process and then forthcoming before the Tribunal.

[83] *Carroll v Dublin Bus* [2005] 4 IR 184 at 212 *per* Clarke J.

[84] High Court, O' Neill J, reported in *The Irish Times*, 23 February 2008.

reported to the Gardaí. The applicant said he felt unable to make a formal complaint in those circumstances. O'Neill J held that the Army's disciplinary procedures were wrongly applied in relation to not recommending a discharge on grounds of reasonable doubt and he ruled the decision to discharge was beyond the provisions of the disciplinary procedures.[85]

Employees will generally be allowed to be represented by others (e.g. a trade union **[10–40]** official), however, it seems this is at the discretion of the decision-maker rather than an entitlement *per se*.[86] The decision-maker must be mindful of the consequences of an adverse outcome for the employee.[87] In *Burns v Governor of Castlerea Prison*[88] the Supreme Court held that "legal representation should be the exception rather than the rule".[89] The Court held that there may be "exceptional cases" in which the Constitution would require legal representation irrespective of the wording of the employer's written procedures. However, representation was "clearly unnecessary" in the instant case, as the issues concerned were factual issues relating to the day-to-day running of the prison. Geoghegan J adopted the criteria identified by Webster J in *R v Secretary of State for the Home Department, Ex p Tarrant*[90] as relevant when considering whether legal representation is desirable in the interests of a fair hearing, namely:

   i.   The seriousness of the charge and of the potential penalty;
   ii. whether any points of law are likely to arise;
   iii. the capacity of a particular person to present his own case;
   iv. procedural difficulty;
   v. the need for reasonable speed in making the adjudication;
   vi. the need for fairness as between the parties.

In *Murphy v College Freight Limited*,[91] where an allegation of theft was at issue, the **[10–41]** EAT held that to allow legal representation in every such case would be over-legalising the workplace which, in its view, would be unhelpful. Although, a "slipshod investigation" by the employer would not be acceptable, equally in such cases "the

---

[85] But see *Rawson v Minister for Defence* [2008] IEHC 404.

[86] However, representation is provided for in the Code of Practice on Grievance and Disciplinary Procedures (SI No 146 of 2000). See *Aziz v Midland Health Board* [1995] ILRM 48, where a solicitor was not allowed accompany the applicant, as the issues to be determined were matters of fact and it was not intended any party would have representation at this stage of procedures. The UK government has provided for a statutory right of "accompaniment" in relation to workplace disciplinary procedures; see the Employment Relations Act 1999, ss 10-14 (as amended by the Employment Relations Act 2004, s 10). An employee who is subject to a disciplinary investigation has a statutory right to be accompanied to any meetings by a fellow colleague or a (trained) member of a trade union.

[87] *Flanagan v UCD* [1988] IR 742.

[88] [2009] IESC 33.

[89] See also the comments, in relation to internal appeals procedures run by commercial companies, of Lord Denning in *Ward v Bradford Corporation* (1971) 70 LGR 27 at 35, where he states: "[w]e must not force these disciplinary bodies to become entrammelled in the nets of legal procedure. So long as they act fairly and justly, their decision should be approved".

[90] [1985] 1 QB 251.

[91] UD 867/2007.

FBI cannot be called in".[92] Two recent decisions of the UK Court of Appeal are of interest here, however. In both *Kulkarni v Milton Keynes NHS Trust*[93] and *R (on the application of G) v Governors of X School*[94] the Court of Appeal (in two cases involving allegations of sexual misconduct on the part of the employee) stated that employees *do* have a right to legal representation for the purpose of workplace disciplinary procedures. In both cases, the Court referred to Art 6 of the European Convention on Human Rights (ECHR) on the right to a fair trial and noted that the Article could be engaged, in the workplace, at a disciplinary hearing on one or two occasions: if the consequences for the employee of an adverse outcome would be extremely serious and/ or if the claimant could lose the right to practise a profession.[95] These cases involved, respectively, a doctor and a teacher, so it is not clear if the decisions can be said to be limited only to *professional* employees. It should be noted, however, that the Court in *Kulkarni* also discussed the possibility that the implied term of trust and confidence between the employer and employee could require the employer to "keep open a discretion to allow an employee to be represented if the employee asked the employer for this discretion to be exercised".[96]

[10–42] The "burden of proof" in these circumstances is on the balance of probabilities (not the criminal standard).[97] In *Madden v Clodagh Ironworks Ltd*[98] there was a conflict of evidence as to the content of a conversation between the plaintiff (who felt he had been dismissed) and a company director (who said he told the plaintiff to merely take some time off) but, on the balance of probabilities, the EAT unanimously accepted the claimant's version of the conversation. Ordinary rules of evidence are generally not applicable. Therefore, the fact that the employee has been acquitted in a criminal prosecution does not mean that he or she cannot be the subject of further disciplinary hearings in respect of the same facts.[99] However, in *Garvey v The Minister for Justice, Equality and Law Reform*[100] the Supreme Court emphasised that:

> "[i]t may in any given circumstances be unfair and oppressive to conduct a disciplinary inquiry into the same issues in respect of which there has been an

---

[92] See also *Stoskus v Goode Concrete* [2007] IEHC 432, where the High Court found that, even if the employee in the case had a right to be legally represented, he had waived it by signing a contract precluding such representation. See also Duffy, "Lawyers in the Workplace- When Are the Services of a Lawyer Appropriate?" (2006) 3(1) IELJ 4; Farrell, "Opening the Door to Injunctions- Refusing Legal Representation at Disciplinary Hearings" (2006) 3(1) IELJ 7; Hayes, "Lawyers in the Workplace" (2006) 3(1) IELJ 7.
[93] [2009] IRLR 829.
[94] [2010] IRLR 222.
[95] See Sanders, "A 'Right' to Legal Representation (in the Workplace) During Disciplinary Proceedings?" (2010) 39(2) ILJ 166, at p 169.
[96] *ibid* at p 178.
[97] *Georgopoulus v Beaumont Hospital Board* [1998] 3 IR 132. See also Tapper and Cross, *Cross and Tapper on Evidence* (11th ed, Oxford University Press, Oxford, 2007), p 26.
[98] UD 557/2004.
[99] *Mooney v An Post* [1998] ELR 238 (SC). Note that the developing jurisprudence on the mutual duty to maintain trust and confidence in the employment relationship may have an impact here. Employees who commit criminal offences (even outside of work) may be said to have breached this duty.
[100] [2006] 1 IR 548.

acquittal on the merits at a criminal trial but this will depend on the particular surrounding circumstances and in particular their cumulative effect. There is no necessary preclusion *per se* of such a double process".[101]

The Court found that there could be circumstances where such a disciplinary inquiry is oppressive and impermissible. In this case, which related to allegations of violence by a prison officer against a prisoner, the Court felt that every aspect of the case must have been discussed within the prison service whether at Governor level or prison officer level. The fact that there had been a lengthy trial (five weeks) leading to an acquittal must have given rise to a flow of arguments and opinions throughout the prison. In what the Court described as "this claustrophobic atmosphere", it was held that it would be a basically unfair procedure to conduct a disciplinary inquiry on what, in effect, were identical allegations to the criminal charges, based on essentially the same evidence and the same witnesses.[102]

[10–43]

In *Minnock v Irish Casing Company Limited*[103] the plaintiff obtained an injunction restraining the continuance of the investigation being conducted by the employer, who claimed this was only to determine whether a full disciplinary hearing was warranted. Clarke J affirmed that the courts will not intervene *in the course of* a disciplinary process unless a clear case has been made out that there is a serious risk that the process is sufficiently flawed and incapable of being resolved, so that irreparable harm would be caused to the plaintiff if the process were permitted to continue. Clarke J detailed the varying types of investigations that can take place in employment situations and the approach the court will adopt if asked to intervene in such investigations. He noted that where the investigation is one in which no findings are made by the investigator other than to determine whether there is sufficient evidence to warrant a formal disciplinary process, then it is not an investigation to which the rules of natural and constitutional justice apply and, therefore, is not an appropriate case for the courts to intervene. On the other hand, other types of investigations result in formal findings being made and it is to these types of investigations that the rules of natural justice apply and which may warrant the court intervening through the making of interlocutory orders. The obligation is on the employer generally to set out the process on which it intends to embark in advance, particularly when requested to do so; in the instant case it had failed to do this.[104]

[10–44]

Note that, in *Hickey v The Eastern Health Board*,[105] the Supreme Court held that the rules of natural justice regulating dismissal for misconduct had no application where the dismissal was for reasons *other than* misconduct. Similarly, in *Sheehy v Ryan*[106] the High Court reaffirmed that an employer was not obliged to have regard to fair procedures in dismissing an employee, other than where there was an issue of

[10–45]

---

[101] *ibid* at 556 per Geoghegan J.

[102] *ibid* at 558 per Geoghegan J.

[103] *Irish Times Law Report, The Irish Times,* 11 June 2007.

[104] See also *Becker v Board of Management of St Dominic's School* [2006] IEHC 130. See Cox *et al, op.cit,* p 858 on the granting of injunctions in relation to workplace disciplinary action.

[105] [1991] 1 IR 208.

[106] [2004] ELR 87. This finding was not disturbed, on appeal, by the Supreme Court; [2008] 4 IR 258.

misconduct. However, in *Cahill v DCU*[107] Clarke J in the High Court held that there had been a breach of fair procedures as a result of an Associate Professor at DCU not being given an opportunity to make representations as to why his contract of employment should not have been terminated. There was no allegation of misconduct in this case; Professor Cahill had merely been given the three months' notice required under the contract of employment.[108] In *Naujoks v National Institute of Bioprocessing Research and Training Ltd*[109] Laffoy J rejected the defendant's position that, as the plaintiff's contract was not terminated on the grounds of misconduct, the latter's contention that he should have been, but was not, afforded fair procedures was irrelevant. The reason given for the termination of the plaintiff's employment was that the Board had lost confidence in his ability to manage the Institute. Laffoy J was of the view that this was not far removed from making a judgment that there was a failure on the part of the plaintiff to properly discharge his duties, which would, under the contract of employment, have entitled the defendant to summarily dismiss the plaintiff, but only subject to affording him fair procedures. Thus, there may some room for arguing that, notwithstanding reaffirmations of the traditional position that fair procedures are not required where no misconduct is at issue, recent decisions raise the spectre that the presence of misconduct may not be required in all circumstances.[110]

VI. Unfair Dismissal

[10–46]   Dissatisfaction with the mode of redress at common law for dismissal led to pressure for statutory intervention in the area. It was felt that the common law, with its all-consuming concern with the employment contract, did not adequately take account of the inherent inequality of bargaining power in the employment relationship and that, for an employee who felt he or she was wrongly dismissed, the route to success through the courts was unduly slow and expensive.[111] It was also felt that legislation in this area would reduce the number of industrial disputes that were occurring as a result of real or perceived injustices related to dismissals.[112] Furthermore, the International Labour Organisation's (ILO) Recommendation concerning Termination of Employment at the Initiative of the Employer[113] was highly influential in prompting Ireland (and many other legal systems) to legislate for unfair dismissal.[114] However, there was also a concern on the part of business groups that the law should not interfere unduly with managerial prerogative; as a result, according to Kerr, "the 1977 Act does not permit a high degree of intrusion into managerial decision-making".[115]

---

[107] [2007] IEHC 20.

[108] On appeal, the Supreme Court upheld the decision; [2009] IESC 80. Professor Cahill is an officer, working in a public sector organisation, which may particularise the findings here.

[109] [2007] 18 ELR 25.

[110] See, however, Laffoy J in *Nolan v Emo Oil Services Ltd* [2009] ELR 122 and *Buckley v National University of Ireland, Maynooth* [2009] IEHC 58.

[111] See Collins, *Justice in Dismissal* (Clarendon Press, Oxford, 1992); Pitt, "Justice in Dismissal: A Reply to Hugh Collins" (1993) 22 ILJ 251.

[112] Murphy, "The Impact of the Unfair Dismissals Act in Workplace Industrial Relations" (1987) 6 JISLL 36.

[113] No 19 of 1963.

[114] Napier, "Dismissal - The New ILO Standards" (1983) 12 ILJ 17.

[115] Kerr, *Termination of Employment Statutes* (3rd ed, Round Hall, Dublin, 2006), p J-4.

Dismissal is defined in s 1 of the Unfair Dismissals Act 1977 as: **[10–47]**

> "(a) the termination by his employer of the employee's contract of employment with the employer, whether prior notice of the termination was or was not given to the employee,
>
> (b) the termination by the employee of his contract of employment with his employer, whether prior notice of the termination was or was not given to the employer, in circumstances in which, because of the conduct of the employer, the employee was or would have been entitled, or it was or would have been reasonable for the employee, to terminate the contract of employment without giving prior notice of the termination to the employer, or
>
> (c) the expiration of a contract of employment for a fixed term without its being renewed under the same contract or, in the case of a contract for a specified purpose (being a purpose of such a kind that the duration of the contract was limited but was, at the time of its making, incapable of precise ascertainment), the cesser of the purpose".

As regards the onus of proof, where the fact of dismissal is not in dispute,[116] the onus is on the *employer* to justify the dismissal. If constructive dismissal (s 1(b) in the definition above) is alleged, the *employee* must prove either contractual entitlement or reasonable response.

It is important to note that the legislation in Ireland governing unfair dismissal from **[10–48]** employment (the Unfair Dismissal Acts 1977–2007) does not actually protect an employee from dismissal; rather, it provides a system of appeal whereby the employee can question the fairness of the dismissal *after* it has occurred.[117] The starting point for a claim under the legislation is that the plaintiff must have been dismissed. The definition refers to, first, unilateral termination by the employer; the employer makes it clear that the contract of employment has, or shall, come to an end. The employee does not have to be given due notice of the dismissal. Secondly, the legislation addresses "forced resignations" or constructive dismissal, where the employee is entitled to terminate the contract due to the employer's conduct. Thirdly, the legislation refers to fixed-term or specified purpose contracts; dismissal is deemed to have taken place once a contract has expired and has not been renewed. Now, of course, fixed-term contracts are also governed by the Protection of Employees (Fixed-Term Workers) Act 2003.[118] Fourthly, dismissals of employees who have taken statutory leave will be deemed unfair unless there are substantial grounds for justifying such dismissals.[119]

Dismissal is deemed to be *fair* under s 6(4) of the 1977 Act where it relates to: capability; **[10–49]** competence or qualifications; the conduct of the employee; redundancy; statutory requirements; or the catch-all justification of "other substantial grounds". Dismissal is deemed *unfair* (ss 5–6) where it relates to: participation in industrial action; trade union

---

[116] See below.

[117] See Deakin and Morris, *op.cit*, p 388.

[118] See chapter 3. Note that relief cannot be granted under *both* the Unfair Dismissals Acts and the Fixed-Term Workers legislation; Protection of Employees (Fixed-Term Workers) Act 2003, s 18.

[119] See chapter 6 on "family-friendly" legislation.

membership; religious or political opinion; involvement in civil or criminal proceedings involving an employer; the exercise of rights under certain "family friendly" legislation; race, colour, sexual orientation, age or membership of the travelling community; pregnancy-related matters; and unfair selection for redundancy.[120]

Express Exclusions and Qualifications

[10–50]   The legislation applies to "employees", i.e. to those working under a contract of service (see chapter 3). The Unfair Dismissals (Amendment) Act 1993 amended the principal Act to provide that agency workers are deemed "employees" for the purposes of the legislation and can claim a right of redress for unfair dismissal against the third party to whom they are supplied by their agency; the Act does not deem the third party in question to be the "employer".[121] However, there are a number of categories of worker not covered by the Act (ss 2–4 of the 1977 Act, as amended):

> i.   Employees who have reached normal retirement age for employees of the same employer in similar employment or who, on the date of dismissal, were under 16 years of age;
> ii. persons employed by a family member, employed in the family home or farm where both employer and employee normally reside;
> iii. members of the Gardaí and Defence Forces;
> iv. FÁS trainees and apprentices;
> v.   persons employed by or under the State and dismissed by the Government;
> vi. managers (not servants) of local authorities (see s 144 of the Local Government Act 2001);
> vii. officers of a health board (other than temporary officers) or a vocational education committee established by the Vocational Education Act 1930;
> viii. the Chief Executive Officer of the Health Services Executive (see s 17 of the Health Act 2004);
> ix. an employee who is dismissed during a period starting with the commencement of the employment when he or she is on probation or undergoing training, if the contract of employment is in writing, and the duration of the probation or training is one year or less and is specified in the contract, or when he or she is undergoing training for the purpose of becoming qualified or registered, as the case may be, as a nurse, pharmacist, health inspector, medical laboratory technician, occupational therapist, physiotherapist, speech therapist, radiographer, or social worker.

Civil servants were excluded until the passing of the Civil Service Regulation (Amendment) Act 2005.

[10–51]   As regards "normal retiring age", there is no single, fixed retirement age in Ireland. Some contracts will contain a mandatory retirement age and some statutory rules exist

---

[120] Note that other legislation also deems dismissals unfair in certain circumstances; e.g. the Safety, Health and Welfare at Work Act 2005 (see chapter 8) and the Employees (Provision of Information and Consultation) Act 2006 (see chapter 11).

[121] See Kimber, "Agency Workers and Employers' Responsibilities" (2005) 2(2) IELJ 79; Regan, "Agency Workers: An Analysis of Key Legal Developments" (2010) 1 ELRI 3; and chapter 3.

for parts of the public sector, but the "usual" age in a factual sense is 65.[122] The changing context of contemporary employment, where life-expectancy and, as a result, expectations regarding the duration of working life, are changing,[123] has meant an increasing focus has come onto the issue of mandatory retirement ages. In *Reilly v Drogheda Borough Council*[124] a part-time fire-fighter challenged a decision by Drogheda Borough Council, which had attempted to force him to retire at age 58. At the time of his appointment, the retirement age for part-time fire-fighters in the employment of the defendant was 65. However, a long and protected set of negotiations between a number of trade unions (including the plaintiff's union, SIPTU) and the employers resulted in an agreement, ultimately consolidated in a collective agreement in 2002, which stated that the retirement age for part-time fire-fighters would be fixed at 55 (with an option to remain on until 58). Laffoy J held that the retirement age of 65 was a term of the plaintiff's contract, that he was not bound by the terms of the collective agreement and granted a declaration that Mr Reilly should not be required to retire until reaching the age of 65, providing he remained in good health as stated in his original employment contract.

The issue of mandatory retirement age has also come before the ECJ in recent times. In the *Heyday* case[125] the ECJ ruled that national legislation making termination of employment automatic on the reaching of a specified age did fall within the scope of Directive 2000/78.[126] The Court held that such provisions could be justified under Art 6(1) of the Directive, if they were objectively and reasonably justified in the context of national law by a legitimate aim relating to employment or social policy and it was not apparent that the means put in place to achieve that aim were inappropriate and unnecessary for the purpose.[127] Three recent ECJ decisions have sought to clarify the issue of when age restrictions are acceptable under EU law.[128] In *Wolf*[129] the applicant sought to challenge a German law restricting applicants seeking to join the fire service to those under the age of 30. The ECJ held that, given the nature of the duties involved in this work, the possession of especially high physical capacities could be regarded as a "genuine and determining occupational requirement" within the meaning of the

[10–52]

---

[122] See Bruton, "Retirement Age and the Unfair Dismissals Act" (2008) 5(4) IELJ 121, where the author notes (at p 124) that "in the absence of the provision of a retirement age in employment contracts, an employee may be able to claim an entitlement to continue in employment for as long as they remain capable of working".

[123] See, generally, Boucher and Collins (eds), *The New World of Work* (Liffey Press, Dublin, 2005).

[124] [2008] IEHC 357.

[125] Case C-388/07 *R. (on the application of Incorporated Trustees of the National Council on Ageing (Age Concern England)) v Secretary of State for Business, Enterprise and Regulatory Reform* [2009] IRLR 373.

[126] Directive 2000/78 of 27 November 2000 establishing a general framework for equal treatment in employment and occupation [2000] OJ L303/16.

[127] See also Case C-411/05 *Palacios de la Villa v Cortefiel Servicios SA* [2007] ECR I-8531; Connolly, "Forced Retirement, Age Discrimination and the *Heyday* Case" (2009) 38(2) ILJ 233; Connolly, "Compulsory Retirement Ages - a Thing of the Past?" (2009) 6(1) IELJ 4. See also chapter 5.

[128] Wanambwa and Birtwistle, "You Can Make Assumptions About the Old But Not the Young" (2010) 108 *Emp LJ 2010* 18.

[129] Case C-229/08 *Wolf v Stadt Frankfurt am Main*.

Directive. It further held that the age limit of 30 was a proportionate means of ensuring the proper functioning of the professional fire service, as recruitment at an older age would mean that the fire-service might be short of officials who could carry out the most physically demanding duties and would also mean those recruited would not be able to be assigned to those duties for a sufficiently long period. In *Peterson*[130] the applicant challenged a German law which prohibited her practicing as a dentist in the German National Health Service after the age of 68. The ECJ held that the objective of maintaining a high-quality medical service, achieved in part by ensuring the competence of medical staff, as well as that of preventing the risk of serious harm to the financial balance of the social security system, are covered by the objective of protection of public health under the Directive. These aims might be achieved by protecting the public from the declining performance of older medical staff and by preventing an oversupply of such staff. The ECJ held that the encouragement of recruitment also constitutes a legitimate social policy, or employment policy, objective of the Member States. A measure intended to promote the access of young people to the profession of dentist in the panel system that existed in the German public health system could, therefore, be regarded as an employment policy measure, as long as this was proportionate taking into account the state of the labour market. In *Kucukde-veci*[131] a German law on the calculation of notice periods in the event of dismissal, which excluded employment completed before the age of 25, was at issue. The applicant, who had been working since she was 18, was dismissed. The employer calculated the notice period as if the employee had three years' length of service, although she had been in its employment for 10 years. The German government argued that the difference in treatment could be justified here by a legitimate employment and labour market policy, i.e. that the measure gives more flexibility to employers in dismissing younger workers, who, due to their age and/or their lesser social, family and private obligations, are assumed to have greater occupational and personal flexibility and mobility. The ECJ accepted there was a legitimate policy objective here but held that the national legislation was not appropriate for achieving that objective, since it applied to *all* employees who joined the undertaking before the age of 25, whatever their age at the *time of dismissal*. The national legislation also affected young employees unequally, in that it affected young people who enter active life early after little or no vocational training but not those who started work later after a long period of training.[132]

[10–53] Section 34(4) of the Employment Equality Act 1998 states that it shall not constitute discrimination on the age ground to fix different ages for the retirement (whether voluntarily or compulsorily) of employees or any class or description of employees. In *Calor Teoranta v Mc Carthy*[133] the Labour Court noted that there were serious questions concerning the proper interpretation of s 34(4) of the Act having regard to the jurisprudence of the ECJ. The Labour Court would have given very serious

---

[130] Case C-341/08 *Petersen v Berufungsausschuss fur Zahnarzte fur den Bezirk Westfalen – Lippe.*

[131] Case C-555/07 *Kucukdeveci v Swedex GmbH & Co KG.*

[132] See the decision of the English Administrative Court in *R. (on the application of Age UK) v Secretary of State for Business, Innovation and Skills* [2009] EWHC 2336 (Admin), which upheld the UK Government's policy of imposing a default retirement age, as long as the measure was used for a legitimate social aim and was proportionate.

[133] ED 089/2008, upheld on appeal to the High Court on a point of law; [2009] IEHC 139.

consideration to making a reference to the ECJ on the issue were it not for the fact that the case before it could be properly decided on its particular facts.[134]

To benefit from statutory rights the employee must have been in continuous employment on a full-time basis by the employer for a specified period. Under the Unfair Dismissals Acts, 52 weeks' continuous service is required (s 2(1)(a) of the 1977 Act, as amended). Under the Redundancy Payments Acts, the requisite continuous service period is 104 weeks (s 4(1) of the Redundancy Payments Act 1967). The 52 weeks' service is not required where the employee is dismissed for trade union membership or activities,[135] acting to uphold the provisions of the minimum wage legislation,[136] pregnancy, maternity or related matters,[137] or where the dismissal results from "penalisation" under the Safety, Health and Welfare at Work Act 2005.[138]   **[10–54]**

Calculating the period of continuous service, therefore, is highly significant for determining eligibility to claim under the legislation. The first thing to establish is the date of commencement, i.e. when did the employment relationship begin. In determining when employment came to an end, the key factor is not when the employee actually stopped working but when the employment *relationship* came to an end. The legislation focuses on two questions; the requisite notice for dismissal (the contract ends when the notice expires or, if valid notice is not given, would have expired) and the position of fixed-term contracts (dismissal occurs on the date the contract expires or its purpose ceases).[139] There is a statutory presumption of continuous employment from the date employment commenced to the date it ceased.[140]   **[10–55]**

There are a number of specified circumstances which are deemed not to break the continuity of service.[141] There is no break in continuity where a dismissal is followed by immediate re-employment.[142] Paragraph 10 of the First Schedule to the 1973 Act provides that if an employee is absent for not more than 26 weeks due to illness, lay-off[143] or an agreement with the employer, such a period will count towards service.[144] If, in any week or part of a week, an employee is absent from his or her employment because he or she was taking part in a strike in relation to the trade or business in which he or she is employed, that week shall not count as a period of service.[145] Where   **[10–56]**

---

[134] On appeal, Clarke J, in the High Court, confirmed the Labour Court was correct in this finding; [2009] IEHC 139.

[135] Unfair Dismissals (Amendment) Act 1993, s 14.

[136] National Minimum Wage Act 2000, s 36(2).

[137] Unfair Dismissals Act 1977, s 6(2)(A) as inserted by the Maternity Protection Act 1994, s 38(5).

[138] s 27(2)(a).

[139] Unfair Dismissals Act 1977, s 1. In cases of constructive dismissal, notice entitlements are not taken into account for the purposes of determining the date of dismissal.

[140] See Forde, *op.cit,* p 190.

[141] See Minimum Notice and Terms of Employment Act, First Schedule (as amended).

[142] First Schedule to the 1973 Act, para 6.

[143] A "lay-off" is a temporary severing of relations in anticipation that the worker will be re-employed in the not too distant future; Forde, *op.cit,* p 191.

[144] Not more than 26 weeks' absence on these grounds, between consecutive periods of employment, can be so counted.

[145] First Schedule to the 1973 Act, para 11.

the employer decides to sell or transfer all/part of the business (a "transfer of undertaking"), continuity will be carried over to the new employer.[146]

Where the aim of dismissal is, in fact, to avoid liability under the legislation it will not be held to have broken continuity. As a result of s 3 of the Unfair Dismissals (Amendment) Act 1993, if a dismissed employee is re-employed by the same employer within 26 weeks of dismissal, his continuity of service is not regarded as broken if it is shown that the employer's objective was wholly or partly to avoid liability under the legislation.

[10–57]   The Acts contain special provisions in respect of contracts for a fixed-term or for a specified purpose[147] of limited duration, which could not be ascertained exactly at the time the contract was made. Section 2(2) of the 1977 Act stipulates that a dismissal consisting only of the expiry of the fixed-term (without renewal) or the completion of the specified purpose shall not be covered by the Acts, provided that the contract is in writing, signed by both parties and contains a clause that the Acts shall not apply to such dismissal. In *Sheehan v Dublin Tribune*[148] the claimant was employed under a fixed-term contract of employment. The contract specifically excluded any claim for loss of office on the termination of contract. However, the EAT found that the wording of this clause was insufficient because it did not specifically state that the Unfair Dismissals Acts would not apply.[149] As a result of s 3 of the Unfair Dismissals (Amendment) Act 1993, protection is afforded to those on successive fixed-term contracts of less than one year, where the entry into such contracts by the employer was wholly or partly to avoid liability under the Unfair Dismissals Acts.

[10–58]   Since the 1993 amendment, a Rights Commissioner (or the Employment Appeals Tribunal or the Circuit Court) may examine any second or subsequent fixed-term or fixed-purpose contract of employment where there was no more than a three-month break between contracts and take a view as to whether the fixed-nature or fixed-purpose of the contract was wholly or partly for, or connected with, the avoidance of liability under the Acts. If this is found to be the case, the length of the various contracts can be added together for the purpose of determining the length of service for eligibility under the Acts and the service is deemed to be continuous. In *Duijne v Irish Chamber Orchestra*[150] the claimant was a cellist with the Irish Chamber Orchestra. His first contract started in February 1999 and was for an 11-month period. The contract finished in January 2000 and then, after a one-month break, the Orchestra and Mr Duijne entered into another 11-month contract. Before the contract

---

[146] First Schedule to the 1973 Act, para 7, as amended by Unfair Dismissals Act 1993, s 15. See also European Communities (Protection of Employees on Transfer of Undertakings) Regulations 2003 (SI 131 of 2003).

[147] Note that specific rules apply to contracts where the specified purpose is to cover for employees on protective leave or natal care absence; see Redmond, (2007), *op.cit*, pp 497-501. See also chapter 6.

[148] [1992] ELR 239.

[149] See the similar case of *Donnelly v BGE* (UD 947/2004), where the claimant was awarded €55,000 under the Acts as the fixed-term contract in question had not contained any express waiver in relation to the legislation on expiry.

[150] [2002] ELR 255.

expired in Feb 2001, the claimant was informed that his contract would not be renewed. He successfully brought a claim for unfair dismissal. As there had been less than a three-month break between contracts, the EAT believed that the employer had entered into the second contract at least partly for the purpose of avoiding liability for unfair dismissal (it could not prove a genuine commercial justification). Joining the two 11-month contracts together meant that the twelve-month continuous service requirement was met.

In *Hooper v Mary Immaculate College*[151] a lecturer working in the UK left his **[10–59]** permanent job there to take up a fixed-term position with the respondents on the basis of certain representations made to him by staff (including the Head of Department) of the respondent. He was, basically, led to believe that he would be made permanent, taking up a position that would arise as another staff member was due to retire. He was employed under a 10-month contract followed by two further one-year contracts. He then applied for the position that arose following the staff member's retirement but was unsuccessful. The EAT held that s 3(a)(iv) of the 1993 Act was applicable and that the contracts were formulated by the University for the purposes of avoiding liability under the Acts. The Tribunal then referred to the representations made to Mr Hooper which it said had the effect of establishing an expectation that the fixed-term contracts were merely a preliminary to a permanent position. The Tribunal were satisfied that Mr Hooper had been led to believe that he would be offered a permanent position and awarded him €123,938. The College is currently appealing the Tribunal's decision.[152]

Note that s 9(2) of the Protection of Employees (Fixed Term Work) Act 2003 provides **[10–60]** that, where an employer proposes to renew a fixed-term contract, the employee shall be informed in writing, not later than the date of renewal, of the objective grounds justifying the renewal of the fixed-term contract and the failure to offer a contract of indefinite duration.[153] Note, also, that prior to 20 December 2001, the Unfair Dismissal Acts did not apply to a person who was normally required to work for the employer for fewer than eight hours a week. However, from that date the Protection of Employment (Part-Time Work) Act 2001 has removed the exclusion as to the number of hours worked.

Under s 14(4) of the 1977 Act, an employee must be given written particulars of the principal grounds for dismissing him or her. These reasons must be given within 14 days of an employee's request for reasons.

Grounds for Dismissal under the Acts—Reasonableness

All dismissals are presumed to be unfair and it is up to the employer to prove fairness **[10–61]** by reference to a listed ground in the Act (the exception is for constructive dismissal cases, examined below). Under s 6 of the 1977 Act, the employer must show that in all the circumstances there were "substantial grounds" justifying the dismissal. However, it is crucial to bear in mind that the issue that the EAT and the courts will focus on is

---

[151] UD 1167/2006.

[152] See also *Martin v University of Limerick* (UD 191/2004) where a similar award of over €120,000 was made by the EAT, again as a result of representations made to an employee at the pre-employment stage.

[153] See chapter 3.

not whether the employee *deserved* to be dismissed but whether a *reasonable* employer would have dismissed the employee in the same circumstances: *Bunyan v United Dominions Trust (Ireland) Ltd.*[154] The burden of proof is on the employer to show that there were substantial grounds for justifying the dismissal (and these should be set out in the written particulars supplied to the employee under s 14(4) of the 1977 Act). As a result, a dismissal can be lawful (in the sense that the contract has been complied with) but unfair; moreover, a dismissal may be unlawful (in that the contract has been breached) but fair according to the legislation.[155] Given this approach, much emphasis is placed on the employer following fair procedures; "be they the actual grievance procedures obtaining at the workplace or the more general principles of fair play".[156] As a result, employers should be cognisant of the provisions of the Code of Practice on Grievance and Disciplinary Procedures.[157]

[10–62]   In *Hennessy v Read and Write Shop*[158] the EAT (deciding that the dismissal in question was fair) applied a test of reasonableness to the *nature and extent* of the enquiry carried out by the respondent prior to the decision to dismiss the claimant and to the *conclusion reached* on the basis of the information available from that enquiry. This is similar to the approach taken in the UK, as laid down in *British Home Stores v Burchell.*[159] This test requires the employer to show it had a reasonable belief, based on reasonable grounds, following a reasonable investigation that the employee was guilty of the conduct alleged.

[10–63]   The EAT has stated on many occasions that it is merely determining what is reasonable in relation to the employer's response to the misconduct of the employee and not whether the employee was *in fact* guilty of such misconduct. The EAT does not ask whether the employee should have been dismissed but is concerned with testing the decision taken against what it considers the reasonable employer would have done and concluded. So, the EAT looks at a number of factors, including[160]:

    i.   was the matter fully investigated without undue delay?[161];
    ii.   was the employee made aware of the allegations and complaints which formed the basis of the dismissal?[162];

---

[154] [1982] ILRM 404.

[155] Lockton, *op.cit*, p 230. The rationale behind this is that this approach recognises that the dismissed employee has a "property right" in his or her job; Deakin and Morris, *op.cit*, p 388.

[156] Forde, *op.cit*, p 203.

[157] SI 146 of 2000. See Redmond, (2007), *op.cit*, pp 254-258 for an excellent practical account of how employers can approach the issue of disciplinary procedures. Note that, in the UK, s 3 of the Employment Act 2008 allows an employment tribunal to increase or decrease an employee's award by up to 25 percent if either the employer or the employee has "unreasonably" failed to comply with the Advisory, Conciliation and Arbitration Service (ACAS) Code on Disciplinary and Grievance Procedures 2009 (the equivalent of the Irish SI 146 of 2000).

[158] UD 192/1978.

[159] [1978] IRLR 1379.

[160] Kerr, *op.cit*, p J-20.

[161] *Hennessy v Read and Write Shop* (UD 192/1978).

[162] *O'Reilly v Dodder Management* (UD 311/1978).

iii. was the employee given an adequate opportunity to challenge the allegations and explain his or her conduct prior to a decision to dismiss being taken?[163];
iv. is there anything which suggests that the matter was prejudged prior to the eventual hearing?[164];
v. whether the employer had a belief that the employee was guilty of the alleged misconduct and whether such belief was based on reasonable grounds[165];
vi. whether the penalty of dismissal was proportionate to the alleged misconduct.[166]

The approach of the EAT is summarised well in the decision of the English Court of Appeal in *British Leyland UK Ltd v Swift*[167]: **[10–64]**

> "It must be remembered that in all these cases there is a band of reasonableness, within which one employer might reasonably take one view: another quite reasonably take a different view. One would quite reasonably dismiss the man. The other would quite reasonably keep him on. Both views may be quite reasonable. If it was quite reasonable to dismiss him, then the dismissal must be upheld as fair: even though some other employers may not have dismissed him".

In *Derryquin Hotels Ltd v Savage*[168] the EAT overturned a Rights Commissioner recommendation that the respondent be reinstated. The Tribunal stated that:

> "It may well be that the members of the Tribunal would wish to have seen a lesser sanction imposed, especially given the seniority of the employee and the fact that he had been unwell, but they are conscious that the role of the Tribunal is prescribed by law and the Tribunal is in no doubt but that dismissal is well within the range of penalties imposed by reasonable employers for working for remuneration elsewhere while on sick leave, claiming social welfare allowance and being paid at the same time by the principal employer".

It is important to note that protection from unfair dismissal means that, even where gross misconduct is proven, the employer still has to consider the gravity of the offence, look at alternatives to dismissal and give proper weight to any mitigating factors.[169] **[10–65]**

Unfair Dismissals

Dismissal is deemed *unfair* (ss 5-6 of the1977 Act, as amended) where it results from: trade union membership or activities[170]; religious or political opinion; involvement in civil or criminal proceedings involving an employer; the exercise of rights under certain **[10–66]**

---

[163] *Daly v Somers* (UD 495/2005).
[164] Note that it is advisable that the employer continues to pay the claimant pending the final hearing; otherwise the employer may be said to be prejudging; *Ni Bheolain v City of Dublin VEC* Unreported, High Court, 28 January 1983.
[165] *Devlin v Player and Wills (Ireland) Ltd* (UD 90/1978).
[166] *Employee v Employer* (UD 490/2007).
[167] [1981] IRLR 91 at 93 *per* Denning MR (as he then was).
[168] UD 273/2007.
[169] Craig, "The Stolen Child: A Discussion on the Ramifications of the Death of Baby P With Regard to Employment Law" (2009) 6(1) IELJ 16.
[170] See Cox *et al*, *op.cit*, pp 753-756.

"family friendly" legislation; race, colour, sexual orientation, age, or membership of the travelling community; pregnancy-related matters; and unfair selection for redundancy. These grounds are "inexcusables" as far as an employer is concerned and the dismissal must result *wholly or mainly* from one of the grounds. Most of these grounds are considered elsewhere in the book in the relevant chapters. One ground that has not been invoked regularly relates to religious or political opinion.[171] In *Loscher v Mount Temple Comprehensive School*[172] the complainant argued that he was victimised because of his views on abortion. It was held there was not enough evidence to sustain this. Whilst the EAT did not expressly reject the contention that views taken on the general issue of abortion could not come within the ambit of dismissal on grounds of religious or political opinions as provided for in the legislation, it would appear that a high standard of proof would have been required of such treatment before impugning a dismissal on those grounds.

"Fair" Dismissals

[10–67] Section 6(4) of the 1977 Act sets out generally the acceptable grounds for dismissal (again the "wholly or mainly" test applies). A dismissal is fair where it relates to the employee's capability, competence or qualifications; the conduct of the employee; redundancy; statutory requirements; or other substantial grounds.

Capability, Competence and Qualifications

[10–68] The issue of capability tends to emerge most usually in the area of medical unfitness.[173] The employee is obliged to be fully fit to perform all the functions required under the contract and if he or she becomes unfit to carry out such functions then the employer may have grounds to dismiss. In *Bolger v Showerings Limited*,[174] where it was claimed the employee's ill-health rendered him incapable of doing his job as a fork-lift driver, Lardner J said that for the employer to demonstrate the dismissal was fair it must show that ill-health was the substantial reason for the dismissal, that the employee got fair notice that dismissal for incapacity was being considered and that the employee had been afforded a right to be heard. Again, the EAT will not look to whether the employee is, or is not, in fact, capable or competent to do the job; it will merely assess whether the employer honestly *believes* that the employee is incapable or incompetent and the *reasonableness* of such a belief.

[10–69] The employer is not legally obliged to redeploy the employee to lighter duties of which he or she is capable but would be well advised to at least explore the possibility of redeployment. In *Burns v St James's Hospital Board*[175] the claimant had an accident at work, which adversely affected his ability to undertake some physical work. The claimant approached the deputy human resources manager about a different position but the manager appeared hesitant to accept him. He provided a letter from Beaumont

---

[171] *Quaere* whether this will change in light of the enactment of the European Convention on Human Rights Act 2003.
[172] [1994] ELR 284.
[173] Regard must also be had here to equality legislation relating to disability; see chapter 5. Medical issues may also result in a contract being frustrated: above, section III.
[174] [1990] ELR 184.
[175] UD 15/2004.

Hospital which recommended that the claimant could commence some duties. The deputy human resources manager said that this was not enough and the position was not open to him. The Tribunal held that a reasonable employer was under an obligation to fully investigate whether an employee, who may be unsuitable for medical reasons for one form of employment, might be suitable for alternative employment. This obligation was not complied with and, consequently, the dismissal was unfair.

In *Carroll v Dublin Bus*[176] the High Court (at the interlocutory stage) found that an **[10–70]** employer is not under any legal obligation to seek alternative work for an employee who is no longer medically fit to perform the duties for which he or she was originally employed. This is subject to two caveats. The first caveat concerns the materiality of the difference between the work that an employee may now be able to do compared with the work for which he or she was employed. An overly narrow or technical objection to his or her ability to carry out such duties might well disentitle an employer to treat the employee as being unfit for the duties for which he or she was employed. The second caveat concerns express terms in the contract of employment. No term would ordinarily be implied into a contract of employment to the effect that an employer would be under an obligation to make light work available. Such a position could, however, be displaced by the existence of an express term or a well-established custom and practice amounting to a term of the contract.[177]

Alcoholism is not automatically a cause for either dismissal or disciplinary action (but **[10–71]** must be distinguished from alcohol-related *conduct*).[178] However, where an employer has made substantial efforts to deal with the issue, yet it remains and is known to be a problem, dismissal may be fair; *Mahony v Department of Defence.*[179] In 2006, the Labour Court upheld the principle that alcoholism is a disability under the Employment Equality Acts. The decision in *A Government Department v An Employee*[180] crystallises the principle that alcoholics cannot be treated less favourably at work. Under equality legislation, alcoholics are entitled to "reasonable accommodation" (e.g. access to independent counselling).

The issue of qualifications rarely arises but an employer should be very careful about **[10–72]** dismissing an employee for an absence of qualifications when he or she had not been sent on training schemes where he or she could have picked up such qualifications. One instance where a dismissal could be valid is where a person is employed on the precondition that qualifications will be upgraded within a reasonable period and he or she has failed to do so; *Ryder and Byrne v Commissioner of Irish Lights.*[181]

Incompetence refers to the fact that the employee is incapable of applying the necessary **[10–73]** skills to the job for which he or she was employed. This must be measured against the employer's expectations of what the employee can achieve in their work. In *Maher v*

---

[176] [2005] 4 IR 184.
[177] See Shubotham, "Illness and Incapacity in the Workplace" (2004) 1(1) IELJ 6.
[178] Redmond, (2007), *op.cit,* p 307.
[179] UD 28/1989.
[180] EDA 062/2006.
[181] UD 81/1977.

Jabil Global Services[182] Clarke J noted that an employer is entitled to set targets for employees that are ambitious, as long as they are not such as would make them unachievable having regard to conditions prevailing in the workplace. Dismissal for incompetence must be predicated on previous warnings where faults are identified and an opportunity given to redress the balance.[183] The warning should be clear in its terms and also in how the employee is expected to improve and, where applicable, it should set out what the employer's commitment is to assisting improvement, e.g. via training and agreed targets to be achieved.[184] Dismissals on the grounds of incompetence, therefore, will generally not arise on the basis of one negligent act but after a succession of acts with warnings and disciplinary procedures, operating within the terms of the contract and a gradual staged disciplinary process listed therein.

Conduct

[10–74]   The employee's conduct is a matter of fact to be determined by the EAT. Generally, the misconduct will need to be of a highly gross or offensive nature to justify dismissal.[185] The High Court has provided a list of "premises" to be established to support a decision to dismiss for misconduct[186]:

i.   The complaint must be a *bona fide* complaint unrelated to any other agenda of the complainant.

ii.   Where the complainant is a person or body of intermediate authority, it should state the complaint factually, clearly and fairly without any innuendo or hidden inference or conclusion.

iii. The employee should be interviewed and his or her version noted and furnished to the deciding authority contemporaneously with the complaint and again without comment.

iv.   The decision of the deciding authority should be based on the balance of probabilities flowing from the factual evidence and in the light of the explanation offered.

v.   The actual decision as to whether a dismissal should follow should be a decision proportionate to the gravity of the complaint, and of the gravity, and effect, of dismissal on the employee.

---

[182] [2005] IEHC 130.

[183] *Richardson v H Williams & Co Ltd* (UD 17/1979). The employer should not leave the employee in blissful ignorance of the latter's failings, as otherwise the employee will not have the opportunity to try and improve. In *Winterhalter Gastronom v Webb* [1973] IRLR 120, Donaldson J pointed out that many do not know they are capable of jumping the five-barred gate until the bull is close behind them!

[184] *Kirwisa v National Association for Deaf People* (UD 393/2007).

[185] It may be the case, however, that an act of misconduct, while not especially gross in its own right, can justify a dismissal when combined with preceding incidences of misconduct. The EAT has referred to this as a "last straw" dismissal, in which a final incident can be said to have "tipped the employer over the edge" in circumstances where, taken in isolation, dismissal would not ordinarily have been the result; *Curtin v An Post* (UD 1409/2005).

[186] *Frizelle v New Ross Credit Union* [1997] IEHC 137.

Instances of misconduct can arise both inside and outside of employment.[187] It is **[10–75]**
impossible to assess all the forms of misconduct that could justify dismissal.[188]
However, it is important to note that, as is true of all justifications of dismissal, it is the
employer's honest and reasonable belief in the employee's guilt that is key; the role of
the EAT is to consider what a reasonable employer in the same position and
circumstances at that time would have done and decided and to set this up as a
standard against which the employer's action and decision should be judged.[189]

Inside employment, *dishonesty* on the part of the employee might justify dismissal. This **[10–76]**
can range from conduct that could be characterised as criminal (theft or falsification of
records, for example) to conduct that involves misleading statements, sly practices and
so on. Even if the conduct could be classed as criminal, the employer does not have to
prove the case to the criminal standard of beyond reasonable doubt. Clear examples of
dishonesty can be dealt with harshly by employers; a falsification of business expenses,
for example, has been held to be grounds for dismissal even where no warning had been
issued to the employee and he had no representation at meetings with management
prior to dismissal.[190] Similarly, a dismissal was upheld as being fair in *Connolly v Carey
Glass Ltd*,[191] where the EAT accepted the employer's reasonable belief that an
employee claiming sick pay from the company's disability scheme was capable of work,
as he had been seen on a number of occasions leaving his house with his tool box.

An important duty under the contract of employment is that the employee should *obey* **[10–77]**
the lawful, reasonable orders of the employer. Refusal to do so could amount to
misconduct. The order must, however, be clear and understood by the employee and
the starting point for assessing this will be the contractual duties. So, for example, a
refusal by an employee to work overtime where provision for this is stipulated in the
contract could justify a finding of misconduct,[192] whereas the employee's refusal to do
so may be reasonable where overtime working is voluntary.[193] In *Sialys v JC Savage
Supermarket Ltd*[194] the EAT held that an employee, who refused to take his break
when told to by his supervisor as he wanted his break to coincide with that of his

---

[187] Although it should be noted that conduct outside of the workplace may fall within the sphere
of an employee's "private and family life" as protected by Art 8 of the European Convention on
Human Rights. For an interesting account of a dismissal of an English probation officer for
activities which included performing shows in hedonist and fetish clubs see Mantouvalou and
Collins, "Private Life and Dismissal: *Pay v UK* [2009] IRLR 139 (ECtHR)" (2009) 38(1) ILJ 133.
[188] Note that misconduct relating to breaches of health and safety laws and bullying and
harassment are dealt with in chapters 8 and 9.
[189] *Looney & Co Ltd v Looney* (UD 843/984).
[190] *McDonald v Flanagan and Co* (UD 648/1990).
[191] UD 45/2003. Here, the employer had retained the services of a private investigator in order to
monitor the movements of the claimant. Such practice is relatively common in cases where the
employer suspects "double-jobbing" is going on, but can, due to data protection and privacy
laws, be controversial; see Redmond (2007), *op.cit*, p 273. In *Gibbons v Essilor Ireland Sales Ltd*
(UD 447/2008) a claim for unfair dismissal was successful in a situation where the employer had
placed the employee (who was on sick leave) under private investigator surveillance, despite having
been provided with medical documentation by the employee's doctor.
[192] *McKenna v Farrell Bros* [1991] ELR 77.
[193] *Sweeney v Otis Elevator (Ire) Ltd)* (UD 587/1988).
[194] UD 50/2009.

girlfriend, was guilty of misconduct. The Tribunal noted that "no company can be expected to make its arrangements to facilitate relationships on the shop floor".

[10–78] Dismissal for smoking in breach of company rules can be justified; however, the EAT, in *Honeywell International Technologies*,[195] found a dismissal for smoking in a non-smoking area of the workplace disproportionate, as there was no agreement between the union and management regarding a defined disciplinary procedure for such a breach.

[10–79] Employees owe their employers a duty of *loyalty and fidelity*; there is also an implied term in the contract of employment of mutual trust and confidence between the parties.[196] As a result, the contract of employment will often contain a term stating that the employee cannot work for another employer. Situations of potential disloyalty could arise where an employee does work for a competitor of the employer or where the employee actually sets up in competition with the employer. A difficulty can arise where an employee intends to leave a job and does some form of "preparatory" work for the prospective employer. In *Miller v Post Publications Ltd*,[197] for example, the EAT found that the actions of a sub-editor, who wanted to leave his employer, did not amount to gross misconduct in a situation where the employee had done a shift with a competitor newspaper to be assessed by them as to whether he was suitable for employment. In *McDermott v Kemek Ltd*,[198] however, the EAT made it clear that, while it would be contrary to public policy to prevent an employee from attempting to set up in business competing with the employer, there is a point at which preparations to set up a new business can be incompatible with working for the existing employer.

[10–80] In recent years, the proper use of *email and internet facilities* by employees has become an issue before the tribunals. Employers should have a clear policy on what constitutes appropriate use of these facilities and should be compliant with data protection legislation. In *Kiernan v A Wear Ltd*[199] a sales assistant dismissed after she posted an expletive message about her employer on the "Bebo" social networking site was awarded compensation for unfair dismissal by the EAT, which found that the decision by the company to dismiss Ms Kiernan was disproportionate. While her conduct had deserved strong censure and possible disciplinary action it did not constitute gross misconduct in the circumstances. The use of such a public forum as the internet means that the employee's conduct can cause significant damage to the employer's reputation, given the possibility of wide dissemination of materials posted. In this case, it was a customer of the respondent retail outlet that drew attention to the derogatory comments posted by the employee.[200]

---

[195] UD 1090/2005.

[196] *Berber v Dunnes Stores* [2009] 20 ELR 61.

[197] UD 572/2001.

[198] [1996] ELR 233.

[199] UD 643/2007.

[200] See also *Employee v Employer* (UD 651/2007), where the claimant sent emails from the employer's computer to a third party, the content of which were offensive. The third party complained to the employer that it would take legal action against the employer if the latter did not resolve the matter.

As a general rule, *absenteeism and illness* will not amount to gross misconduct. The **[10–81]** employer should investigate the reasons for both and issue appropriate warnings to staff before contemplating dismissal.

Difficult issues arise in relation to misconduct, especially that of a criminal nature, that arises *outside* employment. Although such crimes may not impact on employers directly, there are the issues of trust and confidence to consider. In *Noonan v Dunnes Stores (Mullingar) Ltd*[201] the claimant was convicted of assaulting a Garda, being drunk and being a danger to traffic. He was dismissed because of that conduct and because of his failure to inform his employers of the case. The EAT found that the offences were not sufficiently serious to warrant dismissal and ordered reinstatement. The Tribunal was not convinced by arguments that publicity in the local press about the case would adversely affect the image and trade of the company. The Circuit Court upheld the finding but substituted damages for the re-instatement order. Generally, the EAT will look for some form of "work nexus" in these types of cases. In *Martin v Dunnes Stores (Enniscorthy) Ltd*[202] the dismissal followed a conviction for breaking and entering and theft from a retail store. The EAT found it greatly significant that the claimant himself was working for another retail store. The EAT found that trust was an essential ingredient of the employment relationship and that the claimant's involvement in burgling a neighbouring premises breached that trust.

A difficult situation might arise where it is alleged that the employee's conduct outside **[10–82]** the workplace makes him or her unsuitable for the job or unacceptable to other employees. This could arise in situations where the employee has been convicted of conduct that attracts particular moral opprobrium. For example, in *Kavanagh v Cooney Jennings Ltd*,[203] the EAT upheld the right of an employer to dismiss an employee convicted of indecent assault. In *Whitlow v Alkanet Construction Ltd*[204] the English EAT held it reasonable to dismiss an employee for having a sexual relationship with the wife of a director of the employer company.

Redundancy

Where properly made out, the dismissal of an employee by reason of redundancy is a **[10–83]** full defence to a claim for unfair dismissal.[205] Under the Redundancy Payments Acts 1967–2007, there are five possible grounds for dismissal by way of redundancy:

---

[201] Unreported, Circuit Court, 14 July 1989.

[202] UD 571/1988.

[203] UD 175/1983.

[204] [1975] IRLR 321.

[205] Although note that dismissal for redundancy is subject to the general principle outlined in s 6(1) of the 1977 Act that a dismissal is deemed unfair unless there are substantial grounds justifying dismissal. It could be the case, therefore, that a dismissal on the grounds of statutory redundancy could be unfair, having regard to all the circumstances. Redmond suggests a possible example of where the redundancy is effected in a particularly harsh manner, where an employee is given five minutes to clear out his or her desk; (2007), *op.cit*, p 363. Note, too, that the focus here is on redundancy only in the context of dismissal. For an excellent and comprehensive overview of the law on redundancy see Higgins and McCrann, "Redundancy" in *Employment Law* (Regan ed, Tottel, Dublin, 2009), chapter 15.

i. The employer has ceased or intends to cease to carry on the business for the purposes for which the employee was employed by him, or has ceased, or intends to cease, to carry on that business in the place where the employee was so employed;

ii. The requirements of that business for employees to carry out work of a particular kind in the place where the employee was so employed have ceased or diminished or are expected to cease or diminish;

iii. The employer has decided to carry on the business with fewer or no employees, whether by requiring that work for which the employee had been employed (or had been doing before his dismissal) to be done by other employees or otherwise;

iv. The employer has decided that the work for which the employee had been employed (or had been doing before his dismissal) should henceforward be done in a different manner for which the employee is not sufficiently qualified or trained;

v. The employer has decided that the work for which the employee has been employed (or had been doing before dismissal) should henceforward be done by a person who is also capable of doing other work for which the employee is not sufficiently qualified or trained.

[10–84] The first two factors, then, are impersonal as they refer to the requirements of the business. The EAT has consistently referred to the importance of impersonality; it is the position that is being made redundant, rather than the employee.[206] The other three, however, involve elements of employee selection and an examination of qualifications and training. As a result of s 6(4)(c) of the 1977 Act, the dismissal must result wholly or mainly from one of the above factors to be deemed fair. However, under s 6(3) the dismissal will be presumed unfair if there has been an unfair selection for redundancy.

[10–85] The fact of redundancy must be established in accordance with the definition; so, for example, one could challenge this by adducing evidence that the redundant employee was subsequently replaced. The employee should try to get close intelligence on what has happened at the job post-dismissal. So, in *Melroy v Floraville Nurseries Ltd*[207] the claimant was able to demonstrate that, while part of her duties had ceased, other areas of her work continued and other employees had been recruited to do this work on a part-time basis. If the argument is economic, the employer should produce figures to substantiate that argument. In *Crowe v Farrington*,[208] for example, the publican employer cited the introduction of the smoking ban in the workplace, and the resulting decline in trade, as the justification for letting the claimant go. The EAT found no evidence that a redundancy situation existed. If redundancy is on the basis of lack of qualifications or training, one must ascertain whether the employee was given the opportunity to access training. In *McGeehan v Park Developments*[209] the respondent recruited sub-contractors at a time when the market was buoyant and it found it difficult to recruit labour. Subsequently, when business dipped, the respondent

---

[206] *Daly v Hanson Industry Ltd* (UD 719/1986).
[207] UD 703/1993.
[208] UD 763/2005.
[209] UD 950/2008.

dismissed the claimant employees by reason of redundancy. The respondent gave evidence of market changes and the decline in available work and submitted that it could not breach its contractual arrangement with the sub-contractors. The EAT, however, noted the respondent had demand for plastering work to be done after it had let go its own employees and that it had given no consideration to temporary lay-off or short week options or to renegotiating its contract with the sub-contractor. Damages for unfair dismissal were awarded, although the EAT took account of the fact that a redundancy situation would have, in fact, occurred in any event in the months following the dismissals.

Central to the definition of redundancy is the idea of *change*. According to the EAT in *St Ledger v Frontline Distribution*[210]: **[10–86]**

> "... [t]he most dramatic change is a complete close down. Change may also mean a reduction in needs for employees, or a reduction in numbers...change in the way work is done, or some other form of change in the nature of the job...change in the job must be of a qualitative kind...partly, at least, work of a different kind".

Here, the claimant, a warehouse supervisor, was replaced by another person the employer deemed better able to cope with an increased volume of work. This was held not to be a valid redundancy as the amount of work to be done had not decreased but had, in fact, increased. Moreover, it was irrelevant that the replacement was simply better able to do the work, as this related not to training or qualifications but to individual ability. To consider this would be to "deny the essential impersonality" of a genuine redundancy, which focuses on the *job* and not the *individual*. In *Kelleher v St James Hospital*[211] management decided work was to be done by one full-time, rather than two part-time, nurses. The claimant was told, as she was replaced by a full-time nurse, she would henceforth work "on call". The EAT held (even though the volume of work to be done was unchanged) that part-time work was different from on-call work and so the claimant was entitled to a redundancy payment.

It might also be shown that the dismissal was not brought about wholly or mainly for reasons of redundancy; in such cases, the employee seeks to deny the causal link. In *Daly v Hanson Industry Ltd*[212] the employee was dismissed just after acting as a witness in litigation involving the employer. The decision suggests that, although a redundancy situation was established, that situation was not wholly or mainly the reason for dismissal. The EAT suggested that, in such cases, it must be considered, first, whether the dismissal was genuine and, secondly, whether there was a cause and effect relationship between the redundancy and the dismissal. Such situations can arise when it is discovered that there are other factors at play in the employment relationship. For example, in *Ponisi v JVC Europe Ltd*[213] the General Manager of JVC Ireland was informed that, due to restructuring, his position would be lost but that a new position of "Sales Manager Ireland" would be created, for which he could apply. The claimant felt **[10–87]**

---

[210] [1995] ELR 160.
[211] UD 59/1977.
[212] UD 719/1986.
[213] UD 949/2009.

that the new position was, effectively, his old job but with reduced pay and conditions, refused to apply and was made redundant. While the EAT accepted that a downturn in business had occurred that would justify a redundancy situation, it upheld the claim on the basis that it appeared, in effect, that the company was attempting to disguise as a redundancy what was really a cost-cutting measure. The claimant was awarded 14 months' salary (over €161,000). On appeal, the Circuit Court increased Mr Ponisi's award by more than €53,000 to €214,000. Linnane J held that there was no question of a genuine redundancy here, as the company had already decided Mr Ponisi's fate before entering the "sham" consultation process. This case demonstrates that employers need to be careful in effecting a reorganisation of their business, particularly in times of economic downturn.[214] This point is reinforced by the decision of the EAT in *Drelichowski v Heatons*.[215] Here, the claimant had been employed as a retail associate with the respondent and had subsequently been promoted to the position of morning pack supervisor. Owing to an economic downturn he had been informed that he had been selected for redundancy. The decision to make him redundant was not related to his work performance. The claimant maintained that he would have preferred to have been offered his previously held position rather than being made redundant. The EAT recognised that the respondent company was entitled to reorganise and re-structure its business to avoid making losses. However, the particular circumstances of the position holders made redundant (including the claimant) had not been taken into consideration when making the decision to make the positions redundant. The decision was made centrally and applied locally without any attempt to look at what re-structuring options might be open to management, such as offering the claimant his previous position. As a result, the dismissal was held to be unfair.

[10–88] Section 6(7) of the 1977 Act (as amended by the 1993 Act) requires that the reasonableness or otherwise of the conduct (whether by act or omission) of the employer in relation to the dismissal be taken into account in determining whether the dismissal was unfair. In *Hickey v Eastern Health Board*[216] the Supreme Court held that rules relating to natural and constitutional justice did not apply. However, as Connolly notes:

> "... [a]lthough the full 'constitutional and natural justice' rights which would be required in a misconduct-related dismissal do not apply to a redundancy dismissal, the Employment Appeals Tribunal is increasingly examining the manner in which the employer conducted itself. This may require consultation with the employee before a decision is made to make the position redundant and consideration of alternative positions within the workplace".[217]

[10–89] This can be seen in *Barry v Precision Software Ltd*.[218] Here, the EAT found that the employer had acted unreasonably by not notifying the employee of his precarious

---

[214] See Hyde, "In the Line of Fire" (2008) 102(8) GLSI 22; Walshe, "When the Axe Falls" (2009) 103(6) GLSI 26.
[215] UD 919/2009.
[216] [1990] ELR 177.
[217] Connolly, "Management of Employment in an Economic Downturn" (2009) 6(2) IELJ 48, at p 54.
[218] [2007] ELR 190.

position in a situation where the employee had, by virtue of his contract, an expectation regarding an alternative position within the company. The EAT found that there had been a total lack of fair procedures, as the situation regarding the claimant had been allowed to drift on and the claimant had to "prise information from the respondent on a piecemeal basis". Similarly, in *Sheehan and O'Brien v Vintners Federation of Ireland Ltd*,[219] the EAT accepted that a redundancy situation existed but was critical of the manner in which the respondent dealt with the redundancy situation, having regard to the ages of the claimants (64 and 59, respectively) and their length of service (approximately 12 years). In particular, the employer did not give any genuine consideration to the proposals put forward by one of the claimants (especially in failing to consider earnestly the claimants' proposals regarding reorganisation of work), did not offer any training to the claimants and did not properly consider either of them for a role in head office. Employers, therefore, might well be advised that procedural fairness should be followed in redundancy situations. In particular, consultation with the employees in question and redeployment,[220] especially in large organisations, should be considered before dismissal.[221]

Whether or not redundancy is actually established, s 6(3) of the 1977 Act envisages a situation ("unfair selection") where a dismissal is due to redundancy but circumstances apply equally to other employees in similar employment with the same employer who were not dismissed and either: **[10–90]**

a. the selection of that employee for dismissal resulted wholly or mainly from one or more of the matters specified in subsection (2) of this section or another matter that would not be a ground justifying dismissal, or

b. he was selected for dismissal in contravention of a procedure (being a procedure that has been agreed upon by or on behalf of the employer and by the employee or a trade union, or an excepted body under the Trade Union Acts 1941 and 1971, representing him or has been established by the custom and practice of the employment concerned) relating to redundancy and there were no special reasons justifying a departure from that procedure.

In such circumstances, the dismissal is deemed unfair. The grounds referred to in s 6(2) are trade union membership or activities; religious or political opinion; involvement in civil or criminal proceedings involving an employer; the exercise of rights under certain "family friendly" legislation; race, colour, sexual orientation, age, or membership of the travelling community; and pregnancy-related matters.[222] **[10–91]**

As regards unfair selection, then, the issue is why did the employer select a particular employee for redundancy ahead of others in similar employment? The procedures referred to in s 6(3) normally refer to an agreement with trade unions, an established custom and practice (such as "first in, last out") or those incorporated into the contract of employment. If procedures exist, departure from them by the employer will **[10–92]**

---

[219] [2009] ELR 155.
[220] See *Boucher v IPC* [1990] ELR 205.
[221] See *Drelichowski v Heatons* (UD 919/2009).
[222] See Glynn, "Redundancy Payments and their Application to People on Sick and Maternity Leave" (2009) 27(16) ILT 227.

require careful justification.[223] If there is no procedure or custom in place, and s 6(2) does not apply, the EAT will examine whether the employer acted reasonably in all the circumstances. The employer may have an obligation, depending on the particular circumstances, to give prior warnings to employees, to consult with trade unions, to consider redeployment and alternative employment, to consider the timing of the redundancy, or to allow employees to appeal any decision taken.[224] In practice, it is advisable for the employer to have objective selection criteria in place *before* selection is made. These could include length of service, experience, skill levels, technical competence, qualifications and training and future business needs. The employer should avoid the use of subjective criteria. In *Fox v Des Kelly Carpets*[225] the employer tried to justify selection on the grounds of the employee's alleged misconduct. While the EAT expressly did not decide whether or not conduct could be a factor in selecting somebody for redundancy, the dismissal was held to be unfair as the employee had remained in the job for a period after the alleged misconduct. Furthermore, the use of objective criteria will not amount to a blanket defence. If one of the selection criteria relates to attendance records, for example, the employer, in selecting persons with poor records, should seek to ascertain the reasons behind the absences.[226] Where redundancies follow a pay reduction programme, selection of employees only on grounds of objection to the pay cuts would seem to be an unfair process; this would appear to be the case even if the effect is that employees who have voluntarily accepted the pay cut are selected for redundancy because of the application of the selection criteria.[227] Obviously, selection criteria that are prohibited as discriminatory (selecting only part-time workers, female workers, etc) are unacceptable. In choosing length of service as a criterion, employers will also need to be careful not to discriminate on the grounds of age. In *Rolls Royce v Unite*[228] the English High Court upheld a provision in a collective agreement that took into account length of service for the purposes of fair selection for redundancy. While the Court held that such a provision would need to be objectively justified, it held that this requirement was satisfied here as it sought to achieve the legitimate aim of the advancement of an employment policy that achieves a peaceable process of selection agreed with the recognised union. The Court held that the criterion of length of service respects the loyalty and experience of the older workforce and protects the older employees from being put onto the labour market at a time when they are particularly likely to find alternative employment hard to find. However, Morrison J noted that the situation may have been different had the Court been concerned with a scheme which was "last in, first out" alone.[229]

---

[223] See *Mole v Pierse Contracting Ltd* (UD 637/2008), where the complainant successfully argued that there was nothing in the employer's terms and conditions of employment that suggested that seniority would not apply in respect of shop stewards who would escape redundancy.

[224] See Deakin and Morris, *op.cit,* p 548 and the decision of the English EAT in *Williams v CompAir Maxam Ltd* [1982] IRLR 83. Certain obligations arise under employee consultation legislation; see chapter 11.

[225] [1992] ELR 182.

[226] *Paine and Moore v Grundy (Teddington) Ltd* [1981] IRLR 267.

[227] Connolly, *op.cit*, p 58.

[228] [2009] IRLR 49.

[229] Interestingly, in this case it was the *employer* that argued that the scheme may have been discriminatory on the grounds of age.

Other Substantial Grounds

The final ground for a fair dismissal under the Unfair Dismissals Act 1977 is where the employer can show "substantial grounds" other than those listed elsewhere under s 6(4) for justifying dismissal. This is a residual category and, according to Redmond, is particularly relevant where the employer's interests or requirements (e.g. reorganisation of the business, contracting out) result in dismissals.[230]

[10–93]

Given the residual nature of this category, almost any reason could potentially fall under its ambit. For example, the employer's financial security was involved in *Brennan v Bluegas Ltd*.[231] The claimant was a taxi driver who was allegedly involved in three accidents in a six-month period. The insurance company would not insure his employers unless *his* driving was to be excluded from the policy. He was dismissed and this was upheld by the EAT, as the employer was able to present substantial evidence from the insurance broker to support its case.

[10–94]

Maintaining the "ethos" of the employer can also be important. In *Flynn v Power*[232] the claimant teacher in a religious school was dismissed because she was cohabiting with a married man. Costello J held that a religious school was entitled to take into account its religious aims and objects, which differed from those of secular institutions, and was entitled to conclude that claimant's behaviour amounted to a rejection of religious tenets that the school tried to promote.[233]

[10–95]

Pressure can be put on the employer by third parties to dismiss someone and this may amount to a justifiable reason. In *McSweeney v OK Garages Ltd*[234] a faction fight broke out between two groups of employees. One group said that if the other (those in the minority) were not sacked then it would resign, which would have had the effect of debilitating the company. The company did sack the minority group and justified this by saying that it had no other option. The dismissals were found to be unfair, as the employer was not justified in dismissing employees simply as a "self-defence mechanism".[235]

[10–96]

The business needs of the employer may also come into play under this ground, in situations where the employer wants to impose change that may effectively alter the terms of employment. In general, the employer must show there is sound business logic behind any reorganisation; that change was necessary; and that the changes might reasonably have been expected to improve the business or alleviate the problem.[236]

[10–97]

---

[230] Redmond, (2007), *op.cit*, p 365.

[231] UD 591/1993.

[232] [1985] IR 648.

[233] See now s 37 Employment Equality Act 1998 and see Coen, "Religious Ethos and Employment Equality: A Comparative Irish Perspective" (2008) 28(3) *Legal Studies* 452.

[234] UD 107/1978.

[235] See also *Kavanagh v Cooney Jennings Ltd* (UD 175/1983).

[236] Lockton, *op.cit*, p 269.

[10-98]   Failure to implement a procedure can be detrimental to an employer in attempting to argue that any dismissal of an employee is fair.[237] In *McNamara v DCU*[238] the employee made an informal complaint to management, as he was reluctant to go through the formal grievance procedure. Nevertheless, the EAT found that, in circumstances where the claimant's perception of mistreatment through various incidences and over time was such as to justify his conclusion that he was unable to continue in the job following a significant illness and medical treatment, the respondent *employer* should have invoked the grievance procedure that was in place. The respondent had been aware of the claimant's difficulties but had failed to activate its own procedures in his favour.[239]

Constructive Dismissal

[10-99]   The term "constructive dismissal" is not itself used in the legislation but has become common parlance. This is a form of indirect dismissal where, because of the employer's action or conduct, the employee has virtually no choice but to resign. There are two limbs; either an employee is entitled to terminate his or her contract and/or it is otherwise reasonable, due to the employer's conduct, to do so. Constructive dismissal is defined in s 1 of the 1977 Act as:

> "the termination by the employee of his contract of employment with his employer, whether prior notice of the termination was or was not given to the employer, in circumstances, in which, because of the conduct of the employer, the employee was or would have been entitled, or it was or would have been reasonable for the employee, to terminate the contract of employment without giving prior notice of the termination to the employer".

Claims for constructive dismissal are slightly unusual, given that it is the *employee* who must bear the burden of proving that the dismissal has occurred and that it was unfair. This can be a difficult burden to discharge. The EAT stated in *Tierney v DER Ireland Ltd*[240] that the employee:

> "... [m]ust show that it was reasonable for her to consider herself dismissed owing to the conduct of her employer. Central to this is that she shows that she has pursued to a reasonable extent all internal avenues of appeal without a satisfactory or reasonable outcome having been achieved".

[10-100] Thus, just as an employer should follow appropriate grievance and disciplinary procedures before deciding to dismiss, it is incumbent on employees, wherever possible,

---

[237] See Bolger and Bruton, "Recent Developments in Employment Litigation" (2008) 5(1) IELJ 19.

[238] UD 381/2005.

[239] See also *Porter v Atlantic Homecare Limited* [2008] ELR 95, where the claimant stated that she was too afraid to use the grievance procedure in the company handbook furnished to her and, in any event, that when she had spoken to her manager about her difficulties, no mention was made of the procedure. Bolger and Bruton conclude that recent EAT decisions seem to suggest that a failure to invoke a grievance procedure furnished to an employee is not necessarily detrimental to a claim of constructive unfair dismissal, as long as there is evidence justifying that failure to invoke the procedure, *op.cit*, p 19.

[240] UD 866/1999.

to utilise the employer's grievance procedure to its fullest prior to resigning.[241] However, the employee may be able to justify a failure not to invoke disciplinary procedures. In *McNamara v DCU*[242] the employee's failure to invoke the employer's grievance procedure was not fatal in circumstances where the EAT found the *employer* should have had recourse to its own procedures. In *Dinner v Finglas Child and Adolescent Centre*[243] the claimant was successful in alleging constructive dismissal where the employer had initiated a mediation service but had failed to fully implement the service.[244] In *Harrold v St Michael's House*[245] the claimant expressed concerns about a culture of bullying in the respondent organisation. He refused to co-operate with two separate internal grievance processes on the grounds that he felt they would be biased and ultimately resigned as he felt he had exhausted all avenues of communication and did not have anywhere left to go with the issues of bullying. He also felt that he was being targeted for having raised these issues. The EAT held that the test for the claimant to satisfy is whether it was reasonable for him to terminate his contract. The Tribunal determined that the totality of the evidence produced by the claimant, his fellow employees and other relevant witnesses did not establish the existence of bullying within the respondent organisation. Having regard to the claimant's own evidence, it found that the claimant did not act reasonably in refusing to engage with the two processes made available to him by the respondent. This was particularly so as, if the claimant considered the outcome of the internal managerial enquiry unsatisfactory, he had a right of appeal to a Rights Commissioner or the Labour Relations Commission.

There are many grounds under which the employee can claim it was reasonable for him or her to terminate the contract. These can relate to the employer breaching a core express or implied term of the contract, in circumstances where the employee feels that he or she can no longer continue in employment.[246] This would include breaching the implied duty of trust and confidence between employer and employee.[247] Other cases can relate to mistreatment by the employer directed at a particular characteristic of the employee (e.g. race or disability) that may be proscribed by equality law.[248] Many cases, however, relate to a situation where the employee resigns on the basis that he or she is "frozen out" by the employer. This can amount to bullying or harassment and might lead to a claim for psychiatric injury or distress.[249] **[10–101]**

In *Byrne v RHM Food*[250] the claimant was secretary to a marketing manager. When the manager was suspended, the claimant was assured that her job was safe. However, thereafter, her filing cabinet was removed, times for her breaks were altered, she was given very little or no work to do and her telephone was disconnected. The EAT held **[10–102]**

---

[241] See *Conway v Ulster Bank* (UD 474/1981). The EAT noted, however, that the employee is not required to "jump through hoops" to follow a grievance procedure.
[242] UD 381/2005.
[243] UD 141/2006.
[244] See also above, n 239.
[245] [2008] ELR 1.
[246] See above, section IV and Redmond, (2007), *op.cit*, pp 399-403.
[247] *Berber v Dunnes Stores* [2009] ELR 61. See chapter 4.
[248] See chapter 5.
[249] See chapter 9.
[250] UD 69/1979.

that her "continuous isolation" without knowledge of what was going on or contact by any person made it reasonable and understandable that her trust and confidence in her employer should be undermined to the extent that she could tolerate it no longer. In *Allen v Independent Newspapers*[251] the claimant successfully brought a case before the EAT, arguing that the bullying she had been subjected to amounted to grounds for constructive dismissal. The bullying included isolation, being undermined in her job, attempts to unilaterally change agreed working conditions and a failure to tackle her complaints. The Tribunal found that the claimant's conclusion that she could have no confidence in the respondent to properly or effectively address her grievances was a reasonable conclusion in the circumstances.

[10–103] It is important to note that these cases depend very much on the particular circumstances. The Tribunal will need to consider the extent to which the employer's conduct was serious or outrageous, whether the latest conduct complained of was in the nature of the "last straw" for the claimant, whether the workplace environment was so oppressive that the employee had no choice but to resign, and so on.[252] The employee will be expected to bear the normal "rough and tumble" of the average workplace, with its disagreements and misunderstandings, without having recourse to resignation. In *Curtin v Primark*[253] the claimant was the manager of a large department store, who resigned following a disagreement with his area manager. The EAT found that the employer had made genuine and sustained efforts to get the claimant to return to work and dismissed his claim. The Tribunal noted that the claimant, given his position, should have been able to handle the pressure he found himself under. The Tribunal also noted that those in a position of area manager have great demands made upon them, which necessitates that they, in turn, must make demands of those in positions like the claimant's. Clearly, then, the degree of responsibility that an employee takes on (assuming both employer and employee are satisfied the employee is capable of so doing) will affect the Tribunal's determination of what that employee should expect to endure.

In *Leeson v Glaxo Wellcome Ltd*[254] the claimant was private secretary to a managing director (MD) who retired in 1996. A new MD was appointed and the claimant was retained as private secretary. There were problems with the relationship and three meetings were identified where the MD criticised the claimant. The claimant went on holidays and never returned. Subsequently, the employer convened a meeting and suggested re-training. The claimant was unsatisfied with this and resigned. The EAT upheld the clam of constructive dismissal but, on appeal to the Circuit Court, the decision was overturned. It was noted that the MD was heavily reliant on the claimant as his private secretary and so it was entirely appropriate that he should offer criticism of her performance. The Judge found that the employer's criticism came well within the

---

[251] [2002] ELR 84.

[252] See Stewart and Dunleavy, *op.cit*, pp 46-52. A successful claim for constructive dismissal was made in *McKenna v Pizza Express Restaurants Ltd* [2008] ELR 234, for example, where an employee with over 10 years' service was frog-marched out of the workplace in full view of customers and other staff after a dispute about takings. For a good example of a "last straw" resignation see *Kennedy v Foxfield Inns Ltd* [1995] ELR 216.

[253] UD 306/1980.

[254] UD 1002/1997 (EAT); Circuit Court, Smyth J, 16 June 1998.

boundaries of acceptable criticism and did not constitute conduct that would make it reasonable for the employee to terminate her employment.

In certain circumstances, the employee may be told to "resign or be dismissed". [10–104] Generally, this indicates that the resignation is made under duress and so unlikely to be held to be a genuine resignation.[255] Note that a claim for constructive dismissal is not automatically ruled out by virtue of the fact that an employee does not resign immediately after the alleged misconduct; however, undue or unjustifiable delay may result in a finding that the contract has been affirmed.[256] In general, practitioners will be slow to advise an employee to relinquish his or her position. While in situ the employer remains under continuing obligations to the employee. Furthermore, in situations where the relationship appears to have broken down and the employee is not expected to return to work, the weapon of threatening to do just that might be the only one the employee has to invoke.

VII. Procedural Election

Under s 15 of the Unfair Dismissals Act 1977 (as amended), a claimant must choose [10–105] between pursuing a claim for wrongful dismissal at common law or a statutory claim under the Act (this is known as "procedural election").[257] Election is deemed to have been made once a recommendation or determination under the legislation is issued, or the Tribunal has begun hearing a claim under the Acts, or, alternatively, when common law proceedings have been commenced. Obviously, in a termination situation, this is a hugely important tactical question. The factors that the employee will need to consider have been discussed throughout this chapter. These include the existence of preconditions for taking a claim (particularly service periods)[258]; the potential remedies available[259]; the cost and likely duration of taking the claim to the courts as against the employment tribunals; the burden of proving the claim (under the legislation, dismissals are generally deemed to be unfair and the employer must justify the decision; in the courts it is for the plaintiff to prove the case); the different procedural requirements of the courts as against the tribunals (time-limits, evidential requirements); and so on.[260]

---

[255] *O'Reilly v Minister for Industry and Commerce* [1997] ELR 48. See *Employee v Employer* (UD 651/2007), where the claimant was told to resign or he would be sacked. The claimant did resign after having consulted his shop steward. The EAT, by majority, rejected his claim of duress or undue influence and found that he resigned from his job having had the benefit of advice from his union representative.

[256] *Western Excavating (ECC) Ltd v Sharp* [1978] All ER 713.

[257] Laffoy J in *Nolan v Emo Oil Services Ltd* [2009] ELR 122 noted that, under Irish law, an employee has two potential avenues to secure redress for dismissal; one at common law for wrongful dismissal in breach of contractual or constitutional rights, the other under the Unfair Dismissal Acts. The Judge emphasised that the two are mutually exclusive.

[258] Discussed above; one year's service is required for an unfair dismissal action. No such period is required for a wrongful dismissal action.

[259] See chapter 12.

[260] See Stewart and Dunleavy, *op.cit,* chapter 9. An important difference is that claims for unfair dismissal must be initiated within six months of the date of the dismissal (this can be extended to 12 months if the Rights Commissioner or the EAT finds there are "exceptional circumstances"); Unfair Dismissals Act 1977, s 8(2). An action for wrongful dismissal is subject to a limitation period of six years; Statute of Limitations 1957, s 11.

[10–106] It is important to note that this is not the only decision to be made. A number of other statutes also insist on procedural election, most importantly: the Protection of Employees (Fixed Term Work) Act 2003[261]; the Protection of Employees (Part-Time) Work Act 2001[262]; the Employees (Provision of Information and Consultation) Act 2006[263]; and the Employment Equality Act 1998.[264] Many of the tactical issues outlined above apply equally in relation to these statutes. One important innovation in relation to claims of discriminatory dismissal under the equality legislation, introduced by the Equality Act 2004, is that the Director of the Equality Tribunal can recommend (after an investigation is complete) that the case proceed under the unfair dismissals legislation; this may occur where the Director feels that the claimant was unfairly dismissed but not discriminated against.[265]

VIII. Fact of Dismissal

[10–107] As already seen, an employee can claim that his or her dismissal is invalid because it was unfair (by reference to statute) or wrongful at common law. However, in both cases the employee will need to satisfy the tribunals that a dismissal has occurred in a factual sense.[266] This will require demonstrating that the employer has unequivocally communicated to the employee that the contract of employment has come to an end or that this can be reasonably inferred, with a degree of certainty, from the circumstances. In *Casey v Dunnes Stores*[267] the EAT noted that, while "dismissal" appears to be a word with little difficulty attached to its meaning, "in the matrix of employment law its definitive character is less than straightforward". The EAT defined "dismissal" as:

> "... [s]ome act brought about by one party contrary to the wishes of the other party which renders the contract of employment to cease to exist and all the duties and obligations thereunder are no longer binding and as such the employment relationship has plainly come to an end".

[10–108] In this case, there was a conflict of evidence between the parties as to whether or not the claimant was exempted from working Mondays. The EAT reached a majority decision in favour of the employer. However, in an unusually detailed determination, the Tribunal addressed the issue of the burden of proof. The Tribunal noted that normal standard of proof in matters before it is on the balance of probabilities. In finding for the employer the EAT held:

> "... [i]t is fundamental to that standard that it involves weighing the evidence to see if the required standard has been achieved. If it has not, the party bearing the persuasive burden loses, however little evidence his opponent has adduced...it would be wrong for the Tribunal to elevate the testimony of the

---

[261] s 18(1).

[262] s 15(3).

[263] s 13(7).

[264] s 101(4).

[265] Employment Equality Act 1998, s 101(2)(b) (as amended by Equality Act 2004, s 42(a)).

[266] This section, therefore, applies to both common law and statutory actions.

[267] [2003] ELR 313.

claimant, when she claims that she had an arrangement with the respondent, to the stratosphere of icy evidential certainty simply because the respondent is unable to refute the assertion".

Thus, the EAT, in a situation of a conflict of evidence between the parties, will decide the issue on the basis of which evidence seems more credible. [10–109]

The act of dismissal will, oftentimes, be obvious; for example, where the employer writes to the employee informing him or her that he or she has been dismissed. Where problems can arise, however, is when the words used are not clear or when comments are made in the "heat of the moment". The basic rule is that the EAT will ask how would a *reasonable person* understand the words used; if the reasonable person would perceive the words as amounting to a dismissal, a dismissal will be deemed to have occurred.[268]

In *J & J Stern v Simpson*[269] the employee was ordered to leave the workplace and not to return. The words used were "go, get out, get out". The employer happened to be in an agitated state at the time and such an outburst was uncharacteristic. It was held that, even though there was an element of vehemence and bad feeling in the words of the employer, it ought, in the circumstances, to have been evident to the applicant that no actual dismissal was intended. [10–110]

On occasion, doubts can exist on the part of the employee as to the true meaning of the statement. If the employee is in doubt as to its meaning he or she may not be justified in leaving and then claiming unfair dismissal. An example is the case of *Tanner v Kean*,[270] where the employer, in an outburst of rage, said to an employee "you're finished with me". On appeal to the English EAT it was held that the words, though offensive, ought not to have been construed by the applicant as signifying an intention on the part of his employer to dismiss him. Similarly, in the English case of *Futty v Brekkes*,[271] a works foreman remarked to an employee that if he did not like his job he could "fuck off". The Tribunal had to decide upon the precise significance of the words used and held that what they actually meant was: [10–111]

> "If you are complaining about the fish you are working on; or the quality of it, or if you do not like what in fact you are doing, then you can leave your work, clock off, and you will be paid up to the time when you do so. Then you can come back when you are disposed to start work again the next day."

Therefore, there was no dismissal but only, as the Tribunal put it, a "general exhortation". The Tribunal decided that, as the employees were dockworkers, such language would not have been unusual at the workplace and should not have been taken to mean a dismissal. A mistaken interpretation, then, on the part of the employee could well prove to be fatal to his or her claim since, if the tribunal holds the words or acts do not constitute a dismissal, the employee will be held to have resigned. [10–112]

---

[268] See *Devaney v DNT Distribution Co* (UD 412/1993).

[269] [1983] IRLR 52.

[270] [1978] IRLR 110.

[271] [1974] IRLR 130.

Bad language, terms of abuse and even outright exhortations to leave the workplace may not always constitute a dismissal.[272]

IX. Public Law

[10–113] The distinction between ordinary employees, office-holders and those whose employment is governed by statute was discussed in chapter 3. A final issue to consider in relation to dismissal is the possibility of challenging the decision to dismiss by way of public law principles. Particular remedies are available to employees, whose employment is governed by such principles, which will be discussed in chapter 12. For now, it needs to be established which employment decisions are subject to *judicial review*. This is a procedure by which the courts can review the decision of a public body.[273]

[10–114] The first question is when is an employment sufficiently "public" for the decision-making process to be susceptible to judicial review? The courts have tended to look at the source of the power being exercised and the nature of that power.[274] Most obviously, "public employments" are those where the State or a public body is the employer; for example, civil servants[275] or the Gardaí. More difficult cases arise in relation to bodies that exercise some public law function but are not directly controlled by the State.[276] In *Eoghan v University College Dublin*[277] Shanley J in the High Court set out some of the matters to be considered in deciding if judicial review proceedings are appropriate:

> (a) whether the decision was made pursuant to a statute;
> (b) whether the decision-maker, by his decision, was performing a duty relating to a matter of particular and immediate public concern and therefore falling within the public domain;
> (c) where the decision affected a contract of employment, whether that employment had any statutory protection so as to afford the employee any "public rights" upon which he might rely;

---

[272] It should be noted that similar principles will apply where the employee purportedly resigns in the "heat of the moment"; see *Kwik-Fit GB v Lineham* [1992] IRLR 156; discussed above.

[273] See, generally, Hogan and Morgan, *Administrative Law in Ireland* (3rd ed, Round Hall, Dublin 1998). Note that in *Byrne v Furniture Link International* [2008] ELR 229, a €35,000 EAT award against a private company was quashed by the High Court because the Tribunal cited constructive dismissal, even though all agreed the employee had been dismissed by the company. Solicitors for the company challenged this decision in the High Court by way of judicial review, arguing that at no stage had the claimant claimed constructive dismissal, as acknowledged at all times by her. While acknowledging that an appeal to the Circuit Court was possible, it was argued that a judicial review was more appropriate in the circumstances, since the applicant (the employer) ought not to be deprived of a fair hearing at the Tribunal. The High Court, under Peart J, quashed the EAT's determination.

[274] Redmond, (2007), *op.cit*, p 147.

[275] The Civil Service Regulation (Amendment) Act 2005 for the first time brought civil servants within the scope of the Unfair Dismissals Acts; previously, civil servants only had remedies under public law principles.

[276] See *Geoghegan v Institute of Chartered Accountants in Ireland* [1995] 3 IR 86.

[277] [1996] 2 ILRM 302 at 309.

(d) whether the decision was being made by a decision-maker whose powers, though not directly based on statute, depended on approval by the legislature or the Government for their continued exercise. [278]

In *Beirne v Commissioner of An Garda Síochána*[279] it was held that the burden is on the respondents to show that the contract between the parties is a matter of private law. An employee can seek judicial review and at the same time claim for damages at common law or initiate a claim under the Unfair Dismissals Acts.[280] **[10–115]**

A final issue to consider is whether a dismissal can fall foul of the doctrine of legitimate expectation. This was confirmed as part of Irish law in *Webb v Ireland*,[281] where it was recognised as an aspect of the concept of promissory estoppel, which precludes a person from asserting or denying a fact in which he has by words or conduct led others to believe.[282] In *Abrahamson and Ors v Law Society of Ireland*[283] McCracken J held that: **[10–116]**

> "... [i]t is now well established in our law that the courts will, as a general rule, strive to protect the interest of persons or bodies who have a legitimate expectation that a public body will act in a certain way".

If a representation or promise is made in the context of employment, it may, therefore, in certain circumstances, be binding on the maker.[284] In *Eogan v University College Dublin*[285] the applicant, a distinguished academic in archaeology, was unable to get a special exemption in his case. Here, the question was whether he could continue in his post of Professor of Archaeology beyond the age of 65. He had joined the staff in UCD in 1965 and became a professor in 1979. Under the Statutes of UCD, made under the Irish Universities Act 1908, a professor could be continued in that post after the age of 65 and up to the age of 70 if the Governing Body made a recommendation to that effect. This had been done a number of times up to 1987. In 1987, the Governing Body had decided that no person should, in future, be allowed continue in a post after 65. The applicant had objected to this decision but it nevertheless stood. In September 1995, the applicant reached the age of 65. He was informed that the Governing Body would not be recommending that he continue in his post. He then applied for judicial review of that decision. He argued that, at the time he joined UCD, he had a legitimate expectation that he could continue in his post until he was 70. Shanley J decided against the applicant. He held that the Governing Body was entitled to change its policy on retirement. Since the decision it made in 1987 was rational and not **[10–117]**

---

[278] See also *Beirne v Commissioner of An Garda Síochána* [1993] ILRM 1; *Murphy v Turf Club* [1989] IR 171; *Heneghen v Eastern Regional Fisheries Board* [1986] ILRM 225; and *In re Malone's Application* [1988] NI 67.

[279] [1993] ILRM 1.

[280] See Rules of the Superior Courts, Ord 84, r19 and *O'Donnell v Tipperary (South Riding) County Council* [2005] 2 ILRM 168.

[281] [1988] IR 353.

[282] See Enright, *Principles of Irish Contract Law* (Clarus Press, Dublin, 2007), chapter 9.

[283] [1996] 1 IR 403 at 423.

[284] See Crompton and Dillon, "Practice and Procedure" (2009) 6(1) IELJ 25 on some recent decisions involving representations made to potential and existing employees.

[285] [1996] 1 IR 390.

discriminatory and since the applicant had opportunities to make a case against it, he could not claim to have continued to have a legitimate expectation after the 1987 decision. On this basis, his claim was dismissed.

[10–118]   It had been thought, as evinced by McCracken's dicta above, that the doctrine applied only to decisions of public bodies. In *Hennessy v St Gerard's School*,[286] however, Haugh J rejected this idea. The Judge held that:

> "... while there is a formidable body of legal opinion suggesting that entitlements arising under the doctrine of legal expectancy apply only in relation to dealings with public bodies, rather than private ones, it is clear from the judgment of Finlay CJ in *Webb v Ireland* that the said concept is but an aspect of the well recognised equitable doctrine of promissory estoppel, whereby a promise or representation as to intention may, in certain circumstances be held binding on the representor".

Haugh J could not see any rational reason why the doctrine would not apply to private bodies. Whether this decision expands the scope of the doctrine to encompass ordinary employees in a private contract situation remains to be seen.

---

[286] *Irish Times Law Report, The Irish Times,* 13 March 2006.

CHAPTER 11
Collective Employment Law

I. Introduction

Throughout this book, the focus has primarily been on the relationship between the individual employer and the individual employee. However, it is somewhat artificial to reduce the employment relationship to this level. The vast majority of employers (ranging from large corporations to small "corner-shop" businesses) employ a number of employees and employers need, on a day-to-day-basis, to interact with employees as a group. In any case, any interaction by an employer with a particular employee will often have implications for relations with the latter's colleagues. Thus, the realm of collective employment relations or, as it has been traditionally termed, industrial relations, needs to be considered. Up until relatively recently, a look at collective employment relations involved little more than an examination of the law relating to trade unions and collective bargaining. However, as already seen, given the decline across the Western world in trade union membership and density levels, unions play a much-reduced role in employment relations than was previously the case. As a result, more recent attention has focused on how the law governs collective employment relations where unions are *not* present in a workplace. As with other areas of employment law, the law of the European Union has also come to play a larger role in what has traditionally been an area regulated, almost exclusively, by domestic law. **[11–01]**

This chapter begins by looking at how the law regulates the relationship between trade unions and employers focusing, in particular, on the law relating to collective bargaining and collective disputes. It will then move on to look at collective relations in the non-union sphere, focusing on employee rights to "voice" and involvement at work. Throughout the chapter, the impact of EU law on the regulation of collective employment relations will be examined. **[11–02]**

II. Trade Unions and Industrial Relations

As outlined in chapter 1, the Irish system of employment relations has traditionally been classified as "voluntarist", meaning that there is a preference for joint trade union and employer regulation of employment relations and the relative absence of legal **[11–03]** intervention. The role of the State (and, in particular, the legislature) in such a system is to provide the parameters within which the labour market actors (traditionally employer representative groups and trade unions) can operate and to aid the parties in their efforts at dispute-resolution. This is usually through State-established, but independent, third party bodies, such as those examined in chapter 2 (the Labour Court, the Labour Relations Commission and so on). In this section, the legal framework within which collective employment relations are conducted will be examined. In particular, there will be a focus on the legal rights afforded to workers to form and join trade unions and those that are afforded to trade unions to represent the interests of their members.[1]

Collectivism and the Constitution

[11–04] Under Art 40.6.1°(iii) of the Irish Constitution, the State guarantees liberty for the exercise (subject to public order and morality) of the right of citizens to form associations and unions. However, the Article also provides that laws may be enacted for the regulation and control in the public interest of the exercise of this right. The constitutional guarantee of freedom of association underpins the rights of citizens to form trade unions and provides the framework for regulating the right to be a member of a union (although the latter right comes with some significant qualifications). However, litigation involving the role of trade unions under Art 40.6.1°(iii) has:

> "...[a]lmost invariably concerned the protection of individuals in their relations with trade unions, rather than the protection of organised labour in its relationship with the State, or with employers pursuing anti-union policies. This may reflect the fact that unions have a traditional distrust of the law, preferring instead to rely on their industrial muscle in order to achieve their objectives".[2]

Right to Join a Union

[11–05] So, for example, in *NUR v Sullivan*[3] the Supreme Court held that the State could not unduly restrict an individual's freedom to choose between joining different trade unions. The Court declared unconstitutional Part III of the Trade Union Act 1941, which provided that a particular union (or two or more specified unions) could be granted the sole right to organise workers of a particular class. The plaintiff union, the National Union of Railwaymen, successfully argued this to be an unconstitutional restriction on freedom of association as, where a union was so recognised, other unions would not have the right to accept into membership workers in the class affected.[4] However, the Constitution does not guarantee an unqualified right to individuals to join a union of their choice. In *Tierney v Amalgamated Society of Woodcutters*[5] the

---

[1] This chapter does not look at the law regulating the relationship between trade union members and the unions themselves. For a comprehensive treatment of the issues involved see Maguire, *Trade Union Membership and the Law* (Round Hall, Dublin, 1999).

[2] Hogan and Whyte, *JM Kelly: The Irish Constitution* (4th ed, Butterworths, Dublin, 2003), p 1793.

[3] [1947] IR 77.

[4] Note, however, that trade unions themselves can impose restrictions on this freedom to choose; paragraph 46 of the Irish Congress of Trade Unions Constitution provides for restrictions on the transfer of members between unions. Breach of the paragraph could result in an offending union being expelled from Congress.

[5] [1959] IR 254.

plaintiff sought an order directing the union to accept him into membership. He had been refused membership on the grounds that he was not a "genuine carpenter". Although the right to freedom of association was not expressly argued, the High Court (and, on appeal, the Supreme Court) rejected the plaintiff's arguments on the grounds that to hold otherwise would be to force *existing* members of the union to associate with the plaintiff against their will. Budd J (in the High Court) held that "the essence of a voluntary organisation (is that) the members, and they alone, should decide who should be their fellow members".[6] This decision was confirmed in *Murphy v Stewart*,[7] where the Supreme Court held that Art 40.6.1°(iii) of the Constitution did not guarantee a right to join a union but merely a right to form one. However, in the case, recognising that the Constitution does guarantee the unenumerated right to work, Walsh J stated *obiter* that there could be circumstances where the vindication of that right might require a union to accept an individual into membership.[8] The Judge gave the example of a situation where a union had a monopoly in a particular field, the right to work in that field was reserved exclusively to the members of such a union and the union was abusing its monopoly to effectively prevent a person from exercising his or her right to work by refusing to accept the person into membership.

Trade unions, however, are subject to non-discrimination laws. Therefore, unions cannot refuse membership on any of the grounds under which discrimination is prohibited by the Equality Acts 1998–2008[9] or on the grounds of nationality, where the applicant is an EU citizen.[10] [11–06]

Right to Dissociate

It is important to note that Art 40.6.1°(iii) of the Constitution has also been interpreted by the courts as encompassing the right of an individual to abstain from membership of a union and the right not to be forced into membership against his or her will. In *Educational Co of Ireland v Fitzpatrick (No 2)*[11] trade union members employed by the plaintiff began picketing the plaintiff's premises in an effort to force it to insist other employees, who were not members, join the union. The plaintiffs successfully sought an injunction to restrain the picketing. Kingsmill Moore J held that the implicit corollary of any right to *associate* must be a right to *dissociate*: [11–07]

> "I think a guarantee of a right to form associations and unions is only intelligible where there is an implicit right to abstain from joining such associations or unions or, to put it another way, to associate and unite with those who do not join such unions".[12]

---

[6] *ibid* at 263 *per* Budd J.
[7] [1973] IR 97.
[8] *ibid* at 117 *per* Walsh J.
[9] See chapter 5.
[10] Regulation 1612/68 of 15 October 1968 on freedom of movement for workers within the Community [1968] OJ L257/2, Art 8. Note that trade union membership or involvement in trade union activities also attracts certain protections under the unfair dismissals legislation; see chapter 10.
[11] [1961] IR 345.
[12] *ibid* at 395 *per* Kingsmill Moore J.

[11–08]   In *Meskell v CIE*[13] the defendant company agreed with a group of four trade unions that it would only employ union members. In order to effect the agreement, the defendant dismissed all employees and offered them immediate re-employment on the same terms and conditions as before, subject to their becoming a member of one of the four unions. The plaintiff refused to accept the offer of re-employment as he objected to being forced to join a trade union. The Supreme Court upheld the plaintiff's argument that the agreement amounted to a conspiracy to deprive him of his constitutional right of dissociation.

[11–09]   It should be noted that this interpretation of freedom of association has been criticised. Kerr and Whyte argue that, given that the constitutional right to *form* a trade union (as noted above, Art 40.6.1°(iii) does not protect an unqualified right to join a union) is by its nature a collective right, it is difficult to see how its corollary can be a right not to *join* a union, which is an individual right.[14] Davies notes that, from a collectivist rights perspective, the decision to join a trade union need not be a matter of individual choice at all.[15] Such a viewpoint would argue that laws or agreements requiring union membership preserve the strength of a union and, therefore, the individual's interests are best served by joining a strong union that can guarantee better terms and conditions of employment, whether he or she wants to join or not. Furthermore, recognising a freedom to dissociate exacerbates the problem of "free riders", workers who do not join the union or pay subscriptions but who benefit from terms and conditions negotiated by unions, which are applicable to all workers in an organisation, sector (in the case, for example, of a Registered Employment Agreement) or nationally (e.g. where unions negotiate a minimum wage).[16] Nevertheless, the right to dissociate has subsequently been reaffirmed in cases such as *Cotter v Ahern*[17] and *Nolan Transport (Oaklands) Ltd v Halligan.*[18] In *Sørensen and Rasmussen v Denmark* the European Court of Human Rights held that Art 11 of the European Convention on Human Rights, which protects freedom of association, had to be viewed as encompassing a right not to be forced to join an association as well as the right to join an association.[19]

---

[13] [1973] IR 121.

[14] Kerr and Whyte, *op.cit*, pp 12-13.

[15] Davies, *Perspectives on Labour Law* (2nd ed, Cambridge University Press, Cambridge, 2009), p 201.

[16] See Crouch, *Trade Unions: The Logic of Collective Action* (Fontane, Glasgow, 1982), especially pp 59-62.

[17] [1976-7] ILRM 248.

[18] [1999] 1 IR 128.

[19] [2008] 46 EHRR 572. Note that the Court did not, in principle, exclude the view that the positive and the negative aspects of Art 11 should be afforded the *same* level of protection; the Court found that this was a matter that could only be properly addressed in the circumstances of a particular case. In *Olafsson v Iceland* (Application No 20161/06, 27 April 2010) the Court was invited by the applicant to consider whether the negative aspect of the right to freedom of association should be considered on an equal footing with the positive aspect of that right, but, again, did not expressly pronounce on the issue. The Court reiterated, however, that "the notion of personal autonomy is an important principle underlying the interpretation of the Convention guarantees. This notion must therefore be seen as an essential corollary of the individual's freedom of choice implicit in Art 11 and confirmation of the importance of the negative aspect of that provision" (para 46).

The Closed Shop

A closed shop is an agreement between an employer and a union that all employees, or   **[11–10]**
employees of a particular class or grade, will become union members.[20] Closed shops
take two basic forms.[21] A *pre-entry* closed shop exists where a worker must become a
union member in order to be considered for employment. A *post-entry* closed shop
requires employees to join a specified union shortly (or immediately) after taking up a
job.[22] Given the protection of the constitutional right to dissociate discussed above,
closed shops cannot be imposed on existing employees as they cannot be forced to join
a trade union against their will. The situation in relation to requiring perspective
employees to join specified unions is less clear-cut. The *dicta* of Henchy J in the
Supreme Court in *Becton Dickinson v Lee*[23] suggested that a pre-entry closed shop did
not interfere with an individual's freedom of choice, in that a prospective employee had
the choice, prior to accepting the employment, whether or not to accept the condition
relating to union membership. However, imposing such a requirement may be unlawful
where the trade union has an effective monopoly in a particular area of work.[24] In
Sørensen and Rasmussen v Denmark[25] the two applicants successfully claimed that the
existence of closed shop agreements in Denmark in their respective areas of
employment violated their rights under Art 11 of the Convention. The European
Court of Human Rights noted that the trend in the Contracting States was towards
eliminating entirely the use of closed shop agreements, on the basis that such
agreements were not an essential means for securing the interests of trade unions
and their members, and that due weight had to be given to the right of individuals to
join a union of their own choosing, without fear of prejudice to their livelihood. The
Court also held that it was not tenable to make a distinction between pre-entry closed
shop agreements and post entry closed-shop agreements in terms of the scope of the
protection guaranteed by Art 11.

Right to Recognition

While Art 40.6.1°(iii) of the Constitution protects the right of freedom of association,   **[11–11]**
unlike in many other Western democracies, trade unions in Ireland have no right to be
recognised for bargaining purposes by an employer.[26] Thus, while employees are free to
join a trade union, they cannot insist their employer negotiate with that union
regarding their pay and conditions.[27] Employees and trade unions have traditionally
gained the right to negotiate collectively with employers through the use, or threat, of

---

[20] Maguire, "Trade Unions" in *Employment Law* (Regan ed, Tottel, Dublin, 2009), p 645.
[21] See Deakin and Morris, *Labour Law* (5th ed, Hart, Oxford, 2009), p 736; von Prondzynski,
"Freedom of Association and the Closed Shop: The European Perspective" (1982) 41(2) CLJ 256.
[22] Kerr and Whyte, *op.cit*, p 7.
[23] [1973] IR 1.
[24] *Murphy v Stewart* [1973] IR 97.
[25] [2008] 46 EHRR 572.
[26] See Lind *et al*, *Labour and Employment Regulation in Europe* (PIE - Peter Lang, Brussels, 2004);
von Prondzynski, *Freedom of Association and Industrial Relations: A Comparative Study* (Mansell,
London, 1987).
[27] Hogan and Whyte, *op.cit*, p 1803; Kerr and Whyte, *Irish Trade Union Law* (Professional Books
Ltd, Abingdon, 1985), chapter 1.

collective action. This, of course, depends to a large extent on trade unions mobilising a "critical mass" of employees to join and to participate in trade union action.[28]

[11–12] The principle that an employer is not constitutionally bound to negotiate with a union has been affirmed on many occasions. In *Abbot and Whelan v ITGWU*,[29] for example, it was held that there was no duty placed on any employer to negotiate with any particular citizen or body of citizens. In *Ryanair v Labour Court*[30] Geoghegan J in the Supreme Court noted that it was "not in dispute that as a matter of law Ryanair is perfectly entitled not to deal with trade unions": indeed the Judge went further in suggesting that neither could a "law be passed compelling it to do so".[31] It should be noted that the Supreme Court decision would appear to be somewhat at variance with the decision of the European Court of Human Rights in *Demir and Baykara v Turkey*.[32] There, the European Court of Human Rights ruled that the right to collectively bargain with an employer in principle had become one of the "essential elements" of the right to form and join trade unions, guaranteed under Art 11 of the ECHR.[33]

The Collective Bargaining System

[11–13] Trade unions have many functions.[34] However, their principal function within the Anglo-Saxon industrial relations system has traditionally been to engage in collective bargaining with employers. There are many definitions of collective bargaining (some of which are laid down in statute)[35] and differing views on how to conceptualise what is encompassed by the term.[36] However, the essence of the process is well captured by defining collective bargaining as:

---

[28] Twice, in 1967 and again in 1996, groups charged with reviewing the Constitution have considered whether a constitutional amendment was necessary in the area of freedom of association. In both cases, the view expressed was that this matter would be best dealt with by legislation; see *Report of the Committee on the Constitution* (1967) and *Report of the Constitution Review Group* (1996). See below for a further discussion of trade union recognition laws. See, also, Howlin and Fitzpatrick, "The Feasibility of Mandatory Trade Union Recognition in Ireland" (2007) 29(1) DULJ 178.

[29] (1982) 1 JISLL 56.

[30] [2007] 4 IR 199.

[31] *ibid* at 215. This interpretation would seem to suggest that a *legislative* right to trade union recognition, such as exists, for example, in the UK, would be constitutionally prohibited. This will be discussed further below.

[32] Application No 34503/97, 12 November 2008.

[33] See O' Mara, "European Developments— The Right to Strike and Collectively Bargain" (2010) 7(2) IELJ 62.

[34] Ewing, "The Functions of Trade Unions" (2005) 34(1) ILJ 1; Wedderburn, "Collective Bargaining or Legal Enactment: the 1999 Act and Union Recognition" (2000) 29(1) ILJ 1.

[35] Kerr, "Industrial Relations" in *Employment Law* (Regan ed, Tottel, Dublin, 2009), p 667. Kerr notes that while the term "collective bargaining" is used in many statutes, it is not always expressly defined. There are also international law instruments that define the expression, for example *ILO Convention No 98 Concerning the Application of the Principles of the Right of Organise and to Bargain Collectively.*

[36] See, for example, Kahn-Freund, *Labour and the Law* (Stevens, London, 1977), p 124; Crouch, *op.cit*, p 109.

"...[t]he process through which agreement on pay, working conditions, procedures and other negotiable issues are reached between organised employees and management representatives".[37]

While it was traditionally felt that collective bargaining had a particular meaning in the industrial relations context,[38] in *Ryanair v Labour Court*[39] the Supreme Court was of the view that the expression should be given its "ordinary dictionary meaning". The Court held that collective bargaining, under the Industrial Relations (Amendment) Act 2001, did not necessarily bear any trade union connotations but referred to any situation where machinery existed in an organisation whereby employees had their own independent representatives who sat around the table with representatives of the organisation with a view to reaching agreement if possible.[40] This issue will be discussed further below.

[11–14]

Collective Agreements

The result of bargaining between employers and employees can oftentimes be seen in the form of a collective agreement. As negotiations between labour market actors can take place at different levels (between workers and a single employer or a number of employers; at the level of the enterprise or at Sectoral or national level)[41] so too can agreements be concluded at different levels. As was seen in chapter 4, terms of collective agreements tend to be "normative" in so far as these agreements will set out certain terms and conditions of the contract of employment that are aspirational in nature, for example, productivity targets or industrial peace clauses. As a result, although it has not been definitively decided, the dominant view is that collective agreements are not legally enforceable, as they do not generally intend to create legal relations.[42] However, as noted in chapter 4, collectively agreed terms may be incorporated, impliedly or expressly, into individual contracts of employment.[43] However, this is only where such terms are apt or suitable for incorporation.[44]

[11–15]

---

[37] Gunnigle and Flood, *Personnel Management in Ireland: Practice, Trends and Developments* (Gill & Macmillan, Dublin, 1990), p 227.

[38] See *Ashford Castle v SIPTU* [2004] ELR 214 at 217.

[39] [2007] 4 IR 199 at 218 *per* Geoghegan J.

[40] Both Kerr, "Industrial Relations" in *Employment Law* (Regan ed, Tottel, Dublin, 2009), p 668 and Doherty, "Union Sundown? The Future of Collective Representation Rights in Irish Law'" (2007) 4(4) IELJ 96 point out the Oxford English Dictionary definition of "collective bargaining" refers to "a mode of fixing the terms of employment by means of bargaining power between an organised body of employees and an employer, or association of employers". The common understanding of the expression is, therefore, bound up in its usage with a particular model of industrial relations that generally includes trade unions. It is not clear to which "non-union" dictionary definition of collective bargaining the Court was referring.

[41] Wallace *et al*, *Industrial Relations in Ireland* (3rd ed, Gill & Macmillan, Dublin, 2004), pp 251 *et seq.*

[42] *O'Rourke v Talbot* [1984] ILRM 587.

[43] *Goulding Chemicals Ltd v Bolger* [1977] IR 211; *Reilly v Drogheda Borough Council* [2009] ELR 1. See also the Terms of Employment (Information) Act 1994, s 3(3).

[44] Kerr, "Industrial Relations" in *Employment Law* (Regan ed, Tottel, Dublin, 2009), p 670. The author refers to *Kaur v MF Rover Group* [2005] IRLR 40, where the English Court of Appeal held that a term in a collective agreement prohibiting "compulsory redundancy" was not apt for incorporation into individual employment contracts and nor was it intended to be so incorporated.

[11–16] It should be noted that the Irish (and UK) system differs substantially from that in many other EU countries. In states like France and the Netherlands, for example, collective agreements are commonly extended to all workers in a particular sector, while in some Nordic States (like Sweden and Denmark) comprehensive labour market regulation is based on voluntary agreements between strong collective employer and employee organisations.[45] Under various pieces of EU legislation, too, minimum standards are left to be agreed by the social partners at national level. As noted in chapter 7, for example, Art 3 of the Posted Workers Directive[46] requires that Member States ensure that posted workers are guaranteed the same terms and conditions of employment as apply to domestic employees in a number of areas, including maximum work periods and minimum rest periods and minimum rates of pay. However, the Directive only covers such matters where they are laid down by law, regulation or administrative provision, and/or by collective agreements or arbitration awards which have been declared universally applicable in the Member State.

Registered Employment Agreements

[11–17] Collective agreements can be given legal effect if such agreements are registered with the Labour Court. Under s 25 of the Industrial Relations Act 1946, an "employment agreement" is defined as:

> "...an agreement relating to the remuneration or the conditions of employment of workers of any class, type or group made between a trade union of workers and an employer or trade union of employers or made, at a meeting of a registered joint industrial council, between members of the council representative of workers and members of the council representative of employers".[47]

[11–18] Under s 27 of the 1946 Act, any party to such an employment agreement can apply to the Labour Court to register the agreement. There are currently 68 REAs on the Register required to be maintained by the Labour Court.[48] Some of the agreements are definitively not of recent vintage (the REA applying to Shop and Clerical Assistants working in the Grocery and Provision Trade in Clonmel dates from 1956, for example) but over 20 agreements relating to working in the Mushroom Harvesting industry have

---

[45] See Teague, "Deliberative Governance and EU Social Policy" (2001) 7(1) *European Journal of Industrial Relations* 7.

[46] Directive 96/71 of 16 December 1996 concerning the posting of workers in the framework of the provision of services [1996] OJ L18/1.

[47] Joint Industrial Councils (JICs) are voluntary negotiating bodies for an industry or part of an industry and are designed to facilitate collective bargaining at industry level in certain sectors. They generally exist where a high level of unionisation exists. Three such Councils were registered, in 1948, 1964 and 1965, and still exist though two (Construction and Footwear) have been suspended since 1982 and 1983, respectively, and the third (Dublin Wholesale Fruit and Vegetable Trade) has not met for many years. There are also eleven Joint Industrial Councils, which have not sought registration; see www.lrc.ie.

[48] This requirement derives from the Industrial Relations Act, s 26. The Register can be accessed via www.labourcourt.ie.

been registered since 2008 (almost all with individual employers). The Labour Court will register an agreement where it is satisfied[49]:

i. that, in the case of an agreement to which there are two parties only, both parties consent to its registration and, in the case of an agreement to which there are more than two parties, there is substantial agreement amongst the parties representing the interests of workers and employers, respectively, that it should be registered;

ii. that the agreement is expressed to apply to all workers of a particular class, type or group and their employers where the Court is satisfied that it is a normal and desirable practice or that it is expedient to have a separate agreement for that class, type or group;

iii. that the parties to the agreement are substantially representative of such workers and employers;

iv. that the agreement is not intended to restrict unduly employment generally or the employment of workers of a particular class, type or group or to ensure or protect the retention in use of inefficient or unduly costly machinery or methods of working;

v. that the agreement provides that if a trade dispute occurs between workers to whom the agreement relates and their employers a strike or lock-out shall not take place until the dispute has been submitted for settlement by negotiation in the manner specified in the agreement; and

vi. that the agreement is in a form suitable for registration.

Registered agreements, therefore, apply to all employers and employees working in a **[11–19]** particular sector or industry irrespective of whether such employers or employees were, in fact, parties to the agreement or wished to be subject to its terms.[50] Although individual contracts of employment of workers subject to REAs can provide for terms and conditions in *excess* of those stipulated, such contracts cannot contain terms less favourable to workers. Thus, REAs are particularly suited to, and indeed conceived in terms of, labour intensive industries where labour costs form a large portion of overall costs.[51] The rationale behind REAs is to ensure uniform minimum standards apply across the relevant industry in order to prevent a "race to the bottom" amongst employers, who may seek to compete by cutting labour costs.[52] The Labour Court, however, when considering an application for registration cannot simply "rubber-stamp" an agreement: the Court must be satisfied that the agreement overall seeks to create harmony in the industry as a whole and that the parties to the agreement are substantially representative of workers and employers in the industry.[53]

---

[49] Industrial Relations Act 1946, s 27(3).

[50] Industrial Relations Act 1946, s 30(1). REAs can also cover sole traders within a relevant industry; *O'Boyle v TEEU* (REA 0757/2007).

[51] Kerr, "Industrial Relations" in *Employment Law* (Regan ed, Tottel, Dublin, 2009), p 672.

[52] Although Wallace *et al*, *op.cit*, p 111 make the point that regulating industry-wide pay and conditions becomes difficult to maintain, and even redundant, in industries which are open to international competition. This has been a key argument in recent challenges to the operation of REAs; see below.

[53] *National Union of Security Employers v Labour Court* (1994) 10 JISLL 97.

[11–20] Section 28 of the 1946 Act provides that, where a registered employment agreement allows for the variation of the agreement, any party to the agreement may apply to the Court to vary it in its application to any worker or workers to whom it applies.[54] Section 29 of the Act allows for the Labour Court, on the joint application of all parties thereto, to cancel the registration of an agreement. Section 29(2) also allows cancellation where the Court is satisfied that there has been such "substantial change" in the circumstances of the trade or business to which it relates since the registration of the agreement that it is undesirable to maintain registration.[55] This section has been recently invoked in relation to an increasingly bitter dispute in the Electrical Contracting sector which, at the time of writing, has had, and continues to have, important implications for the REA system. In *National Electrical Contractors of Ireland v TEEU*[56] an application was made by two new employer groupings in the electrical contracting industry (the National Electrical Contractors of Ireland (NECI) and a non-aligned group of over 500 electrical contractors) to strike out the REA that had set minimum pay and conditions in the sector since 1990. The REA was defended by the only union in the sector (the TEEU) and two employer bodies (the Electrical Contractors' Association (ECA) and the Association of Electrical Contractors in Ireland (AECI), albeit the latter wanted significant changes in the agreement). The Labour Court ruled that it was for the applicants against the agreement to establish, as a matter of probability, that the three tests under s 29(2) were satisfied. The Court also ruled that "substantial change" under s 29(2) stood in contrast to "ordinary or ongoing change, which is a normal feature of all industry and employment". In respect of whether any "substantial change" made it "undesirable" to maintain registration of the agreement, the Court felt the use of the word "undesirable" suggested that there must be evidence of some weight to indicate that, because of changed circumstances, the "overall or dominant effect of the agreement has become deleterious to the interests of all parties in the sector or that some other compelling reason exists as to why the registration of the agreement should be cancelled".

[11–21] The Court ultimately concluded that the sector *had* experienced substantial change since the REA was registered (in particular, in respect of the number of entities carrying on business to some degree in electrical contracting and the extent of external competition from outside the jurisdiction) but it did not feel these changes rendered it undesirable to maintain the REA. However, three separate High Court challenges, being held concurrently, involving the REA are now awaiting decision: two challenges to the REA lodged in 2008 and 2009 by the non-aligned group of over 500 electrical contractors and a case stated from Longford District Court arising from one local contractor's alleged non-compliance with the REA. The non-aligned group is challenging the representativeness of the employer and union bodies that are party to the REA, the negotiating rights of the two employer bodies involved and the

---

[54] See *Serco Services v Labour Court* [2002] ELR 1; *National Electrical Contractors of Ireland v TEEU* (REP 091/2009).

[55] This does not require an application by any party to the agreement but allows the Court, on its own motion, to consider if the maintenance of an REA on the register is no longer desirable (including where changed circumstances have been brought to the Court's attention by a third party affected by the REA); *National Electrical Contractors of Ireland v TEEU* (REP 091/2009).

[56] REP 091/2009.

constitutionality of those sections of the 1946 Industrial Relations Act that govern REAs in general.[57] As this book was going to press, it was reported that Hedigan J, in the High Court, had dismissed the bid by the non-aligned group to overturn the REA, although the judgment was not yet available.[58] The High Court reportedly found that the Labour Court had not erred in law in its conclusions (outlined above) and found that, as the non-aligned group had delayed excessively in taking judicial review proceedings, it was out of time with its claim. Crucially, therefore, the High Court did not address the key constitutional challenges to the REA system, meaning that a further challenge remains a possibility.

Where a contract of employment provides for terms and conditions less favourable than those contained in an applicable REA, the terms of the REA are deemed to substitute for the contractual terms.[59] A breach of a worker's entitlements under an REA can be pursued by the worker in civil proceedings or by an inspector, on behalf of a worker, under the Industrial Relations Act 1990 (s 54). Trade unions can also apply to the Court in respect of alleged breaches of REAs and the Court may direct the employer to do such things (including the payment of any sum due to a worker for remuneration in accordance with the agreement) as will in the opinion of the Court result in the said agreement being complied with by the said employer.[60]   [11–22]

Joint Labour Committees

Joint Labour Committees (JLCs) are statutory bodies established under Part IV of the Industrial Relations Acts 1946–2001 to provide for the fixing of minimum rates of pay and the regulation of employment.[61] They typically exist in employments where there is little or no collective bargaining and are designed to protect vulnerable workers. The Labour Court has the power, under s 35 of the Industrial Relations Act 1946, to establish such bodies, on the application of the Minister, a trade union or any organisation or group of persons claiming to be representative of a group of workers or employers.[62] The Court must be satisfied, before making an establishment order that, in respect of an application by an organisation or a group of persons claiming to be representative of workers or employers, that the claim is well-founded. Furthermore, there must be *either* substantial agreement between such workers and their employers to the establishment of a joint labour committee *or* the Court must be satisfied that the existing machinery for effective regulation of remuneration and other conditions of employment of such workers is inadequate or is likely to cease or to cease to be adequate *or* the Court must be satisfied, having regard to the existing rates of   [11–23]

---

[57] See Morgan, "Implied Terms in the Employment Contract: New Questions From Emerging Litigation" (2009) 3/4 ELRI 192.
[58] "Electrical Contractors' Challenge to REA Dismissed by High Court" (2010) IRN 25.
[59] Industrial Relations Act 1946, ss 30(2) and (3).
[60] *ibid*, s 32(1). Section 32(2) allows an employer or employers' association to apply to the Court to complain of industrial action taken by a union in contravention of the terms of an REA.
[61] See Meenan, "Regulation of Pay and Conditions of Employment" (2009) 6(4) IELJ 92.
[62] Industrial Relations Act 1946, s 36.

remuneration or conditions of employment of such workers or any of them, it is expedient that a joint labour committee should be established.[63]

[11–24] The Constitution and proceedings of JLCs are provided for in the Fifth Schedule to the Industrial Relations Act 1990. A JLC comprises of an independent chairperson appointed by the Minister and representative members (of such number as the Labour Court shall think fit) of employers and employees following consultation with the social partners. The most important function of a JLC is to submit proposals to the Labour Court on fixing minimum wages and regulating conditions of employment for workers covered.[64] If such proposals are confirmed by the Labour Court, through the making of an Employment Regulation Order (ERO), they become statutory minimum remuneration and statutory conditions of employment, which employers are not permitted to undercut in the contract of employment.[65] Where a worker's contract provides for less than the terms of an ERO, the ERO terms are effectively read into the contract and replace the provisions relating to pay and/or conditions contained therein.[66] Failure by an employer to comply with the terms of an ERO is an offence and, on conviction, the employer may be ordered to alter the terms and conditions of the employee in question, as well as compensate him or her for the period of employment in which terms and conditions fell below the ERO minimum.[67] The worker may issue proceedings on his or her own behalf, or under s 49 of the 1990 Act, an inspector may institute, on behalf of a worker, civil proceedings for the enforcement of any right of action of the worker against his employer in respect of the failure of the employer to comply with an ERO.[68]

[11–25] As with the REA system discussed above, recent events have posed a challenge to the operation of the JLC system. In 2008, a group of hoteliers challenged a decision of the Labour Court to approve JLC proposals for a minimum wage for 25,000 staff in the hotel sector. The applicants sought a declaration that the provisions of ss 42 and 43 of the Industrial Relations Act 1946 and s 48 of the Industrial Relations Act 1990 were invalid as they allowed an impermissible delegation of legislative functions (the setting of minimum wages) to a body other than the Oireachtas and on the grounds that they unduly interfered with constitutionally protected property rights.[69] The case was

---

[63] *ibid*, s 37. Formulated proposals must be available for inspection and representations in respect of these can be made to the JLC; Industrial Relations Act 1990, s 48(1). The Supreme Court in *Burke v Minister for Labour* [1979] IR 354 had stipulated that JLCs must exercise their functions, not only with constitutional propriety and due regard to natural justice but also within the framework of the terms and objects of the Act and with basic fairness, reasonableness and good faith. The careful exercise of powers was required, in particular, as "once such an order is made (no matter how erroneous, ill-judged or unfair it may be) a joint labour committee is debarred from submitting proposals for revoking or amending it until it has been in force for at least six months" (at 359 *per* Henchy J; the six-month period is stipulated in s 42(3) of the 1946 Act).

[64] Industrial Relations Act 1946, s 42. The procedures to be followed once a JLC has formulated proposals is set out in the Industrial Relations Act 1990, s 48.

[65] Kerr, *The Trade Union and Industrial Relations Acts* (3rd ed, Round Hall, Dublin, 2007), p 225.

[66] Cox *et al*, *Employment Law in Ireland* (Clarus Press, Dublin, 2009), p 57.

[67] Industrial Relations Act 1946, s 45.

[68] The onus is on the employer to show that the statutory minimum compensation has been paid and that it has complied with the statutory conditions of employment; Industrial Relations Act 1946, ss 45(5) and (6).

[69] See Meenan, *op.cit*, for a discussion of the claim.

ultimately decided on procedural grounds and the constitutional challenge did not proceed. However, a recent constitutional challenge to the operation of JLCs has been mounted by a number of businesses in the "quick food" sector calling itself the "Quick Food Alliance".[70] In addition, a number of challenges to the coverage of EROs have been mounted recently under the hitherto rather obscure s 57 of the Industrial Relations Act 1946, which allows the Labour Court to interpret whether or not an ERO applies to certain persons.[71]

These challenges to both the REA and JLC systems have prompted the publication of   [11–26] the Industrial Relations (Amendment) Bill 2009.[72] The Bill aims to strengthen the existing system for the making of both EROs and REAs and to provide for their continued operation. In particular, the Bill seeks to address the problem of a body other than the Oireachtas stipulating legally binding terms and conditions of employment. So, the Bill proposes amending s 27 of the 1946 Act (REAs) and s 43 of the 1946 Act (EROs) so that agreements and orders will in future be confirmed and made by Ministerial Order (laid before Parliament in the usual manner).[73] Section 42 of the 1946 Act will be amended in that JLCs, when formulating proposals, are now to explicitly consider the legitimate interests of: the workers and employers; the prevailing economic circumstances (and those of the workers and employers); and the terms of any national agreement in force relating to pay and conditions.[74] Furthermore, EROs will be capable of being revoked or amended before the six-month limit (set out in s 42) has expired where "exceptional circumstances" exist.[75] Finally, s 11 of the Bill provides for improved procedures to be followed when formulating proposals for an ERO.

---

[70] See Morgan, *op.cit,*; "Catering JLCs Face High Court Challenge" (2009) 6 IRN.

[71] The Court has found that door supervisors ("bouncers") are not covered by the security industry ERO (*Irish Security Industry Association v NERA* (DEC 101/2010)) but that coffee shops also selling goods for consumption off the premises, such as boxes of chocolates, gifts, take-away drinks and food, and food outlets which are part of a "food court" in a shopping centre were covered by the catering JLC (*Butlers Chocolate Ltd v NERA* (DEC 091/2009) and *Busy Bee Bagels Ltd v NERA* (DEC 092/2009)). It is interesting to note that all these cases arose subsequent to NERA inspections (indeed the *Butlers* case was the first time NERA appeared before the Labour Court). This might suggest that the various challenges to the ERO and REA systems are, in part, driven by employers' reactions to a more rigorous enforcement regime (undertaken by NERA) than has hitherto existed. In *P Mulrine & Sons Sales v SIPTU* (DEC 102/2010) the Labour Court rejected a claim by an unfermented sweet drinks manufacturer that it should be excluded from the Aerated Waters & Wholesale Bottling Trade Joint Labour Committee. The claimant unsuccessfully argued for an exclusion on the basis that the pure fruit juice it produces was not fizzy (aerated). The company has been given permission to challenge the Labour Court decision by way of judicial review.

[72] Review of the JLC and JIC systems was agreed as part of the social partnership agreement *Review and Transitional Agreement 2008-2009* of *Towards 2016*. However, the court challenges to the systems have undoubtedly expedited the publication of the legislation.

[73] Industrial Relations (Amendment) Bill 2009, ss 4 and 9. Although the Bill differentiates between REAs and EROs made before and after its enactment, existing agreements and orders remain valid. Sections 5 and 6 provide for the same procedure as under s 4 in respect of an order to vary an agreement or to cancel an agreement, respectively.

[74] Industrial Relations (Amendment) Bill 2009, s 8.

[75] *ibid.*

[11–27] In *Burke v Minister for Labour*[76] Henchy J referred to the JLC in question as "an unelected body, functioning behind closed doors". The provisions of the 2009 Bill attempt to address this alleged "democratic deficit". It is undoubtedly the case that the JLC and REA systems are in need of modernisation. Meenan argues that:

> "...[t]here must be a mechanism devised where there is full transparency in respect of the adoption of pay rates at joint labour committees... Bearing in mind that employers may be held criminally liable in respect of a breach of an employment regulation order, there should be some method of wider employer representation to prevent deliberation behind 'closed doors' or indeed the perception of such decision making. Employers should be able to plead 'inability to pay' and have at least the similar entitlements to an application under the National Minimum Wage Act 2000 which provides for a once-off only application for such exemption".[77]

However, other authors caution against any further undermining of collective rights to minimum terms and conditions of employment, particularly in respect of classes of workers in low-skill, low-pay work that may be deemed particularly vulnerable.[78] It might also be noted that the "inability to pay" mechanism under the National Minimum Wage Act has never actually been used.

The Industrial Relations (Amendment) Acts 2001–2004

[11–28] As we have seen, there is no right under the Constitution or at common law for workers to have their trade unions represent their interests in negotiations with employers, reflecting Ireland's voluntarist system of industrial relations. According to O' Hanlon J in *Association of General Practitioners Ltd v Minister for Health*[79]:

> "I do not consider that there is any obligation imposed by ordinary law or by the Constitution on an employer to consult with or negotiate with any organisation representing his employees or some of them, when the conditions of employment are to be settled or reviewed. The employer is left with freedom of choice as to whether he will negotiate with any organisation or consult with them on such matters, and is also free to give a right of audience to one representative body and refuse it to another, if he chooses to do so".

[11–29] Employees and trade unions have traditionally gained the right to negotiate collectively with employers through the use, or threat, of collective action. Unions can, however, process "recognition" claims under s 20 of the Industrial Relations Act 1969. This section allows workers (or their unions) concerned in a trade dispute to request the Labour Court to investigate the dispute as a whole or allows the parties to a dispute to request the Court to investigate specified issues within the dispute. This would include disputes relating to union recognition.

---

[76] [1979] 1 IR 354.

[77] Meenan, *op.cit,* p 97.

[78] Doherty, "Institutional Challenge: Tribunals, Industrial Relations and the Law" (2009) 2 ELRI 70.

[79] [1982] IR 382 at 391.

Recommendations are binding on the party referring the dispute to the Court (i.e. the [11-30] union) but not on the employer. As a result, recommendations under the 1969 Act that the employer should recognise the union in respect of those workers it had in membership were often ignored by employers.[80] In the context of declining trade union density in the 1980s and 1990s, the issue of statutory recognition rights for trade unions became a key point of discussion during social partnership talks. Under the fourth social partnership agreement, *Partnership 2000*, a high-level group comprising trade union and employer representatives was set up to examine the issue. The result was the drawing up of the Code of Practice on Voluntary Dispute Resolution[81] and the passing of the Industrial Relations (Amendment) Act 2001 (which was further amended in 2004).[82] The Code of Practice and the 2001 Act explicitly exclude the imposition of any "arrangements for collective bargaining" on the grounds of protecting Ireland's voluntarist tradition.[83] The general philosophy behind both is that disputes relating to union recognition should be dealt with within the context of voluntary collective bargaining (with parties offered recourse to the advisory and conciliation services of the Labour Relations Commission - LRC).[84] Thus, the 2001 Act does not provide for union recognition but for a range of procedures to allow unions to seek to have specific disputes with regard to pay, terms and conditions of employment and dispute resolution procedures addressed.[85]

The provisions of the Act are used as a fallback measure whereby, in a situation where [11-31] the parties cannot come to agreement under the "voluntary leg" of the process, a union or excepted body[86] may request a further investigation by the Labour Court, which can issue a recommendation and, where appropriate, give its view as to the action that should be taken having regard to terms and conditions of employment and dispute resolution and disciplinary procedures in the employment concerned.[87] Should the issue remain unresolved, the Court has the power to issue a legally binding determination on pay and terms of employment.[88] In practice, the Court's recommendations and determinations have tended to revolve principally around pay issues,

---

[80] Higgins, "The Right to Bargain Law: Is it Working?" (2001) 45 IRN. However, such a recommendation still allowed a union taking industrial action in support of recognition to show that it had done its best to abide by procedures.

[81] SI No 145 of 2000.

[82] See Purdy, "The Industrial Relations (Amendment) Act 2001 and the Industrial Relations (Miscellaneous Provisions) Act 2004 - Have they helped?" (2004) 1(5) IELJ 142; Redmond, "The Future of Labour Law" (2004) 1(1) IELJ 3. Kerr notes that referrals under the 1969 Act continued even after the passing of the 2001 Act; Kerr, "Industrial Relations" in *Employment Law* (Regan ed, Tottel, Dublin, 2009), p 676.

[83] Industrial Relations (Amendment) Act 2001, s 5(2).

[84] Kerr, *The Trade Union and Industrial Relations Acts* (3rd ed, Round Hall, Dublin, 2007), pp 279-280.

[85] Ryan, "Leaving it to the Experts - In the Matter of the Industrial Relations (Amendment) Act 2001" (2006) 3 IELJ 118.

[86] "Excepted body" is defined by s 6(3)(h) of the Trade Union Act 1941 (as inserted by s 2 of the Trade Union Act 1942) and refers to "a body all the members of which are employed by the same employer and which carries on negotiations for the fixing of wages or other conditions of employment of its own members (but no other employees)".

[87] Industrial Relations (Amendment) Act 2001, ss 2 and 5.

[88] *ibid*, s 6.

including rates of pay, sick pay and overtime, as well as grievance and disciplinary procedures.[89] If the employer does not comply with a Labour Court determination, the trade union may apply to the Circuit Court for an order directing the employer to carry out the determination in accordance with its terms.[90]

[11-32] Changes to the legislation were agreed under the *Sustaining Progress* partnership agreement[91] and resulted in the passing of the Industrial Relations (Miscellaneous Provisions) Act 2004. SI No 145 was repealed and replaced by the Industrial Relations Act 1990 (Enhanced Code of Practice on Voluntary Dispute Resolution) (Declaration) Order 2004.[92] The 2004 Act provided that the processing of disputes under the Voluntary Dispute Resolution Code should take place within an indicative overall time frame of 26 weeks, with the possibility of extending it to a maximum of 34 weeks. Under the Acts, therefore, an employer may be compelled to grant union representatives the right to represent unionised employees on workplace issues relating to pay and terms and conditions of employment but cannot be forced to make arrangements for collective bargaining.[93] To this end, the proposals amount to a set of dispute resolution procedures, rather than a means of promoting recognition *per se*.[94] Nevertheless, some commentators, and employers, expressed concern that the Acts effectively promoted a form of "back door" union recognition by allowing unions to get their "foot in the door" and force employers to deal with them on some level and, undoubtedly, the unions hoped that this would be the case.[95] This outcome seems now less likely in the light of the Supreme Court decision in *Ryanair v Labour Court*.[96]

Interpreting the "Right to Bargain" Legislation

[11-33] Section 2 of the 2001 Act (as amended by s 2 of the 2004 Act) sets out the prerequisites that must be satisfied before the Labour Court can consider a dispute with a view to issuing a recommendation. The Court can investigate a trade dispute where:

---

[89] Doherty, "Representation, Bargaining and the Law: Where Next For the Unions?" (2009) 60(4) NILQ 383 at 387. The author notes that the Court's radical powers under ss 5 and 6 have generally been exercised where it can be demonstrated that pay or conditions of employment in the organisation are out of line with accepted norms and standards in the industry in question; pp 396-399. This can be seen in cases like *Bank of Ireland v IBOA* (LCR 17745/2004) and *Ashford Castle v SIPTU* [2004] ELR 214 (see also the High Court decision; *Ashford Castle v SIPTU* [2007] 4 IR 70).

[90] Industrial Relations (Amendment) Act 2001, s 10 (as substituted by Industrial Relations (Miscellaneous Provisions) Act 2004, s 4).

[91] See article 8.9 of *Sustaining Progress*.

[92] SI No 176 of 2004.

[93] Doherty, "Union Sundown? The Future of Collective Representation Rights in Irish Law" (2007) 4 IELJ 96.

[94] Contrast, for example, the statutory procedure for gaining recognition rights that now exists in the UK under the Employment Relations Act 1999; see Dukes, "The Statutory Recognition Procedure 1999: No Bias in Favour of Recognition?" (2008) 37(2) ILJ 236; and Oxenbridge *et al*, "Initial Responses to the Statutory Recognition Provisions of the Employment Relations Act 1999" (2003) 41(2) *British Journal of Industrial Relations* 315.

[95] See, for example, Dobbins, "Union Recognition Law Used for Benchmarking Private Sector Pay" (2005) 36 IRN; Doherty, "Representation, Bargaining and the Law: Where Next For the Unions?" (2009) 60(4) NILQ 383.

[96] [2007] 4 IR 199.

a. it is not the practice of the employer to engage in collective bargaining negotiations and the internal dispute resolution procedures normally used by the parties concerned have failed to resolve the dispute;

b. either the employer has failed to observe a provision of the Code of Practice on Voluntary Dispute Resolution, or the dispute having been referred to the LRC for resolution in accordance with the provisions of such Code, no further efforts on the part of the LRC will, in the opinion of the LRC, advance the resolution of the dispute;

c. the trade union or the excepted body or the employees, as the case may be, have not acted in a manner which, in the opinion of the Court, has frustrated the employer in observing a provision of such code of practice; and

d. the trade union or the excepted body or the employees, as the case may be, have not had recourse to industrial action after the dispute in question was referred to the Commission in accordance with the provisions of such code of practice.

These pre-requisites to the Labour Court having jurisdiction have been analysed in some detail in a number of recommendations issued by the Labour Court.[97]

The term "trade dispute" for the purposes of the 2001 Act is set out in s 3 of the Industrial Relations Act 1946:   **[11–34]**

> "Any dispute or difference between employers and workers or between workers and workers connected with the employment or non employment, or the terms of the employment, or with the conditions of employment, of any person".[98]

In order to exercise jurisdiction under the legislation, the Labour Court must be satisfied that it is "not the practice of the employer to engage in collective bargaining negotiations in respect of the relevant grade, group or category of workers who are parties to the trade dispute". There is no definition of "collective bargaining" in the legislation. Whether or not it is the practice of the employer to engage in collective bargaining was one of the key issues at the centre of the Supreme Court's decision in *Ryanair v Labour Court*.[99] The *Ryanair* case centred on a dispute between a number of pilots, members of the Irish Airline Pilots Association (IALPA, a branch of the Irish Municipal Public and Civil Trade Union, IMPACT), who sought to have the union negotiate with Ryanair about various issues on their behalf. Ryanair refused to negotiate with the union and, as a result, the union invoked the procedures under the Acts. When both the Labour Court and the High Court found against it, Ryanair appealed to the Supreme Court.[100]

---

[97] See Doherty, "Representation, Bargaining and the Law: Where Next For the Unions?" (2009) 60(4) NILQ 383 for a comprehensive analysis of key Labour Court recommendations.

[98] The Labour Court had interpreted this definition as encompassing a "dispute" but also a "difference" between the parties; the latter being something falling short of the former. The Supreme Court in *Ryanair*, however, held that it did not follow from the section that a "difference" was something distinct from a "dispute"; see Cox *et al*, *op.cit*, p 23.

[99] [2007] 4 IR 199.

[100] See Turner, "Cases and Comment: *Ryanair v The Labour Court and Irish Municipal Public and Civil Trade Union (IMPACT)*" (2007) 4(1) IELJ 24.

[11–35]   The significance of the decision in terms of Labour Court procedures and in terms of the interaction between an expert body, like the Labour Court, and the regular courts was examined in chapter 2. However, the decision also laid down some definitive and controversial interpretations of the 2001–2004 Acts.[101] Ryanair contended that it did engage in "collective bargaining" as employees, including pilots, elected employee representatives to Employee Representative Committees (ERCs), which negotiated directly with the company on an ongoing basis in relation to all terms and conditions of employment. The Labour Court's view was that if a group of employees unilaterally withdraws from the internal negotiating procedures (as had occurred in the instant case) it could not thereafter be said that the employer had a "practice" of engaging in collective bargaining with them.[102] The Supreme Court, however, interpreted the provision as requiring a decision on whether or not there was in place any permanent machinery, which would have obliged the management of Ryanair to sit around the table with representatives of the Dublin pilots and discuss matters of pay and conditions. Such machinery would need to have been established, in place and not *ad hoc*: however, the "practice" did not cease to exist simply because the employees unilaterally abandoned it.[103]

[11–36]   As noted above, the Supreme Court held that an "ordinary dictionary" meaning (not any distinctive meaning as understood in trade union negotiations) of collective bargaining was to be read into the legislation. In *Ashford Castle v SIPTU*[104] the Labour Court had decided that the expression should be assigned the meaning that it would normally bear in an industrial relations context:

> "Collective bargaining comprehends more than mere negotiation or consultation on individual employment related issues including the processes of individual grievances in relation to pay or conditions of employment. In the industrial relations context in which the term is commonly used it connotes a process by which employers or their representatives negotiate with representatives of a group or body of workers for the purpose of concluding a collective agreement fixing the pay and other conditions of employment applicable to the group of workers on whose behalf the negotiations are conducted.
> Normally the process is characterised by the involvement of a trade union representing workers but it may also be conducted by a staff association, which is an excepted body within the meaning of the Trade Union Act, 1941, as amended. However an essential characteristic of collective bargaining, properly

---

[101] See Connolly, "Industrial Relations (Miscellaneous Provisions) Act 2004 - Implications for Industrial Relations Law and Practice of the Supreme Court Decision in *Ryanair v Labour Court and IMPACT*" (2007) 4 IELJ 37; Doherty, "Representation, Bargaining and the Law: Where Next For the Unions?" (2009) 60(4) NILQ 383; Doherty, "Union Sundown? The Future of Collective Representation Rights in Irish Law" (2007) 4 IELJ 96; Gilvarry and Hunt, "Trade Union Recognition and the Labour Court: Picking Up the Pieces after Ryanair" in *The State of the Unions* (Hastings ed, The Liffey Press, Dublin, 2008).

[102] *Ryanair v Impact/IALPA* (LCR 18075/2005).

[103] *Ryanair v Labour Court* [2007] 4 IR 199 at 217 *per* Geoghegan J. See also *Iarnród Éireann v Holbrooke* [2001] 1 IR 237.

[104] [2004] ELR 214 at 217.

so called, is that it is conducted between parties of equal standing who are independent in the sense that one is not controlled by the other".

The Supreme Court in *Ryanair,* however, objected to the view "arguably hinted at" in the definition that collective bargaining in a non-unionised company must take the same form and adopt the same procedures as would apply in collective bargaining with a trade union. The Court reiterated that, if machinery existed in Ryanair whereby the pilots had their own independent representatives who sat around the table with representatives of Ryanair with a view to reaching agreement if possible, that would seem to be collective bargaining within an ordinary dictionary meaning.[105] In *Demir and Baykara v Turkey*[106] the European Court of Human Rights held that Art 11 of the ECHR encompasses a right *not* to have prohibitions imposed on the freedom of trade unions to engage in collective bargaining. The Court seemed to suggest that the absence of legislation necessary to give effect to provisions of international law (in particular ILO Conventions) protecting collective bargaining rights might be in breach of the ECHR. According to Ewing and Hendy, this could have serious problems for states like Ireland where "the Supreme Court appears to be inching its way towards a position where the implied constitutionally protected right not to associate means ... that employers have a right not to recognise [a union]".[107] **[11–37]**

The Supreme Court in *Ryanair* also addressed the question of who were the "grade, group or category" of workers who were "parties" to the dispute. It was held that this referred to the parties to the dispute itself, rather than the parties before the Court (one of which, inevitability, will be a trade union). In *Ashford Castle*, the Labour Court held that "parties" refers to the specific employees involved in the particular dispute rather than referring to the employer and its employees generally.[108] **[11–38]**

In order to begin an investigation, the Labour Court must be satisfied that the internal dispute resolution procedures normally used by the parties concerned have failed to resolve the dispute. In *Radio Kerry v Mandate*[109] the Court made it clear that what is at issue here are *collective* dispute resolution procedures (rather than *individual* grievance procedures) as the Act is primarily concerned with resolving group or category disputes. Such procedures must be normally used, that is "routinely and consistently resorted to".[110] **[11–39]**

The Labour Court must decline jurisdiction under the legislation where the employer has been frustrated in observing a provision of the Code of Practice on Voluntary **[11–40]**

---

[105] For criticism of this interpretation as being difficult to reconcile with international obligations see D'Art and Turner, "Ireland in Breach of ILO Conventions on Freedom of Association, Claim Academics" (2006) IRN 11; Doherty, "Union Sundown? The Future of Collective Representation Rights in Irish Law" (2007) 4 IELJ 96.
[106] Application No 34503/97, 12 November 2008.
[107] Ewing and Hendy, "The Dramatic Implications of *Demir and Baykara*" (2010) 39(1) ILJ 2, pp 30-31.
[108] *Ashford Castle v SIPTU* (DEC 032/2003).
[109] LCR 17919/2004.
[110] *Ashford Castle v SIPTU* (DEC 032/2003). Here, a staff forum was newly instigated only after the union became involved in trying to negotiate with the employer and only met on four occasions. This was not sufficient to satisfy the statutory requirement.

Dispute Resolution. This was considered by the Court in its recommendation in *Ashford Castle*.[111] The employer in that case argued that the provision should be read as applying only where it can be shown that the employer's refusal to observe a provision in the Code was made in bad faith. The Court declined to accept that analysis and rejected the employer's submission that some of the employees had sought to frustrate the employer in resolving disputes by making unreasonable demands; the Court held that the statutory provision is not about whether or not the parties acted *reasonably* in their dealings with each other but about whether or not the employer was frustrated in observing the Code of Practice.[112]

Industrial Action and the Law

[11–41] The right of workers to withdraw labour or engage in other forms of action deleterious to their employer's interests is one that is protected in most democratic legal systems. The right to strike, in particular, is guaranteed in many economic and social rights instruments.[113] It may seem odd that such a "right" would be protected. As Kahn-Freund and Hepple point out, a strike (or a potential strike) is "an event which of necessity entails a waste of resources and damage to the economy" yet remains "by general consent an indispensible element of a democratic society".[114] Various justifications have been put forward for this state of affairs. For some, the right to withdraw labour is seen as a fundamental human right, linked with civil and political rights such as the right not to be subjected to forced labour.[115] For others, the right should be viewed specifically within the industrial relations context. This can be seen in the view that only workers acting in concert can counter the "concentrated power of capital" to hire and sack workers and close down businesses or in the view that the right to have recourse to industrial action is integral to the operation of an autonomous collective bargaining system, as workers must have some "muscle" to back up bargaining positions.[116] Of course, from an economic perspective, the right to strike can be seen as producing strongly negative outcomes in terms of damage to the employer's business, loss of productivity in the economy and even, potentially, harm to the workers themselves (for example, if the employer or its suppliers are forced to shed jobs).[117] Legal systems also vary in how they treat to right to strike. There is no express right to strike in the Irish Constitution, for example, while such a right is contained

---

[111] *ibid.*

[112] For example, where a union failed to make itself available for meetings at specified times; *Kildare Hotel and Golf Club v Amicus* (LCR 18672/2006).

[113] See, for example, Art 8(1)(d) of the International Covenant on Economic, Social and Cultural Rights and Art 28 of the EU Charter of Fundamental Rights. The right to strike is recognised as a fundamental principle of EU law; Case C-438/05 *International Transport Workers' Federation and Finnish Seamen's Union v Viking Line* [2008] IRLR 14. The right is also protected by Art 11 ECHR; *Enerji Yapi-Yol Sen v Turkey* (Application No 68959/01, 21 April 2009). See also Novitz, *International and European Protection of the Right to Strike* (Oxford University Press, Oxford, 2003).

[114] Kahn-Freund and Hepple, *Laws Against Strikes* (Fabian Research Series 302, London, 1972), p 4.

[115] Davies, *op.cit*, p 220.

[116] Deakin and Morris, *op.cit*, p 890. See also the judgment of the European Court of Human Rights in *Enerji Yapi-Yol Sen v Turkey* (Application No 68959/01, 21 April 2009).

[117] Davies, *op.cit*, p 225.

in the Constitutions of other EU countries, like France, Italy, Spain, Greece and Sweden.[118]

This section will attempt to pick a path through the "minefield" of the law of industrial action.[119] This is a notoriously technical and difficult area of employment law. The Irish system derives from that of the UK, where the legal framework has developed in a "ramshackle, ad hoc manner, which is all but incomprehensible to those coming from outside"[120]; despite the rationalisation of the law in Ireland in 1990, this continues to be largely true of this area of Irish employment law too. Recent developments in relation to EU law, discussed below, have served to further complicate this position.

[11–42]

The "Immunities" and the Industrial Relations Act 1990

Those who organise, or participate in, industrial action have historically been vulnerable to legal liability of some kind. In the normal course of events, engaging in industrial action could involve the commission of a crime (e.g. criminal conspiracy) or any number of torts (e.g. interference with contractual relations, conspiracy, etc). Furthermore, trade unions organising the action could be sued (e.g. for inducing breaches of contract) as a result of the unlawful acts of their officials, on the grounds that the latter were acting as agents of the union.[121] In order to legitimise trade union action, therefore, in the first half of the 20th Century, "immunities" in relation to trade union action were recognised and enacted in the Trade Union Act 1871 and updated in the Trade Disputes Act 1906. This legislation did not give unions the status of corporate entities[122] but protected trade union action from amounting to a tort or a crime. The general intention was to allow trade unions to exist within the law but to prevent legal regulation of their affairs. In other words, the "voluntarist" system that emerged granted immunities but did not grant positive rights.

[11–43]

The legal regulation of trade union and industrial action remained for many years governed by the Act of 1871 and the Industrial Relations Act of 1946 (and their various amendments). As Kerr notes, reform of Irish trade union and industrial relations legislation was high on the agenda of successive Ministers for Labour for many years (especially since the establishment of the Department of Labour in 1966) [123] but it only arrived, somewhat belatedly, with the enactment of the Industrial Relations Act 1990. The 1990 Act involved some of the most far-reaching changes in Irish labour law since the 1940s and effected major modification of the law both in the area of trade disputes and industrial relations generally.[124] The 1906 Trade Disputes Act was repealed in its entirety and the Labour Relations Commission (LRC) was established.[125] Prior to the 1990 Act, the Oireachtas legislated separately for trade

[11–44]

---

[118] See Jacobs, "The Law of Strikes and Lockouts" in *Comparative Labour Law and Industrial Relations in Industrialised Market Economies* (Blanpain ed, Kluwer, The Netherlands, 2007).
[119] O' Neill, "Navigating the Minefield - An Overview of the Law of Industrial Action" (2009) 2 ELRI 91.
[120] Deakin and Morris, *op.cit*, p 893.
[121] *Taff Vale Railway Co v Amalgamated Society of Railway Servants* [1901] AC 426.
[122] Trade Union Act 1871, s 5.
[123] Kerr, *The Trade Union and Industrial Relations Acts* (3rd ed, Round Hall, Dublin, 2007), p 183.
[124] Kerr, "Irish Industrial Relations Legislation: Consensus Not Compulsion" (1991) 20(4) ILJ 240.
[125] See chapter 2.

union law and industrial relations law. The 1990 Act amended or repealed all previous law by means of a single consolidated piece of legislation. The purpose of the Act, as set out in the Long Title, is to "make further and better provision for promoting harmonious relations between workers and employers and to amend the law relating to trade unions". Part III of the Act deals with industrial relations generally, including the role of the dispute resolution bodies and codes of practice[126] and updates and amends the law relating to JLCs and REAs.[127] Here, the focus is on Part II of the Act, which relates to the law on trade disputes, the "minefield, through which the lawyer can tread with great caution and very little assurance of safety".[128]

Definitions Under Section 8 of the 1990 Act

[11–45]   Section 8 of the Act provides definitions for the key terms relating to trade union law. Trade dispute is defined as "any dispute between employers and workers which is connected with the employment or non-employment or the terms or conditions of or affecting the employment of any person". Clearly, this is not limited to disputes solely between an employer and its workers, as "worker" is defined as "any person who is or was employed whether or not in the employment of the employer with whom a trade dispute arises".[129] It seems that persons seeking work for the first time do not come within the definition.[130] The definition does not cover disputes *between* workers but would cover any disputes "connected with" with terms and conditions of, or affecting, employment or non-employment.[131] It also covers disputes involving "any person", so can cover disputes between employers and workers over the employment of persons who are not workers.

[11–46]   A trade union is defined as "a trade union, which is the holder of a negotiation licence under Part II of the Trade Union Act 1941".

Industrial action is defined as:

> "any action, which affects, or is likely to affect, the terms or conditions, whether express or implied of a contract and which is taken by any number or body of workers in compelling their employer, to accept or not to accept terms or conditions of or affecting employment".

A strike is defined as:

> "a cessation of work by any number or body of workers in combination or a concerted refusal under a common understanding of any number to continue to work for their employer done as a means of compelling their employer to accept or not to accept terms and conditions of or affecting employment".

---

126 See chapter 2.

127 Discussed above.

128 McMahon and Binchy, *Irish Law of Torts* (3rd ed, Butterworths, Dublin, 2000), p 843.

129 Members of the Defence Forces and the Garda Síochána are excluded from the definition.

130 *Goulding Chemicals Ltd. v Bolger* [1977] IR 211 at 230 *per* O' Higgins CJ.

131 "Non-employment" can be wide enough to cover disputes arising out of the employment or dismissal of any person and a dispute over an employer's hiring policy; Kerr, *The Trade Union and Industrial Relations Acts* (3rd ed, Round Hall, Dublin, 2007), p 188. See also *J Bradbury Ltd v Duffy* (1984) 3 JISLL 86.

Both definitions are framed in terms of *collective* action: action by an individual **[11–47]**
worker would not be covered.[132] The action must be taken to compel an employer
(or aid other workers in compelling their employer) to accept or not to accept terms
or conditions of, or affecting, employment. This would not cover "political" strikes or
industrial action (e.g. action in protest against State support for military action
abroad).[133] Industrial action might include an overtime ban, a work-to-rule, a go-slow,
blacking of machinery, and so on.[134]

The Immunities and the "Golden Formula"

Under s 9(2) of the 1990 Act, where there are agreed procedures in existence, by **[11–48]**
custom, practice or collective agreement, for the resolution of *individual* grievances, the
immunities under ss 10–12 only apply where those procedures have been resorted to
and exhausted. Exhausting remedies includes having resort to State dispute resolution
bodies (the Labour Court, the LRC, etc) but does not refer to an "appeal to a court".
Under s 9 (1), the immunities relating to peaceful picketing (s 11), inducing another or
threatening to induce another to break his or her contract of employment, threatening
to break one's own contract of employment or interfering with the trade, business or
employment of another person (s 12) and actions in tort (s 13) apply only to authorised
trade unions holding a negotiating licence and their members and officials. Workers
who are not members of such unions are only entitled to the protection under s 10
(relating to acts done in contemplation or furtherance of a trade dispute). Under s 17,
however, immunities under ss 10–12 are lost if action is carried out contrary to, or in
disregard of, the result of a secret ballot.

Section 10 refers to the tort, and the crime, of conspiracy. Unlike the immunities in ss **[11–49]**
11–13, the immunities here are not confined to members or officials of authorised trade
unions. Immunity, however, is only available where the "golden formula" applies,[135]
that is where action is taken "in contemplation or furtherance of a trade dispute". The
interpretation of this phrase, therefore, determines the boundaries of lawful industrial
action. Clearly, the use of the word "contemplation" means that it is not necessary
there be a dispute in existence at the time of the action. However, the mere anticipation
of a possible dispute will not suffice: there must be a dispute "either imminent or
actual".[136] In *Express Newspapers v MacShane*[137] a majority in the House of Lords
accepted that "furtherance" was to be given a subjective interpretation. The immunity
is to depend on the bona fides of the defendant. Once a trade dispute is shown to exist,
the person who acts, and not the court, is the judge of whether the acts will further the
dispute.

---

[132] Kerr, *The Trade Union and Industrial Relations Acts* (3rd ed, Round Hall, Dublin, 2007),
p 190.
[133] See Ewing and Hendry, *op.cit*, p 16, where the authors suggest that recent decisions of the
European Court of Human Rights seem to be moving towards a "human rights" conception of
strike action that would extend beyond the narrow employment context to encompass, for
example, protest strikes directed against the government.
[134] Wallace *et al*, *op.cit*, p 207. Remember, too, that industrial action can be taken by the
employer; a "lock-out" of workers, for example.
[135] Wedderburn, *The Worker and the Law* (Penguin Books, London, 1965), p 222.
[136] *Crazy Prices (NI) v Hewitt* [1980] NI 150 at 167 *per* Gibson LJ.
[137] [1980] AC 672.

[11–50]   The issue of whether ulterior motives could compromise the categorisation of a dispute as a genuine "trade dispute" under the 1990 Act was addressed by the Supreme Court in *Nolan Transport (Oaklands) Ltd v Halligan*.[138] The case involved the issue of union recognition in a small transport company, the alleged dismissal of two employees and a picket organised by SIPTU. The key issues revolved around the conduct of a ballot for strike action and the question of the existence of a trade dispute. In the High Court, Barron J issued a permanent injunction against the defendant union from participating in any industrial action against the plaintiff and awarded damages of nearly £600,000 (Irish pounds).[139] Barron J felt that the "so-called" trade dispute did not fall within the scope of the Act as it was not bona fide. He felt the union was not engaged in a trade dispute but simply trying to gain recognition rights. On appeal, the High Court finding was overturned and the damages award was vacated.

[11–51]   Murphy J, in the Supreme Court, was in disagreement with Barron J as to the inferences drawn in relation to the motivation and purpose of the union and the legal principles that are applicable where industrial action is undertaken with a view to achieving more than one objective. Barron J had adverted to a number of factors (including, *inter alia,* the publication of slanted and dishonest communications by union officials and the failure of previous efforts by the union to organise within the company) and concluded that the real purpose of the union's actions was to represent the entire workforce. Murphy J did not agree that those factors would justify the inference that a trade union was attempting, or would attempt, to institute industrial action for the purpose of coercing an employer and its employees into a closed shop agreement. He found that the dispute between the appellants and the company was bona fide in the sense that Mr. Halligan had "an honest belief, for which there were reasonable grounds, and further that the dispute was genuine in the sense that it represented the immediate quarrel between the parties".[140] Even if recognition could be identified as the ultimate goal of the union, it did not represent the current dispute. At worst, the irregular and improper conduct in which the union was engaged might have suggested a willingness by it to take industrial action in the *future* for an improper purpose but no future plan could render unlawful a dispute which was protected by the relevant legislation. Thus, whereas Barron J's judgment had contained a *subjective element* by suggesting a trade dispute had to be bona fide, the Supreme Court test could be seen as objective or pragmatic: whether there was a reasonable basis for an *honest belief* in the existence of a trade dispute.

Picketing

[11–52]   Picketing is permissible under s 11(1) of the 1990 Act. This section was a major amendment to the law and is generally seen as the most important section in the Act.[141] Even prior to the 1990 Act, judicial dicta had averted to the impact of pickets:

>   "The power of a picket comes from the refusal of workmen employed by other employers, or the fellow employees of those picketing, to pass it unless they are

---

[138] [1999] 1 IR 128. See de Vries, "Industrial Disputes and Secret Ballots" (1999) 17 ILT 58.
[139] [1995] ELR 1.
[140] [1998] ELR 177 at 193. Thus, a dispute may well be bona fide if one party denies that there is a dispute but the other believes that he or she has been wronged and is in dispute as a result.
[141] McMahon and Binchy, *op.cit*, p 856.

directed to do so by their unions. It is thus an immensely powerful weapon which closes the businesses of those against whom it is used".[142]

Section 11(1) covers "primary" picketing (picketing one's own employer) and s 11(2) deals with "secondary" picketing (picketing another employer, where there is a reasonable belief that the latter is assisting the employer that is party to the trade dispute in the frustration of the industrial action being undertaken).[143] For the latter, it seems merely "filling a gap in the market" would not suffice: the picketed employer would need to take some active steps to assist the employer in dispute (e.g. filling orders on its behalf).

[11–53]

It is lawful under s 11 to picket where the employer works or carries on business or approaches to that place (not necessarily where the workers themselves work), provided the picketing is for the purpose of peacefully obtaining or communicating information or of peacefully persuading any person to work or not to work.[144] There are no limits as to the numbers of pickets but if more pickets are employed than are reasonably necessary for the stated purpose the court may infer a lack of bona fides on the part of the picketers.[145] The courts have been keen to stress that the activities protected be done in a "peaceful manner". Thus, the use of abusive language (such as "scab") or physical force,[146] the publication (on placards, for example) of misleading false-hoods,[147] and the recommending of alternative outlets to potential customers or clients of the employer[148] have all been deemed non-peaceable methods of picketing. What is deemed reasonable in a picket situation is a matter of degree and depends upon, *inter alia*, the size of the premises and the workforce, the number of persons calling to a premises, the number of entrances and uses of the area before the picket takes place.[149] Persons are, however, entitled to pass a picket without having to listen to any of the picketers, if they do not wish to do so.[150] A particular issue arises in relation to "multi-employment" locations (e.g. industrial estates where there are many different companies). In *Rayware Ltd v TGWU*[151] the plaintiff carried on business in a private trading estate. A dispute arose and a picket was placed at the gate leading from the main road to the estate. The English Court of Appeal refused to restrain the picket as

[11–54]

---

[142] *Goulding Chemicals Ltd v Bolger* [1977] IR 211 at 239 *per* Kenny J.

[143] It is not, therefore, necessary for the picketed employer to have actually assisted the picketers' employer; it is sufficient that the picketers had a reasonable belief that this was the case from the outset of the placing of the picket.

[144] See O' Neill, *op.cit*, pp 92-99.

[145] *EI Company Ltd v Kennedy* [1968] IR 69. See also *News Group Newspapers Ltd v SOGAT* [1986] IRLR 337 on potential liability for those who organise a picket despite knowing from experience it may constitute a tortuous act.

[146] *EI Company Ltd v Kennedy* [1968] IR 69.

[147] *Esplanade Pharmacy Ltd v Larkin* [1957] IR 285.

[148] *Ryan v Cooke* [1938] IR 512.

[149] *Brendan Dunne Ltd v Fitzpatrick* [1958] IR 29.

[150] *P Elliott & Co Ltd v BATU* (Unreported, High Court, Clarke J, 20 October 2006). See also *Broome v DPP* [1974] AC 587.

[151] [1989] 1 WLR 675 at 677 *per* May LJ.

this was "the nearest practicable point" at which the picket could take place without a trespass being committed: it was "at or near" the employees place of work.

Section 11(1) fell to be interpreted for the first time since the 1990 Act was passed recently in *Dublin City Council v TEEU.*[152] In the case, pickets had been placed following a dispute between the defendant union and Pickerings, a lift maintenance company, over the redundancy of seven employees. A month or so later, the company had its contract with Dublin City Council (the owners of the flats in which the lifts were located) terminated. The pickets, however, continued and the City Council took action against the TEEU arguing that, as the union was not engaged in an industrial dispute with the City Council and Pickerings were no longer working on the site, the picketing was unlawful. The case centred around the interpretation of "where the employer works or carries on business" in s 11(1). Laffoy J held that:

> "in applying s 11(1), the relevant date at which the test whether the picketers' employer 'works or carries on business' at the location of the picketing is the *date when the picketing commences* and, if the test is satisfied at that date, the picketing is lawful, provided the other requirements of s 11(1) are complied with, *even if the picketers' employer is no longer working or carrying on business at the location at the time the Court is considering the application of s 11(a)"* (emphasis added).

Thus, while "picketing cannot lawfully be engaged in at a place where the targeted employer had worked or carried on business, say, a week, or a month or a year previously", the test was satisfied in this case.[153] Laffoy noted that this interpretation must be assumed to be in line with the intention of the Oireachtas when passing the Act, which was to "exclusively link the location of lawful picketing to the work or business environment of the relevant employer". The requirement that the employer works or carries on business at the picketed location, combined with the requirement that the objective of the picketing must be the furtherance of the trade dispute and the peaceful obtaining or communicating of information "must, even as a matter of common sense, narrow the circumstances in which lawful picketing may continue once the picketers' employer has departed the scene, and must reduce, if not entirely eliminate, the possibility of picketing for a useless or illegitimate purpose."

[11–55] Under s 11(5), it is lawful for trade union officials and branch officers to accompany any union member whom they represent, provided that their purpose is the contemplation and furtherance of a trade dispute and is for the purposes of obtaining or communicating information or peacefully persuading any person to work or not to work. In *P Elliott & Co Ltd v BATU*[154] Clarke J noted that it would generally be a useful safeguard to have senior union officials present at a picket.

---

[152] Unreported, High Court, Laffoy J, 9 June 2010.

[153] Note that this would seem to indicate that a union faced with an employer that intends to cease trading would need to have any pickets in place *before* the closure of the operation takes place.

[154] Unreported, High Court, 20 October 2006. Clarke J also felt it would be desirable for the union to have picketing guidelines for the future.

Immunity from Other Tortious Acts

Section 12 protects persons against legal action for acts (done, of course, in **[11–56]** contemplation or furtherance of a trade dispute) consisting of inducing another or threatening to induce another to break his or her contract of employment, threatening to break one's own contract of employment, or the interference with the trade, business or employment of another person or that person's right to freely dispose of capital and labour. There is no immunity for the actual breach of an employment contract.[155]

Section 13 grants immunity to trade unions (and their officials and members sued in a representative capacity) from liability in tort for acts done in contemplation or furtherance of a trade dispute. Trade union officials, however, may still face an action in relation to their *personal* tortious liability. The section does not apply to actions in contract (for restitution, for example) or for breach of constitutional rights.[156] As the section refers to "acts committed" the question of whether injunctive relief may be granted against trade unions in respect of *future* tortious acts not yet committed remains moot.

Secret Ballots

Section 14 of the 1990 Act has been described as "perhaps the most revolutionary **[11–57]** provision" of Part II of the Act.[157] Under this section, trade unions are required to make provisions in their rules for the conduct of secret ballots in order to sanction industrial action. Failure to do so will result in the loss of the union's negotiating licence and, as a result, the loss of the protections of ss 11–13 of the Act.[158] Furthermore, engaging in a strike or another form of industrial action contrary to, or in disregard of, the result of a secret ballot means that the immunities under ss 10–12 are lost.[159] Finally, failure to comply with secret ballot requirements has implications for the granting of injunctions to employers under s 19 (see below).

Therefore, pursuant to s 14(2) of the Act, the rules of every union must contain a **[11–58]** provision to the effect:

a. that no strike or other industrial action take place without a secret ballot;
b. that all members whom it is reasonable for the union to believe at the time of the ballot are likely to be called upon to engage in the strike or industrial action be given a fair opportunity of voting;

---

[155] Kerr, *The Trade Union and Industrial Relations Acts* (3rd ed, Round Hall, Dublin, 2007), p 197. See also that the author notes the section does not deal with the developing generic tort of "unlawful interference with trade or business" nor does it give definitive guidance on whether *indirect* inducement of a breach of a commercial contract is actionable. This arises where a defendant (e.g. a group of workers in company A) induces a third party (e.g. workers in company B, which has a contract with company A) to do an act so wrongful (break their employment contracts) as to prevent the performance of a contract by a fourth party (company B) with the plaintiff (company A).
[156] However, see McMahon and Binchy, *op.cit*, p 853 for an extensive discussion of the relationship between s 13 and actions for interference with constitutional rights.
[157] *Nolan Transport (Oaklands) Ltd v Halligan* [1999] 1 IR 128 at 154 *per* Murphy J.
[158] Industrial Relations Act 1990, ss 9 and 16.
[159] Industrial Relations Act 1990, s 17(1). The immunity conferred by s 13 is not forfeited in such a circumstance; *Nolan Transport (Oaklands) Ltd v Halligan* [1999] 1 IR 128.

c.   that the controlling authority of the union shall not call, organise or participate in industrial action without a majority of votes having being cast in favour of industrial action;

d.   that the governing body of the union shall have full discretion in relation to the calling, organisation of, or participation in, industrial action where the majority of votes cast favour industrial action;

e.   that the trade union make known to the members entitled to vote in the ballot the results of a secret ballot as soon as practicable after the vote;

f.   that the governing body of the trade union may set aside a majority vote against industrial action *only when* the aggregate majority of the members of all unions balloted favours industrial action. This deals with the situation of multi-union workplaces where one union votes against action, but a majority of all employees vote in favour. The union that votes against will be entitled to call on its members to support the action. A formal aggregation arrangement is not necessary;

g.   that the union must ballot before calling on its members to support a strike (but not other industrial action) by another union. Where the decision is to support another union, that decision shall not be implemented without sanction by the Irish Congress of Trade Unions.

[11–59]   Thus, all unions are required to hold secret ballots and adhere to strict procedures before sanctioning a strike or another form of industrial action.[160] The union must ensure that any members entitled to vote in any ballot are able to do so without interference or constraint imposed by any member or officer of the union and that every member wishing to vote is given a fair opportunity to vote. In terms of secondary action, this may require a second ballot including union members employed in the business to be secondarily picketed.[161]

[11–60]   In *G & T Crampton Ltd v BATU*[162] a dispute arose over the termination of the employment of a number of bricklayers at a site on which the plaintiffs were the main contractor. When one sub-contractor completed work, it terminated the employment of the bricklayers and the new sub-contractor did not re-employ them. The men claimed they were, in fact, employees of the plaintiff and picketed the site. The plaintiff obtained a High Court injunction restraining the picketing, as Laffoy J concluded there was "no evidence whatever" before the Court as to the outcome of any secret ballot. The case revolved around the balloting procedures under the 1990 Act and whether they had been complied with. The Supreme Court noted that the ballot papers had not contained the proposal on which the members were being called to ballot but simply asked whether members were prepared to engage in "a strike or other industrial action". The Court seemed to suggest it would be necessary for a union to particularise

---

[160] Ewing and Hendy, *op.cit*, p 21, note that in the light of recent European Court of Human Rights jurisprudence on Art 11 ECHR, extremely restrictive obligations in relation to strike ballots and notice, which may be said to frustrate union attempts to take collective action, might give rise to questions of compatibility with the ECHR (as well as ILO Convention 87 and the European Social Charter).

[161] See Kerr, *The Trade Union and Industrial Relations Acts* (3rd ed, Round Hall, Dublin, 2007), pp 200-202.

[162] [1998] 1 ILRM 430.

the nature of the action sought to be taken more carefully in order to comply with the terms of s 14.[163]

In *Nolan Transport (Oaklands) Ltd v Halligan*[164] Murphy J noted that s 14 does *not* **[11–61]** require that industrial action should be authorised by a secret ballot but that the statute requires that the *rules* of the trade union should contain provisions in relation to such ballots and imposes sanctions for the failure either to have such rules or to observe them. On the face of it, the Supreme Court decided that the participation by a trade union in, or its support for, a strike or other industrial action without the authority of a secret ballot of its members would be a matter of internal management of the affairs of the union and would constitute a breach of contract between the executive of the *union* and the *membership* rather than a breach of statutory duty. As noted above, under s 17 of the Act, immunities granted by ss 10–12 are lost if action is carried out contrary to, or in disregard of, the result of a secret ballot. In the present case, the Court concluded that either no secret ballot was held or else the secret ballot "in its outcome" authorised the industrial action, so that there was no question of the individual appellants acting in *disregard* of the resolution of their colleagues. Even if the evidence justified the Court's conclusion that the majority of the employees or members of the union voted against industrial action, the decision of the Court could hardly be regarded as "the outcome" of the ballot and certainly it could not be suggested that the striking members acted in disregard thereof.

Murphy J also stressed that secret ballots should be conducted "not merely in **[11–62]** accordance with the terms of such rules but also under professional and independent guidance which will guarantee that all appropriate conditions are complied with": this would also facilitate unions in proving that such was the case.[165] O'Flaherty J concluded:

> "If there is one lesson that can be learned from this litigation it is surely that the requirements for having a proper secret ballot should always be observed...I reject the submission that once such a shambles as is disclosed as regards the 'ballot' that was held here occurs that we should simply turn a blind eye to it... there is a serious obligation on union management to give proper example... legislation solidifies and expands the privileged position afforded by the law to trade unions. Privileges carry duties as well as rights... the union cannot avoid blame...This will have to be dealt with in deciding on costs".[166]

Maguire distils the key points made in the leading cases on secret ballots to make the **[11–63]** following points in relation to union compliance with the balloting provisions[167]:

a. ballot papers should clearly state the issue involved;
b. ballot papers should clearly state the exact form of industrial action to be pursued;

---

[163] See also *P Elliott & Co Ltd v BATU* (Unreported, High Court, Clarke J, 20 October 2006).
[164] [1999] 1 IR 128.
[165] *ibid* at 161.
[166] *ibid* at 136.
[167] Maguire, "Trade Unions" in *Employment Law* (Regan ed, Tottel, Dublin, 2009), p 645. See also the decision of the Court of Appeal of England and Wales in *British Airways v Unite* [2010] EWCA Civ 669.

c. an independent person should supervise the conduct of the ballot;
d. the union should be able to demonstrate that it balloted all members that might reasonably be expected to be involved in the action;
e. the union should be able to confirm details of compliance with s 14(2)(f) (to give details of the number of ballots, the number of spoilt votes and the number of votes cast for and against the motion);
f. if circumstances change, and/or the form of action to be taken changes, the union should re-ballot.

Injunctions

[11–64]   Section 19 of the 1990 Act provides extensive protection to trade unions against the granting of injunctions restraining industrial action, as long as the unions fulfil certain conditions.[168] This issue is one of particular importance as, prior to the 1990 Act, it was relatively easy for employers to secure interlocutory injunctions. This was because the courts applied the standard principles on injunctions laid down in *Campus Oil v Minister for Industry and Energy*,[169] namely that the court is satisfied there is a serious question to be tried and that the balance of convenience favours the granting of the injunction. As any action would obviously impact monetarily on the employer, it would usually be able to satisfy the second limb of the test. In the context of trade disputes, however, injunctions have a particular effect, as noted by McCarthy J (in a dissenting judgment) in *Bayzana Ltd. v Galligan*[170]:

> "It is notorious that in actions of this kind, the resolution of the interlocutory motion is, effectively, the resolution of the action…if an interlocutory injunction is granted, either at first instance or on appeal, by the time the trial takes place, however relatively short the interval may be, the bloom has gone off the steel of industrial action; men give up-seek other jobs-go elsewhere for that purpose-emigrate. Worst of all, they may well settle for less than what are their true rights because, they think, however mistakenly, that the dice are loaded against them in the Law Courts".

[11–65]   Under s 19(1) of the 1990 Act, an employer cannot get an injunction *ex parte* as long as the union fulfils certain conditions, namely that a secret ballot has been held, that the outcome favours a strike or other form of industrial action and that the union gives notice of not less than one week. Under s 19(2), a court shall *not* grant an injunction restraining the strike or other industrial action where the respondent establishes a fair case that he or she was acting in contemplation or furtherance of a trade dispute. If the rules on ballots are not fulfilled, however, the benefits of s 19 are lost.

[11–66]   In *G & T Crampton Ltd v BATU*[171] it was noted by Keane J, in the High Court, that, prior to the 1990 Act, frequent use of the injunction procedure by employers had often meant that the use of what were otherwise legitimate methods of protest by employees and unions were effectively neutralised by the way in which the law operated. In

---

[168] For an overview on the law relating to injunctions, see Delany, *Equity and the Law of Trusts in Ireland* (4th ed, Round Hall, Dublin, 2007).
[169] [1983] IR 88.
[170] [1987] IR 238 at 252-253.
[171] [1998] 1 ILRM 430.

particular, he noted that s 19(1) was enacted to deal with the quite common occurrence where an employer would apply to the court for an interim, but not always an interlocutory, injunction restraining picketing, the object being to take the heat out of the situation in the hope that support for the action would dissipate.

As Kerr points out, given that the question of whether the union has complied with balloting requirements is considered in the context of an interlocutory application, the questions of the onus and standards of proof are crucial.[172] It seems clear that the onus of proof that balloting procedures were complied with rests on the party resisting the injunction, i.e. the union.[173] What standard of proof is required, though, is unclear and has given rise to much discussion.[174] In *Malincross v BATU*[175] McCracken J granted an injunction restraining picketing at a premises that was once that of the employer but which it had subsequently vacated. The Judge felt there was a serious issue to be tried as to whether the action was authorised by the secret ballot and therefore the union was held not to be entitled to the protection of s 19(2). In *Daru Blocklaying Ltd v BATU*[176] a far greater number of workers picketed the plaintiff's premises than had been balloted. As the union, therefore, had not complied with the requirements of s 14, it lost the benefit of protection under s 19(2) and an injunction was granted restraining the picketing. In *Chieftan Construction v Ryan*[177] the defendants had had been dismissed by the plaintiff and believed they were to be replaced by agency workers. They picketed the employer's premises, without authorisation, and the employer sought an injunction arguing that, as those picketing were no longer its employees, s 11 did not apply to their action. Edwards J considered the strength of the plaintiff's case and decided that that the plaintiff's prospects of success were remote:

[11–67]

> "In considering the question as to whether or not the plaintiff has established a fair or substantial or serious issue to be tried I feel bound to take into account my view that the plaintiffs' case, though arguable, is weak. In all the circumstances of the case I am not satisfied that the plaintiffs' point has sufficient substance, in the broad sense, to persuade me that there is a fair or substantial or serious issue to be tried".

As a result, he refused to grant the injunction. Maguire argues that the case is significant in that it suggests that employers will need to show prospect of success at trial in order to secure an injunction: this could mean those engaging in industrial action, even without a ballot, will have greater success at resisting interlocutory injunctions than in the past.[178]

[11–68]

---

[172] Kerr, *The Trade Union and Industrial Relations Acts* (3rd ed, Round Hall, Dublin, 2007), p 205.

[173] *Daru Blocklaying Ltd v BATU* [2002] 2 IR 619.

[174] See McMahon and Binchy, *op.cit*, pp 863-866; Maguire, "Trade Unions" in *Employment Law* (Regan ed, Tottel, Dublin, 2009), pp 658-664.

[175] [2002] ELR 78.

[176] [2002] 2 IR 619.

[177] [2008] IEHC 147.

[178] Maguire, "Trade Unions" in *Employment Law* (Regan ed, Tottel, Dublin, 2009), p 664. Note that O' Neill, *op.cit*, p 102, refers to a successful application for an injunction by Coca-Cola in late 2009 that sought, not to restrain picketing, but to ensure that the pickets were conducted in an orderly manner.

Industrial Action and the Employment Contract

[11–69]　Finally in this section, we will consider briefly the legal issues that arise in relation to the contract of employment when workers engage in industrial action. At common law, the view traditionally was that workers who went on strike had terminated their contracts of employment. However, in *Becton Dickinson & Co Ltd v Lee*[179] a majority of the Supreme Court agreed that it was to be implied into every contract that, where a strike takes place after due notice has been given, the contract is not breached but suspended. Such an implied term would not be read in where there was an express provision to the contrary (i.e. a "no-strike clause").

[11–70]　While the "suspension" theory might not hold striking workers to be in breach of their contracts, there is no obligation on employers to continue to pay workers who are on strike. In *Fuller v Minister for Agriculture*[180] Gilligan J held that, while on strike, an employee is negotiating for better working conditions and, therefore, as a result is aware that by going on strike he or she will be unavailable for work. Once an employee is unavailable for work, he or she is not entitled to be paid or to receive any pension entitlements for the relevant period. Gilligan J also refused to accept the proposition that an employee who goes on strike and is therefore unavailable for work, but who subsequently may succeed in having the particular grievance rectified, is entitled to be paid wages and pension entitlements during the strike period.

[11–71]　The issue of whether industrial action affects continuity of employment is governed by the First Schedule to the Minimum Notice and Terms of Employment Act 1973. A week, or part of a week, in which an employee is on strike does not count in calculating the length of continuous employment. It will not, therefore, be counted as service for the calculation of statutory redundancy entitlements or service for the purposes of the Unfair Dismissals Acts. Section 5(2) of the Unfair Dismissals Act 1977[181] provides that if the employer dismisses some, but not others, involved in a strike or industrial action dispute, or dismisses all those involved but subsequently allows some, but not all, to resume their employment (what are termed "selective dismissals") the dismissal will be deemed to be unfair. Non-selective dismissals are subject to the general principle of unfairness, provided for in s 6 of the 1977 Act.[182] Section 5(2)(A) of the 1977 Act[183] provides that, without prejudice to s 6 of the 1977 Act, in determining whether a non-selective dismissal in the context of a trade dispute is unfair, regard will be had to: the reasonableness of the parties; the extent to which the employer complied with dismissals procedure under the legislation; the extent to which the parties have complied with codes of practice relating to procedures for dismissal; and whether the parties have adhered to grievance procedures.[184]

---

[179]　[1973] IR 1.

[180]　[2008] IEHC 95.

[181]　As amended by the Unfair Dismissals (Amendment) Act 1993, s 4.

[182]　See chapter 10. Dismissals for taking part in unlawful industrial action are also subject to this presumption; Kerr, "Industrial Relations" in *Employment Law* (Regan ed, Tottel, Dublin, 2009), p 685.

[183]　As inserted by the Protection of Employment (Exceptional Collective Redundancies and Related Matters) Act 2007, s 26.

[184]　See O' Neill, *op.cit*, p 101.

Collective Action and EU Law

A series of recent decisions by the European Court of Justice (ECJ) has brought a new   [11–72]
dimension to the law on industrial action, where disputes relating to free movement
rights under the EU Treaties are at issue. The regulation of the right to engage in
industrial action, as with many other areas of collective labour law, has traditionally
not been within the competence of the Union, but has been a matter for the Member
States' individual laws and practices. While Art 28 of the Charter of Fundamental
Rights protects the right to take collective action, the legal status of the Charter is
somewhat ambiguous.[185] In a series of cases, *Laval, Viking, Rüffert and Luxembourg*,[186]
the ECJ has severely restricted the rights of trade unions (and Member States) to act in
order to protect collective agreements in cases where the rights of free movement of
services or establishment are involved. In the *Viking* case, the International Transport
Workers' Federation (ITF) and the Finnish Seamen's Union threatened industrial
action over Viking Line's plans to reflag one of its Finnish vessels to Estonia and
replace the crew with cheaper workers from that country. The ECJ ruled that a trade
union's threat to strike in order to force an employer to conclude a collective agreement
may constitute a restriction on the freedom of establishment (under Art 49TFEU,
ex-Art 43EC), if the terms of the agreement are liable to deter the company from
exercising its freedom of establishment (as was the case here). The Court did,
significantly, recognise the right to take collective action (including the right to strike)
as a fundamental right, forming part of the general principles of EU law. However, Art
49TFEU did confer rights on private undertakings, which could be relied on against a
trade union or an association of trade unions to render unlawful collective action that
would unduly restrict establishment rights. The ECJ went on to say that collective
action may be legitimate, however, if its aim is to protect workers' jobs or working
conditions and if all other ways of resolving the conflict were exhausted. Action could:

> "[b]e justified by an overriding reason of public interest, such as the protection
> of workers, provided that it is established that the restriction is suitable for
> ensuring the attainment of the legitimate objective pursued and does not go
> beyond what is necessary to achieve that objective".[187]

Collective action in these circumstances, then, is to be subject to a proportionality test.   [11–73]
A week after the judgment in *Viking*, the ECJ gave its judgment in *Laval*.[188] The ECJ
ruled that the blockage of a building site in order to force a foreign service provider to
enter into negotiations on pay and sign collective agreements is illegal under EU rules
on the freedom to provide services under Art 56TFEU (ex-Art 49EC). The Court
accepted that action could be justified in cases where the public interest of protecting
workers prevailed. According to the Court, however, this was not the case in the *Laval*

---

[185] Article 6 of the new Treaty on European Union (TEU) provides that the provisions of the
Charter shall not extend in any way the competences of the Union as defined in the Treaties.
[186] Case C-341/05 *Laval v Svenska Byggnadsarbetareförbundet* [2007] ECR I-11767; Case C-438/
05 *International Transport Workers' Federation and Finnish Seamen's Union v Viking Line ABP*
[2008] IRLR 14; Case C-346/06 *Rüffert v Land Niedersachsen* [2008] IRLR 467; and Case C-319/
06 *European Commission v Luxembourg* [2009] IRLR 388.
[187] At para 90.
[188] For a review of the facts of the case, see chapter 7.

situation. The ECJ accepted, following on from *Viking*, that the right to take collective action must be recognised as a fundamental right which forms an integral part of the general principles of EU law but stated that the exercise of that right may be subject to certain restrictions, namely that it pursues a legitimate objective compatible with the Treaty and is justified by overriding reasons of public interest. The Court went on to state that the right to take collective action for the protection of the workers of the host State against possible "social dumping" may constitute an overriding reason of public interest. However, this was not the case here. Thus, while the ECJ explicitly recognised the right to strike or to take collective action as a fundamental principle of EU law, the Court emphasised the necessity to balance this right of collective action with the needs of EU law to uphold the core economic freedoms guaranteed by the Treaty, such as freedom of establishment and the right to provide services.

[11–74]   These cases have provoked much comment.[189] Two points are worth noting here. First, the cases have disappointed many (especially those in the trade union movement) concerned about a "race to the bottom" in labour standards in that, while they recognise that the right to take collective action is a fundamental right under EU law (be it in social, political or human rights terms),[190] it seems to be one that is secondary to the economic rights of free movement.[191] Secondly, as Davies notes, the impact of the *Viking* and *Laval* decisions in practice will turn on the application of the proportionality test, which, while common to labour lawyers in Continental Europe, is somewhat alien to those in the UK and Ireland:

> "This test may work perfectly well where it is applied by specialist labour courts with a good understanding of the industrial relations context. However, for an English [or Irish] lawyer, this is a remarkable new development. [Our] approach to the regulation of industrial action seeks to avoid 'politicising' the courts by preventing them from ruling on the merits of the dispute. The court's task is simply to ascertain whether the union has acted in 'contemplation or furtherance of a trade dispute'...the harm caused to the employer by the action is not considered provided that the action is lawful...The rulings in

---

[189] See Deakin, "The Labour Law Perspective: the Economic Implications of the Decisions" (2007-08) 10 *CYELS* 463; Barnard, "Viking and Laval: A Single Market Perspective" in *The New Spectre Haunting Europe- The ECJ, Trade Union Rights and the British Government* (Ewing and Hendy (eds), Institute of Employment Rights, Liverpool, 2009); Davies, "One Step Forward, Two Steps Back? The Viking and Laval Cases in the ECJ" (2008) 37(2) ILJ 126; Peijpe, "Collective Labour Law after Viking, Laval, Rüffert and Commission v Luxembourg" (2009) 25(2) *International Journal of Comparative Labour Law and Industrial Relations* 81.

[190] Davies, *op.cit*, p 220; Deakin and Morris, *op.cit*, p 890; Joerges and Rodl "Informal Politics, Formalised Law and the 'Social Deficit' of European Integration: Reflections After the Judgments of the ECJ in Viking and Laval" (2009) 15(1) ELJ 1.

[191] See Dølvik and Visser, "Free Movement, Equal Treatment and Workers' Rights: Can the European Union Solve its Trilemma of Fundamental Principles?" (2009) 40(6) *Industrial Relations Journal* 491; Barnard, "The UK and Posted Workers: The Effect of Commission v Luxembourg on the Territorial Application of British Labour Law" (2009) 38(2) ILJ 122; Eldring and Eldring, "Labour Mobility and Wage Dumping: The Case of Norway" (2008) 14(4) *European Journal of Industrial Relations* 441. Also, contrast the manner in which the ECJ balanced the competing rights of freedom of expression and free movement of goods in Case C-112/00 *Schmidberger v Austria* [2003] ECR I-5659.

Viking and Laval have the potential to involve the courts in a much more politically sensitive set of questions as they seek to apply the proportionality test to unions' strike action".[192]

However, recent jurisprudence of the European Court of Human Rights must also be noted here. In cases such as *Demir and Baykara v Turkey*[193] and *Enerji Yapi-Yol Sen v Turkey*,[194] decided after the ECJ decisions in *Laval* and *Viking*, the Court has held that the right to collective bargaining is protected by Art 11 of the ECHR and that the right to strike constitutes an important aspect in the protection of trade union members. In *Enerji* the Court held that, while the right to strike is not absolute, State restrictions on this right would need to be justified as being necessary in a democratic society. Ewing and Hendy contend that the ECJ decisions cannot be reconciled with the European Court of Human Right's requirements of a legal regime that "(i) recognises the right to collective bargaining (and the duty to take steps to promote it), (ii) respects the right to take collective action, and does so (iii) in accordance with international labour conventions and regional labour standards".[195]

[11–75]

III. Employee Voice at Work

In recent years, in the context of rapid industrial change and restructuring, a major focus of EU and Member State policy debate has been on increasing employee "voice" and participation at the workplace.[196] From a business perspective, the Lisbon Strategy (and its successor, Europe2020) seek to make Europe the most competitive and dynamic knowledge-based economy in the world by better utilising and exploiting the advantage of comparatively well-educated European workforces.[197] At the same time, there have been significant EU legislative developments in relation to employee rights

[11–76]

---

[192] Davies, "One Step Forward, Two Steps Back? The Viking and Laval Cases in the ECJ" (2008) 37(2) ILJ 126, p 146. The author also notes (p 147) that the use of a proportionality test may also make it easier for employers to injunct industrial action, by adding another set of arguments for them to deploy in cross-border situations; see also Barnard, "'British Jobs for British Workers': the Lindsey Oil Refinery Dispute and the Future of Local Labour Clauses in an Integrated EU Market" (2009) 38(3) ILJ 245.

[193] Application No 34503/97, 12 November 2008.

[194] Application No 68959/01, 21 April 2009.

[195] Ewing and Hendy, *op.cit*, p 40. The authors conclude, with undisguised relish, that the European Court of Human Rights is "pulling in different directions from its Luxembourg counterpart [the ECJ], with the mouth-watering possibility of a high noon conflict between the two" (p 4).

[196] The term "employee voice" is used here, but it should be acknowledged that this (like terms such as "participation", "involvement" etc.) is a multi-faceted and complex concept. Therefore, this section does not seek to unpack precise voice and involvement arrangements and how they might, or might not, be supported but uses the catch-all term "employee voice" as shorthand for the various voice and participation mechanism that can be identified in the literature; see, for example, Dundon *et al*, "Conceptualising the Dynamics of Employee Information and Consultation: Evidence from the Republic of Ireland" (2006) 37(5) *Industrial Relations Journal* 492; Dundon *et al*, "The Meanings and Purpose of Employee Voice" (2004) 15(6) *International Journal of Human Resource Management* 1150; Marchington *et al*, *Management Choice and Employee Voice* (CIPD Publishing, London, 2001).

[197] Doherty, "Hard Law, Soft Edge? Information, Consultation and Partnership" (2008) 30(6) *Employee Relations* 603.

and the protection of employees' dignity, and opportunities for personal development, at work.[198] Title IV of the Charter of Fundamental Rights explicitly protects workers' rights to information and consultation within the undertaking (Art 27), while the EU has also been keen to promote "social dialogue" (see Arts 152-155TFEU, ex-Arts 137-139EC). After all, the knowledge-based economy that the EU is so keen to establish is inconceivable without the active involvement of individual employees.[199] The vast majority of the "old" EU15 has long had in place mechanisms providing for information and consultation of employees at the workplace. These range from statutory works councils (for example, in Germany and France), to encompassing collective agreements which, although backed by legislation, are the primary means of regulating information and consultation in countries like Denmark and Belgium, to the hybrid Italian model, where a statutory framework allows for sectoral agreements to flesh out the detailed operations of works councils.[200] Ireland and the UK are the odd ones out here, reflecting their voluntarist traditions, as neither country has a general, permanent and statutory system of information and consultation or employee representation. Traditionally, it was the job of trade unions to interact with management on behalf of their members. However, given that, as we have seen above, there is no obligation on employers to recognise trade unions, and given the decline in union density, attention has recently shifted to obligations that exist on employers in non-union settings to negotiate, inform and consult with their workers.[201]

[11–77]   This section will begin by briefly looking at the implications for non-union employee representation of the decision in the *Ryanair* case, discussed in detail above.[202] As has been shown, a key plank of the company's case against the Labour Court exercising jurisdiction under the Industrial Relations (Amendment) Acts 2001–2004 was its contention that the pilots as a category constituted an "excepted body". "Excepted body" is defined by s 6(3)(h) of the Trade Union Act 1941 and refers to "a body all the members of which are employed by the same employer and which carries on negotiations for the fixing of wages or other conditions of employment of its own members (but no other employees)".[203] In *Ryanair* the Supreme Court decided that if it could be

---

[198] Note that other international law instruments also seek to protect these rights; in the context of the Council of Europe, for example, see Birk and Maack, "The Council of Europe and Employee Involvement in Private Enterprises" (2009) 25(2) *International Journal of Comparative Labour Law and Industrial Relations* 123.

[199] Sissen, *The Information and Consultation Directive: Unnecessary "Regulation" or an Opportunity to Promote "Partnership"?* (Warwick Papers in Industrial Relations No 67, Warwick, 2002).

[200] Broughton, "European Comparative Practice in Information and Consultation" in *Adding Value Through Information and Consultation* (Storey ed, Palgrave, Basingstoke, 2005).

[201] Connolly, *op.cit*, notes that the distinction at European level between obligations to consult and obligations to negotiate has become increasingly blurred, citing the judgment of the ECJ in Case C188/03 *Wolfgang Kühnel v Junk* [2005] ECR I-885 (discussed below). However, notwithstanding the importance of that ECJ decision, the distinction is one that is encountered (and reconciled) on a daily basis by employers, employees and unions in Continental Europe, especially where works councils exist. In this case, as in so many others, the peculiarities of the voluntarist model make some concepts that are second nature to Continental labour lawyers somewhat alien to those in Ireland and the UK; see Hyman, "Industrial Relations in Europe: Theory and Practice" (2005) 1(1) *European Journal of Industrial Relations* 17.

[202] *Ryanair v Labour Court* [2007] 4 IR 199.

[203] As inserted by the Trade Union Act 1942, s 2.

demonstrated that the company's Employee Representative Committee (ERC) was an instrument in place, whereby pilots could enter into collective bargaining negotiations with Ryanair, then it would constitute an excepted body. The purpose of the 1941 Act was to deal with a situation where both employer and employees in a small firm wanted to negotiate terms and conditions in a situation where the employees would not be acting illegally for not having a negotiation licence under the 1941 Act. However, according to the Court, what is required under these statutory provisions is simply that the employer has in place an appropriate system for such negotiations to take place.

It is clear, therefore, from the Supreme Court judgment that employers would be free to **[11–78]** determine the form, structure and organisation of any internal, non-union collective bargaining units, as long as these have a degree of permanency and are not ad hoc. Thus, if an employer were to set up some sort of "Employee Council", it could presumably decide on issues such as how employees would be elected or chosen to be members, the remit of the Council and the terms of office of its members. While the Council would need to operate in a fair and reasonable manner, and this would need to involve a clearly defined set of rules and procedures, the nature and extent of these remain in question, as the Supreme Court did not set down precise rules or offer guidelines for the operation of such a unit.[204] The extent to which the Council would be merely *consultative*, or whether *negotiations* would need to be with a view to reaching agreement on wages and conditions, remains moot.

We will now go on to assess two important (EU mandated) pieces of legislation relating **[11–79]** to the information and consultation of employees, the Transnational Information and Consultation of Employees Act 1996 and the Employees (Provision of Information and Consultation) Act 2006. It should be noted that other statutory obligations to inform and consult with workers arise from the requirements of EU law and we should note the principal pieces of legislation here. The Protection of Employment Act 1977 (as amended by the Protection of Employment Order 1996 and the European Communities (Protection of Employment) Regulations 2000)[205] and the Protection of Employment (Exceptional Collective Redundancies and Related Matters) Act 2007[206] both oblige employers to consult with employee representatives with a view to reaching agreement on how collective redundancies should be effected.[207] The European Communities (Protection of Employees on Transfer of Undertakings) Regulations 2003[208] give effect to the Transfer of Undertakings Directive,[209] which

---

[204] See Doherty, "Representation, Bargaining and the Law: Where Next For the Unions?" (2009) 60(4) NILQ 383; Doherty, "Union Sundown? The Future of Collective Representation Rights in Irish Law'" (2007) 4(4) IELJ 96.

[205] Respectively, SI No 370 of 1996 and SI No 488 of 2000.

[206] Both of which take account of the Consolidated Collective Redundancies Directive; Directive 98/59 of 20 July 1998 on the approximation of the laws of the Member States relating to collective redundancies [1998] OJ L225/98.

[207] See Higgins and McCrann, "Redundancy" in *Employment Law* (Regan ed, Tottel, Dublin, 2009), chapter 15; Cox *et al, op.cit,* p 789 *et seq.*

[208] SI No 131 of 2003.

[209] Directive 2001/23 of 12 March 2001 on the approximation of the laws of the Member States relating to the safeguarding of employees' rights in the event of transfers of undertakings, businesses or parts of undertakings or businesses [2001] OJ L82/01.

requires the appointment of employee representatives for information and consultation purposes in advance of the transfer, or sale as a going concern, of a business.[210] The European Company Statute[211] provides for board-level employee involvement in certain, specified circumstances, while the European Communities (Cross-Border Mergers) Regulations 2008[212] give effect to Directive 2005/56 on cross-border mergers of limited liability companies.[213] Also, the Safety, Health and Welfare at Work Act 2005 requires consultation with employee representatives on various matters relating to health and safety in the workplace.[214]

[11–80]   What is distinctive about virtually all of the above situations where employee involvement is legislatively mandated is that the worker rights are activated in the context of a specific *employer-initiated* event (e.g. redundancy, sale of a business, etc) and therefore information and consultation rights tend to be temporary and ad hoc: what can be termed an "event-driven disclosure model".[215] This model tends to focus on procedural justice in a specific context, is palliative rather than preventative and rights granted under such a model have no continuous impact on the employment relationship. This contrasts with an "agenda-driven disclosure model",[216] whereby the trigger lies within a bargaining/consultation *agenda* and where information and consultation rights cover a range of interlinked issues and involve an ongoing relationship between employers and employees.[217] What we will see, however, in focusing on the legislation outlined below, is an attempt to mandate a general culture of requiring employees to be kept informed about significant developments within the undertaking in which they work.[218]

European Works Councils

[11–81]   The Transnational Information and Consultation of Employees Act 1996 implements the European Works Councils Directive[219] and requires works councils to be set up for information and consultation purposes in specified large, transnational organisations.[220] The Act provides for the establishment of European Works Councils (EWCs)

---

[210] See Byrne, "Transfer of Undertakings" in *Employment Law* (Regan ed, Tottel, Dublin, 2009), chapter 19; Cox *et al, op.cit,* p 789 *et seq,* and chapter 23.

[211] Directive 2001/86 of 8 October 2001 supplementing the Statute for a European company with regard to the involvement of employees [2001] OJ L294/01.

[212] SI No 157 of 2008.

[213] [2005] OJ L310/01.

[214] This Act further implements Directive 89/391 of 12 June 1989 on the introduction of measures to encourage improvements in the safety and health of workers at work [1989] OJ L183/89. See chapter 8.

[215] Gospel *et al,* "A British Dilemma: Disclosure of Information for Collective Bargaining and Joint Consultation" (2003) 22 *Comparative Labour Law and Policy Journal* 327, p 346.

[216] *ibid.*

[217] Doherty, "It's Good to Talk ... Isn't It? Legislating for Information and Consultation in the Irish Workplace" (2008) 15 DULJ 120.

[218] Cox *et al, op.cit,* p 503.

[219] Directive 94/45 of 22 September 1994 on the establishment of a European Works Council or a procedure in Community-scale undertakings and Community-scale groups of undertakings for the purposes of informing and consulting employees [1994] OJ L254/64.

[220] See, generally, Whittall *et al, Towards a European Labour Identity: The Case of the European Works Council* (Routledge, London, 2007); Kerckhofs, *European Works Councils: Facts and Figures* (ETUI, Brussels, 2006).

in multinational companies that have 1000 or more workers and employ at least 150 employees in two or more Member States.[221] The purpose of an EWC is to bring together employee representatives from the different European countries in which a multinational has operations, ensuring that local representatives get the opportunity to engage with both central management and colleagues in other countries and ensuring that these representatives can be informed and consulted by central management on transnational issues of concern to the company's employees.[222] According to the European Trade Union Congress (ETUC), as of May 2008, some 828 (or 34 percent) of the estimated 2,264 companies covered by the legislation had EWCs in operation; as many of these firms are large multinationals, the proportion of employees represented by EWCs is estimated to be much higher (more than 64 percent or 14.5 million workers across Europe).[223] Although, on the face of it, this looks like impressive coverage, research has cast doubts on the how successful the EWC Directive has been in achieving its aims: "an array of factors, particularly language, disagreement over the objectives of such an institution and parochialism, continue to undermine the competence of EWCs".[224] In the Irish context, data shows that, as of June 2005, just 43 Irish-owned companies headquartered in Ireland were covered by the EWC Directive, of which only six had established EWCs: a "compliance rate" of 14 percent, compared with an overall EU average of 35 percent for companies headquartered in respective Member States.[225] Additionally, as Cox *et al* point out, the importance of the EWC legislation has been considerably reduced given the changes introduced by the 2006 Act (discussed below).[226]

The 2006 Act applies to a "Community-scale undertaking", defined as any under-   **[11–82]**
taking with at least 1,000 employees within the Member States and at least 150 employees in each of at least two Member States or a "Community-scale group" of undertakings, defined as a group of undertakings with at least 1,000 employees within the Member States, and at least one group undertaking with at least 150 employees in one Member State and at least one other group undertaking with at least 150 employees in another Member State.[227] The number of employees employed in the undertaking or group of undertakings is calculated as the average number of

---

[221] Note that the location of the headquarters of a multinational (or group) has no influence on the application of the Directive; many companies registered in the US or Japan that meet these criteria are covered by the Directive; Casey et al, "Employee Involvement" in *Employment Law* (Regan ed, Tottel, Dublin, 2009), p 612.

[222] *ibid.*

[223] www.etuc.org.

[224] Whittall *et al*, "The Frontiers Within: Why Employee Representatives Fail to Set Up European Works Councils" (2009) 40(6) *Industrial Relations Journal* 546, p 546. The authors go on to point out that surprisingly "in light of the number of enterprises failing to set up an EWC, currently estimated at around 65 percent...the question of implementation rates has neither played a significant role in the revision of the Directive or for that matter EWC research. In short, the non-implementation of the Directive remains, for whatever reasons, unnavigated territory" (p 547).

[225] Dobbins, "Irish Multinationals have 14% European Works Council Compliance Rate" (2006) 37 IRN.

[226] Cox *et al, op.cit*, p 503.

[227] Transnational Information and Consultation of Employees Act 1996, s 3.

employees, including part-time employees, employed in the undertaking or group of undertakings during the previous two years: part-time employees must have been in the continuous service of an employer for not less than 13 weeks and must normally be expected to work not fewer than eight hours each week.[228]

[11–83] Section 8 of the 1996 Act requires that EWCs, or arrangements for the information and consultation of employees, be established in undertakings or groups of undertakings that fall within its scope. Section 10 provides that central management *may* on its own initiative or *must* at the written request of at least a total of 100 employees or their representatives spread over at least two undertakings or establishments, one or more of which are in one Member State and the other or others of which are in at least one other Member State, establish a "Special Negotiating Body" (SNB).[229] The role of the SNB is to negotiate with central management for the establishment of a European Employees' Forum or an information and consultation procedure. An SNB shall have not fewer than three but not more than 17 elected or appointed members.[230] The main function of the SNB is to negotiate with central management for a written agreement for the establishment of arrangements for the information and consultation of employees.[231] This agreement may provide for the establishment of a European Employees' Forum or the parties may agree to establish one or more information and consultation procedures but, either way, the agreement must specify[232]:

    a.   the undertakings or establishments of the Community-scale undertaking covered by the agreement;

    b.   the duration of the agreement and the procedure for its re-negotiation, and

    c.   the method for transmitting information to employees and for relaying their opinions back to central management.

[11–84] Where an agreement requires the establishment of a European Employees' Forum, it must also specify: the composition of the Forum; the number of members; the allocation of seats and the term of office; the functions and the procedure for information and consultation of the Forum; the venue, frequency and duration of meetings of the Forum; and the financial and other resources to be allocated to the Forum. Where an agreement requires the establishment of another type of information and consultation procedure, it must also specify: what that procedure shall be; the issues for information and consultation; the methods according to which the

---

[228] Transnational Information and Consultation of Employees Act 1996, s 4.

[229] s 6 of the Act exempts from its scope undertakings or groups of undertakings that, at the date of commencement of the Act (22 September 1996), had a subsisting and valid pre-existing agreement in place, covering the entire workforce, that provided for the transnational information and consultation of employees.

[230] Although extra members are to be added depending on the percentage of employees employed in particular Member States; Transnational Information and Consultation of Employees Act 1996, ss 10(4)(b-c). Members are to be elected or appointed by employees, or by central management on a basis agreed with employees; s 14.

[231] Transnational Information and Consultation of Employees Act 1996, s 11. s 11(7) provides that the reasonable expenses relating to the negotiations are to be borne by central management so as to enable the SNB to carry out its functions in an appropriate manner.

[232] Transnational Information and Consultation of Employees Act 1996, s 12(3).

employees' representatives in the different Member States can meet for exchange of views regarding the information conveyed to them; and the financial and other resources to be allocated to ensure the operation of the procedure and the holding of meetings.[233]

Where neither a European Employees' Forum nor a different procedure under s 12 has **[11–85]** been established, an EWC will be formed. This can be where central management and the SNB so agree or, by default, where central management refuses to commence negotiations within six months of a request to do so or where, after the expiration of a period of three years from the date of the request, the parties are unable to conclude an agreement.[234] The rules and procedures for the establishment and operation of an EWC are set out in the Second Schedule to the Act. This grants the EWC the right to meet with central management once a year in order to be informed and consulted on the progress of the business of the undertaking or group of undertakings and its prospects. In particular, information and consultation should focus on: the structure, economic and financial situation and probable trends in employment, investments and substantial changes concerning the organisation; the introduction of new working methods or production processes; the transfer of production, mergers, cutbacks or closures of undertakings, establishments or important parts thereof; and collective redundancies. Where there are exceptional circumstances affecting the employees' interests to a considerable extent, particularly in the event of relocation, the closure of establishments or undertakings or collective redundancies, either the EWC or a select committee has the right to be informed and the right to meet central management so as to be informed and consulted on measures significantly affecting employees' interests.[235] Section 15 of the 1996 Act obliges all parties not to reveal confidential information and central management may withhold commercially sensitive information, *inter alia*, where it can be shown that disclosure would be likely to prejudice significantly and adversely the economic or financial position of an undertaking or group of undertakings. Section 17 provides that employees' representatives who perform functions in accordance with the Act shall not be dismissed or suffer any unfavourable change in their conditions of employment or any unfair treatment, including selection for redundancy, or suffer any other action prejudicial to their employment because of their status or reasonable activities as employees' representatives.[236]

In 2009, a recast of the EWC Directive[237] was agreed, "mainly in response to a few **[11–86]** high-profile cases in which the EWC appeared ineffective, such as Renault (Vilvoorde,

---

[233] Transnational Information and Consultation of Employees Act 1996, ss 12(4) and (5).

[234] Transnational Information and Consultation of Employees Act 1996, s 13.

[235] Transnational Information and Consultation of Employees Act 1996, Second Schedule.

[236] Transnational Information and Consultation of Employees Act 1996, s 17. The section also provides that such representatives shall be afforded such reasonable facilities, including time off, as will enable them to carry out their functions promptly and efficiently.

[237] Directive 2009/38 of 6 May 2009 on the establishment of a European Works Council or a procedure in Community-scale undertakings and Community-scale groups of undertakings for the purposes of informing and consulting employees [2009] OJ L122/28. The Directive should be transposed by the Member States by June 2011.

Belgium) and Nokia (Bochum, Germany), plus the need to accommodate the geographical expansion of the European Union (EU) eastwards".[238] The Directive aims, in particular, to: enhance the effectiveness of employees' transnational information and consultation rights; resolve legal uncertainties and problems in the practical application of the Directive; and harmonise the EWC Directive with other recent directives on employee representation. So, for example, a definition of information is introduced and the meaning of consultation is clarified and a right to paid training is introduced for EWC members.[239] Whether the amendments made will be effective in strengthening the rights of affected workers to information and consultation remains to be seen.[240]

Information and Consultation at Work: The 2006 Act

[11–87] Although the 1996 Act and EWC Directive did seek to move beyond information and consultation rights tied to the event-driven disclosure model outlined above, the Act only affected employees working in multinational companies. Despite its enactment, legally grounded employee rights to information and consultation, or to input into organisational decision-making, in Ireland remained rather limited. In this context, the passing, in 2002, of the Information and Consultation Directive[241] opened up the possibility of considerable adjustment to the Irish model of industrial relations.[242] The Directive contains a general framework setting out minimum requirements for employee rights to information and consultation. Article 4 requires that employees have rights to: *information* on the recent and probable development of the undertaking or establishment's activities and economic situation; rights to be *informed and consulted* on the situation, structure and probable development of employment within the undertaking or establishment and on any anticipatory measures envisaged, in particular, where there is a threat to employment; and a right to be *informed and consulted* on decisions likely to lead to substantial changes in work organisation or in contractual relations, *with a view to reaching agreement*.[243] The Directive was to be implemented by the Member States by March 2005 but for countries with no "general, permanent and statutory" system of information and consultation or employee representation (essentially Ireland and the UK) a phased introduction was permitted, with full application by March 2008.

---

[238] Whittall *et al*, "The Frontiers Within: Why Employee Representatives Fail to Set Up European Works Councils" (2009) 40(6) *Industrial Relations Journal* 546, p 546.

[239] Arts 2 and 10, respectively, of Directive 2009/38.

[240] See Laulom, "The Flawed Revision of the European Works Councils Directive" (2010) 32(9) ILJ 202.

[241] Directive 2002/14 of 11 March 2002 establishing a general framework for informing and consulting employees in the European Community [2002] OJ L80/02.

[242] See Hayes, "Informing and Consulting Employees-Irish and EU Developments" (2005) 2 IELJ 89; Sissen, *op.cit*, Ewing and Truter, "The Information and Consultation of Employees Regulations: Voluntarism's Bitter Legacy" (2005) 68 MLR 626.

[243] In Case C-188/03 *Wolfgang Kühnel v Junk* [2005] ECR I-885, the ECJ, in the context of the collective redundancies legislation, held that consultation "imposes an obligation to negotiate" and emphasised that consultation "with a view to reaching agreement" involves the possibility of compromise and change (at paras 43-44); see O' Mara, "Calling Time on Collective Dismissals-the Junk Case" (2005) 2 IELJ 68.

The Employees (Provision of Information and Consultation) Act 2006 came into force   **[11–88]**
for undertakings[244] with at least 150 employees from 4 September 2006, for
undertakings with at least 100 employees from 23 March 2007 and for undertakings
with at least 50 employees from 23 March 2008.[245] The legislation, therefore, only
applies to employees working in organisations with at least 50 employees. Some
concern has been expressed in the UK about the exclusion of businesses with as many
as, for example, 40 or 45 employees[246] and this is especially relevant for Ireland, where
there are well in excess of 200,000 small and medium enterprises, which typically each
employ 27 people (and about half the national workforce in total).[247] An "employee" is
defined in s 2 as someone "who has entered into or works under a contract of
employment" and does not explicitly cover agency workers or others engaged in
"atypical work". Under s 1 of the Act, "information" is defined as the transmission by
the employer to one or more employees or their representatives (or both) of data in
order to enable them to acquaint themselves with the subject matter and to examine it;
"consultation" means the exchange of views and establishment of dialogue between the
employer and either one or more employees or the employees' representative(s). The
Act provides for three types of information and consultation agreements but,
significantly, rights under the Act must be "triggered".[248] Section 7 provides that the
employer may initiate negotiations or employees may request negotiations with the
employer to establish information and consultation arrangements. The employer is
only obliged to set up information and consultation structures where requested to do
so by 10 percent of the workforce, subject to a minimum of 15 employees and a
maximum of 100 employees.[249] There is no obligation on the employer to be proactive
in establishing information and consultation structures.[250] Where an application is
made to the employer for the establishment of information and consultation
arrangements to be put in place and the 10 percent threshold is not met (that is,
where an insufficient number of employees support the request) two years must pass
before a further request can be made.[251] It should also be noted that while the

---

[244] The Directive offered a choice to Member States of applying its requirements to
"undertakings" employing at least 50 employees or "establishments" employing at least 20
employees. An "undertaking" is defined as a public or private undertaking carrying out an
economic activity, whether or not operating for gain; Employees (Provision of Information and
Consultation) Act 2006, s 2.

[245] Employees (Provision of Information and Consultation) Act 2006, s 4.

[246] Ewing and Truter, *op.cit.*

[247] See http://www.skillsireland.ie/press/reports/pdf/egfsn060512_sme_report_webopt.pdf. Note
that the obligation to negotiate with employee representatives under the collective redundancies
legislation applies to companies with 20 or more employees; Protection of Employment Act 1977,
s 6(a) (as amended).

[248] Doherty, "Hard Law, Soft Edge? Information, Consultation and Partnership" (2008) 30(6)
Employee Relations 603, p 615.

[249] Employees (Provision of Information and Consultation) Act 2006, s 7(2).

[250] Therefore, where employers do not initiate the process it seems employees may have to fight
to secure rights under the Act. In non-union workplaces (or, indeed, where unions do not
promote the legislation) it seems unlikely many employees will be aware of their rights; Doherty,
"It's Good to Talk...Isn't It? Legislating for Information and Consultation in the Irish
Workplace" (2008) 15 DULJ 120, p 127. Indeed, Hayes has argued that the Directive itself does
not support the introduction of this "trigger mechanism"; Hayes, *op.cit*, p 93.

[251] Employees (Provision of Information and Consultation) Act 2006, s 7(8).

legislation contains protection against victimisation for employee representatives,[252] it is silent on protection for those seeking to establish arrangements.

[11–89]　As noted, provision is made for three types of information and consultation agreements. *Pre-existing agreements* allow employers and employees and/or their representatives to customise information and consultation arrangements, either through the retention of existing arrangements or the establishment of new arrangements, prior to the date the Act comes into force for the relevant undertaking.[253] Such agreements must be in writing and available for inspection by employees.[254] The agreement must be approved by a majority of voting employees, (or through some other agreed mechanism)[255] but, again, only where rights under the Act are "triggered" and may be for a specified term or open-ended.[256] The agreement must make reference to: duration and procedures for renegotiation (if applicable); the subjects for information and consultation; the method and timeframe by which information is to be provided and by which consultation is to be conducted (including, in both cases, whether this is to be directly or through representatives, see below); and the procedure for dealing with confidential information.[257] Section 8 provides for *negotiated agreements* (following an employee request or an employer's initiative), providing the employer and the employees and/or their representatives with the opportunity to devise their own tailor-made information and consultation agreement through negotiations. The agreement must be approved by a majority of voting employees or their representatives elected or appointed under the Act or through some other agreed mechanism.[258] The agreements must make reference to the same issues as those outlined above in respect of pre-existing agreements.[259]

[11–90]　Both of these agreements fall some way short of the "Standard Rules" provisions of section 7, which, arguably, embody more accurately the spirit of the Directive.[260] This is a fallback position for setting up an information and consultation arrangement where the employer refuses to enter into negotiations or where the parties have entered into negotiations but cannot reach agreement within the specified time limit.[261] The key element in the Standard Rules is the establishment of an Information and Consultation Forum. Ballots for election to the Forum are to be organised by the employer[262] or, in the absence of elections, representatives are to be appointed by employees by means of a

---

[252] *ibid*, s 13.

[253] *ibid*, s 9.

[254] *ibid*, s 9(2).

[255] *ibid*, s 9(3).

[256] *ibid*, s 9(5).

[257] *ibid*, s 9(7). Although some commentators (see Connolly, "Consultation With Employees" (2004) 1 IELJ 36) had expressed the view that the publication of the draft legislation would lead to many employers commencing the process of preparing a consultation agreement applicable to the needs of the local enterprise, this did not, in fact, happen to any appreciable extent; Dobbins, "Unions Hold Workshops on Consultation Law" (2007) 25 IRN.

[258] Employees (Provision of Information and Consultation) Act 2006, s 8(3).

[259] *ibid*, s 8(5).

[260] Hall, "Assessing the Information and Consultation of Employees Regulations" (2005) 34 ILJ 103.

[261] This limit is six months, but this can be extended by agreement between the parties; Employees (Provision of Information and Consultation) Act 2006, ss 7(6) and (7).

[262] Employees (Provision of Information and Consultation) Act 2006, Schedule 2.

procedure agreed with the employer.[263] This Forum (detailed procedural rules for which are laid out in Schedule 1 to the Act) would meet at least twice a year, would be resourced by the employer[264] and, as such, would approximate in many ways a works council-type arrangement. Information must be supplied by the employer at the time, in the fashion and with the content appropriate to enable the Forum to prepare for consultation. Unlike agreements under ss 8 and 9, the subjects for information and consultation are specified as including:

a. information on the recent and probable development of the undertaking's activities and economic situation;
b. information and consultation on the situation, structure and probable development of employment within the undertaking and on any anticipatory measures envisaged, in particular where there is a threat to employment;
c. information and consultation on decisions likely to lead to substantial changes in work organisation or in contractual relations...

Furthermore, the Standard Rules explicitly require the engagement by the employer with employee representatives and rule out the "direct involvement" systems provided for in s 11. This section provides that, for both negotiated and pre-existing agreements, employees may receive information and consultation either through representatives *or* directly.[265] To make a change from a system of direct involvement to one involving representatives, at least 10 percent of employees who operate under the direct involvement system in the undertaking are required to make a written request to the employer or to the Labour Court.[266] Any change must then be approved by a majority of the employees who operate under the direct involvement system.[267] The inclusion of a direct involvement procedure has been criticised as being out of step with the spirit, if not the letter, of the Directive, which seems to promote a more process-driven, trust-based and representative model of employee voice.[268] Practically speaking, it is also difficult to see how a meaningful exchange of views and dialogue (the essence of consultation) can take place, or agreement be reached, *directly* in a medium or large-sized organisation.[269]

[11–91]

---

[263] Employees (Provision of Information and Consultation) Act 2006, Schedule 1.

[264] In one of only two recommendations made by the Labour Court under the Act (at the time of writing), the Court considered, in *Nortel (Ireland) Limited v Information and Consultation Forum Nortel (Ireland) Limited* (RIC 101/2010), what type of expenses an employer was bound to bear under the terms of the legislation. In the instant case, the Court decided that the employer was not bound to bear certain costs incurred by the Forum in obtaining legal advice on employment related issues.

[265] For example, by way of email or through face-to-face meetings with individual employees; Doherty, "It's Good to Talk...Isn't It? Legislating for Information and Consultation in the Irish Workplace" (2008) 15 DULJ 120, p 129.

[266] Employees (Provision of Information and Consultation) Act 2006, s 11(2).

[267] *ibid*, s 11(4).

[268] Doherty, "It's Good to Talk...Isn't It? Legislating for Information and Consultation in the Irish Workplace" (2008) 15 DULJ 120, p 130. The clause has become known as the "Intel clause" as it is rumoured to have been furiously lobbied for by the American Chamber of Commerce Ireland on behalf of US multinationals based in the country; Doherty, "Hard Law, Soft Edge? Information, Consultation and Partnership" (2008) 30(6) *Employee Relations* 603, p 618.

[269] See Hayes, *op.cit*, p 96.

[11–92] Section 6 of the Act defines employees' representatives as employees of the undertaking, elected or appointed for the purposes of the Act. The employer is obliged to arrange for the election or appointment of representatives.[270] Where it is the practice of the employer to conduct collective bargaining negotiations with a trade union or excepted body that represents 10 percent or more of the employees in the undertaking, the Act provides that employees who are members of that trade union or excepted body are entitled to elect or appoint from amongst their members one, or more than one, employees' representative(s).[271] The parties themselves can determine the overall number of representatives except in relation to the Standard Rules, which prescribe the number of representatives allowed in relation to the Information and Consultation Forum.[272] This is one area where the Irish trade unions have fared better than their UK counterparts as, unlike in the UK, the Irish legislation does grant a privileged position to workplace representatives of recognised trade unions. However, the definition of employee representatives does not seem to allow any role for external union officials (as is provided for by the legislation on European Works Councils)[273] nor does it seem to allow for external expert assistance when the original information and consultation arrangements are negotiated. Employee representatives are entitled to "reasonable facilities, including time off" to fulfil their functions. [274]

[11–93] Section 14 imposes an obligation of confidence on employee representatives and participants in information and consultation arrangements in relation to the disclosure of confidential information. The employer is not required to disclose information or undertake consultation where to do so would seriously harm the functioning of the undertaking or be prejudicial to the undertaking.[275] Disputes as to how information is classified are to be referred to the Labour Court and, in coming to a decision, the Court may be assisted by a panel of experts.[276] The interpretation of what is to be classed as confidential is likely to be crucial in determining the parameters of the legislation and its practical impact in terms of employee involvement in the enterprise.[277]

[11–94] The legislation is to be policed by inspectors with wide-ranging powers of entry and examination and failure to comply with the requests or direction of such an inspector is an offence.[278] Disputes concerning negotiations for an information and consultation

---

[270] Employees (Provision of Information and Consultation) Act 2006, s 6(2).

[271] *ibid*, s 6(3). This is to be done on a pro-rata basis with other elected or appointed representatives; s 6(4). Note that, in *Ryanair v Labour Court* [2007] 4 IR 199, the Supreme Court ruled that where an employer has an internal, non-union collective bargaining unit in place, which has a degree of permanency and is not ad hoc, this unit could constitute an "excepted body". Therefore its members could have rights to sit in any alternate information and consultation forum; see Doherty, "Union Sundown? The Future of Collective Representation Rights in Irish Law" (2007) 4 IELJ 96 and Cox *et al, op.cit,* p 493.

[272] The Forum shall have at least 3 but not more than 30 members; Employees (Provision of Information and Consultation) Act 2006, Schedule 1.

[273] Transnational Information and Consultation of Employees Act 1996, s 3.

[274] Employees (Provision of Information and Consultation) Act 2006, s 13.

[275] *ibid*, s 14(4).

[276] *ibid*, s 15(8).

[277] Doherty, "It's Good to Talk...Isn't It? Legislating for Information and Consultation in the Irish Workplace" (2008) 15 DULJ 120, p 132.

[278] Employees (Provision of Information and Consultation) Act 2006, s 18.

agreement under ss 8 or 10, the interpretation or operation of agreements under ss 8, 9, and 10 or the interpretation or operation of a direct involvement system under s 11 are to be referred to the Labour Court.[279] Such referrals are to be made only once internal dispute resolution procedures have failed to resolve the dispute and the matter has been referred to the Labour Relations Commission.[280] Disputes relating to matters of confidentiality under s 14 are also to be referred to the Labour Court[281] and any determination can be enforced through the Circuit Court.[282] In terms of criminal sanctions for those in breach of the legislation,[283] the Act provides for fines of up to €3,000 and/or a prison sentence of up to six months for a summary conviction and fines of up to €30,000 and/or a prison sentence of up to 36 months for a conviction on indictment. There has been some concern as to the extent to which the penalties provided for can be said to be "effective, proportionate and dissuasive", as required by the Directive.[284] The first draft of the Directive provided for injunctive relief where employers proceeded with decisions in breach of their obligations but this was removed from the final version.[285] It is questionable whether a fine of €30,000 would be "dissuasive" to a medium, or large, sized organisation (it stretches credibility to think it might be so in the case of a large multinational, for example) and such a fine, in any case, would only apply in respect of the most serious of breaches. There is no provision in the Irish Act for the compensation of *employees* affected by an employer's breach of the legislation. To date, only two recommendations have been made by the Labour Court under the legislation.[286]

The transposition of the 2002 Directive has disappointed many who had felt it might plug the "voluntarist gaps" in the Irish IR system and grant robust collective involvement and participation rights to Irish employees.[287] Several particular problems have been noted, for example, the requirement for employees to trigger rights, the exclusion from the scope of the law of many organisations and certain categories of employee, the lack of protection given to those seeking to establish information and consultation arrangements, the provision for direct involvement systems and the question mark over the adequacy of penalty provisions. As a result, since the Act came into force, there has not been much evidence of activity in relation to it; it seems that most employers to date have, at best, adopted a strategy of "risk assessment" rather than active compliance.[288]

[11–95]

---

[279] *ibid*, s 15(1).

[280] *ibid*, s 15(2).

[281] *ibid*, s 15(4).

[282] *ibid*, s 17.

[283] Primarily employers, but also those who breach confidentiality requirements.

[284] See Case C-382-92 *Commission v United Kingdom* [1994] ECR I-2435, where the ECJ found the existing UK regime for consultation of employees in the case of collective redundancies to be inadequate.

[285] Ewing and Truter, *op.cit*, p 634.

[286] *Health Service Executive v Health Service Staff Panel* (RIC 081/2008) and *Nortel (Ireland) Limited v Information and Consultation Forum Nortel (Ireland) Limited* (RIC 101/2010).

[287] Doherty, "Hard Law, Soft Edge? Information, Consultation and Partnership" (2008) 30(6) *Employee Relations* 603, p 618.

[288] Hall, *op.cit*, p 124.

CHAPTER 12
Remedies

I. Introduction: "Regular" and "Specialist" Remedies

As has been noted throughout this book, employment law is a quite distinctive area of law in that it derives from a considerable number of sources (both formal and informal) and the balance between these various sources is continuously changing.[1] This reflects the reality that the employer-employee relationship itself is one that is constantly developing, often in response to prevailing labour market, economic and societal trends. A significant factor that contributes to the complexity of employment law is the fact that, in addition to the regular courts, there is a variety of specific institutions and tribunals that deal with claims relating to employment disputes.[2] As there is a multiplicity of fora to which claims may be brought, it can be very difficult for all but the most experienced practitioners to navigate a path through the maze of potential employment law remedies. The employment relationship is primarily founded on contract and, as a result, traditional principles of contract law apply. Employees and employers also, of course, enjoy the same rights of access to the courts of the land under Art 40.3 of the Constitution as do all potential litigants.[3] Therefore, many employment claims will proceed through the "regular" courts as "regular" cases. A claim for wrongful dismissal, for example, will proceed as an ordinary, common law claim for breach of contract and the usual rules of court will apply.[4] Furthermore, as noted in chapter 2, where an issue of European Union law is in question, the Irish courts and tribunals may wish to, or be required to, refer the matter to the European Court of Justice under Art 267TFEU (ex-Art 234EC). A ruling of the ECJ on the interpretation or application of any provision of EU law is binding on all national courts and tribunals.[5] However, the Irish legislature has also established a specific institutional framework for the resolution of particular employment disputes and has prescribed that certain "specialist" remedies will apply in specific employment dispute contexts.

[12–01]

---

[1] Regan, "Sources and Institutions" in *Employment Law* (Regan ed, Tottel, Dublin, 2009), p 3.

[2] See chapter 2.

[3] *Tuohy v Courtney* [1994] 3 IR 1.

[4] See, generally, Enright, *Principles of Irish Contract Law* (Clarus Press, Dublin, 2007); Stewart and Dunleavy, *Compensation on Dismissal* (FirstLaw, Dublin, 2007), chapter 9.

[5] See Craig and de Búrca, *EU Law: Text, Cases and Materials* (4th ed, Oxford University Press, Oxford, 2008), chapter 13.

[12–02] This chapter will examine some of the principal remedies that are available to claimants in employment law disputes. It is not the intention here to provide an exhaustive guide to every possible remedy that could be sought for every possible breach of employment law, which would be an improbable, if not impossible, task. Instead, the focus will be on the primary remedies that can be granted in the areas focused on in earlier chapters.[6] The next section, therefore, will look at the main remedies laid down by the relevant legislation applicable to areas of the employment relationship described in chapters 3-11.[7] Readers will find it useful to refer back to the relevant chapters when considering the remedies described. The description of the role and functions of the various employment law tribunals, as well as the practice and procedure before them, outlined in chapter 2, should also be noted. The final section of this chapter will look in more detail at a relatively recent development in employment litigation, which is the increasing use of what has become known as the "employment injunction".

II. Legislative Remedies

The Employment Relationship: Fixed-Term and Part-Time Workers

[12–03] In 1997, the Part-Time Workers Directive was adopted[8] and subsequently transposed into Irish law by means of the Protection of Employees (Part-Time Work) Act 2001. The Directive and the Act have the twofold aim of providing for the removal of discrimination against part-time workers and improving the quality of part-time work. Similarly, the Fixed-Term Workers Directive,[9] transposed into Irish law by means of the Protection of Employees (Fixed-Term Work) Act 2003, aimed to improve the quality of fixed-term work by ensuring the application of the principle of non-discrimination and establishing a framework to prevent abuse arising from the use of successive fixed-term employment contracts or relationships. As the remedies granted under both pieces of legislation are similar, and many common principles apply, they can be considered together here.

[12–04] Disputes under the Acts can be referred by an employee (or a trade union of which he or she is a member) to a Rights Commissioner within six months of the date of the contravention of the Act. This period may be extended by a further 12 months where the Commissioner is satisfied that the failure to present the complaint within that period was due to "reasonable cause".[10] It is for the claimant to establish the reasonable cause justifying the delay; the length of the delay and any possible

---

[6] As this chapter is concerned with "specific" employment law remedies, the various remedies that can be pursued in common law claims (in the "regular" courts) will not be examined in any detail.

[7] This chapter will largely discuss remedies relating to *individual* claims; the specialist nature of collective law remedies is discussed throughout chapter 11.

[8] Directive 97/81 of 15 December 1997 concerning the Framework Agreement on part-time work concluded by ETUC, UNICE and CEEP [1997] OJ L14/9.

[9] Directive 1999/70 of 28 June 1999 concerning the framework agreement on fixed-term work concluded by ETUC, UNICE and CEEP [1999] OJ L175/43.

[10] Protection of Employees (Part-Time Work) Act 2001, ss 16(3) and (4); Protection of Employees (Fixed-Term Work) Act 2003, ss 14(3) and (4).

prejudicial effects on the other party, as well as the conduct of the latter, will be important factors.[11]

A decision of the Rights Commissioner can do one or more of the following: declare that the complaint was, or was not, well founded; require the employer to comply with the relevant provision of the Act; and/or require the employer to pay the employee compensation that is just and equitable having regard to all the circumstances, but not exceeding two years' remuneration.[12] Additionally, under s 14(2)(c) of the 2003 Act, the Rights Commissioner can require the employer to re-instate or re-engage the employee (including on a contract of indefinite duration).[13]

[12–05]

Either party can appeal to the Labour Court within six weeks of the date of the Rights Commissioner's decision for a legally binding determination.[14] A further appeal, on a point of law only, to the High Court is permitted and the determination of the High Court is "final and conclusive".[15] The Superior Courts have traditionally been extremely reluctant to overturn decisions of specialist tribunals, such as the Labour Court, and will only do so where such a decision is based on a mistake in law or the drawing of inferences so unreasonable that no reasonable decision maker would have arrived at that decision.[16] This was emphasised by Hamilton CJ in *Henry Denny and Sons (Ireland) Limited v Minister for Social Welfare,*[17] where he stated that it:

[12–06]

"...should be recognised that (where) tribunals which have been given statutory tasks to perform and exercise their functions, as is now usually the case, with a high degree of expertise and provide coherent and balanced judgments on the evidence and arguments heard by them it should not be necessary for the courts to review their decisions by way of appeal or judicial review."

It should also be noted that "save in the most exceptional circumstances" the High Court, on appeal from the Labour Court, will neither entertain arguments nor give consideration to a point which had not been taken in the Labour Court and in respect of which the respondent had not been given an opportunity to rebut.[18] In *National University of Ireland Cork v Ahern*[19] the Supreme Court accepted that, as a general

[12–07]

---

[11] *Minister for Finance v CPSU* [2007] ELR 36.

[12] Protection of Employees (Part-Time Work) Act 2001, s 16(2); Protection of Employees (Fixed-Term Work) Act 2003, s 14(2).

[13] The remedies of "re-instatement" and "re-engagement" will be discussed further below.

[14] Protection of Employees (Part-Time Work) Act 2001, s 17; Protection of Employees (Fixed-Term Work) Act 2003, s 15. In *Bus Eireann v SIPTU* (PTD 8/2004) the Labour Court held that a "decision" in this context referred to "a complete or final decision, which determines whether or not there has been an infringement of the Act"; the Court, did, however, consider that there may exceptionally be questions of "pure law" that require to be determined on appeal by the Labour Court as a preliminary point.

[15] Protection of Employees (Part-Time Work) Act 2001, s 17(6); Protection of Employees (Fixed-Term Work) Act 2003, s 15(6).

[16] *Russell v Mount Temple Comprehensive School* [2009] IEHC 533.

[17] [1998] 1 IR 34 at 37.

[18] *Russell v Mount Temple Comprehensive School* [2009] IEHC 533. See also *Minister for Finance v McArdle* [2007] 2 ILRM 438.

[19] [2005] 2 IR 577.

principle, matters of fact as found by the Labour Court must be accepted by the superior courts. However, the Supreme Court held that the *basis upon which* the Labour Court found certain facts (for example, the relevance or admissibility of the matters relied on by the Labour Court in determining the facts) is a question of law, which can be examined on appeal.

[12–08] Where a decision of a Rights Commissioner in relation to a complaint under the Acts has not been carried out by the employer concerned in accordance with its terms, the time for bringing an appeal against the decision has expired and no such appeal has been brought, the employee may bring the complaint before the Labour Court and the Labour Court, without hearing the employer concerned or any further evidence, shall make a determination to the like effect as the Rights Commissioner's decision.[20] Similarly, where an employer fails to carry out in accordance with its terms a determination of the Labour Court, the Circuit Court shall, on application to it by either the employee, the employee's trade union, or the Minister, and without hearing the employer or any further evidence, make an order directing the employer to carry out the determination in accordance with its terms.[21]

[12–09] Redress for claims for penalisation amounting to dismissal cannot be granted under both the 2001 Act and the unfair dismissals legislation[22] and recovery cannot be granted under both the 2001 Act and the equality legislation.[23] Similarly, relief cannot be granted under both the 2003 Act and the unfair dismissals legislation in the event of penalisation resulting in dismissal.[24] Neither can recovery be granted under both the 2003 Act and the equality legislation.[25] Where the employee is *both* a part-time worker under the 2001 Act *and* a fixed-term worker under the 2003 Act, recovery cannot be granted under both pieces of legislation in respect of complaints arising from the same circumstances.[26] As Kerr points out, given that both pieces of legislation are concerned with the principle of "non-discrimination", it may have been more appropriate to

---

[20] Protection of Employees (Part-Time Work) Act 2001, s 17(8); Protection of Employees (Fixed-Term Work) Act 2003, s 15(8).

[21] Protection of Employees (Part-Time Work) Act 2001, s 18; Protection of Employees (Fixed-Term Work) Act 2003, s 16. Note that the formulation of how orders are to be enforced outlined here is repeated throughout the various pieces of employment legislation discussed in this chapter; as a result where "enforcement" of a decision is referred to below, this should be taken to refer to a situation where a decision of a court or tribunal in relation to a complaint has not been carried out by the employer concerned in accordance with its terms, the time for bringing an appeal against the decision has expired and no such appeal has been brought, the employee may bring the complaint before a specified higher court or tribunal, which will, without hearing the employer concerned or any further evidence, make a determination to the like effect as the initial decision.

[22] Protection of Employees (Part-Time Work) Act 2001, s 15(3).

[23] Employment Equality Act 1998, s 101.

[24] Protection of Employees (Fixed-Term Work) Act 2003, s 18(1). Note that there seems to be no bar to an employee bringing a common law claim for dismissal.

[25] Employment Equality Act 1998, s 101A. However, there does not appear to be anything to prevent two separate claims being *processed* under the equality legislation and either the 2001 or 2003 Act. The prohibition appears to relate to "double recovery"; see Ryan, "Fixed-Term Workers" in *Employment Law* (Regan ed, Tottel, Dublin, 2009), p 334.

[26] Protection of Employees (Fixed-Term Work) Act 2003, s 18(2).

provide for complaints to be referred to the Director of the Equality Tribunal in the first instance.[27] It is perhaps unfortunate that this option was not exercised.

The Employment Contract

As noted in chapter 4, the Terms of Employment (Information) Act 1994 puts certain obligations on employers that relate to, first, the provision of a written statement of the terms and conditions of employment, secondly, the notification of changes to terms and conditions of employment and, thirdly, situations where the employee is required to work outside the state. Complaints by employees under the Act are to be referred to a Rights Commissioner.[28] A Rights Commissioner shall not entertain a complaint if it is presented more than six months after the date of termination of the employment concerned.[29] A decision of the Rights Commissioner can do one or more of the following: declare that the complaint was, or was not, well founded; confirm all or any of the particulars contained or referred to in any statement furnished by the employer or alter or add to any such statement in order to correct inaccuracies or omissions; require the employer to give to the employee concerned a written statement containing such particulars as may be specified by the Commissioner; and/or require the employer to pay the employee compensation that is just and equitable having regard to all the circumstances, but not exceeding four weeks' remuneration.[30] The parties have a right to appeal the Rights Commissioner's recommendation to the Employment Appeals Tribunal within six weeks of the date on which the recommendation was communicated to the party in question.[31] There is a further right of appeal to the High Court from a determination of the Tribunal on a point of law and the determination of the High Court shall be final and conclusive.[32] Decisions of a Rights Commissioner in relation to a complaint under the Acts may be enforced by the EAT[33] and determinations of the EAT may be enforced, on application to it by either the employee, the employee's trade union or the Minister, by the District Court.[34]

[12–10]

Pay and Working Time

Enforcement of the provisions of the Payment of Wages Act 1991 occurs at both a civil and criminal level.[35] In the civil context, an employee may bring a complaint to a Rights Commissioner that his or her employer has contravened s 5 of the Act (regulating deductions from pay).[36] The complaint must be brought within six months from the date of the contravention of s 5: this period can be extended by a further six

[12–11]

---

[27] Kerr, *Employment Rights Legislation* (2nd ed, Round Hall, Dublin, 2006), p H-74.

[28] Terms of Employment (Information) Act 1994, s 7(1).

[29] *ibid*, s 7(3). This means that there is no time limit for bringing a complaint while the employee is still employed by the employer. Cox *et al* note that there is no provision as things stand for the Rights Commissioner to extend the time limits and deal with cases outside the six-month time period; Cox *et al*, *Employment Law in Ireland* (Clarus Press, Dublin, 2009), p 116.

[30] Terms of Employment (Information) Act 1994, s 7(2).

[31] *ibid*, ss 8(1-2).

[32] *ibid*, s 8(3).

[33] *ibid*, s 8(6).

[34] *ibid*, s 9.

[35] Cox *et al*, *op.cit*, p 438. Note that the enforcement of pay provisions in the collective context (Registered Employment Agreements, for example) is discussed in chapter 11.

[36] The issue of unlawful deductions from pay is also discussed in chapter 4.

months, if the Rights Commissioner is satisfied that exceptional circumstances prevented the presentation of the complaint within the prescribed period.[37] Proceedings will generally be held in public. Where the Rights Commissioner decides that the complaint is well-founded, he or she shall order the employer to pay to the employee compensation of such amount (if any) as he or she thinks reasonable in the circumstances. However, this will not exceed the net amount of the wages (after any lawful deduction has been made) that would have been paid to the employee in respect of the week immediately preceding the date of the deduction if the deduction had not been made (or, as the case may be, the payment to the employer had not been made). If the amount of the deduction or payment is greater than the net amount of the wages, the Rights Commissioner cannot order the employer to pay more than double the amount of the deduction or payment.[38] The parties have a right to appeal the Rights Commissioner's recommendation to the EAT within six weeks of the date on which the recommendation was communicated to the party in question.[39] There is a further right of appeal to the High Court from a determination of the Tribunal on a point of law and the determination of the High Court shall be final and conclusive.[40] Under s 8 of the 1991 Act, a decision of a Rights Commissioner, or a determination of the Tribunal, may be enforced as if it were an order of the Circuit Court made in civil proceedings.

[12–12]   There is a number of provisions in the 1991 Act that provide for summary criminal offences. In particular, it is an offence under s 2 to pay wages to an employee otherwise than by a mode specified in that section and an offence for an employer not to comply with s 4, which requires a statement in writing to be given to the employee specifying clearly the amount of the wages payable and the nature and amount of any deduction therefrom. The Minister may appoint an "authorised officer" to monitor the enforcement of the legislation and it is an offence to obstruct or impede an authorised officer in the exercise of his or her powers.[41] Proceedings for offences under the Act may be brought and prosecuted by the Minister and must be instituted within 12 months from the date of the offence.[42]

[12–13]   The means of enforcement of the National Minimum Wage Act 2000 also have both civil and criminal aspects. Under s 24 of the Act, where an employee and an employer cannot agree on the appropriate entitlement to pay of the employee in accordance with the Act, resulting in an alleged under-payment to the employee, either party (or a representative of either of them) may refer the dispute to a Rights Commissioner. Such a referral cannot be made unless the employee either obtained a statement of his or her average hourly rate of pay in respect of the relevant pay reference period under s 23 of the Act, or has requested the statement and has not been provided with it within the time limit laid down by that section (four weeks), at some point within the six-month period before the reference was made.[43] The same section provides that a Rights Commissioner cannot

---

[37]   Payment of Wages Act 1991, s 6(4).

[38]   *ibid*, s 6(2).

[39]   *ibid*, ss 7(1-2).

[40]   *ibid*, s 7(4).

[41]   *ibid*, s 9.

[42]   *ibid*, s 10.

[43]   National Minimum Wage Act 2000, s 24(2). This can be extended by the Rights Commissioner to a maximum period of 12 months.

deal with a reference where, in respect of an alleged under-payment, the employer is or has been the subject of investigation by an inspector or prosecuted for a criminal offence. A referral in the same manner as under s 24 can also be made where an employee alleges that he or she is being prejudiced by a reduction in hours of work *without* a concomitant reduction in duties or amount of work: the employer has two weeks (after being requested by the employee or the employee's representative) to restore the employee's working hours to those obtaining immediately before the reduction.[44]

The Rights Commissioner may award arrears (i.e. the difference between any amount paid or allowed by the employer to the employee for pay and the minimum amount the employee was entitled to be paid or allowed) and any reasonable expenses of the employee in connection with the dispute. The parties have a right to appeal the Rights Commissioner's decision to the Labour Court within six weeks of the date on which the recommendation was communicated to the party in question.[45] The Labour Court shall, as soon as practicable after hearing the appeal, either confirm the decision of the Rights Commissioner or substitute for that decision any decision of its own that the Rights Commissioner could have made on hearing the dispute.[46] There is a further right of appeal to the High Court from a determination of the Labour Court on a point of law.[47] A decision of a Rights Commissioner in relation to a complaint under the Acts may be enforced by the Labour Court.[48] Where an employer fails to carry out in accordance with its terms a determination of the Labour Court, the determination may be enforced by the Circuit Court.[49]   [12–14]

In addition to the above, s 39 of the 2000 Act allows civil proceedings to be instituted by the Minister on behalf, and in the name, of the employee. This can occur where the Minister (on advice from an inspector) is of the opinion that it is not reasonable in the circumstances to expect the employee (or the representative of the employee) to either refer a dispute or allegation to a Rights Commissioner or to institute civil proceedings on the employee's own behalf for the recovery of the amount.   [12–15]

Various criminal offences are also created by the 2000 Act. Sections 33 and 34 outline the role and powers of labour inspectors, who have a key role in enforcing the provisions of the Act.[50] Section 35 makes it an offence for an employer to refuse, or fail, to remunerate a qualifying employee at the minimum wage rate.[51] Section 36 prohibits victimisation of employees who access, or attempt to access, their rights under the Act or who oppose, or attempt to oppose, an unlawful act under the legislation. Where the employer causes or suffers any action prejudicial to an employee   [12–16]

---

[44] *ibid*, s 25.

[45] *ibid*, s 27(1). Under s 28, the powers of the Labour Court in hearing the appeal are set out in some detail.

[46] *ibid*, s 29.

[47] *ibid*, s 30(2).

[48] *ibid*, s 31.

[49] *ibid*, s 32.

[50] See the discussion of the National Employment Rights Authority (NERA) in chapter 2.

[51] Under s 35(2), where the employer charged is found guilty of this offence, evidence may be given of any like contravention on the part of the employer in respect of any period during the three years immediately preceding the date of the offence.

under this section that amounts to a dismissal, this shall be deemed to be an unfair dismissal for the purposes of the Unfair Dismissals Acts, except that it is not necessary for the employee to have at least one year's continuous service with the employer.[52] Section 37 provides for both summary prosecution and prosecution on indictment, depending on the nature of the alleged offence. There is, however, a defence for the employer to proceedings for an offence under the Act, where the employer proves that it exercised due diligence and took reasonable precautions to ensure that the Act and any relevant regulations made under it were complied with by the employer and any person under its control.[53]

[12–17]   The provisions of the Organisation of Working Time Act 1997 can also be enforced by means of a civil or a criminal claim. This reflects the dual concerns of the legislation, namely to foster safety in the workplace and to vindicate the interests of employees.[54] Taking civil remedies first, employee complaints in relation to s 6(2), ss 11 to 23, s 26[55] or the breach of relevant provisions of regulations, a collective agreement, registered employment agreement or employment regulation order are to be referred to a Rights Commissioner.[56] The complaint must be made within six months of the date of the contravention to which the complaint relates: this period can be extended for a further 12 months if the Rights Commissioner is satisfied that the failure to present the complaint within the period specified was due to "reasonable cause". In *Cementation Skanska v Carroll*[57] the Labour Court held that the claimant's explanation for a delay must be reasonable (i.e. not irrational or absurd) and that a causal connection between the circumstances cited and the delay must be established. The length of any delay will be a significant factor to be considered. A decision of a Rights Commissioner shall do one or more of the following: declare that the complaint was, or was not, well founded; require the employer to comply with the relevant provision; and/or require the employer to pay to the employee compensation of such amount (if any) as is just and equitable having regard to all the circumstances, but not exceeding two years' remuneration. Note that, where an employer fails to keep records as required under s 25(4) of the Act, the onus of proving, in proceedings before a Rights Commissioner or the Labour Court, that it is in compliance with a particular provision of the Act in relation to an employee lies with the employer; this makes it very difficult for an employer to defend a claim in the absence of such records.[58]

---

[52]   National Minimum Wage Act 2000, s 6(2).

[53]   *ibid*, s 38.

[54]   Cox *et al*, *op.cit*, p 410. The authors point out that the enforcement regime under the Act is somewhat unsophisticated in that, whilst logic would suggest issues of health and safety would best be the subject of a criminal prosecution and those relating to the employees' interest a civil claim, this distinction is not consistently maintained in the legislation.

[55]   s 26 states that an employer shall not penalise an employee for having, in good faith, opposed, by lawful means, an act which is unlawful under the 1997 Act. Where such a penalisation occurs and amounts to a dismissal, this shall constitute an unfair dismissal within the meaning of the Unfair Dismissals Acts. Relief cannot be granted to the employee in respect of such penalisation under both pieces of legislation.

[56]   Organisation of Working Time Act 1997, s 27.

[57]   DWT 0338/2003.

[58]   Lyons and Whelan, "Working Time" in *Employment Law* (Regan ed, Tottel, Dublin, 2009), p 106. See also *Goode Concrete Ltd v Munro* (DWT 051/2005).

The parties have a right to appeal the Rights Commissioner's recommendation to the Labour Court within six weeks of the date on which the recommendation was communicated to the party in question.[59] There is a further right of appeal to the High Court from a determination of the Labour Court on a point of law and the determination of the High Court shall be final and conclusive.[60] A decision of a Rights Commissioner may be enforced by the Labour Court.[61] Where an employer fails to carry out, in accordance with its terms, a determination of the Labour Court, this can be enforced by the Circuit Court.[62] Furthermore, under s 31, where it appears to the Minister that an employer is not complying with a relevant provision but a complaint has not been presented to a Rights Commissioner by the employee (or any trade union of which he or she is a member) and the circumstances touching the matter are, in the opinion of the Minister, such as to make it unreasonable to expect the employee or trade union to present such a complaint, the Minister may present a complaint on behalf of the employee (which is to be treated as if it were a complaint presented by the employee).

[12–18]

The 1997 Act also creates a number of criminal offences. The most important relate to inspections. Inspectors appointed pursuant to s 8 have a wide range of powers, including: the right to enter workplaces and make such examinations or inquires as are necessary for ascertaining whether an employer is in compliance with the Act; require the production of records, which the employer is obliged to keep under the Act; require employers or employees to furnish such information as the inspector may reasonably request; examine employers or employees and require them to answer such questions (other than questions tending to incriminate the employers or employees) as the inspector may put relative to matters relevant to the legislation; and require such employers or employees to sign a declaration of the truth of the answers.[63] It is a criminal offence under s 8(8) of the 1997 Act to: obstruct, or fail to comply with, the work of such an inspector; to refuse to produce any record which an inspector lawfully requires; to produce or knowingly allow to be produced to an inspector any record which is false or misleading in any material respect (where it is known by the producer that the record is false or misleading); or to knowingly give to an inspector any information which is false or misleading in any material respect.[64] It is an offence under s 25 not to keep such records as are necessary to determine compliance with the legislation or to fail to retain such records for at least three years from the date of their making.[65] A person guilty of an offence under the Act is open to a summary conviction and, if found guilty, to a fine. Moreover, if the contravention of the Act grounding the conviction is continued after the conviction, the person is guilty of a further offence on

[12–19]

---

[59] Organisation of Working Time Act 1997, s 28(2).

[60] *ibid*, s 28(6).

[61] *ibid*, s 28(8).

[62] *ibid*, s 29.

[63] *ibid*, s 8(3).

[64] The powers outlined in this section are a good summation of the powers accorded to inspectors in the employment legislation generally; therefore, unless otherwise stated, such powers can be taken as applying to the various other Acts referred to below.

[65] This section was amended by the European Communities (Organisation of Working Time) (Activities of Doctors in Training) Regulations 2004 (SI No 494 of 2004).

every day on which the contravention continues and for each such offence the person shall be liable, on summary conviction, to a fine.[66]

[12–20] An important decision in relation to the powers of inspection under the National Minimum Wage Act and the Organisation of Working Time Act was handed down by the Supreme Court in the *Gama* case.[67] Here, statements were made in the Dáil by Joe Higgins TD, alleging that the applicant company was acting in breach of its obligations under the minimum wage and working time legislation. On foot of the allegations, the Labour Inspectorate was directed by the Minister to investigate the matter and produce a report. The resulting report, it appeared, was intended for general publication. The company successfully sought an interlocutory injunction restraining its publication and then a full judicial review into its legitimacy. The High Court (with which the Supreme Court concurred) held that the powers under which the Labour Inspectorate had operated were provided under the 2000 and 1997 Acts expressly and only for the purposes of those Acts. As a result, the powers did not permit the Inspectorate to produce a general report on a particular workplace (including matters outside of those relating to minimum wages or working time), which could be circulated or published generally. Nonetheless, the Supreme Court decided that neither the investigation nor the report were compromised by the fact that the Inspectorate had been directed by the Minister to produce a report that was intended to be published more widely than was permitted under the terms of the legislation. The Supreme Court did, however, endorse the principle laid down in *Desmond v Glackin (No 2)*[68] that a private and limited circulation of the Inspector's report to the *relevant* statutory authorities was permissible. In this case, the relevant authorities were those State bodies with a prosecutorial function in relation to the matters identified in the report.[69] Indeed, Kearns J went on to state that he felt that this was both "desirable and indeed necessary" if effective enforcement of the relevant employment legislation was to be assured.

Equality and Bullying and Harassment

[12–21] The Equality Tribunal, the Labour Court and the Circuit Court all have roles in relation to the enforcement of the provisions of the Employment Equality Act 1998 and the Equality Act 2004. Complainants can refer their claim in the first instance to the Equality Tribunal.[70] Under s 77(3) (as amended), persons with claims relating to *gender*

---

[66] Organisation of Working Time Act 1997, s 34. Sections 39 and 40 also make important procedural changes with a view to ensuring increased administrative convenience in the enforcement of employment law; see Cox *et al*, *op.cit*, p 418.

[67] *Gama Construction & Gama Endustri v Minister for Enterprise, Trade and Employment* [2009] IESC 37. The Court largely upheld the High Court decision of Finlay Geoghegan J [2007] 3 IR 472. See chapters 2 and 4 for further discussion of the Gama dispute.

[68] [1993] 3 IR 67.

[69] Named as The Competition Authority, the Department of Finance (Taxation and Government Contracts), the Department of Transport, the Director of Corporation Enforcement, the Garda Fraud Squad, the Garda National Immigration Bureau, the Incorporated Law Society, the Irish Auditing & Accounting Supervisory Authority, the Irish Financial Services Regulatory Authority, the Joint Body of Local Authorities, the National Roads Authority and the Revenue Commissioners.

[70] Employment Equality Act 1998, s 77 (as amended by the Equality Act 2004, ss 34 and 46).

discrimination have the option of referring the claim to the Circuit Court in the first instance. This may be appropriate, for example, where the level of compensation sought exceeds that which the Director of the Equality Tribunal can award.[71] A complaint under the 1998 Act must be made within six months of the date of occurrence of the discrimination or victimisation to which the case relates or, as the case may be, the date of its most recent occurrence.[72] Application can be made to have this limit extended up to a maximum of 12 months on the grounds of "reasonable cause". In *Department of Finance v IMPACT*[73] the Labour Court said it was for the applicant to explain the delay and afford an excuse, which should be reasonable (not irrational or absurd). The Court held that this question is one of fact and degree to be decided by applying common sense and normally accepted standards of reasonableness; while the standard is therefore an objective one, it must be applied to the facts known to the applicants at the material time. It seems the Court will also address any countervailing factors (for example, the degree of prejudice suffered by the respondent, the length of the delay, whether the applicant was culpable in the delay, etc) in deciding whether to grant an extension. The six-month limit does not apply to equal pay cases.[74] A parent, guardian or other person acting in place of a parent can be the complainant where a person is unable by reason of an intellectual or psychological disability to pursue a claim effectively.[75] Cases can be struck out after a year if the Director decides they are not being pursued. The Director may also dismiss a claim at any stage if of the opinion that it has been made in bad faith or is frivolous, vexatious or misconstrued or relates to a trivial matter (a decision that can be appealed to the Labour Court).[76]

If attempts at mediating the dispute fail,[77] s 82(1) of the 1998 Act (as amended) outlines the forms of redress that are available. In equal pay claims, the Director may make an order for equal pay from the date of referral and arrears in respect of a period not exceeding three years before that date. The Director may also make: an order for equal treatment in whatever respect is relevant to the case; an order that a specified course of action be taken by named person(s); an order for compensation for the effects of acts of discrimination or victimisation, which occurred not earlier than six years before the date of referral; and, in cases where unequal treatment under the Act has resulted in dismissal, an order for reinstatement or re-engagement with or without an order for compensation. In the case of the last two orders mentioned, compensation can be ordered of up to a maximum of two years' pay or €12,697.38 (where the complainant is not an employee).[78] In gender discrimination claims that are initiated in

[12–22]

---

[71] s 82(3) of the Employment Equality Act 1998 (as amended) provides that there is no limit to the amount of compensation that may be ordered by the Circuit Court in gender equality cases.

[72] Employment Equality Act 1998, s 77(5) as amended by the Equality Act 2004, s 32.

[73] EET 2/2004.

[74] Employment Equality Act 1998, s 77(5)(c) as substituted by the Equality Act 2004, s 32.

[75] Employment Equality Act 1998, s 77(4) as inserted by the Equality Act 2004, s 32.

[76] Employment Equality Act 1998, s 77A as inserted by the Equality Act 2004, s 33.

[77] See chapter 2.

[78] Employment Equality Act 1998, s 82(4). The maximum compensation limit applies notwithstanding that there may have been discrimination on more than one ground or that there was discrimination on one or more of the grounds and harassment or sexual harassment; s 82(6)(a) as inserted by the Equality Act 2004, s 36.

the Circuit Court, the Court (in equal pay claims) may make an order for equal pay from the date of referral and order compensation in the form of arrears of pay in respect of a period not exceeding six years before that date. The Circuit Court can also make the same orders as the Director in relation to acts of discrimination or victimisation, equal treatment, specifying a course of action to be followed and dismissal cases.[79] Section 82(3) of the Employment Equality Act 1998 (as amended) provides that there is no limit to the amount of compensation that may be ordered by the Circuit Court in gender equality cases.

[12–23] The Labour Court has affirmed that, in assessing compensation, regard must be had to all the effects that flowed from the discrimination: these include, in addition to financial loss, "distress and indignity...including the effects of bringing these proceedings".[80] Note that the European Court of Justice has held that where a Member State chooses to penalise the prohibition of gender discrimination by way of compensation, the latter must be such as to guarantee "real and effective" judicial protection, have a real deterrent effect on employers and be adequate in relation to the damage sustained.[81] Bolger and Kimber note that, in practice, awards are not commonly made of two years' pay. They point out that awards tend to range from around €3,000 (discrimination in access to employment or promotion) to around €20,000 (discrimination whilst in the job); awards for discriminatory dismissal can be higher (as they depend on salary level)[82] and where victimisation is involved, awards tend to be higher again.[83]

[12–24] All decisions (including decisions on time limits and striking out of the claim) may be appealed to the Labour Court not later than 42 days from the date of a decision of the Director.[84] The Labour Court has the same powers of redress as the Tribunal[85]: it may also require the Director of the Tribunal to investigate, further investigate or re-investigate any aspect of the case and submit a report thereon to the Court.[86] Note that the Labour Court had previously heard cases of discriminatory dismissal as a tribunal of first instance: this jurisdiction was removed by s 46 of the Equality Act 2004. Where a determination is made by the Labour Court on an appeal, either party may appeal to the High Court on a point of law.[87] In considering whether to allow such an appeal, the High Court must consider whether the Tribunal based its decision on an identifiable

---

[79] Employment Equality Act 1998, s 82(3).

[80] *Citibank v Ntoko* [2004] ELR 116.

[81] Case C-271/91 *Marshall v Southampton & SW Hants AHA* [1993] ECR I-4367.

[82] See *Kavanagh v Aviance UK Ltd* (DEC-E2007-39), where the complainant was awarded compensation for both discriminatory dismissal and the effects of discriminatory treatment, leading to stress, where both awards resulted from the same set of facts.

[83] Bolger and Kimber, "Employment Equality" in *Employment Law* (Regan ed, Tottel, Dublin, 2009), p 519. See also *Dublin City Co v McCarthy* (EDA 2/2002), where it was noted that "the victimisation of a person for having in good faith taken a claim under the equality legislation is very serious as it could have the impact of undermining the effectiveness of the legislation and is completely unacceptable".

[84] Employment Equality Act 1998, s 83(1).

[85] *ibid*, s 83(4).

[86] *ibid*, s 84(2).

[87] *ibid*, s 90(1).

error of law or an unsustainable finding of fact.[88] A decision cannot be challenged merely on the grounds of irrationality, if there is relevant material to support it. In *Thompson v Tesco (Ireland)*[89] the appellant worked as a sales assistant and sought to have her working hours amended to suit child-minding arrangements. The request was refused and the appellant, a lone parent, claimed that similar requests were favourably received from men and married women. Both the Equality Tribunal and the Labour Court rejected the appellant's complaint of unlawful sex discrimination. Lavan J held that it was well-settled law that, where a quasi-judicial function was delegated to an expert administrative tribunal, the decision of such a tribunal could not be challenged on the grounds of irrationality, if there was any relevant material to support it. In the instant case, the Labour Court acknowledged that, while the fact that the appellant's request for shorter working hours was not acceded to might amount to unfairness in an industrial relations sense, it could not avail her complaint of discrimination. The employer was entitled, owing to sound, non-discriminatory business reasons, to refuse such requests and was found to have done so on a non-discriminatory basis. All findings of fact were sustainable based on the relevant material before the Labour Court.

Section 85A of the 1998 Act[90] deals with the burden of proof in discrimination cases and states that where, in any proceedings, facts are established by, or on behalf of, a complainant from which it may be presumed that there has been discrimination in relation to him or her, it is for the respondent to prove the contrary. In *Southern Health Board v Mitchell*[91] the Labour Court considered the issue: **[12–25]**

> "The first requirement is that the claimant must 'establish facts' from which it may be presumed that the principle of equal treatment has not been applied to them. This indicates that a claimant must prove, on the balance of probabilities, the primary facts on which they rely in seeking to raise a presumption of unlawful discrimination. It is only if these primary facts are established to the satisfaction of the Court, and they are regarded by the Court as being of sufficient significance to raise a presumption of discrimination, that the onus shifts to the respondent to prove that there was no infringement of the principle of equal treatment".

In that case, the "primary facts" upon which the complainant sought to rely were that he was continually assigned more work than other financial administrators with whom he worked and that different standards of scrutiny and supervision were applied to his work relative to that of others. The complainant was not able to satisfy the test here, as witnesses on behalf of the respondent gave evidence of the methods by which work was allocated within the employment (and as to the supervisory structures and practices) and they told the Court that the manner in which the complainant was treated in respect of those matters was identical to that afforded to all other employees with whom he worked. **[12–26]**

Finally in this section, a brief note on bullying and harassment in the workplace. The approach of the law has been to treat this issue essentially as one of employment equality. **[12–27]**

---

[88] *Henry Denny & Sons v Minister for Social Welfare* [1998] 1 IR 34.
[89] [2003] ELR 21.
[90] As inserted by the Equality Act 2004, s 38.
[91] [2001] ELR 201.

As a result, the equality legislation does not concern itself solely with issues of pay and other direct and indirect forms of less favourable treatment on the prohibited grounds, but also deals with what Eardley refers to as "more aggressive, predatory conduct" that exists in the workplace.[92] Thus, claims for harassment on any of the prohibited grounds or sexual harassment under s 14A of the 1998 Act (as inserted by s 8 of the 2004 Act) may be processed in the manner described above. However, it is also the case that, depending on the context, harassment actions may be taken pursuant to the unfair dismissals legislation or the health and safety legislation.[93] Importantly, there is a growing line of case law concerning common law actions against employers in the area of workplace harassment and bullying, focusing on liability in tort (negligence) and breach of contract, as well as important case law to do with vicarious liability.[94]

Family Friendly Working

[12–28] The general manner in which the various pieces of "family friendly" legislation described in chapter 6 are enforced is the same in all the different Acts.[95] As a result this can be dealt with together here.

Disputes under the legislation can be referred, in the first instance, to a Rights Commissioner.[96] Referrals must be made within six months of the date:

a. (under the adoptive leave legislation) of placement or, in circumstances where no placement takes place, on which the employer receives the first notification of the adopting parent's intention to take leave under the Act[97];
b. (under the carer's leave legislation) of the contravention of the legislation[98];
c. (under the parental leave legislation) of the occurrence of the dispute[99];
d. (under the maternity protection legislation) on which the employer is informed of the initial circumstances relevant to the dispute, i.e that the employee is pregnant, has recently given birth or is breastfeeding or, in the case of an employee who is the father of a child, that the child's mother has died.[100]

---

[92] Eardley, *Sex Discrimination at Work* (FirstLaw, Dublin, 2002), p 129.

[93] Ryan, "Bullying, Harassment and Stress at Work" in *Employment Law* (Regan ed, Tottel, Dublin, 2009), p 231.

[94] See Ryan, *ibid*, chapter 7; Cox *et al*, *op.cit*, chapter 10; Ryan and Ryan, "Vicarious Liability of Employers - Emerging Themes and Trends and Their Potential Implications for Irish Law" (2007) 4(1) IELJ 3; Cox, "Recent Developments in the Rules Relating to Workplace Stress: the Supreme Court Decision in *Berber v Dunnes Stores*" (2008/9) 3(3) QRTL 17.

[95] An important exception relates to the question of whether the criteria are fulfilled for the employee to take carer's leave; these are matters to be decided by the Deciding Officer or Appeals Officer under the Social Welfare (Consolidation) Act 2005. Also, disputes in relation to dismissal or redundancy, or relating to minimum notice, must be dealt with, respectively, under the unfair dismissals and minimum notice legislation; Cox *et al*, *op.cit*, p 481.

[96] Adoptive Leave Acts 1995 and 2005, s 34(1); Carer's Leave Act 2001, s 19(1); Parental Leave Acts 1998 and 2006, s 18(2); Maternity Protection Act 1994, s 30(4).

[97] Adoptive Leave Acts 1995 and 2005, s 34(1).

[98] Carer's Leave Act 2001, s 19(3).

[99] Parental Leave Acts 1998 and 2006, s 18(5).

[100] Maternity Protection Act 1994, s 31.

If the Rights Commissioner is satisfied that exceptional circumstances prevented the referral within the period specified, he or she can extend the period up to a maximum of 12 months from the date specified: this is not permitted, however, under the parental leave legislation.[101] A decision of a Rights Commissioner shall do one or more of the following: give to the parties concerned such directions as the Rights Commissioner considers necessary or expedient for the resolution of the dispute (this provision does not exist under the carer's leave legislation)[102]; either require the employer to grant the relevant leave[103]; and/or pay to the employee compensation of such amount (if any) as is just and equitable having regard to all the circumstances, but not exceeding 20 weeks' remuneration under the Adoptive Leave, Parental Leave and Maternity Protection Acts and not exceeding 26 weeks' remuneration under the Carer's Leave Acts.[104]

[12–29]

The parties have a right to appeal the Rights Commissioner's decision to the EAT within four weeks of the date on which the decision was communicated to the party in question.[105] There is a further right of appeal to the High Court from a determination of the Tribunal on a point of law.[106] A decision of a Rights Commissioner, or a determination of the Tribunal, may be enforced by the Circuit Court.[107]

[12–30]

Health and Safety

Health and safety in the workplace is another area of employment where the traditional importance of common law remedies remains a feature. As Deakin and Morris note, much of health and safety law operates by imposing regulatory duties upon employers, which are enforced through the powers of a designated health and safety inspectorate and, ultimately, the sanction of the criminal courts.[108] In terms of remedies for the individual, an employer may be liable at common law in negligence for breaching a duty of care to an employee (either personally or vicariously).[109] However,

[12–31]

---

[101] Adoptive Leave Acts 1995 and 2005, s 34(1); Carer's Leave Act 2001, s 19(8); Maternity Protection Act 1994, s 31(1).

[102] Adoptive Leave Acts 1995 and 2005, s 33(1); Parental Leave Acts 1998 and 2006, s 21(1); Maternity Protection Act 1994, s 32(1).

[103] Carer's Leave Act 2001, s 21(1); Parental Leave Acts 1998 and 2006, s 21(2); Maternity Protection Act 1994, s 32(2). This is not specifically provided for in the Adoptive Leave Acts 1995 and 2005.

[104] Adoptive Leave Acts 1995 and 2005, s 33(3); Carer's Leave Act 2001, s 21(2); Parental Leave Acts 1998 and 2006, s 21(3); Maternity Protection Act 1994, s 32(3).

[105] Adoptive Leave Acts 1995 and 2005, s 35(2); Carer's Leave Act 2001, s 20(2); Parental Leave Acts 1998 and 2006, s 19(2); Maternity Protection Act 1994, s 33(2). Under the Carer's Leave Act 2001, s 20(1) this can be extended by the EAT, if it considers this reasonable, for a further six weeks.

[106] Adoptive Leave Acts 1995 and 2005, s 36(2); Carer's Leave Act 2001, s 23(2); Parental Leave Acts 1998 and 2006, s 20(2); Maternity Protection Act 1994, s 34(2).

[107] Adoptive Leave Acts 1995 and 2005, s 39; Carer's Leave Act 2001, s 22; Parental Leave Acts 1998 and 2006, s 22; Maternity Protection Act 1994, s 37.

[108] Deakin and Morris, *Labour Law* (5th ed, Hart, Oxford, 2009), p 294.

[109] See *Dalton v Frendo* (Unreported, Supreme Court, 15 December 1977), where the common law duty of the employer "to take reasonable care for the servant's safety in all the circumstances of the case" was identified. See McMahon and Binchy, *Irish Law of Torts* (3rd ed, Butterworths, Dublin, 2000), chapters 18 and 43. The duty of an employer to provide a safe working environment for the employee is also an implied term of the employment contract. See, generally, Shannon, *Health and Safety: Law and Practice* (2nd ed, Round Hall, Dublin, 2007).

there is a significant overlap between the principles developed at common law in relation to the employer's duties and those outlined under health and safety legislation. As a result, the provisions of the Safety, Health and Welfare at Work Act 2005, and their interpretation by the courts, are likely to be highly significant in informing the development of the common law position.[110] Furthermore, it seems that all the duties in the 2005 Act may found a cause of action in tort for breach of statutory duty.[111] Here, the plaintiff must demonstrate: that the statute was intended to create civil liability; that the statutory duty was owed to the individual claimant; that the statute imposed the duty on the defendant; that the defendant was in breach of the duty; and that the claimant suffered damage as a result, which was of a type contemplated by the statute.[112] It should be noted that an action for breach of statutory duty might succeed in a situation where a common law claim in negligence (arising out of the same facts) does not.[113] This can be seen in *Everitt v Thorsman Ireland Ltd*,[114] where the employer was found not to have acted unreasonably in not detecting a latent defect in equipment supplied to the employee but was found to have breached its duty under the Safety, Health and Welfare at Work (General Application) Regulations 1993.[115] Kearns J found that while the provision in question (Regulation 19 of the 1993 Regulations) imposed virtually an absolute duty on employers in respect of the safety of equipment provided for the use of their employees, and while there was no "blameworthiness in any meaningful sense of the word" on the part of the employer, the Regulations nevertheless existed for "sound policy reasons", namely, to ensure that an employee who suffers an injury at work through no fault of his or her own by using defective equipment should not be left without a remedy.[116]

[12–32]   Generally, the 2005 Act provides for criminal offences where an employer is in breach of its duties. Section 27, however, prohibits an employer from penalising or threatening to penalise an employee with respect to any term or condition of his or her employment to his or her detriment, if the employee is acting in accordance with health and safety legislation or performing any duty, or exercising any right, under health and safety legislation. The prohibition extends to penalisation related to the employee making a complaint or a representation about safety, health or welfare at work, giving evidence in enforcement proceedings or leaving or refusing to return to the place of work when he or she reasonably considers that there is serious or imminent

---

[110] Cox *et al*, *op.cit*, p 552.

[111] Byrne, *Safety, Health and Welfare at Work Act 2005* (Round Hall, Dublin, 2006), p 21. Under the Safety, Heath and Welfare at Work Act 1989, civil actions for a breach of the general duties under ss 6-11 of the Act were expressly excluded (s 60). However, it seemed the specific regulations made under the Act were assumed to give rise to a civil action, unless the regulations expressly indicated otherwise (s 60(2)).

[112] For an overview of the law relating to breach of statutory duty see McMahon and Binchy, *op.cit*, chapter 21.

[113] Cox *et al* note that the inverse is also the case; an employer might have fulfilled its statutory duties but breached its common law duty of care in negligence; *op.cit*, p 519.

[114] [2000] 1 IR 256.

[115] SI No 44 of 1993.

[116] [2000] 1 IR 256 at 263 *per* Kearns J. See, generally, Ichino, "The Changing Structure and Contents of the Employer's Legal Responsibility for Health and Safety at Work in Post-Industrial Systems" (2006) *International Journal of Comparative Labour Law and Industrial Relations* 603.

danger, with which the employee could not reasonably have dealt. Penalisation by an employer includes: suspension, layoff or dismissal; demotion or loss of opportunities for promotion; transfer or a change of location; reduction in wages or change in working hours; imposition of any discipline, reprimand or other penalty; and coercion or intimidation.[117] The dismissal of an employee will be a dismissal under the Unfair Dismissals Acts if it results from penalisation under s 27; such dismissal shall not be deemed to be unfair if the employer shows that the steps taken or proposed to be taken were so negligent that it was reasonable to dismiss the employee.[118]

Complaints under s 27 should be notified to a Rights Commissioner (within six months of the date of the contravention to which the complaint relates; this can be extended to a maximum of 12 months),[119] who can order a specific course of action or such compensation as is just and equitable having regard to all the circumstances.[120] A right of appeal lies to the Labour Court (within six weeks of the communication to the party of the decision),[121] and to the High Court on a point of law.[122] A decision of a Rights Commissioner may be enforced by the Labour Court.[123] Where an employer fails to carry out, in accordance with its terms, a determination of the Labour Court, the determination may be enforced by the Circuit Court.[124] The Labour Court will take claims of penalisation extremely seriously. In *LW Associates v Lacey*,[125] for example, a pregnant worker who asked for a risk assessment to be carried out was placed immediately on paid leave. She resigned, claiming penalisation. The Labour Court found that, if a risk assessment identifies the necessity for a pregnant worker to avoid certain physical tasks, the employer should either find alternative employment or place the employee on health and safety leave. Here, the employer did not adequately explore alternatives to paid leave; the "precipitous manner" in which it decided to place the employee on health and safety leave, without affording the complainant the benefit of representation, amounted to penalisation.[126]

[12–33]

---

[117] In *Kelly v Algirdas Girdzius* (HSD 081/2008) the Labour Court rejected a claim that a failure to provide proper health and safety training in an appropriate language which the employee could understand amounted, in and of itself, to penalisation under s 27 of the 2005 Act. The Court found that, in order to succeed in an action grounded on s 27, the claimant must establish not only that he or she suffered a detriment of a type referred to in subsection (1), but also that the detriment was imposed because of, or was in retaliation for, the employee having raised safety issues.

[118] Safety, Health and Welfare at Work Act 2005, s 27(7). Under s 27(5) of the 2005 Act, relief may not be granted to the employee in respect of a penalisation resulting in dismissal under both the 2005 Act and the Unfair Dismissals Acts 1997-2007.

[119] Safety, Health and Welfare at Work Act 2005, s 28(4).

[120] *ibid*, s 28(3).

[121] *ibid*, s 29(2)

[122] *ibid*, s 29(6)

[123] *ibid*, s 29(8).

[124] *ibid*, s 30.

[125] HSD 085/2008.

[126] In *Toni & Guy Blackrock Ltd v O' Neill* (HSD 095/2009) the Labour Court awarded €20,000 compensation to an employee of a hair salon who was penalised as a result of complaining about protective gloves. See also *Department of Justice, Equality and Law Reform v Kirwan* (HSD 082/2008); Curran, "Victimisation: A New Remedy for Employees" (2008) 5(1) IELJ 4.

[12–34]   As noted, however, the primary means of enforcement under the Act is through the use by the Health and Safety Authority (HSA) of its regulatory powers.[127] A key function of the HSA (in conjunction with the Minister) under s 34 of the Act is to make adequate arrangements for the enforcement of all legislation on occupational health and safety, particularly through workplace inspections. The HSA basically adopts a model of "persuasion backed by sanction".[128] Section 62 of the 2005 Act provides that the Authority may authorise persons as inspectors to enforce the relevant statutory provisions.[129] Section 63 empowers the Authority to designate inspectors or other persons, who are registered medical practitioners, to receive any notice, report or certificate required under health and safety legislation to be sent by a registered medical practitioner to the Authority. Sections 65–69 of the 2005 Act essentially cover the powers the HSA possesses to try and cajole or force the employer into compliance with the legislation prior to a criminal prosecution; as Byrne notes, at each stage of the progression "the nature and consequence of the various powers increase, in accordance with the risk to which each remedy is to be applied".[130] These powers can be summarised as follows:

   a.   an inspector may give a written direction to an employer requiring the submission of an *improvement plan* in the case of an activity involving, or likely to involve, a risk to the safety, health or welfare of persons (s 65);

   b.   a continuing contravention of health and safety legislation, or the failure to submit or revise an improvement plan as directed, can result in the service of an *improvement notice* on the person in control of the work activity concerned[131];

   c.   a *prohibition notice* requires either the immediate cessation of an activity at a place of work that involves, or could involve, a risk of serious personal injury to any person, or cessation from the effective date and time specified on the prohibition notice[132];

   d.   where activities are carried on in contravention of a prohibition notice served under s 67, the High Court may, on an application by an inspector, by order prohibit the continuance of the activities[133];

---

[127] See Shannon, "Safety, Health and Welfare at Work Act 2005 - Offences and Penalties" (2005) 4(3) IELJ 68 and chapter 2.

[128] Byrne, *op.cit*, p 112.

[129] The inspectors have a wide range of powers, *inter alia*, to enter a workplace, request and retain records and direct relevant persons to provide information and assistance; Safety, Health and Welfare at Work Act 2005, s 64.

[130] Byrne, *op.cit*, p 119.

[131] A person on whom a notice is served may appeal to the District Court within 14 days and the judge may confirm, vary, or cancel the notice. When making an appeal, the person must also notify the HSA, which is entitled to appear and give evidence in court; Safety, Health and Welfare at Work Act 2005, s 66(7).

[132] Safety, Health and Welfare at Work Act 2005, s 67. A person may, within seven days of the service of a prohibition notice, appeal to the District Court and the judge may confirm, vary, or cancel the notice; Safety, Health and Welfare at Work Act 2005, s 67(7). An inspector may withdraw a prohibition notice at any time if satisfied that the activity no longer involves a risk of serious personal injury to any person or if he or she is satisfied that the notice was issued in error or is incorrect; Safety, Health and Welfare at Work Act 2005, s 67(12).

[133] *ibid*, s 68. The application to the High Court may be *ex parte* and the court may make an interim or interlocutory order and set down terms and conditions regarding the payment of costs; Safety, Health and Welfare at Work Act 2005, s 68(2).

e. a person on whom an improvement notice or a prohibition notice is served must bring it to the attention of any person whose work is affected by the notice and display the notice or a copy of it in a prominent place at or near the place of work or article or substance affected by the notice (s 69).

Section 71 of the 2005 Act applies where the Authority considers that the risk to the safety, health or welfare of persons is so serious that the use of a place of work or part of it should be restricted or immediately prohibited until specified measures have been taken to reduce the risk to a reasonable level. The section enables the Authority to apply *ex parte* to the High Court for an order restricting or prohibiting the use of the place of work or part thereof.

[12–35]

Section 77 of the 2005 Act provides for two broad ranges of offences. The first category applies to offences that may only be tried by the Authority summarily in the District Court[134] and the second category covers offences that may be tried either summarily or on indictment; in the case of summary disposal by the Authority and on indictment by the Director of Public Prosecutions.[135] The section provides for several other offences covering contraventions of particular sections or other specific matters. This section also provides that, in addition to the imposition of a fine in respect of an offence, a convicted person may also be ordered to take steps to remedy health and safety matters within a specific time.[136] An employer does not have a defence in a case taken for breach of health and safety legislation by reason of any act or default by an employee or by a competent person appointed under s 18 of the 2005 Act.[137] One of the innovations in the Act is the power to make regulations for the imposition of on-the-spot fines for breaches of the health and safety code.[138] In *People (DPP) v Roseberry Construction Ltd*[139] fines of €315,000 were imposed on the defendant company arising from a double fatality on a building site. The Court of Criminal Appeal pointed out that a fine is neither lenient nor harsh in itself but only in terms of the circumstances of the person who must pay. The Court outlined certain aggravating factors (death resulting from a statutory breach, failure to heed warnings and risks run in order to save money) and mitigating factors (prompt admission of responsibility or a guilty plea, remedial steps and a good prior record) that would be taken into consideration in assessing the level of the fine. Section 80 of the 2005 Act provides that when an offence under health and safety legislation is committed by an undertaking and the acts involved were authorised or consented to, or were attributable to connivance or neglect

[12–36]

---

[134] Some summary offences can only result in a fine of up to €3,000; others can result in a fine of up to €3,000 and/or imprisonment (for a period of up to six months); Safety, Health and Welfare at Work Act 2005, s 78(2)(i).

[135] These can result in a fine of up to €3m and/or imprisonment for a period of up to two years; Safety, Health and Welfare at Work Act 2005, s 78(2)(ii). s 82 of the Act empowers the Authority to initiate summary proceedings for offences within 12 months from the date an offence was committed. s 83 specifies that any person (including the Authority) may appeal to a judge of the Circuit Court and the decision of the judge of the Circuit Court shall be final and conclusive.

[136] Safety, Health and Welfare at Work Act 2005, s 77(8).

[137] *ibid*, s 77(12).

[138] *ibid*, s 79.

[139] [2003] 4 IR 338.

on the part of either a director, manager or other similar officer, that person as well as the undertaking will be guilty of an offence and liable to be proceeded against and punished as if the person was guilty of the offence committed by the undertaking.[140] Under s 85 of the 2005 Act, the Authority may, from time to time, compile and publish lists of names and addresses and the description of business or other activity of persons on whom fines or other penalties were imposed by a court under health and safety legislation, or to whom prohibition notices were issued, or in respect of whom interim or interlocutory orders were made. This "name and shame" list must include details, as the Authority thinks fit, of the matter involved and the fine, penalty, notice or order concerned.

Termination of Employment

[12–37] The employment relationship can be lawfully terminated on the giving of proper notice.[141] The Minimum Notice and Terms of Employment Act 1973 lays down minimum periods of notice to be given by employers when terminating a contract of employment. Section 11 of the 1973 Act provides that any dispute arising on any matter under the Act shall be referred to the Employment Appeals Tribunal; the decision of the Tribunal shall be final and conclusive, save that any person dissatisfied with the decision may appeal to the High Court on a question of law.

[12–38] It was shown in chapter 10 that an action for wrongful dismissal is essentially an action for breach of contract and ordinary contract law and equitable remedies can be sought.[142] Most usually, the remedy sought is damages, which are traditionally related to the period of notice to which the employee was entitled but did not receive.[143] The High Court or Supreme Court may also declare a purported dismissal invalid or unconstitutional if it can be established that the dismissal contravened the Constitution or any of its provisions.[144] The influence of the European Convention on Human Rights is also likely to grow more pronounced as a result of its incorporation into Irish law by means of the European Convention on Human Rights Act 2003.[145]

[12–39] Remedies for unfair dismissal are laid down in the Unfair Dismissals Acts 1977–2007.[146] The primary purpose of the legislation in this context is to compensate the

---

[140] Note that the Law Reform Commission has recommended the creation of a new statutory offence of "corporate manslaughter"; see its report on "Corporate Killing" (LRC CP 26-2005).
[141] Note that remedies for dismissal under other pieces of legislation discussed elsewhere in the chapter (e.g. under legislation relating to health and safety, part-time work and so on) will not be covered in this section.
[142] See, generally, Enright, *Principles of Irish Contract Law* (Clarus Press, Dublin, 2007); Redmond, *Dismissal Law in Ireland* (2nd ed, Tottel, Dublin, 2007), chapters 10 and 11; Stewart and Dunleavy, *op.cit*, chapter 9.
[143] Stewart and Dunleavy, *op.cit*, p 141. See the discussion, in chapter 11, of the interaction between a breach of an implied term of trust and confidence and remedies for dismissal. Note that a claim for unfair dismissal under the Unfair Dismissal Acts will preclude an action for damages at common law; *Nolan v Emo Oil Services Ltd* [2009] ELR 122.
[144] Stewart and Dunleavy, *op.cit,* chapter 15 and Redmond, *op.cit*, chapter 8.
[145] See Allen *et al*, *Employment Law and Human Rights* (2nd ed, Oxford University Press, Oxford, 2002), Part 3.
[146] See, generally, Redmond, *op.cit*, chapter 24.

worker for the loss of security, the loss of earnings and benefits and the uncertainty and anxiety of a change of job (which can be present even where a new job is relatively quickly secured). One of the key rationales behind setting up the statutory unfair dismissals regime was to provide a process under which redress could be sought in a speedy and cost-effective manner.[147] As a result, the legislation provides for claims to be brought to a Rights Commissioner or, if either party objects to such a hearing, to the EAT.[148] The Rights Commissioner hearings are held in private; EAT hearings are usually held in public.[149] Any claim must be initiated within six months of the date of the dismissal (this can be extended to 12 months if the Rights Commissioner or the EAT finds there are "exceptional circumstances"; e.g. serious illness).[150] There is a right of appeal from a decision of the Rights Commissioner to the EAT (within six weeks of the date the decision was given to the parties)[151] and from the EAT to the Circuit Court (within six weeks of the date the determination was given to the parties) by way of full re-hearing of the case.[152] There is also a further right of appeal from the Circuit Court to the High Court on a point of law.

Section 7 of the Unfair Dismissals Act 1977 (as amended) sets out the available remedies. Section 7(1)(a) provides for *re-instatement* of the employee in the position held immediately prior to dismissal, on the terms and conditions on which he or she was employed immediately at that time. This means that the employee is to be treated, to all intents and purposes, as if he or she had never been dismissed. The employee is entitled to any arrears of salary from the date of dismissal to the date of reinstatement and continuity of service is deemed not to have been broken. Furthermore, if the terms or conditions of workers in comparable positions (for example, where workers are on an incremental salary scale), or the terms or conditions generally of the employer's other employees, have improved the re-instatement will be on those improved terms.[153] An order for re-instatement, therefore, essentially renders the employee blameless; however, even if this is the case, there may be situations (due to the employment context leading to the dismissal) where such an order is impractical. Section 7(1)(b) provides for *re-engagement* of the employee *either* in the position held immediately prior to dismissal *or* in a different position, which would be reasonably suitable on such terms and conditions as are reasonable having regard to all the circumstances. This can mean that the employee is re-employed but in a slightly different job. The order for re-engagement can specify the terms and operative dates. Therefore, there is no automatic entitlement to loss of earnings or guarantee of continuity of service. Re-engagement, therefore, is an order more likely where the employee has *not* been totally blameless.

[12–40]

---

[147] See chapter 2 on the operation of the EAT and the Rights Commissioner Service and note, in particular, the discussion of increased legalism at the employment tribunals.

[148] Unfair Dismissals Acts 1977, s 8(1).

[149] See *Report of the Working Group of the Employment Appeals Tribunal 2007* (available at www.deti.ie/publications). Determinations are now published on the EAT website, www.eattribunal.ie.

[150] Unfair Dismissals Act 1977, s 8(2)(b).

[151] *ibid*, s 9.

[152] Unfair Dismissals (Amendment) Act 1993, s 11(1).

[153] Unfair Dismissals Act 1977, s 1 as amended by the Unfair Dismissals (Amendment) Act 1993, s 2.

[12–41]   The EAT has held it has absolute discretion in choosing which remedy to award.[154] Restoring the employee to his or her position may be undesirable where, for example, it would result in compelling an employer to continue a relationship with an employee in whom it had no trust or confidence or where restoring the employee would require constant supervision on the part of the employer to ensure adequate performance of duties.[155] Redmond notes that, in fact, the vast majority of claimants before the EAT who are declared to be unfairly dismissed do *not* get their jobs back.[156] This is similar to the situation in the UK, where research has shown that a primary reason for this is that the employment tribunals pay a lot of attention to employers' views regarding the practicality and acceptability of re-employment and rarely make such an order in the face of employer opposition.[157]

[12–42]   It is not surprising, therefore, that the most common remedy awarded in unfair dismissals claims is that of *compensation*. Section 7(1)(c) of the 1977 Act (as amended) allows the employee to be compensated for financial loss incurred, which is attributable to the dismissal, subject to a maximum of 104 weeks' remuneration. If the employee incurred no financial loss, compensation may be awarded as is just and equitable having regard to all the circumstances but not exceeding four weeks' remuneration.[158] The employee may have suffered no real financial loss, for example, where he or she got another job more or less immediately. It is clear from the factors outlined in s 7(2) of the 1977 Act (as amended) that there must be a direct link between the financial loss incurred and the unfair dismissal; these include consideration of the conduct of both parties, including any (non-)compliance with relevant procedures or codes of practice. The Supreme Court outlined, in *Carney v Balken Tours Ltd*,[159] that, when determining compensation, the EAT must take into account all the circumstances of the case; this would include the conduct of the parties *prior* to dismissal.[160] If the employee's conduct contributed "wholly or substantially" to the dismissal, there would no right to compensation.

[12–43]   The employee is required to mitigate his or her loss.[161] This is a question of fact to be proven by the party alleging mitigation did not take place.[162] This would include spending time job-seeking, registering with an employment agency and, of course, getting another job. The employee is not necessarily obliged to take the first job that comes along; the test is one of "reasonableness". An employee should not, therefore, use the time where he or she is not in work to no purpose but should use the time to seek a

---

[154] Although, as a matter of practical reality, it will consider the wishes of the parties; *McArdle v Kingspan* (UD 1342/2003).

[155] *Sheehan v Continental Administration Co Ltd* (UD 858/1999).

[156] Redmond, *op.cit*, p 515.

[157] Deakin and Morris, *op.cit*, p 472, quoting Dickens *et al, Dismissal: A Study of Unfair Dismissal and the Industrial Tribunal System* (Blackwell, Oxford, 1985).

[158] Unfair Dismissals Act 1977, s 7(1)(c) as amended by Unfair Dismissals (Amendment) Act 1993, s 6. "Remuneration" includes allowances in the nature of pay and benefits in lieu of, or in addition to, pay; Unfair Dismissals Act 1977, s 7(3).

[159] [1997] 1 IR 153.

[160] See also *Allen v Independent Newspapers (Ireland) Ltd* [2002] ELR 84.

[161] Unfair Dismissals Act 1977, s 7(2)(c).

[162] *Bessenden Properties v Corness* [1970] ICR 821.

"better paid job" which will reduce the overall loss and the amount of compensation which the previous employer has to pay.[163] In *Employee v Employer*[164] the EAT recognised that the failure of a former employer to furnish a suitable reference may be a factor in reducing a former employee's ability to mitigate losses arising from dismissal.

Finally, where a decision involving a dismissal can be challenged by way of judicial review, particular remedies are available.[165] An employee may seek a *declaration* that a dismissal is null and void or that the employee, in fact, never ceased to hold employment; the precise nature and content of the declaration will be crucial in how effective a remedy it is for the worker.[166] An order of *certiorari* may be granted quashing a decision of a public body that has been arrived at in excess of jurisdiction. An application for this order is often sought in conjunction with an order of *mandamus* seeking to require the body in question to make the decision again. Injunctions can also be sought by way of judicial review; this will be examined further in the next section.

[12-44]

III. The Employment Injunction

A feature of employment litigation in recent years has been the increasing tendency of plaintiffs to seek injunctions, both to restrain dismissal and conduct by the employer short of dismissal. This development has provoked much comment.[167] The reasons for this increase in the seeking of injunctions are many and varied, probably reflecting changing attitudes on the part of the judiciary,[168] as well as a greater tendency towards litigiousness in employment matters generally. This has led, as was shown in chapter 2, to a backlog of cases to be dealt with by the various employment tribunals and the courts. As a result, where there is a significant delay in getting a wrongful or unfair dismissal claim adjudicated upon and the plaintiff is not being paid, he or she may be at serious risk of poverty. As Redmond notes, however, there are also clearly tactical concerns at play; plaintiffs who have sought injunctions in recent times have, in the main, been senior executives, who do not want to face the delays of going to the EAT and who often seek to "embarrass" employers (through the bad publicity generated by such hearings) and discomfort them (through the threat of high legal costs).[169]

[12-45]

---

[163] *AG Bracey Ltd v Iles* [1973] IRLR 210.

[164] UD 163/2008.

[165] Rules of the Superior Courts, Order 84. See also Stewart and Dunleavy, *op.cit*, chapter 14; Redmond, *op.cit*, chapter 9.

[166] Redmond, *op.cit*, p 152.

[167] See, for example, Charleton, "Employment Injunctions: An Over-Loose Discretion" (2009) 2 *Judicial Studies Institute Journal* 1; Mallon, "Recent Developments in Employment Injunctions" (2008) 5(2) IELJ 48; Delany, "Employment Injunctions: The Role of Mutual Trust and Confidence" (2006) 13(1) DULJ 260; Horan, "Employment Injunctions: Current Status and Future Developments" (2006) 1 ELR 8.

[168] Traditionally, injunctions were felt to be inappropriate in this area as, first, the employee had no *right* to be employed, simply an entitlement to a period of notice before termination; secondly, because employment law derived from the old law of master and servant, it was felt that the close nature of the relationship was such as to make it obnoxious to grant injunctive relief; and, thirdly, there was the notion that no injunction should be granted if constant supervision was needed to ensure compliance therewith; Charleton, *op.cit*, p 3.

[169] Redmond, *op.cit*, p 173. The author also notes that the one year's service requirement under the Unfair Dismissals Acts 1997-2007 does not apply in this context.

Frequently, indeed, the disputes at issue never come to full trial. As Clarke J noted in *Bergin v Galway Clinic Doughiska Ltd*[170]:

> "It is the frequent experience of the court dealing with such matters that a great many of the cases which are the subject of an interlocutory ruling are resolved by agreement between the parties before the matter comes to trial. It would be somewhat naïve not to surmise that a significant feature of the interlocutory hearing is concerned with both parties attempting to establish the most advantageous position from which to approach the frequently expected negotiations designed to lead to an agreed termination of the contract of employment concerned. The employee who has the benefit of an interlocutory injunction can approach such negotiations from a position of strength as can the employer who has successfully resisted an interlocutory application".

[12–46]   A comprehensive treatment of the principles governing the grant of employment injunctions is beyond the scope of this work.[171] However, the following section will briefly examine some of the main issues that have emerged.

An injunction is a court order directing a party to do, or refrain from doing, a specified thing.[172] Most employment injunctions are either *interlocutory* or *interim* injunctions, "holding orders" that are sought and granted prior to the full hearing of the case. At the outset, it should be noted that the "normal" rules governing the granting of injunctions apply in the employment context also; namely that the plaintiff establishes that there is a fair issue to be tried; that damages are not an adequate remedy for the party seeking the injunction if he or she were successful at the trial; and that the "balance of convenience" favours the granting of the injunction at the interlocutory stage.[173] Cox *et al* note that there are four categories into which applications for employment injunctions tend to fall.[174] These will be considered in turn.

[12–47]   First, the plaintiff may seek an order that a dismissed employee be re-instated. This is the most difficult order to obtain as it is severely restrictive of the employer's right to run its business as it sees fit; it also requires the re-instatement of the employee in a situation where the mutual trust and confidence inherent in the employment

---

[170] [2008] 2 IR 205 at 212.

[171] See Redmond, *op.cit*, chapter 10; Stewart and Dunleavy, *op.cit*, chapter 12; Cox *et al*, *op.cit*, chapter 24. For an interesting comparative take on the issue, see O' Connell, "The Evolution of the Employment Injunction in Ireland and the United Kingdom: Analysing a Divergent Approach" (2009) 3/4 ELRI 147.

[172] See, generally, Delany, *Equity and the Law of Trusts in Ireland* (4th ed, Round Hall, Dublin, 2007).

[173] *Campus Oil v Minister for Industry* (No 2) [1983] IR 88. However, in *Maha Lingam v HSE* [2006] ELR 137 the High Court found that, where the employment injunction being sought is mandatory (requiring action to be taken), as opposed to prohibitory (restraining action), in nature the plaintiff would need to show a *strong* case that is likely to succeed at trial. This has been affirmed in many cases since; see, for example, *Khan v HSE* [2009] ELR 178. On the "balance of convenience" test, see *Keenan v Iarnród Éireann* [2010] IEHC 15 and *Yap v Children's University Hospital (Temple St Ltd)* [2006] 4 IR 298.

[174] *op.cit*, p 835.

relationship may have irretrievably broken down. As a result, such orders are rarely granted.[175] Secondly, the plaintiff may seek an order restraining his or her dismissal (but not requiring his or her re-instatement). This is commonly referred to as a *"Fennelly* order", following the decision of Costello J in *Fennelly v Assicurazione Generali SPA*[176] where an interlocutory injunction was granted restraining the purported dismissal of the employee and requiring the employer to continue paying his salary pending the trial. The terms of the order were that the plaintiff would need to be available to carry out duties as requested by the employer, although the Court recognised that the employer might prefer in such circumstances to place the plaintiff on a leave of absence. The plaintiff, however, was not re-instated. This type of order is often granted where the plaintiff would otherwise be left in a precarious financial position.[177] Thirdly, the plaintiff may seek an order restraining the employer from replacing him or her. This may be an order restraining the appointment of a direct replacement or an order restraining the employer from substantially reorganising the business in such a manner that the plaintiff is effectively frozen out. In *Bergin v Galway Clinic Doughiska Ltd*[178] the High Court granted the plaintiff (the chief executive of the defendant) an order restraining the defendant from dismissing the plaintiff and from appointing another chief executive, *save* on terms sufficient to allow the plaintiff to return to his duties should the court ultimately make such an order at trial. Finally, an order may be sought preventing the employer from carrying out disciplinary proceedings other than in accordance with the terms of the employment contract, agreed procedures, or the principles of constitutional justice and fair procedures outlined in chapter 10. Typically, this will arise where the employee alleges he or she was not afforded a proper disciplinary hearing at all, or where such a hearing was held but the procedures adopted were not sufficiently fair.[179] In *Minnock v Irish Casing Company Limited*[180] Clarke J affirmed that the court will not intervene in the *course of* a disciplinary process unless a clear case has been made out that there is a serious risk that the process is sufficiently flawed and incapable of being resolved, so that irreparable harm would be caused to the plaintiff if the process were permitted to continue.

---

[175] See, for example, *Orr v Zomax Ltd* [2004] ELR 161; *Philpott v Ogilvy & Mather Ltd* [2000] 3 IR 206. Note, however, that Mallon, *op.cit,* points out that interlocutory injunctions *have* been granted in cases where the essential trust and confidence between the parties was damaged to a greater or lesser extent; he cites, for example, *Harte v Kelly & Others* [1997] ELR 125; *Boland v Phoenix Shannon Plc* [1997] ELR 113; *Moore v Xnet Information Systems Ltd & Others* [2002] 13 ELR 65.

[176] [1985] 3 ILT 37.

[177] See *Shortt v Data Packaging* [1994] ELR 251. Cox *et al* note that in times of economic difficulty for *employers* it may be argued that the reverse logic should apply, i.e. that it may be unduly burdensome on the employer to have to continue paying an employee who is on leave; *op.cit,* p 855.

[178] [2008] 2 IR 205.

[179] See, for example, *Carroll v Dublin Bus* [2005] 4 IR 184; *Maher v Irish Permanent plc (No 1)* [1998] ELR 77; *Giblin v Irish Life & Permanent plc* [2010] IEHC 36 (where Laffoy J deemed it an appropriate situation for court intervention, notwithstanding the fact that the employee had a right of appeal under the disciplinary procedures themselves).

[180] *Irish Times Law Report,* 11 June 2007.

[12–48] Redmond has identified various situations in which employment injunctions have, and have not, been granted.[181] Among the most important in the former category is where the plaintiff is alleging the breach of a substantive limitation regarding termination in the contract[182] or, as discussed, a breach of an express or implied term relating to procedural fairness. In terms of the latter, it seems that, where an employee is dismissed having been given the requisite notice, there is no issue to be tried even where the employer has acted unreasonably or maliciously.[183] It seems that even where there is a doubt as to whether notice requirements have been complied with, injunctive relief may not be granted. In *Philpott v Ogilvy & Mather Ltd*[184] the High Court refused to grant interim relief:

> "The traditional relief at common law for unfair (sic) dismissal was a claim for damages. The plaintiff may also have been entitled to declarations in certain circumstances such as, for instance, that there was an implied term in his contract entitling him to fair procedures before he was dismissed. But such declarations were in aid of his common law remedy and had no independent existence apart from it. If the plaintiff loses his right to sue for damages at common law the heart has gone out of his claim and there is no other free standing relief which he can claim at law or in equity".[185]

[12–49] Thus, the logic appears to be that, as the plaintiff's remedy under the common law would be damages, damages will be, by definition, an adequate remedy and injunctive relief should not be granted.

Finally, one important suggestion for reform of the system involving injunctive relief has been made by Mallon.[186] He considers it to be a serious flaw in the unfair dismissals legislation that the EAT cannot make interim or interlocutory orders and suggests that, while the granting of employment injunctions should only occur in limited circumstances, the EAT or the Circuit Court might be given power to grant interim or interlocutory reliefs, including the continuation of payment of salary, in unfair dismissals cases.

---

[181] Redmond, *op.cit*, pp 181-200.

[182] *Fennelly v Assicurazione Generali SPA* [1985] 3 ILT 37.

[183] *Orr v Zomax Ltd* [2004] ELR 161; *Sheehy v Ryan* [2004] ELR 87 (HC); [2008] IESC 14 (SC).

[184] [2000] 3 IR 206.

[185] *ibid* at 212 *per* Murphy J, who was relying on the Supreme Court judgment in *Parsons v Iarnród Éireann* [1997] ELR 203.

[186] Tom Mallon BL, speaking at the Round Hall Employment Law Conference, Dublin, 24 May 2006, cited in Redmond, *op.cit*, p 200.

INDEX